The Sunday

GOLF COURSE GUIDE
—— TO ——
BRITAIN & IRELAND
DONALD STEEL

CollinsWillow
An Imprint of HarperCollins*Publishers*

To Graham

Happy Birthday

Best wishes

John, Hayley +
Emily

P.S. If I'd known that Scottish
courses were included, I'
wouldn't have bought it!

This edition published 1994 by
Collins Willow
an imprint of HarperCollins*Publishers*
London

First published 1968
Eleventh revised edition 1994

A CIP catalogue record for this book
is available from the British Library

ISBN 0-00-218454-0

This edition produced by
Robert MacDonald Publishing, London SW1

Typeset by Peter MacDonald, Twickenham
Printed and bound in Great Britain by
Butler & Tanner Ltd, Frome and London

CONTENTS

KEY TO THE MAPS

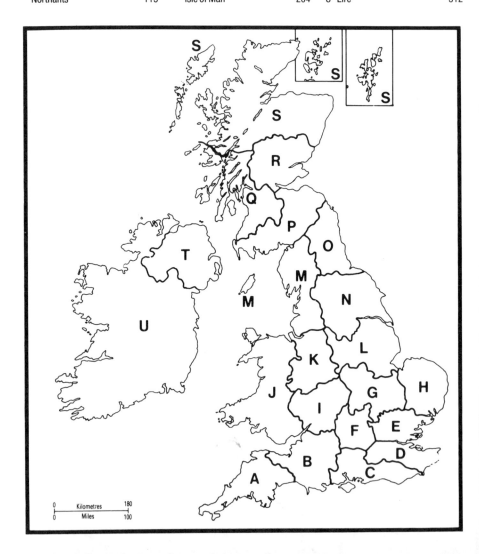

FOREWORD

There are few golfers whose education in the matter of courses may be considered complete who have seen, in their own country at any rate, all the courses that are worth the seeing. The aim of this Guide has always been to draw the attention of readers to the unique variety that Britain and Ireland have to offer; and to help them with as much information as possible — not least in giving directions as to how to find their destinations.

If I had to compile a list of the hardest courses to locate, the list would be headed by Woking followed closely by Little Aston, St George's Hill, Huddersfield, County Louth, Formby, Bingley St Ives and Southerndown, with an honourable mention in dispatches for Sandy Lodge, Camberley Heath, Moor Allerton and Eaton G.C. at Waverton. Our motorways have, at least, made the task of finding courses easier, notably the M25 which now has exits at strategic points, at least as far as the golfer is concerned.

Since the first edition was published in 1968, the number of entries included in the Guide has risen by something like eight hundred and fifty, the increase in the last two years alone amounting to more than a hundred and fifty. The last two editions have accounted for nearly five hundred additional courses between them; and while a number of these are multi-million pound ventures, the basic need hasn't changed. Value for money for the golfer is the thing which is most important.

Few new projects can afford palatial clubhouses, but most British and Irish golfers are happy as long as there is somewhere to hang their coats, have a drink and get something to eat. Some place greater priority on these comforts than on their actual round of golf, but it is to the courses themselves that the main attention must always be turned, and to which proper finance must be directed, in order to present them as all golfers love to see them.

Exploring new avenues, and playing different courses, are therefore among the delights of the game which this Guide has done its best to promote. The 11th edition is no exception.

Donald Steel
March 1994

INTRODUCTION

This book is intended primarily to be of use to the travelling or holidaying golfer, or to parties and golfing societies looking for somewhere new and interesting for a day's outing. Since an increasing number of courses are allied to hotel, country club and conference facilities, it should also find a place in the libraries of companies whose executives like to leaven serious business with a round of golf.

This 11th revised edition of the guide retains the same structure and general organisation as its predecessor, the 10th. However, since the last edition involved several major changes of presentation, the book may well look unfamiliar to those whose previous acquaintance is with the 9th or earlier editions. It is, therefore, worth summarising the changes that have been made.

The most obvious is the introduction of colour into the maps, adding considerably to the ease with which courses can be located and identified. At the same time, the geographical organisation of the book has been radically altered; and, for the first time, a separate section devoted to a selection of driving ranges and other practice facilities has been included.

Organisation. The book is divided into 21 areas or county groupings, as opposed to the 28 used in previous editions. The areas have been chosen on the basis of golfing affinities and familiarity of use rather than cartographical convenience or bureaucratic definition. In particular, the purely administrative boundaries created by local government reorganisation have been ignored where they conflict with County Golf Union affiliations; thus the golf courses of Humberside have been reallocated to Lincolnshire and Yorkshire, those of the West Midlands to Warwickshire or Staffordshire, those of Avon to Gloucestershire and Somerset. Middlesex has been resurrected. This is not just in recognition of the fact that the new counties and metropolitan areas were little loved; it anticipates similar action on the part of the government itself.

As before, the areas are labelled alphabetically, from A to U. Each area has a map indicating the location of courses within it (see page 4 for a key to the county groupings and pages on which individual area maps are to be found). Within each section, courses are listed alphabetically, and numbered, and the combination of letter and number is used to identify each course in the overall index (page 342).

Course Information. For each golf course in the book, we have tried to provide the following information: the name; telephone number; address; travel directions to the course; a brief description of the type of course; the number of holes, length and Standard Scratch Score; the course architect and date of foundation if known; restrictions on visiting golfers — when they may play and whether reservations, club membership, handicap certificates are required, for example; green fees; whether parties or visiting societies are permitted and, if so, when; what catering and other facilities (for example swimming pools, tennis courts, putting greens or driving ranges) are available; and finally local hotels (particularly where golfing holidays can be arranged). Where no information is given for a particular category — eg Societies or Catering — it can be assumed that the facilities are not available to visitors or don't exist.

Conversely, the absence of hotel information does not mean that there are no local hotels. Details of accommodation facilities are normally only given where hotels are scarce, or where specific attention is paid to the requirements of golfers or where there is a recommendation from the golf course concerned. In other cases, there will generally be an abundance of local hotels or of bed and breakfast accommodation, of which details can be found from one of the many guide books on the market, or from the local tourist board.

The information in this book has been compiled with the help of club secretaries and course managers, whose assistance is gratefully acknowledged.

DALRIADA SPORTS HOLIDAYS
IRELAND, FRANCE, PORTUGAL, SPAIN AND UK

We have selected areas of each country to offer you golf with choices of courses, starting times, hotel accommodation and car hire.

Phone, fax or write to us for details and receive our brochure.

DALRIADA SPORTS HOLIDAYS, P.O. BOX 24, PERTH. PH2 0SZ
Tel: 0738 22716 Fax: 0738 39392

Courses in Eire. It should be noted that telephone numbers in the Republic of Ireland should be dialled in exactly the same way as any other international calls. The numbers given are those for use when telephoning from within Eire itself. From all other countries (including the UK) the area code (without the initial zero) should be prefixed with the international dialling code (010 353).

Green fees for courses in Eire should be assumed to be in Irish pounds (punts).

Green Fees. All the information in this book has been compiled with the help of club secretaries and was valid at the time of going to press (January 1994). However, many clubs set green fees for the coming year in the spring, and information may not have been available during the period of compilation of this book. Intending golfers would generally be wise to ring the golf course concerned to check before setting out. It should also be noted that some green fees are subject to VAT, in addition to the fees quoted, and that weekend rates often apply on public holidays also, even if this is not specifically stated in the Guide.

Abbreviations. As the number of new courses continues to grow, it is inevitable that some abbreviations should be required. These should be self-evident:
  G & CC = Golf and Country Club
  LC = Leisure Centre
  GC = Golf Centre or Golf Complex
  WD = weekday(s) — Monday to Friday
  WE = weekend(s) — Saturday, Sunday
  BH = Bank (or Public) Holidays
  GH = Guest House
Standard abbreviations are also used for months and days of the week.

Driving Ranges. Despite the considerable number of new golf courses, it still remains difficult for the casual golfer in many areas to spend an hour or two improving his or her game. No doubt in response to this, a plethora of driving ranges and other types of practice facility have appeared. We have therefore included a selection of these at the end of the book (between pages 336 and 341). Space limitations have made it impossible to give more than the most basic information; however, it should be noted that the great majority offer P.G.A. professional tuition, as well as club repair, club hire and, often, a full range of retail services.

Comments. The publishers of this Guide would welcome any information about courses that are not in the book — and indeed about any errors or alterations relating to the current contents, so that they can be incorporated in the next edition. Any comments and suggestions should be sent to: Robert MacDonald Publishing, c/o The Sunday Telegraph, 1 Canada Square, Canary Wharf, London E14 5DT, where they will be gratefully received.

PASTURES NEW

Golf courses are no different from paintings in giving rise to likes and dislikes. There are those who rave about the extravagance of multi-million pound ventures although they may be far beyond their financial reach; and there are others who believe that the soundly designed and sensibly built creations highlighting the natural look, represent far better value for money.

The last two years in Britain and Ireland have seen examples of both but it has also been a period in which new courses have made the news for all the wrong reasons. Dreams all too quickly turned to nightmares, hopes to disillusionment.

Even making allowance for the recession, much of the damage was self-inflicted through a lack of proper understanding of the market, insufficient research, application of the wrong principles and scant knowledge of what British golfers need and can afford.

Developers, armed with a copy of the Royal & Ancient's pamphlet "Demand for Golf", and a vision of what they had seen and heard about the game in America and Japan, leapt to the conclusion that what works there would work here. Nothing could be further from the truth. However, rescue packages have come to the aid of several afflicted courses which undoubtedly deserved a reprieve — none more so than Loch Lomond on whose bonny, bonny banks Tom Weiskopf, one of the best professional golfers turned architect, has produced an eye catching 18-holes to test and dazzle the best.

Admittedly, his canvas is flanked by a frame of gold although wise heads warn of midges in summer — if ever summer returns. A stunning setting anywhere in the world is a great asset for a new course, a fact that raises the thought as to what opinion would have made of the actual courses at Pebble Beach, Gleneagles or Killarney if they had been created in Hackney Marshes instead.

Be that as it may, Loch Lomond will stand comparison in any context, the first golfing requirement being definite cont-rol from the tee to hit largely well-guarded fairways. Since the hardest part of the game is to aim straight and hit straight, those finding the fairways should always have a decided advantage over those who do not. Weiskopf, in his time, was as handsome a player as there was and, not surprisingly, his design at Loch Lomond owes nothing to gimmickry.

It would be hard to find a challenge to Loch Lomond in terms of beauty but Skibo on the Dornoch Firth in Sutherland manages it easily. Featured later in the book, it is the first links course to be built in Scotland or England for half a century and, considering the demands of ecologists and environmentalists, could well be one of the last.

As the Highland home of Andrew Carnegie, you would expect a special place and visitors are never disappointed but Scotland features prominently in the list of new courses opened since the last edition of this Guide. The Strathtyrum, St Andrews' sixth course, is a particularly welcome addition.

It caters principally for those seeking a more modest challenge than the celebrated Old, New, Eden and Jubilee. At little over 5,000 yards, the Strathtyrum provides the lesson that the market for the majority lies more at this end of the scale but, along with the 9-hole Balgove, it forms part of the exciting new Golf Centre which was long overdue at the Home of Golf, a complex which includes a splendid driving range on what used to be the first two and last two holes on the old Eden.

Another Golf Centre to open its doors in 1994 is that at Leeds which rubs shoulders with Alwoodley and Moor Allerton — vintage territory. Besides a driving range and David Leadbetter Academy, it provides a full 18-hole course and a short 9, an excellent formula that offers something for everyone.

Puckrup Hall near the historic town of Tewkesbury is another new course to make its bow in the last couple of years along with Overstone Park (Northampton), West Park, Brocket Hall, Hever,

Kilworth Springs, Pine Ridge Golf Centre and Lambourne. These are just a few of the 150 odd new entries, Ireland staking its claim with The European Club in County Wicklow, Faithlegg in County Waterford and St Helens Bay in Rosslare.

Most represent Clubs or courses, designed by British or Irish architects, directed at the majority of golfers, but the last few years have also seen the unveiling of a number of projects founded by Japanese, designed by Americans, and aimed at an altogether richer clientele.

The monopoly of American architects in expensive projects was broken by Nick Faldo, whose first steps as a designer were taken at Chart Hills. It will be interesting to see how it settles down and whether Faldo expects as much of others in the challenge he poses as he does of himself. In general, the Japanese prefer palatial style clubhouses and courses built in what can be described as the American manner involving major earth moving to introduce a reshaped landscape.

This is in keeping with the Japanese golfing culture although it is an easy form of golf course architecture provided that there is a substantial budget. An architect's skill is tested far more if the budget is limited and the course has to be fitted into the existing landscape with due regard given to proper environmental issues and wild life conservation.

It was the Americans who fostered this type of modern course building with extensive land shaping, many large lakes, fairway irrigation, huge flat bunkers and the importation of specialist grasses for fairways, tees and greens. This forms the basic pattern behind the Oxfordshire, Monarch's Course at Gleneagles, the London Club and Stockley Park, courses which have recently opened their doors and were designed by Americans, although it has to be said that European architects are just as capable of following that style if that is what clients want and must have.

The Oxfordshire near Thame is the best, Rees Jones having moulded a varied challenge by excavating vast lakes in order to provide the material to indulge in the formation of the myriad of mounds and hills. Water is very much part of the challenge notably on the par 5 17th which

offers the choice of a long shot across the lake or the longer, safer dry-land route around it. Appropriately, the fairway is in the shape of a question mark.

It is the type of course on which sponsors will cast covetous eyes for major tournaments as they will the Monarch's at Gleneagles which, like the Heritage course at The London Club, was designed by Jack Nicklaus. The International course at The London Club is the work of Ron Kirby, a respected name.

Gleneagles' decision to add another course to their stable was a significant one although the Oxfordshire, The London and The Monarch's are confined strictly to members and guests, in the case of Gleneagles their hotel guests.

Today's professionals have, by now, become very used to courses in which everything is predictable and measurable, beautifully manicured with the help of fairway irrigation systems, and favouring greens which can only be reached through the air. Such courses couldn't have been built even 30 or 40 years ago; yet they are changing, indeed, have already changed, the character of the game.

Whether this is a passing fashion I somehow doubt, but there are signs that opinion amongst many of the leading players favours courses typifying more traditional values, courses that remind you that a good deal of golf should be played along the ground.

When the U.S. Open returned to Shinnecock Hills on Long Island in 1986, there was a chorus of approval for a course which is amongst the oldest and most influential in America. Reaction to it amongst the younger professionals varied from mild surprise to open eyed amazement that the greens, for instance, were all open in front. Lee Trevino saw its greatness in lying in the fact that it favoured nobody. In his words, "you can go high, low, hook, fade, do what you want".

Ingenuity, improvisation and imagination are not as big a part of the modern players' armoury as they should be but that is the fault of many new courses and the policy of architects. Definitions of a great course vary but one essential ingredient is that they must be capable of giving challenge and enjoyment to all classes of golfer. The emphasis here is on the word enjoyment which is more likely to result on holes which invite thought as opposed to fear.

Variety is as desirable in a layout as it is in a piano concerto or a box of chocolates but increasing concern is being expressed over the impact of some new golf courses on the countryside, a concern that voices the need for new courses to make a positive contribution to landscape enhancement.

It will be interesting to see, when the 12th Edition of this Guide is published, what effect this policy will have had in determining the number and type of new courses then under review.

ACCIDENT OR DESIGN?

In December 1993, Nick Price won the Sun City Million Dollar Challenge on a course measuring around 7,600 yards with a total of 264, 24 under par. Admittedly, allowance has to made for the ball going further in the thinner air at high altitude, but it showed unmistakably how length alone poses few barriers to the leading players these days.

Sixteen years earlier, Al Geiberger's 59 in the Memphis Classic, the only round under 60 in the history of the U.S. Tour, was achieved on a course of 7,200 yards and there are countless other examples in between of low scoring on long courses which many might have thought were impregnable.

Naturally enough, most new courses have had to be stretched to accommodate the dramatic advances in technique and equipment which have resulted in every golfer achieving extra length.

Something of the same has been seen in rugby, where goals are now kicked from everywhere, and in tennis, where the speed of serving has revolutionised the game. However, the search to combat power in golf has led to a regrettable fashion amongst some developers and architects, who maintain that every new course must have a par of 72 with four par 5s, four par 3s and a championship label irrespective of whether a championship is ever housed on it. This desire for uniformity is as senseless as trying to restrict the world to a single variety of cheese or wine.

What lifts golf onto a higher plane than games that are played on courts or pitches with prescribed dimensions is that golf courses come in all shapes and sizes. Statistics cannot distinguish between the good and the bad. True judgement is based on interest, enjoyment and use of the terrain which, in turn, is a reflection of the skill and ingenuity of the architect.

The architect is cheered — or should be — by the comfort that there are no rights and wrongs, particularly with regard to the make-up and balance of his designs. How could there be?

Let me elaborate. The Old course at St Andrews — still hailed as a model for all architects — has only two par 3s and two par 5s. It has the 11th hole crossing the 7th and is unique in having many of its holes sharing fairways.

At Royal Worlington and Newmarket which no less a judge than Bernard Darwin described as "The Sacred Nine", you drive on three occasions over the green which you have just played. Even at Royal Porthcawl, venue of the 1995 Walker Cup, the opening tee shot plays straight across the 18th fairway. Elsewhere in Britain, it is not uncommon to drive over roads and, less commonly, fast flowing rivers or streams.

There maybe a few unwritten "rules" to which golf course architects conform, but all an architect can try to do is to make the best use of the land available within his allotted budget and, since no two pieces of land are the same, his scope is endless.

Clearly, the scale of a course is dictated by the quantity and character of land at his disposal. He must cut his coat according to his cloth, a fact that leads to all sorts of different balances between the pars of holes and the make-up of new 18, 27 or 36-hole courses.

Where possible, the par 3s, 4s and 5s are arranged so that they don't all come at once, but the list of design oddities which follows has been drawn up to counter some of the suggestions so frequently put forward, and so often received as conventional wisdom, about the par and SSS of courses, courses beginning or ending with a par 3, courses having consecutive par 3s or par 5s and those maintaining a roughly equal balance in length between the two 9s on an 18-hole course.

It is not meant to be a comprehensive catalogue, but it does show that there are precedents for practically everything that a golf course architect might think of incorporating in his designs. Before that, however, it is worth reflecting that, of our seven current Open Championship Links courses, only St Andrews and Royal Troon have a par of 72.

18-hole courses over 5,800 yards beginning with a par 3

Aboyne
Accrington
Addington
Anglesey
Ashburnham
Ballards Gore
Berkshire (Blue)
Churston
City of Derry
Cochrane Castle
Colville Park
Crow Wood
Dartford
Davenport
Davyhulme Park
Deer Park
Easingwold
Eastham Lodge
Falkirk Tryst
Hayling
Hollingbury Park
Horam Park
Houldsworth
Huntercombe
Kettering
Kingsknowe
Knole Park
Largs
La Moye
Liphook
Llandudno (Maesdu)
Llanymynech
Longcliffe
Macroom
Meyrick Park
Monkstown
Peebles
Preston
Purley Downs
Royal Lytham and St
   Annes
Royal Mid-Surrey
Royal Norwich
Southport and Ainsdale
Thetford
Upton by Chester
Wearside
Wellow
West Bowling
West Cornwall
Whitchurch (Cardiff)
Withington
Yelverton

18-hole courses over 5,800 yards ending with a par 3

Aberystwyth
Airdrie
Alloa
Arkley

Ashford (Kent)
Bandon
Barnard Castle
Beadlow Manor
Berkshire (Red)
Boyce Hill
Breightmet
Bremhill Park
Brinkworth
Brora
Carlyon Bay
Cawder (Cawder)
Chapel-en-le-Frith
Chelmsford
Cold Ashby
Courtown
Darenth Valley
Deeside
Dewsbury
Dougalston
Downes Crediton
Dunstable Downs
Dunwood Manor
East Herts
Ellesmere
Erewash Valley
Fairlop Waters
Forest of Arden (Arden)
Fortrose and Rosemarkie
Glamorganshire (Penarth)
Goodwood
Great Barr
Hayston
Hoebridge
Howley Hall
Ilfracombe
Kennilworth
Killarney (Mahony's
   Point)
Kilsyth Lennox
Kirkcaldy
Lancaster
Langley Park
Leasowe
Leeds
Lindrick
Lochwinnoch
Louth
Milford Haven
Moor Park (High)
Mount Oswald
Northcliffe
Nottingham City
Old Padeswood
Old Ranfurly
Padeswood and Buckley
Parkstone
Penwortham
Piltdown
Prestwick St Nicholas
Royal Eastbourne
Royal Guernsey
Royal St David's
Ryton

Saffron Walden
St Pierre
Saltburn-by-the-Sea
Sandy Lodge
Shanklin and Sandown
Sickleholme
Stocksfield
Stoke by Nayland (both)
Stone
Tredegar Park
Wallsend
Welwyn Garden City
West Linton
Wetherby
Whitburn
Woodbury (Oaks)
Woodhall Hills (both)
Worksop

18-hole courses beginning and ending with a par 3

Aboyne
Aldwark Manor
Bala
Bearsted
Bingley St Ives
Didsbury
Eltham Warren
Harpenden Common
Hawick
Peacehaven
Southwold
Upminster

18-hole courses over 5,800 yards with two consecutive par 3s

Ashford Manor
Ballybunion (Old)
Balmoral
Bandon
Barnard Castle
Bawburgh
Birr
Bishop Auckland
Brancepeth Castle
Brough
Burntisland
Chester-le-Street
Clonmel
Consett and District
Cruden Bay
Elgin
Erewash Valley
Harburn
Hartsbourne
Hayston
Holywood
Ganstead Park
Glamorganshire (Penarth)

Haywards Heath
Ilkley
Kidderminster
Killymoon
Knott End
Lee-on-the-Solent
Leyland
Linlithgow
Loudoun (twice)
Lurgan
Machrihanish
Market Rasen
Millport
North Oxford
Potters Bar
Royal Eastbourne
Royal Jersey
Rushmere
Sandy Lodge
Stoneham
Tain
Thurlestone
The Manor, Laceby
Tredegar Park
Waterlooville
West Linton
West Monmouthshire
West Sussex
Willesley Park

18-hole courses over 6,000 yards with fewer than 3 par 3s

St Andrews (Old) — 2
Golf House Club, Elie — 2

18-hole courses over 5,900 yards with more than five par 3s

Barnard Castle — 6
Bershire (Red) — 6
Bigbury — 6
Darlington — 6
Downes Crediton — 6
Killymore — 6
Sandy Lodge — 6
Tredegar Park — 6
Note: The Red Course at The Berkshire has six par 3s six par 4s and six par 5s.

Courses with holes over 600 yards

Aldenham G & CC (13th, 636 yards)
Belton Woods (Wellington) (18th, 613 yards)

East Dorset (6th, 604 yards)
Gedney Hill (2nd, 671 yards)
Portal (6th, 603 yards)
Welwyn Garden City (17th 601 yards)

Courses over 7,000 yards

Austin Lodge (7,118 yards)
Ballards Gore (7,062 yards)
Barkway Park (7,000 yards)
Bidford Grange (7,233 yards)
The Belfry (Brabazon) (7,177 yards)
Belton Woods (Lancaster) (7,021 yards)
Bowood (7,317 yards)
Bright Castle (7,143 yards)
Carnoustie (7,272 yards)
Chart Hills (7,086 yards)
Dartmouth (7,012 yards)
East Dorset (7,027 yards)
East Sussex (West) (7,154 yards)
Forest of Arden (Arden) (7,102 yards)
Gleneagles (The Monarch's Course) (7,081 yards)
Hanbury Manor (7011 yards)
Killarney (Killeen) (7,079 yards)
Loch Lomond (7,053 yards)
The London Club (Heritage 7,208 yards) (International 7,005 yards)
Millbrook (7,100 yards)
Moatlands (7,060 yards)
Mount Juliet (7,100 yards)
The Oxfordshire (7,143 yards)
Notts (Hollinwell) (7,020 yards)
Perton Park (7,007 yards)
Portal (7,145 yards)
Royal Liverpool (7,100 yards)
Slaley Hall (7038 yards)
Stocks Hotel (7,016 yards)
Thorpe Wood (7,086 yards)
Waterville (7,184 yards)

West Berkshire (7,059 yards)
Loch Lomond (7,053 yards)

18-hole courses with holes under 100 yards

Bridport and West Dorset (2nd, 81 yards)
Dun Laoghaire (7th, 95 yards)
Erewash Valley (4th, 89 yards)
Ilfracombe (4th, 81 yards)
Tilsworth (13th, 97 yards)

Courses with par 3s numbered all odds or all evens

Addington
Auchterarder
Cape Cornwall
Cirencester
County Armagh
County Louth
Hoebridge
Liphook
Lyme Regis
Oake Manor
Scunthorpe
Stockwood Park
Sundridge Park (West)
West Cornwall
Uttoxeter

18-hole courses with notable differences between the lengths of their two nines

Chapel-en-le-Frith (821 yards)
Davids Heath (786 yards)
Flackwell Heath (615 yards)
Kings Lynn (584 yards)
Kirkhill (648 yards)
Old Ranfurly (507 yards)
Reddish Vale (534 yards)
Thurlestone (821 yards)
Woodhall Hills (754 yards)
Worcestershire (655 yards)

A

CORNWALL, DEVON, CHANNEL ISLANDS

There is about the courses in this region an unmistakable air of holiday golf although it is thoroughly easy to appreciate how the members of Clubs heave a sigh of relief when the holiday-makers have gone for the year and they are left in peace.

For the historical contribution that its golfers have made to the game it is appropriate to start in Jersey where Harry Vardon and Ted Ray were born, Vardon in a cottage on the edge of Royal Jersey's Links at Grouville. It is remarkable that, of the tiny handful of British winners of the US Open, two were born within a mile or so of each on an island that represents a mere dot on the world map. Vardon, who did not take up the game until he was 21 and yet was Open champion four years later, forged his game on a course that begins along the shore of Grouville Bay under the watchful, distant eye of Mont Argeuil.

Elsewhere, particularly on the second nine, recent change has eliminated one or two architectural shortcomings but nothing compared to the new broom that has transformed La Moye, set on Jersey's exposed western headland. In less than 20 years, it has been turned from a test of sporting eccentricities into one which, given the aid of a stiff breeze, can have a field of top class professionals at full stretch.

Les Mielles, on St Ouen's Bay, is relatively new and there are plans for a Jersey Golf Centre just down the road from La Moye. Over the water on Guernsey, there has been no such upheaval on the charming Royal Guernsey which has to shoulder and satisfy almost the entire golfing demand of the community.

On the mainland, St Mellion and Bodmin have boosted the courses in Cornwall, a county whose traditional delights surround West Cornwall at Lelant, Trevose and St Enodoc, the latter with a fine new clubhouse on land purchased from the Duchy in their centenary year in 1990.

Local interest in Devon was given a boost when their men's team won the English Counties championship for the first time in 1985, a tribute to the courses on which many were raised.

East Devon, a sort of elevated seaside Sunningdale, is the pick in the South, the Manor House at Moretonhampstead dominates the central heart while Saunton and Royal North Devon guard the northern coast with justifiable pride. Saunton, which has always been one of my favourite spots, boasts arguably the best pair of courses in Britain, the West upgraded a year or two back to rival its neighbour — a regular and deserved choice for championships.

Across the estuary at Westward Ho!, Royal North Devon is an ageless monument, the oldest seaside course in England although one where invasion of the sea is proving hard to repel. Nevertheless, ground that may appear plain from a distance comes compellingly to life as the holes penetrate land that is full of character down nearer the famous Pebble Ridge. No golfer with a grain of romance in his soul should pass it by, particularly as journeys to that part of the world have been made so much simpler by a new road from Tiverton and by a new bridge that crosses the estuary at Bideford.

A hearty word, too, for Yelverton on the edge of Dartmoor, north of Plymouth and for Thurlestone and Churston; and there are the comparatively recent complexes at Dartmouth and Woodbury Common near Budleigh Salterton which both lend a nice, modern balance to a south western tip of Britain which has so many good things to offer.

A1 Alderney

☎(0481) 822835
Routes des Carriers, Alderney,
Channel Islands
1 mile E of St Annes.
Undulating seaside course.
9 holes, 2528 yards, S.S.S.32;
double rounds for 18, S.S.S.65
Designed by Frank Pennink.
Visitors: welcome at all times,
except competition days.
Green Fee: apply for details.
Societies: catered for on weekdays
by arrangement and weekends for
special events.
Catering: bar foods served on
weekdays, Sun lunch, special parties
or lunches by arrangement.
Hotels: Bellevue; Sea View.

A2 Ashbury

☎(0837) 55453, 55468 Fax
Higher Maddaford, Southcott,
Okehampton, Devon EX20 4NL
4 miles W of Okehampton, 0.5 mile N
of A3079 to Ashbury.
Moorland course.
18 holes, S.S.S.68; 18 holes Par 3,
2000 yards
Designed by D.J. Fenson.
Founded 1991

Visitors: welcome at all times; busy
most days, must book tee-off times.
Green Fee: £12 WD, £15 WE.
Societies: small societies welcome,
preferably pm; free golf at all times
for residential societies (see below).
Catering: full clubhouse facilities;
bar and bar snacks to 6pm every day.
Indoor pool, sauna, solaria, snooker,
indoor bowls, 10-pin bowling.
Hotels: Ashbury GC; Manor House
Hotel (Okehampton); both offer free
golf for residents booking 3 nights.

A3 Axe Cliff

☎(0297) 20499, 24371 Sec
Squires Lane, Axmouth, Seaton,
Devon EX12 4AB
Through village of Axmouth, along
riverside, turn left just before
Axmouth bridge and straight up lane.
Coastal course one side, country the
other.
18 holes, 4867 yards, S.S.S.64
Founded 1892
Visitors: h/cap cert and membership
of recognised club required; own
clubs, no sharing; course closed until
11am Wed; with member only
12am-2pm Sat and 1pm-2pm Sun;
competitions Sun before 11.30am.

Green Fee: £10 WD, £12 WE & BH.
Societies: welcome, must book in
advance.
Catering: bar and catering
arrangements.
Hotels: Shrubbery (Rousdon).

A4 Ballpark Golf and Leisure

☎(0326) 572518
Wendron, Helston, Cornwall TR13
0LX
1 mile N of Helston on B3297 Redruth
road.
Short park and downland course,
holes ranging from 70 to 190 yards,
duration 2 hrs.
18 holes, 2030 yards, Par 3
Founded 1988
Visitors: welcome any time, open
daily year round 9am to dusk (7am
summer)
Green Fee: £4-5/round, pay & play.
Societies: Mon-Sat before 11am or
after 5pm, book in advance.
Catering: at Jolly Farmer freehouse
pub and restaurant.
Crazy golf, tennis, croquet, boule,
horseshoes, skittles, crown bowls.
Hotels: Angel; Gweandues; Nansloe
Manor.

A beautiful 18 hole course overlooking the sea in South Devon

BIGBURY GOLF CLUB LIMITED
Bigbury, Kingsbridge, South Devon TQ7 4BB (0548) 810207

No golfer visiting the South Hams should miss the opportunity of playing at Bigbury. It's an ideal holiday course – challenging enough for low handicappers but not too daunting for the average golfer. There are outstanding views from almost everywhere on the course – with Dartmoor to the North, the river Avon running near a number of holes and breathtaking scenes of Bantham Beach and Burgh Island.

A5 Bigbury
☎(0548) 810207, 810557 Sec, 810412 Pro
Bigbury-on-Sea, Kingsbridge, Devon TQ7 4BB
Take A379 Plymouth-Kingsbridge road; turn right 2 miles from Modbury at Harraton Cross, signposted Bigbury-on-Sea; club is a further 5 miles from here.
Undulating seaside course.
18 holes, 6048 yards, S.S.S.69
Designed by J.H. Taylor.
Founded 1926
Visitors: welcome.
Green Fee: £20/day, half price after 5pm.
Societies: welcome by arrangement.
Catering: full facilities.
Hotels: Thurlestone; Cottage Hotel (Hope Cove).

A6 Bowood
☎(0840) 213017
Bowood Park, Valley Truckle, Camelford, Cornwall PL32 9RT
A39 through Camelford to Valley Truckle, then right onto B3266 Boscastle-Tintagel road, 1st left after garage towards Lanteglos; entrance 0.5 mile on left.
Parkland course with woodland and numerous ponds and lakes.
18 holes, 6692 yards, S.S.S.72
Founded June 1992
Visitors: welcome, starting times can be booked.
Green Fee: £23/round WD, £25/round WE; £30 for 36 holes Mon-Fri.
Societies: catered for by prior arrangement.
Catering: full facilities.
Driving range, practice areas.
Hotels: accomodation at Club.

A7 Bude and N Cornwall
☎(0288) 352006 Sec, 353176 Catering, 353635 Pro, 356855 Fax
Burn View, Bude, Cornwall EX23 8DA
A39, 1 minute from town centre.
Seaside links course.
18 holes, 6202 yards, S.S.S.70
Designed by Tom Dunn.
Founded 1891

Visitors: 1st tee reserved for members 8-9.30am, 12.30-2pm, 5-6.30pm; times may be booked in advance.
Green Fee: £20/day WD, £25/day WE & BH.
Societies: welcome; 1st tee can be reserved (Mon-Fri).
Catering: wide selection of meals available throughout the day.
Hotels: Camelot; Grosvenor; Falcon; Penarvor; Burn Court; Chough; Cliff; Langfield Manor; Stamford Hill.

A8 Budock Vean Hotel
☎(0326) 250288
Nr Mawnan Smith, Falmouth, Cornwall TR11 5LG
On main road between Falmouth and Helston; head for Mabe then go through Mawnan Smith; golf course approx 1.5 miles on right.
Undulating parkland course.
9 holes (18 tees), 5222 yards, S.S.S.65
Designed by James Braid, D. Cook and P.H. Whiteside.
Founded 1932
Visitors: welcome any time with h/cap certs; phone for start time am only.
Green Fee: £14/day Mon-Sat, £18/day Sun & BH.
Societies: on application.
Catering: snacks, lunch and table d'hôte or à la carte dinner.
Snooker, swimming, tennis.
Hotels: Budock Vean.

A9 Cape Cornwall G & CC
☎(0736) 788611
Cape Cornwall, St Just, Penzance, Cornwall TR19 7NL
A3071 to St Just-in-Penwith, left at memorial clock, club 1 mile on left.
Coastal parkland course.
18 holes, 5650 yards, S.S.S.68
Founded May 1990
Visitors: welcome except Sat and Sun between 8am and 11.30am.
Green Fee: £16/round, £25/day WD, £20/round, £25/day WE & BH.
Societies: welcome by arrangement any time.
Catering: full bar all week, lunch 12-2pm, dinner 7-10pm Wed-Sat

(winter), every day (summer).
Indoor heated pool, sauna, solarium, snooker, gym, practice area, putting green, on site accommodation.

A10 Carlyon Bay Hotel
☎(0726) 812304, 814228 Tee times
Carlyon Bay, St Austell, Cornwall PL25 3RD
Main Plymouth-Truro road 1 mile W of St Blazey.
Clifftop/parkland course.
18 holes, 6463 yards, S.S.S.71
Designed by J. Hamilton Stutt.
Founded 1926
Visitors: h/cap certs required; ring for starting times.
Green Fee: on application
Societies: welcome by arrangement.
Catering: full facilities.
Hotels: Carlyon Bay.

A11 China Fleet CC
☎(0752) 848668
Saltash, Cornwall PL12 6LJ
1 mile from Tamar Bridge, leave A38 before tunnel and follow signs.
Parkland course.
18 holes, 6551 yards, S.S.S.72
Designed by Martin Hawtree.
Founded June 1991
Visitors: by prior arrangement only.
Green Fee: £20 WD, £25 WE.
Societies: by arrangement with Sec (golf).
Catering: full facilities.
Driving range.
Hotels: accommodation available; off-peak packages.

A12 Chulmleigh
☎(0769) 80519
Leigh Rd, Chulmleigh, N Devon EX18 7BL
From Barnstaple follow "Tourist Route Exeter" signs; from Exeter follow A377 Crediton road, continue through Crediton, after approx 12 miles turn right into Chulmleigh.
Meadowland course.
18 holes, 1450 yards, S.S.S.54; winter (Dec-Mar), 9 holes, 2360 yards, S.S.S.56
Designed by J.W.D. Goodban OBE.
Founded 1976

Visitors: welcome.
Green Fee: £5/round, (£4 jnrs), £7.50/2 rounds (£6 jnrs), £10/day (£8 jnrs).
Societies: welcome by prior arrangement.
Catering: light snacks, licensed bar.
Hotels: Thelbridge Cross Inn; luxury apartment available at golf club, sleeps 6.

A13 Churston
☎(0803) 842751 Sec, 842218 Club, 845738 Fax
Churston, Nr Brixham, Devon TQ5 0LA
On A379 3 miles from Paignton.
Downland course overlooking Torbay.
18 holes, 6219 yards, S.S.S.70
Designed by H.S. Colt.
Founded 1890
Visitors: members of recognised golf clubs only; h/cap certs required.
Green Fee: £22/day WD, £27/day WE.
Societies: by arrangement.
Catering: bar and dining room facilities available all day.
Hotels: Broadsands Links.

A14 Clovelly G & CC
☎(0237) 431442, 431448
Woolsery, Bideford, Devon EX39 5RA
6 miles S of Clovelly off A39.
Parkland course.
9 holes (18 tees), 5648 yards, S.S.S.67
Designed by John Hepplewhite.
Founded 1987
Visitors: no restrictions except acceptable standard of golf.
Green Fee: apply for details.
Societies: by prior arrangement
Catering: bar and restaurant.
Swimming, snooker, pool, tennis, fishing, children's play area.
Hotels: lodge accommodation available on site.

A15 Dainton Park
☎(0803) 813812
Ipplepen, Newton Abbot, Devon TQ12 5TN
On A381 Newton Abbot-Totnes road.
Parkland course.
18 holes, 6207 yards, S.S.S.70
Designed by Adrian Stiff.
Founded 1993
Visitors: welcome, pay-as-you-play, booking advisable up to 4 days in advance; usual dress standards apply.

Green Fee: £12 WD, £15 WE.
Societies: welcome.
Catering: full facilities.

A16 Dartmouth G & CC
☎(080 421) 650, 628 Fax
Blackawton, Totnes, Devon TQ9 7DG
Off A3122 between Totnes and Dartmouth, 5 miles W of Dartmouth.
Moorland/parkland course.
18 holes, 7012 yards, Par 72; 9 holes, 2614 yards, Par 33
Designed by Jeremy Pern.
Founded 1992
Visitors: requested to book starting times at the club and produce h/cap certs.
Green Fee: apply for details.
Societies: Mon-Fri, phone for confirmation of date, start times, fees etc.
Catering: bar meals, restaurant, lounge/spike bar; function room for 240.
Hotels: Fingals (Dittisham).

A17 Dinnaton
☎(0752) 892512, 892452, 691288
Golf shop
Dinnaton Sporting and Country Club, Ivybridge, Devon PL21 9HU
At A38 Ivybridge follow Dinnaton Golf signs.
Parkland course.
9 hole, twin tee, 4100 yards, S.S.S.59
Founded 1989
Visitors: welcome at all times.
Green Fee: £10.
Societies: welcome at all times by arrangment.
Catering: Club bar, coffee lounge, Haywain restaurant.
Driving range, badminton, squash, volleyball, solarium, sauna, multi-gym, pool, tennis, snooker.
Hotels: phone above number for accommodation on site for up to 18.

A18 Downes Crediton
☎(0363) 773025 Sec, 773991 Clubhouse, 774464 Pro
The Clubhouse, Hookway, Crediton, Devon EX17 3PT
Off A377 Exeter-Crediton road, 8 miles NW of Exeter; turn off at Crediton railway station (by Shell garage), then left at crossroads towards Hookway.
Parkland/meadowland course with water features.
18 holes, 5920 yards, S.S.S.69
Founded 1976

Visitors: welcome, telephone Sec or Pro; h/cap cert required or proof of membership of recognised club.
Green Fee: £16 WD, £22 WE & BH (approx).
Societies: welcome by appointmenti.
Catering: coffee, breakfast, lunch, dinners available.
Hotels: Rosemont, Fair Park Guest House; Medland Manor.

A19 East Devon
☎(0395) 443370
North View Rd, Budleigh Salterton, Devon
5 miles E of Exmouth on A376.
Heathland seaside course.
18 holes, 6214 yards, S.S.S.70
Founded 1902
Visitors: welcome with letter of intro.
Green Fee: apply for details.
Societies: by arrangement.
Catering: full facilities every day from 10am.

A20 Elfordleigh G & CC
☎(0752) 336428 Pro, 348425 Sec
Colebrook, Plympton, Plymouth, Devon PL7 5EB
Off A38, 5 miles NE of Plymouth, 2 miles from Marsh Mills roundabout.
Undulating parkland course.
9 holes (18 tees), 5664 yards, S.S.S.67
Designed by J.H. Taylor.
Founded 1932
Visitors: weekdays unrestricted, weekends phone first; h/cap cert required.
Green Fee: on application
Societies: weekdays, phone first.
Catering: full facilities.
Swimming, snooker, squash, tennis etc.
Hotels: Elfordleigh.

A21 Exeter G & CC
☎(0392) 874139 Tel/Fax
Countess Wear, Exeter, Devon EX2 7AE
Topsham road off Countess Wear roundabout.
Parkland course.
18 holes, 6000 yards, S.S.S.69
Designed by James Braid.
Founded 1929
Visitors: welcome on weekdays with h/cap cert.
Green Fee: £22.
Societies: Thurs only by arrangement.

SALSTON MANOR HOTEL
Ottery St Mary, Near Exeter
Devon EX11 1RQ

A FIVE COURSE MENU IN EAST DEVON
Woodbury Park, Honiton, Sidmouth, Budleigh Salterton, Axe Cliff

A warm welcome awaits with En suite Rooms,
Indoor Heated Swimming Pool, Squash, Sauna, Solarium
and plenty of interest for Golfing Widows.

For Golfing Breaks, phone or Fax us now on: (0404) 815581

Catering: lunch and evening meals all week.
Snooker, indoor and outdoor swimming pools, tennis courts.
Hotels: Devon Motel; Countess Wear Lodge; Buckerell Lodge.

A22 **Falmouth**
☎(0326) 311262 Sec, 316229 Pro
Swanpool Road, Falmouth, Cornwall TR11 5BQ
0.5 mile W of Swanpool Beach, Falmouth, on road to Maenporth.
Seaside parkland course.
18 holes, 5680 yards, S.S.S.68
Founded 1928
Visitors: welcome, h/caps required.
Green Fee: £20/round, £25/day, £90/week; jnrs under 18 £10/round.
Societies: welcome by written application; min 4 weeks notice required.
Catering: bar, lunch and tea all week, evening meals by arrangement.
Practice fields.
Hotels: Royal Duchy; St Michael's; Penmere Manor; Greenlawns; Falmouth Beach; Meudon Vean; Park Grove; Falmouth: all offer reduced fees or free golf and golfing breaks/packages.

A23 **Fingle Glen**
☎(0647) 61817
Fingle Glen Family Golf Centre, Tedburn St Mary, Nr Exeter, Devon EX6 6AF
4 miles from Exter on A30 to Okehampton, 400 yards from Fingle Glen junction.
Public parkland course.
9 holes, 2466 yards, S.S.S.63
Designed by W. Pile.
Founded July 1989
Visitors: welcome.
Green Fee: £7 (9 holes), £12.50 (18 holes) WD; £9 (9 holes), £14 (18 holes) WE.
Societies: welcome.
Catering: bar, lounge, restaurant, 10am-10pm.
Driving range, fishing by arrangement.
Hotels: own 9-bed hotel; golfing breaks/packages available.

A24 **Great Torrington**
☎(0805) 22229, 472792 Sec
Weare Trees, Torrington, Devon EX38 7EZ
1 mile from Torrington on Weare Giffard road.
Undulating commonland course.
9 holes, 4418 yards, S.S.S.61
Founded 1932
Visitors: welcome except Sat and Sun am.
Green Fee: £12.50 WD, £14 WE & BH.
Societies: by arrangement except Sat and Sun am.
Catering: full meals by arrangement.

A25 **Highbullen Hotel**
☎(0769) 540561
Chittlehamholt, Umberleigh, Devon EX19 8TB
10 mins W on A361 from South Molton.
Parkland course.
9 holes, 2210 yards, S.S.S.29
Designed by Hugh Neil.
Founded 1960
Visitors: welcome.
Green Fee: £8/day.
Catering: full hotel facilities.
Full leisure facilities.
Hotels: Highbullen.

A26 **Holsworthy**
☎(0409) 253177
Kilatree, Holsworthy, N Devon, EX22 6XU
1.5 miles W of Holsworthy on A3072 Bude road.
Parkland course.
18 holes, 6059 yards, S.S.S.69
Founded 1937
Visitors: welcome except Sun am.
Green Fee: £15 WD, £20 WE & BH.
Societies: by arrangement.
Catering: bar; dining facilities.
Practice area.
Hotels: Coles Mill; Court Barn (Clawton).

A27 **Honiton**
☎(0404) 44422 Sec, 42943 Pro, 47167 bar and catering
Middlehills, Honiton, Devon EX14 8TR
2 miles S of Honiton on minor road from town centre, past railway

station and up steep hill signposted Northleigh and Seaton; caravans should approach from A35.
Parkland course.
18 holes, 5940 yards, S.S.S.68
Founded 1896
Visitors: members of a recognised golf club welcome any time except competition days and Bank Holidays.
Green Fee: £18/day WD, £23 WE.
Societies: Thurs
Catering: lunch, high tea and dinner, except Sun.
Touring caravan park for golfers.
Hotels: Honiton Motel; Heathfield.

A28 **Hurdwick**
☎(0822) 612746
Tavistock Hamlets, Tavistock, Devon PL19 8PZ
1 mile N of Tavistock on road to Brentnor.
Parkland course.
18 holes, 4553 yards, S.S.S.62
Designed by Hawtree.
Founded Aug 1990
Visitors: welcome.
Green Fee: £14/round, £20/day WD; £16/round, £25/day WE & BH.
Societies: Tues-Fri inclusive.
Catering: bar and bar snacks.
Hotels: Bedford (Tavistock); Castle Inn (Lydford).

A29 **Ilfracombe**
☎(0271) 862176, 367731 Fax
Hele Bay, Ilfracombe, N Devon EX34 9RT
On A399 Ilfracombe to Combe Martin road.
Undulating heathland course with views over sea and moors.
18 holes, 5893 yards, S.S.S.69
Designed by T.K. Weir
Founded 1892
Visitors: welcome; start sheets May-Oct; h/cap certs preferred.
Green Fee: £17/day WD, £20/day WE & BH; £75/5 day ticket (Mon-Fri).
Societies: by arrangement with Sec.
Catering: bar; full time catering, rebuilt clubhouse. Pool tables.
Hotels: Collingdale, Darnley, Floyd, Wembley, Abbeydale, Maranatha, St Helier, Avalon, Seven Hills, Woodlands

A30 Isles of Scilly
☎(0720) 22692
St Mary's, Isles of Scilly, TR21 0NF
1.5 miles from Hugh Town in St
Mary's.
Moorland/seaside course.
9 holes, 6001 yards, S.S.S.69
Designed by Horace Hutchinson.
Founded 1904
Visitors: welcome Mon-Sat.
Green Fee: £14.
Catering: available.

A31 Killiow
☎(0872) 70246
Killiow, Kea, Truro, Cornwall TR3 6AG
Leave Truro on A39 Truro/Falmouth
road; turn right at 1st roundabout 3
miles from Truro, clearly signposted
thereafter.
Picturesque parkland course.
18 holes, 3542 yards, S.S.S.57
Founded 1987
Visitors: welcome at all times;
course restricted for members' use
until 10.30am weekends and Bank
Holidays; in main season advisable to
ring for availability.
Green Fee: apply for details.
Hotels: Hospitality Hotels (St Agnes).

A32 La Moye
☎(0534) 43401 Sec/Manager,
47166 Course Ranger, 43130 Pro
La Moye, St Brelade, Jersey, Channel
Islands
From airport turn right at crossroads,
follow main road to main junction,
turn right at crossroads; club about 1
mile down road, private lane on right.
Links course.
18 holes, 6741 yards, S.S.S.72
Founded 1902
Visitors: welcome 9.30-11.30am,
2.30-4pm except competition days;
must have h/cap cert.
Green Fee: £35/round, £55/day
(incl. lunch).
Societies: on request.
Catering: full restaurant facilities.
Practice ground, indoor practice net.
Hotels: Atlantic; L'Horizon; Le
Chalet.

A33 Lanhydrock
☎(0208) 73600, 77325 Fax
Lostwithiel Rd, Bodmin, Cornwall
PL30 5AQ.
1 mile S of Bodmin, easy access from
B3268 via A38/A30 Bodmin/Liskeard
road.
Parkland course.

18 holes, 6142 yards, S.S.S.69
Designed by J. Hamilton Stutt.
Founded 1990
Visitors: welcome.
Green Fee: on application.
Societies: welcome on application
(weekend dates available).
Catering: full facilities.
Driving range (opening 1994).

A34 Launceston
☎(0566) 773442
St Stephens, Launceston, Cornwall
PL15 8HF
1 mile N of Launceston on Bude road
(B3254).
Parkland course.
18 holes, 6407 yards, S.S.S.71
Designed by J. Hamilton Stutt.
Founded 1927
Visitors: welcome weekdays by
arrangement.
Green Fee: £20.
Societies: welcome Mon-Fri by
arrangement.
Catering: available by arrangement.
Hotels: White Hart; Eagle House.

A35 Les Mielles Golf Centre
☎(0534) 82787
The Mount, Valde la Mare, St Ouen's,
Jersey, Channel Islands
Located in the middle of St Ouen's
Bay.
Public seaside course
12 holes, 4,200 yards, S.S.S.60
Founded 1976
Visitors: welcome.
Green Fee: apply for details.
Societies: welcome weekdays by
prior arrangement.
Catering: cafeteria.
Driving range.
Hotels: Lobster Pot; La Place.

A36 Libbaton
☎(0769) 60269, 60167 Pro
High Bickington, Umberleigh,
N Devon EX37 9BS
On B3217 1 mile through High
Bickington towards Winkleigh,
adjacent to A377 Barnstaple to
Crediton road.
Parkland course.
18 holes, 6494 yards, S.S.S.72
Founded 1988
Visitors: welcome.
Green Fee: £12/round, £15/day WD;
£15/round, £18/day WE.
Societies: welcome Mon, Tues,
Wed, Fri; society package (golf and
food) £27.50 per head.

Catering: food all day, bar except
Sun when licensing laws apply.
Driving range, trout fishing.
Hotels: Bedford House; Northcote
Manor.

A37 Looe
☎(050 34) 239
Bin Down, Looe, Cornwall PL13 1PX
3 miles E of Looe.
Downland/parkland course.
18 holes, 5940 yards, S.S.S.68
Designed by Harry Vardon.
Founded 1934
Visitors: welcome 7 days per week.
Green Fee: on application, 5 and 7
day tickets available.
Societies: welcome, arranged to suit
requirements.
Catering: refreshments all day.

A38 Lostwithiel G & CC
☎(0208) 873550
Lower Polscoe, Lostwithiel, Cornwall
PL22 0HQ
On A390 12 miles W of Liskeard,
signposted.
Parkland course.
18 holes, 6098 yards, S.S.S.71
Designed by Stewart Wood R.I.B.A.
Founded 1991
Visitors: welcome with current
h/cap cert; booking advised for
starting time.
Green Fee: apply for details.
Societies: most welcome, not
weekends or Bank Holidays.
Catering: bar and bar snacks all day;
restaurant evenings and Sun lunch.
Tennis.
Hotels: Lostwithiel G & CC on
course; golf inclusive bargain breaks.

A39 Manor House Hotel
☎(0647) 40355
Moretonhampstead, Newton Abbot,
Devon TQ13 8RE
M5-A30-A382 or M5-B3212, on
Dartmoor National Park, 17 miles
from Exeter.
Parkland/moorland course.
18 holes, 6016 yards, S.S.S.69
Designed by J.F. Abercromby.
Founded 1934
Visitors: welcome by arrangement.
Green Fee: £22.50/round.
Societies: catered for 7 days by
arrangement.
Catering: full facilities.
Fishing, game and lake, croquet,
tennis, snooker, driving range, Par 3
6 hole practice ground.
Hotels: Manor House Hotel and GC.

Lanteglos Country House Hotel

The Lanteglos Country House Hotel has long been established as one of the major golfing centres in Cornwall with a very real understanding and appreciation of the holiday golfer's requirements.

Tucked away in a secluded valley in one of the most beautiful and unspoilt parts of Cornwall, yet situated on the very edge of the superb Bowood Park Golf Club, our aim is to provide quality accommodation, good food and friendly service in a relaxed and enjoyable atmosphere.

We have special arrangements and concessionary rates at most of the leading courses – ranging from glorious parkland courses such as Bowood, Launceston and Lanhydrock to some of the finest links outside Scotland including St Enodoc, Trevose and Perrenporth the

ultimate challenge in the south west of the Jack Nicklaus Championship course at St Mellion.

You can choose from our golf packages or for any length of stay with a golf itinary tailor made to suit your own requirements. We make all the tee reservations for you so all you have to do is just turn up to play whether it is a party of two or a society of 22.

On the days when perhaps you want a rest from breaking par, there is an abundance of other attractions: golden beaches, picture postcard fishing villages, lovely gardens and great historic houses, coastal and moorland walks, not to mention the facilities of the hotel which include; squash and tennis courts, swimming pool, a snooker lounge and a delightful conservatory lounge.

Lanteglos Country House Hotel & Villas Ltd
Camelford, Cornwall PL32 9RF
Tel & Fax: (0840) 213551

A40 **Merlin**
☎(0841) 540222, (0637) 881057 Fax
Mawgan Porth, Newquay, TR8 4AD
Mawgan Porth to St Eval road.
Links type course.
9 holes, 2300 yards, S.S.S.32
Designed by Ross Oliver
Founded July 1991
Visitors: welcome any time.
Green Fee: £6 (9 holes), £9 (18 holes).
Societies: parties of 12 or more by arrangement.
Catering: at Merrymoor Inn and Falcon Inn.
Floodlit driving range.
Hotels: White Lodge, Tredragon (Golf packages).

A41 **Mortehoe & Woolacombe**
☎(0271) 870225 Course Owners, 870745 Sec
Easewell, Mortehoe, N Devon
Take Mortehoe turning on main Mullacott Cross to Woolacombe road; course approx 1 mile on right, just before village of Mortehoe.
Open parkland course, views of sea from every tee and green.
9 holes, S.S.S.63

Designed by Hans Ellis.
Founded Jan 1992
Visitors: welcome at all times; no restrictions.
Green Fee: £6 (9 holes), £10 (18 holes).
Societies: welcome at all times, terms by negotiation.
Catering: full catering March-Oct, other times by negotiation.
Practice nets, putting green, indoor swimming pool.
Hotels: Woolacombe Bay; The Cleave; camping facilities on site.

A42 **Mullion**
☎(0326) 240685 Sec, 240276 Clubhouse, 241176 Pro
Cury, Helston, Cornwall TR12 7BP
5 miles from Helston on A3083 Lizard road.
Links and clifftop course.
18 holes, 6022 yards, S.S.S.69
Founded 1895
Visitors: welcome, h/cap required.
Green Fee: £20/day £70 5 days
Societies: welcome.
Catering: bar, bar snacks, restaurant.
Hotels: Polurrian; Mullion Cove; Mullion Holiday Park; Cornwallis (St Ives).

A43 **Newquay**
☎(0637) 874354 Tel/Fax, 874830
Tower Rd, Newquay, Cornwall TR7 1LT
From ring road down Tower Rd to end, adjacent to Fistral beach.
Seaside course.
18 holes, 6136 yards, S.S.S.69
Designed by H.S. Colt.
Founded 1890
Visitors: welcome.
Green Fee: £20 WD & WE
Societies: weekdays, min 12.
Catering: full facilities.
Tennis, snooker, gym.
Hotels: Bristol; Barrowfield; Palma Nova.

A44 **Newton Abbot (Stover)**
☎(0626) 52460
Bovey Rd, Newton Abbot, S Devon TQ12 6QQ
On A382 Newton Abbot-Bovey Tracey road, N of Newton Abbot.
Parkland course.
18 holes, 5899 yards, S.S.S.68
Designed by James Braid
Founded 1931
Visitors: must be introduced or have proof of membership of recognised club.

Green Fee: £22/day.
Societies: Thurs only, minimum 24.
Catering: full catering daily from 11am.
Hotels: Edgemoor, Dolphin (Bovey Tracey).

A45 Northbrook
☎(0392) 57436, 460546 Fax
Topsham Rd, Exeter, Devon EX2 6EU
From M5 junction 30 take A379; at 1st roundabout take 3rd exit onto B3182 Topsham road, course 0.5 mile on left.
Public, wooded parkland course.
18 holes, 1078 yards, S.S.S.54
Founded 1968
Visitors: open to all, Pay-as-you-Play.
Green Fee: £1.65/round (clubs provided).
Catering: vending and confectionery.

A46 Okehampton
☎(0837) 52113
Okehampton, Devon EX20 1EF
A30 to Okehampton centre from where club is clearly signposted.
Undulating moorland course.
18 holes, 5307 yards, S.S.S.67
Founded 1913
Visitors: welcome, no athletes' shorts, ankle socks or denim.
Green Fee: on application, special winter rates.
Societies: welcome.
Catering: available.

A47 Padbrook Park (Cullompton)
☎(0884) 38286
Padbrook Park, Cullompton, Devon EX15 1RU
1 mile from M5 Junction 28.
Parkland course; pay-as-you-play.
9 holes (double tees), 6108 yards, S.S.S.70.
Designed by Bob Sandow
Founded 1991
Visitors: welcome at all times.
Green Fee: £7 (9 holes), £10 (18 holes), WD; £8 (9 holes), £16 (18 holes) WE.
Societies: welcome by prior arrangement.
Catering: full bar and catering all day.
Full practice facilities, 3-rink indoor bowling arena, tennis, outdoor pool, fishing lake and nature trail.
Hotels: can be arranged through manager.

A48 Perranporth
☎(0872) 573701 Sec, 572454, 572317 Pro
Budnic Hill, Perranporth, Cornwall TR6 0AB
A3075 from Newquay then B3285; club on fringe of town adjacent to beach.
Links course with sea views.
18 holes, 6208 yards, S.S.S.70
Designed by James Braid.
Founded 1929
Visitors: welcome but ring before arrival.
Green Fee: £20/day WD; £25 WE.
Societies: welcome.
Catering: 7 days a week from 7am.
Hotels: Beach Dunes; Dunsmore.

A49 Praa Sands
☎(0736) 763445, 763399 Fax
Germoe Crossroads, Praa Sands, Penzance, Cornwall TR20 9TQ
7 miles E of Penzance on A394.
Scenic seaside parkland course.
9 holes, 4104 yards, S.S.S.60
Founded May 1971
Visitors: welcome 8.30am-11pm any day except Fri after 5pm and Sun am.
Green Fee: £14/round (£9 with member).
Societies: welcome by prior arrangement.
Catering: open all day for meals or snacks. Pool, darts.
Hotels: Tarbert, Mount Prospect (Penzance); Lobster Pot (Mousehole); Praa Sands.

A50 Radnor Golf Centre
☎(0209) 211059
Radnor Road, Redruth, Cornwall.
2 miles NE of Redruth, signposted from A3047 – old Redruth by-pass and North Country Cross roads.
Public heathland type course created on derelict land.
9 holes Par 3, 1326 yards.
Designed by Gordon Wallbank.
Founded 1988
Visitors: no restrictions but own clubs required; phone first.
Green Fee: £4.50 (9 holes), £7 (18 holes).
Catering: bar.
Driving range, indoor ski training machine, snooker.

A51 Royal Guernsey
☎(0481) 47022
L'Ancresse Vale, Guernsey, Channel Islands

3 miles from St Peter Port.
Seaside course.
18 holes, 6206 yards, S.S.S.70
Designed by Mackenzie Ross.
Founded 1890
Visitors: not after 12am Thurs and Sat; not Sun: must have h/cap cert.
Green Fee: £25/day (£15 with member).
Societies: small societies on application between Oct and Mar.
Catering: morning coffee, afternoon tea, lunch, evening meals Tues, Wed, Thurs, Fri and Sat.
Driving range, snooker.
Hotels: Pembroke; L'Ancresse Lodge.

A52 Royal Jersey
☎(0534) 854416, 851042 Sec, Steward and Members, 854684 Fax
Grouville, Jersey, Channel Islands
4 miles E of St Helier on road to Gorey.
Seaside course.
18 holes, 6059 yards, S.S.S.70
Founded 1878
Visitors: welcome weekdays after 10am, weekends & Bank Holidays after 2.30pm (BST), 12.30pm (GMT).
Green Fee: £30 WD, £35 WE.
Societies: small parties only.
Catering: full facilities by prior arrangement with Steward.
Hotels: Beachcomber; Grouville Bay.

A53 Royal Naval Air Station Culdrose
☎(0326) 574121 extn 2413/7543
RNAS Culdrose, Helston, Cornwall TR12 8QY
2.5 miles from Helston on Lizard road.
Part of military airfield; members only.
11 holes (18 tees), S.S.S.71
Founded 1962
Visitors: through Sec or as guest of member, daily play restricted to weekends and leave periods.
Green Fee: £6.

A54 Royal North Devon
☎(0237) 473817 Sec, 473824 Clubhouse
Westward Ho!, Bideford, Devon EX39 1HD
From Northam village take the road down Bone Hill past the P.O. keeping left; clubhouse is visible as you come down the hill.
Links course.
18 holes, 6449 yards, S.S.S.72

Designed by Tom Morris.
Founded 1864
Visitors: welcome; booking required.
Green Fee: on application.
Societies: by booking.
Catering: full facilities.
Snooker.
Hotels: Culloden House; Durrant House; Anchorage.

A55 St Austell
☎(0726) 74756 Sec, 72649 Clubhouse
Tregongeeves Lane, St Austell, Cornwall PL26 7DS
On A390 St Austell-Truro road, 1 mile W of St Austell; the Tregongeeves Lane junction is clearly signposted just below St Mewan school.
Heathland/parkland course.
18 holes, 6089 yards, S.S.S.69
Founded 1911
Visitors: welcome with reservation; must be club members and hold h/cap certs.
Green Fee: £15/round/day, £18 WE.
Societies: catered for weekdays by arrangement.
Catering: full service; hot meals, bar snacks daily; evening meals available, phone first.
Hotels: Cliff Head; Carlyon Bay.

A56 St Clements
☎(0534) 21938
Jersey Recreation Grounds Co Ltd, Graeve d'azette, St Clements, Jersey, Channel Islands JE2 6QN
Close to St Helier.
Public meadowland course
9 holes, 2244 yards, Par 30
Founded 1913
Visitors: open to public every day except Sun am
Green Fee: £12 (18 holes).
Societies: any day except Sun am.
Catering: buffet bar and restaurant.
Tennis (16 courts), bowling, putting green etc.
Hotels: Hotel de Normandy

A57 St Enodoc
☎(0208 86) 3216 Sec, 2402 Pro
Rock, Wadebridge, Cornwall PL27 6LB
From Wadebridge take B3314 Port Isaac road for 3 miles and then turn left to Rock.
Classic links course.
Church Course, 18 holes, 6207 yards, S.S.S.70; Holywell Course, 18 holes, 4166 yards, S.S.S.61

Designed by James Braid.
Founded 1890
Visitors: h/cap cert required for Church course, 24 max.
Green Fee: Church course, £22/round, £35/day WD; £27/round, £40/day WE: Holywell course, £12/round, £18/day WD & WE.
Societies: all year round, but avoid public holidays and main holiday periods.
Catering: full facilities available every day.
Practice ground with driving, bunker and putting facilities.
Hotels: St Enodoc; St Moritz; Bodare; Port Gaverne.

A58 St Mellion International
☎(0579) 50101, 50116 Fax
St Mellion, Saltash, Cornwall PL12 6SD
3 miles S of Callington on A388.
Parkland course.
Nicklaus course, 18 holes, 6626 yards, S.S.S.72; Old course, 18 holes, 5927 yards, S.S.S.68
Designed by Jack Nicklaus (International course), J. Hamilton Stutt (Old Course).
Founded 1976
Visitors: welcome.
Green Fee: on application.
Societies: welcome.
Catering: restaurant, coffee shop, grill room; banqueting, conferences. Swimming pool, sauna, solarium, mulitgym, badminton, tennis, snooker,
Hotels: St Mellion.

A59 St Pierre Park Hotel
☎(0481) 727039, 728282 Hotel
Rohais, St Peter Port, Guernsey, Channel Islands
1 mile W of St Peter Port on Rohais road.
Hilly course with water hazards.
9 holes, 1500 yards, S.S.S.48
Designed by Tony Jacklin.
Founded 1984
Visitors: welcome except during competitions (Sun am).
Green Fee: £10 (9 holes), £17 (18 holes) WD; £12 (9 holes), £20 (18 holes) WE; special rates for Hotel guests.
Societies: by arrangement.
Catering: full facilities at St Pierre Park Hotel.
Driving range, indoor swimming pool, health suite, etc.
Hotels: St Pierre Park.

A60 Saunton
☎(0271) 812436, 814241 Fax
Saunton, Nr Braunton, N Devon EX33 1LG
On B3231 from Braunton to Croyde, 7 miles from Barnstaple.
Traditional links course.
East, 18 holes, 6708 yards, S.S.S.73; West, 18 holes, 6356 yards, S.S.S.71
Designed by Herbert Fowler (East), Frank Pennink (West).
Founded 1897
Visitors: must be members of clubs with h/cap certs.
Green Fee: £28/day WD, £33/day WE & BH.
Societies: any time booked in advance.
Catering: full restaurant all day.
Hotels: Saunton Sands; Kittiwell House; Preston House; Croyde Bay House.

A61 Sidmouth
☎(0395) 513451 Sec, 513023 Club, 516407 Pro
Cotmaton Road, Peak Hill, Sidmouth, Devon EX10 8SX
Take Exeter Station Rd to Woodlands Hotel, then right on Cotmaton Rd.
Undulating parkland course.
18 holes, 5109 yards, S.S.S.65
Founded Oct 1889
Visitors: welcome by arrangement with Sec.
Green Fee: £18 any day.
Societies: by arrangement.
Catering: no catering Mon; all-day bar Sat.

A62 Staddon Heights
☎(0752) 402475
Staddon Heights, Plymstock, Plymouth, Devon PL9 9SP
Leave Plymouth city on Plymstock road; club is 5 miles S of city near Royal Navy aerial towers.
Seaside course.
18 holes, 5869 yards, S.S.S.68
Founded 1895
Visitors: welcome weekdays with h/cap cert.
Green Fee: £15 WD, £20 WE & BH.
Societies: weekdays.
Catering: every day.

A63 Tavistock
☎(0822) 612049 Clubhouse, 612344 Sec
Down Rd, Tavistock, Devon PL19 9AQ
Take Whitchurch road, turn into Down Rd, and onto Whitchurch Down.
Moorland course.

TREVOSE GOLF & COUNTRY CLUB
Constantine Bay, Padstow, North Cornwall PL28 8JB
Telephone: (0841) 520208 Fax: (0841) 521057

Trevose offers not only great Golf (Championship 18 hole Course, a 9 hole full length (3,100 yds) par 35 plus a 9 hole Short Course) but also; a first class Club House and Restaurant, 3 hard all weather Tennis Courts, a heated outdoor Swimming Pool in the summer, a Childrens Games Room and a Gift Shop. Accommodation is available in Bungalows, Chalets, Luxury Flats and Dormy Suites. Send for our detailed full colour brochure.

---

18 holes, 6250 yards, S.S.S.70
Founded 1890
Visitors: welcome, telephone in advance.
Green Fee: £17 WD, £22 WE & BH.
Societies: by arrangement.
Catering: lunch, bar snacks, evening meals.
Hotels: Bedford; Moorland Links; Arundel Arms.

A64 Tehidy Park
☎(0209) 842208
Nr Camborne, Cornwall TR14 0HH
Off A302, 2 miles NE of Camborne on the Portreath road.
Parkland course.
18 holes, 6241 yards, S.S.S.70
Founded 1922
Visitors: h/cap cert required.
Green Fee: £21/round, £27/day WD; £26/round, £32/day WE & BH.
Societies: weekdays only.
Catering: full range bar snacks, à la carte restaurant mornings and evenings. Snooker.
Hotels: Penventon, Glenfeadon, Old Shire Inn, Tyacks.

A65 Teignmouth
☎(0626) 774194 Sec, 772894 Pro, 773614 Club
Exeter Rd, Teignmouth, Devon TQ14 9NY
2 miles from Teignmouth on Exeter road B3192.
Moorland course.
18 holes, 6142 yards, S.S.S.69
Designed by Dr Alister Mackenzie.
Founded 1924
Visitors: must be members of a club and have h/cap cert.
Green Fee: £22 WD & WE.
Societies: by appointment, not weekends or Wed.
Catering: full service every day.
Hotels: London; Venn Farm.

A66 Thurlestone
☎(0548) 560405, 560715 Pro
Thurlestone, Nr Kingsbridge, S Devon TQ7 3NZ
Take Thurlestone turning from A379 Plymouth-Salcombe road; club situated 4 miles S of Kingsbridge.
Downland course.
18 holes, 6337 yards, S.S.S.70
Founded 1897
Visitors: must produce a current h/cap cert from recognised club.
Green Fee: £24/day any day.
Societies: not catered for.
Catering: full facilities all day.
12 tennis courts (3 hard, 9 grass).
Hotels: Thurlestone.

A67 Tiverton
☎(0884) 252187
Post Hill, Tiverton, Devon EX16 4NE
5 miles from junction 27 on M5 towards Tiverton on A373; take 1st exit left on dual carriageway through Samford Peverell to Halberton.
Parkland/meadowland course.
18 holes, 6263 yards, S.S.S.71
Designed by James Braid.
Founded 1931
Visitors: letter of intro. or h/cap cert required; no visitors Wed pm, weekends or Bank Holidays, or during Championship, Club and Open meetings.
Green Fee: £20 WD, £26 WE.
Societies: no, unless already a standard fixture.
Catering: lunch, teas available.
Hotels: Tiverton; Green Headland; Hartnoll.

A68 Torquay
☎(0803) 314591
Petitor Rd, St Marychurch, Torquay, Devon TQ1 4QF
N of Torquay on A379 Teignmouth road, on outskirts of town.

Parkland course.
18 holes, 6192 yards, S.S.S.70
Founded 1910
Visitors: welcome, h/cap certs required.
Green Fee: £20 WD, £25 WE & BH.
Societies: by arrangement.
Catering: available daily except Mon.

A69 Tregenna Castle Hotel
☎(0736) 795254
St Ives, Cornwall TR26 2DE
In grounds of Tregenna Castle Hotel, signposted to left just before St Ives on A3074 from Hayle.
Parkland course
18 holes, 3549 yards, S.S.S.57
Founded 1982
Visitors: welcome; ring for tee times.
Green Fee: apply for details.
Societies: welcome by prior arrangement.
Catering: full bar and restaurant facilities at hotel.
Tennis, squash, badminton, swimming etc.
Hotels: Tregenna Castle.

A70 Treloy
☎(0637) 878554
Newquay, Cornwall TR7 4JN
On A3059 St Columb Major to Newquay road, 3 miles from Newquay.
Public heathland/parkland course.
9 holes, 2143 yards, S.S.S.31
Designed by M.R.M. Sandow
Founded 1991
Visitors: welcome.
Green Fee: £7.50 (9 holes), £11.50 (18 holes).
Societies: welcome.
Hotels: Barrowfield, Hotel California (Newquay); White Lodge, Tredragon (Mawgan Porth).

Thurlestone

Thurlestone is by the sea but it is not a course of mighty dunes. With the exception of the 1st hole, its character is best described as clifftop and downland. It is certainly exposed to the wind and that is its main defence. At the same time, an elevated setting is its greatest attraction, with views that are as fine and varied as any in the land.

The approach, through narrow, high-hedged lanes, so typical of many small towns in Devon, has a timeless air about it, reinforced by the excellent hotel and by the simple welcome to the Golf Club, which has kept hospitable doors open since the last century.

There is challenge here as well as a welcome, although there are no impossible carries or a series of lakes to engulf a dozen balls. Old fashioned it may be in parts but that is its strength.

Not that it all dates back to the age of hickory when a brewer, a doctor and a solicitor discussed plans for a course on an area of scrub, gorse and brambles alive with rabbits. Nine holes was the limit then, with a stone wall marking the western boundary — rather like the one at Prestwick which marked the end of the famous old 12-hole course. No doubt there was fierce debate at Thurlestone as to whether to obtain land beyond the wall to extend to 18 holes; but the progressives won the argument, even if the acquisition introduced an altogether different type of golf. Further land was obtained fairly recently to complete the course as it is today; but it is a curious fact that the 1st hole remains the only one at sea level.

It provides an unusual opening, a short par 4 from a high tee above the clubhouse, the drive having to cross the road and avoid a number of bunkers. There is then an awkward pitch to a green broader than it is deep, a green that can on occasions be driven by those with the necessary daring.

Ambitions on the first tee are inclined to be more modest and Thurlestone's 1st might be a more enticing hole later in the round, but the drive at the 2nd has the face of a hill to scale and must be soundly struck to have any hope of a four. The force of the wind is increasingly felt, and rare are the days in the year when there is none.

Flighting the ball well is the key to success at the seaside and nowhere is that truer than on the short 3rd which heads towards the point of the cliff. By now, the full flavour of the setting can be experienced, the splendour of the Devon coast in both directions, the quaintly shaped rock on Thurlestone beach and always sight and sound of the sea.

The first seven holes are not overlong but they are the best and most varied in terms of strokemaking and appeal. After a splendid par four at the 4th, consecutive short holes at the 5th and 6th call for widely differing tee shots. At the 5th, the emphasis is on power, on the 6th it is more a case of art and judgement to clear the bunker and hold the green.

An inviting drive on the 7th is the prelude to a demanding second beside the original boundary wall but, as a further climb takes us on to more open territory, the yardages on the card show a marked uplift. The second nine is over 800 yards longer than the first.

Stout hitting, and the stouter the better, is increasingly the order of the day, the 9th and 11th nevertheless falling within the range of most in two shots. The line from the tee at the 9th is down the left while the revised 11th offers advantage from that side as well. However, the position of the 11th green is the most spectacular of all, Bigbury Bay and Burgh Island adding a new dimension to the panorama.

Starting with the 12th, the longest par 4, the finish poses stern demands with three par 5s in the last six holes and a par 3 of over 200 yards. It lacks the charm of the earlier holes, but the 17th is an attractive short hole in spite of being encircled by bunkers and the 18th poses the threat of out of bounds in the gardens of houses down the left. But it is hardly likely that their occupants would resent any intrusion, for they look out on a truly memorable sight that is, mercifully, unchanging.

A71 Trevose Country Club

☎(0841) 520208
Constantine Bay, Padstow, Cornwall
PL28 8JB
4 miles W of Padstow off B3276.
Seaside links course.
18 holes, 6608 yards, S.S.S.71; 9
holes, 3108 yards, Par 35; short
course 1357 yards, Par 29
Designed by H.S. Colt.
Founded 1925
Visitors: welcome; 3 and 4 ball
matches restricted; phone first.
Green Fee: on application
Societies: any time except July-Sept.
Catering: all meals, good restaurant.
Outdoor pool, tennis, snooker.
Hotels: Treglos; own self-catering
accommodation available.

A72 Truro

☎(0872) 78684
Treliske, Truro, Cornwall TR1 3LG
From Truro follow A390 to Redruth,
after 2 miles turn right at small
roundabout; course signposted.
Undulating parkland course.
18 holes, 5357 yards, S.S.S.66
Designed by Colt, Alison & Morrison.
Founded 1937
Visitors: welcome, phone to
ascertain any tee reservations.
Green Fee: £18/day/round WD, £22
WE & BH, (half price with member).
Societies: welcome except
weekends and Tues.
Catering: full bar and restaurant
facilities every day.
Snooker.
Hotels: special arrangements with
Hospitality Hotels.

A73 Warren

☎(0626) 862255
Dawlish Warren, Dawlish, Devon EX7
0NF
Take A379 from Exeter to Dawlish
Warren.
Links course.
18 holes, 5968 yards, S.S.S.69
Founded 1892
Visitors: welcome with h/cap certs.
Green Fee: £21 WD, £24 WE
Societies: weekdays by
arrangement with Sec.
Catering: bar, snacks, meals daily.
Hotels: Langstone Cliff; Dawlish
Warren.

A74 Waterbridge

☎(0363) 85111
Down St Mary, Nr Crediton, Devon
EX17 5LG

Off A377 Barnstaple-Exeter road
between Down St Mary and
Copplestone.
Parkland course.
9 holes, 3908 yards, Par 62
Designed by David Taylor.
Founded July 1992
Visitors: welcome; times bookable
24 hrs in advance.
Green Fee: £5 (9 holes), £9 (18
holes) WD; £6.50 (9 holes), £12 (18
holes) WE & BH.
Societies: welcome.
Catering: light snacks, meals by
arrangement.
Hotels: Fox & Hounds (Eggesford).

A75 West Cornwall

☎(0736) 753401 Sec, 753177 Pro,
753319 Members
Lelant, St Ives, Cornwall TR26 3DZ
Take A30 to Hayle, then A3074 to St
Ives.
Seaside links course.
18 holes, 5884 yards, S.S.S.69
Founded Dec 1889
Visitors: h/cap cert required.
Green Fee: £20/day WD, £25/day
WE.
Societies: on application to Sec.
Catering: lunch and dinner except
Mon. Snooker.
Hotels: Badger Inn (Lelant); Pedn
Olva (St Ives); Boskerris (Carbis Bay).

A76 Whitsand Bay Hotel Golf and Country Club

☎(0503) 30276 Club, 30329 Fax
Portwrinkle, Torpoint, Cornwall PL11
3BU
On B3247, 6 miles off A38 from
Plymouth.
Clifftop course.
18 holes, 5800 yards, S.S.S.69
Designed by William Fernie of Troon.
Founded 1905
Visitors: welcome, h/cap cert
required.
Green Fee: £15 WD, £17.50 WE,
residents £35/week.
Societies: welcome all year by
arrangement.
Catering: 2 bars, 3 restaurants.
Indoor swimming pool, sauna,
solarium etc.
Hotels: Whitsand Bay; special golf
rates for residents.

A77 Woodbury Park Golf & Country Club

☎(0395) 233382, 233384
Woodbury Castle, Woodbury, Exeter
EX5 1JJ

From M5 junction 30 take A3052
Sidmouth road, turn right onto
B3180, after approx 1 mile turn right
to Woodbury Salterton, then
immediately turn right to course.
Public parkland/moorland/heathland
course.
Oaks course: 18 holes, 6707 yards,
S.S.S.72; Acorns course: 9 holes,
2297 yards, Par 32.
Designed by J. Hamilton Stutt
Founded 1992
Visitors: welcome, h/cap cert
required.
Green Fee: 18 hole course,
£20/round WD, £25/round WE;
9 hole course, £8/round WD,
£9/round WE.
Societies: welcome at all times by
arrangement.
Catering: catering available, 2 bars.
Driving range, practice area.

A78 Wrangaton

☎(0364) 73229 Sec, 72161 Pro
Wrangaton, South Brent, S Devon
TQ10 9HJ
Turn off A38 between South Brent
and Bittaford at Wrangaton Post
Office.
Moorland/parkland course.
18 holes, 6041 yards, S.S.S.69
Designed by Donald Steel.
Founded 1895
Visitors: welcome; h/cap cert or
proof of competence required.
Green Fee: £16/day WD, £20/day
WE & BH.
Societies: welcome Tues and Thurs
by arrangement.
Catering: bar and catering daily
except Mon.
Hotels: The Coach House Inn;
Glazebrook.

A79 Yelverton

☎(0822) 852824, 852864
Sec/Manager, 853593 Pro
Golf Links Rd, Yelverton, Devon PL20
6BN
8 miles N of Plymouth and 5 miles S
of Tavistock on A386.
Moorland course.
18 holes, 6363 yards, S.S.S.70
Designed by Herbert Fowler.
Founded 1904
Visitors: accredited golfers
welcome; h/cap cert required.
Green Fee: £20/day
Societies: welcome by
arrangement.
Catering: daily (0822) 855658.
Hotels: Manor House; Moorland
Links; Rosemont.

B

SOMERSET, DORSET, WILTSHIRE, SOUTH AVON

Some of the most enjoyable golf in Britain can be found around Bournemouth, an area rich in natural heathland characterised by heather, gorse, pines and silver birch. Ferndown, Parkstone and Broadstone are the pick although Isle of Purbeck is the best from a scenic point of view. Both Queen's Park and Meyrick Park also feature some of the finest public facilities in the country and, as a result, are highly popular.

Dorset has seen its share of new developments in recent years, one being Dudsbury at Longham which has a splendid clubhouse position looking down on the River Stour. Converted from farmland and boasting lakes, well established trees and pleasant contours, it fills an obvious need in an area where the demand is great. A few miles away are even newer ventures at Crane Valley and Hamptworth. Slightly more remote are the settings of Sherborne in the midst of rural splendour and Lyme Regis on its clifftop perch close to the border with Devon. However, both of them typify the variety that exists on British courses.

Wiltshire is among our smaller counties in golfing terms, although both Marlborough and High Post deserve mention, together with Broome Manor at Swindon which is certainly among the busiest courses. A public complex, it operates a booking system to cater for the enormous demand. New attractions include Bowood, the longest course in Britain, and Castle Combe. But the one true championship course in Dorset, Wiltshire, Somerset and Avon is Burnham and Berrow, looking out on the

Bristol Channel and the distant coastline of Wales.

Its dunes used to be among the most mountainous, the arrangement of holes taking somewhat eccentric benefit of them until modern amendments ironed out a few quirks and kinks. Burnham's most recent changes surrounded the loss of the Church hole and the old 13th which is now a housing estate. In consequence, the 14th is a short hole in the opposite direction but, for all its undoubted challenge, Burnham and Berrow is unchanging in its appeal.

Weston Super Mare is worth a visit, one memory of my first acquaintance of it thirty years ago being the comparison of one hole with the Road Hole at St Andrews. In spite of the persuasiveness of my guide, I remained unconvinced but that is no criticism of a course whose original design was by Tom Dunn, one of the early professionals who was among the first to turn his hand to golf course architecture.

There is nothing really outstanding in the region of Bristol or Bath but pleasant rounds await at Long Ashton, Bristol & Clifton, Knowle, and, in the Gloucestershire area, Lansdown and Tracy Park. Mendip, north of Shepton Mallett, displays the best of Frank Pennink's art.

Crossing over into Wiltshire again, North Wilts represents some of the finest elements of downland golf while the courses of Salisbury and South Wiltshire rub shoulders with Salisbury racecourse. Chippenham — extended from twelve holes — has been greatly improved and Shrivenham Park keeps a welcome for all.

B1 The Ashley Wood

☎(0258) 452253 Sec, 480379 Pro
Wimborne Rd, Blandford, Dorset
DT11 9HN
From Blandford 1 mile S along B3082
Wimborne road.
Undulating meadowland course.
18 holes, 6230 yards, S.S.S.70
Designed by Patrick Tallack.
Founded 1896
Visitors: welcome except Tues am.
Green Fee: £17/day WD (£10 with
member), £24 WE & BH (£12 with
member).
Societies: welcome by arrangement
with Sec.
Catering: Stewardess welcomes
applications.
Hotels: Crown (Blandford Forum).

B2 Bath

☎(0225) 425182, 463834 Sec,
466953 Pro
Sham Castle, North Rd, Bath, Avon
BA2 6JG
Take A36 Bath to Warminster road,
turn up North Rd and club is about
800 yards on left, 1.5 miles SE of
Bath.
Downland course.
18 holes, 6369 yards, S.S.S.70
Founded 1880
Visitors: must have h/cap; welcome
weekdays and weekends, subject to
course availability.
Green Fee: £25 WD, £30 WE.
Societies: catered for Wed and Fri.
Catering: every day; bar snacks on
Thurs.
Hotels: Bath; Beaufort; Dukes; Spa.

B3 Blue Circle

☎(0373) 822481
Trowbridge Rd, Westbury, Wilts
Parkland course; part of Blue Circle
Works Sports Complex.
9 holes, 5500-6000 yards, S.S.S.66
Visitors: with member only, or on
county card system.
Green Fee: apply for details.
Societies: by arrangement.
Catering: by arrangement.

B4 Bournemouth & Meyrick Park

☎(0202) 290307 Office, 290862 or
290871 Bookings
Central Drive, Meyrick Park,
Bournemouth BH2 6LH
In centre of Bournemouth.
Municipal parkland course (Meyrick
Park), very picturesque.
18 holes, 5663 yards, S.S.S.68

Founded 1890
Visitors: welcome any time;
advisable to book previous day.
Green Fee: £10/round WD,
£11/round WE; £6 jnrs.
Societies: welcome by prior
arrangement.
Catering: café and bar.
Squash.

B5 Bowood Golf & Country Club

☎(0249) 822228, (0249) 822218
Fax
Calne, Wilts SN11 9PQ
Follow signs off M4 and A4 to
Bowood House.
Public course in Grade 1 listed
parkland.
18 holes, 7317 yards, S.S.S.74 (from
Championship tees)
Designed by Dave Thomas
Founded May 1992
Visitors: open to anyone with proof
of h/cap.
Green Fee: £27/round, £40/day WD;
£32 WE (after 12 noon only).
Societies: weekdays and weekend
after 12 noon.
Catering: private dining room,
restaurant, lounge bar.
Driving range, 3 Academy holes
£5/hour.
Hotels: fully serviced house in centre
of course (sleeps 8) for rent, free golf;
apply for details.

B6 Bradford-on-Avon

☎(0225) 868268
Avon Close, Trowbridge Rd,
Bradford-on-Avon, Wilts
From Bradford towards Trowbridge,
on left near Police Station.
Parkland course alongside River
Avon.
9 holes, 2109 metres, S.S.S.61
Founded June 1991
Visitors: welcome, not Sat/Sun am.
Green Fee: apply for details.
Catering: clubhouse due for
completion mid-summer 1992.
Hotels: Lea Park.

B7 Brean

☎(0278) 751570 Pro shop/bookings
Coast Rd, Brean, Burnham-on-Sea,
Somerset TA8 2RF
Leave M5 at junction 22, follow signs
for Brean Leisure Park, course 4
miles N of Burnham, 6 miles M5.
Level moorland course.
18 holes, 5714 yards, S.S.S.68
Founded 1975

Visitors: members of other golf
clubs welcome, not Sat or Sun am.
Green Fee: £12 WD, £15 WE.
Societies: welcome weekdays with
prior notice.
Catering: bar and snacks, meals can
be arranged in adjacent Leisure
Centre.
Course adjoins Leisure Park and
6-mile sandy beach.
Hotels: Dunston House; Queens
(Burnham-on-Sea); caravan park
(touring & static) adjacent.

B8 Bridport & West Dorset

☎(0308) 422597 Members, 421095
Sec, 421491 Pro shop
East Cliff, West Bay, Bridport, Dorset
DT6 4EP
Off A35, 1.5 miles S of Bridport on
B3157.
Clifftop links course.
18 holes, 5246 yards, S.S.S.66
Designed by G.S.P. Salmon.
Founded 1891
Visitors: welcome.
Green Fee: £18/day (£12 after 2pm)
WD, £22 (£18 after 2pm) WE.
Societies: as arranged.
Catering: full, plus licensed bar.
9 hole Pitch & Putt.
Hotels: Haddon House.

B9 Brinkworth

☎(0666) 510277
Longmans Farm, Brinkworth,
Chippenham, Wilts SN15 5DG
Between Swindon and Malmesbury
on B4042.
Meadowland course.
18 holes, 5884 yards, S.S.S.69
Founded 1984
Visitors: welcome any time.
Green Fee: £5 WD, £7 WE.
Societies: by arrangement.
Catering: available.

B10 Bristol & Clifton

☎(0275) 393474, 393031 Pro,
393117 House Manager, 392723
Catering
Beggar Bush Lane, Failand, Nr
Clifton, Bristol BS8 3TH
Junction 19 off M5, 4 miles along
A369 to Bristol turn right at traffic
lights, then further 1.5 miles.
Parkland course.
18 holes, 6294 yards, S.S.S.70
Founded 1891
Visitors: welcome weekdays with
club h/cap cert; weekends during
restricted times.
Green Fee: £30 WD, £35 WE.

Societies: by arrangement, not weekends.
Catering: normal golf club catering.
Hotels: Redwood Lodge; Beggar Bush Land; Failand.

B11 **Broadstone**
☎(0202) 692595
Wentworth Drive, Broadstone, Dorset
Off A349 half-way between Wimborne and Poole.
Heathland course.
18 holes, 6151 yards, S.S.S.70
Designed by George Dunn & H.S. Colt.
Founded 1898
Visitors: weekdays after 9.30am.
Green Fee: apply for details.
Societies: weekdays only.
Catering: by arrangement.
Hotels: King's Head; Fairlight.

B12 **Broome Manor**
☎(0793) 532403
Piper's Way, Swindon, Wilts SN3 1RG
2 miles from M4 junction 15 to Swindon; follow signs for Golf Complex.
Public parkland course.
18 holes, 6359 yards, S.S.S.70; 9 holes, 2745 yards, S.S.S.67
Designed by Hawtree & Son.
Founded 1976
Visitors: welcome; booking system in operation throughout the year.
Green Fee: apply for details.
Societies: welcome Mon-Thurs.
Catering: full facilities all week.
Driving range.
Hotels: Holiday Inn; Crest; Goddard Arms.

B13 **Bulbury Woods**
☎(0929) 459574
Halls Rd, Lytchett Matravers, Nr Poole, Dorset BH16 6EP
Off Poole-Bere Regis road A35.
Parkland course.
18 holes, 6100 yards, S.S.S.68
Designed by J. Sharkey.
Founded 1989
Visitors: welcome.
Green Fee: £15/round, £25/day WD; £18/round, £30/day WE.
Societies: welcome.
Catering: full facilities.
Practice ground.
Hotels: on site accommodation.

B14 **Burnham & Berrow**
☎(0278) 785760
St Christopher's Way,
Burnham-on-Sea, Somerset TA8 2PE
M5 junction 22, 1 mile N of Burnham.
Seaside links, championship course.
18 holes, 6447 yards, S.S.S.72; 9 holes, 6332 yards, S.S.S.70
Founded 1890
Visitors: must be members of recognised club with h/caps of 22 or under (ladies 30) for championship course; book in advance.
Green Fee: £28 WD, £40 WE; 9-hole course, £8/day.
Societies: as for visitors.
Catering: every day 11am-6pm; breakfast and evening meals available on prior booking.
Hotels: Dormy House at club, golf inclusive prices; Batch Farm (Lympsham); Lulworth GH.

B15 **Came Down**
☎(0305) 812531 Steward/club, 813494 Manager/Fax, 812670 Pro
Came Down, Dorchester, Dorset DT2 8NR
2 miles S of Dorchester off A354.

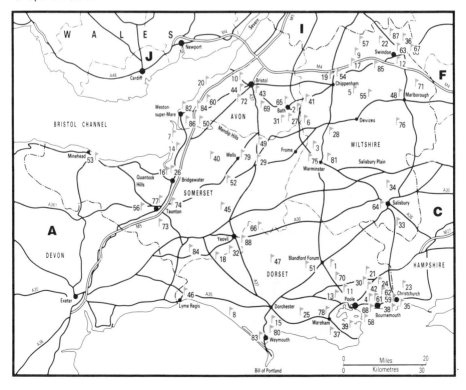

Undulating downland course, chalk base, good drainage.
18 holes, 6224 yards, S.S.S.71
Designed by J.H. Taylor.
Founded 1896
Visitors: midweek from 9am, Sat from 9am, Sun from 11am, h/cap required, please phone.
Green Fee: £20/day WD, £25/day Sat and after 11am Sun.
Societies: society day Wed, coffee, lunch, 36 holes approx £30.
Catering: bar, restaurant, refreshments.
Driving/practice area, putting green.

B16 Cannington
☎(0278) 652394
Cannington College, Nr Bridgewater, Somerset TA5 2LS
M5 junction 23; course 3 miles W of Bridgewater.
Parkland course.
9 holes, S.S.S.68
Designed by Martin Hawtree.
Founded July 1993
Visitors: welcome, no restrictions; reservations for matches and societies.
Green Fee: £10 (18 holes) WD, £12 (18 holes) WE.
Societies: welcome by arrangement with golf course manager/pro.
Catering: bar and restaurant.

B17 Castle Combe G & CC
☎(0249) 782982, (0249) 782992 Fax, 783101 Pro
Castle Combe, Wilts SN14 7PL
Off B4039 to N of Castle Combe village.
Ancient woodland/parkland course
18 holes, 6340 yards, Par 73
Designed by Peter Alliss & Clive Clark.
Founded 1992
Visitors: welcome any time, no jeans, trainers, bermuda shorts, shell suits etc.
Green Fee: £25/round (approx).
Societies: mainly Tues and Thurs, small societies (under 20 players) any weekday, packages from £30.
Catering: 2 bars, restaurant, private dining facilities, bar snacks all day.
Snooker room, practice range.
Hotels: Manor House; Lucknam Park.

B18 Chedington Court
☎(0935) 891413 Bookings, 891265 Manager
South Perrott, Beaminster, Dorset DT8 3HU

0.5 mile E of South Perrott on A356 Crewkerne-Dorchester road.
Parkland course.
9 holes, 3320 yards, S.S.S.72
Designed by D. Hemstock, P. & H. Chapman.
Founded 1991
Visitors: welcome; proper dress required.
Green Fee: 9 holes, £7.50 WD, £10 WE; 18 holes, £12 WD, £15 WE.
Societies: by arrangement.
Catering: refreshments available.
Basic Pitch & Putt course, driving and practice areas.
Hotels: Chedington Court (0935 891265), bargain breaks all year, half board with unlimited golf available.

B19 Chippenham
☎(0249) 652040 Sec, 655519 Pro
Malmesbury Rd, Chippenham, Wilts SN15 5LT
Junction 17 off M4, 1 mile from town centre on A429.
Meadowland course.
18 holes, 5540 yards, S.S.S.67
Founded 1896
Visitors: welcome with restrictions.
Green Fee: £20 WD, £25 WE.
Societies: welcome weekdays only.
Catering: lunch (limited catering Mon).
Hotels: Old Bell (Malmesbury).

B20 Clevedon
☎(0275) 874057 Sec, 874704 Pro, 873140 Steward, 341228 Fax
Castle Rd, Clevedon, Avon BS21 7AA
Leave M5 at junction 19 (junction 20 from S), follow signs to Clevedon; on outskirts of Clevedon turn right into Holly Lane, at top of hill turn right into private lane to golf club and castle.
Undulating parkland course.
18 holes, 5887 yards, S.S.S.69
Designed by Sandy Herd.
Founded 1908
Visitors: every day, not Wed am; must be playing members of a golf club and must produce h/cap certs.
Green Fee: £22 WD, £35 WE & BH.
Societies: Tues only, not Bank Holidays.
Catering: every day (bar snacks only Mon). Snooker.
Hotels: Wellington; Walton Park.

B21 Crane Valley
☎(0202) 814088
West Farm, Romford, Verwood, Dorset BH31 6LE

From A31 take B30181 signposted Verwood, course is on left hand side on northern outskirts of Verwood.
Parkland course, part public.
18 holes, 6424 yards, S.S.S.71; 9 holes (public course), 2060 yards, S.S.S.60.
Designed by Donald Steel.
Founded 1992
Visitors: members of recognised clubs with h/cap certs on 18 hole course; all welcome on 9 hole course.
Green Fee: phone for details.
Societies: by appointment.
Catering: full restaurant and bar, spikes bar and snacks.
Driving range.

B22 Cricklade Hotel & Country Club
☎(0793) 750751
Common Hill, Cricklade, Wilts SN6 6HA
B4040 Cricklade-Malmesbury road, 15 mins from M4 junctions 15/16.
Parkland course.
9 holes, 1830 yards, S.S.S.62
Designed by Ian Bolt.
Founded 1992
Visitors: welcome Mon-Fri.
Green Fee: £16 (18 holes), £25/day.
Societies: welcome by arrangement.
Catering: full facilities, à la carte restaurant.
Indoor swimming pool, snooker, tennis, health and fitness facilities.
Hotels: Cricklade.

B23 Dudmoor Farm
☎(0202) 483980
Dudmoor Farm Rd, Christchurch, Dorset BH23 6AQ
Off A35 W of Christchurch.
Woodland course.
9 holes, 1428 metres, Par 31
Founded 1974
Visitors: welcome 7 days.
Green Fee: £4.50 for 18 holes.
Societies: advisable to phone.
Catering: snacks and soft drinks.
Squash, fishing.
Hotels: Avon Causeway; B&B on site.

B24 Dudsbury
☎(0202) 593499
Christchurch Rd, Ferndown, Dorset BH22 8ST
From A31 at Ferndown take A348 for approx 2 miles, then turn left down B3073, entrance on right after approx 500 yards.

Parkland course.
18 holes, 6200 yards, S.S.S.71; 5 hole Academy course.
Designed by Donald Steel.
Founded April 1992
Visitors: phone for information.
Green Fee: on application.
Societies: welcome any weekday (if free), packages negotiable.
Catering: Spike bar, lounge bar, restaurant (open to non-members), function suite. Driving range.

B25 **East Dorset**
☎(0929) 472244 Sec, 472272 Golfshop/reservations, 471294 Fax
Hyde, Wareham, Dorset BH20 7NT
Take A352 from Wareham (by-pass), take 1st junction right past Worgret Manor Hotel, enter Puddletown Rd, Worgret Heath, after 3-4 miles turn right at Hyde junction, then 300 yards to club: from Bere Regis take Wool road; after 4.5 miles past Bovington Tank Museum sign, turn left into Puddletown Rd; club signposted 0.5 miles.
Parkland course, part in rhododendron woodland.
Lakeland, 18 holes, 7027 yards, S.S.S.75; Woodland, 9 holes, 2440 yards, Par 33
Designed by Martin Hawtree.
Founded 1978
Visitors: welcome weekdays and weekends subject to availability (prior reservation).
Green Fee: £18/round, £23/day WD; £25/round, £30/day WE.
Societies: welcome any day on application.
Catering: full bar and restaurant service, open to non-golfers.
Driving range, large golf shop, dormy bungalow.
Hotels: Springfield County; Kemps.

B26 **Enmore Park**
☎(0278) 671481, 671519 Pro/bookings
Enmore, Bridgewater, Somerset TA5 2AN
3 miles W of Bridgewater on Durleigh road.
Undulating parkland course.
18 holes, 6406 yards, S.S.S.71
Designed by Hawtree and Son.
Founded 1932, redesigned 1971
Visitors: welcome weekdays, check weekends.
Green Fee: £18/round, £25/day WD; £25/round, £30/day WE & BH.
Societies: welcome Mon, Thurs, Fri by arrangement with Sec.

Catering: available, restricted catering on Mon.
Hotels: Walnut Tree, North Petherton (3 miles).

B27 **Entry Hill**
☎(0225) 834248
Entry Hill, Bath, Avon BA2 5NA
Take A367 Wells road from city centre, fork left into Entry Hill Rd after 1 mile; course is about 0.5 mile on right.
Compact, hilly parkland course (private club playing on public course).
9 holes, 2103 yards, S.S.S.61
Founded 1985
Visitors: no restrictions but pre-booking up to 7 days in advance essential for weekends, Bank Holidays and peak periods.
Green Fee: apply for details.
Societies: weekdays by arrangement with Pro
Hotels: Bear.

B28 **Erlestoke Sands**
☎(0380) 831069 Office/Fax, 831027 Pro shop/bookings, 830507 Catering Steward
Erlestoke, Devizes, Wiltshire SN10 5GA
On B3098 off A350 at Westbury signposted Bratton, course 6 miles on left before village of Erlestoke: or, on B3098 off A360 at West Lavington signposted Erlestoke (3 miles) on right after Erlestoke village.
Parkland course.
18 holes, 6649 yards, S.S.S.72
Designed by Adrian Stiff.
Founded May 1992.
Visitors: welcome.
Green Fee: £12 WD, £16 WE.
Societies: weekdays preferably, phone Steward.
Catering: full facilities.
3 Academy holes and 5 acre driving/practice area
Hotels: local B&B.

B29 **Farrington**
☎(0761) 241274
Marsh Lane, Farrington Gurney, Bristol BS18 5TS
On A37/A39 from Bath and Bristol towards Wells.
Undulating downland course with spectacular views.
9 holes (18 from Sept 1994), 1440 yards, S.S.S.27
Designed by Peter Thompson.
Founded Aug 1993

Visitors: welcome, advance booking required; no jeans.
Green Fee: £5.50/round.
Societies: welcome at all times, please book.
Catering: full facilities every day.
Driving range, practice bunker, putting green.

B30 **Ferndown**
☎(0202) 874602
119 Golf Links Rd, Ferndown, Dorset BH22 8DU
A31 to Trickett's Cross and A348 to Ferndown.
Heathland course.
Old Course, 18 holes, 6462 yards, S.S.S.71; New Course, 9 holes, 5604 yards, S.S.S.68
Designed by Harold Hilton (Old Course).
Founded 1913
Visitors: prior permission, h/cap cert required; limited weekends.
Green Fee: Old: £35 WD, £40 WE; New: £15 WD, £20 WE.
Societies: Tues and Fri only.
Catering: full facilities all week.
Hotels: Coach House Motel; Dormy; Bridge House.

B31 **Fosseway Country Club**
☎(0761) 412214, 418357 Fax
Charlton Lane, Midsomer Norton, Bath, Somerset BA3 4BD
Off A367 10 miles S of Bath, through Radstock and turn left at Charlton roundabout.
Parkland course.
9 holes, 4246 yards, S.S.S.61
Founded 1971
Visitors: members only on Sat until 12am, Sun until 2pm and Wed after 5pm.
Green Fee: £10 WD and Sun pm, £15 Sat pm & BH.
Societies: details on application.
Catering: full facilities in Centurion Restaurant; bar meals. Conferences, banqueting, swimming, bowls, squash, snooker.
Hotels: Centurion (part of Fosseway complex).

B32 **Halstock**
☎(0935) 891689
Halstock Golf Enterprises, Common Lane, Halstock, Somerset BA22 9SF
300 yards from centre of Halstock village; turn right at green, from Quiet Woman pub, 50 yards on left past village shop/P.O., signposted.

18 holes, 4351 yards, S.S.S.63
Founded 1988
Visitors: welcome.
Green Fee: £9/round WD, £11/round
WE.
Societies: by arrangement.
Catering: limited at present to light
refreshments.

B33 Hamptworth Golf & Country Club

☎(0794) 390155, 390022 Fax
Hamptworth Rd, Landford, Wilts SP5
2DU
6 miles from M27 junctions 1 and 2,
off A36 to Salisbury, follow Landford
and then Downton road signs.
Parkland, ancient woodlands, lakes
and river throughout.
18 hole championship quality
course; 4 hole practice academy.
Designed by Brian Pierson and D.
Saunders.
Founded May 1994
Visitors: by prior arrangment only;
h/cap certs required.
Green Fee: £25/round (approx).
Societies: by prior arrangement;
h/cap certs required for all in group.
Catering: bar and light refreshments.
Croquet, lawn tennis.
Hotels: Chewton Glen (Highcliffe);
Dormy (Ferndown).

B34 High Post

☎(072 273) 356, 219 Pro
Great Durnford, Salisbury, Wilts SP4
6AT
Half-way between Salisbury and
Amesbury on the A345, opposite the
Inn at High Post.
Downland course.
18 holes, 6267 yards, S.S.S.70
Founded 1922
Visitors: welcome weekdays
without restriction; h/cap cert
required weekends.
Green Fee: £20/round, £25/day WD;
£25/round WE & BH.
Societies: catered for weekdays,
bookings via Pro
Catering: full catering facilities.
Hotels: The Inn; High Post; Milford
Hall (Salisbury).

B35 Highcliffe Castle

☎(0425) 272210
107 Lymington Rd, Highcliffe on Sea,
Dorset BH23 4LA
A35 to Hinton Admiral, follow
signpost to Highcliffe, approx 1 mile;
on A337 3 miles E of Christchurch.
Seaside course.

18 holes, 4732 yards, S.S.S.63
Founded 1913
Visitors: welcome if member of
recognised golf club.
Green Fee: £18 WD, £27 WE & BH.
Societies: Tues only.
Catering: bar and restaurant.
Hotels: Avonmouth; Waterford
Lodge.

B36 Highworth Golf Centre

☎(0793) 766014
Highworth Community Golf Centre,
Swindon Rd, Highworth, Wilts SN6
7SJ
A361 Swindon Highworth road, in
village.
Public, undulating downland course.
9 holes, 3230 yards, S.S.S.35
Founded 1990
Visitors: welcome.
Green Fee: apply for details.
Societies: welcome.
9 hole Pitch & Putt, practice ground.
Hotels: Blunsdon House, Jesmond
House.

B37 Hyde House Country Club

☎(081) 940 7782 Head Office
Forest Lodge, Hyde, Nr Wareham,
Dorset
Woodland/parkland courses with
river and lakes.
Old, 18 holes, 6450 yards, S.S.S.72;
New, 18 holes, 6230 yards, S.S.S.72
Designed by J. Hamilton Stutt & Chris
Reynard.
Visitors: no casual visitors, bookings
only through head office for golf and
multi-adventure activities.
Green Fee: on application.
Societies: welcome weekdays and
weekends.
Catering: available
Hotels: accommodation available.

B38 Iford Bridge Sports Complex

☎(0202) 473817
Iford Bridge Sports Centre, Barrack
Rd, Iford, Christchurch, Dorset BH23
2BA
Off A35 between Bournemouth and
Christchurch, then signposted.
Public parkland/meadowland course
next to River Stour.
9 holes, 4852 yards, S.S.S.63
Founded 1977
Visitors: welcome.
Green Fee: £5.40 WD, £6.10 WE &
BH, reduced rates for OAPs and jnrs.

Societies: welcome.
Catering: bar facilities and snacks
served.
Driving range, tennis, bowling.
Hotels: for bargain breaks contact
Christchurch Information Centre
(0202 471780).

B39 Isle of Purbeck

☎(0929) 44361, 44354 Pro, 44501
Fax
Studland, Dorset BH19 3AB
Either by ferry from Sandbanks or by
road through Wareham, turning left
onto B3351 signposted Studland at
Corfe Castle.
Undulating heathland course.
Purbeck Course, 18 holes, 6248
yards, S.S.S.71; Dene Course, 9
holes, 2022 yards, S.S.S.30
Designed by H.S. Colt.
Founded August 1892
Visitors: welcome; h/cap cert
required for Purbeck Course.
Green Fee: Purbeck Course,
£22.50/round, £30/day WD;
£27.50/round, £35/day WE; Dene
Course, £10/day WD, £12/day WE.
Societies: welcome by
arrangement.
Catering: bar open from 11am daily,
restaurant open Tues-Sun.
Hotels: Knoll House; Pines
(Swanage).

B40 Isle of Wedmore

☎(0934) 712452
Lineage, Lascots Hill, Wedmore,
Somerset BS28 4QT
1st right past church in Wedmore,
0.5 mile on right.
Parkland course.
18 holes, 5900 yards, S.S.S.68
Designed by Terry Murray.
Founded July 1992
Visitors: welcome, usual standards
of dress, no jeans T-shirts etc.
Green Fee: £12/round WD,
£15/round WE.
Societies: welcome, groups up to
100, weekdays only.
Catering: full bar and restaurant
facilities
Hotels: Webbington (Loxton)

B41 Kingsdown

☎(0225) 742530
Kingsdown, Corsham, Wilts SN14
9BS
Turn off A4 onto A363, turn left at
Crown Inn 250 yards, uphill for 2
miles.
Heathland course.

18 holes, 6445 yards, S.S.S.71
Founded 1880
Visitors: welcome with h/caps, not weekends.
Green Fee: £22 WD.
Societies: by arrangement with Sec.
Catering: dining room meals or bar snacks.
Hotels: Beaufort (Bath); Conigre Farm (Melksham); Orchard (Bathford).

B42 Knighton Heath
☎(0202) 572633
Francis Ave, Bournemouth, Dorset BH11 8NX
On main A348 Poole-Ringwood road, junction with A3049 at Wallisdown roundabout.
Heathland course.
18 holes, 5987 yards, S.S.S.69
Founded 1976
Visitors: after 9.30am weekdays, not weekends or Bank Holidays, h/cap cert required.
Green Fee: on application.
Societies: weekdays by prior arrangement.
Catering: lunch daily except Mon.
Hotels: Bridge House (Longham).

B43 Knowle
☎(0272) 770660
Fairway, Brislington, Bristol BS4 5DF
3 miles S of city centre on the A4 to junction with West Town Lane, entrance on left 800 yards along West Town Lane.
Parkland course.
18 holes, 6016 yards, S.S.S.69
Designed by Hawtree & J.H. Taylor.
Founded 1905
Visitors: welcome weekdays, weekends by special arrangement; h/cap certs required.
Green Fee: £22/round, £27/day WD; £27/round, £32/day WE.
Societies: Thurs only.
Catering: lunch daily, evening meals by arrangement.
Hotels: Grange (Keynsham).

B44 Long Ashton
☎(0275) 392316 Sec, 392265 Pro, 394395 Fax
Long Ashton, Bristol BS18 9DW
Leave M5 at junction 19, take A369 to Bristol, turn right into B3129 at traffic lights and then left onto B3128; club is 0.5 mile on right.
Undulating moorland/parkland course.
18 holes, 6077 yards, S.S.S.70

Designed by Hawtree & Taylor.
Founded 1893
Visitors: must have official club h/cap.
Green Fee: £22 WD, £30 WE.
Societies: by arrangement.
Catering: full facilities daily until 6pm; evening meal by arrangement.
Hotels: Redwood Lodge.

B45 Long Sutton
☎(0458) 241017
Long Load, Nr Langport, Somerset TA10 9JU
Take Langport road from A303, after 3 miles turn left into Long Sutton, course 1 mile on left.
Parkland course.
18 holes, 6148 yards, S.S.S.69
Designed by Patrick Dawson.
Founded Sept 1991
Visitors: pay-as-you-play course, tees must be booked at weekends.
Green Fee: £12/round WD, £16 WE.
Societies: by prior arrangement.
Catering: bar and restaurant.
Driving range.
Hotels: can be arranged through Sec.

B46 Lyme Regis
☎(0297) 442963, 442043 Catering
Timber Hill, Lyme Regis, Dorset DT7 3HQ
Off A3052 Charmouth road 1 mile E of town.
Undulating meadowland course.
18 holes, 6220 yards, S.S.S.70
Founded 1893
Visitors: welcome, must have h/cap cert or proof of membership of recognised club; restrictions on Thurs and Sun.
Green Fee: £24/day (£20 after 2pm).
Societies: apply for booking; Mon, Tues, Wed and Fri.
Catering: full à la carte, hot and cold snacks all day.
Hotels: Alexander; Bay; Buena Vista; Devon; Fairwater Head; Tudor House; The Cedars (Axminster); all offer reduced green fees.

B47 Lyons Gate
☎(03005) 239
Lyons Gate Farm, Lyons Gate, Dorchester DT2 7AZ
3 miles N of Cerne Abbas on A352 Sherborne-Dorchester road.
Wooded farmland course.
9 holes, 2000 yards, S.S.S.60
Designed by Ken Abel.
Founded 1991

Visitors: welcome 8am-5pm summer, 8.30am-4.30pm Oct-Mar.
Green Fee: £4.50 (9 holes), £7.50 (18 holes).
Societies: unrestricted
Catering: light refreshments; new clubhouse due Jan 1994.
Practice nets.
Hotels: Kings Arms.

B48 Marlborough
☎(0672) 512147
The Common, Marlborough, Wilts SN8 1DU
0.75 mile from town centre on A345 to Swindon.
Downland course.
18 holes, 6505 yards, S.S.S.71
Founded 1888
Visitors: welcome weekdays and weekends on non-competition days, ring in advance; h/cap certs required.
Green Fee: apply for details.
Societies: with prior booking, weekdays only.
Catering: full catering facilities all week.
Hotels: Castle & Ball; Ivy House.

B49 Mendip
☎(0749) 840570 Sec, 840793 Pro, 841439 Fax
Gurney Slade, Bath, Somerset BA3 4UT
3 miles N of Shepton Mallet off A37.
Undulating downland course.
18 holes, 6330 yards, S.S.S.70
Designed by H. Vardon with an extension by F. Pennink.
Founded 1908
Visitors: with member only at weekends unless member of affiliated club; phone Pro to check availability.
Green Fee: £20/round, £25/day WD; £30/day WE.
Societies: welcome Mon-Fri.
Catering: full facilities every day.
Hotels: White Hart.

B50 Mendip Spring
☎(0934) 853337
Honeyhall Lane, Congresbury, Avon BS19 5JT
From M5 junction 21 take A370 towards Bristol, turn right in Congresbury onto B3133.
Parkland course with hill views.
Brinsea, 18 holes, 6500 yards, S.S.S.72; Lakeside, 9 holes, 2,300 yards
Designed by Terry Murray.
Founded 1991

Visitors: start times may be reserved.
Green Fee: apply for details.
Societies: apply to director of golf.
Catering: bar and restaurant.
Extensive leisure facilities, driving range, swimming pool, health club.

B51 Mid-Dorset
☎(0258) 861386, 861184 Pro, 860656 Fax
Belchalwell, Blandford Forum, Dorset DT11 0EG
9 miles SW of Blandford between Okeford Fitzpaine and Ibberton.
Parkland course.
18 holes, 6503 yards
Designed by Project Golf (D.W. Asthill).
Founded 1990
Visitors: all welcome.
Green Fee: apply for details.
Societies: welcome by prior arrangement.
Catering: lunches, tea, evening meals, 7-day bar open all day.
Large practice facilities.
Hotels: Swan (Sturminster Newton); Anvil (Pimperne Blandford).

B52 Millfield School
☎(0458) 42291 ext.279
Nr Glastonbury, Somerset
1 mile SE of Butleigh.
Parkland course.
9 holes, 4516 yards, S.S.S.62
Founded 1970
Visitors: members and guests only and when not required by school.
Green Fee: £4.

B53 Minehead & West Somerset
☎(0643) 702057, 704378 Pro
The Warren, Minehead, Somerset TA24 5SJ
E end of sea front.
Links course.
18 holes, 6130 yards, S.S.S.70
Designed by Johnny Alan.
Founded 1882
Visitors: welcome.
Green Fee: £19.50 WD, £23 WE & BH.
Societies: welcome on written application.
Catering: by prior arrangement with caterer; snacks always available.
Hotels: York; Northfield; Marshfield.

B54 Monkton Park Par 3
☎(0249) 653928 Tel/Fax
Monkton Park, Chippenham, Wilts SN15 3PE

Into Chippenham, past railway station, turn right.
Parkland course.
9 holes, Par 3 (longest hole 175 yards)
Designed by M. Dawson.
Founded 1960
Visitors: welcome.
Green Fee: £2.75 9 holes (£2 OAP); £4 18 holes.
Catering: refreshments available.

B55 North Wilts
☎(0380) 860627 Sec, 860330 Pro
Bishops Cannings, Devizes, Wilts SN10 2LP
1 mile from A4 E of Calne.
Downland course.
18 holes, 6484 yards, S.S.S.71
Founded 1890
Visitors: welcome, h/cap cert required at weekends.
Green Fee: £18/round, £25/day WD, £30 WE.
Societies: welcome by prior arrangement.
Catering: full facilities available.
Hotels: Bear (Devizes); Lansdowne Strand (Calne).

B56 Oake Manor
☎(0823) 461993
Oake, Taunton, Somerset TA4 1BA
M5 northbound, exit 26, then A38 to Taunton, follow signs to Oake; 10 mins from motorway. From M5 southbound, exit 25 onto B3227, 5 miles W of Taunton.
Parkland course with lakes.
18 holes, 6109 yards, S.S.S.69
Designed by Adrian Stiff.
Founded July 1993
Visitors: welcome 7 days, phone for start times.
Green Fee: £12/round, £20/day WD; £15 WE.
Societies: golf days and societies welcome weekdays by arrangement.
Catering: bar and bar snacks, restaurant, 8am-10pm daily.
Driving range.
Hotels: Rumwell Manor.

B57 Oaksey Park
☎(0666) 577995, 577174 Fax
Oaksey, Malmesbury, Wilts SN16 9SB
Off A419 between Swindon and Cirencester, W of Cotswold Water Park.
Public parkland course.
9 holes, 2904 yards, S.S.S.68
Designed by Chapman & Warren.
Founded 1991

Visitors: welcome.
Green Fee: £8/day WD, £13/day WE.
Societies: welcome.
Catering: full facilities.
Driving range, practice ground, clay pigeon shoot, rare breeds, children's play area, archery, hot air ballooning.
Hotels: Oaksey Park Country Cottages Hotel (10 farm cottages).

B58 Parkstone
☎(0202) 707138, 708092 Pro
Links Rd, Parkstone, Poole, Dorset BH14 9JU
A35 Bournemouth-Poole road, turn S at St Osmond's Church.
Undulating heathland course.
18 holes, 6250 yards, S.S.S.70
Designed by Willie Park and James Braid.
Founded 1910
Visitors: welcome on weekdays (book in advance); h/cap certs required.
Green Fee: £25/round, £34/day WD; £30/round, £40/day WE & BH.
Societies: catered for on weekdays.
Catering: lunch available every day.

B59 Parley
☎(0202) 593131
Parley Green Lane, Hurn, Christchurch, Dorset BH23 6BB
Opposite Bournemouth International Airport.
Parkland course.
6 holes (9 from June 1994), 5112 yards, Par 69
Designed by Paul Goodfellow.
Founded 1992
Visitors: welcome.
Green Fee: £3 (6 holes), £6 (18 holes).
Societies: advisable to contact in advance.
Catering: bar and snacks.

B60 Puxton Park
☎(0934) 876942
Woodspring Golf & Leisure Park, Puxton, Nr Weston-Super-Mare, Avon BS24 6TA
2 miles E of M5 junction 21 on A370 Bristol-Weston road.
Moorland course.
18 holes, 6559 yards, Par 72
Founded 1992
Visitors: pay-and-play course, all welcome.
Green Fee: £8/round WD, £10/round WE.
Societies: welcome.
Catering: bar.

Sherborne

Sherborne belongs to that category of courses that provides the right degree of testing quality, without in any way impairing the enjoyment of a round in an incomparable setting — views, on a good day, across two or three counties. Taking the road up the hill out of a town famous for its abbey and its schools, you reach the club down a narrow country lane. Before the club's founding in 1894, the whole area was part of the fertile agricultural plain that surrounds it, but the second nine in particular covers some gently rolling land of which Harry Colt would certainly have approved. He believed that undulations and hummocks are of great value through the green as they provide difficult stances and lies, without which no golf course can be deemed to be perfect.

Judged from the first six holes, Sherborne suggests a non-stop assault with woods and long irons. The first nine is, in fact, more than 800 yards longer than the second, though that does not necessarily mean that the second nine is any easier in relation to par. What it does mean is that the first six holes, including three par 5s, hold the key to a good score, the 1st and 3rd being notable par 4s.

It is easy enough though to have your card in tatters almost before you have started. There is plenty of scope for going out of bounds with an opening drive to a fairway which tapers cleverly to ensure that the further you hit the ball, the straighter you have to be. Control is essential too with the second shot to the 2nd, doglegging round the practice ground, while the 3rd and 4th, running up and back, are two of the best.

The 5th is the first of an excellent batch of short holes which vary in length and character, as all good short holes should, the 5th being perhaps the finest and the 7th the most daunting. In between, the par 5 6th demands a well positioned drive to allow a flat stance for what is most likely to be a long second; and the second, too, requires both care and thought in order to leave the easiest pitch when the pin is tucked away at the back of the green.

Nothing less than the most truly-hit tee shot will suffice at the 7th but there is a little respite at the 8th and 9th which epitomises the compact nature of the layout on a limited acreage. It accommodates one more hole, the third par 3, before crossing back and passing the clubhouse and on down the excellent 459 yard 11th where the sloping terrain demands that, to hold both fairway and green, there is a very definite, if narrow, line to adopt.

It is from the tee that the full panorama of the view unfolds, an unmistakable slice of England at its greenest and best. There are other chances to stand and stare but not until the business in hand is complete and the ridge up the 18th fairway has been safely scaled.

In the meantime, the tiny 12th is not to be taken lightly. It is an admirable illustration that short holes don't have to be 200 yards to give a sense of achievement at hitting the green; and, though of modest length also, the 13th and 14th, one up and one back down again, permit little error in judging the pitches comprising the second shots.

The 15th has much in common with the 7th, a tee shot with the emphasis on carry, while the drive at the 16th must be well flighted to clear the trees guarding the wooded menace on the right. It may be wiser to take the safer line to the left and to rub shoulders with those turning back up the 17th with its hopes of a birdie. But, by now, thoughts are on negotiating the final slope to the 18th.

This is done preferably with a drive and crisp iron but, for those flagging physically and in spirit, the sight of the clubhouse has the same effect as an oasis in the desert and it's no mirage. It has splendid reviving powers and if, on reflection, your golf is best forgotten, look not on the dark side. A further glimpse at the scenic splendour will promptly persuade you that it has been amply worthwhile.

B61 Queen's Park (Boscombe)

☎(0202) 302611, 36198 (Boscombe GC)
Queen's Park West Drive, Bournemouth, Dorset BH8 9BY
From Ringwood, proceed along Wessex Way (A338), leave by 1st junction, turn right at roundabout and right again into Queens Park West Drive.
Undulating public parkland course
18 holes, 6505 yards, S.S.S.72
Founded 1906
Visitors: welcome any time.
Green Fee: apply for details.
Societies: by prior arrangement.
Catering: bar and restaurant facilities.

B63 RMCS Shrivenham

☎(0793) 785725
RMCS Shrivenham, Swindon, Wilts SN6 8LA
In grounds of Royal Military College of Science on A420 1 mile NE of Shrivenham.
Parkland course
18 holes, 5547 yards, S.S.S.69
Founded 1953
Visitors: restricted access; with member only; entry to grounds must be arranged with Manager.
Green Fee: £8 WD, £10 WE.
Societies: limited access weekdays, green fees + £1/day.
Catering: coffee/tea/soft drinks.

B62 Riversmeet

☎(0202) 477987
Two Riversmeet Leisure Centre, Stony Lane South, Christchurch, Dorset BH23 1HW
Left at mini-roundabout at end of Christchurch High St, on to crossroads, turn right to Leisure Centre.
Picturesque public seaside course.
18 holes, 1455 metres, Par 3
Visitors: welcome any time.
Green Fee: £4.50 adults, £2.25 jnrs.
Catering: bar and restaurant.
Squash, badminton, swimming pool, gym etc.

B64 Salisbury & South Wiltshire

☎(0722) 742645 Sec, 742929 Pro
Netherhampton, Salisbury, Wilts SP2 8PR
On A3094 2 miles from Salisbury and from Wilton.
Parkland course.
18 holes, 6528 yards, S.S.S.71; 9 hole course.
Designed by J.H. Taylor.
Founded 1888
Visitors: welcome; h/cap cert required weekends.
Green Fee: £25 WD, £40 WE & BH.
Societies: welcome by arrangement.
Catering: full bar and catering facilities.
Snooker.
Hotels: Rose & Crown (Salisbury); Pembroke Arms (Wilton).

B65 Saltford

☎(0225) 873513
Golf Club Lane, Saltford, Bristol BS18 3AA
Off A4 between Bath and Bristol.
Meadowland course.
18 holes, 6081 yards, S.S.S.69
Founded 1904
Visitors: welcome; h/cap cert required.
Green Fee: £21/round, £26 2 rounds.
Societies: Mon and Thurs by arrangement.
Catering: meals served daily.
Snooker.
Hotels: Grange (Keynsham); Crown; Tunnel House.

B66 Sherborne

☎(0963) 814431
Higher Clatcombe, Sherborne, Dorset DT9 4RN
1 mile N of Sherborne off B3145 to Wincanton.
Parkland course.
18 holes, 5758 yards, S.S.S.68
Designed by James Braid.
Founded 1894
Visitors: weekdays and weekends dependent on Club Diary.
Green Fee: £20 WD, £25 WE & BH.
Societies: Tues and Wed by arrangement.
Catering: comprehensive range of facilities available.
Hotels: Post House; Half Moon; Antelope.

B67 Shrivenham Park

☎(0793) 783853
Pennyhooks, Shrivenham, Swindon, Wilts SN6 8HH
A420 Swindon-Oxford road 6 miles from Swindon, leave by-pass for Shrivenham; on E edge of village.
Public undulating parkland course.
18 holes, 6000 yards, S.S.S.70
Designed by Roger Mace, Glen Johnson.
Visitors: welcome, pay-as-you-play.
Green Fee: £9/round, £15.50/day WD; £12/round, £18.50/day WE; reductions for jnrs, OAPs, students & unemployed; gradually reducing twilight fees.
Societies: at all times.
Catering: full bar and restaurant facilities.

B68 Solent Meads Par 3

☎(0202) 420795
Rolls Drive, Nr Hengistbury Head, Bournemouth, Dorset
In Selfridge Avenue, off Broadway at Hengistbury Head.
Public seaside course.
18 holes, Par 3, 2235 yards
Visitors: welcome at all times.
Green Fee: apply for details.
Catering: light refreshments, café.
Driving range.

B69 Stockwood Vale

☎(0272) 866505
Stockwood Lane, Keynsham, Bristol BS18 2ER
In Stockwood Lane off A4.
Public, undulating parkland course.
9 holes, 4020 yards, S.S.S.61
Designed by J. Wade & M. Ramsay.
Founded 1991
Visitors: welcome, tee times bookable 7 days in advance.
Green Fee: apply for details.
Societies: by prior arrangement.
Driving range.
Hotels: The Grange.

B70 Sturminster Marshall

☎(0258) 858444
Moor Lane, Sturminster Marshall, Dorset BH21 4AH
Off A350 Poole-Blandford road, signposted from middle of village.
Meadowland course.
9 holes, 4650 yards, S.S.S.63
Designed by John Sharkey.
Founded 1992
Visitors: welcome, no restrictions.
Green Fee: £5 (9 holes), £8 (18 holes).
Societies: welcome.
Catering: cafeteria, soft drinks.

B71 Swindon

☎(067 284) 327
Ogbourne St George, Marlborough, Wilts SN18 1TB
Junction 15 off M4, on A345 to Marlborough.

Undulating downland course.
18 holes, 6226 yards, S.S.S.70
Designed by Taylor, Hawtree and Cotton.
Founded 1907
Visitors: welcome on weekdays.
Green Fee: £17/round, £23/day.
Societies: weekdays.
Catering: restaurant, bar snacks.

B72 Tall Pines
☎(0275) 472076 Tel/Fax
Cooks Bridle Path, Downside, Backwell, Bristol BS19 3DJ
0.5 mile N of Bristol Airport.
Public parkland course.
18 holes, 5827 yards, S.S.S.68
Designed by Terry Murray.
Founded 1990
Visitors: welcome, booking at weekends only.
Green Fee: £10 WD, £12.50 WE.
Societies: Mon-Fri.
Catering: Bar and restaurant.
Hotels: Towns Talk.

B73 Taunton & Pickeridge
☎(0823) 421537 Sec, 521742 Fax
Corfe, Taunton, Somerset TA3 7BY
B3170, 4 miles S of Taunton, through Corfe village, then 1st left.
Undulating course.
18 holes, 5927 yards, S.S.S.68
Designed by Hawtree.
Founded 1892
Visitors: welcome weekdays by prior arrangement, h/cap cert required.
Green Fee: on application
Societies: welcome by prior arrangement
Catering: full catering facilities available.
Hotels: Forte Crest; County; Taunton; Travel Inn.

B74 Taunton Vale
☎(0823) 412220 Sec, 412880 Pro/reservations
Creech Heathfield, Taunton, Somerset TA3 5EY
Just off A361 at junction with A38, exits 24 or 25 from M5.
Parkland course.
18 holes, 6072 yards, Par 70; 9 holes, 2000 yards, S.S.S.60
Designed by John Pyne.
Founded July 1991
Visitors: welcome, appropriate dress and etiquette.
Green Fee: 18 holes, £14 WD, £17.50 WE; 9 holes, £7 WD, £8.75 WE.

Societies: welcome weekdays.
Catering: full bar and catering in clubhouse.
Driving range.
Hotels: Walnut Tree (N Petherton – Best Western packages); Post House, County, Castle(Taunton); Falcon (Henlade).

B75 Thoulstone Park
☎(0373) 832825, (0373) 832821 Fax
Chapmanslade, Nr Westbury, Wilts BA13 4AQ
2.5 miles W of Warminster on A36.
Parkland course with spectacular views.
18 holes, 6384 yards, S.S.S.71
Designed by M.R.M. Sandow
Founded Oct 1991
Visitors: welcome.
Green Fee: £13/round, £17.50/day WD; £19.50/round, £28/day WE
Societies: welcome weekdays; special arrangements for weekends, contact General Manager.
Catering: Restaurants, bars; conference facilities, function rooms, offices.
Driving range, sauna, solarium.

B76 Upavon (RAF)
☎(0980) 630787 Club Manager, 630281 Pro
Douglas Avenue, Upavon, Nr. Pewsey, Wilts SN9 6BQ
2 miles SE of Upavon village on A342 Andover-Devizes road.
Undulating downland course.
9 holes, 5116 metres (5589 yards), S.S.S.67
Founded 1918
Visitors: welcome on weekdays, weekends with member or after 11am with h/cap certificate.
Green Fee: £15/day WD, £20/day WE; £8 with member.
Societies: welcome, call for details.
Catering: by special arrangement.
Hotels: Shears; Crown; Woodbridge Inn.

B77 Vivary
☎(0823) 289274, 333875 Bookings/Manager
Taunton, Somerset
In centre of Taunton.
Municipal parkland course.
18 holes, 4620 yards, S.S.S.63
Designed by Herbert Fowler.
Founded 1928
Visitors: welcome.
Green Fee: £7.50/round.

Societies: welcome weekdays only; special rates for groups of 16+; Company days available.
Catering: available.
Hotels: County; Castle; Corner House; Rumwell Manor.

B78 Wareham
☎(0929) 554147
Sandford Rd, Wareham, Dorset BH20 4DH
On A351 near railway station, 8 miles from Poole.
Undulating parkland course with fine views.
18 holes, 5603 yards, S.S.S.67
Designed by C. Whitcombe
Founded 1924
Visitors: welcome 9.30am to 5pm Mon-Fri, phone in advance; h/cap certs required.
Green Fee: £15/round, £20/day.
Societies: by arrangement.
Catering: full bar and catering facilities.
Hotels: Springfield.

B79 Wells (Somerset)
☎(0749) 675005, 679059 Pro
East Horrington Rd, Wells, Somerset BA5 3DS
1.5 miles from city centre off B3139.
Meadowland/parkland course.
18 holes, 6015 yards, S.S.S.69
Founded 1893 (extended 1993)
Visitors: welcome, current h/cap card required weekends; no visitors before 9.30am weekends.
Green Fee: £16/round, £19/day WD; £20/round, £22/day WE & BH.
Societies: welcome with advance booking, weekdays only.
Catering: bar, midday and evening meals available 7 days.
Hotels: Caravan facilities adjacent.

B80 Wessex Golf Centre
☎(0305) 784737
Radipole Lane, Weymouth, Dorset
Behind Weymouth football ground.
9 holes, Par 3
Visitors: welcome any time.
Green Fee: £3.50/round (£5 inc. club hire). Driving range.

B81 West Wilts
☎(0985) 212702 Steward, 212110 Pro, 213133 Sec
Elm Hill, Warminster, Wilts BA12 0AU
Towards Westbury, on edge of town, on old road, not on the new by-pass; 1 mile from centre of Warminster.

Downland course, scenic views.
18 holes, 5709 yards, S.S.S.68
Designed by J.H. Taylor.
Founded 1891
Visitors: welcome with h/cap cert,
except Sat and Sun am.
Green Fee: £22 WD, £33 WE.
Societies: accepted Wed/Thurs/Fri,
contact Sec.
Catering: available.
Hotels: The Bell.

B82 Weston-super-Mare
☎(0934) 626968 Office, 633360 Pro
Uphill Rd North, Weston-super-Mare,
Avon BS23 4NQ
M5 or A370 from Bristol.
Seaside links course.
18 holes, 6225 yards, S.S.S.70
Designed by T. Dunn.
Founded July 1892
Visitors: welcome, h/cap cert
required at weekends and Bank
Holidays.
Green Fee: £20 WD, £28 WE & BH.
Societies: by arrangement.
Catering: bar and restaurant, snacks
and meals daily. Snooker.
Hotels: Grand Atlantic; Beachlands;
Arosfa; Rozel.

B83 Weymouth
☎(0305) 773981
Links Rd, Weymouth, Dorset DT4 0PF
From Dorchester take A354, at
Wessex roundabout take Town
Centre exit, signposted at next exit.
Seaside/parkland course.
18 holes, 6009 yards, S.S.S.69
Designed originally by James Braid;
redesigned by J. Hamilton Stutt.
Founded 1909
Visitors: welcome with h/cap cert or
proof of club membership.
Green Fee: £22 WD, £28 WE & BH.
Societies: Tues and Thurs by
arrangement.
Catering: full bar and restaurant
facilities. Practice area.
Hotels: Moonfleet Manor, weekday
packages.

B84 Windwhistle
☎(0460) 30231, (0460) 30055 Fax
Windwhistle, Cricket St Thomas, Nr
Chard, Somerset TA20 4DG
On N side of A30 5 miles from
Crewkerne, 3 miles from Chard,
opposite wildlife park; follow signs
from M25 junction 25.
Downland/parkland course.

18 holes, 6500 yards, S.S.S.71; 9
holes, 3200 yards.
Designed by J.H. Taylor (1932),
Leonard Fisher (1992).
Founded 1932
Visitors: welcome but advisable to
phone first.
Green Fee: apply for details.
Societies: welcome by appointment,
phone for information.
Catering: comprehensive catering
facilities.
International standard squash
courts.
Hotels: information on request.

B85 Wootton Bassett
☎(0793) 849999
Wootton Basset, Swindon, Wilts SN4
7PB
Parkland course with 10 large lakes.
18 holes, 6,600 yards, SSS73
Designed by Peter Alliss & Clive Clark.
Founded April 1992
Visitors: phone for availability.
Green Fee: apply for details.
Societies: phone for availability.
Catering: full bar and restaurant
facilities.

B86 Worlebury
☎(0934) 623214 Clubhouse,
625789 Sec
Monks Hill, Worlebury,
Weston-super-Mare, Avon BS22 9SX
2 miles from M5 at top of hill (off
A370); 2 miles from centre of
Weston-super-Mare.
Seaside meadowland course.
18 holes, 5921 yards, S.S.S.69
Designed by W. Hawtree & Son.
Founded 1908
Visitors: welcome on weekdays
after 9am; h/cap certificate and
membership of recognised club or
society.
Green Fee: £20 WD (£12 with
member), £30 WE (£17 with
member).
Societies: catered for on weekdays,
other days by special arrangement.
Catering: licenced bar, restaurant
serving snacks, lunch and evening
meal. Snooker.
Hotels: Beachlands; Commodore;
Rozel; Queenswood.

B87 Wrag Barn Golf & Country Club
☎(0793) 861327 Sec, 766027 Pro,
861325 Fax

Shrivenham Rd, Highworth, Wilts
SN7 7QQ
10 miles from M4 junction 15; take
A419 towards Cirencester, left turn
to Highworth, follow A316 to
Highworth then 3rd exit at
roundabout onto B4000 to
Shrivenham; course is 0.5 mile on
right.
Undulating, scenic, parkland course.
18 holes, 6548 yards, S.S.S.71
Designed by Hawtree & Sons.
Founded July 1990
Visitors: welcome; some restrictions
at weekends, advisable to ring Pro.
Green Fee: £15/round WD,
£20/round WE & BH.
Societies: by arrangement with Sec.
Catering: full bar and restaurant
facilities; catering for companies,
parties, receptions.
Hotels: Blunsden House Hotel &
Leisure Centre (Blunsden); Jesmond
House (Highworth).

B88 Yeovil
☎(0935) 22965 Sec, 75949
Clubhouse, 73763 Pro
Sherborne Rd, Yeovil, Somerset
BA21 5BW
1 mile E of Yeovil on A30 Yeovil to
Sherborne.
Undulating parkland course.
Old course, 18 holes, 6144 yards,
S.S.S.70; Newton course, 9 holes,
5016 yards, S.S.S.66
Designed by 18 hole, Fowler &
Alison; 9 hole, Sports Turf Research
Institute.
Founded 1919
Visitors: welcome weekdays, both
courses 9.30am-12.30pm and 2pm
onwards (h/cap cert required for Old
Course).
Green Fee: Old Course: £20/round,
£30/day WD, £30/day WE. Newton
Course: £12/day WD, £15/day WE (to
be confirmed).
Societies: must be affiliated to EGU
or bona-fide members of a golf club.
Catering: full bar and restaurant.
Driving/practice area, snooker.
Hotels: Yeovil Court, Manor House
(Yeovil); Northover House (Ilchester);
Post House (Sherborne).

C

HAMPSHIRE, SUSSEX, ISLE OF WIGHT

The connoisseur, making his way east from Brokenhurst Manor in the New Forest to Rye on the East Sussex border with Kent, passes through as good and varied a golfing tapestry as could be imagined — a veritable Aladdin's Cave. Compared with other parts of the country, the volume of courses is none too dense but any shortcomings in quantity are more than absorbed by quality.

For the purposes of playing qualification at county level, Hampshire embraces the Channel Islands, the Isle of Wight and Hayling Island, the latter a links, or part links, which Tom Simpson rated enormously highly. I also remember Henry Longhurst singing its praises and I can join in the chorus but Hampshire's inland gems are North Hants at Fleet, Blackmoor and Liphook — all extensions of the rich seam of heather, gorse and silver birch country which starts with Wentworth and Sunningdale in the east and continues down through Swinley Forest and Camberley Heath.

Liphook, straddling the busy A3 and involving one or two mad dashes to cross it, has had strong naval connections in view of its proximity to Portsmouth but it has remained essentially a refuge for the Club golfer in spite of being able to test the best.

Hockley and Royal Winchester typify downland golf at its best, while Stoneham at Southampton is more in the mould of Liphook. Sussex, too, is full of variety with something for everyone. West Sussex at Pulborough is a particular favourite, ideal for any occasion and giving the chance of a good score with its five short holes although, like Rye, the par of 68 can be tantalisingly elusive.

Straight hitting has more merit than unharnessed power, for the heather is punishing but the unique charms of Rye centre more on a battle with the winds that sweep off the sea or across the chilly reaches of Romney Marsh.

There is a charm about Rye that never varies or fades. Expectation begins with departure from the ancient town and its cobbled streets and heightens as the road to Camber twists and turns through fields of grazing sheep. The character of the golf is distinctive in the range of shots it demands, the ability to flight the ball and gauge how it will run on landing being infinitely more valuable than memorising yardage charts and clubbing by numbers.

Rye is a monument to the links style of British golf but the new East Sussex National is the opposite, an expensive machine-shaped exercise in creating a new landscape over which the European Open was played in 1993. There are those who prefer courses which preserve nature rather than fighting it and nowhere is that aspect better illustrated than Royal Ashdown Forest or Crowborough which run hither and thither across the Sussex Downs, Ashdown Forest notably without bunkers.

Goodwood is another from whose highest points scenic splendour unfurls, a contrast to its neighbour, the Goodwood Park Hotel Golf & Country Club which occupies a large part of the grounds of Goodwood House. Bognor Regis, Selsey and Littlehampton lie a few miles to the south while Chichester Golf Centre is a recently opened venture at Hunston — ideal for those wishing to learn the ropes.

Worthing, Brighton and Eastbourne are well served while Cooden Beach has a host of admirers, along with a particular favourite in Seaford, another downland course overlooking the Channel.

C1 Aldershaw

☎(0424) 870898
Sedlescombe, E Sussex TN33 0SD
On main A21 near Sedlescombe.
Parkland course.
18 holes, 6400 yards, S.S.S.71
Founded 1991
Visitors: Mon-Fri on production of
current h/cap cert.
Green Fee: apply for details.
Societies: on application.
Catering: bar and snacks.
Driving range.
Hotels: Brickwall.

C2 Alresford

☎(0962) 733746 Sec, 736040 Fax
Tichborne Down, Alresford, Hants
SO24 0PN
1 mile S of A31 Winchester-Alton
road, 2 miles N of A272
Winchester-Petersfield road.
Undulating parkland course.
18 holes, 5905 yards, S.S.S.68
Designed by Scott Webb Young
Founded 16 Nov 1890
Visitors: welcome; not before 12am
weekends and Bank Holidays.
Green Fee: £15/round, £23/day WD;
£30/round WE & BH (reductions with
member).

Societies: Tues, Wed, Thurs;
bookings via Sec.
Catering: full catering every day
except Mon.
Hotels: Swan; Bell.

C3 Alton

☎(0420) 82042
Old Odiham Rd, Alton, Hants GU34
4BU
2 miles N of Alton on A32 turn right at
Golden Pot public house, 1st right
again, 0.5 mile on right.
Undulating parkland course.
9 holes, 5744 yards, S.S.S.68
Founded 1908
Visitors: welcome Mon-Fri;
weekends 18 h/cap or with member.
Green Fee: £12/round, £16/day WD;
£16/round, £20/day WE & BH.
Societies: by prior arrangement
weekdays.
Catering: bar.
Hotels: Alton House; Swan.

C4 Ampfield Par 3

☎(0794) 368480, 368750 Pro
Winchester Rd, Ampfield, Romsey,
Hants SO51 9BQ
On A31 2.5 miles W of Hursley

village, next door to White Horse
public house.
Parkland course.
18 holes, 2478 yards, S.S.S.53
Designed by Henry Cotton.
Founded 1963
Visitors: welcome but advisable to
telephone first; h/cap cert required
weekends and Bank Holidays.
Green Fee: on application.
Societies: small societies welcome
weekdays by prior arrangement.
Catering: light lunch, snacks and
society dinners by prior
arrangement.
Hotels: Potters Heron (Ampfield);
White Horse (Romsey).

C5 Andover

☎(0264) 358040 Sec, 323980
Members, 324151 Pro
Winchester Rd, Andover, Hants SP10
2EF
Just off A303 on Andover by-pass,
entrance to club about 500 yards
after leaving A303 on A3057.
Undulating parkland course.
9 holes, 5933 yards, S.S.S.68
Designed by J.H. Taylor.
Founded 1907
Visitors: welcome.

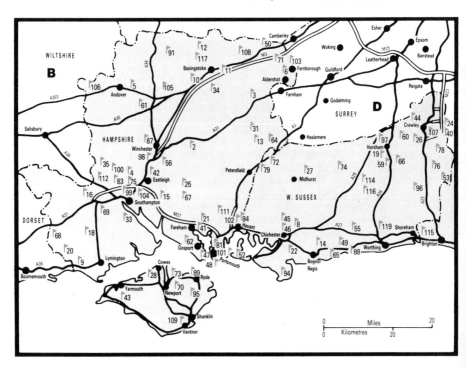

Green Fee: £12 (£8 with member) WD, £22 after 12am (£11 with member) WE; full day £17.50 (£11 with member) WD.
Societies: welcome Mon-Wed.
Catering: snacks, lunch, evening meal.
Hotels: Danebury; White Hart.

C6 Army

☎(0252) 540638 Sec, 541104 Club, 547232 Pro
Laffans Rd, Aldershot, Hants GU11 2HF
Access from Eelmoor Bridge off A323 Aldershot-Fleet road.
Heathland course.
18 holes, 6550 yards, S.S.S.71
Designed by Frank Pennink.
Founded 1883
Visitors: welcome Mon-Fri, 18 holes only, h/cap cert required.
Green Fee: £22/round.
Societies: Mon, Thurs only.
Catering: available 9am to 5pm.
Hotels: Queens

C7 Ashdown Forest Hotel

☎(0342 82) 4866
Chapel Lane, Forest Row, E Sussex RH18 5BB
3 miles S of East Grinstead on A22 in village of Forest Row, E on B2110; Chapel Lane 4th on right.
Heathland/woodland course.
18 holes, 5510 yards, S.S.S.67
Designed by Horace Hutchinson (1930s); Henry Luff (1965).
Founded 1985 (Anderida Golfers).
Visitors: welcome but advisable to check, particularly at weekends.
Green Fee: on application.
Societies: catered for 7 days.

Catering: full restaurant service and bar snacks 7 days. Banqueting facilities up to 100.
Hotels: Ashdown Forest.

C8 Avisford Park

☎(0243) 554611
Avisford Park Country Hotel, Walberton, Arundel, W Sussex BN18 0LS
On A27 4 miles W of Arundel, 6 miles E of Chichester.
Parkland course.
9 holes, 6418 yards, S.S.S.71
Visitors: welcome, pay-as-you-play system.
Green Fee: winter; £12/day, £10 (18 holes) WD; £15/day, £13 (18 holes) WE: summer; £15/day, £12 (18 holes) WD, £18/day, £15 (18 holes) WE.
Societies: any time, terms on application.
Catering: bar and restaurant. Tennis, swimming, squash, snooker etc.
Hotels: own hotel on site; subsidised golf for residents.

C9 Barton-on-Sea

☎(0425) 615308 Sec, 611210 Pro, 610189 Members, 639092 Steward
Marine Drive, Barton-on-Sea, New Milton, Hants BH25 7DY
Off A337 at the extreme E end of Marine Drive at Barton.
Seaside course.
27 holes, 3 loops of 9; A+B, 6505 yards, S.S.S.71; A+C, 6289 yards, S.S.S.70; B+C, 6444 yards, S.S.S.71
Designed by H.S. Colt.
Founded 1898

Visitors: welcome weekdays after 8.30am and weekends and Bank Holidays after 11.15am; advisable to ring to ascertain programme for day.
Green Fee: £25 (£8.50 with member) WD, £30 (£10 with member) WE.
Societies: societies 12 and over accepted Wed and Fri.
Catering: snacks and teas, evening catering for societies by arrangement.
Hotels: Chewton Glen; Old Coastguard; Passford House.

C10 Basingstoke

☎(0256) 465990
Kempshott Park, Basingstoke, Hants RG23 7LL
On A30 3 miles W of Basingstoke, M3 junction 7.
Parkland course.
18 holes, 6284 yards, S.S.S.70
Designed by James Braid.
Founded 1928
Visitors: weekdays with h/cap cert, weekends with member.
Green Fee: on application.
Societies: welcome Wed and Thurs.
Catering: full every day except Mon.
Hotels: Wheatsheaf; Audley Wood.

C11 Basingstoke Golf Centre

☎(0256) 50054
Worting Rd, West Ham, Basingstoke, Hants RG23 0TY
M3 junction 7; 0.5 mile from Basingstoke town centre in Basingstoke Leisure Park.
Public parkland course.
9 holes Par 3, 908 yards.
Visitors: welcome.
Green Fee: apply for details.
Driving range.

C12 Bishopswood

☎(0734) 815213, 812200
Bishopswood Lane, Tadley, Basingstoke, Hants RG26 6AT
6 miles N of Basingstoke, off A340.
Public parkland course.
9 holes, 6474 yards, S.S.S.71
Designed by Blake and Phillips.
Founded 1976
Visitors: welcome, Mon to Fri, no h/cap cert required.
Green Fee: £8 (9 holes), £13 (18 holes).
Societies: welcome by arrangement (weekdays only)
Catering: bar snacks and restaurant. Driving range.

C13 **Blackmoor**

☎(0420) 472775
Golf Lane, Whitehill, Bordon, Hants
GU35 9EH
Off A325 between Farnham and
Petersfield, turn into Firgrove Rd at
Whitehill crossroads.
Parkland/heathland course.
18 holes, 6213 yards, S.S.S.70
Designed by H.S. Colt.
Founded 1913
Visitors: welcome weekdays with
h/cap cert.
Green Fee: apply for details.
Societies: Wed, Thurs and Fri.
Catering: full, available every day.
Hotels: Silver Birch, Greatham.

C14 **Bognor Regis**

☎(0243) 821929
Downview Rd, Felpham, Bognor
Regis, W Sussex PO22 8JD
A259 Littlehampton-Bognor road,
from Bognor Regis to traffic lights,
turn left, club 0.5 mile at end of road.
Parkland course
18 holes, 6238 yards, S.S.S.70
Designed by James Braid.
Founded 1 Jan 1892
Visitors: welcome with h/cap cert,
weekends April-Oct with member
only.
Green Fee: on application
Societies: by arrangement only.
Catering: meals by arrangement.

C15 **Botley Park Hotel & Country Club**

☎(0489) 780888, 789242 Fax
Winchester Road, Boorley Green,
Botley, Hants SO3 2UA
NW of Botley on B3354 Winchester
road, within easy reach of M27
junction 7, or M3/A33.
Parkland course.
18 holes, 6026 yards, S.S.S.70
Designed by Charles Potterton.
Founded Feb 1990
Visitors: phone bookings required;
also h/cap cert.
Green Fee: apply for details.
Societies: available Wed and Thurs.
Catering: full restaurant facilities,
bars and bar snacks; banqueting.
Driving range, indoor swimming
pool, squash, tennis, croquet,
snooker, petanque, sauna etc.
Hotels: Hotel in complex.

C16 **Bramshaw**

☎(0703) 813433 Manager, 813434
Pro, 812214 Hotel
Brook, Lyndhurst, Hants SO4 7HE

Exit from M27 (Cadnam) at junction
1, take B3078 for 1 mile, club on
right behind Bell Inn.
Manor course, parkland; Forest
course, undulating.
Manor, 18 holes, 6233 yards,
S.S.S.70; Forest, 18 holes, 5774
yards, S.S.S.69
Founded 1880
Visitors: not weekends unless
playing with member or Bell Inn
resident.
Green Fee: £20/round, £30/day.
Societies: any weekday, bookings
only.
Catering: full catering.
Hotels: Bell Inn within Golf Complex
(golf inclusive breaks available with
reserved tee times at Bramshaw and
Dunwood Manor, see C35).

C17 **Brighton & Hove**

☎(0273) 556482 Sec, 540560 Pro
Dyke Rd, Brighton, E Sussex BN1 8YJ
N of Brighton centre, 2.5 miles up
Dyke Rd on left side.
Downland course.
9 holes, 5722 yards, S.S.S.68
Designed by James Braid.
Founded 1887
Visitors: welcome; not before 12am
Wed, 10am Fri, 12am Sun.
Green Fee: £12.50 (18 holes) WD,
£21 WE.
Societies: catered for weekdays.
Catering: full service available.
Snooker.
Hotels: Old Ship.

C18 **Brokenhurst Manor**

☎(0590) 23332 Sec, 23092 Pro,
24140 Fax
Sway Rd, Brockenhurst, Hants SO42
7SG
A337 to Brockenhurst, then B3055 S
from village centre, club 1 mile on
right.
Gently undulating forest/parkland
course.
18 holes, 6222 yards, S.S.S.70
Designed by H.S. Colt, with recent
alterations by J. Hamilton Stutt.
Founded 1919
Visitors: phone booking in advance;
must have current h/cap cert.
Green Fee: £25/round, £35/day WD;
£40/round/day WE & BH.
Societies: Thurs; book with Sec;
small parties can be accommodated
on Mon, Wed and Fri, details from
Sec.
Catering: bar and meals available
every day.
Hotels: information on request.

C19 **Brookfield**

☎(0403) 891568, 891891
answerphone, 891499 Fax
Winterpit Lane, Plummer's Plain,
Horsham, W Sussex RH13 6LU
From M23 take A279 to Handcross,
through village, then 2nd right and
1st left; from Horsham take A281
towards Brighton, at Manning's
Heath Dun Horse pub turn left, over
crossroads into Waterpit Lane.
Public parkland course.
6 holes, S.S.S.53
Designed by P. Webster and
Associates.
Founded March 1991
Visitors: welcome at all times, no
restrictions.
Green Fee: £10.
Societies: always welcome, also
corporate day brochure available.
Catering: 2 bars, lounge,
restaurants.
Driving range, pool/games room,
sauna, gardens, children's play area.
Hotels: Brookfield Farm

C20 **Burley**

☎(0425) 402431 Sec
Cott Lane, Burley, Ringwood, Hants
BH24 4BB
Leave A31 Ringwood-Cadnam road
at Picket Post, through Burley Street
and Burley; club at top of hill, 400
yards from village centre on
Lymington road.
Undulating heathland course.
9 holes, 6149 yards, S.S.S.69
Founded 1905
Visitors: welcome with h/cap cert
and required standard of dress; not
Wed until 1.45pm (Ladies Day);
members only most Sat and some
Sun.
Green Fee: £14/day (£8 with
member), £16 WE & BH (£9 with
member).
Catering: bar and catering available
lunch time most days.
Hotels: Moorhill House; Burley
Manor; White Buck; Toad Hall.

C21 **Cams Hall**

☎(0329) 827222
Cams Hall, Fareham, Hants PO16 8UP
200 yards from M27 exit 11.
Parkland and coastal courses.
18 holes, 6000 yards, Par 71; 9
holes, 2500 yards, Par 69.
Designed by Peter Alliss, Clive Clark.
Founded 1993
Visitors: welcome, h/cap certs
required, phone in advance;
restricted at weekends.

Green Fee: 18 hole course, £25; 9 hole course £12.50, WD, £15 WE.
Societies: arranged in advance.
Catering: full facilities.
Sauna

C22 Chichester Golf Centre
☎(0243) 533833 Reservations, 536666 Admin, 539922 Fax
Hoe Farm, Hunston, Chichester, W Sussex PO20 6AX
3 miles S of Chichester (A27) on B2145 to Selsey, on left hand side after village of Hunston.
Public course with membership; parkland with lakes.
Tower, 18 holes, 6204 yards, S.S.S.69; Cathedral, new 'Florida' style course, 6461 yards, Par 72, open May 1994
Designed by Philip Sanders
Founded August 1990
Visitors: welcome, h/cap required on Cathedral course; tee reservations required; strict dress code.
Green Fee: £13/round, £25/day WD; £18.50/round, £30/day WE: Par 3, £3.50 WD, £4.50 WE (inc. clubs and ball).
Societies: welcome by prior arrangement, society clubroom available.
Catering: temporary catering and refreshments available.
Driving range, Academy hole, 825 yard Par 3 course.
Hotels: Millstream (Bosham); Hunston Mill B&B (Hunston); Post House (Hayling Island).

C23 Cooden Beach
☎(0424) 842040 Sec, 843936 Catering, 843938 Pro
Cooden Sea Rd, Nr Bexhill-on-Sea, E Sussex TN39 4TR
A259 Eastbourne-Hastings road, follow Cooden Beach sign at Little Common roundabout.
Seaside course.
18 holes, 6450 yards, S.S.S.71
Designed by Herbert Fowler.
Founded 1912
Visitors: h/cap certs required; prior arrangement preferred.

Green Fee: £26 WD, £33 WE & BH.
Societies: Mon, Thurs, Fri by arrangement.
Catering: full services available.
Snooker.
Hotels: Cooden Resort.

C24 Copthorne
☎(0342) 712508, 712405 Pro, 717682 Fax
Borers Arms Rd, Copthorne, Crawley, W Sussex RH10 3LL
On A264, 4 miles E of Crawley; 2 miles E of exit 10 from M23.
Heathland course.
18 holes, 6505 yards, S.S.S.71
Designed by James Braid.
Founded 1892
Visitors: welcome weekdays and afternoons at weekends.
Green Fee: £25/round, £32/day WD; £40/round WE after 1pm.
Societies: Thurs and Fri.
Catering: lunch Mon-Fri and Sun.
Hotels: Copthorne.

C25 Corhampton
☎(0489) 877279
Sheeps Pond Lane, Droxford, Southampton, Hants SO3 1QZ
Right off A32 at Corhampton on B3135 for 1 mile.
Downland course.
18 holes, 6444 yards, S.S.S.71
Founded 1891
Visitors: welcome weekdays, with member at weekends.
Green Fee: £20/round, £30/day.
Societies: welcome Mon and Thurs.
Catering: lunch, tea, dinners except Tues.
Hotels: Little Uplands Country Guest House; Coach House Motel.

C26 Cottesmore
☎(0293) 528256
Buchan Hill, Pease Pottage, Crawley, Sussex RH11 9AT
M23 exit to Pease Pottage, 1 mile down Horsham road from Pease Pottage, on right.
Undulating meadowland course.
Old, 18 holes, 6280 yards, S.S.S.70; New, 18 holes, 5800 yards, S.S.S.68
Designed by M.D. Rogerson.

Founded 1974
Visitors: welcome.
Green Fee: Old; £30 WD, £40 WE; New £20 WD, £26 WE.
Societies: weekdays only; weekend breaks in club accommodation.
Catering: full facilities.
Tennis, squash, indoor swimming pool, health club, saunas etc.
Hotels: accommodation available at club.

C27 Cowdray Park
☎(0730) 813599 Sec
Midhurst, W Sussex GU29 0BB
Situated about 1 mile E of Midhurst on A272.
Parkland course.
18 holes, 5972 yards, S.S.S.70
Founded 1920
Visitors: welcome.
Green Fee: apply for details.
Societies: catered for on weekdays except Tues and Fri.
Catering: bar snacks daily, evening meals by arrangement.
Hotels: Angel; Spread Eagle.

C28 Cowes
☎(0983) 292303
Crossfield Ave, Cowes, PO31 8HN
Make for Cowes High School; course is at far end of school playing field.
Parkland course, Solent views.
9 holes, 2967 yards, S.S.S.68
Founded 1908
Visitors: welcome by arrangement; not before 11.30am Sun or 10.30am-3pm Thurs.
Green Fee: on application.
Societies: on application to Sec.
Catering: bar snacks from 11.30am to 1pm except Sun, summer only.
Hotels: Fountain; New Holmwood.

C29 Crowborough Beacon
☎(0892) 661511
Beacon Rd, Crowborough, E Sussex TN6 1UJ
8 miles S of Tunbridge Wells on A26.
Heathland course.
18 holes, 6318 yards, S.S.S.70
Founded 1895
Visitors: weekdays; h/cap cert or letter of intro required.

Green Fee: £22.50/round, £34/day WD; £16.50/round with county card.
Societies: Mon, Tues, Wed, Fri by prior arrangement with Sec.
Catering: for up to 60; breakfast available by prior arrangement.
Hotels: Winston Manor.

C30 Dale Hill Hotel
☎(0580) 200112, 201249 Fax
Ticehurst, Wadhurst, E Sussex TN5 7DQ
35 mins Gatwick Airport; A21 to Flimwell crossroads, then B2087 towards Ticehurst.
Parkland course.
18 holes, 6150 yards, S.S.S.69; new course under construction
Founded 1974
Visitors: visitors welcome after 10am, ring to book times.
Green Fee: £20 WD, £25 WE.
Societies: welcome weekdays, ring for Society form.
Catering: clubhouse bar/restaurant and hotel restaurant.
Snooker, practice area, health club (residents only)
Hotels: Dale Hill, golf breaks and packages; all day golf £15

C31 Dean Farm (Kingsley)
☎(0420) 489478, 472313
Main Rd, Kingsley, Bordon, Hants GU35 9NG
Off A325 Farnham-Petersfield road, 3 miles E of Bordon on the B3004.
Public pay-and-play parkland course.
9 holes, 1797 yards, S.S.S.27
Founded 1984
Visitors: welcome any time.
Green Fee: £4 (9 holes), £6.50 (18 holes).
Catering: bar and snacks.

C32 Dewlands Manor Golf Course
☎(0892) 852266, 853308, 853015 Fax
Cottage Hill, Rotherfield, E Sussex, TN6 3JN
0.5 mile S of village of Rotherfield just off B2101 to Five Ashes; 10 miles from Tunbridge Wells.
Pay-and-play parkland/woodland course with water hazards.
9 holes, 3186 yards, S.S.S.70
Designed by R.M. and Nick Godin.
Founded 1991
Visitors: welcome all playing days; course open Mar-Nov 15th, thereafter Fri, Sat and Sun.

Green Fee: summer £12.50 (9holes), £23 (18 holes) WD; £14.50 (9 holes), £27.50 (18 holes) WE: winter £12.50 (9 holes), £20 (18 holes).
Societies: small business groups welcome at all times, limit 20.
Catering: fully licensed bar, light snacks at all times, special orders by pre-arrangement.
Practice net, putting green, practice hole.
Hotels: Soa, Royal Wells (Tunbridge Wells); Winston Manor (Crowborough).

C33 Dibden
☎(0703) 207508 Bookings, 845596 Shop, 845060 Catering
Main Rd, Dibden, Southampton, Hants SO4 5TB
Turn off A326 at Dibden roundabout, course 0.5 mile on right hand side.
Public parkland course.
18 holes, 6206 yards, S.S.S.70; 9 holes, 1520 yards Par 29
Designed by J. Hamilton Stutt.
Founded 1974
Visitors: welcome, no restrictions.
Green Fee: £6.50 WD, £9.50 WE.
Societies: by arrangement with Pro.
Catering: full catering facilities available.
Driving range.

C34 Dummer
☎(0256) 397888
Dummer, Hants
M3 exit 7.
Parkland course.
18 holes, Par 72
Designed by Peter Alliss & Clive Clark.
Founded 1992
Visitors: details on application.
Green Fee: £21.
Societies: details on application.
Catering: full facilities.
Sauna
Hotels: Audley's Wood; Hilton National (Basingstoke).

C35 Dunwood Manor
☎(0794) 340549 Office, 340663 Pro shop, 341215 Fax
Shootash Hill, Romsey, Hants SO51 0GF
Off A27 Romsey to Salisbury road, after 2 miles turn right at Shootash crossroads into Danes Rd, club is on left.
Undulating parkland course.
18 holes, 6004 yards, S.S.S.69
Founded 1972

Visitors: welcome weekdays by arrangement.
Green Fee: £20/round, £28/day WD; £30/round WE & BH.
Societies: by arrangement.
Catering: bar meals 12am-2pm and 7-9.30pm or by arrangement.
Snooker and pool table.
Hotels: Bell Inn (discounts available).

C36 Dyke
☎(0273) 857296, 857260 Pro, 857078 Fax
Devil's Dyke, Dyke Rd, Brighton, E Sussex BN1 8YJ
5 miles N of Brighton between A23 and A27, 2 miles off Brighton by-pass.
Premier downland course.
18 holes, 6611 yards, S.S.S.72
Founded 1906
Visitors: welcome by appointment.
Green Fee: £21/round, £31/day WD; £31/round WE & BH; contact Pro.
Societies: full day inc meals £45.
Catering: licensed bar and restaurant. Snooker.
Hotels: Old Ship (Brighton).

C37 East Brighton
☎(0273) 604838
Roedean Rd, Brighton, E Sussex BN2 5RA
Follow A259 from Brighton towards Newhaven, then signs for Marina; over 1st set of traffic lights; club 50 metres on left.
Downland course.
18 holes, 6346 yards, S.S.S.70
Designed by James Braid
Founded 1893
Visitors: welcome on weekdays, weekends by appointment; h/cap cert required.
Green Fee: £21/day WD, £30/day WE.
Societies: by arrangement Mon, Tues pm, Thurs, Fri.
Catering: full bar, lunch/tea served every day, evening meals by arrangement. Snooker
Hotels: Old Ship, golf inclusive packages; Grand; Metropole; Brighton Thistle.

C38 East Sussex National
☎(0825) 880088
Little Horsted, Uckfield, East Sussex TN22 5ES
2 miles S of Uckfield on A22.
Part (18 holes) public course: England's "Augusta" – bent grass tees, fairways and greens.

East, 18 holes, 7158 yards, S.S.S.74; West, 18 holes, 7154 yards, S.S.S.74; National Academy, 3 holes, 1155 yards, S.S.S.12
Designed by Bob Cupp.
Founded 1989
Visitors: welcome; reservations advised.
Green Fee: in season; £59.50/round, £75/day: out of season; £49.50 unlimited golf inc brunch or lunch.
Societies: welcome daily by arrangement.
Catering: bar and restaurant facilities.
Academy of Golf Teaching Centre; 2 double ended practice ranges; chipping, pitching, putting greens.
Hotels: Horsted Place Hotel on site (golfers privileges).

C39 Eastbourne Downs
☎(0323) 720827
East Dean Rd, Eastbourne, E Sussex BN20 8ES
On A259 W of Eastbourne.
Downland course.
18 holes, 6635 yards, S.S.S.72
Designed by J.H. Taylor.
Founded 1907
Visitors: welcome.
Green Fee: £18/day.
Societies: welcome.
Catering: Tues-Sun.
Hotels: Queens; Princes; Lansdowne; Wish Tower.

C40 Effingham Park
☎(0342) 716528
West Park Rd, Copthorne, W Sussex RH10 3EU
From M23 junction 10 onto A264.
Parkland course.
9 holes, 3498 yards, S.S.S.57
Designed by Francisco Escario.
Founded 1980
Visitors: welcome, not before 1pm Sat/Sun, not after 4pm Tues.
Green Fee: £9 (9 holes), £12.50 (18 holes) WD; £10, £14.50 WE.
Societies: on application.
Catering: 2 restaurants, clubhouse bar. Leisure Club; swimming, sauna, gym; Golf academy, corporate days.
Hotels: Effingham Park; Copthorne Gatwick (American Express weekend break).

C41 Fleetlands
☎(0705) 822351 extn 44384 Sec
R.N.A.Y. Fleetlands, Gosport, Hants PO13 0AW
Off A32 2 miles S of Fareham.

9 holes, 4852 yards, S.S.S.64
Founded 1963
Visitors: with members only.
Green Fee: on application.
Societies: by appointment.
Catering: bar.

C42 Fleming Park
☎(0703) 612797 Pro, 612692 catering
Magpie Lane, Eastleigh, Hants SO5 3LH
A27/M27, turn off at Eastleigh sign, 1 mile to course.
Parkland course.
18 holes, 4402 yards, S.S.S.62
Designed by Charles Lawrie.
Founded 1973
Visitors: welcome, phone in advance.
Green Fee: on application
Societies: apply to Pro.
Catering: bar snacks and meals.

C43 Freshwater Bay
☎(0983) 752955
Afton Down, Freshwater Bay, Isle of Wight PO40 9TZ
3 miles from Yarmouth on A3055 overlooking Freshwater Bay.
Seaside downland course with extensive views over Solent and English Channel.
18 holes, 5662 yards, S.S.S.68
Founded 1893
Visitors: welcome after 9.30am on weekdays and 10am on Sun.
Green Fee: £18 WD, £22 WE & BH.
Societies: welcome at times shown for visitors; advance bookings required.
Catering: full catering facilities, licenced bar
Hotels: Albion; Country Garden; Farringford.

C44 Gatwick Manor Hotel
☎(0293) 26301
London Rd, Lowfield Heath, Nr Crawley, W Sussex
0.75 miles S of Gatwick Airport on A23.
Refurbished parkland course.
9 holes, 1118 yards, Par 28
Designed by Patrick Tallack.
Visitors: welcome; priority to guests of Hotel.
Green Fee: apply for details.
Societies: societies and Company days welcome by prior arrangement.
Catering: full facilities; 2 bars and 2 restaurants.
Hotels: Gatwick Manor.

C45 Goodwood
☎(0243) 774968
Goodwood, Chichester, W Sussex PO18 0PN
On A286 5 miles N of Chichester.
Downland/parkland course.
18 holes, 6401 yards, S.S.S.71
Designed by James Braid.
Founded 1891
Visitors: not before 9am weekdays and 10am weekends; phone Pro shop for details.
Green Fee: £25 WD, £35 WE.
Societies: Wed, Thurs; essential to book early.
Catering: full catering by booking except Mon. Snooker.
Hotels: Goodwood Park; Chichester Resort; Dolphin & Anchor.

C46 Goodwood Park Hotel Golf & Country Club
☎(0243) 775987
Goodwood, Nr Chichester, W Sussex PO20 0QB
A27-M27 E of Chichester, in the grounds of Goodwood House.
Parkland course.
18 holes, 6525 yards, S.S.S.72
Designed by Donald Steel.
Founded 1989
Visitors: welcome with h/cap cert and correct attire.
Green Fee: £17/round WD, £25/round WE (no day tickets).
Societies: welcome by arrangement Tues-Thurs.
Catering: full catering and bar facilities, inc. private rooms.
Tennis, swimming, squash, snooker, gym, sauna etc.
Hotels: Goodwood Park, golf and leisure breaks, conference venue.

C47 Gosport & Stokes Bay
☎(0705) 527941 Sec, 581625 Club
Fort Rd, Haslar, Gosport, Hants PO12 2AT
S on A32 from Fareham, E to Haslar.
Links course.
9 holes, 5966 yards, S.S.S.69
Founded 1885
Visitors: welcome except Sun am.
Green Fee: £12 WD, £15 WE.
Societies: by arrangement.
Catering: bar snacks, meals by arrangement.
Hotels: Anglesey.

C48 Great Salterns
☎(0705) 664549, 699519
Portsmouth Golf Centre, Eastern Rd, Portsmouth PO3 6QB

2 miles from A27 on A2030 into Southsea.
Public seaside/parkland course.
18 holes, 5600 yards, S.S.S.68
Founded 1914
Visitors: welcome, booking system 7 days.
Green Fee: apply for details.
Societies: welcome by prior arrangement.
Catering: at Farmhouse pub adjacent to course.
Driving range.
Hotels: Hilton; Inn Lodge next to Farmhouse.

C49 Ham Manor
☎(0903) 783288, 783732 Pro
Angmering, W Sussex BN16 4JE
3 miles E of Littlehampton.
Gently undulating parkland course.
18 holes, 6269 yards, S.S.S.70
Designed by H.S. Colt.
Founded 1936
Visitors: welcome after 8.45am by prior arrangement; h/cap certs required.
Green Fee: on application
Societies: by arrangement.
Catering: lunch except Mon.
Snooker.

C50 Hartley Wintney
☎(0252) 844211 Sec, 843779 Pro, 842214 Club
London Rd, Hartley Wintney, Hants RG27 8PT
On A30 8 miles NE of Basingstoke.
Parkland course.
9 holes, 6096 yards, S.S.S.69
Founded 1891
Visitors: weekdays; Bank Holidays and weekends with member only; restrictions on Wed.
Green Fee: £17/round, £25/day
Societies: full catering except Mon, snacks 7 days.
Catering: snacks and full catering 6 days.
Hotels: Lismoyne; Lamb.

C51 Hastings
☎(0424) 852981
Battle Rd, St Leonards-on-Sea, E Sussex TN38 0TA
A2100 from Battle to Hastings, 3 miles NW of Hastings.
Municipal parkland course.
18 holes, 6284 yards, S.S.S.71
Designed by Frank Pennink.
Founded 1973
Visitors: no restrictions; tee booking system.

Green Fee: apply for details.
Societies: welcome Mon-Fri.
Catering: full facilities.
Driving range
Hotels: Beauport Park.

C52 Hayling
☎(0705) 464446 Sec, 464491 Pro, 463712 Steward
Links Lane, Hayling Island, Hants PO11 0BX
5 miles S of Havant off M27 to A3023, situated at W end of the seafront.
Links course.
18 holes, 6489 yards, S.S.S.71
Designed by Tom Simpson.
Founded 1883
Visitors: private club h/cap cert required and letter of intro from Home Club appreciated.
Green Fee: £27/day, £35 WE (prior arrangement).
Societies: Tues and Wed only by prior arrangement.
Catering: not Mon.
Hotels: Post House (Northney); Newtown House.

C53 Haywards Heath
☎(0444) 414866
High Beech Lane, Haywards Heath, W Sussex RH16 1SL
2 miles NE of Haywards Heath, follow B2112 towards Lindfield, then left towards Ardingly into Summerhill Lane; High Beech Lane is 4th on left.
Parkland course.
18 holes, 6206 yards, S.S.S.70
Founded 1922
Visitors: welcome subject to tee reservations.
Green Fee: on application
Societies: Wed and Thurs only.
Catering: bar, lunch, evening catering by arrangement.

C54 Highwoods
☎(0424) 212625 Sec, 212770 Pro
Ellerslie Lane, Bexhill-on-Sea, E Sussex TN39 4LJ
Off A259 from Eastbourne or Hastings, 2 miles from Bexhill; from Battle A269 via Ninfield, turn right in Sidley.
Parkland course.
18 holes, 6218 yards, S.S.S.70
Designed by J.H. Taylor.
Founded 1925
Visitors: welcome with h/cap cert; no visitors Sun before 12am unless with member.
Green Fee: £25 WD, £30 WE & BH.

Societies: by arrangement.
Catering: lunch by arrangement, snacks, tea.
Hotels: Cooden Resort; White Friars.

C55 Hill Barn
☎(0903) 237301
Hill Barn Lane, Worthing, Sussex BN14 9QE
N of Worthing off London & Edinburgh Building Soc roundabout on A27, take exit directly before Brighton exit, signposted.
Municipal downland course.
18 holes, 6224 yards, S.S.S.70
Designed by Hawtree & Son.
Founded 1935
Visitors: welcome, no restrictions.
Green Fee: £10.50/round WD, £12.50/round WE & BH.
Societies: weekdays only; min 20.
Catering: breakfasts, snacks, hot meals available all day.
Hotels: Beach; Ardington & Chatsworth.

C56 Hockley
☎(0962) 713165, 714572 Steward, 713678 Pro
Twyford, Winchester, Hants SO21 1PL
2 miles S of Winchester on A335 (Twyford road).
Downland course
18 holes, 6279 yards, S.S.S.70
Designed by James Braid.
Founded 1915
Visitors: welcome weekdays, and at weekends with member or by arrangement with Secretary.
Green Fee: £25.
Societies: not Mon.
Catering: snacks, lunch and evening meals; other requirements contact Steward.

C57 Hollingbury Park
☎(0273) 552010
Ditchling Rd, Brighton, Sussex BN1 7HS
1 mile from Brighton, astride the Downs between A23 London Rd and A27 Lewes Rd.
Public undulating downland course.
18 holes, 6502 yards, S.S.S.71
Designed by J. Braid and J.H. Taylor.
Founded 1908
Visitors: welcome anytime.
Green Fee: municipal rates.
Societies: weekdays only.
Catering: full restaurant facilities open 7 days.
Hotels: Old Ship; Preston Resort.

C58 Horam Park
☎(0435) 813477, 813677 Fax
Chiddingly Rd, Horam, E Sussex
TN21 0JJ
0.5 mile S of Horam on road to
Chiddingly; Horam is 13 miles N of
Eastbourne on A267.
Parkland course with lakes.
9 holes, 5864 yards, S.S.S.68
Designed by Glen Johnson.
Founded 1985
Visitors: welcome, ring for
bookings.
Green Fee: ring for details.
Societies: ring for brochure.
Catering: carvery, bar meals.
Driving range.
Hotels: Boship Farm (Hailsham).

C59 Horsham Golf Park
☎(0403) 271525, 274528 Fax
Worthing Rd, Horsham, W Sussex
RH13 4AX
A24 Horsham bypass at Southwater
roundabout with Shell garage,
signposted to golf course and
Horsham; course entrance 200 yards
on right.
Public parkland course.
9 holes, S.S.S.30
Founded July 1993
Visitors: welcome; bookable on day
of play.
Green Fee: £6 (9 holes), £10 (18
holes) WD; £8 (9 holes), £13 (18
holes) WE.
Societies: welcome, not weekends;
36 holes, lunch and evening meal
£29.95.
Catering: bar and restaurant.
Practice ground.

C60 Ifield G & CC
☎(0293) 520222, 523088 Pro
Rusper Rd, Ifield, Crawley, W Sussex
RH11 0LN
M23 Crawley junction; follow signs to
Brighton and A23; after 3
roundabouts take right turning; left
into Ifield Drive, 2nd right after
shops, 1st left into Rusper Rd 0.5
mile then signposted.
Parkland course.
18 holes, 6314 yards, S.S.S.70
Designed by Bernard Darwin;
constructed by F. Hawtree and J.H.
Taylor.
Founded 1927
Visitors: welcome weekdays only or
with member at weekends.
Green Fee: £20/round, £27/day.
Societies: welcome Mon, Tues pm,
Wed pm, Thurs.
Catering: full facilities all week.

C61 Leckford & Longstock
☎(0264) 810320
Leckford, Stockbridge, Hants
2.5 miles N of Stockbridge on
Andover road.
Downland course
9 holes, 3251 yards, S.S.S.71; 9
holes, 2500 yards, Par 32
Designed by John Morrison.
Visitors: employees of John Lewis
Partnership and guests only.
Green Fee: on application

C62 Lee-on-the-Solent
☎(0705) 551170 Manager, 550207
Members, 551181 Pro
Brune Lane, Lee-on-the-Solent,
Hants PO13 9PB
3 miles due S of M27 junction 11.
Heathland course.
18 holes, 5959 yards, S.S.S.69
Founded 1905
Visitors: welcome on weekdays;
h/cap cert required.
Green Fee: £25/round/day WD, £30
WE.
Societies: Thurs, bookable in
advance.
Catering: full facilities available all
week.
Hotels: Belle Vue.

C63 Lewes
☎(0273) 473245, 483823 Pro shop
Chapel Hill, Lewes, Sussex BN7 2BB
On A27 Lewes-Eastbourne road
opposite junction of Cliffe High St and
South St.
Downland course.
18 holes, 6204 yards, S.S.S.70
Founded 1896
Visitors: welcome weekdays and
weekends after 2pm; golf shoes
required; no denims.
Green Fee: £16.50/round/day WD,
£27/round WE.
Societies: welcome as for visitors by
arrangement.
Catering: licensed bar; restaurant
(7/8am to 6pm), evening meals by
arrangement.
Practice ground.

C64 Liphook
☎(0428) 723271 Pro, 723785 Sec
Wheatsheaf Enclosure, Liphook,
Hants GU30 7EH
1 mile S of Liphook off old A3.
Heath/heatherland course.
18 holes, 6250 yards, S.S.S.70
Designed by Arthur Croome.
Founded 1921

Visitors: h/cap cert required; phone
in advance; not before 2pm Sun &
Bank Holidays.
Green Fee: £25/round, £35/day WD;
£35/round, £45/day Sat; £40/round
Sun & BH.
Societies: Wed, Thurs & Fri, min 16,
max 36.
Catering: bar and bar snacks snacks
daily; 3 course lunch and dinner
available.
Hotels: Links; Angel.

C65 Littlehampton
☎(0903) 717170, 726629 Fax
170 Rope Walk, Riverside,
Littlehampton, W Sussex BN17 5DL
From Littlehampton take Bognor
Regis road; take 1st left after bridge
over river, marked To Golf Club.
Seaside links course.
18 holes, 6244 yards, S.S.S.70
Founded 1898
Visitors: welcome 7 days; after
12am weekends.
Green Fee: £24 WD, £30 WE.
Societies: not weekends.
Catering: full catering facilities daily.
Hotels: Bailiff's Court.

C66 Mannings Heath
☎(0403) 210228
Goldings Lane, Mannings Heath,
Horsham, W Sussex RH13 6JU
3 miles SE of Horsham on A281; 4
miles from M25, exit at Pease
Pottage or Handcross.
Undulating parkland course, many
feature holes.
18 holes, 6404 yards, S.S.S.71
Founded 1908
Visitors: welcome by prior
arrangement.
Green Fee: £27/round WD,
£35/round WE
Societies: weekdays.
Catering: full catering facilities.
Hotels: South Lodge (Lower
Beeding).

C67 Meon Valley Hotel Golf & Country Club
☎(0329) 833455, 834411 Fax
Sandy Lane, Shedfield, Southampton
S03 2HQ
On A334 8 miles E of Southampton
between Botley and Wickham.
Parkland courses.
Meon course, 18 holes, 6519 yards,
S.S.S.71; Valley course, 9 holes,
2714 yards, S.S.S.68
Designed by J. Hamilton Stutt.
Founded 1978

Liphook

For most golfers charm is a more important quality in a course than challenge. Liphook is the type which combines the two in equal measure. 6207 yards is not long these days but matching the par of 70 is another matter when the heather and trees, the hallmark of the best Surrey and Hampshire courses, place such a premium on controlled shot-making.

You certainly appreciate the lovely setting rather more if you keep straight, the countryside possessing more normal contouring than the valleys, plateaux and gulleys that characterise the land surrounding the Devil's Punchbowl at Hindhead just up the Portsmouth Road, and in terms of golf course architecture, Liphook has rightly been hailed as an example for the connoisseur.

My late senior partner, Ken Cotton, was always singing its praises but the remarkable part of the story is that its designer, A.C. Croome, was first and foremost a schoolmaster. Liphook was the only new course for which he was entirely responsible. Jack Neville keeps him notable company in this regard, Neville's lone masterpiece being Pebble Beach. It was ill health rather than lack of demand that prevented Croome pursuing the final chapter of a working life that had more variety than most.

In addition to being a housemaster at Radley College, he wrote about cricket and golf for several newspapers, both games at which he excelled himself. He was founder member of the Oxford and Cambridge Golfing Society donating the Croome Shield for annual competition among College pairs at the President's Putter, and was a regular competitor in the Amateur and other championships.

It was J.F. Abercromby, the designer of Addington, among others, who persuaded him to join forces in the firm of Fowler, Abercromby, Simpson and Croome — as elite a quartet as anyone could muster. At first, Croome's role was mainly administrative, but inside every golfer is a golf course architect clamouring to get out, and Liphook was the ultimate expression of Croome's talents.

No clubhouse gets a better view of its 1st and 18th holes, the work of John Morrison who wanted to provide a fine, long short hole to get players moving, but, apart from the difficulty of the opening tee shot, Liphook is quick to let golfers know what is expected of them. There are three par 4s of well over 400 yards in the first six holes, the 4th, High View, being particularly demanding. It leads to the first crossing of the busy road and on to the first of three par 5s where thorn trees feature in the drive.

The 6th, with its little grassy hollow behind the green, doubles back on the 5th, the attractive short 7th starting the section of 10 holes on the other side of the railway. The railway is not the feature it is on some courses although the 7th and 8th run roughly parallel to it. The 9th, 438 yards, another demanding 4, prompts a long uphill second over a road and a heathery dell but the 10th offers a more inviting drive even if a ditch lurks on the approach to the green.

A large central bunker dominates the short 11th in a visual sense, the 12th, Forest Mere, completing the long par 4s and always with a victim or two. A nice downhill drive and a slightly uphill second give the longer hitters a chance of a birdie at the 13th, and, for those negotiating the dogleg successfully, a good pitch can do the same at the 14th.

Then it is a deep breath and a mad dash to the 15th where the drive takes us up over a steep ridge with the temptation to cut off more than is good for us. The 16th is the reverse of the 15th, a quarry and the corner of a wood awaiting any poorly struck or mis-directed second. The walk to the 17th is a last reminder of the Portsmouth Road which explains in part the club's traditionally strong links with the Navy; the 17th's tee shot across a diagonal, corrugated bank of gorse and heather makes the fifth and last short hole difficult to judge, enhancing Liphook's reputation that it's not just nautical men who are all at sea.

Visitors: welcome with h/cap cert.
Green Fee: Meon course, £25/round WD, £30/round WE & BH; Valley course, £18/round WD, £25/round WE & BH (18 holes)
Societies: by arrangement, residents only at weekends.
Catering: meals and snacks available.
Squash, tennis, snooker, indoor swimming pool, health and beauty facilities (residents only).
Hotels: Meon Valley, residential golf packages available.

C68 Moors Valley Country Park

☎(0425) 479776
Moors Valley Country Park, Horton Rd, Ashley Heath, Nr Ringwood, Hants BH24 2ET.
A31 through Ringwood, right at roundabout signposted Ashley Heath, 2 miles on right of entrance to parkland, course inside Country Park.
Municipal parkland/heathland course.
18 holes, 6270 yards
Designed by Martin Hawtree.
Founded 1988, extended 1992
Visitors: no restrictions, bookings one week in advance.
Green Fee: £5 (9 holes) £8.50 (18 holes) WD; £6 (9 holes), £11 (18 holes) WE.
Societies: contact Pro shop
Catering: tea room in visitor centre; new clubhouse.
Driving range.

C69 New Forest

☎(0703) 282752 Office, 282752 Pro shop
Southampton Rd, Lyndhurst, Hants SO43 7BU
On A35 Southampton-Bournemouth road between Ashurst and Lyndhurst.
Heathland course.
18 holes, 5742 yards, S.S.S.68
Designed by Peter Swann.
Founded 1888
Visitors: from 8.30am Mon-Fri, from 10am Sat, from 1.30pm Sun.
Green Fee: £12/round/day WD; £14 WE & BH.
Societies: welcome Tues, Wed & Thurs; to be booked and confirmed in advance.
Catering: bar from 11am Mon-Sat, from 12am to 3pm Sun; snacks and meals 11.30am-4pm Mon-Sat.
Hotels: Crown; Lyndhurst Park; Carey's Manor.

C70 Newport

☎(0983) 525076
St George's Down, Newport, Isle of Wight PO30 3BA
A3056 Newport-Sandown road 0.5 mile from Newport.
Undulating parkland course.
9 holes, 5704 yards, S.S.S.68
Designed by Guy Hunt.
Founded 1896
Visitors: welcome except Sat and Sun am.
Green Fee: £15 WD, £17.50 WE.
Societies: Mon-Fri by arrangement with Sec.
Catering: bar meals on request to Stewardess before round.

C71 North Hants

☎(0252) 616443, 811627 Fax
Minley Rd, Fleet, Hants GU13 8RE
0.5 mile N of Fleet Station on B3013, M3 junction 4a.
Heathland course.
18 holes, 6257 yards, S.S.S.70.
Designed by James Braid.
Founded 1904
Visitors: by prior arrangement with Sec; letter of intro and h/cap cert required.
Green Fee: on application.
Societies: Tues and Wed by arrangement.
Catering: lunch, tea, dinner; pre-booking required.
Hotels: various in Fleet, Camberley and Farnborough.

C72 Old Thorns

☎(0428) 724555, 725036 Fax
London Kosaido Co Ltd, Old Thorns, Longmoor Rd, Griggs Green, Liphook, Hants GU30 7PE
Take Griggs Green exit off A3 (1st exit past Liphook from London); Old Thorns is situated 500 yards on right of Longmoor Rd.
Public parkland course.
18 holes, 6533 yards, S.S.S.71
Designed by Commander John Harris, adapted by Peter Alliss and Dave Thomas
Founded 1982
Visitors: all welcome.
Green Fee: £25/round, £40/day WD & BH; £35 WE.
Societies: Society Day £55, Sat £58; min 12.
Catering: full à la carte menu, terrace buffet and Japanese restaurant.
Driving range, putting green, indoor swimming, sauna, tennis, shiatsu.
Hotels: Old Thorns.

C73 Osborne

☎(0983) 295421 Sec/Manager, 295649 Pro
Osborne, East Cowes, Isle of Wight PO32 6JX
A3052 Newport to East Cowes road, situated in grounds of Osborne House.
Parkland course.
9 holes, 6304 yards, S.S.S.70
Founded 1903
Visitors: not before 12am Sat & Sun or 1.30pm Tues.
Green Fee: £14 WD, £19 WE & BH.
Societies: by arrangement with Sec/Manager.
Catering: available.
Hotels: Padmore House, Crossway; Clarence House.

C74 Osiers Farm

☎(0798) 44097
Petworth, W Sussex GU28 9LX
2.5 miles N of Petworth on A283 Guildford road.
Public course over farmland, hedges, trees etc.
9 holes, 5220 yards, S.S.S.64
Designed by Chris Duncton.
Founded 1991
Visitors: welcome at any time.
Green Fee: apply for details.
Societies: as required, not Sun, Bank Holidays or Sat am.
Catering: light refreshments only at present.
Driving range.
Hotels: B&B on course; Angel, Masons Arms (Petworth).

C75 Paultons Golf Centre

☎(0703) 813345, 813993 Fax
Old Salisbury Rd, Ower, Nr Romsey, Hants SO51 6AN
Exit 2 off M27 in direction of Ower, left at 1st roundabout, then right at Heathlands Hotel; then signposted.
Parkland course.
18 holes, S.S.S.72
Founded 1993
Visitors: all welcome at all times.
Green Fee: approx £6 (9 holes), £15 (18 holes).
Societies: welcome by arrangement.
Catering: bars and restaurant.
Driving range.
Hotels: Heathlands (500 yards).

C76 Paxhill Park

☎(0444) 484467
East Mascalls Lane, Lindfield, W Sussex RH16 2QN
Parkland course.
18 holes, 6174 yards, S.S.S.69

Designed by Patrick Tallack.
Founded Oct 1990
Visitors: welcome; not before 12am weekends.
Green Fee: £15/round, £25/day WD; £20/round WE.
Societies: cated.
Catering: full restaurant and bar facilities; banqueting.
Hotels: Birch Hotel (Haywards Heath).

C77 Peacehaven
☎(0273) 514049
Brighton Rd, Newhaven, E Sussex BN9 9UH
On A259 1 mile W of Newhaven.
Undulating downland course.
9 holes, 5305 yards, S.S.S.66
Designed by James Braid.
Founded 1895
Visitors: welcome weekdays, after 11.30am weekends and Bank Holidays.
Green Fee: £10 WD, £16 WE & BH
Societies: catered for Mon-Fri.
Catering: available weekends, by arrangement Mon-Fri.

C78 Pease Pottage
☎(0293) 521706
Horsham Rd, Pease Pottage, Crawley RH11 9AP
M23 junction 11, then signposted from large roundabout.
Public parkland course.
9 holes, 3511 yards, Par 60
Designed by Adam Lazar.
Founded 1986
Visitors: welcome.
Green Fee: £8.50 (18 holes) WD, £11 WE.
Societies: welcome by prior arrangement.
Catering: bar and restaurant.
Driving range.

C79 Petersfield
☎(0730) 262386 Sec and Fax, 267732 Pro
Heath Rd, Petersfield, Hants GU31 4EJ
Turn off A3 to E at town centre (Red Lion), clubhouse 1 mile past lake.
Heathland/parkland course.
18 holes, 5603 yards, S.S.S.67
Founded 1892
Visitors: welcome weekdays, weekends after 12am.
Green Fee: £15/round, £21/day WD; £21/round, £30/day WE.
Societies: Wed, Thurs and Fri (no evening catering).

Catering: bar and dining area; lunch available Tues-Sat; evening meals by prior booking.
Hotels: Concorde; Red Lion.

C80 Piltdown
☎(0825) 722033, 722389 Pro
Piltdown, Uckfield, E Sussex TN22 3XB
1 mile W of Maresfield off A272 signposted Isfield.
Undulating gorse and heather.
18 holes, 6070 yards, S.S.S.69
Designed by J. Rowe, G.M. Dodd, Frank Pennink.
Founded 1904
Visitors: not before 9.30am (2pm Sun); various other restrictions, essential to phone; h/cap cert or letter of intro required; jacket and tie in clubhouse.
Green Fee: £27.50/round/day.
Societies: by arrangment Mon, Wed and Fri only.
Catering: bar snacks and full catering daily, phone (0825) 722033.
Hotels: Roebuck (Forest Row); Maiden's Head, Horsted Place (Uckfield).

C81 Portsmouth
☎(0705) 372210, 372299
Crookhorn Lane, Widley, Portsmouth, Hants PO7 5QL
Located on the hills overlooking Portsmouth Harbour on N of the city, within 1 mile of A3M.
Municipal undulating parkland course.
18 holes, 6200 yards, S.S.S.69
Founded 1926
Visitors: welcome.
Green Fee: £9.40 summer, £6.90 winter.
Societies: please arrange weekdays.
Catering: full facilities available (0705) 375999.
Hotels: Bear; Corner House.

C82 Pyecombe
☎(0273) 845372
Clayton Hill, Pyecombe, Sussex BN45 7FF
On A273, 0.5 mile from junction with A23 at Pyecombe, 5 to 6 miles N of Brighton.
Downland course.
18 holes, 6234 yards, S.S.S.70
Founded 1894
Visitors: weekdays after 9.15am; Sat after 2pm; Sun after 3pm.
Green Fee: £16 weekday, £25 WE.

Societies: catered for Mon, Tues pm, Wed, Thurs.
Catering: full services available.

C83 Romsey
☎(0703) 734637 Manager, 732218 Steward
Romsey Rd, Nursling, Southampton, Hants SO1 9XW
2 miles SE of Romsey on A3057 Southampton road; near M27/M271 junction 3.
Wooded parkland course.
18 holes, 5851 yards, S.S.S.68
Designed by Charles Lawrie.
Founded 1925
Visitors: welcome Mon-Fri.
Green Fee: £19.50/round, £24/day.
Societies: Mon, Tues and Thurs.
Catering: full licensed bar, full restaurant facilities.
Hotels: White Horse (Romsey); Travel Inn (Nursling).

C84 Rowlands Castle
☎(0705) 412784 Sec, 412785 Pro
Links Lane, Rowlands Castle, Hants PO9 6AE
7 miles S of Petersfield; leave A3(M) junction left to Havant/Rowlands Castle.
Parkland course.
18 holes, 6381 yards, S.S.S.70
Founded 1902
Visitors: welcome weekdays; not Sat; restricted numbers Sun, advisable to ring.
Green Fee: £22/round/day WD; £27 Sun & BH.
Societies: catered for Tues and Thurs, details on application.
Catering: service until 6pm.
Hotels: Brookfield (Emsworth); Bear (Havant); Fountain Inn (Rowlands Castle).

C85 Royal Ashdown Forest
☎(0342) 822018, 822247 Pro shop
Chapel Lane, Forest Row, East Grinstead, E Sussex RH18 5LR
A22 East Grinstead-Eastbourne road, 4.5 miles S of East Grinstead turn left in Forest Row opposite church onto B2110, after 0.5 mile turn right into Chapel Lane, top of hill turn left, over heath to clubhouse.
Undulating moorland course with views over forest.
18 holes, 6477 yards, S.S.S.71
Founded 1888
Visitors: welcome, restricted weekends, Bank Holidays; essential to phone beforehand.

Green Fee: £27/round, £35/day WD; £32/round, £40/day WE.
Societies: Wed-Fri normal catering; Mon limited catering.
Catering: lunch, tea; casual visitors requested to book in advance or before teeing off.
Hotels: Ashdown Forest; Chequers.

C86 Royal Eastbourne
☎(0323) 729738 Sec, 736986 Pro
Paradise Drive, Eastbourne, Sussex
BN20 8BP
0.5 mile from Town Hall.
Parkland/downland course.
18 holes, 6109 yards, S.S.S.69; 9 holes, 4294 yards, S.S.S.61
Founded 1887
Visitors: h/cap cert required for 18 hole course, advisable to telephone 3-4 days in advance.
Green Fee: on application.
Societies: by arrangement.
Catering: full facilities daily. Snooker.
Hotels: Grand; Lansdowne; self catering golf cottage (sleeps 4) adjacent to clubhouse, includes free golf.

C87 Royal Winchester
☎(0962) 852462
Sarum Rd, Winchester, Hants SO22 5QE
Leave Winchester on Romsey road.
Downland course.
18 holes, 6218 yards, S.S.S.70
Designed by H.S. Colt and A.P. Taylor.
Founded 1888
Visitors: weekdays, h/cap cert required.
Green Fee: £26/round.
Societies: Mon, Tues, Wed.
Catering: every day, liaise with Manager.
Hotels: Royal; Wessex.

C88 Rustington Golf Centre
☎(0903) 850790, 850982 Fax
Golfers Lane, Rustington, W Sussex
BN16 4NB
A259 at Rustington, between Worthing and Chichester.
Public parkland course.
9 hole Par 3 course opening summer 1994; full Par 70 course starting construction spring 1994
Designed by David Williams Partnership.
Visitors: 9am to 9pm 7 days a week.
Green Fee: £4.95 for Par 3 course.

Catering: coffee shop serving hot and cold lunches.
Driving range.

C89 Ryde
☎(0983) 614809
Binstead Rd, Ryde, Isle of Wight
PO33 3NF
Main Ryde-Newport road.
Parkland course.
9 holes, 5200 yards, S.S.S.66
Founded 1921
Visitors: not Wed pm, Sun am.
Green Fee: £15 WD, £20 WE.
Societies: Weekdays except Wed, contact Sec for details.
Catering: meals and snacks.
Hotels: Newlands.

C90 Rye
☎(0797) 225241
Camber, Rye, E Sussex TN31 7QS
A259 from Rye towards Folkestone, turn right after 0.5 mile at signpost Camber, course 3 miles on right.
Links course.
18 holes, 6310 yards, S.S.S.71; 9 holes, 6141 yards, S.S.S.70
Designed by H.S. Colt.
Founded 1894
Visitors: only on introduction by a member.
Green Fee: £34.50/round, £52.50/day WD.
Catering: lunch daily except Tues.
Hotels: George; Mermaid; Broomhill Lodge; Playden Oasts; Hope Anchor; Top of the Hill; Queens Head.

C91 Sandford Springs
☎(0635) 297881, 2978833 Tee Bookings, 298065 Fax
Wolverton, Nr Basingstoke, Hants
RG26 5RT
Beside A339 at Kingsclere between Basingstoke and Newbury.
Picturesque and varied course overlooking 5 counties.
27 holes, 3 courses of 6143, 6222, 6005 yards, S.S.S.69, 70, 69
Designed by Hawtree & Son.
Founded 1988
Visitors: welcome weekdays; booking system in operation.
Green Fee: £23/round, £29/day.
Societies: Society and Company Days welcome.
Catering: full bar and restaurant facilities; parties; wedding receptions, business gatherings catered for.
Hotels: Hilton National (Basingstoke and Newbury); special rates agreed.

C92 Seaford
☎(0323) 892442
East Blatchington, Seaford, E Sussex
BN25 2JD
Off A259 N of Seaford.
Downland course.
18 holes, 6241 yards, S.S.S.70
Designed by J.H. Taylor.
Founded 1887
Visitors: welcome weekdays after 9.30am; telephone first.
Green Fee: £20/round, £30/day.
Societies: welcome after 9.30am by prior arrangement.
Catering: breakfast, lunch, tea and dinner available.
Hotels: Dormy House on course.

C93 Seaford Head
☎(0323) 894843 Sec, 890139 Pro
Southdown Rd, Seaford, E Sussex
BN25 4JS
S of A259, 12 miles from Brighton.
Public seaside course.
18 holes, 5812 yards, S.S.S.68
Founded 1887
Visitors: welcome at all times.
Green Fee: on application
Societies: welcome.
Catering: light snacks, Societies catered for.

C94 Selsey
☎(0243) 602029 Sec, 602203 Pro
Golf Links Lane, Selsey, Chichester, W Sussex PO20 9DR
On B2145 7 miles S of Chichester.
Seaside course.
9 holes, 5932 yards, S.S.S.68
Founded 1909
Visitors: welcome if member of recognised club.
Green Fee: on application
Societies: small societies welcome.
Catering: lunch and snacks.

C95 Shanklin & Sandown
☎(0983) 403217, 404424 Pro, 403170 Members
The Fairway, Lake, Sandown, Isle of Wight PO36 9PR
On A3055 to Lake, down The Fairway.
Heathland course.
18 holes, 6063 yards, S.S.S.69
Designed by Dr J. Cowper, James Braid.
Founded 1900
Visitors: members of affiliated clubs only with h/cap certs; after 1pm weekends.
Green Fee: £21/round, £25/day WD; £25/round/day WE. £15 after 3pm WD; half price jnrs.

SHANKLIN
ISLE OF WIGHT
CULHAM LODGE HOTEL
Languard Manor Road, PO37 7HZ
Tel: (0983) 862880

- Delightful small hotel. Well known for good value.
- Facilities include: lovely garden, conservatory room, solarium and **heated swimming pool**.
- Convenient for all seven island golf courses.
- Bed and Breakfast £15 to £19.50. Dinner £7. Most rooms en suite.
- For breaks or main holidays, please send for our colour brochure.

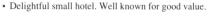

Societies: by arrangement, 20-40 players.
Catering: available from 10am all day; usual Sun bar hours.

C96 Singing Hills Golf Course
☎(0273) 835353, 835444 Fax
Albourne, E Sussex
Beween Henfield and Hurstpierpoint on B2117 adjacent to A23.
Downland courses; Lake 3rd is exact replica of 17th at Sawgrass USA.
3 x 9 holes played in 3 different combinations of 18; Lake/River, Lake/Valley, River/Valley;
6200-6300 yards, S.S.S.71
Designed by Richard Hurd (Sandow).
Founded Easter 1992
Visitors: pay-as-you-play; computerised booking; h/cap certs or membership of recognised club required.
Green Fee: £20/round (includes £2 voucher for bar/restaurant).
Societies: welcome 7 days a week.
Catering: 2 bars, 2 restaurants, conference facilities in Pavillion.
Driving range; extensive practice area.
Hotels: Hickstead Resort.

C97 Slinfold Park G & CC
☎(0403) 791154 Clubhouse, 791555 Shop and Range, 791465 Fax
Stane Street, Slinfold, Horsham, W Sussex RH13 7RE
A29 S of junction with A281.
Wooded parkland course.
18 holes, 6462 yards, Par 72; 9 hole course.
Designed by John Fortune.
Founded Opened 1993
Visitors: welcome, pay-as-you-play.
Green Fee: on application.
Societies: apply for details.
Catering: full facilities.
Driving range, putting green, practice ground.
Hotels: Random Hall.

C98 South Winchester
☎(0962) 877800 Club and Gen Manager, 840469 Pro, 877900 Fax
Pitt, Winchester, Hants SO22 5QW
In village of Pitt on Romsey-Hursley road.
Championship links style course.
18 holes, 6688 yards, Par 72
Designed by Dave Thomas, Peter Alliss, Clive Clark.
Founded 1993
Visitors: by prior arrangement with Pro.
Green Fee: apply to golf Pro.
Societies: by prior arrangement with General Manager.
Catering: golfers' bar, club bar, dining room.

C99 Southampton
☎(0703) 767996, 768407 Pro
Golf Course Rd, Bassett, Southampton, Hants
N end of city, off Bassett Ave, half-way between Chilworth roundabout and Winchester Rd roundabout.
Municipal parkland course.
18 holes, 5683 meters, S.S.S.70;
9 holes, 2185 meters.
Founded 1935
Visitors: welcome.
Green Fee: apply for details.
Societies: by arrangement with Council Municipal Golf Course Manager.
Catering: breakfast, lunch, bar snacks available.
Hotels: Albany (Bassett).

C100 Southampton Manor Course
☎(0703) 740544
Manor Farm, Botley Rd, Chilworth, Southampton, Hants SO1 7JE
On A27 between Southampton and Romsey.
Public parkland course.
9 holes, 2362 yards, S.S.S.32
Founded 1989
Visitors: pay-as-you-play with advance booking system, only 12 players per hour allowed.
Green Fee: apply for details.
Societies: catered for by arrangement.
Catering: light refreshments; full catering by arrangement.
Driving range.
Hotels: Hilton, Crest.

C101 Southsea
☎(0705) 830009
The Mansion, Great Salterns, Eastern Rd, Portsmouth, PO3 6QB
2 miles off M27/A27/A3 on E road into Portsmouth.
Municipal meadowland course.
18 holes, 5800 metres, S.S.S.68
Founded 1935
Visitors: welcome.
Green Fee: apply for details.
Societies: by arrangement with Portsmouth City Council.
Catering: available in adjacent Farmhouse public house.
Driving range at Portsmouth Golf Centre.

C102 Southwick Park
☎(0705) 380131
Pinsley Drive, Southwick, Fareham, Hants PO17 6EL
A333 7 miles N of Portsmouth, follow signs to HMS Dryad.
Parkland course.
18 holes, 5972 yards, S.S.S.69
Designed by Charles Lawrie.
Founded 1977
Visitors: welcome weekdays, weekends guests of members only.
Green Fee: £16.
Societies: welcome Tues by prior arrangement.
Catering: full catering facilities available.
Hotels: Holiday Inn (Cosham).

C103 Southwood
☎(0252) 548700
Ively Rd, Cove, Farnborough, Hants GU14 0LJ
1 mile W of A325 Farnborough.
Public parkland course.
18 holes, 5553 yards, S.S.S.67
Designed by Hawtree & Son.
Founded 1977
Visitors: welcome, bookable at all times.
Green Fee: on application.
Societies: weekdays only by prior arrangement.
Catering: bar snacks, tea and lunch available.
Hotels: Lakeside International (Frimley).

C104 **Stoneham**

☎(0703) 768151, 769272 Sec
Bassett Green Rd, Bassett,
Southampton, Hants SO2 3NE
From A33 turn left at Chilworth
roundabout, 0.5 mile on left side of
A27; from M27 exit 5 follow
signposts to Southampton then
Bassett.
Heather and peat parkland course.
18 holes, 6310 yards, S.S.S.70
Designed by Willie Park.
Founded 1908
Visitors: any time tee is available;
restricted weekends.
Green Fee: apply for details.
Societies: Mon, Thurs, Fri by
arrangement.
Catering: full catering by day, bar
11.30am-10pm; evening meals by
arrangement.
Hotels: Wessex; Northlands; Crest;
Post House; Hilton.

C105 **Test Valley**

☎(0256) 771737
Micheldever Rd, Overton, Nr
Basingstoke, Hants RG25 3DS
2 miles S of Overton village junction
with B3400; or 1.5 miles N of A303
from Overton turn off.
Inland links course.
18 holes, 6811 yards, S.S.S.73
Designed by D. Wright (E. Darcy).
Founded May 1992
Visitors: welcome weekdays and
weekends; prior telephone booking
advisable.
Green Fee: £14/round, £22/day WD,
£20/round, £32/day WE.
Societies: welcome 7 days; from
£18 for golf and meal.
Catering: full bar and dining
facilities; dining room for up to 100.
Extensive practice facilities.

C106 **Tidworth Garrison**

☎(0980) 42301 Sec, 42321 Club,
42393 Pro
Bulford Rd, Tidworth, Hants SP9 7AF
From Salisbury, take A338 to
Tidworth, turn left at traffic lights, 1st
left into Bulford Rd, course 1 mile on
right.
Tree-lined downland course with
scenic views.
18 holes, 6075 yards, S.S.S.69
Founded 1908
Visitors: welcome by arrangement.
Green Fee: £18/day.
Societies: catered for Tues, Thurs.
Catering: hot and cold meals daily
except Mon when sandwiches only.
Hotels: Antrobus Arms; George.

C107 **Tilgate Forest Golf Centre**

☎(0293) 530103, (0293) 523478
Fax
Titmus Drive, Tilgate, Crawley, W
Sussex RH10 5EU
M23, junction Pease Pottage, follow
main road to Crawley, at 1st
roundabout turn right, follow signs.
Public parkland course.
18 holes, 6359 yards, S.S.S.70; 9
holes, 1350 yards.
Designed by Huggett and Coles.
Founded 1983
Visitors: welcome.
Green Fee: £11.50 WD, £15.75 WE.
Societies: Mon-Thurs.
Catering: restaurant and bar all day.
Driving range.

C108 **Tylney Park**

☎(0256) 762079
Rotherwick, Basingstoke, Hants
Off A30 at Nately Scures, follow signs
for Rotherwick; approx 1.5 miles.
Parkland course.
18 holes, 6138 yards, S.S.S.70
Designed by W. Wiltshire.
Visitors: welcome; h/cap cert
required.
Green Fee: £20 WD (£11 with
member), £28 WE (£11 with
member).
Societies: welcome Mon to Fri.
Catering: meals served.
Hotels: Tylney Hall; Raven (Hook).

C109 **Ventnor**

☎(0983) 853326, 853198 Sec
Steephill Down Rd, Ventnor, Isle of
Wight
A3055 to Ventnor, course on downs
above at Upper Ventnor.
Undulating downland course.
9 holes, 5752 yards, S.S.S.68
Founded 1892
Visitors: welcome except
12am-3.30pm Fri, not before 1pm
Sun.
Green Fee: apply for details.
Societies: not Sun am, catering by
arrangement.
Catering: snacks at bar.
Pool table.
Hotels: Eversly; Bonchurch Manor.

C110 **Waterhall**

☎(0273) 508658
Off Devils Dyke Rd, Brighton, E
Sussex BN1 8YN
N of the town, 5 miles from centre,
towards Devil's Dyke.
Hilly downland course.
18 holes, 5775 yards, S.S.S.68
Founded 1923
Visitors: welcome.
Green Fee: £11/round, £17/day WD;
£14/round WE & BH.
Societies: welcome weekdays
except Tues by prior arrangement
with Sec.
Catering: available daily during
summer; limited in winter.

C111 **Waterlooville**

☎(0705) 263388 Sec/Manager,
256911 Pro
Cherry-Tree Ave, Cowplain,
Waterlooville, Hants PO8 8AP
Off A3 in Cowplain, 10 miles N of
Portsmouth.
Tree-lined parkland course.
18 holes, 6647 yards, S.S.S.72
Designed by Henry Cotton.
Founded 1907
Visitors: welcome Mon to Fri.
Green Fee: on application.
Societies: Thurs only.
Catering: 10am to 5pm daily.
Hotels: Post House (Hayling Island);
Bear (Havant).

C112 **Wellow**

☎(0794) 322872 Sec, 323833 Pro
Ryedown Lane, East Wellow,
Romsey, Hants SO51 6BD
M27 exit 2 onto A36 towards
Salisbury, after 1 mile right to East
Wellow, after 1 mile right into into
Ryedown Lane.
Parkland course.
18 holes, 5902 yards, S.S.S.68
Designed by W. Wiltshire.
Founded May 1991
Visitors: welcome 7 days.
Green Fee: £15 WD, £20 WE.
Societies: welcome, not weekends.
Catering: bar and restaurant open all
day.

C113 **Wellshurst Golf & Country Club**

☎(04353) 813636 Office, 813456
Pro, 812444 Fax
North St, Hellingly, E Sussex BN27
4EE
2 miles N of Boship roundabout on
A22 at Hailsham, on A267.
Pay-as-you-play parkland course,
with views of South Downs.
18 hole course in operation; further
18 hole course under construction
Designed by Golf Corporation.
Founded 1991
Visitors: welcome 7 days; must
have golf shoes, no denims.

Green Fee: £12/round WD, £16/round WE.
Societies: welcome, terms agreed on requirements.
Catering: full bar and catering facilities.
Driving range.
Hotels: Boship; many in Eastbourne.

C114 West Chiltington
☎(0798) 813574 Sec, 812115 Pro shop, 812631 Fax
Broadford Bridge Road, West Chiltington, W Sussex RH20 2YA
Turn left off A283 1 mile E of Pulborough; from West Chiltington village take Broadford Bridge Rd opposite Queen's Head public house.
Public course with limited membership; gently undulating parkland.
18 holes, 5890 yards, S.S.S.69; 9-hole Par 3.
Designed by Brian Barnes and Max Faulkner
Founded July 1988
Visitors: welcome at all times.
Green Fee: 18 holes, £15 WD, £20 WE; 9 holes, £5 WD, £7.50 WE.
Societies: welcome by prior arrangement.
Catering: full catering and bar facilities.
Driving range; putting green.
Hotels: The Mill House (Ashington).

C115 West Hove
☎(0273) 419738 Manager, 413494 Pro, 439988 Fax
Church Farm, Hangleton, Hove, Sussex.
New course and clubhouse off new by-pass, 2nd junction from A23 flyover going W.

Undulating downland course overlooking the sea.
18 holes, 6201 yards, S.S.S.70
Designed by Hawtree
Founded 1910
Visitors: weekdays, weekends pm on application.
Green Fee: on application.
Societies: catered for weekdays.
Catering: available daily.
Snooker.
Hotels: Old Ship; Bedford; Sackville (Brighton).

C116 West Sussex
☎(0798) 872563
Pulborough, West Sussex RH20 2EN
1.5 miles E of Pulborough on A283.
Heathland course.
18 holes, 6221 yards, S.S.S.70
Designed by Sir Guy Campbell, Major C.K. Hutcheson.
Founded 1931
Visitors: welcome weekdays only except Tues (members only) with letter of intro. and h/cap cert.
Green Fee: apply for details.
Societies: Wed and Thurs.
Catering: lunch and tea.
Hotels: Abingworth Hall; The Roundabout.

C117 Weybrook Park
☎(0256) 20347
Aldermarston Rd, Sherborne St John, Basingstoke, Hants RG24 9ND
2 miles NW of Basingstoke town centre; situated between A339 and A340 Basingstoke/Newbury road and A340 Basingstoke/Aldermarston road.
Parkland course.
18 holes, 6100 yards, S.S.S.70
Founded 1971

Visitors: welcome except Wed pm; restrictions at weekends during competitions.
Green Fee: £12 WD, £14 WE; £6 OAPs and Jnrs.
Societies: Mon-Fri, not Wed.
Catering: bar.

C118 Willingdon
☎(0323) 410981 Sec, 410984 Pro
Southdown Rd, Eastbourne, E Sussex BN20 9AA
2 miles N of Eastbourne off A22.
Downland course.
18 holes, 6118 yards, S.S.S.69
Designed by J.H. Taylor, modernised by Dr Mackenzie 1925.
Founded 1898
Visitors: welcome weekdays.
Green Fee: £24/1-2 rounds WD, £27 Sat and Bank Holidays.
Societies: weekdays except Tues.
Catering: by arrangement.
Hotels: Grand; Queens; Lansdown.

C119 Worthing
☎(0903) 60801, 694664 Fax
Links Rd, Worthing, W Sussex BN14 9QZ
At top of hill on A27 0.25 mile E of Offington roundabout at junction with A24 London road.
Downland course.
Lower, 18 holes, 5819 yards, S.S.S.72; Upper, 18 holes, 5048 yards, S.S.S.66
Designed by H.S. Colt.
Founded 1906
Visitors: by prior arrangement with Sec, must produce h/cap certificate.
Green Fee: on application
Societies: welcome weekdays except Tues.
Catering: lunch served except Mon.

D

SURREY, KENT, SOUTH LONDON

Whatever geological quirk of fate decreed that Surrey should possess so much ground so utterly perfect for golf, the fact remains that lovers of inland courses regard it as their idea of heaven. Where else in the world (with the exception perhaps of Melbourne) is there such a cluster of first class places to play — most portraying the virtues of the pine, heather and silver birch country?

Until Woking was founded in 1893 "by a few mad barristers", the game around London had largely been confined to public commons and muddy parks. Woking celebrated its centenary in 1993. But, within the space of a few years, at the end of the last century, a whole new dimension opened up introducing names now familiar the world over. Sunningdale, Walton Heath, New Zealand, Worplesdon, West Hill, West Byfleet and St George's Hill were all in existence before the Great War. West Hill owes its creation to a woman, Mrs Geoffrey Lubbock, who tired of being unable to play on Sunday and enlisted Willie Park and Jack White, Open champion in 1904, to pioneer a Club which forms part of the famous trinity of Ws with Worplesdon and Woking.

Everyone has his or her own particular favourite in Surrey although even the worst would be looked upon with envy in other areas of Britain. Their nearness to London and to Heathrow Airport, the pleasant nature of the challenge they offer and the fact that a number have 36-holes, make them enormously popular with visitors and visiting Societies.

Today, Wentworth, not founded until 1924, features prominently on the list, their Edinburgh course, opened in 1990, adding considerably to an already established reputation but the county map is festooned with famous names — Royal Wimbledon, Coombe Hill, Addington,

Hankley Common, Camberley Heath, Farnham, Guildford, Burhill and Effingham. Hoebridge has boosted the public amenities while, at the other end of the scale, Wisley was opened in 1991, funded by an expensive debenture scheme Another notable newcomer is Wildwood; and Royal Mid-Surrey remains the standard bearer of Surrey's relatively small amount of parkland golf.

To illustrate how quickly soil conditions change, Kent enjoys none of the heather courses so widespread in Surrey. Its focal point is centred firmly on the coastal links of Royal St George's, Royal Cinque Ports and Princes; and, to a slightly lesser degree, on Littlestone between Folkestone and Rye. Royal St George's is still the only Open championship venue south of Lancashire.

North Foreland is a course within easy reach of Sandwich and one used for the Open championship qualifying rounds but the Medway coastline has courses in most of its towns while, in addition to Canterbury, that city also has Broome Park, opened in 1979. A more recent addition is Tudor Park Hotel Golf & Country Club, a stone's throw from the more senior Leeds Castle which has undergone something of a facelift. However the most recent addition is The London Club near Brands Hatch which is something of a modern extravaganza. Its facilities include two 18-hole courses.

Knole Park and Wildernesse are highly respected names as well as excellent courses around Sevenoaks; West Kent, Rochester & Cobham, and Langley Park come in the same category along with Sundridge Park at Bromley which has two courses — established Clubs in a county in which West Malling, Poult Wood, Cranbrook and Cherry Lodge are others to have appeared in the last twenty-five years.

D1 **Abbey Moor**
☎(0932) 570741, 570765
Green Lane, Addlestone, Surrey
KT15 2XV
Leave M25 at junction 11 and
proceed on St Peters Way towards
Weybridge; take right turn at large
roundabout towards Addlestone on
A318, then over railway bridge; take
2nd right at small roundabout into
Green Lane; course 0.5 mile on right.
Public pay-and-play parkland course.
9 holes, S.S.S.65
Designed by David Taylor.
Founded Sept 1991
Visitors: welcome weekdays and
weekends; advisable to book early.
Green Fee: £6.50 WD, £7.50 WE & BH
Societies: weekdays only.
Catering: bar and restaurant
facilities.

D2 **The Addington**
☎(081) 777 6057 Sec, 777 1701
Pro, 777 1055 Club
205 Shirley Church Rd, Croydon,
Surrey CR0 5AB
2.5 miles from East Croydon Station.
Heathland course.
18 holes, 6243 yards, S.S.S.71
Designed by J.F. Abercromby.
Founded 1914
Visitors: welcome from 8am; no
single players.
Green Fee: on application
Societies: weekdays; terms on
application.
Catering: bar and restaurant.
Practice hole.

D3 **Addington Court**
☎(081) 657 0281/2/3
Featherbed Lane, Croydon, Surrey
CR0 9AA
Undulating public heathland course
Championship, 18 holes, 5577
yards, S.S.S.67; Falconwood, 18
holes, 5513 yards, S.S.S.66; 9 holes,
1812 yards.
Designed by F. Hawtree Snr.
Founded 1931
Visitors: welcome.
Green Fee: apply for details.
Societies: welcome by arrangement.
Catering: full catering facilities.
18 hole Pitch & Putt,
Hotels: Holiday Inn; Selsdon Park.

D4 **Addington Palace**
☎(081) 654 3061
Gravel Hill, Addington Park, Croydon,
Surrey CR0 5BB
2 miles from East Croydon station.

Parkland course
18 holes, 6262 yards, S.S.S.71
Founded 1923
Visitors: welcome weekdays; with
member weekends.
Green Fee: apply for details.
Societies: Tues, Wed, Fri, Thurs pm.
Catering: snacks and meals except
Mon.

D5 **Aquarius**
☎(081) 693 1626
Marmora Rd, Honor Oak, London
SE22 0RY
Off Forest Hill Rd.
Set around a reservoir.
9 holes, 5426 yards, S.S.S.66
Founded 1912
Visitors: welcome with member only.
Green Fee: £10/round/day.
Catering: restaurant, Sat and Sun
only.

D6 **Ashford (Kent)**
☎(0233) 622655
Sandyhurst Lane, Ashford, Kent
TN25 4NT
Off A20, 1.5 miles W of Ashford.
Parkland course.
18 holes, 6246 yards, S.S.S.70
Designed by C.K. Cotton.
Founded 1924
Visitors: welcome any day except
before 11am weekends and Bank
Holidays; h/cap certs required.
Green Fee: £27/day WD, £42/day
WE & BH after 11.30am.
Societies: Tues and Thurs by
arrangement.
Catering: full facilities (functions,
banquets etc).
Hotels: Eastwell Manor; The Croft.

D7 **Austin Lodge**
☎(0322) 863000, 868944
Bookings, 862406 Fax
Eynsford, Nr Swanley, Kent DA4 0HU
M25 junction 3 and A20 from
London, then A225 to Eynsford
station, past station along cul-de-sac
to course.
Peaceful countryside course, 40
mins from West End of London.
18 holes, 7118 yards, S.S.S.73
Designed by Peter Bevan & Mike
Walsh.
Founded July 1991
Visitors: by telephone booking.
Green Fee: £15/round.
Societies: welcome, bookings
required.
Catering: light meals and bar all day.
Golf academy.

D8 **Banstead Downs**
☎(081) 642 2284
Burdon Lane, Belmont, Sutton,
Surrey SM2 7DD
100 yards E of junction of A217 and
B2230.
Downland course
18 holes, 6169 yards, S.S.S.69
Founded 1890
Visitors: welcome with letter of intro
Mon-Fri; Bank Holidays, Sat, Sun am,
with member only.
Green Fee: apply for details.
Societies: welcome by prior
arrangement.
Catering: 11am-6pm, dinner by
arrangement.
Hotels: Thatched House (Cheam);
Drift Bridge (Epsom).

D9 **Barnehurst**
☎(0322) 523746
Mayplace Rd East, Bexley Heath,
Kent DA7 6JU
To Bexleyheath Clock Tower then
on to Mayplace Rd East, golf club
on left.
Mature inland course in traditional
woodland setting.
9 holes (18 tees), 5320 yards,
S.S.S.66
Designed by James Braid.
Founded 1904
Visitors: welcome.
Green Fee: £5.70 WD, £9.20 WE &
BH; reduced rates OAPs and jnrs.
Societies: welcome.
Catering: full facilities; large
function room.
Hotels: Crest (Bexley).

D10 **Barrow Hills**
☎(0932) 848117
Longcross, Chertsey, Surrey KT16
0DS
4 miles W of Chertsey.
Parkland course.
18 holes, 3090 yards, S.S.S.53
Founded 1970
Visitors: with member only.

D11 **Bearsted**
☎(0622) 738198
Ware St, Bearsted, Kent ME14 4PQ
Off M20 at A249; turn right at large
roundabout, take left slipway to
Bearstead Green, bear left at
mini-roundabout, straight on under
bridge; course 400 yards on left.
Parkland course.
18 holes, 6278 yards, S.S.S.70
Designed by Golf Landscapes.
Founded 1895

Visitors: must be member of bona fide club with h/cap; with member only weekends; advisable to phone.
Green Fee: £22/round, £30/day.
Societies: Tues-Fri by arrangement with Sec.
Catering: bar, restaurant, snacks; business lunches by arrangement.
Hotels: Stakis Country Court; Tudor Park Hotel G & CC; Great Danes.

D12 **Beckenham Place Park**
☎(081) 650 2292
Beckenham Hill Rd, Beckenham, Kent BR3 2BP

1 mile from Catford towards Bromley, right at Homebase.
Parkland course.
18 holes, 5722 yards, S.S.S.68
Founded 1932
Visitors: welcome.
Green Fee: winter, £7.60/round WD, £12.40/round WE; summer, £8.70/round WD, £14/round WE.
Catering: meals and snacks.

D13 **Betchworth Park**
☎(0306) 882052
Reigate Rd, Dorking, Surrey RH4 1NZ
1 mile E of Dorking on A25 to

Reigate, entrance opposite horticultural gardens.
Parkland course
18 holes, 6266 yards, S.S.S.70
Designed by H. Colt.
Founded 1913
Visitors: welcome Mon and Thurs, and Tues and Wed pm; restricted Fri and Sun pm.
Green Fee: £31/day WD, £43/day WE.
Societies: Mon and Thurs.
Catering: lunches and teas available.
Hotels: Burford Bridge; White Horse; Travelodge.

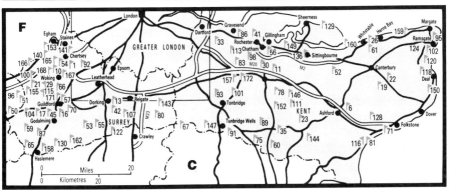

D14 **Bexleyheath**
☎(081) 303 6951
Mount Rd, Bexleyheath, Kent DA6
8JS
1 mile from Bexleyheath station, off
Upton Rd.
Undulating course.
9 holes, 5239 yards, S.S.S.66
Founded 1907
Visitors: welcome 8am-4pm
Mon-Fri.
Green Fee: £20 (£10 with member).
Societies: by arrangement.
Catering: lunch, snacks and evening
meals, except Mon.
Hotels: Crest (Bexley).

D15 **Birchwood Park**
☎(0322) 660554
Birchwood Rd, Wilmington, Dartford,
Kent DA2 7HJ
Off A20 or M25 at Swanley turn off.
Meadowland course.
18 holes, 5826 yards, S.S.S.71; 9
holes, 1356 yards, Par 29
Designed by Howard Swan.
Founded 1990
Visitors: welcome.
Green Fee: £18 WD, £23 WE.
Societies: welcome weekdays,
weekends limited; contact Sec.
Catering: full facilities.
Driving range.

D16 **Bramley**
☎(0483) 892696 Sec, 893042
Steward, 893685 Pro, 894673 Fax
Bramley, Nr Guildford, Surrey GU5
0AL
Situated 4 miles S of Guildford on
A281 Guildford-Horsham road,
between the villages of Shalford and
Bramley.
Parkland course
18 holes, 5990 yards, S.S.S.69
Designed by Charles Mayo,
redesigned by James Braid.
Founded 1913
Visitors: welcome Mon-Fri; guests
of members only at weekends.
Green Fee: £25/round, £30/day.
Societies: Mon-Fri by prior
arrangement with Sec.
Catering: bar snacks and grill menu
daily. Driving range
Hotels: Bramley Grange.

D17 **Broadwater Park**
☎(0483) 429955
Guildford Rd, Farncombe, Nr
Godalming, Surrey GU7 3DD
A3100 between Godalming and
Guildford opposite Manor Inn.
Public parkland course.
9 holes Par 3, 1323 yards.
Designed by K.D. Milton.
Founded 1989
Visitors: no restrictions.
Green Fee: 9 holes, £3.50 WD, £4
WE; 18 holes £6 WD, £7 WE.
Societies: welcome weekdays.
Catering: bar, snacks.
Driving range.
Hotels: Manor Inn.

D18 **Bromley**
☎(081) 462 7014
Magpie Hall Lane, Bromley, Kent BR2
8JF
A21 2 miles S of Bromley.
Public parkland course.
9 holes, 2507 yards, S.S.S.69
Visitors: welcome.
Green Fee: apply for details.
Societies: welcome.
Catering: snacks available.

D19 **Broome Park Country Club**
☎(0227) 831701, 821973 Fax
Barham, Canterbury, Kent CT4 6QX
Off M2 onto A2 then Folkestone road
A260, 700 yards on right hand side, 8
miles from Canterbury.
Parkland course.
18 holes, 6610 yards, S.S.S.72
Designed by Donald Steel.
Founded 1979
Visitors: weekdays with h/cap cert;
start times to be booked in advance.
Green Fee: on application.
Societies: Mon-Fri.
Catering: 2 bars, 2 restaurants, 7
days, Dizzy's Jazz Bar & Creole
Restaurant.
Tennis, squash, snooker, putting
green, croquet, clay pigeon shooting,
health & fitness centre.
Hotels: Woodpeckers Country; The
Gate (Canterbury).

D20 **Burhill**
☎(0932) 227345
Walton-on-Thames, Surrey KT12
4BL
Off A3 on A245 towards Byfleet, right
into Seven Hills Rd and again into
Burwood Rd, entrance is 2nd on
right.
Parkland course
18 holes, 6224 yards, S.S.S.70
Designed by Willie Park.
Founded 1907
Visitors: weekdays by arrangement,
h/cap cert required.
Green Fee: on application.
Societies: catered for Wed and Thur
only.
Catering: lunch, snack bar facilities
available except Mon.
Squash and Badminton.
Hotels: Oatlands Park (Weybridge).

D21 **Camberley Heath**
☎(0276) 23258, (0276) 692505 Fax
Golf Drive, Camberley, Surrey GU15
1JG
On A325 to Camberley, near M3 exit
4, follow signs to Bagshot and
Frimley.
Undulating heathland course.
18 holes, 6337 yards, S.S.S.70
Designed by H. S. Colt.
Founded 1913
Visitors: welcome, but must have
h/cap cert from recognised golf club
and should phone for tee reservation.
Green Fee: on application.
Societies: by arrangement.
Catering: meals and snacks served;
Japanese restaurant.
Hotels: Frimley Hall; One Oak.

D22 **Canterbury**
☎(0227) 453532
Scotland Hills, Canterbury, Kent CT1
1TW
A257 1 mile from Canterbury.
Parkland course.
18 holes, 6249 yards, S.S.S.70
Designed by H.S. Colt.
Founded 1927
Visitors: welcome on weekdays.
Green Fee: £27/round, £36/day WD;
£36/round (after 3pm) Sat and Sun.
Societies: catered for Tues and
Thurs only.
Catering: full menu Mon-Sat.
Hotels: Ebury; Canterbury; Abbots
Barton.

D23 **Chart Hills**
☎(0580) 292222, 292233 Fax
Weeks Lane, Biddenden, Kent TN27
8JX
Off A274 from Leeds Castle to
Tenterden.
Parkland course.
18 holes, 7068 yards, S.S.S.72
Designed by Nick Faldo.
Founded 1993
Visitors: welcome; h/cap cert
requied.
Green Fee: ring for details.
Societies: welcome.
Catering: full facilities.
Snooker, health centre.
Hotels: Chequers (Smarden); Great
Danes.

D24 **Cherry Lodge**
☎(0959) 72550 office, 72989 Pro
Jail Lane, Biggin Hill, Kent TN16 3AX
Off A233 by RAF Biggin Hill.
Undulating downland course.
18 holes, 6652 yards, S.S.S.72
Designed by John Day.
Founded 1969
Visitors: welcome Mon-Fri only by
arrangement.
Green Fee: on application.
Societies: Mon-Fri, min 18; full
catering facilities by prior booking.
Catering: à la carte restaurant
Mon-Sat, Sun lunches, 2 bars.
Banqueting.
Hotels: Kings Arms (Westerham);
Bromley Court (Bromley).

D25 **Chessington**
☎(081) 391 0948 Shop, 974 1705
Office
Garrison Lane, Chessington, Surrey
KT9 2LW
Opposite Chessington South station,
very near to Chessington zoo.
Parkland course.
9 holes, 1400 yards, Par 3 course,
S.S.S.25
Designed by Patrick Tallack.
Founded 1983
Visitors: welcome.
Green Fee: £3.95 WD, £4.50 WE.
Societies: welcome.
Catering: full catering facilities.
Driving range.
Hotels: Seven Hills; Oatlands Park.

D26 **Chestfield**
☎(0227) 794411 Sec/Manager,
793563 Pro
103 Chestfield Rd, Whitstable, Kent
CT5 3LU
0.5 mile S of Thanet Way at
Swalecliffe/Chestfield roundabout.
Parkland/seaside course.
18 holes, 6181 yards, S.S.S.70
Founded 1925
Visitors: must have current h/cap
certs; not weekends or Bank
Holidays.
Green Fee: £20/round, £30/day.
Societies: by arrangement Mon,
Tues, Wed and Fri.
Catering: full facilities.
Hotels: Marine; Hotel St George.

D27 **Chipstead**
☎(0737) 555781
How Lane, Coulsden, Surrey CR3
3PR
Follow signs to Chipstead from A217.
Undulating parkland course.

18 holes, 5454 yards, S.S.S.67
Founded 1906
Visitors: welcome weekdays.
Green Fee: £25/day, £20 after 2pm,
(£10 with member).
Societies: catered for on weekdays.
Catering: lunch served except Mon;
prior booking required.

D28 **Chislehurst**
☎(081) 467 2782
Camden Place, Camden Park Rd,
Chislehurst, Kent BR7 5HJ
0.5 mile from Chislehurst station, on
A222 to Bromley.
Parkland course.
18 holes, 5128 yards, S.S.S.65
Founded 1894
Visitors: welcome weekdays only.
Green Fee: £25 WD (£10 with
member).
Societies: by arrangement with Sec.
Catering: lunch each day.
Hotels: Bromley Court.

D29 **Chobham**
☎(0276) 855584, 856243 Fax
Chobham Rd, Knaphill, Woking,
Surrey GU21 2TU
5 minutes from Woking and M3
junction 3, between Knaphill and
Chobham villages.
Parkland course.
18 holes
Designed by Clive Clark & Peter Alliss.
Opening summer 1994
Visitors: limited for first year of play.
Green Fee: member's guest fees
approx £15.
Societies: no society play for first 2
years.
Catering: bars, restaurant, function
room.

D30 **Cobtree Manor Park**
☎(0622) 753276 Pro shop/Bookings
Chatham Rd, Maidstone, Kent ME14
3AZ
Take A229 from M20.
Municipal parkland course.
18 holes, 5635 yards, S.S.S.68
Designed by F. Hawtree.
Founded 1984
Visitors: welcome.
Green Fee: £8.50 WD, £13.25 WE.
Societies: on application.
Catering: available.

D31 **Coombe Hill**
☎(081) 942 2284
Golf Club Drive, Kingston, Surrey KT2
7DG

0.25 mile W of A3 on A238.
Parkland course.
18 holes, 6286 yards, S.S.S.71
Designed by J.F. Abercromby.
Founded 1911
Visitors: by appointment only, phone
Pro for details.
Green Fee: £45 WD only.
Societies: welcome weekdays,
phone Pro for details.
Catering: lunches served every day.

D32 **Coombe Wood**
☎(081) 942 0388
George Rd, Kingston Hill, Surrey KT2
7NS
1 mile N of Kingston-on-Thames, off
Kingston Hill.
Parkland course.
18 holes, 5210 yards, S.S.S.66
Designed by T. Williamson.
Founded 1904
Visitors: weekdays only.
Green Fee: on application.
Societies: welcome Wed, Thurs and
Fri.
Catering: available.
Hotels: Kingston Lodge (adjoining
course).

D33 **Corinthian**
☎(0474) 707559
Gay Dawn Farm, Fawkham,
Longfield, Kent DA3 8LZ
4 miles S of Dartford Tunnel, E of
Brands Hatch along Fawkham road.
Parkland course (grass greens in
summer, artificial greens in winter).
9 holes (18 tees), 6045 yards,
S.S.S.70
Founded 1987
Visitors: unrestricted weekdays, pm
only weekends and Bank Holidays.
Green Fee: £12.50/day.
Societies: by arrangement with Sec.
Catering: bar evenings, Sat and Sun
lunch.
Tennis, squash, sauna, gymnasium.

D34 **Coulsdon Court**
☎(081) 668 0414 or 660 0468
Coulsdon Rd, Coulsdon, Surrey CR3
2LL
Just off A23, 2 miles S of Croydon, 2
miles N of M25 and M23.
Parkland course.
18 holes, 6037 yards, S.S.S.69
Designed by H.S. Buck.
Founded 1926
Visitors: welcome.
Green Fee: apply for details.
Societies: welcome.
Catering: full facilities.

D35 **Cranbrook**

☎(0580) 712833
Benenden Rd, Cranbrook, Kent TN17 4AL
Take A262 Ashford/Cranbrook turning off A21 just N of Lamberhurst; turn right at Bull public house in Sissinghurst, over crossroads (1.5 miles), club 1 mile on left.
Heavily wooded parkland course.
18 holes, 6351 yards, S.S.S.70
Designed by John D. Harris.
Founded 1969
Visitors: welcome weekdays, times limited at weekends.
Green Fee: £19 WD, £27.50 WE.
Societies: on application; specialists in company golf days.
Catering: full bar and restaurant facilities.
Hotels: Willesley; Kennel Holt; Tudor Court.

D36 **Cray Valley**

☎(0689) 839677 Sec, 837909 Pro shop, 831927 Clubhouse
Sandy Lane, St Paul's Cray, Orpington, Kent BR5 3HY
A20 to Ruxley roundabout, junction with A233.
Undulating meadowland course.
18 holes, 5624 yards, S.S.S.67; 9 hole course.
Designed by Golf Centres Ltd.
Founded 1972
Visitors: weekdays unlimited, weekends restricted.
Green Fee: £10 WD, £15.50 WE.
Societies: welcome weekdays, not weekends.
Catering: telephone above.

D37 **Croham Hurst**

☎(081) 657 5581, 657 7705 Pro
Croham Rd, South Croydon, Surrey CR2 7HJ
1 mile from S Croydon; from M25 exit 6 N onto A22, take B270 to Warlingham at roundabout, then B269 to Selsdon; at traffic lights turn left into Farley Rd, clubhouse 1.75 miles on left.
Parkland course.
18 holes, 6286 yards, S.S.S.70
Designed by Hawtree & Sons.
Founded 1911
Visitors: h/cap cert required; with member only at weekends.
Green Fee: £33/round/day.
Societies: Wed, Thurs, Fri by arrangement.
Catering: full catering every day 10am-6pm; banqueting.

D38 **Cuddington**

☎(081) 393 0952
Banstead Rd, Banstead, Surrey SM7 1RD
200 yards from Banstead station.
Parkland course.
18 holes, 6394 yards, S.S.S.70
Designed by H.S. Colt.
Founded 1929
Visitors: welcome by appointment.
Green Fee: on application.
Societies: Thurs only.
Catering: available weekdays by appointment.
Hotels: Driftbridge.

D39 **Darenth Valley**

☎(0959) 522944 Manager, 522922 Pro, (0959) 525089 Fax
Station Rd, Shoreham, Kent TN14 7SA
Along A225 Sevenoaks-Dartford road, 4 miles N of Sevenoaks.
Public meadowland course.
18 holes, 6195 yards, S.S.S.71
Founded 1973 by M.F.C. Cross.
Visitors: welcome; bookings daily.
Green Fee: £11/round WD, £15/round WE & BH.
Societies: welcome, prices on application to the Manager.
Catering: bar meals, society catering, functions (100).

D40 **Dartford**

☎(0322) 223616, 226455 Sec, 226409 Pro
Dartford Heath, Dartford, Kent DA1 2TN
On Dartford Heath, 2 miles from Dartford town centre.
Heathland course.
18 holes, 5914 yards, S.S.S.68
Founded 1897
Visitors: welcome weekdays if member of recognised club, at weekends only with member; h/cap certs required.
Green Fee: £28 (£12.50 with member)
Societies: Mon and Fri, booked well in advance.
Catering: full restaurant service.
Hotels: Royal Bull; Victoria.

D41 **Deangate Ridge**

☎(0634) 251180
Hoo, Rochester, Kent ME3 8RZ
A228 from Rochester to Isle of Grain, then road signposted to Deangate Ridge, 4 miles NE of Rochester.
Municipal parkland course.
18 holes, 6300 yards, S.S.S.70
Designed by Hawtree & Sons.
Founded 1972
Visitors: welcome any time, bookings essential weekends.
Green Fee: on application.
Societies: welcome.
Catering: lunch and dinner served, bookings essential weekends.
Hotels: Inn on the Lake (on A2).

D42 **Dorking**

☎(0306) 886917, 885914
Chart Park, Dorking, Surrey RH5 4BX
A24 0.5 mile S of Dorking between A25 and North Holmwood roundabouts.
Undulating parkland course.
9 holes (18 tees), 5163 yards, S.S.S.65
Designed by James Braid.
Founded 1897
Visitors: welcome weekdays, members only weekends and Bank Holidays; Ladies' Day Wed am.
Green Fee: £16/day WD.
Societies: welcome by prior arrangement.
Catering: full meals and snacks except Mon.
Hotels: Burford Bridge; White Horse.

D43 **Drift**

☎(0483) 284641
The Drift, East Horsley, Surrey KT24 5HD
Turn off A3 onto B2039 signposted East Horsley, 2 miles on left, signposted.
Woodland course.
18 holes, 6425 yards, S.S.S.72
Designed by H. Cotton
Founded 1975
Visitors: welcome weekdays only.
Green Fee: £30/day
Societies: welcome weekdays except Tues am.
Catering: bar and restaurant facilities.
Hotels: Preston Cross; Thatchers.

D44 **Dulwich & Sydenham Hill**

☎(081) 693 3961
Grange Lane, College Rd, London SE21 7LH
Off S Circular road at Dulwich College and College Rd.
Parkland course.
18 holes, 6051 yards, S.S.S.69
Founded 1894
Visitors: welcome weekdays only by prior booking.
Green Fee: £25/round.

Societies: weekdays by arrangement.
Catering: lunch daily, dinner by arrangement.
Hotels: Queens (Crystal Palace).

D45 Dunsfold Aerodrome
☎(0483) 265472, 276118 Sec
British Aerospace, Dunsfold Aerodrome, Nr Godalming, Surrey GU8 4BS
12 miles S of Guildford on A281.
Parkland course.
9 holes (18 tees), 6090 yards, S.S.S.69
Designed by John Sharkey.
Founded 1965
Visitors: with member only.
Green Fee: £3/round.
Societies: from British Aerospace only.
Catering: bar, snacks.

D46 Edenbridge Golf & Country Club
☎(0732) 865097
Crouch House Rd, Edenbridge, Kent TN8 5LQ
Travelling N through Edenbridge High St, turn left into Stangrove Rd (30 yards before railway station), at end of road turn right, course is short distance on left.
Undulating meadowland course.
Old, 18 holes, 6635 yards, S.S.S.71;
New, 18 holes, 5763 yards, S.S.S.67; 9 hole Beginner's Course, Par 31
Founded 1975
Visitors: welcome, members only on Old Course weekends.
Green Fee: apply for details.
Societies: weekdays only.
Catering: lunch and bar snacks served daily.
Driving range.
Hotels: Oxted (East Grinstead).

D47 Effingham
☎(0372) 452203, 459959 Fax
Guildford Rd, Effingham, Surrey KT24 5PZ
On A246 8 miles E of Guildford.
Downland course.
18 holes, 6550 yards, S.S.S.71
Designed by H.S. Colt.
Founded 1927
Visitors: Mon-Fri only by arrangement, h/cap certs required.
Green Fee: £35/day, £27.50 after 2pm.
Societies: catered for Wed, Thurs and Fri.

Catering: lunch, tea, evening meal, snacks etc.
Tennis, squash, snooker (must be accompanied by member).
Hotels: Thatchers (East Horsley); Preston Cross (Great Bookham).

D48 Eltham Warren
☎(081) 850 1166, 850 4477
Bexley Rd, Eltham, London SE9 2PE
Continuation of Eltham High St, 0.5 mile E.
Parkland course.
9 holes, 5840 yards, S.S.S.68
Founded 1890
Visitors: weekdays only; must be member of recognised club.
Green Fee: £25/day.
Societies: welcome weekdays.
Catering: bar snacks; full catering by arrangement except Mon.
Snooker.
Hotels: Crest Hotel (Bexley).

D49 Epsom
☎(0372) 721666 Sec, 741867 Pro
Longdown Lane South, Epsom, Surrey KT17 4JR
0.5 mile S of Epsom Downs Station, next to Epsom College heading towards the downs.
Downland course.
18 holes, 5701 yards, S.S.S.68
Founded 1889
Visitors: welcome on weekdays from 8am, except Tues from 12.30pm; bookings with Pro on Sat and from 12am Sun.
Green Fee: £16/round, £24/day WD; £18/round WE.
Societies: Wed and Fri on written application, min 12, max 40.
Catering: meals and snacks.
Hotels: Drift Bridge; Chalk Lane.

D50 Farnham
☎(0252) 782109 Sec, 782198 Pro
The Sands, Farnham, Surrey GU10 1PX
1 mile E of Farnham on A31, turning to The Sands signposted.
Parkland/heathland course.
18 holes, 6325 yards, S.S.S.70
Founded 1896
Visitors: welcome weekdays with h/cap cert; guests of members only at weekends.
Green Fee: on application.
Societies: welcome by arrangement Wed and Thurs.
Catering: full catering on request.
Hotels: Hogs Back; Bush; Bishops Table.

D51 Farnham Park
☎(0252) 715216
Folly Hill, Farnham, Surrey
0.75 mile N of Farnham, next to castle in Farnham Park.
Par 3 parkland course.
9 holes, 1161 yards, S.S.S.54
Designed by Henry Cotton.
Founded 1963
Visitors: welcome at all times; weekends and Bank Holidays booking only.
Green Fee: £3.25 WD, £4.10 WE; reductions jnrs and OAPs.
Catering: hot or cold snacks as required.
Hotels: The Bush (Farnham).

D52 Faversham
☎(0795) 890561
Belmont Park, Faversham, Kent ME13 0HB
Leave M2 at junction 6, A251 to Faversham, then A2 to Sittingbourne for 0.5 mile, turn left at Brogdale Rd, and follow signs.
Parkland course.
18 holes, 6030 yards, S.S.S.69
Founded 1902
Visitors: welcome weekdays, only with member weekends and public holidays.
Green Fee: £25/round, £30/day WD; £22/round, £30/day (with member) WE.
Societies: catered for Wed and Fri only by arrangement, £25/round, £32/day.
Catering: by arrangement with Steward.
Hotels: Ship.

D53 Fernfell Golf & Country Club
☎(0483) 268855
Barhatch Lane, Cranleigh, Surrey GU6 7NG
Take A281 out of Guildford; 1 mile through Cranleigh take Ewhurst road, then Shere turn into Barhatch Road/Barhatch Lane.
Parkland course.
18 holes, 5561 yards, S.S.S.68
Founded 1985
Visitors: welcome weekdays.
Green Fee: apply for details.
Societies: welcome weekdays by prior arrangement.
Catering: bar, restaurant, snacks, banquets.
Tennis, snooker, outdoor swimming pool.
Hotels: Post House (Guildford); Bramley Grange (Bramley).

D54 **Foxhills**
☎(0932) 872050, 874762 Fax
Stonehill Rd, Ottershaw, Surrey KT16
0EL
Off A320 at Otter public house, turn
right and right again into Foxhills Rd;
1 mile from M25 exit 11.
Heathland courses.
Chertsey, 18 holes, 6370 yards,
S.S.S.70; Longcross, 18 holes, 6123
yards, S.S.S.69; 9 hole Par 3
Designed by F. Hawtree.
Founded 1973
Visitors: welcome Mon-Fri, after
12am weekends.
Green Fee: £45/round, £65/day WD,
£55/round WE & BH.
Societies: only by appointment.
Catering: 3 restaurants plus bars.
Driving range, tennis courts (10),
squash (4), indoor and outdoor pools,
gym, health suite, snooker,
banqueting, clay shoot, archery.
Hotels: 16 suites on the complex.

D55 **Gatton Manor**
☎(0306) 627555, 627557 Pro shop,
627713 Fax
Ockley, Dorking, Surrey RH5 5PQ
A29 1.5 miles SW of Ockley.
Undulating parkland course.
18 holes, 6145-6902 yards,
S.S.S.69-73
Designed by D.B. & D.G. Heath.
Founded 1969
Visitors: welcome except Sun am.
Green Fee: on application
Societies: weekdays.
Catering: meals and snacks, à la
carte restaurant.
Bowls, tennis, coarse and trout
fishing, practice range and putting
green.
Hotels: Gatton Manor.

D56 **Gillingham**
☎(0634) 853017 Sec, 855862 Pro,
850999 Bar, 574749 Fax
Woodlands Rd, Gillingham, Kent ME7
2AP
On A2 at Gillingham, about 2 miles
from M2 turn off to Gillingham.
Meadowland course.
18 holes, 5863 yards, S.S.S.68
Designed by James Braid.
Founded 1908
Visitors: must be member of another
club or hold current h/cap cert; only
with member weekends.
Green Fee: £22/round/day WD;
£11/round, £16.50/day with member
WD and WE.
Societies: any day except Thurs;
must be 24 or over Mon/Tues.

Catering: Wed-Sun lunch and
evening meals.
Hotels: Park Hotel.

D57 **Goal Farm Par 3**
☎(048 67) 3183, 3205
Gole Rd, Pirbright, Surrey GU24 0PZ
1 mile from Brookwood station off
A322 towards Pirbright
9 holes Par 3, 1273 yards
Founded 1977
Visitors: welcome, not Thurs am or
Sat.
Green Fee: £3.25 WD, £3.50 WE.
Catering: bar and bar snacks.

D58 **Guildford**
☎(0483) 63941 Sec, 66765 Pro,
31842 Steward/Caterer, 453228 Fax
High Path Rd, Merrow, Guildford,
Surrey GU1 2HL
2 miles E of Guildford on A246.
Downland course.
18 holes, 6090 yards, S.S.S.70
Designed by James Braid.
Founded 1886
Visitors: welcome on weekdays,
weekends with member only.
Green Fee: £25/round, £35/day.
Societies: welcome by
arrangement.
Catering: bar snacks, restaurant by
arrangement.
Practice ground, snooker.
Hotels: Angel; White Horse;
Clavadel.

D59 **Hankley Common**
☎(0252) 792493 Sec, 793761 Pro
Tilford Rd, Tilford, Farnham, Surrey
GU10 2DD
4 miles SE of Farnham; from
Farnham dual carriageway A31
southbound, turn left at lights, over
railway crossing, fork right to Tilford.
Heathland course.
18 holes, 6456 yards, S.S.S.71
Designed by James Braid.
Founded 1896
Visitors: welcome weekdays, by
arrangement with Sec weekends;
h/cap cert required.
Green Fee: £28/round, £35/day
Societies: Tues and Wed.
Catering: always available.
Practice ground.
Hotels: Frensham Ponds.

D60 **Hawkhurst**
☎(0580) 752396
High St, Hawkhurst, Cranbrook, Kent
TN18 4JS

On A268, 2 miles from A21 at
Flimwell, 0.5 mile from junction with
A229.
Undulating parkland course.
9 holes, 5791 yards, S.S.S.68
Designed by Rex Baldock.
Founded 1968
Visitors: welcome; only with
member weekends.
Green Fee: £15/day.
Societies: on application; mostly Fri.
Catering: by arrangement.
Hotels: Royal Oak; Tudor Court;
Queens.

D61 **Herne Bay**
☎(0227) 373964
Eddington, Herne Bay, Kent CT6 7PG
Take Thanet Way at Herne Bay
towards Canterbury, immediately
turn right.
Parkland course.
18 holes, 5535 yards, S.S.S.66
Founded 1895
Visitors: welcome, some restrictions
weekends and Bank Holidays.
Green Fee: on application
Societies: welcome any time.
Catering: full facilities, full meals by
prior arrangement.

D62 **Hever**
☎(0732) 700771, 700775 Fax
Hever, Kent TN8 7NG
10 mins from M25 or A21; course
between Sevenoaks and Edenbridge
adjacent to Hever Castle.
Parkland course with 5 lakes.
18 holes, S.S.S.73
Designed by Dr Peter Nicholson.
Founded May 1992
Visitors: welcome any time but must
book; h/cap cert required; no visitors
before 11am weekends.
Green Fee: £25 WD, £40 WE.
Societies: Mon-Fri only; must have
h/caps.
Catering: main bar, spike bar, Silver
Service restaurant (à la carte),
snacks and sandwiches.
Snooker, tennis, health club.
Hotels: The Chaser Inn (Stumble
Hill).

D63 **Hewitts Golf Centre**
☎(0689) 896266, 824577 Fax
Court Rd, Orpington, Kent BR6 9BX
From M4 junction 4 follow A224 to
Orpington; 2 mins from motorway
junction.
Public downland course.
Chelsfield Downs, 18 holes,
S.S.S.69; Warren, 9 holes Par 3

Designed by MRM Leisure.
Founded 1993
Visitors: welcome at all times.
Green Fee: Chelsfield Downs, £13 WD, £16 WE; Warren, £5 WD, £5.50 WE.
Societies: welcome Mon-Fri.
Catering: bar, restaurant, society room (private, seats 40).
Driving range.

D64 High Elms
☎(0689) 858175
High Elms Rd, Downe, Kent
5 miles out of Bromley off the A21 to Sevenoaks.
Public parkland course.
18 holes, 5626 yards, S.S.S.69
Designed by Fred Hawtree
Founded 1969
Visitors: welcome.
Green Fee: £11/round.
Societies: weekdays only.
Catering: full meals and snacks.
Hotels: Bromley Court.

D65 Hindhead
☎(0428) 604614 Tel/Fax, 604458 Pro
Churt Rd, Hindhead, Surrey GU26 6HX
1.5 miles N of Hindhead on A287 towards Farnham.
Heathland course.
18 holes, 6373 yards, S.S.S.70
Founded 1904
Visitors: welcome weekdays, weekends by appointment; h/cap cert required.
Green Fee: £25/round, £33/day WD; £40 WE.
Societies: Wed and Thurs only.
Catering: bar, restaurant, snack bar. Snooker, practice ground, putting green.
Hotels: Devil's Punch Bowl; Pride of the Valley (Churt); Frensham Ponds.

D66 Hoebridge Golf Centre
☎(0483) 722611, 740369 Fax
Old Woking Rd, Old Woking, Surrey GU22 8JH
On B382 Old Woking road between Old Woking and West Byfleet.
Public parkland course.
Hoebridge, 18 holes, 6536 yards, S.S.S.71; Shey Copse, 9 holes, 2294 yards, Par 33; Maybury, Par 3, 9 holes, 2230 yards;
Designed by John Jacobs.
Founded 1982
Visitors: welcome any time, must book at weekends.

Green Fee: £12.50/round
Hoebridge, £6.75/round Shey Copse (9 holes), £6/round Par 3.
Societies: welcome by arrangement.
Catering: restaurant and snack bar open all day.
Driving range; snooker (members only).
Hotels: Post House (Guildford); Hilton International (Cobham).

D67 Holtye
☎(0342) 850635, 850576 Sec
Holtye Common, Cowden, Edenbridge TN8 7ED
On A264 between East Grinstead and Tunbridge Wells, 5 miles W of East Grinstead, 4 miles due S of Edenbridge.
Testing forest/heathland course.
9 holes, 5325 yards, S.S.S.66
Founded 1893
Visitors: welcome weekdays; restricted Thurs am and weekends am; telephone first.
Green Fee: £15/day WD, £18 afternoons only WE.
Societies: Tues and Fri.
Catering: lunchtimes, 7 days a week.
Large practice ground.
Hotels: White Horse Inn (adjacent).

D68 Home Park
☎(081) 977 2423 Office, 977 2658 Pro Shop, 977 4414 Fax
Hampton Wick,
Richmond-upon-Thames, Surrey KT1 4AS
From Kingston over Kingston Bridge, at roundabout turn left, 50 yards on left through iron gates at Old Kings Head public house, straight road to club.
Parkland course in park of Hampton Court Palace.
18 holes, 6598 yards, S.S.S.71
Founded 1895
Visitors: welcome.
Green Fee: apply for details.
Societies: weekdays.
Catering: lunches and bar snacks served; dinner bookings taken.
Hotels: Lion Gate.

D69 Horton Park Country Club
☎(081) 393 8400 office, 394 2626 shop
Hook Road, Epsom, Surrey KT19 8QG
Off Hook Rd through Epsom to Chessington.

Public parkland course.
18 holes, 5208 yards, Par 70
Founded 1987
Visitors: welcome; proper golf shoes, no jeans
Green Fee: apply for details.
Societies: welcome weekdays only.
Catering: 2 bars, restaurant, function suite.
Hotels: Travel Inn (Chessington).

D70 Hurtmore
☎(0483) 426492, 426121 Fax
Hurtmore Rd, Hurtmore, Godalming, Surrey GU7 2RN
Off A3, 3 mile S of Guildford.
Parkland course, 7 lakes.
18 holes, 5500 yards, S.S.S.69
Designed by Peter Alliss & Clive Clark.
Founded 1990
Visitors: welcome; pay-as-you-play on booking system.
Green Fee: £12/round WD, £15/round WE.
Societies: welcome any time.
Catering: restaurant and bar.
Putting green, small practice area.

D71 Hythe Imperial
☎(0303) 267554 Sec, 267441 Pro
Princes Parade, Hythe, Kent CT21 6AE
Turn off M20 to Hythe, to E end of seafront.
Seaside course.
9 holes, 5560 yards, S.S.S.66
Founded 1950
Visitors: welcome, h/cap cert required.
Green Fee: £15 WD, £25 WE.
Societies: by arrangement.
Catering: hotel; hotel/club bar.
Hotels: Hythe Imperial; Stade Court.

D72 Kingswood (Surrey)
☎(0737) 832188
Sandy Lane, Tadworth, Surrey KT20 6NE
4 miles S of Sutton on A217, M25 junction 8.
Parkland course.
18 holes, 6513 yards, S.S.S.71
Designed by James Braid.
Founded 1928
Visitors: welcome when space available.
Green Fee: £30/round WD, £42/round WE.
Societies: welcome weekdays.
Catering: full restaurant facilities.
Snooker, squash.
Hotels: Bridge (Reigate); Heathside (Banstead); Holiday Inn (Sutton).

D73 **Knole Park**
☎(0732) 452150
Seal Hollow Rd, Sevenoaks, Kent
TN15 0HJ
From M25 onto A21 Hastings road,
after 1 mile bear left onto A25
Maidstone road; at 2nd set of lights
turn right into Seal Hollow Rd, 0.5
mile before entering Seal village.
Club 1.25 miles on left.
Parkland course of great beauty.
18 holes, 6249 yards, S.S.S.70
Designed by J.A. Abercromby.
Founded 1924
Visitors: weekdays only by
appointment; h/cap certs required.
Green Fee: £26/round, £37/2 rounds.
Societies: Tues, Thurs, Fri by
appointment only; 2 only per week.
Catering: lunch, tea, dinner.
Squash, snooker.
Hotels: Sevenoaks Park; Royal Oak.

D74 **Laleham**
☎(0932) 564211, 562877 Pro
Laleham Reach, Chertsey, Surrey
KT16 8RP
A320 between Staines and Chertsey,
opposite Thorpe Water Park; follow
signs for Thorpe Park.
Testing meadowland course with
water hazards.
18 holes, 6211 yards, S.S.S.70
Founded 1907
Visitors: welcome weekdays only
before 4.30pm.
Green Fee: on application
Societies: Mon, Tues, Wed and Fri
only.
Catering: full facilities.

D75 **Lamberhurst**
☎(0892) 890241 Clubhouse,
890591 Sec, 890552 Pro, 891140
Fax
Church Rd, Lamberhurst, Kent TN3
8DT
Entrance from A21 on outskirts of
Lamberhurst village to N.
Undulating parkland course.
18 holes, 6232 yards, S.S.S.70
Designed by Frank Pennink.
Founded 1920
Visitors: welcome any day; after
12am at weekends and Bank
Holidays unless accompanied by
member; h/cap certs required.
Green Fee: £20/round, £30/day WD;
£36 WE.
Societies: catered for on Tues, Wed
and Thurs only.
Catering: lunch, dinner and snacks
served.
Hotels: Star and Eagle (Goudhurst).

D76 **Langley Park**
☎(081) 658 6849 or 650 1663 Pro
Barnfield Wood Rd, Beckenham,
Kent BR3 2SZ
At lights near Bromley South station
turn into Westmoreland Rd,
clubhouse 1.75 miles on left.
Gently undulating parkland course.
18 holes, 6488 yards, S.S.S.71
Designed by J.H. Taylor.
Founded 1910
Visitors: not at weekends; telephone
Pro for bookings.
Green Fee: £35.
Societies: Wed only.
Catering: full facilities every day.
Hotels: Bromley Court.

D77 **Leatherhead**
☎(0372) 843966
Kingston Rd, Leatherhead, Surrey
KT22 0EE
From M25 junction 9 take A243
towards London, entrance 500
yards.
Parkland course.
18 holes, 6157 yards, S.S.S.69
Founded 1903
Visitors: welcome by appointment.
Green Fee: £30/round, £35/2 rounds
WD; £42.50/round WE.
Societies: welcome.
Catering: restaurant, brasserie, bar.
Practice ground.
Hotels: Woodlands Park (Oxshott).

D78 **Leeds Castle**
☎(0622) 880467, 765400 ext 4329
Leeds Castle, Maidstone, Kent ME17
1PL
On A20 from Maidstone towards
Ashford, signposted to Leeds Castle.
Public parkland course.
9 holes, 2880 yards, Par 34
Designed by Neil Coles (4 new holes,
1988)
Founded 1928
Visitors: bookings taken (9 holes
only) 6 days in advance; correct
dress, no denim jeans.
Green Fee: £8.50 (9 holes); £6.50
jnrs, disabled, OAPs.
Societies: and company bookings
weekdays only.
Catering: at Park Gate Inn, in golf
course car park.
Practice nets, putting green.
Hotels: Great Danes.

D79 **Limpsfield Chart**
☎(0883) 723405 Sec, 722106
Steward
Limpsfield, Oxted, Surrey RH8 0SL
On A25 between Oxted and
Westerham, over traffic lights 300
yards on right, E of Oxted.
Heathland course.
9 holes, 5718 yards, S.S.S.68
Founded 1889
Visitors: welcome Mon, Tues, Wed
and Fri; weekends by appointment.
Green Fee: £18/day/round
Societies: can be arranged.
Catering: meals served.
Hotels: Kings Arms (Westerham);
White Hart (Brastead).

D80 **Lingfield Park**
☎(0342) 834602
Racecourse Road, Lingfield, Surrey
RH7 6PQ
M25 Junction 6; through Lingfield
village towards Edenbridge; course
is on right next to racecourse before
railway bridge.
Parkland course.
18 holes, 6500 yards, S.S.S.72
Founded May 1987
Visitors: welcome Mon-Fri.
Green Fee: £20/round, £30/day WD.
Societies: welcome by arrangement
with Manager.
Catering: full bar facilities, bar
snacks; other by arrangement.
Driving range.
Hotels: Copthorne; Effingham Park.

D81 **Littlestone**
☎(0679) 63355 Sec, 62310
Clubhouse, 62231 Pro
St Andrews Rd, Littlestone, New
Romney, Kent TN28 8RB
M20 to Ashford, B2070 to New
Romney, 1.5 miles from New
Romney.
Seaside links course.
18 holes, 6460 yards, S.S.S.72
Designed by Laidlaw Purves.
Founded 1888
Visitors: weekdays after 9.30am,
weekends after 3pm; max h/cap 20
(Men), 30 (Ladies); advance booking
necessary.
Green Fee: £26 WD, £32 WE.
Societies: weekdays by
arrangement with Sec.
Catering: bar and restaurant.
Hotels: Stade Court (Hythe); Romney
Bay House (Littlestone); Broadacre
(New Romney).

D82 **London Scottish**
☎(081) 788 0135, 789 7517 Sec
Windmill Enclosure, Wimbledon
Common, London SW19 5NQ
1 mile from Putney Station (S.R.).

 # LEEDS CASTLE GOLF COURSE

'. . . there is nothing to compare with the delightful surroundings of Leeds Castle . . .'
(Donald Steel: The Golf Course Guide)

A round of golf at Leeds Castle offers some unforgettable golfing memories.

You'll find yourself playing alongside the moat, lining up tee shots against the Castle battlements and pausing to watch the black swans and wildfowl which inhabit the 500 acres of parkland.

This 9 hole, 2880 yard course was re-designed by Neil Coles and is open the year round for everyone to enjoy.

The golf Professional, Chris Miller, offers coaching, equipment advice and club and trolley hire, from the Golf Centre.

Golf societies and groups are welcomed and residential golf weekends can be organised.

Please call for further details or reservations. Booking is essential.

Leeds Castle Golf Course, nr. Maidstone, Kent.   Tel (0622)880467

Parkland course.
18 holes, 5436 yards, S.S.S.67
Founded 1865
Visitors: welcome weekdays, except Bank Holidays; must wear red upper garment.
Green Fee: apply for details.
Societies: all year; not weekends or Mon.
Catering: lunch served, evening meals available if ordered, except Mon.

D83 The London
☎(0474) 879899, 879912 Fax
South Ash Manor Estate, Ash, Nr Sevenoaks, Kent TN15 7EN
Leave M25 at junction 3 or M20 at junction 1 and take A20 towards Brands Hatch; after passing under M20, turn left into Stansted lane; from M26 exit 2a, follow signs to Brands Hatch, turn right at Stansted Lane; club is 100 yards on left.
Inland links course.
Heritage, 18 holes, S.S.S.74 (provisional); International, 18 holes, S.S.S.74 (provisional)
Designed by Jack Nicklaus (Heritage), Ron Kirby (International).
Founded Sept 1993

Visitors: members' guests only.
Catering: 2 bars, excellent restaurant. teppanyaki restaurant. Extensive practice facilities.

D84 Lullingstone Park
☎(0959) 533793
Park Gate, Chelsfield, Orpington, Kent BR6 7PX
Signposted from M25 junction 4.
Municipal parkland course.
18 holes, 6068 yards, S.S.S.72; 9 holes, 2432 yards
Designed by Fred Hawtree.
Founded 1923
Visitors: welcome.
Green Fee: summer, £9/round WD, £11/round WE; winter, £5.80 (9 holes) WD, £7.80 WE.
Societies: by arrangement.
Catering: bar, snacks always available; meals by arrangement.

D85 Malden
☎(081) 942 0654 Sec, 942 6009 Pro, 336 2219 Fax
Traps Lane, New Malden, KT3 4RS
0.5 mile from New Malden station, near A3 between Wimbledon and Kingston.

Parkland course.
18 holes, 6295 yards, S.S.S.70
Founded 1926
Visitors: weekdays unrestricted, weekends restricted.
Green Fee: on application to Pro
Societies: Wed, Thurs, Fri.
Catering: all week, bar.

D86 Mid-Kent
☎(0474) 568035, 564218 Fax
Singlewell Rd, Gravesend, Kent DA11 7RB
A2 S of Gravesend, turn off at Tollgate Moathouse Hotel.
Parkland course.
18 holes, 6206 yards, S.S.S.70
Designed by Frank Pennink.
Founded 1909
Visitors: weekdays, weekends with member, h/cap cert required
Green Fee: on application
Societies: Tues only.
Catering: lunch 7 days, dinner by arrangement. Snooker.

D87 Milford
☎(0483) 419200
Milford, Nr Guildford, Surrey GU8 5HS
Off A3 close to Godalming.

Woodland/meadowland course with water hazards.
18 holes, 6224 yards, Par 69
Designed by Peter Alliss & Clive Clark.
Founded 1993
Visitors: contact in advance, h/cap certs required; restricted at weekends.
Green Fee: £20 WD, £25 WE & BH.
Societies: by prior arrangement.
Catering: full facilities.
Practice ground.

D88 **Mitcham**
☎ (081) 648 1508, 640 4280 Pro
Carshalton Rd, Mitcham Junction, Surrey CR4 4HN
A237 off A23, by Mitcham Junction station.
Meadowland course.
18 holes, 5935 yards, S.S.S.68
Founded 1886
Visitors: weekdays, restrictions weekends.
Green Fee: on application, phone Pro.
Societies: Thurs only Apr-Sep.
Catering: full facilities.

D89 **Moatlands**
☎ (0892) 724400
Watermans Lane, Brenchley, Kent TN12 6ND
Take A21 past Sevenoaks, Tonbridge and Tunbridge Wells; turn left at roundabout onto B2160 to Matfield and Paddock Wood; through Matfield, down steep hill, then right at bottom, signposted.
Undulating parkland course with views over weald.
18 hole championship course, 7060 yards, S.S.S.74
Designed by K. Saito.
Founded Nov 1993
Visitors: welcome, ring Pro shop for weekend times.
Green Fee: £30 WD, £40 WE.
Societies: welcome 2 days a week; ring Pro shop for details.
Catering: restaurant (à la carte), bar food all day.
Snooker and health club (members only); driving range for lessons.
Hotels: Pembury Resort.

D90 **Moore Place**
☎ (0372) 463533
Portsmouth Rd, Esher, Surrey KT10 9LN
On A3 Portsmouth road, 0.5 mile from centre of Esher towards Cobham.

Public undulating parkland course.
9 holes, 3512 yards, S.S.S.58
Designed by David Allen.
Founded 1926
Visitors: welcome any time, no restrictions.
Green Fee: £5.50 WD, £7.25 WE & BH.
Societies: weekdays, phone for information.
Catering: full facilities.
Hotels: Ladbroke Hilton Seven Hills.

D91 **Nevill**
☎ (0892) 525818
Benhall Mill Rd, Tunbridge Wells, Kent TN2 5JW
Turn into Forest Rd from A267 out of Tunbridge Wells.
Parkland/heathland course.
18 holes, 6336 yards, S.S.S.70
Designed by C.K. Cotton
Founded 1914
Visitors: accepted with h/cap cert.
Green Fee: £33/day (£12 with member) WD, £17/day with member only WE.
Societies: Wed, Thurs only.
Catering: 7 days a week.
Hotels: Spa; Calverley.

D92 **New Zealand GC**
☎ (0932) 345049
Woodham Lane, Addlestone, Surrey KT15 3QD
At junction of Woodham Lane and Sheerwater Rd in West Byfleet.
Heathland course.
18 holes, 6012 yards, S.S.S.69
Designed by Mure-Fergusson.
Founded 1895
Visitors: by arrangement.
Green Fee: on application.
Societies: weekdays only, by arrangement.
Catering: bar and restaurant (no evening meals).

D93 **Nizels**
☎ (0732) 833138 Club, 838926 Pro shop, 833764 Fax
Nizels Lane, Hildenborough, Nr Tonbridge, Kent TN11 8NX
From A21 take Tonbridge North B245; 5 mins from M25.
Parkland course.
18 holes, C.S.S.71
Designed by Pocock Developments Ltd.
Founded Sept 1992
Visitors: booking up to 3 days in advance.
Green Fee: £25/round, £35/day.

Societies: weekdays.
Catering: bar and restaurant open all day, breakfast from 7.30am.

D94 **North Downs**
☎ (0883) 652057, 653298, 653004, 652832 Fax
Northdown Rd, Woldingham, Caterham, Surrey CR3 7AA
2 miles N of M25 junction 6 to roundabout, 5th exit to Woldingham (2 miles); clubhouse 0.5 mile through village on left.
Downland course.
18 holes, 5843 yards, S.S.S.68
Designed by J.J. Pennink.
Founded 1899
Visitors: welcome weekdays, h/cap cert required or prior enquiry to Manager.
Green Fee: £28/day.
Societies: catered for weekdays, half or full day (half day only Thurs).
Catering: full restaurant facilities, snacks.
Hotels: Kings Arms; Felbridge; Villa Sonia.

D95 **North Foreland**
☎ (0843) 62140 Sec, 69628 Pro
Convent Rd, Broadstairs, Kent CT10 3PU
A28 from Canterbury, or A2/M2/A299 from London to Kingsgate via Broadstairs, course 1.5 miles from Broadstairs station.
Seaside/clifftop course.
18 holes, 6382 yards, S.S.S.71; Short Course, 18 holes, 1752 yards, Par 54
Designed by Fowler and Simpson.
Founded 1903
Visitors: main course by prior booking, h/cap cert required; short course unrestricted.
Green Fee: main course, £23.50/round, £35/day, short course £5.50/round, £6.50/day.
Societies: Wed and Fri.
Catering: available; private functions. Tennis.
Hotels: Castle Keep; Fayreness; Castlemere; Rothsay; Ann Marie; Hotel Lancaster.

D96 **Oak Park (Crondall)**
☎ (0252) 850880, 850066 Pro
Heath Lane, Crondall, Nr Farnham, Surrey GU10 5PB
Off A287 Farnham-Odiham road 3 miles SE of M3 junction 5.
Gently undulating parkland course.
18 holes, 6437 yards, S.S.S.71

Designed by Patrick Dawson.
Founded 1984
Visitors: welcome every day; tee reservations at weekends and public holidays.
Green Fee: £16/round, £25/day WD; £22.50/round, £40/day WE.
Societies: welcome every day by reservation.
Catering: bar, bar snacks, à la carte restaurant every day except Sun/Mon evenings; conference and banqueting facilities.
Driving range.
Hotels: Bush (Farnham), THF Golfing Breaks.

D97 Oaks Sports Centre
☎(081) 643 8363, 770 7303 Fax
Woodmansterne Rd, Carshalton, Surrey SM5 4AN
On the B2032 past Carshalton Beeches station, Oaks Sports Centre signposted N of A2022, half way between A217 and A237.
Public meadowland course.
18 holes, 5975 yards, S.S.S.69; 9 holes, 1590 yards, S.S.S.28
Designed by Alphagreen.
Founded 1972
Visitors: welcome (public course).
Green Fee: 18 hole, £10 WD, £12 WE; 9 hole, £4.50 WD, £5.50 WE.
Societies: by arrangement.
Catering: Licenced restaurant (no smoking), lunchtime Carvery, evening à la carte, refreshments all day, public bar (normal pub hours).
Driving range, 5 squash courts.
Hotels: Greyhound (Carshalton).

D98 Oastpark
☎(0634) 242661
Malling Rd, Snodland, Kent ME6 5LG
A228 West Malling to Rochester road.
Public parkland course.
18 holes, S.S.S.69
Designed by Terry Cullen
Founded June 1992
Visitors: welcome any time, proper dress required.
Green Fee: £9 (18 holes) WD, £12 WE.
Societies: welcome any time.
Catering: bar, restaurant.
Large practice area.
Hotels: Trust House (Wrotham).

D99 Pachesham Golf Centre
☎(0372) 843453, 844076 Fax
Oaklawn Road, Leatherhead, Surrey KT22 0BT

From M25 junction 9 towards Esher on A244.
Public parkland course.
9 holes, 1752 yards, S.S.S.56
Designed by Phil Taylor.
Founded June 1991
Visitors: welcome 7 days, bookings by phone 2 days in advance.
Green Fee: £6.50 WD, £7.50 WE & BH.
Societies: welcome pre-booked.
Catering: bar and restaurant. Driving range, putting green, chipping area.
Hotels: Woodlands Park.

D100 Pine Ridge Golf Centre
☎(0276) 20770 Bookings, 678825 Clubhouse, 678837 Fax
Old Bisley Rd, Frimley, Camberley, Surrey GU16 5NX
5 mins from M3 junction 3; location map available on request.
Public, pine forested course.
18 holes, 6458 yards, S.S.S.71
Designed by Clive D. Smith.
Founded June 1992
Visitors: welcome at all times, bookings taken up to 7 days in advance.
Green Fee: approx £16/day WD, £20/day WE.
Societies: welcome Mon-Fri, min 12; advisable to book well in advance.
Catering: large bar and restaurant; food and drink available all day.
Driving range, putting green.
Hotels: Lakeside; Frimley Hall; Cricketers.

D101 Poult Wood
☎(0732) 364039 Bookings, 366180 Catering/Soc bookings
Higham Lane, Tonbridge, Kent TN11 9QR
1 mile N of Tonbridge off A227.
Municipal wooded course.
18 holes, 5569 yards, S.S.S.67; 9 hole short course from summer 1994
Designed by Fred Hawtree.
Founded 1972
Visitors: welcome weekdays, advance booking for registered users.
Green Fee: £8 WD, £12 WE.
Societies: Mon-Fri with advance booking; £22/day, £11 (18 holes).
Catering: restaurant and lounge bar; spikes snack bar; conference room. 4 squash courts, practice area,
Hotels: Langley; Rose and Crown; Chimneys; Chequers.

D102 Prince's
☎(0304) 611118, 613797 Pro
Sandwich Bay, Sandwich, Kent CT13 9QB
4 miles from Sandwich railway station via St George's Rd and Sandown Rd.
Traditional links course.
3 x 9-hole interconnecting loops, 3 combinations of 18 holes, 6500-7000 yards, S.S.S.72/71/71
Designed by Sir Guy Campbell & John Morrison.
Founded 1904
Visitors: welcome 7 days, no jeans or training shoes.
Green Fee: £31/round, £36/day WD; £35.50/round, £41/day Sat and BH; £35.50/round, £46.50/day Sun; special reduced rates Oct-April.
Societies: by arrangement, no restrictions.
Catering: full bar and restaurant; banqueting.
Driving range, full practice facility, snooker.
Hotels: Bell, golf/accomodation packages on request.

D103 Purley Downs
☎(081) 657 8347 Sec
106 Purley Downs Rd, South Croydon CR2 0RB
3 miles S of Croydon on A235, fork left onto Purley Downs Rd.
Downland course.
18 holes, 6212 yards, S.S.S.70
Founded 1894 (Centenary Year 1994)
Visitors: weekdays, weekends with a member; must have h/cap cert.
Green Fee: £30
Societies: Mon, Thurs, Fri on occasion.
Catering: 19th (informal), lounge bar, dining room.
Hotels: Selsdon Park.

D104 Puttenham
☎(0483) 810498, 810277 Pro shop, 810988 Fax
Heath Rd, Puttenham, Guildford, Surrey GU3 1AL
Just off A31, Farnham to Guildford road (Hog's Back), 4 miles W of Guildford.
Heathland course.
18 holes, 6214 yards, S.S.S.70
Founded 1894
Visitors: welcome weekdays only; accomplished players only.
Green Fee: £26 (36 holes).
Societies: Wed, Thurs only.
Catering: full facilities available.
Hotels: Hog's Back.

D105 **Pyrford**
☎(0483) 723555
Warren Lane, Pyrford, Woking,
Surrey GU22 8XR
From A3 take Ripley junction and
follow signs to Pyrford.
Hilly meadowland course with water
hazards.
18 holes, 6230 yards, S.S.S.70
Designed by Peter Allis & Clive Clark.
Visitors: welcome any time.
Green Fee: £35 WD, £50 WE;
half-price with member.
Societies: by prior arrangement.
Catering: full facilities.
Practice range, chipping area.
Hotels: Hilton (Cobham).

D106 **RAC Country Club**
☎(0372) 276311
Woodcote Park, Epsom, Surrey KT18
7EW
A24, 1.75 miles from Epsom.
Parkland courses.
Coronation, 18 holes, 5474 yards,
S.S.S.67; Old, 18 holes, 6702 yards,
S.S.S.72
Founded 1913
Visitors: no.
Green Fee: apply for details.
Societies: on request.
Catering: full services available.
Hotels: Chalk Lane.

D107 **Redhill & Reigate**
☎(0737) 240777 Sec, 244626
Clubhouse, 244433 Pro
Clarence Lodge, Pendleton Rd,
Redhill, Surrey RH1 6LB
1 mile S of Reigate (A217), at traffic
lights turn left (A2044), after 0.25
mile, turn left into Pendleton Rd.
Moorland course.
18 holes, 5261 yards, S.S.S.66
Designed by James Braid.
Founded 1887
Visitors: welcome Mon-Fri; Sat and
Sun after 11am; not Sun June-Sept.
Green Fee: on application
Societies: Thurs/Fri only.
Catering: bar snacks; meals if
booked.

D108 **Reigate Heath**
☎(0737) 242610, 226793 Sec
Reigate Heath, Reigate, Surrey RH2
8QR
0.5 mile S of A25 to W of Reigate.
Heathland course.
9 holes, 5658 yards, S.S.S.67
Founded 1895
Visitors: welcome weekdays, but
telephone first.

Green Fee: on application.
Societies: Wed and Thurs.
Catering: full facilities except Mon.
Hotels: Reigate Manor; Cranleigh.

D109 **Richmond**
☎(081) 940 4351, 940 1463
Sudbrook Park, Richmond, Surrey
TW10 7AS
On A307 1 mile S of Richmond, look
for Sudbrook Lane on left.
Parkland course.
18 holes, 6007 yards, S.S.S.69
Designed by Tom Dunn.
Founded 1891
Visitors: welcome on weekdays by
prior arrangement.
Green Fee: £38.
Societies: welcome Tues, Thurs and
Fri.
Catering: bar snacks and lunches
available every day.
Hotels: Petersham; Richmond Gate.

D110 **Richmond Park**
☎(081) 876 3205, 1795
Roehampton Gate, Richmond Park,
London SW15 5JR
Just inside Roehampton Gate in
Richmond Park.
Public parkland course
18 holes, 5909 yards, S.S.S.70; 18
holes, 5940 yards, S.S.S.68
Designed by Hawtree & Sons
Founded 1923
Visitors: welcome, dawn to dusk
depending on Park Gate opening
hours; must wear golf shoes;
booking system at weekends.
Green Fee: £9 WD, £12.50 WE.
Societies: welcome weekdays.
Catering: pavilion café.
Driving range, practice area.
Hotels: Richmond Hill.

D111 **The Ridge**
☎(0622) 844382 Sec, 844243 Pro
shop, 844168 Fax
Chartway St, East Sutton, Maidstone,
Kent ME17 3DL
From M20 exit 8, take B2163 and
A274 to Sutton Valence, then 1st left
into Chartway St.
Parkland course.
18 holes, 6254 yards, S.S.S.70
Designed by Tyton Design Ltd.
Founded June 1993
Visitors: h/cap certs required,
weekends by prior arrangement only.
Green Fee: £25/round WD,
£30/round WE.
Societies: welcome, Tues and Thurs
only.

Catering: 3 bars, 80-seat
restaurant, private function room.
Extensive practice facilities; driving
range.
Hotels: Great Danes (Bearstead).

D112 **Riverside**
☎(081) 310 7975, 312 3441 Fax
Summerton Way, Thamesmead,
SE28 8PP
Off A2, 10 mins from Blackheath, 15
mins Bexleyheath; just by Woolwich.
Pay-as-you-play course on
reclaimed marshland.
9 holes, 5604 yards, Par 70
Designed by Heffernan & Heffernan
Founded 1991
Visitors: welcome subject to
reasonable standard of golf.
Green Fee: approx £9.50 (9 holes),
£10 (18 holes).
Societies: welcome weekdays, only
very small societies weekends.
Catering: 2 bars, à la carte
restaurant.
Driving range.
Hotels: Black Prince (Bexleyheath).

D113 **Rochester & Cobham Park**
☎(0474) 823411, 823658 Pro shop,
824446 Fax
Park Pale by Rochester, Kent ME2
3UL
Situated on A2, turn left onto B2009
and follow signs to clubhouse.
Undulating parkland course.
18 holes, 6467 yards, S.S.S.71
Founded 1891
Visitors: weekdays unaccompanied,
h/cap cert required; weekends with
member before 5pm.
Green Fee: £26/round, £36/day.
Societies: Tues and Thurs.
Catering: details on request.
Hotels: Inn on the Lake; Tollgate
Motel.

D114 **Roehampton**
☎(081) 876 1621
Roehampton Lane, London SW15 5LR
Off A306 at bottom of Roehampton
Lane.
Parkland course.
18 holes, 6046 yards, S.S.S.69
Founded 1901
Visitors: with member only.
Green Fee: £16 WD, £22 WE.
Societies: limited 32 players, must
be introduced by a member.
Catering: full 7 day service.
Tennis, croquet, bowls, snooker,
squash and indoor/outdoor pools

Royal Cinque Ports, Deal

Nowhere in Britain, indeed nowhere in the world, do three Open championship courses lie in such close proximity as Prince's, Sandwich and Deal. You can chip a ball from Prince's to Sandwich and you could almost drive a ball from Sandwich onto the furthest reaches of Deal if it were not for the line of buildings that once included the late lamented Guildford Hotel.

Nowadays only Sandwich, reinstated in 1981, meets all the demands imposed by a modern Open, the old version of Prince's being largely demolished during the last war; but no course has remained more untouched by the years than Deal or, to give it its proper title, the Royal Cinque Ports G.C.

The sea has done its best on three occasions to sweep it away, large areas being devastated by floods swept in on angry tides, The most recent invasion was 1978 but it resulted in a gigantic exercise to strengthen the sea wall which is now thought to be man enough to repulse everything the elements might throw at it.

Like many champsionship links, Deal was no doubt more formidable in the days of the gutty ball and hickory shafts, the hummocky nature of the ground on many of the fairways being considerably easier to negotiate with a steel shaft and modern ball.

Its last Open was in 1920 when George Duncan profited from Abe Mitchell's spectacular collapse on the final day, but the tournament that keeps Deal in the forefront of the public eye is the Halford Hewitt whose participating legions descend every April to put themselves through a process of friendly torture.

The drama invariably unfolds on the 18th and 19th and, for that reason, they are the best remembered holes. The 1st is innocent enough as a first hole in spite of the stream in front of the green, and the chance of driving out of bounds or of burying a hook in the clumps of rushes. However, as the 19th, its cloak is far more sinister. The fairway seems to shrink in width and the stream casts some hypnotic power over those who seem to have all strength and coordination drained from their hands.

The 2nd, a stern two-shooter, is the sort of hole you could only find on a British seaside links, a label even more applicable to the 3rd. There are two or three enormous hollows between twin sandhills and the green.

The 4th, Sandy Parlour, is the first of three short holes which make as good a set as you will find, each calling for a different shot with a different club in a different direction. David Blair thought enormously highly of them and was very much what one might term a Deal man, as was Leonard Crawley. Their shotmaking powers were well suited to controlling the ball in moderate winds that for ordinary folk made the fives many and the fours few.

From the 2nd to the 7th, you get used to the wind from the same quarter except for the pitch to the 6th — a stroke that catches many by surprise. First time players on the course never expect to find the green where it is.

The 9th, 10th and 11th are excellent fours, running largely at right angles to the rest of the holes particularly the finish which is easy or difficult according to the wind. The 12th is another old-fashioned shaped green while the 16th and 17th also have their own distinctive contours. The 16th, in fact, is perched up like a gun turret, the steep, guardian bank frequently killing off a long second seeking a birdie four.

On the 17th, the problem for the second shot is finding a predictable landing area but at the 18th the only recommended way of hitting a flat, plateau green is carrying the shot all the way. Here again, the stream crossing the fairway claims its haul of balls although there is less excuse for causing a ripple than on the 1st. Bernard Darwin wrote, many moons ago, that Deal consists of plenty of "fine, straight-ahead, long-hitting golf". It still does.

D115 Roker Park
☎(0483) 236677
Holly Lane, Aldershot Rd, Guildford,
Surrey
3 miles from Guildford on A323
Aldershot road.
Public parkland course.
9 holes, S.S.S.70
Designed by W.V. Roker.
Founded June 1992
Visitors: welcome any day.
Green Fee: £6.50 WD, £7.50 WE.
Societies: weekdays, booking in
advance.
Catering: bar and restaurant.
Driving range.
Hotels: Worplesdon Place;
Forte/Crest (Guildford).

D116 Romney Warren
☎(0679) 63355 Sec, 62231 Pro
St Andrews Rd, Littlestone, New
Romney, Kent TN28 8RB
M20 to Ashford, B2070 to New
Romney, 1.5 miles E of New Romney.
Pay-as-you-Play, links course.
18 holes, 5126 yards, S.S.S.65
Designed by J.D. Lewis, B.M. Evans.
Founded 1993
Visitors: welcome, no restrictions;
all times bookable in advance.
Green Fee: £10 WD, £13 WE.
Societies: welcome weekdays by
arrangement with Sec.
Catering: bar and restaurant
facilities.
Practice ground.
Hotels: Stade Court (Hythe); Romney
Bay House (Littlestone); Broadacre
(New Romney).

D117 Royal Blackheath
☎(081) 850 1795 Club, 850 1763 Pro
Court Rd, Eltham, London SE9 5AF
8 miles from central London; take A2
and turn off for Eltham, club entrance
400 yards left on Court Rd after
leaving Eltham High St; from M25
exit 3 (A20) towards London, right at
2nd lights, club 600 yards on right; 5
mins walk from Mottingham Station.
Parkland course with Georgian
clubhouse.
18 holes, 6219 yards, S.S.S.70
Designed by James Braid.
Founded 1608
Visitors: welcome weekdays only
with h/cap cert.
Green Fee: £40/day.
Societies: Tues-Fri, April-Oct.
Catering: dining room, bar.
Museum of Golf.
Hotels: Bromley Court; Yardley Court
(Eltham).

D118 Royal Cinque Ports
☎(0304) 374007
Golf Rd, Deal, Kent CT14 6RF
Follow coast road through Deal to
end, turn left onto Godwyn Rd, at end
turn right onto Golf Rd to club.
Seaside links course.
Medal, 18 holes, 6406 yards,
S.S.S.71
Designed by Tom Dunn, Guy
Campbell.
Founded 1892
Visitors: welcome weekdays,
reservations required; must be
members of recognised golf club and
have h/cap below 20 (Men), 28
(Ladies); 2 ball play only.
Green Fee: £45/day/round before
1pm, £35 after 1pm.
Societies: by arrangement
weekdays.
Catering: full facilities; jacket and tie
required.
Hotels: Royal; Kings Head (Deal);
Bell (Sandwich).

D119 Royal Mid-Surrey
☎(081) 940 1894 Clubhouse/Office,
940 0459 Pro, 332 2957 Fax
Old Deer Park, Richmond, Surrey
TW9 2SB
On A316, 300 yards before
Richmond roundabout heading into
London.
Parkland courses.
Inner, 18 holes, 5544 yards,
S.S.S.68; Outer, 18 holes, 6385
yards, S.S.S.70
Designed by J.H. Taylor.
Founded 1892
Visitors: weekdays with letter of
intro from own club, membership or
h/cap cert, or playing with member;
weekends and Bank Holidays
members' guests only.
Green Fee: £45/round WD.
Societies: recognised societies
welcome if previously arranged with
Sec.
Catering: lunch served except Mon,
snack lunch served every day.
Hotels: Richmond Hill; Richmond
Gate.

D120 Royal St George's
☎(0304) 613090 Sec, 615236 Pro,
611245 Fax
Sandwich, Kent CT13 9PB
1 mile from Sandwich to Sandwich
Bay.
Links course.
18 holes, 6903 yards, S.S.S.74
Designed by Dr Laidlaw Purves.
Founded 23 May 1887

Visitors: Mon-Fri only.
Green Fee: £50/round, £70/day.
Societies: details available on
request.
Catering: bar, restaurant and snack
bar; dinners by arrangement for large
groups.
Hotels: Bell (Sandwich); St Crispin
Inn (Worth).

D121 Royal Wimbledon
☎(081) 946 2125
29 Camp Rd, Wimbledon, SW19 4UW
0.75 mile W of War Memorial in
Wimbledon village.
Parkland course.
18 holes, 6300 yards, S.S.S.70
Founded 1865
Visitors: none.
Societies: Wed, Thurs only.

D122 Rusper
☎(0293) 871456, 871871 Pro
shop/bookings, 871987 Fax
Rusper Rd, Newdigate, Surrey RH5
5BX
M25 exit 9 towards Dorking and A24;
on A24 at Beare Green roundabout
take signpost to Newdigate; in village
take signpost Rusper, course 2 miles
on right; from Crawley, on Horsham
road at Faygate turn right for Rusper,
course 1.5 miles on left.
Pakland course.
9 holes, 6069 yards, S.S.S.69
Designed by S. Hood.
Founded Aug 1992
Visitors: welcome at all times,
bookable 1 day in advance; no jeans
allowed.
Green Fee: £7.50 (9 holes), £11.50
(18 holes) WD; £9.50 (9 holes),
£15.50 (18 holes) WE.
Societies: welcome weekdays,
packages available on request.
Catering: bar and bar snacks every
day; society meals bookable in
advance.
Driving range, pool table.
Hotels: Russ Hill (reservations
through golf club).

D123 Ruxley
☎(0689) 871490
Sandy Lane, St Paul's Cray,
Orpington, Kent BR5 3HY
A20 to Ruxley roundabout, into
Sandy Lane.
Undulating parkland course.
18 holes, 4964 yards, S.S.S.65
Founded 1973
Visitors: welcome weekdays from
7am, weekends after 11.30am.

Green Fee: apply for details.
Societies: welcome.
Catering: breakfast and lunch daily; evening meals by arrangement.
Driving range.
Hotels: Crest (Bexley).

D124 St Augustine's
☎(0843) 590333 Sec, 590222 Pro
Cottington Rd, Cliffsend, Ramsgate, Kent CT12 5JN
Entrance at railway bridge on B2048 off Ramsgate-Sandwich road.
Parkland course.
18 holes, 5138 yards, S.S.S.65
Designed by Tom Vardon.
Founded 1907
Visitors: welcome with h/cap cert weekdays and after 10.30am weekends.
Green Fee: on application.
Societies: weekdays except Mon; prior booking essential.
Catering: available.

D125 St George's Hill
☎(0932) 842406
St George's Hill, Weybridge, Surrey KT13 0NL
B374 from station towards Cobham, 0.5 mile on left.
Heathland course.
3 x 9 hole courses, 3 combinations of 18; 6569 yards, S.S.S.71; 6097 yards, S.S.S.69; 6210 yards, S.S.S.70
Designed by H.S. Colt.
Founded 1913
Visitors: welcome Wed-Fri only (Mon members and guests only, Tues Ladies Day), must book tee time in advance.
Green Fee: £30/round, £40/day,
Societies: catered for Wed-Fri.
Catering: full restaurant lunch and bar snacks served.

D126 Sandown Golf Centre
☎(0372) 463340, 465921
More Lane, Esher, Surrey KT10 8AN
About 1 mile from Esher station, in centre of Sandown Park racecourse, off Portsmouth road; follow brown signs to Sandown Park Leisure Centre.
Public parkland course.
9 holes, 5656 yards, S.S.S.67; 9 holes Par 3
Designed by John Jacobs.
Founded 1967
Visitors: welcome at any time; booking at weekends.

Green Fee: main course, £5 WD, £6.50 WE; Par 3, £3.40 WD, £4.25 WE.
Societies: by arrangement.
Catering: available.
Driving range, 9-hole Pitch & Putt.
Hotels: Hilton National (Cobham).

D127 Selsdon Park Hotel and Golf Course
☎(081) 657 8811, 651 6171 Fax
Sanderstead, South Croydon, Surrey CR2 8YA
B274 from Croydon, A2022 at Selsdon.
Parkland course.
18 holes, 6407 yards, S.S.S.71
Designed by J.H. Taylor.
Founded 1929
Visitors: welcome, contact golf administration.
Green Fee: £20/round, £30/day WD, £30/round WE.
Societies: welcome by prior arrangement.
Catering: full service available.
Driving range, putting green.
Hotels: Selsdon Park, residential golfing breaks.

D128 Sene Valley
☎(0303) 268513
Sene, Folkestone, Kent CT18 8BL
Off B2065, 1 mile from Hythe.
Undulating downland course with magnificent sea views.
18 holes, 6320 yards, S.S.S.70
Designed by Henry Cotton.
Founded 1888
Visitors: by arrangement with Manager, h/cap cert required.
Green Fee: on application.
Societies: Wed, Thurs, Fri.
Catering: available daily except Mon.
Snooker
Hotels: Imperial (Hythe); Burlington.

D129 Sheerness
☎(0795) 662585
Power Station Rd, Sheerness, Kent ME12 3AE
9 miles from Sittingbourne on A249.
Seaside course.
18 holes, 6460 yards, S.S.S.71
Founded 1906
Visitors: welcome weekdays, weekends with member.
Green Fee: £15 WD.
Societies: welcome Tues-Thurs.
Catering: except Mon.
Hotels: Royal (Sheerness); Abbey (Minster).

D130 Shillinglee Park
☎(0428) 653237, 644391 Fax
Chiddingfold, Godalming, Surrey GU8 4TA
Leave A3 at Milford, S on A283 to Chiddingfold; at top end of Green turn left along local road, after 2 miles turn right signposted Shillinglee; entrance on left after 0.5 mile.
Public, undulating parkland course.
9 holes, 2516 yards, S.S.S.64
Designed by Roger Mace.
Founded 1980
Visitors: welcome, advisable to book; telephone bookings accepted.
Green Fee: £7.50 (9 holes), £10 (18 holes), £12.50/day WD; £8.50 (9 holes), £13 (18 holes), £16/day WE; gradually reducing twilight fees; reductions for jnrs, OAPs etc.
Societies: and company days welcome.
Catering: bar and restaurant facilities available daily from 8.30am-6pm (3pm Sun); evening meals and parties by arrangement.
Pitch & Putt, £3 unlimited play.
Hotels: Lythe Hill; Crown Inn.

D131 Shirley Park
☎(081) 654 1143
194 Addiscombe Rd, Croydon, Surrey CR0 7LB
On A232 approx 1 mile E of East Croydon station, near Shirley.
Parkland course.
18 holes, 6210 yards, S.S.S.70
Founded 1914
Visitors: welcome 8.30-12am, 1.30-4pm weekdays; with member only weekends.
Green Fee: £28/day/round.
Societies: half-day pm, Mon, Thurs, Fri; full day Tues.
Catering: breakfast, snack lunch, afternoon tea daily; banqueting and functions (sponsored by member).
Hotels: Croydon Court; Holiday Inn; Brierley.

D132 Shooters Hill
☎(081) 854 6368
Lowood, Eaglesfield Rd, SE18 3DA Off A207.
Very hilly parkland/woodland course.
18 holes, 5736 yards, S.S.S.68
Founded 1903
Visitors: weekdays only with recognised golf club h/cap.
Green Fee: £24/round, £30/day.
Societies: Tues and Thurs only; £24 per round, £30 per day.
Catering: daily.
Hotels: Clarendon (Blackheath).

D133 **Shortlands**
☎(081) 460 2471
Meadow Rd, Shortlands, Kent BR2
0PB
9 holes, 5261, S.S.S.66
Founded 1894
Visitors: only with member.
Green Fee: apply for details.
Societies: bar and catering for
members and guests.

D134 **Sidcup**
☎(081) 300 2150 Sec, 309 0679 Pro
7 Hurst Rd, Sidcup, Kent DA15 9AE
A222 off A2, 400 yards N of Sidcup
railway station.
Parkland course.
9 holes, 5722 yards, S.S.S.68
Designed by James Braid and H.
Myrtle.
Founded 1891
Visitors: welcome, with member
only weekends; h/cap certs required;
smart casual dress except after 7pm.
Green Fee: £18/round/day.
Societies: welcome.
Catering: bar and restaurant
facilities except Mon. Snooker.
Hotels: Bickley Arms.

D135 **Silvermere**
☎(0932) 867275
Redhill Rd, Cobham, Surrey KT11
1EF
At junction 10 of M25 and A3 take
A245 to Byfleet; Silvermere is 0.5
mile on left.
Woodland/parkland/meadowland
course.
18 holes, 6333 yards, S.S.S.71
Founded 1976
Visitors: welcome, book 7 days in
advance; members only am Sat and
Sun.
Green Fee: £16.50 WD, £21 WE.
Societies: weekdays only, £47 full
day including dinner.
Catering: full facilities from 8am.
Hotels: Hilton National.

D136 **Sittingbourne & Milton Regis**
☎(0795) 842261
Wormdale, Newington,
Sittingbourne, Kent ME9 7PX
1 mile N of exit 5 off M2 on A249.
Undulating course.
18 holes, 6121 yards, S.S.S.69
Designed by Harry Hunter.
Founded 1929
Visitors: welcome weekdays with
letter of intro or h/cap cert.
Green Fee: apply for details.

Societies: catered for Tues and
Thurs.
Catering: Tues to Sat.
Hotels: Coniston (Sittingbourne).

D137 **Springfield Park**
☎(081) 871 2468, 871 2221 Fax
Burntwood Lane, Wandsworth,
London SW18 0AT
Off Garrett Lane between Tooting
and Wandsworth, in former grounds
of Springfield Hospital.
Inland links course in rural setting in
heart of London.
9 holes, 18 tees, S.S.S.62
Designed by Patrick Tallack
Founded 1993
Visitors: welcome except Sat and
Sun am when members only.
Green Fee: £6/9 holes WD, £7 WE &
BH; reduced rates for jnrs and OAPs.
Societies: as for visitors.
Catering: fully licensed bar and
catering facilities.
Bowls club, snooker room, large
function room.

D138 **Sunbury**
☎(0932) 772898, 770298
Clubhouse
Charlton Lane, Shepperton,
Middlesex TW17 8QA
2 miles from M3 junction 1.
Public parkland course.
18 holes, Par 69; 9 holes, Par 33
Visitors: welcome any time, no
restrictions.
Green Fee: £13 WD, £15 WE
Societies: welcome.
Catering: available in 16th century
clubhouse.
Driving range.
Hotels: Moat House.

D139 **Sundridge Park**
☎(081) 460 0278
Garden Rd, Bromley, Kent BR1 3NE
5 mins walk from Sundridge Park
station.
Parkland courses.
East, 18 holes, 6467 yards, S.S.S.71;
West, 18 holes, 6007 yards, S.S.S.69
Designed by James Braid and Jack
Randall.
Founded 1902
Visitors: welcome weekdays only;
official club h/cap required.
Green Fee: £36/day.
Societies: on application.
Catering: full catering facilities every
day.
Hotels: Bromley Court; Bromley
Continental.

D140 **Sunningdale**
☎(0344) 21681
Ridgemount Rd, Sunningdale, Ascot,
SL5 9RW
Ridgemount Rd is 50 yards W of
Sunningdale railway station crossing
on the A30.
Heathland courses.
Old, 18 holes, 6341 yards, S.S.S.70;
New, 18 holes, 6676 yards, S.S.S.72
Designed by Willie Park.
Founded 1901
Visitors: weekdays by prior
arrangement, max h/cap 18.
Green Fee: £80/day.
Societies: Tues, Wed, Thurs by
arrangement.
Catering: full catering facilities
except Mon.
Hotels: Berystede; Runnymede.

D141 **Sunningdale Ladies**
☎(0344) 20507
Cross Rd, Sunningdale, Surrey SL5
9RX
2nd turning left on A30 going W from
Sunningdale level crossing.
Heathland course
18 holes, 3622 yards, S.S.S.60
Designed by Edward Villiers.
Founded 1902
Visitors: welcome, phone first.
Green Fee: on application
Societies: catered for, Ladies only.
Catering: lunch and tea except Sun.

D142 **Surbiton**
☎(081) 398 3101 Club, 339 0992
Fax
Woodstock Lane, Chessington,
Surrey KT9 1UG
From A3 westbound, take
Esher/Chessington fly off, turn left to
Claygate, club 400 yards on right.
Parkland course.
18 holes, 6211 yards, S.S.S.70
Founded 1896
Visitors: welcome weekdays only;
h/cap certs required; members'
guests only at weekends.
Green Fee: £27/round, £40.50/day.
Societies: Mon and Fri only.
Catering: full facilities.
Hotels: Haven (Esher).

D143 **Tandridge**
☎(0883) 712274
Oxted, Surrey RH8 9NQ
Off A25 by Oxted, 2 miles E of
Godstone; junction 6 from M25.
Parkland course.
18 holes, 6260 yards, S.S.S.70
Designed by H.S. Colt.

Founded 1923
Visitors: welcome on Mon, Wed and Thurs only, unless with member; prior arrangement essential.
Green Fee: on application.
Societies: catered for on Mon, Wed and Thurs.
Catering: lunch daily except Tues, Gallery bar food all day
Hotels: Kings Arms (Westerham).

D144 Tenterden

☎(0580) 763987 Club, 762409 Pro
Woodchurch Rd, Tenterden, Kent TN30 7DR
1 mile E of Tenterden on B2067.
Undulating parkland course.
18 holes, 6030 yards, S.S.S.69
Founded 1905
Visitors: welcome except Sat, Sun and Bank Holidays.
Green Fee: £20.
Societies: by arrangement.
Catering: light meals served, other catering by arrangement.
Hotels: Vine Inn; William Caxton; Collina House.

D145 Thames Ditton & Esher

☎(081) 398 1551
Scilly Isles, Portsmouth Rd, Esher, Surrey
Off A3 by Scilly Isles roundabout 0.25 mile from Sandown Park race course.
Parkland course.
9 holes, 5606 yards, S.S.S.65
Founded 1892
Visitors: welcome, Sun after 2pm.
Green Fee: apply for details.
Societies: max 32 booked with Sec.
Catering: snacks, buffet for societies.

D146 Tudor Park Country Club

☎(0622) 734334
Ashford Rd, Bearstead, Maidstone, Kent ME14 4NR
Follow A20, Ashford road, on right, 3 miles from Maidstone centre.
Parkland course.
18 holes, 6041 yards, S.S.S.69.
Designed by Donald Steel.
Founded 1988
Visitors: welcome with h/cap cert.
Green Fee: apply for details.
Societies: weekdays by prior arrangement.
Catering: full facilities.
Leisure club and conference facilities.
Hotels: Tudor Park Hotel.

D147 Tunbridge Wells

☎(0892) 523034, 541386 Pro
Langton Rd, Tunbridge Wells, Kent
Behind Marchants Garage next to Spa Hotel.
Undulating parkland course.
9 holes, 4560 yards, S.S.S.62
Founded 1889
Visitors: welcome weekdays only; h/cap cert required.
Green Fee: on application to Pro.
Societies: by arrangement with Sec.
Catering: 11am-3pm daily; evenings by arrangement.
Hotels: Spa; Periquito; Royal Wells.

D148 Tyrrells Wood

☎(0372) 376025, 375200 Pro shop
Tyrrells Wood, Leatherhead, Surrey KT22 8QP
Exit 9 from M25, follow A24 to Dorking, past permanent AA caravan site, next turn left to Tyrrells Wood, signposted.
Undulating parkland course.
18 holes, 6268 yards, S.S.S.70
Designed by James Braid.
Founded 1922
Visitors: welcome weekdays and Sun pm by prior appointment; h/cap certs.
Green Fee: on application.
Societies: welcome, enquiries to manager.
Catering: available all day.
Hotels: Burford Bridge, White Horse.

D149 Upchurch River Valley

☎(0634) 360626 General/Socs, 379592 Pro/Bookings, 387784 Fax
Oak Lane, Upchurch, Sittingbourne, Kent ME9 7AY
From M2 junction 4 take A278 Gillingham road, right at 3rd roundabout onto A2 to Rainham, course 2.5 miles on left.
Public moorland/seaside course.
18 holes, 6160 yards, S.S.S.69; 9 holes Par 3, 1596 yards.
Designed by David Smart.
Founded June 1991.
Visitors: no restrictions, bookings available daily.
Green Fee: 18 holes, £9.95 WD, £12.95 WE; 9 holes, £5.95 WD, £6.95 WE; reductions for jnrs, OAPs.
Societies: Mon-Fri, min. 12, no max.
Catering: Rivers restaurant, full à la carte, Sun lunches; 19th Hole bars, Driving range, golfers only swimming pool.
Hotels: Newington Manor, Rank Motor Lodge.

D150 Walmer & Kingsdown

☎(0304) 373256
The Leas, Kingsdown, Deal, Kent CT14 8ER
Off A258, 2.5 miles S of Deal; signposted at Ringwould village.
Undulating meadowland course.
18 holes, 6451 yards, S.S.S.71
Designed by James Braid.
Founded 1909
Visitors: welcome weekdays and after 12am weekends and Bank Holidays; must produce h/cap cert.
Green Fee: £22/round, £28/day WD; £24/round, £30/day WE & BH.
Societies: by arrangement weekdays only.
Catering: full facilities.
Hotels: Royal; Clarendon; Guildford House; Dover Moat House.

D151 Walton Heath

☎(0737) 812380 Sec, 812060 Club, 812152 Pro, 812974 Caddies
off Deans Lane, Walton-on-the-Hill, Tadworth, Surrey KT20 7TP
2 miles north of M25 junction 3; off A217 towards Sutton at 3rd roundabout turn left onto B2032 to Dorking; Clubhouse 0.75 mile, signposted off Deans Lane.
Heathland course.
Old, 18 holes, 6801 yards, S.S.S.73; New, 18 holes, 6609 yards, S.S.S.72
Designed by Herbert Fowler/James Braid.
Founded 1904
Visitors: Mon-Fri, not WE or BH; h/cap certificate required, advance bookings must be made by phone or letter.
Green Fee: £57 before 11.30am, £47 after 11.30am.
Societies: Mon-Fri only, standard package, terms on request from Sec.
Catering: 2 lounge bars, dining room (140), private dining room (36). Large practice area, small target practice ground.
Hotels: Heathside; Bridge House; Chalk Lane.

D152 Weald of Kent

☎(0622) 890866 Club, 863163 Pro
Maidstone Rd, Headcorn, Kent TN27 9PT
On A274 5 miles S of Maidstone.
Parkland course.
18 holes, 6169 yards, S.S.S.69
Designed by John Millen.
Founded 1991
Visitors: welcome, bookings taken 3 days in advance.

Green Fee: £14 WD, £18.50 WE.
Societies: welcome except Sat/Sun.
Catering: full facilities all day;
conferences, banqueting.
Shooting, fishing, riding.
Hotels: Shant (East Sutton).

D153 Wentworth
☎(0344) 842201, 842804 Fax
Wentworth Drive, Virginia Water,
Surrey GU25 4LS
21 miles SW of London at A30/A329
junction; M25 exit 13, 8 miles.
Heathland courses.
West, 18 holes, 6945 yards,
S.S.S.74; East, 18 holes, 6176 yards,
S.S.S.70; Edinburgh, 18 holes, 6979
yards, S.S.S.73; 9 holes, 1902 yards,
Par 27
Designed by H.S. Colt (East and
West); J.R.M. Jacobs (Edinburgh).
Founded 1924
Visitors: weekdays only with prior
booking; h/cap certs required.
Green Fee: West £80/round, East
£55/round, Edinburgh £65/round.
Societies: Mon-Fri, limited to 50
max per course.
Catering: breakfast, lunch, dinner
and banqueting.
Tennis, outdoor heated swimming
pool.
Hotels: Pennyhill Park; Royal
Berkshire; Runnymede.

D154 West Byfleet
☎(0932) 343433 Sec, 345230 Club,
346584 Pro
Sheerwater Rd, West Byfleet, Surrey
KT14 6AA
M25 exit 10 onto A245 to about 0.75
mile W of West Byfleet.
Heathland/parkland course.
18 holes, 6211 yards, S.S.S.70
Designed by Cuthbert Butchart.
Founded 1904
Visitors: welcome weekdays only.
Green Fee: on application.
Societies: by arrangement on Tues
and Wed only.
Catering: snacks, lunch and tea
served; evening meals by
arrangement; lunch only on Sun.
Hotels: Northfleet (Woking); Hilton
International (Cobham).

D155 West Hill
☎(0483) 474365, 474252 Fax
Bagshot Rd, Brookwood, Surrey
GU24 0BH
On A322 Guildford-Bagshot road,
club entrance just by railway bridge
at Brookwood.

Heathland course.
18 holes, 6368 yards, S.S.S.70
Designed by Willie Park and Jack
White.
Founded 1909
Visitors: Mon-Fri only.
Green Fee: £32/round, £42/day.
Societies: Mon-Fri by application to
Sec.
Catering: full catering facilities
available.
Hotels: Worplesdon Place
(Worplesdon); Northfleet (Woking).

D156 West Kent
☎(0689) 851323
West Hill, Downe, Orpington, Kent
BR6 7JJ
A21 to Orpington, head for Downe
village; leave on Luxted Lane for 300
yards then right into West Hill.
Parkland/downland course.
18 holes, 6399 yards, S.S.S.70
Founded 1916
Visitors: welcome weekdays with
letter from Sec or h/cap cert; must
phone in advance.
Green Fee: £24/round, £36/day.
Societies: by arrangement Tues,
Wed, Thurs.
Catering: full facilities.
Hotels: Bromley Continental.

D157 West Malling
☎(0732) 844785 Sec, 844795
Enquiries, 844022 Pro
London Rd, Addington, Maidstone,
Kent
Off A20 from London, 8 miles NW of
Maidstone.
Parkland course.
Spitfire Course, 18 holes, 6142
yards, Par 70; Hurricane Course, 18
holes, 6011 yards, Par 70
Founded 1974
Visitors: welcome weekdays; after
12am weekends.
Green Fee: £20/round, £28/day;
£30/round WE after 12am.
Societies: welcome by prior
arrangement.
Catering: full facilities.
Hotels: Larkfield; Trusthouse Forte.

D158 West Surrey
☎(0483) 421275
Enton Green, Godalming, Surrey GU8
5AF
0.5 mile from Milford station.
Parkland course.
18 holes, 6247 yards, S.S.S.70
Designed by Herbert Fowler.
Founded 1909

Visitors: welcome preferably by
arrangement to avoid reservations or
restrictions (including weekends);
collar and tie in dining room.
Green Fee: £35/day WD, £42 (1 or 2
rounds) WE.
Societies: normally Wed (pm), Thurs
and Fri by arrangement.
Catering: full restaurant facilities
available by arrangement.
Hotels: Inn on the Lake; Pride of the
Valley.

D159 Westgate & Birchington
☎(0843) 831115
176 Canterbury Rd,
Westgate-on-Sea, Kent CT8 8LT
A27, 0.25 mile from Westgate station.
Seaside links course.
18 holes, 4926 yards, S.S.S.64
Founded 1892
Visitors: welcome if members of
recognised clubs.
Green Fee: £15 WD, £18 WE & BH.
Societies: by arrangement.
Catering: by arrangement.
Hotels: Edgewater; Ivyside; White
Lodge.

D160 Whitstable & Seasalter
☎(0227) 272020
Collingwood Rd, Whitstable, Kent
CT5 1EB
From A299 Thanet Way turn off at
Long Reach roundabout, drive down
Borstal Hill, under railway bridge,
take 2nd left into Nelson Rd and 2nd
left again along unmade road.
Seaside links course.
18 holes, 5276 yards, S.S.S.63
Founded 1910
Visitors: welcome weekdays;
weekends only with member.
Green Fee: apply for details.
Catering: bar snacks.
Hotels: Marine.

D161 Wildernesse
☎(0732) 761199
Seal, Sevenoaks, Kent TN15 0JE
Off A25 in Seal village.
Rolling parkland course.
18 holes, 6438 yards, S.S.S.72
Designed by W. Park.
Founded 1890
Visitors: letter of intro. required.
Green Fee: £26/round, £37/day.
Societies: Mon and Thurs.
Catering: bar and restaurant.
Hotels: Post House; Royal Oak;
Sevenoaks Park.

D162 Wildwood

☎(0403) 753255, 752005 Fax
Horsham Rd, Alfold, Surrey GU6 8JE
On A281, 10 miles S of Guildford, 10
miles NW of Horsham, on
Surrey/Sussex border.
Wooded parkland course.
18 holes, 6655 yards, S.S.S.72; 9
hole extension under development.
Designed by Martin Hawtree.
Founded 1992
Visitors: Mon-Fri, weekends
aftrnoons only.
Green Fee: £25/round, £35/day.
Societies: welcome weekdays only;
ring for details.
Catering: breakfast, lunch and
dinner available in restaurant.
Teaching Academy; driving range.
Hotels: Random Hall, golfing
packages available.

D163 Wimbledon Common

☎(081) 946 7571 Sec, 946 0294 Pro
Camp Rd, Wimbledon Common,
London SW19 4UW
1 mile NW of War Memorial, past Fox
& Grapes on right in Camp Rd.
Moorland course.
18 holes, 5438 yards, S.S.S.66
Designed by Tom and Willie Dunn.
Founded 1908
Visitors: welcome weekdays.
Green Fee: £13.50/round, £20/day.
Societies: Tues-Fri by arrangement.
Catering: light meals available.

D164 Wimbledon Park

☎(081) 946 1002
Home Park Rd, Wimbledon, London
SW19 7HR
250 yards from Wimbledon station
(District Line).
Parkland course.
18 holes, 5492 yards, S.S.S.66
Founded 1898
Visitors: with h/cap cert or letter of
intro from club; only after 3pm
weekends.
Green Fee: £25/day WD, £25/round
WE.
Societies: welcome, usually Tues
and Thurs.
Catering: full facilities available
except Mon.
Hotels: Canizaro Park.

D165 Windlemere

☎(0276) 858727
Windlesham Rd, West End, Woking,
Surrey GU24 9QL
Take A322 from Bagshot towards

Guildford; turn left on A319 towards
Chobham; course is on left opposite
the Gordon Boys' School.
Gently undulating public parkland
course.
9 holes, 2673 yards, S.S.S.34
Designed by Clive D. Smith.
Founded 1978
Visitors: open to public on payment
of green fees.
Green Fee: apply for details.
Societies: as arranged with Pro at
club.
Catering: bar snacks always
available.
Driving range, pool tables.

D166 Windlesham

☎(0276) 452220, 452290 Fax
Grove End, Bagshot, Surrey GU19
5HY
At junction of A30 and A322.
Parkland course.
18 holes, S.S.S.72
Designed by Tommy Horton.
Founded Opening July 1994
Visitors: contact club for details,
h/cap certs required.
Green Fee: contact club.
Societies: contact club.
Catering: full bar and restaurant
facilities.
Practice range.

D167 The Wisley

☎(0483) 211022
Mill Lane, Ripley, Nr Woking, Surrey
GU23 6QU
From M25 juncion 10 take A3 to
Guildford, off at exit marked Ockham,
Send and Ripley, 3rd exit from
roundabout, 1st left into Mill Lane;
signs to club.
Parkland course (members only).
3 x 9 holes; Church, 3355 yards;
Garden 3385 yards; Mill, 3473 yards;
any combination gives 18 hole
course, S.S.S.73
Designed by Robert Trent Jones Jr.
Founded Jan 1990
Visitors: with member only.
Green Fee: apply for details.
Catering: bar, restaurant.

D168 Woking

☎(0483) 760053 Sec/Bookings,
769582 Pro
Pond Rd, Hook Heath, Woking,
Surrey GU22 0JZ
Just S of 1st road bridge over
railway, W of Woking station
(Woking-Brookwood line), take
Hollybank Rd; then immediately right

into Golf Club Rd and right at end to
clubhouse; avoid Woking town
centre.
Heathland course.
18 holes, 6322 yards, S.S.S.70
Designed by Tom Dunn.
Founded 1893
Visitors: book in advance; not
weekends and public holidays.
Green Fee: £30/round, £45/day WD.
Societies: book in advance.
Catering: lunch available every day
if ordered in advance.
Hotels: Mayford Manor; Glen Court.

D169 Woodcote Park

☎(081) 668 2788 Tel/Fax
Meadow Hill, Bridleway, Coulsdon,
Surrey CR5 2QQ
At far end of Meadow Hill, off
Woodcote Grove Road (A237),
Purley, main road from Coulsdon to
Wallington.
Slightly undulating parkland course.
18 holes, 6669 yards, S.S.S.72
Founded 1912
Visitors: welcome on weekdays with
h/cap cert.
Green Fee: £25/round, £35/day.
Societies: weekdays by
arrangement.
Catering: bars, bar snacks, à la carte
menu daily.
Snooker.

D170 Woodlands Manor

☎(09592) 3806
Tinkerpot Lane, Sevenoaks, Kent
TN15 6AB
Off A225, 4 miles NE of Sevenoaks, 5
miles S of M25 junction 3.
Undulating parkland course in AONB.
18 holes, 6000 yards, S.S.S.68
Designed by N. Coles, J. Lyons.
Founded 1928
Visitors: welcome weekdays;
weekends after 1pm, with h/cap
cert.
Green Fee: on application
Societies: welcome Mon-Fri by
arrangement.
Catering: meals served.
Practice ground, tennis.
Hotels: Thistle (Brands Hatch).

D171 Worplesdon

☎(0483) 472277 Sec
Heath House Rd, Woking, Surrey
GU22 0RA
Leave Guildford on A322 to Bagshot,
after 6 miles turn right into Heath
House Rd.
Heathland course.

18 holes, 6422 yards, S.S.S.71
Designed by J.F. Abercromby.
Founded 1908
Visitors: welcome with introduction
from Club Sec; weekdays only.
Green Fee: £40/round, £50/day.
Societies: Mon, Wed, Thurs, Fri by
arrangement.
Catering: bar every day, lunch
served except Tues.

D172 **Wrotham Heath**
☎(0732) 884800
Seven Mile Lane, Comp, Sevenoaks,
Kent TN15 8QZ
Off A20 near junction with A25.
Woodland/heathland course.
18 holes (from autumn 1994), 6010
yards, S.S.S.69
Designed by Donald Steel (new 9
holes).

Founded 1906
Visitors: welcome weekdays with
h/cap cert; not bank holidays.
Green Fee: £22/round, £32/day, £11
with member.
Societies: catered for by
arrangement Fri only.
Catering: full catering facilities by
arrangement with Steward.
Hotels: Post House.

E

HERTFORDSHIRE, ESSEX, MIDDLESEX, NORTH LONDON

Essex has seen a significant number of new courses in the last few years and even more applications for permission to build. It is a big county but the greatest demand lies around the fringe of London where the supply of land is scarcer. West Essex, Romford, Ilford, Wanstead and Chigwell are all bastions of suburbia while public facilities are exemplified by Hainault Forest, Chingford and Belhus Park (Thurrock), but the increasing sense of freedom that the country brings is reflected in the character of the golf.

Clacton-on-Sea, Frinton and Quietwaters remind travellers how far Essex's limits extend from the sound of Bow Bells, but the best of the county's golf focuses on Chelmsford, Thorndon Park and Orsett. Thorpe Hall at Southend has the proud boast of having for years been the home Club of Michael Bonallack; and a word for Skips, newly extended and renamed Stapleford Abbots, and Channels, both less than 20 years old.

Neighbouring Hertfordshire is more densely populated with golf courses, even if the majority of them are in the south. Most are parkland in character although two of the exceptions are undoubtedly among the best. Ashridge and Berkhamsted enjoy a lofty perch on the Hertfordshire ridge of the Chilterns, Ashridge where Henry Cotton was once the professional and Berkhamsted, a course on a delightful common famous for the absence of sand bunkers.

In keeping with many Clubs which started life in an exposed, open environment, Berkhampsted is now much more enclosed, making accuracy from the tee a definite prerequisite of good scoring. It is rightly popular. The northern boundary of Hertfordshire is marked by Royston on undulating heathland on which little has changed in a hundred years. The Club's annual fixture with Cambridge is the University's oldest in continuous existence.

Letchworth and Knebworth are divided by the Great North Road which also took land from Welwyn Garden City, the course on which Nick Faldo's talents were shaped. It highlights what can be achieved on a limited acreage. Nearer to London, Sandy Lodge, Hadley Wood, Porters Park, Brookmans Park and Moor Park (with its 36-holes) are among the best known.

There are South Herts, Mid-Herts, East Herts and West Herts with a worthy mention for Verulam and Batchwood Hall on opposite sides of St Albans. Elstree offers a variety of facilities, particularly for beginners and, at the other end of the scale, is the new Hanbury Manor. Brickendon Grange, even if now 25 years old, is more modern than most, and there are two courses full of character at Harpenden.

The Middlesex courses, as you might expect, are altogether more confined although wonderful oases for the city dweller. From planes approaching Heathrow, it is all too clear how great are their land values. So too further north, where Enfield, Crews Hill and Bush Hill Park, once out in the countryside, are close to the Hertfordshire border.

Middlesex, county champions for the first time in 1989, won the title again in 1991 and have been indebted for some time to several fine golfers from Ealing. Ricky Willison, who won the 1981 English championship, later turned professional. Ealing fronts the A40 Western Avenue, a stone's throw from Sudbury and West Middlesex. Highgate, Hampstead and Hendon form as tight a cluster but Ashford Manor and Fulwell, almost into Surrey, are perhaps Middlesex's finest, along with Northwood.

E1 **Abbey View**
☎(0727) 41973
Holywell Hill, Westminster Lodge, St
Albans, Herts
In centre of St Albans.
Public parkland course.
9 holes, 2162 yards
Designed by Jimmy Thomson.
Founded 1990
Visitors: open to public at all times.
Green Fee: apply for details.

E2 **Abridge Golf & Country Club**
☎(0708) 688396
Epping Lane, Stapleford Tawney,
Essex RM4 1ST
M11 from London exit 5 via Abridge;
from the N, M11 exit 7 via Epping.
Parkland course.
18 holes, 6070 yards, S.S.S.72
Designed by Henry Cotton.
Founded 1964
Visitors: weekdays only; h/cap cert
required.
Green Fee: apply for details.
Societies: Mon and Wed.
Catering: every day except Fri (no
evening meals).
Hotels: Post House, Epping.

E3 **Airlinks**
☎(081) 561 1418
Southall Lane, Hounslow, Middx TW5
9PE
Off M4 at junction 3 onto A312 and
A4020; next to David Lloyd Tennis
Centre.
Public meadowland/parkland
course.
18 holes, 6001 yards, S.S.S.69
Designed by P. Alliss.
Founded 1984
Visitors: welcome, some restrictions
at weekends.
Green Fee: on application.
Societies: welcome Mon-Fri; fees by
negotiation.
Catering: licensed bar, snacks, hot
and cold meals.
Diving range.

E4 **Aldenham Golf & Country Club**
☎(0923) 853929, 857889 Pro,
858472 Fax
Church Lane, Aldenham, Nr Watford,
Herts WD2 8AL
Leave M1 at junction 5, take A41
towards S Watford, turn left at 1st
roundabout towards Radlett, club
0.25 mile.
Parkland course.

18 holes, 6445 yards, S.S.S.71; 9
holes, 2500 yards, S.S.S.29
Founded 1975
Visitors: welcome weekdays, after
1pm weekends.
Green Fee: £20/round WD, £28 WE;
£10 9-hole course.
Societies: Mon-Fri by arrangement.
Catering: snack bar, restaurant.
Hotels: London Hilton; Spiders Web.

E5 **Arkley**
☎(081) 449 0394
Rowley Green Rd, Barnet, Herts EN5
3HL
Off A1 at Stirling Corner to A411;
signposted at Rowley Lane on left.
Parkland course.
9 holes, 6045 yards, S.S.S.69
Designed by James Braid.
Founded 1909
Visitors: weekdays restricted;
weekends with member; (Tues
Ladies Day).
Green Fee: £15/round/day.
Societies: Wed, Thurs, Fri, max 40.
Catering: meals served daily except
Mon.
Hotels: Elstree Moat House.

E6 **Ashford Manor**
☎(0784) 257687
Fordbridge Rd, Ashford, Middx TW15
3RT
Staines by-pass A308, 2 miles E of
Staines.
Parkland course.
18 holes, 6343 yards, S.S.S.70
Founded 1898
Visitors: must be member of
recognised golf club; weekends only
by prior arrangement.
Green Fee: on application
Societies: welcome weekdays by
prior arrangement.
Catering: available.

E7 **Ashridge**
☎(0442) 842244, 843770 Fax
Little Gaddesden, Berkhamsted,
Herts HP4 1LY
A41 to Berkhamsted, turn right at
Northchurch on B4506.
Parkland course.
18 holes, 6508 yards, S.S.S.71
Designed by Sir Guy Campbell,
Colonel Hotchkin and Cecil
Hutchinson.
Founded 1932
Visitors: telephone Sec for booking.
Green Fee: on application.
Societies: telephone Sec for
booking.

Catering: morning coffee, lunch,
afternoon tea, sandwiches always
available; evening dinners for
societies.
Large practice ground.
Hotels: Bell Inn.

E8 **Ballards Gore**
☎(0702) 258917 Sec, 258924 Pro
Gore Rd, Canewdon, Rochford, Essex
SS4 2DA
From London via A127 to Southend
Airport, then through Rochford onto
Great Stambridge road; course 1.5
miles from Rochford centre.
Parkland course.
18 holes, 7062 yards, S.S.S.74
Designed by D. and J.J. Caton.
Founded July 1980
Visitors: welcome weekdays;
weekends guest of member only;
after 12.30pm summer, 11.30am
winter.
Green Fee: £22 WD.
Societies: weekdays by
arrangement with Sec, subject to
availability.
Catering: bar and restaurant
facilities; private functions.
Hotels: Renouf.

E9 **Basildon**
☎(0268) 533297
Clay Hill Lane, Basildon, Essex SS16
5HL
On A176 off A13 or A127, Kingswood
roundabout, Sparrows Herne.
Public undulating parkland course.
18 holes, 6153 yards, S.S.S.69
Designed by Cottons.
Founded 1967
Visitors: welcome at all times,
booking weekends.
Green Fee: £7.50/round WD, £14.50
WE.
Societies: weekdays.
Catering: full facilities.
Hotels: Crest; Campinile.

E10 **Batchwood**
☎(0727) 844250, 850586 Fax
Batchwood Tennis and Golf Centre,
Batchwood Drive, St Albans, Herts
AL3 5XA
NW corner of St. Albans; 5 miles S of
M1 junction 9.
Public parkland course.
18 holes, 6487 yards, S.S.S.71
Designed by J.H. Taylor.
Founded 1935
Visitors: Mon-Fri 8am-twighlight;
Sat/Sun summer 9.40am-twighlight,
winter 10am-twighlight.

Green Fee: £8 and £10.50 (approx).
Societies: catered for by arrangement between Oct and April, Mon-Fri only.
Catering: Public bar and restaurant. 4 indoor, 5 outdoor tennis courts, 2 squash courts, putting green, fitness gym, dance studio.
Hotels: Aubrey Park.

E11 Belfairs Park (Southend-on-Sea)

☎(0702) 525345 Starter, 526911 Club members
Starter's Hut, Eastwood Rd North, Leigh-on-Sea, Essex SS9 4LR

4.5 miles from Southend centre; Eastwood Rd links A127 and A13. Private clubs playing on public course set in Belfairs Park. Parkland front 9, heavily wooded back 9.
18 holes, 5871 yards, S.S.S.68
Designed by H.S. Colt.
Founded 1926
Visitors: unrestricted but bookings Thurs am, weekends and public holidays.
Green Fee: £11.20 WD, £16.80 WE and BH; 9 holes 2 hrs before dark, £5.10 WD, £7.90 WE & BH.
Societies: no facilities.
Catering: Public restaurant.

E12 Belhus Park (Thurrock)

☎(0708) 854260
Belhus Park, South Ockendon, Essex RM15 4QR
A13 to Avely.
Public parkland course.
18 holes, 5439 yards, S.S.S.68
Designed by Frank Pennink.
Founded 1972
Visitors: bookings at course weekdays, by telephone weekends
Green Fee: apply for details.
Societies: telephone manager.
Catering: bar and restaurant.
Driving range, squash, swimming pool, leisure centre.

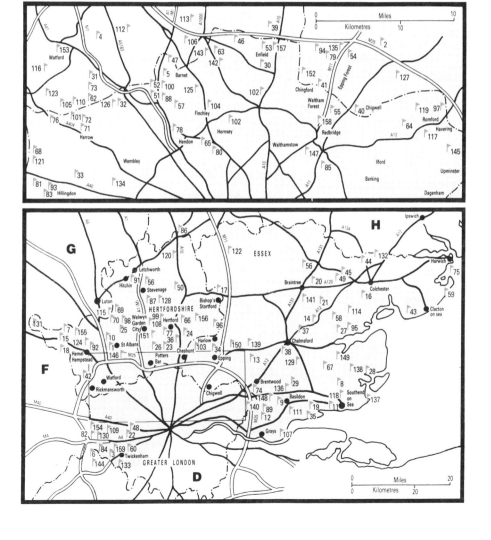

E13 **Bentley**
☎(0277) 373179
Ongar Rd, Brentwood, Essex CM15 9SS
4 miles from Brentwood on A128 to Ongar.
Parkland course.
18 holes, 6709 yards, S.S.S.72
Designed by Alec Swan.
Founded 1972
Visitors: welcome Mon-Fri with letter of intro. or h/cap cert.
Green Fee: £20/round, £26/day.
Societies: welcome weekdays with prior arrangement.
Catering: snacks all day, hot food lunch times, evening meals by arrangement.
Hotels: Post House.

E14 **Benton Hall**
☎(0376) 502454, 521050 Fax
Wickham Hill, Witham, Essex CM8 3LH
2 mins from Witham exit off A12.
Parkland course.
18 hole Championship course, 9 hole Par 3 course
Designed by Alan Walker and Charlie Cox.
Founded Jan 1990
Visitors: pre-booking times.
Green Fee: £16/round WD, £20/round WE.
Societies: midweek information package on request.
Catering: bar snacks, à la carte restaurant overlooking lake; all functions catered for.
Driving range.
Hotels: Rivenhall Resort; White Hart; Marks Tey.

E15 **Berkhamsted**
☎(0442) 865832 Manager, 865851 Pro
The Common, Berkhamsted, Herts HP4 2QB
Take junction 8 off M1 to Hemel Hempstead, at roundabout take Leighton Buzzard road; after about 3 miles take Potten End turn and follow road for approx 3 miles to club.
Heathland course, not suitable for novice golfers.
18 holes, 6605 yards, S.S.S.72
Designed by G.H. Gowring (1890/2 Founder), 1912 C.J. Gilbert with advice from Harry Colt, 1927 extension with advice from James Braid.
Founded 1890
Visitors: welcome, must be member of a golf club with h/cap; not before 12.30pm Tues, not before 11.30am Sat, Sun and Bank Holidays.
Green Fee: £20/round, £35/day WD; £35 WE.
Societies: Wed and Fri.
Catering: full facilities except Mon and Tues (limited catering); new clubhouse 1993.
Hotels: Post House; Pennyfarthing; Most House.

E16 **Birch Grove**
☎(0206) 734276
Layer Rd, Colchester CO2 0HS
2 miles S of Colchester on B1026.
Meadowland course.
9 holes, 4108 yards, S.S.S.60
Founded 1970
Visitors: welcome except Sun am.
Green Fee: £10 WD, £12 WE & BH.
Societies: welcome weekdays, catering for 60.
Catering: meals available during opening hours; parties by prior arrangement.

E17 **Bishop's Stortford**
☎(0279) 654715 Sec, 651324 Pro
Dunmow Rd, Bishop's Stortford, Herts CM23 5HP
Exit 8 from M11, follow signs to town centre/hospital, course is on left next to Nag's Head on E edge of town.
Parkland course.
18 holes, 6440 yards, S.S.S.71
Founded 1912
Visitors: weekdays only; weekends with member.
Green Fee: £21.
Societies: by appointment weekdays only.
Catering: lunch and dinner by appointment; bar meals until 9.30pm.
Hotels: Hilton (Stanstead Airport).

E18 **Boxmoor**
☎(0442) 242434
18 Box Lane, Hemel Hempstead, Herts HP3 0DH
0.75 mile from Hemel Hempstead station on A41.
Undulating parkland course.
9 holes, 4854 yards, S.S.S.64
Founded 1890
Visitors: welcome weekdays, not Sun; suitable attire and golf shoes required.
Green Fee: £10/round WD, £15 WE.
Societies: welcome with 4 weeks notice.
Catering: limited service.
Pool table.

E19 **Boyce Hill**
☎(0268) 793625
Vicarage Hill, South Benfleet, Essex SS7 1PD
7 miles W of Southend-on-Sea; A127 to Rayleigh Weir (3 miles from course); A13 to Victoria House Corner (1 mile from course).
Undulating parkland course.
18 holes, 5882 yards, S.S.S.68
Designed by James Braid.
Founded 1922
Visitors: welcome weekdays; weekends with member.
Green Fee: £20/round, £30/day.
Societies: Thurs only.
Catering: service throughout day.
Hotels: Crest; Airport.

E20 **Braintree**
☎(0376) 324117 Members, 346079 Sec, 343465 Pro
Kings Lane, Stisted, Braintree, Essex CM7 8DA
A120 eastbound after Braintree bypass, 1st left, 1 mile to course, signposted.
Parkland course.
18 holes, 6161 yards, S.S.S.69
Designed by Hawtree and Son.
Founded 1891 (1971 at present location).
Visitors: welcome except Sat & Sun; h/cap cert required Fri.
Green Fee: £25/day WD (£15/day with member).
Societies: welcome by arrangement Mon, Wed, Thurs (Tues Ladies Day).
Catering: meals served.
Hotels: White Hart.

E21 **Braxted Park**
☎(0621) 892305
Braxted Park, Witham, Essex CM8 3EN
M25-A12 between Chelmsford and Colchester; left at sign to Silver End and Great Braxted, right at T-junction, 0.5 mile to brick wall, follow round to main gates marked Golf Course.
Parkland course in 18th century listed park with lake, pay-and-play course Mon-Fri.
9 holes, 1980 yards, Par 30
Founded 1958
Visitors: welcome all daylight hours.
Green Fee: £8 (9 holes), £11 (18 holes).
Societies: £450 exclusive use of course, otherwise as for visitors.
Catering: soup sandwiches, teas, coffee etc from Oct 1994.
Hotels: Rivenhall Resort.

E22 Brent Valley

☎(081) 567 4230
Church Rd, Hanwell, London W7 3BE
A4020 Uxbridge Rd, Hanwell, on to
Church Rd by Brent Lodge Animal
Centre.
Public meadowland course.
18 holes, 5440 yards, S.S.S.66
Designed by P. Alliss and D. Thomas.
Founded 1938
Visitors: welcome 7 days.
Green Fee: apply for details.
Societies: organised via the Pro.
Catering: restaurant from 8am.

E23 Brickendon Grange

☎(0992) 511258 Sec/Manager,
511228 Bar, 511218 Pro, 511411 Fax
Brickendon, Nr Hertford, Herts SG13
8PD
3 miles S of Hertford near Bayford BR
station.
Undulating parkland course.
18 holes, 6315 yards, S.S.S.70
Designed by C.K. Cotton.
Founded 1968
Visitors: welcome weekdays, h/cap
cert required.
Green Fee: £24/round, £30/day.
Societies: welcome weekdays
except Wed.
Catering: bar lunches
Hotels: White Horse; Salisbury Arms.

E24 Briggens House Hotel

☎(0279) 793742 Pro, 792416 Hotel
Stanstead Abbots, Ware, Herts
Just off A414 between St Albans and
Harlow.
Parkland course.
9 holes, 5800 yards, S.S.S.72
Founded 1988
Visitors: welcome, not Sun am;
usual dress rules apply.
Green Fee: apply for details.
Societies: apply to Pro.
Catering: full facilities.
Putting green, croquet, tennis,
swimming pool.
Hotels: Briggens House, free golf for
residents, golfing weekends/breaks
available.

E25 Brocket Hall

☎(0707) 390055
Brocket Hall, Welwyn Garden City,
Herts AL8 7XG
A1(M) exit 4, then via A6129 and
B653 to course.
Picturesque parkland course, set in
18th century listed estate.
Melbourne course, 18 holes, 6569
yards, S.S.S.72

Designed by Peter Alliss & Clive Clark.
Founded 1992
Visitors: members and guests only;
no societies.
Catering: full facilities.

E26 Brookmans Park

☎(0707) 652487 Sec, 652468 Pro,
661851 Fax
Golf Club Rd, Hatfield, Herts AL9 7AT
Junction 24 off M25 (Potters Bar);
course located at top of Mymms
Drive, off A1000, 1 mile N of Potters
Bar, 3 miles S of Hatfield.
Parkland course.
18 holes, 6454 yards, S.S.S.71
Designed by Hawtree & Taylor.
Founded 1930
Visitors: welcome weekdays by
arrangement with Pro, h/cap certs
required; weekends only as guest of
member.
Green Fee: £27/round, £32/day (£14
with member).
Societies: Wed, Thurs, some Fri, by
arrangement with Sec's office.
Catering: bar and restaurant.
Hotels: Crest (S Mymms).

E27 Bunsay Downs

☎(0245) 222648
Little Baddow Rd, Woodham Walter,
Nr Maldon, Essex CM9 6RW
Leave A414 at Danbury (signposted
Woodham Walter), course 0.5 mile to
W of village.
Public, gently undulating
meadowland course.
9 holes, 2932 yards, S.S.S.68; 9
holes Par 3, 1319 yards
Founded 1982
Visitors: welcome.
Green Fee: £7.50 (9 holes), £9.50
(18 holes) WD; £8.50 (9 holes),
£10.50 (18 holes) WE; Par 3 £8; 9
holes on each course £10.
Societies: weekdays only, not BH
Catering: all week from 8am.
Driving range, petanque.

E28 Burnham-on-Crouch

☎(0621) 782282 Sec, 785508 Club
Ferry Rd, Creeksea,
Burnham-on-Crouch, Essex CM0
8PQ
Turn right off B1010 2 miles after
Althorne (at 40mph limit for
Burnham-on-Crouch).
Undulating meadowland course
along R Crouch.
18 holes, 6056 yards, S.S.S.68
Designed by Howard Swann (2nd 9).
Founded 1923

Visitors: welcome; start
9.30am-2pm; not Thurs am,
weekends or Bank Holidays; proof of
h/cap or club membership required.
Green Fee: £20/day.
Societies: catered for Tues, Fri.
Catering: lunches, bar snacks
except Mon.
Hotels: White Hart.

E29 The Burstead

☎(0277) 631171, 632766 Fax
Tythe Common Rd, Little Burstead,
Billericay, Essex CM12 9SS
Off A127 at Fortunes of War
roundabout towards Billericay, turn
left just before entering Billericay at
wooden sign into Laindon Common
Rd; at centre of Little Burstead follow
road round to right of War Memorial,
entrance 200 yards.
Farmland course with woods,
hedgerows, ponds and streams.
18 holes, 6177 yards, S.S.S.69
Designed by Patrick Tallack.
Founded 1993
Visitors: welcome Mon-Fri with
proof of membership of bona fide golf
club.
Green Fee: £18/round.
Societies: to be decided; check with
Sec.
Catering: bar and bar snacks;
restaurant for members and guests
only.
Practice ground.

E30 Bush Hill Park

☎(081) 360 5738
Bush Hill, Winchmore Hill, London
N21 2BU
0.5 mile S of Enfield town.
Parkland course.
18 holes, 5825 yards, S.S.S.68
Founded 1895
Visitors: welcome weekdays.
Green Fee: £22/round, £30/day.
Societies: on application except
Wed.
Catering: bar snacks, full restaurant.
Hotels: West Lodge; Royal Chase.

E31 Bushey Golf & Country Club

☎(081) 950 2283 Manager,
9502215 Pro
High St, Bushey, Herts WD2 1BJ
On A411 1.5 miles from M1/A411
junction.
Parkland course.
9 holes, 3000 yards, S.S.S.69
Designed by Donald Steel.
Founded 1980

Visitors: weekdays before 6pm; weekends and Bank Holidays after 2pm; no visitors Wed.
Green Fee: £8 (9 holes), £15 (18 holes) WD; £10 (9 holes), £20 (18 holes) WE.
Societies: max 50 by arrangement, not Wed.
Catering: meals served.
Driving range, squash, function room.
Hotels: Ladbrokes; Spiders Web; Hilton National.

E32 Bushey Hall
☎(0923) 222253 Sec, 225802 Pro shop, 229759 Fax
Bushey Hall Drive, Bushey, Herts WD2 2EP
1 mile SE of Watford.
Undulating parkland course.
18 holes, 6099 yards, S.S.S.69
Designed by Robert Stewart Clouston.
Founded 1886
Visitors: welcome, must book with Pro shop; h/cap certs required.
Green Fee: £14/round WD, £19/round WE.
Societies: welcome Mon, Tues, Thurs only.
Catering: full facilities.

E33 C & L Golf & Country Club
☎(081) 845 5662/3/4, (081) 841 5515 Fax
Junction of West End Road & A40, Northolt, Middlesex UB5 6RD
A40 from London; opposite Northolt Airport.
Parkland course.
9 holes, 4438 yards, S.S.S.62
Designed by Patrick Tallack.
Founded Jan 1991
Visitors: Public days Mon, Wed, Fri; no jeans or T-shirts; golf shoes only.
Green Fee: apply for details.
Societies: any day during the week; very competitive rates.
Catering: main bar, restaurant; banqueting hall.
Tennis, snooker, bowls, squash and health and fitness facilities.

E34 Canons Brook
☎(0279) 421482
Elizabeth Way, Harlow, Essex CM19 5BE
M11 to Harlow, Edinburgh Way then Elizabeth Way.
Parkland course.
18 holes, 6745 yards, S.S.S.73

Designed by Sir Henry Cotton.
Founded 1963
Visitors: welcome weekdays.
Green Fee: £25/round/day.
Societies: welcome weekdays.
Catering: lunch, dinners except Sun.
Hotels: Churchgate; Moat House.

E35 Castle Point
☎(0268) 510830
Somnes Avenue, Canvey Island, Essex SS8 8BH
A13 to Southend, right on A130 to Canvey Island at Saddler's Farm roundabout, over Waterside Farm roundabout to Somnes Ave, course on left.
Public seaside links course.
18 holes, 5627 yards, S.S.S.69
Designed by Golf Landscapes.
Founded June 1988
Visitors: no restrictions.
Green Fee: £9 WD, £12 WE.
Societies: on request in advance.
Catering: bar and restaurant facilities.
Driving range.
Hotels: Crest (Basildon).

E36 Chadwell Springs
☎(0920) 463647
Hertford Rd, Ware, Herts SG12 9LE
On A119 half way between Hertford and Ware.
Parkland course.
9 holes, 3209 yards, S.S.S.71
Designed by J.H. Taylor.
Founded 1975
Visitors: welcome weekdays, guests of member only weekends.
Green Fee: apply for details.
Societies: welcome on weekdays.
Catering: lunchtime food served.
Hotels: Salisbury Arms (Hertford); Moat House (Ware).

E37 Channels
☎(0245) 440005, 441056 Pro, 443311 Starter/tee reservations, 442032 Fax
Belsteads Farm Lane, Little Waltham, Chelmsford, Essex CM3 3PT
2 miles NE of Chelmsford on A130.
Undulating course on restored gravel workings, lakes and wildlife.
18 holes, 6211 yards, S.S.S.70
Designed by Henry Cotton & Assoc.
Founded 1974
Visitors: welcome weekdays, weekends with member only.
Green Fee: £28/day.
Societies: weekdays only.

Catering: excellent table d'hôte, à la carte. Restored Essex barn available for weddings and corporate days.
Hotels: County; South Lodge.

E38 Chelmsford
☎(0245) 256483, 257079 Pro/Bookings
Widford Rd, Chelmsford, Essex CM2 9AP
A1016 to Wood St roundabout, Chelmsford, turn right (from London) and right again.
Undulating parkland course.
18 holes, 5944 yards, S.S.S.68
Founded 1893
Visitors: welcome weekdays if members of recognised club; weekends with member only.
Green Fee: on application.
Societies: limited number by arrangement; Wed, Thurs only.
Catering: lunch except Mon, dinners Fri, Sat only, bar snacks daily.
Hotels: South Lodge; Miami.

E39 Cheshunt
☎(0992) 24009 bookings, 29777 Clubhouse
Park Lane, Cheshunt, Herts EN7 6QD
From M25 junction 25 towards Hertford, at 2nd lights turn left to mini-roundabout, turn right then signposted.
Municipal parkland course.
18 holes, 6608 yards, S.S.S.71
Founded 1976
Visitors: welcome weekdays and by arrangement at weekends.
Green Fee: £8 WD (£4 OAPs and Borough residents), £10.50 WE.
Societies: catered for any time by arrangement.
Catering: cafeteria service all day.
Hotels: Marriott.

E40 Chigwell
☎(081) 500 2059
High Rd, Chigwell, Essex IG7 5BH
On A113, 13.5 miles NE of London.
Undulating parkland course.
18 holes, 6279 yards, S.S.S.70
Founded 1925
Visitors: by prior appointment; weekdays only unless accompanied by member.
Green Fee: £28/round, £35/day, not weekends.
Societies: Mon, Wed and Thurs; early booking essential.
Catering: full bar and catering facilities.
Hotels: Prince Regent; Roebuck.

E41 Chingford
☎(081) 529 5708, 529 2195 (Royal Epping Forest GC)
Bury Rd, Chingford, London E4
Off Station Rd, 300 yards S of Chingford station.
Public parkland course.
18 holes, 6432 yards, S.S.S.70
Designed by James Braid.
Founded 1888
Visitors: welcome, red outer garment must be worn.
Green Fee: apply for details.
Societies: by appointment.
Catering: snacks, no bar.

E42 Chorleywood
☎(0923) 282009
Common Rd, Chorleywood, Herts WD3 5LN
0.5 mile from Chorleywood station near Sportsman Hotel.
Well-wooded heathland course on common land.
9 holes, 5676 yards, S.S.S.67
Founded 1890
Visitors: welcome weekdays except Tues and Thurs am.
Green Fee: £14 WD.
Societies: small societies, limited.
Catering: bar and catering; snooker.
Hotels: The Sportsman.

E43 Clacton-on-Sea
☎(0255) 421919
West Rd, Clacton-on-Sea, Essex CO15 1AJ
On A133 16 miles from Colchester, 1 mile W of pier next to old Butlins Holiday Camp.
Undulating seaside course.
18 holes, 6494 yards, S.S.S.71
Designed by Jack White.
Founded 1892
Visitors: weekdays subject to availability; Sat am, Sun pm and Bank Holidays on application; h/cap certs required at all times.
Green Fee: £20/round, £26/day WD; £30 WE & BH.
Societies: by prior arrangement with Sec.
Catering: full except Mon.
Hotels: Royal; Glengarry.

E44 Colchester
☎(0206) 853396 Sec, 852946 Club
Braiswick, Colchester, Essex CO4 5AU
0.75 mile up Bergholt Rd from Colchester North station.
Parkland course.
18 holes, 6319 yards, S.S.S.70
Designed by James Braid.
Founded 1907
Visitors: welcome weekdays, weekends only with member.
Green Fee: £22/day.
Societies: weekdays by arrangement.
Catering: available.
Hotels: Marks Tey; George; Mill.

E45 Colne Valley (Essex)
☎(0787) 224233, (0787) 224452 Fax
Station Road, Earls Colne, Essex CO6 2LT
Leave A12 at Colchester, take A604 for 8 miles through Earls Colne village, Station Rd is 1st on right.
Parkland course in the Colne valley, river and 6 lakes.
18 holes, 6272 yards, S.S.S.70
Designed by Howard Swan.
Founded May 1990
Visitors: welcome weekdays and after 10am weekends and Bank Holidays.
Green Fee: apply for details.
Societies: welcome weekdays by arrangement.
Catering: limited, temporary clubhouse; ploughman's, sandwiches and licensed bar.

E46 Crews Hill
☎(081) 363 6674, 364 5641 Fax
Cattlegate Rd, Crews Hill, Enfield, Middx EN2 8AZ
Off A1005 Enfield to Potters Bar road into East Lodge Lane, turn right into Cattlegate Rd.
Parkland course.
18 holes, 6230 yards, S.S.S.70
Designed by H. Colt.
Founded 1921
Visitors: must be members of recognised club; weekends and Bank Holidays only with member.
Green Fee: on application
Societies: advance booking.
Catering: lunch except Mon.
Hotels: Royal Chase; Ridgeway

E47 Dyrham Park
☎(081) 440 3361 Sec, 440 3904 Pro
Galley Lane, Barnet, Herts.
2 miles outside Barnet near Arkley, off A1 and M25.
Parkland course.
18 holes, 6369 yards, S.S.S.70
Designed by C.K. Cotton.
Founded 1963
Visitors: only as guest of member or member of Golf Society.

Green Fee: £19 WD, £26.50 WE.
Societies: Wed only; two rounds golf, light lunch and dinner or lunch and afternoon tea.
Catering: full restaurant facilities.
Hotels: Elstree Moathouse; Post House.

E48 Ealing
☎(081) 997 0937, 997 3959 Booking
Perivale Rd, Greenford, Middx UB6 8SS
Off A40 W opposite Hoover building (Tesco).
Parkland course.
18 holes, 6216 yards, S.S.S.70
Designed by H. Colt.
Founded 1898
Visitors: welcome weekdays only phone for advance booking.
Green Fee: £30 (£15 with member).
Societies: Mon, Wed and Thurs only.
Catering: bar snacks, lunches every day; evening meal by arrangement.
Hotels: Caernarvon; Kempton House; Bridge (Greenford).

E49 Earls Colne Golf & Country Club
☎(0787) 224466
Earls Colne, Nr Colchester, Essex CO6 2NS
On B1024 Earls Colne-Coggeshall road, 4 miles N of A12, 1 mile S of A604.
Landscaped and tree-planted course on converted farmland.
18 hole championship course, 6842 yards, Par 73; 9 holes, 1520 yards, Par 30; 4 hole Academy course for tuition.
Designed by Reg Plumbridge.
Founded 1991
Visitors: welcome.
Green Fee: £15/round (£10 OAPs) WD, £18/round WE.
Societies: welcome.
Catering: full bar and restaurant facilities.
Driving range; leisure, health and beauty facilities, tennis, bowls, flying school, business and conference facilities.
Hotels: Marks Tey; Anchor; White Hart (Coggeshall), Forte (Eight Ash Green).

E50 East Herts
☎(0920) 821978 Sec
Hamels Park, Buntingford, Herts SG9 9NA
A10 between Buntingford and Ware, just N of Puckeridge roundabout.

ENFIELD GOLF CLUB
Old Park Road South, Enfield, Middlesex EN2 7DA Tel: 081-363 3970
A warm welcome awaits you at Enfield. Course designed by James Braid.
Casual green fees (with Handicap Certificate) and Society Days welcome.
Call secretary for details.

1893

Parkland course.
18 holes, 6455 yards, S.S.S.71
Founded 1898
Visitors: Mon-Fri only; h/cap cert required.
Green Fee: £23/round, £30/day.
Societies: larger Mon and Fri; restricted to 35 on Tues, none Wed and 20 at other times.
Catering: facilities available.
Hotels: Vintage Corner Motel.

E51 Edgewarebury
☎(081) 958 3571
Edgeware Way, Edgeware, Middx HA8
On A41 between Edgeware and Elstree.
Par 3 Pitch & Putt course.
9 holes, 1045 yards, Par 27
Founded 1946
Visitors: welcome 9am until dusk; no booking necessary.
Green Fee: apply for details.

E52 Elstree
☎(081) 953 6115 Office, 207 5680 Booking, 207 6390 Fax
Watling St, Elstree, Herts WD6 3AA
On A5183 (A5) just outside Elstree village; close to M1, M25, A41, A1; nearest rail station Elstree & Borehamwood.
Parkland course.
18 holes, 6603 yards, S.S.S.72
Founded 1984
Visitors: welcome weekdays, after 2pm weekends.
Green Fee: £20/round, £30/day WD, £25 WE after 2pm.
Societies: Mon, Tues, Thurs, Fri by prior arrangement; phone for details.
Catering: restaurant, bar, conservatory all day.
Driving range.
Hotels: Elstree Moat House; Hilton International; Edgewarebury.

E53 Enfield
☎(081) 363 3970, 366 4492 Pro, 342 0381 Fax
Old Park Rd South, Enfield, Middx EN2 7DA
Leave M25 at Junction 24 (Potters Bar); take A1005 to Enfield (4 miles)
to roundabout with Church on left; turn right down Slades Hill, then 1st left into Old Park View; Club at end of road on right in Old Park Road South.
Parkland course.
18 holes, 6154 yards, S.S.S.70
Designed by James Braid
Founded 1893
Visitors: welcome weekdays (excl Bank Holidays); 24 hours notice, with h/cap and if member of another club.
Green Fee: on application.
Societies: Mon, Wed and Fri, excluding Bank Holidays.
Catering: meals available every day.
Hotels: Royal Chase; West Lodge Park.

E54 Epping Forest Golf & Country Club
☎(081) 500 2549 Dir of Golf, 559 8272 Pro shop, 559 8409 Fax
Woolston Hall, Abridge Rd, Chigwell, Essex IG7 68X
Alongside M11; take Loughton/Debden exit 5 (northbound only) to Chigwell and Abridge.
Parkland course with numerous water hazards.
18 holes, 6435 yards, Par 72
Designed by Neil Coles.
Founded 1994
Visitors: members and guests only; no casual visitors or societies.

E55 Fairlop Waters
☎(081) 500 9911
Forest Rd, Barkingside, Ilford, Essex IG6 3JA
Signposted from M11 and along A12; near Fairlop underground station (Central Line).
Public heathland course.
18 holes, 6018 yards, S.S.S.69; 9 hole Par 3, 1167 yards
Designed by John Jacobs.
Founded Jan 1988
Visitors: welcome, tidy dress required.
Green Fee: £7.50 WD, £10 WE.
Societies: weekdays by arrangement.
Catering: bar, Daltons American Diner, 2 banqueting suites.
Driving range, sailing, children's play area, country park.

E56 The Family Golf Centre
☎(0462) 482929
Jack's Hill, Graveley, Herts SG4 7EQ
Just off Junction 8 or 9 of A1(M), approx. 1.5 miles along B197 N of village of Graveley.
Pay-as-you-play, inland links/downland course.
Chesfield Downs, 18 holes, 6630 yards, S.S.S.72; Lannock Links, 9 holes Par 3, 975 yards, S.S.S.27
Designed by Jonathan Gaunt.
Founded Jan 1991
Visitors: welcome; advance booking system to reserve tee-off times, 1 week's notice preferred.
Green Fee: Chesfield Downs, £13.25 WD, £19.25 WE; Lannock Links, £2 WD, £3 WE.
Societies: catered for by arrangement.
Catering: "19th Hole" bar and bistro; coffee shop.
Driving range.
Hotels: Novotel (Knebworth Park, Stevenage); special rates available.

E57 Finchley
☎(081) 346 2436 Sec, 346 5086 Pro
Nether Court, Frith Lane, Mill Hill, London NW7 1PU
Near junction of A1 and A41, Mill Hill East underground 5 min walk.
Parkland course.
18 holes, 6411 yards, S.S.S.71
Designed by James Braid.
Founded 1929
Visitors: welcome weekdays, pm weekends.
Green Fee: £28 WD, £37 WE.
Societies: Wed and Fri.
Catering: every day except Mon.
Hotels: Hendon Hall.

E58 Forrester Park
☎(0621) 891406 Bookings, 893456 Pro shop
Beckingham Rd, Great Totham, Nr Maldon, Essex CM9 8EA
5 miles NE of Maldon on B1022, between S and N villages of Great Totham; from A12, turn off at Rivenhall End, follow signs to Great Braxted, at B1022 turn right towards Maldon, after 1.8 miles turn left.

Parkland course.
18 holes, 6073 yards, S.S.S.69
Designed by D.A.H. Everett & T.R.
Forrester-Muir.
Founded 1975
Visitors: to look like golfers, not
before 12.30pm Sat, Sun.
Green Fee: £15/round (approx).
Societies: with prior reservation
Mon, Thurs, Fri.
Catering: bar 8am until dark, snacks
8am-6pm daily; lunches
10.30am-2pm Mon-Sat; dinners for
parties on request.
4 all-weather tennis courts,
banqueting/conferences for 80.

E59 Frinton

☎(0255) 674618 Tel/Fax, 671618
Pro
1 The Esplanade, Frinton-on-Sea,
Essex CO13 9EP
A133 Colchester to Weeley village,
B1033 to Frinton and turn right at
seafront.
Seaside links course.
18 holes, 6259 yards, S.S.S.70; 18
hole short course, 2508 yards, Par
66
Designed by Tom Dunn.
Founded 1895
Visitors: welcome weekdays and
weekends by arrangement with Sec;
h/cap cert for main course.
Green Fee: £22/day; short course
£7.50/day.
Societies: catered for Wed and
Thurs only.
Catering: meals available except
Mon.
Snooker.
Hotels: Maplin.

E60 Fulwell

☎(081) 977 2733, 977 3844 Pro
Shop
Wellington Rd, Hampton Hill, Middx
TW12 1JY
2 miles S of Twickenham on A311,
opposite Fulwell railway station.
Meadowland course.
18 holes, 6490 yards, S.S.S.71
Designed by D. Morrison.
Founded 1904
Visitors: welcome weekdays, book
through Pro shop.
Green Fee: £25/day WD, £35/day
WE (£12 with member).
Societies: catered for Wed, Thurs
and Fri.
Catering: full service for societies
but advisable to phone.
Hotels: Cardinal Wolsey (Hampton
Court).

E61 Gosfield Lake

☎(0787) 474747
Hall Drive, Gosfield, Halstead, Essex
CO9 1SE
1 mile W of village of Gosfield which
is 7 miles N of Braintree on A1017.
Parkland course.
Lakes, 18 holes, 6649 yards,
S.S.S.72; Meadows, 9 holes, 4037
yards (for 18)
Designed by Sir Henry Cotton,
Howard Swan.
Founded 1988
Visitors: h/cap cert required for
Lakes course; with member only
from 12am weekends.
Green Fee: Lakes, £20/day (£10
with member), Meadows £10/day
(£5 with member).
Societies: welcome by
arrangement.
Catering: full bar, snack bar,
restaurant facilities from 12am;
conference facilities, private
functions, company days.
Hotels: Bull.

E62 Grim's Dyke

☎(081) 428 4539
Oxhey Lane, Hatch End, Pinner,
Middx HA5 4AL
Between Harrow and Watford on
A4008.
Parkland course.
18 holes, 5598 yards, S.S.S.67
Designed by James Braid.
Founded 1910
Visitors: weekdays; h/cap cert
required.
Green Fee: on application
Societies: catered for Tues-Fri by
arrangement.
Catering: lunch except Mon; dinner
by arrangement.

E63 Hadley Wood

☎(081) 499 4328, 449 3285 Pro,
364 8633 Fax
Beech Hill, Barnet, Herts EN4 0JJ
From M25 junction 24 take A111
towards Cockfosters, 3rd turning
right into Beech Hill, entrance 400
yards on left.
Parkland course with water hazards.
18 holes, 6457 yards, S.S.S.71
Designed by Alister Mackenzie.
Founded 1922
Visitors: weekdays, require h/cap
cert or proof of club membership; at
weekends only between 12am and
1pm Sun..
Green Fee: on application.
Societies: welcome by
arrangement.

Catering: morning coffee, lunch,
dinner for functions and societies,
breakfast by arrangement.
Large practice area.
Hotels: West Park Lodge; Hadley.

E64 Hainault Forest

☎(081) 500 2097, 500 0385 Sec
Chigwell Row, Hainault, Essex 0JJ
On A217 12 miles from Central
London.
Public parkland course.
18 holes, 5754 yards, S.S.S.67; 18
holes, 6445 yards, S.S.S.71
Founded 1912
Visitors: welcome.
Green Fee: apply for details.
Catering: meals served.

E65 Hampstead

☎(081) 455 0203, 455 7089 Pro
Winnington Rd, Hampstead, London
N2 0TU
1 mile down Hampstead Lane from
Highgate Village or Hampstead,
course adjacent to Spaniards Inn
public house.
Undulating parkland course.
9 holes, 5812 yards, S.S.S.68
Founded 1893
Visitors: welcome weekdays (not
Tues) by prior booking with Pro;
restricted times weekends.
Green Fee: £23/round (18 holes),
£28/day WD; £30/round WE & BH.
Societies: small societies by
arrangement.
Catering: bar, bar snacks, teas
served.
Hotels: La Gaffe; Central (Golders
Green).

E66 Hanbury Manor Golf & Country Club

☎(0920) 487722, 487692 Fax
Ware, Herts SG12 0SD
22 miles N of London on A10, 8 miles
N of M25 junction 25.
Parkland course.
18 holes, 7011 yards, S.S.S.74
Designed by Jack Nicklaus II.
Founded 1990
Visitors: hotel and member's guests
only; h/cap certs required.
Green Fee: £35 WD, £40 WE.
Catering: bars, 3 restaurants
(overseen by Albert Roux).
Practice ground, tennis, squash,
gymnasium, swimming pool and full
range of leisure club facilities.
Hotels: Hanbury Manor, special
golfing packages available; details
on request.

E67 **Hanover**
☎(0702) 232377
Hullbridge, Rayleigh, Essex SS6 9QS
Undulating course.
18 hole championship course, Par
73; 18 hole pay-and-play course, Par
63
Designed by Reg Plumbridge.
Founded 1991
Visitors: guests of members only.
Societies: PGA associated society
enquiries only.

E68 **Harefield Place (Uxbridge)**
☎(0895) 231169, 237287, 810262
Fax
The Drive, Harefield Place, Uxbridge,
Middx UB10 9PA
2 miles N of Uxbridge; off M40 at
B467.
Public parkland course.
18 holes, 5711 yards, S.S.S.68
Visitors: welcome 7 days.
Green Fee: £9.50 WD, £13.50 WE
(approx).
Societies: welcome 7 days, pm only
at weekends.
Catering: full facilities; function
rooms, weddings etc.
Hotels: all airport hotels.

E69 **Harpenden**
☎(0582) 712580, 767124 Pro,
712725 Fax
Hammonds End, Redbourn Lane,
Harpenden, Herts AL5 2AX
Off A1081 4 miles N of St Albans on
B487 Redbourn road.
Parkland course.
18 holes, 6363 yards, S.S.S.70
Designed by Hawtree and Taylor.
Founded 1894
Visitors: weekdays except Thurs.
Green Fee: on application
Societies: weekdays except Thurs.
Catering: by arrangement.

E70 **Harpenden Common**
☎(0582) 715959
East Common, Harpenden, Herts AL5
1BL
Adjacent A1081, 4 miles N of St
Albans, 1 mile S of Harpenden.
Heathland course.
18 holes, 5664 yards, S.S.S.67
Founded 1931
Visitors: welcome Mon, Wed, Thurs,
Fri; h/cap certs required.
Green Fee: £20/round, £25/day.
Societies: Thurs and Fri.
Catering: full bar facilities; lunches,
teas and snacks; dinner to order.

Hotels: Gleneagles, Moat House
(Harpenden); Aubrey Park
(Redbourne).

E71 **Harrow Hill**
☎(081) 864 3754
Kenton Road, Harrow, Middlesex
HA1
Off Harrow main by-pass road at
Northwick Park roundabout.
Public parkland course.
9 holes Par 3, 950 yards
Designed by S. Teahan.
Founded 1982
Visitors: welcome.
Green Fee: apply for details.
Catering: soft drinks.

E72 **Harrow School**
Harrow School, 5 High Street,
Harrow-on-the-Hill, Middlesex HA1
3JE
Parkland course.
9 holes, 3690 yards, S.S.S.57
Designed by Donald Steel.
Founded 1979
Visitors: no visitors.
Green Fee: apply for details.

E73 **Hartsbourne Golf & Country Club**
☎(081) 950 1133
Hartsbourne Ave, Bushey Heath,
Herts WD2 1JW
Turn S off A411 at entrance to
Bushey Heath village 5 miles SE of
Watford.
Parkland course.
18 holes, 6000 yards, S.S.S.70; 9
holes, 5432 yards, S.S.S.66
Designed by Hawtree and Taylor.
Founded 1946
Visitors: with member only.
Societies: welcome Mon and Fri by
arrangement.
Catering: daily catering and bar.
Hotels: Hilton National.

E74 **Hartswood**
☎(0277) 218850 Sec
King George's Playing Fields, Ingrave
Rd, Brentwood, Essex
1 mile S of Brentwood on A128.
Municipal parkland course.
18 holes, 6160 yards, S.S.S.69
Founded 1964
Visitors: welcome.
Green Fee: £7.25 WD, £11 WE.
Societies: welcome weekdays, not
weekends.
Catering: lunch, bar snacks except
Sun (members only).

E75 **Harwich & Dovercourt**
☎(0255) 503616
Station Rd, Parkeston, Harwich,
Essex CO12 4NZ
A120 towards Parkeston Quay, after
last roundabout 200 yards on left.
Meadowland course.
9 holes, 5742 yards, S.S.S.68
Founded 1903
Visitors: welcome, h/cap cert
required.
Green Fee: on application.
Societies: welcome by
arrangement.
Catering: bar snacks or full catering
as required.
Hotels: Cliff, Towers (Dovercourt).

E76 **Haste Hill**
☎(09274) 26485
The Drive, Northwood, Middx HA6
1HN
On A404.
Public parkland course.
18 holes, 5787 yards, S.S.S.68
Founded 1930
Visitors: welcome.
Green Fee: apply for details.
Societies: by arrangement.
Catering: meals served daily.

E77 **Hatfield London Country Club**
☎(0707) 42624, 42626
Bedwell Park, Essendon, Hatfield,
Herts AL9 6JA
A1000 from Potters Bar, B158
towards Essendon.
Undulating parkland course.
18 holes, 6854 yards, S.S.S.73
Designed by Fred Hawtree.
Founded 1976
Visitors: welcome; by advance
booking only.
Green Fee: apply for details.
Societies: welcome.
Catering: bar snacks at lunchtime.

E78 **Hendon**
☎(081) 346 6023, 346 8990 Pro,
343 1974 Fax
Off Sanders Lane, Mill Hill, London
NW7 1DG
From Hendon Central take Queens
Rd through Brent St, continue to
roundabout, take 1st exit on left, club
0.5 mile on left in Devonshire Rd;
from junction 2 M1 southbound, turn
left at 1st traffic lights and continue
to roundabout, then as above.
Parkland course.
18 holes, 6266 yards, S.S.S.70

Designed by H.S. Colt.
Founded 1903
Visitors: Sat, Sun, Mon limited;
Tues-Fri all day.
Green Fee: £25/round, £30/day WD;
£35 WE & BH.
Societies: Tues-Fri by arrangement.
Catering: snacks only Mon; other
days lunch, snacks, high tea to 6pm.
Hotels: Hendon Hall; Holiday Inn
(Brent Cross).

E79 High Beech
☎(081) 508 7323
Wellington Hill, Loughton, Essex IG10
4AH
B1393 (old A11) to Robin Hood
roundabout take turning signed to
Conservation Centre and Youth
Hostel; follow YH sign, course just
past YH next to Duke of Wellington
pub.
Public parkland course
Red course, 9 holes Par 3; yellow
course, 9 holes Par 3
Founded 1963
Visitors: Red course open to public 7
days a week, yellow course
members only weekends and Bank
Holidays and after 5pm.
Green Fee: Red course £2.70 (9
holes); yellow course £3 (9 holes),
membership fees £15 pa, £10 joining
fee.
Catering: café
5 practice nets.

E80 Highgate
☎(081) 340 1906
Denewood Rd, London N6 4AH
Off Hampstead Lane near Kenwood
House, turn into Sheldon Ave then 1st
left into Denewood Rd.
Parkland course.
18 holes, 5982 yards, S.S.S.69
Founded 1904
Visitors: Mon, Tues, Thurs, Fri only;
no visitors weekends.
Green Fee: apply for details.
Societies: Tues, Thurs, Fri by
arrangement.
Catering: full, 12am-8pm.

E81 Hillingdon
☎(0895) 233956 Sec, 251980 Pro
18 Dorset Way, Hillingdon, Middx
UB10 0JR
Turn off A40 to Uxbridge, past RAF
Station, up Hillingdon Hill to left turn
at Vine public house into Vine Lane,
club gates 0.75 mile on left.
Undulating parkland course.
9 holes, 5459 yards, S.S.S.67

Designed by Harry Woods & Chas E.
Stevens.
Founded 1892
Visitors: welcome Mon, Tues, Wed
and Fri; not Sat, Sun or Bank Holidays
unless with full member after
12.30pm; must be members of golf
club with h/cap cert.
Green Fee: apply for details.
Societies: Mon only.
Catering: bar and catering facilities.
Hotels: Master Brewer Motel; The
Old Cottage.

E82 Holiday Inn Golf Course
☎(0895) 444232
Stockley Rd, West Drayton, London
In grounds of Holiday Inn Hotel.
Open parkland course.
9 holes, 3236 yards, S.S.S.62
Founded 1975
Visitors: welcome.
Green Fee: apply for details.
Catering: at Holiday Inn Hotel.

E83 Horsenden Hill
☎(081) 902 4555
Woodland Rise, Greenford, Middx
UB6 0RD
Signposted off Whitton Ave East, rear
of Sudbury Golf club.
Public undulating parkland course.
9 holes, 3236 yards, S.S.S.56
Founded 1935
Visitors: welcome, no restrictions.
Green Fee: £3.95 WD, £5.95 WE.
Societies: any time
Catering: bar, restaurant

E84 Hounslow Heath
☎(081) 570 5271
Staines Rd, Hounslow, Middx TW4
5DS
A315 main road between Hounslow
and Bedfont, on left hand side.
Public parkland course.
18 holes, 5901 yards, S.S.S.68
Designed by Fraser.
Founded 1979
Visitors: welcome.
Green Fee: £7.30/round WD,
£10.20/round WE.
Societies: welcome by
arrangement.
Catering: snacks, soft drinks.
Hotels: Hounslow.

E85 Ilford
☎(081) 554 2930
291 Wanstead Park Rd, Ilford, Essex
IG1 3TR

0.5 mile from Ilford railway station.
Parkland course.
16 holes, 5414 yards, S.S.S.68
Founded 1906
Visitors: welcome; Sat, Sun and
Bank Holidays limited to members
and guests.
Green Fee: apply for details.
Societies: weekdays.
Catering: restaurant and meals
available most days.

E86 Kingsway Golf Centre
☎(0763) 262727
Cambridge Road, Melbourn,
Royston, Herts SG8 6EY
On main A10 N of Royston.
Landscaped farmland course.
9 holes, c. 2500 yards, Par 33;
(further 18 holes opening
end 1994)
Founded 1991
Visitors: welcome any time.
Green Fee: £5/round WD, £6/round
WE.
Societies: welcome by
arrangement.
Catering: bar and restaurant.
Driving range, 9 hole Par 3 Pitch &
Putt
Hotels: Cambridgeshire Motel.

E87 Knebworth
☎(0438) 812752
Deards End Lane, Knebworth, Herts
SG3 6NL
1 mile S of Stevenage on B197.
Parkland course.
18 holes, 6492 yards, S.S.S.71
Designed by Willie Park.
Founded 1908
Visitors: weekdays unaccompanied;
weekends, Bank Holidays with
member only; club h/cap cert
required.
Green Fee: on application.
Societies: Mon, Tues, Thurs only.
Catering: facilities daily.
Hotels: Roebuck Inn; Heath Lodge;
Clock Motel (Welwyn).

E88 Laing Sports Club
☎(081) 441 6051
Rowley Lane, Arkley, Barnet, Herts.
Off A1 S at Borehamwood.
9 holes, 4178 yards, S.S.S.60
Designed by employees of John
Laing and members only.
Visitors: only if accompanied by a
member.
Green Fee: £6.
Catering: limited.
Tennis, bowls, hockey, snooker

E89 Langdon Hills

☎(0268) 548444, 548065 Fax
Lower Dunton Road, Bulphan, Essex
RM14 3TY
8 miles from M25 junction 30, A13 E
towards Tilbury, after approx 7 miles
turn off on B1007 towards Horndon
on the Hill; after approx 1 mile turn
left into Lower Dunton Rd.
Parkland course.
18 holes, 6485 yards, S.S.S.71; 9
hole course
Designed by MRM Sandow.
Founded June 1991
Visitors: 18 hole course, welcome
with h/cap cert, not before 12am
weekends; 9 hole course
unrestricted.
Green Fee: 18 hole course,
£18.50/round, £26.50/day WD;
£25/round WE after 12am: 9 hole
course £4 (9 holes), £6 (18 holes)
WD; £7.50 (18 holes) WE.
Societies: welcome weekdays.
Catering: bars and restaurant;
function suite.
Driving range, practice ground, 3
practice holes played as 9-hole Par
34; home of European School of Golf.
Hotels: Langdon Hills.

E90 Lee Valley

☎(081) 803 3611, 345 6666
Lee Valley Leisure Golf Course,
Picketts Lock Lane, Edmonton,
London N9 0AS
1 mile N of North Circular road,
junction with Montagu Rd.
Public parkland course with large
lake and river hazard.
18 holes, 4902 yards, S.S.S.64
Founded 1974, extended 1993
Visitors: open to public every day, no
restrictions except dress code in
operation.
Green Fee: £10/round WD (£5 OAPs
and jnrs), £12 WE.
Societies: welcome weekdays only,
30 max.
Catering: breakfast until midday, bar
and bar snacks daily.
Driving range, full sporting facilities
at leisure centre.

E91 Letchworth

☎(0462) 683203 Sec, 682713 Pro,
484567 Fax
Letchworth Lane, Letchworth, Herts
SG6 3NQ
2 miles from A1(M) near village of
Willian, adjacent to Letchworth Hall
Hotel.
Parkland course.
18 holes, 6181 yards, S.S.S.69
Designed by Harry Vardon.
Founded 1905
Visitors: weekdays, h/cap cert
required; weekends accompanied by
member only.
Green Fee: £23.50/round,
£32.50/day.
Societies: Wed, Thurs, Fri.
Catering: except Mon.
Hotels: Letchworth Hall.

E92 Little Hay Golf Complex

☎(0442) 833798
Box Lane, Bovingdon, Hemel
Hempstead, Herts HP3 0DQ
Just off A41, turn left at 1st traffic
lights, past Hemel Hempstead
station, up hill; course on right,
signposted.
Public parkland course.
18 holes, 6610 yards, S.S.S.72
Designed by Hawtree & Son.
Founded 1977
Visitors: welcome.
Green Fee: £6.75/round WD, £10
WE.
Societies: by arrangement.
Catering: full meal facilities.
Driving range.
Hotels: Bobsleigh.

E93 London Golf Centre

☎(081) 845 3180
Ruislip Rd, Northolt, Middx UB5 6QZ
500 yards S of Polish War Memorial
roundabout on A40.
Public parkland course.
9 holes (18 tees), 5627 yards,
S.S.S.71
Founded 1975
Visitors: welcome any time, no
restrictions.
Green Fee: apply for details.
Societies: welcome.
Catering: 2 bars and bistro; function
hall.
Driving range,

E94 Loughton

☎(081) 502 2923
Clay's Lane, Loughton, Essex IG10
2RZ.
From M25 junction 26 take A121
towards Loughton; 3rd exit at
roundabout, 1st turning on left.
Public parkland course.
9 holes, 4700 yards, S.S.S.63
Founded 1981
Visitors: welcome, book after Thurs
for weekends.
Green Fee: £5 (9 holes) WD, £6 WE
(reductions for members).
Societies: welcome, limited
catering.
Catering: bar.
Hotels: Swallow; Bell (Epping).

E95 Maldon

☎(0621) 853212
Beeleigh, Langford, Maldon, Essex
CM9 6LL
2 miles NW of Maldon on B1019, turn
off at Essex Waterworks in Langford.
Meadowland course.
9 holes, 6197 yards, S.S.S.69
Founded 1891
Visitors: welcome weekdays with
h/cap cert.
Green Fee: £15 (£10 with member).
Societies: Mon and Thurs by
arrangement.
Catering: bar; catering by
arrangement.
Hotels: Blue Boar.

E96 Manor of Groves Golf & Country Club

☎(0279) 722333 Club, 726972 Fax
High Wych, Sawbridgeworth, Herts
CM21 0LA
1 mile N of Harlow.
Parkland course.
18 holes, 6200 yards, S.S.S.70
Designed by S. Sharer.
Founded 1991
Visitors: welcome at any time
weekdays, no restrictions; after
11am at weekends.
Green Fee: £16 WD, £20 WE.
Societies: any day; numbers
restricted weekends; corporate days
a speciality.
Catering: restaurant, function room
for 200, banqueting.
Snooker, swimming pool.
Hotels: Own hotel on site; weekend
golfing breaks available, reduced
rates for residents.

E97 Maylands Golf & Country Club

☎(0708) 373080, 346466
Colchester Rd, Harold Park, Romford,
Essex RM3 0AZ
On A12 between Romford and
Brentwood; M25 exit 28 towards
London, take next U-turn for
entrance.
Undulating parkland course.
18 holes, 6172 yards, S.S.S.70
Designed by Colt, Alison and
Morrison.
Founded 1936
Visitors: welcome weekdays with
member or if member of other club.

Green Fee: £20/round, £30/day WD. **Societies:** Mon, Wed, Fri; min 20, max 40; includes meals and 36 holes. **Catering:** bar snacks all day, lunch daily; some evening April-Oct. **Hotels:** Post House, Moat House (Brentwood); Hilton National.

E98 Mid-Herts
☎(058 283) 2242
Gustard Wood, Wheathampstead, St Albans, Herts AL4 8RS
On B651 6 miles N of St Albans.
Heathland/parkland course.
18 holes, 6094 yards, S.S.S.69
Founded 1893
Visitors: Tues not before 1pm, Wed not after 1pm; weekends, Bank Holidays only with member.
Green Fee: apply for details.
Societies: Thurs, Fri only.
Catering: every day except Sun.
Hotels: St Michaels Manor.

E99 Mill Green
☎(0707) 276900
Gypsy Lane, Welwyn Garden City, Herts AL7 4TY
Between Welwyn and Hatfield via A1(M), A404 and A1000.
Parkland/woodland course.
18 holes, 6615 yards, Par 72; 9 holes Par 3 (from July 1994)
Designed by Peter Alliss & Clive Clark.
Founded 1994
Visitors: welcome but restricted at present; please phone for details.
Green Fee: £30/round WD (£15 with member) WD; £40/round (£20 with member) WE & BH.
Societies: as for visitors; prices on application.
Catering: bar and bar snacks, à la carte restaurant.

E100 Mill Hill
☎(081) 959 2282 Clubhouse, 959 2339 Sec, 959 7261 Pro, 906 0731 Fax
100 Barnet Way, Mill Hill, London NW7 3AL
From junction of A1/A41; going N, immediately filter right and cross into Marsh Lane, after 0.5 mile turn left

into Hankins Lane, leading to clubhouse; going S, 1 mile from Stirling Corner turn left into clubhouse.
Parkland course.
18 holes, 6286 yards, S.S.S.70
Designed by J.F. Abercromby (1931 remodelled by H.S. Colt)
Founded 1925
Visitors: welcome weekdays, weekends reservations only.
Green Fee: £20/round, £25/day WD, £35 WE.
Societies: Mon, Wed and Fri.
Catering: daily.
Snooker, practice ground.
Hotels: Jarvis; Hilton National; Elstree Moat.

E101 Moor Park
☎(0923) 773146 Sec/reservations, 774113 Pro, 777109 Fax
Rickmansworth, Herts WD3 1QN
Situated on A404 between Rickmansworth and Northwood, 0.75 mile from Moor Park tube station (Metropolitan Line).
Undulating parkland course.
High, 18 holes, 6713 yards, S.S.S.72; West, 18 holes, 5815 yards, S.S.S.68
Designed by H.S. Colt.
Founded 1923
Visitors: welcome but must book in advance, h/caps required; Mon/Wed/Fri all day, Tue after 1pm, Thurs after 10am, not weekends.
Green Fee: High £30, West £25, £50 all day.
Societies: welcome weekdays.
Catering: snacks and lunch available Mon to Fri.
Hotels: Bedford Arms.

E102 Muswell Hill
☎(081) 888 1764 Sec, 888 8046 Pro
Rhodes Ave, Wood Green, London N22 4UT
1 mile from Bounds Green tube station, 1.5 miles from N Circular Rd.
Undulating course.
18 holes, 6474 yards, S.S.S.71
Founded 1893
Visitors: weekdays restricted; weekends and Bank Holidays limited bookings through Pro.

Green Fee: £23/round, £33/day WD; £35/round WE & BH.
Societies: Mon, Wed, Thurs, Fri booked through Sec.
Catering: meals and snacks, bar.
Hotels: Ragland Hall.

E103 The Nazeing
☎(0992) 893798 Bookings, 893915 Clubhouse
Middle St, Nazeing, Essex EN9 2LW
From M25 exit 26 take B194 N to Nazeing, then right at lights, course is on left; from A10 at Broxbourne lights, take Nazeing road to course, approx 10 mins.
Parkland course.
18 holes, S.S.S.71
Designed by Martin Gillett.
Founded 1990
Visitors: Mon-Thurs, experienced golfers only; strict dress-code.
Green Fee: £20 WD, £28 WE.
Societies: Mon, Tues, Thurs and Fri, details on application.
Catering: lounge bar, spike bar, restaurant, snacks available all day. Driving range, 9-hole putting green.
Hotels: Moat House (Harlow).

E104 North Middlesex
☎(081) 445 1604 Manager, 445 3060 Pro
The Manor House, Friern Barnet Lane, Whetstone, London N20 0NL
A1000 5 miles N of Finchley; 5 miles S of M25 junction 23 via A1081.
Undulating parkland course.
18 holes, 5611 yards, S.S.S.67
Designed by Willie Park Jnr.
Founded 1928
Visitors: welcome, h/cap cert desirable.
Green Fee: £22/round, £27.50/day.
Societies: Tues and Thurs.
Catering: full facilities (old manor house with terrace overlooking 18th).
Hotels: Raglan Hall (Muswell Hill).

E105 Northwood
☎(0923) 821384
Rickmansworth Rd, Northwood, Middx HA6 2QW
On main road between Northwood Hills and Rickmansworth A404.

Moor Park and Sandy Lodge

In one of the popular television programmes which John Betjeman narrated towards the end of his life, he highlighted the Metropolitan line and the station of Moor Park and Sandy Lodge, shared in its earliest days largely for the convenience of golfers. While the walk to Moor Park involves quite a lengthy climb, Sandy Lodge is no more than a long pitch shot from the station which, until it was elaborately modernised, was a somewhat odd looking basic wooden structure.

Sandy Lodge is a most pleasant course remembered by most golfers for the carry over large, deep bunkers to the 1st green, a prominent sleeper-faced bunker at the 2nd, consecutive short holes at the 7th and 8th and a short hole to finish across a quarry that is much less stark than it used to be.

It also has its 16th green beside the railway and a par 5 17th alongside a wood. Laddie Lucas and Alec Hill were its best known members, and John Jacobs its best known professional. It was at Sandy Lodge that he built up his considerable reputation as a teacher but, in the days when he was a regular figure on the tournament circuit, the opening tournament of what was then a more truncated season was invariably at Moor Park.

The architectural splendour of the clubhouse makes it one of the most photographed in the world but, in addition to the professional tournaments which were always attractions for school boys in the Easter holidays, the Carris Trophy was certainly one of the blue riband events of junior golf.

It involved a round on each of the High and West courses, the High regarded as the sterner of the tests, like Sandy Lodge ending with a short hole, at which Harold Henning once earned £1000 for holing-in-one, a small fortune in the 1960s, during the Esso Round Robin event.

The High and West epitomise the characteristics of parkland golf, but the High is unusually undulating, a factor that adds to the problems it presents. The West dominates the front of the clubhouse, the 1st tee and 18th green on the High being quite a step from its noble pillars. The 1st, crossing the road, has a narrow-looking fairway lined on the right by stately trees, while the 2nd has another demanding drive. If it is not held up sufficiently on the left, it will fall to the right, adding suitable problems to the second shot. But the problem of guardian bunkers to the green is nothing compared to the short 3rd, whose green is virtually encircled.

From the 4th green, one of the lowest points, the next couple of fairways run beside elegant houses into which it is easy to slice. The 8th green lies beside a pond which, before water features became so fashionable, caused quite a stir. The 9th is one of the best holes, with an awkward green to hit and an expensive one to miss, the inward 9 beginning near one of the main entrances to the park with a short hole where I once saw Arthur Havers, the local professional, hole-in-one in a tournament.

The 11th, 12th and 13th confront some of the severer slopes and hollows, while the 14th green is remembered for being very much wider than it is deep. There is an inviting downhill second to the 15th, an up and back element about the 16th and 17th and finally a downhill short hole where out of bounds lurks on the right.

It is a hole which, mercifully, cannot be lengthened more than a few yards and the modern giants rarely need more than a lofted iron from the tee, but it is not always easy to judge, the fear of being big often leading to being short.

Parkland course.
18 holes, 6553 yards, S.S.S.71
Designed by James Braid.
Founded 1891
Visitors: welcome weekdays only.
Green Fee: £21/round, £28/day.
Societies: Mon, Thurs and Fri.
Catering: lunchtime catering daily.
Hotels: Tudor Lodge (Eastcote);
Long Island (Rickmansworth).

E106 Old Fold Manor
☎(081) 440 9185, 440 7488 Pro
Hadley Green, Barnet, Herts EN5 4QN
On Potters Bar road (A1000) 0.25
mile from Barnet; M25 junction 23.
Parkland course.
18 holes, 6449 yards, S.S.S.71
Founded 1910
Visitors: welcome on weekdays,
with member only at weekends;
Public Days Mon and Wed; h/cap
certs required.
Green Fee: £27/round, £30/day (£10
with member) WD; £12 (with
member only) WE
Societies: Thurs, Fri only.
Catering: meals served except Mon
and Wed; snooker room.
Hotels: Hadley; West Lodge Park.

E107 Orsett
☎(0375) 891352
Brentwood Rd, Orsett, Essex RM16
3DS
On A128 400 yards from A13
towards Chadwell St Mary.
Heathland course.
18 holes, 6614 yards, S.S.S.72
Designed by James Braid.
Founded 1899
Visitors: weekdays by arrangement.
Green Fee: on application.
Societies: catered for Mon, Tues,
Wed.
Catering: restaurant 7 days by
arrangement.
Hotels: Plough Motel; Stifford Moat
House; Orsett Hall.

E108 Panshanger
☎(0707) 333350
Old Herns Lane, Welwyn Garden City,
Herts AL7 2ED.
Off B1000 close to A1, 1 mile NE of
town.
Public undulating parkland course.
18 holes, 6538 yards, S.S.S.70
Founded 1976
Visitors: unrestricted.
Green Fee: on application
Societies: welcome.
Catering: lunch every day.

E109 Perivale Park
☎(081) 575 7116
Stockdove Way, Argyle Road,
Greenford, Middx
On Ruislip Rd East between
Greenford and Perivale, entrance
from Argyle Rd.
Public parkland course.
9 holes, 2667 yards, S.S.S.65
Founded 1932
Visitors: welcome, no restrictions.
Green Fee: £3.95 (9 holes) WD;
£5.95 (9 holes), £11 (18 holes) WE.
Societies: not practical but apply to
Pro.
Catering: cafeteria serving meals,
tea, coffee etc.
Hotels: Kenton (Hanger Hill).

E110 Pinner Hill
☎(081) 866 0963 club, 866 2109 Pro
Southview Rd, Pinner Hill, Middx HA5
3YA
From Pinner Green take Pinner Hill
Rd and follow signs into residential
estate.
Hilly parkland course with views over
London and Harrow on the Hill.
18 holes, 6266 yards, S.S.S.70
Designed by Taylor and Hawtree.
Founded 1928
Visitors: Wed and Thurs
unrestricted; Mon, Tues, Fri with
h/cap cert; Sat h/cap 23 or less, by
arrangement.
Green Fee: Wed and Thurs
£8.10/round; Mon, Tues and Fri
£25/day; Sat £32/day.
Societies: Mon, Tues, Fri by
arrangement; full catering inc
evening meal.
Catering: full except Wed and Thurs
(stud bar only).

E111 Pipps Hill
☎(0268) 523456
Cranes Farm Rd, Basildon, Essex
A127 or A13, Basildon turnoff; off
A1235.
Public meadowland course; part of
Pipps Hill Leisure Complex.
9 holes, 2829 yards, S.S.S.67
Visitors: welcome, 18 holes only at
weekends.
Green Fee: £5.50 (9 holes), £9.50
(18 holes).
Societies: welcome weekdays.
Catering: full catering facilities
available; bars, restaurant, private
rooms seating up to 750.
Driving range, swimming, squash,
snooker, tennis.
Hotels: Forte Posthouse (in same
complex)

E112 Porters Park
☎(0923) 854127 Manager
Shenley Hill, Radlett, Herts WD7 7AZ
From M25 junction 22 to Radlett via
A5183, turn at rail station, 0.5 mile to
top of Shenley Hill.
Undulating parkland course.
18 holes, 6313 yards, S.S.S.70
Founded 1899
Visitors: welcome weekdays; h/cap
cert required, telephone in advance.
Green Fee: £28/round, £42/day.
Societies: Wed, Thurs only, min 20
max 50, £66 inclusive.
Catering: own chef, full catering for
societies; breakfast (ordered in
advance), comprehensive bar menu.
2 Practice grounds
Hotels: Red Lion; Water Splash.

E113 Potters Bar
☎(0707) 652020, 655051 Fax
Darkes Lane, Potters Bar, Herts EN6
1DE
M25 exit 24, follow signs Potters Bar;
turn right at 2nd traffic lights into
Darkes Lane; entrance 400 yards on
left.
Undulating parkland course.
18 holes, 6273 yards, S.S.S.70
Designed by James Braid.
Founded 1923
Visitors: welcome weekdays, must
have current h/cap cert.
Green Fee: £18.50/round, £28/day.
Societies: Mon, Tues and Fri by
arrangement.
Catering: lunches served every
day.
Hotels: Brookmans Park; South
Mimms Crest.

E114 Quietwaters
☎(0621) 868888
Colchester Rd, Tolleshunt Knights,
Maldon, Essex CM9 8HX
B1026 S of Colchester.
Seaside courses.
Links, 18 holes, 6250 yards,
S.S.S.70; Lakes, 18 holes, 6767
yards S.S.S.72
Founded 1974 (extended 1990)
Visitors: welcome at most times.
Green Fee: on application.
Societies: catered for weekdays
only.
Catering: full facilities, bars and
dining room.
Indoor and outdoor tennis, bowls,
squash, health and fitness,
banqueting.
Hotels: own 58-bed hotel; details of
bargain breaks and golf packages on
application.

E115 Redbourn

☎(0582) 793493 Pro, 792150 Sec,
793363 bar
Kinsbourne Green Lane, Redbourn,
Herts AL3 7QA
S of MI at junction 9 to A5, turn left
after 1 mile down Luton Lane.
Parkland courses.
18 holes, 6407 yards, S.S.S.71; 9
holes, 1361 yards, Par 27 (public
course)
Designed by H. Stovin.
Founded 1971
Visitors: welcome weekdays.
Green Fee: £14 WD (£11 with
member); WE & BH £18 with
member.
Societies: Mon, Tues, Wed, Thurs.
Catering: fully licensed bar, bar
snacks; restaurant meals daily by
arrangement; functions catered for.
Driving range.
Hotels: Aubrey Park.

E116 Rickmansworth

☎(0923) 775278
Moor Lane, Rickmansworth, Herts
WD3 1QL
A4145, 0.5 mile S of town.
Undulating municipal parkland
course.
18 holes, 4493 yards, S.S.S.62
Visitors: welcome.
Green Fee: £8 WD, £11.50 WE.
Societies: catered for weekdays.
Catering: meals served all day,
licensed.

E117 Risebridge (Havering)

☎(0708) 741429
Risebridge Chase, Lower Bedfords
Rd, Romford, Essex
2 miles from Gallows Corner and
Romford station.
Public parkland course.
18 holes, 5237 yards, S.S.S.70
Visitors: welcome; bookings for
weekends.
Green Fee: apply for details.
Societies: by arrangement.
Catering: snacks daily.
Pitch & Putt.
Hotels: Brentwood Post Hotel.

E118 Rochford Hundred

☎(0702) 544302
Rochford Hall, Hall Rd, Rochford,
Essex SS4 1NW
A127 to Southend, follow signs to
airport, then to Rochford; bypass
Rochford, turn left under railway
bridge, club 400 yards on left.

Parkland course
18 holes, 6255 yards, S.S.S.69
Designed by James Braid.
Founded 1893
Visitors: welcome weekdays, with
member only at weekends.
Green Fee: apply for details.
Societies: by arrangement on Wed
or Thurs.
Catering: lunch only Mon-Fri.
Hotels: Airport.

E119 Romford

☎(0708) 740986
Heath Drive, Gidea Park, Romford,
Essex RM2 5QB
1.5 miles from Romford town centre,
off A12.
Parkland course
18 holes, 6365 yards, S.S.S.70
Designed by Mackintosh (redesigned
by H.S.Colt 1921)
Founded 1894 (centenary year 1994)
Visitors: weekdays if member of golf
club and by arrangement with Pro.
Green Fee: £23/round, £30/day.
Societies: welcome by arrangement.
Catering: available.

E120 Royston

☎(0763) 242696
Baldock Rd, Royston, Herts SG8 5BG
On A505 on outskirts of town to E,
course on Therfield Heath.
Undulating heathland course.
18 holes, 6032 yards, S.S.S.69
Founded 1892
Visitors: welcome weekdays;
weekends with member only.
Green Fee: £20/day WD, £12.50
with member only WE & BH.
Societies: by arrangement with Sec.
Catering: full facilities available.
Snooker.
Hotels: Old Bull Inn; The Banyers.

E121 Ruislip

☎(0895) 638835
Ickenham Rd, Ruislip, Middx HA4 7DQ
1 mile N of A40, Hillingdon.
Public parkland course.
18 holes, 5702 yards, S.S.S.68
Designed by Sandy Herd.
Founded 1936
Visitors: welcome, telephoned tee
bookings can be made.
Green Fee: £9 WD, £12 WE & BH.
Societies: catered for every day;
booking essential.
Catering: breakfast, lunch, snacks,
à la carte menu daily until 10pm.
Driving range, snooker (8 tables).
Hotels: Master Brewer.

E122 Saffron Walden

☎(0799) 522786 Sec, 527728 Pro
Windmill Hill, Saffron Walden, Essex
CB10 1BX
Take B184 from Stumps Cross
roundabout on M11 (junction 9),
entrance just before entering town.
Parkland course.
18 holes, 6617 yards, S.S.S.72
Founded 1919
Visitors: welcome weekdays, with
member weekends and Bank
Holidays.
Green Fee: on application.
Societies: Mon, Wed, Thurs.
Catering: lunch available weekdays;
evening meals for societies.
Hotels: Saffron.

E123 Sandy Lodge

☎(09274) 25429
Sandy Lodge Lane, Northwood,
Middx HA6 2JD
2 miles S of Watford and 2 miles N of
Northwood, immediately adjoining
Moor Park station, Metropolitan Line.
Links course.
18 holes, 6340 yards, S.S.S.71
Designed by Harry Vardon.
Founded 1910
Visitors: weekdays; weekends and
Bank Holidays with member; h/cap
cert required.
Green Fee: on application
Societies: Mon, Thurs, Fri.
Catering: full facilities.

E124 Shendish House

☎(0442) 251806
Shendish House, Apsley, Hemel
Hempstead, Herts HP3 0AA
M25 junction 20, just before Apsley
on A4125.
Parkland course.
9 holes (extending to 18), 6076
yards, S.S.S.69
Designed by Henry Cotton, extension
1994 by Donald Steel.
Founded 1989
Visitors: welcome Mon-Fri, after
12pm weekends
Green Fee: £10 WD, £14 WE.
Societies: welcome, from £32.
Catering: full facilities.
9 hole Pitch & Putt, tennis, practice
ground.

E125 South Herts

☎(081) 445 2035
Links Drive, Totteridge, N20 8QU
In Totteridge Lane (A5109), 0.5 mile
W of junction with High Rd,
Whetstone (A1000).

Undulating parkland course.
18 holes, 6432 yards, S.S.S.71; 9 hole short course.
Designed by Harry Vardon.
Founded 1899
Visitors: weekdays only, recognised h/cap cert required; weekends only with member.
Green Fee: £25/round, £30/day.
Societies: Wed, Thurs and Fri; apply in writing.
Catering: lunch 12.30-1.45pm; bar snacks.

E126 Stanmore
☎(081) 954 2599
Gordon Ave, Stanmore, Middx HA7 2RL
E of Harrow; entrance off Gordon Ave, via Old Church Lane.
Parkland course.
18 holes, 5860 yards, S.S.S.68
Founded 1893
Visitors: Public days Mon and Fri; Tues, Wed, Thurs h/cap certs or club membership required; not weekends or Bank Holidays.
Green Fee: £8.10/round, £11.15/day Mon and Fri; £25/round, £32/day Tues, Wed, Thurs.
Societies: Wed and Thurs only.
Catering: full facilities daily.
Hotels: Grimsdyke.

E127 Stapleford Abbotts
☎(0708) 370040 Abbotts tee reservations, (0277) 373344 Priors tee
Horseman's Side, Tysea Hill, Stapleford Abbotts, Essex RM4 1JU
3 miles from M25 Junction 28, off B175 Romford to Ongar, left at Stapleford Abbotts up Tysea Hill.
Parkland course.
Abbotts: 18 holes, 6476 yards, S.S.S.71. Priors: 18 holes, 5828 yards, S.S.S.69. Friars: 9 holes, 1140 yards, Par 3
Designed by Howard Swan.
Founded 1972
Visitors: welcome by phoning starter.
Green Fee: Abbotts £40, Priors £15, Friars £5.
Societies: welcome any day.
Catering: bar and other facilities, function room. Sauna.
Hotels: Post House, Brentwood.

E128 Stevenage
☎(0438) 880424
Aston Lane, Aston, Stevenage, Herts SG2 7EL

Leave A1(M) Stevenage South, then on A602 to Hertford, course signposted about 1.5 miles.
Public parkland/meadowland course.
18 holes, 6451 yards, S.S.S.71
Designed by John Jacobs.
Founded 1980
Visitors: welcome every day, but necessary to book in advance at weekends.
Green Fee: £8.40 WD, £10 WE.
Societies: welcome weekdays.
Catering: full facilities, meals and bar snacks.
Hotels: Roebuck; Stevenage Moat House; Hertford Park; Novotel (Knebworth Park).

E129 Stock Brook Manor Golf & Country Club
☎(0277) 653616, 633063
Queens Park Avenue, Stock, Billericay, Essex CM12 0SP
M25 exit 28, then A12 to Galleywood/Stock exit, then B1007 to Stock.
Parkland course.
18 holes, 6728 yards, S.S.S.72; 8 holes, 2997 yards, S.S.S.69.
Designed by Martin Gillett.
Founded 1992
Visitors: apply for details.
Green Fee: on application.
Societies: apply for information pack.
Catering: available
Country club, bowls, tennis, croquet from 1994.
Hotels: Heybridge Moat House (Ingatestone).

E130 Stockley Park
☎(081) 813 5700
Uxbridge, Middx UB11 1AQ
5 mins from Heathrow, 2 mins M4 junction 4 towards Uxbridge.
Hilly parkland championship course with young trees.
18 holes, 6548 yards, S.S.S.71
Designed by Robert Trent Jones Snr.
Founded June 1993
Visitors: welcome 7 days, pay-as-you-play; correct dress, no denims, golf shoes required.
Green Fee: £25, reduced rates for members and residents of Hillingdon.
Societies: and corporate days, welcome weekdays booked in advance.
Catering: bar and restaurant.
Hotels: Holiday Inn; Novotel; Hilton; Sheraton Skyline.

131 Stocks Hotel & Country Club
☎(0442) 851341, 851491 Pro shop, 851253 Fax
Stocks Rd, Aldbury, Nr Tring, Herts HP23 5RX
In village of Aldbury, 2 miles E of Tring.
Parkland course.
18 holes, 7016 yards, S.S.S.73
Designed by Mike Billcliffe.
Founded 1993
Visitors: welcome weekdays, guest of member after 12am weekdays.
Green Fee: £30 WD, WE on application.
Societies: only by appointment.
Catering: 2 restaurants and bar; breakfast, lunch, dinner, banqueting. Health suite, gymnasium, tennis, riding, outdoor heated pool (May-Sept), snooker; practice academy.
Hotels: 18 bed (6 suites) hotel on site.

E132 Stoke-by-Nayland
☎(0206) 262836
Keepers Lane, Leavenheath, Colchester, Essex CO6 4PZ
A134 from Colchester for 7 miles, turn off onto B1068 to Stoke-by-Nayland.
Parkland/meadowland course.
18 holes, 6471 yards, S.S.S.71, 18 holes, 6498 yards, S.S.S.71
Founded 1972
Visitors: unrestricted during week; after 10.30am weekends; must have h/cap cert and club membership.
Green Fee: apply for details.
Societies: weekdays only by arrangement.
Catering: full catering facilities available.
Hotels: The Mill; The Bull; The Swan.

E133 Strawberry Hill
☎(081) 894 0165 Club, 898 2082 Pro
Wellesley Rd, Twickenham, Middx TW2 5SD
Adjacent to Strawberry Hill station.
Parkland course.
9 holes, 2381 yards, S.S.S.62
Designed by J.H. Taylor.
Founded 1900
Visitors: welcome weekdays only.
Green Fee: £18/round (18 holes), £25/day.
Societies: 24 max number considered on application.
Catering: bar snacks except Mon and Tues.

E134 Sudbury

☎(081) 902 3713 Sec, 902 7910 Pro
Bridgewater Rd, Wembley, Middx
HA0 1AL
At the junction of Bridgewater Rd
(A4005) and Whitton Ave East
(A4090).
Undulating parkland course.
18 holes, 6282 yards, S.S.S.70
Designed by H. Colt.
Founded 1920
Visitors: must produce h/cap cert or
be introduced by a member;
weekends with member only.
Green Fee: £20/round, £30/2
rounds.
Societies: Tues pm, Wed, Thurs and
Fri by appointment.
Catering: full catering service and
bar facilities.
Hotels: Caernarvon (Ealing
Common); Cumberland (Harrow);
Kenton (Ealing).

E135 Theydon Bois

☎(0992) 813054 Sec/Fax, 812460
Pro
Theydon Rd, Epping, Essex CM16
4EH
Off B172 1 mile S of Epping; M25 exit
26 Waltham Abbey (3 miles).
Undulating woodland course.
18 holes, 5472 yards, S.S.S.68
Designed by James Braid.
Founded 1897
Visitors: must have proof of
membership of recognised golf club
or society; not Wed, Thurs am.
Green Fee: £23/round WD;
£20/round WE after 2pm phone Pro.
Societies: Mon, Tues, £32 per day,
£20 after 2pm.
Catering: full catering facilities
available.
Hotels: The Bell; Trust House Forte.

E136 Thorndon Park

☎(0277) 811666 Club, 810345 Sec,
810736 Pro
Ingrave, Brentwood, Essex CM13
3RH
2 miles SE of Brentwood on A128.
Parkland course.
18 holes, 6455 yards, S.S.S.71
Designed by H. Colt.
Founded 1920
Visitors: welcome weekdays and
with member weekends.
Green Fee: £25/round, £40/day.
Societies: catered for Tues and Fri
by arrangement.
Catering: meals served on
weekdays.
Hotels: Post House.

E137 Thorpe Hall

☎(0702) 582205
Thorpe Hall Ave, Thorpe Bay, Essex
SS1 3AT
On seafront, about 2 miles E of
Southend Pier.
Parkland/meadowland course.
18 holes, 6286 yards, S.S.S.71
Founded 1907
Visitors: welcome weekdays with
club h/cap.
Green Fee: on application
Societies: catered for Fri only.
Catering: lunch served except Mon.
Snooker, squash, sauna.

E138 Three Rivers Golf and Country Club

☎(0621) 828631, 828060 Fax
Stow Rd, Cold Norton, Nr
Chelmsford, Essex CM3 6RR
10 miles from Chelmsford on B1012
via A12, A130, A132.
Parkland course.
Kings 18 holes, 6609 yards,
S.S.S.72; Queens 9 holes, 2142
yards, Par 54
Designed by Fred Hawtree.
Founded 1973
Visitors: welcome weekdays and
weekends.
Green Fee: on application
Societies: apply to Director of golf.
Catering: at all times.
Squash, tennis, snooker, sauna.
Hotels: Three Rivers Country Club

E139 Toothill

☎(0277) 365747
School Road, Toot Hill, Ongar, Essex
CM5 9PU
Between Ongar and Epping.
Parkland course.
18 holes, 6014 yards, S.S.S.69
Designed by Martin Gillet.
Founded Sept 1991
Visitors: welcome, h/cap card
necessary.
Green Fee: £25/round, £35/day WD.
Societies: catered for Tues and
Thurs.

E140 Top Meadow

☎(0708) 852239
Fen Lane, North Ockendon, Essex
RM14 3PR
Off B186 in North Ockendon.
Parkland course.
9 holes Par 3, 2000 yards; from Oct
1992, 18 holes, 5500 yards, Par 69
Founded 1986
Visitors: welcome with member.
Green Fee: apply for details.

Societies: welcome by advance
booking.
Catering: bar and restaurants.
Driving range.

E141 Towerlands

☎(0376) 326802
Panfield Rd, Braintree, Essex CM7
5BJ
Course on B1053 out of Braintree.
Undulating meadowland course.
9 holes, 2698 yards, S.S.S.66; 18
holes, 5406 yards, S.S.S.66
Designed by G.R. Shiels.
Founded 1985
Visitors: welcome anytime, not
before 12.30pm Sat, Sun.
Green Fee: £8.50 (9 holes), £10.50
(18 holes) WD; £12.50 (18 holes) WE
& BH.
Societies: welcome any time by
arrangement.
Catering: full bar and restaurant.
Driving range, 3 squash courts,
sports hall, equestrian centre, indoor
bowls.

E142 Trent Park

☎(081) 366 7432
Bramley Rd, Oakwood, N14 4XS
Near Oakwood tube station
(Piccadilly Line).
Public parkland course.
18 holes, 6008 yards, S.S.S.69
Founded 1973
Visitors: welcome any time; booking
required.
Green Fee: £10 WD, £12 WE
Societies: Mon-Fri only; brochure
available on request.
Catering: bar, snacks, meals by
arrangement. Diving range.
Hotels: Royal Chase (Enfield).

E143 Tudor Park Sports Ground

☎(081) 441 2261, 449 0282 ticket
office
Clifford Rd, East Barnet, Herts
Off Potters Rd.
Public parkland course.
9 holes, 1836 yards, S.S.S.57
Visitors: welcome.
Green Fee: apply for details.
Catering: clubhouse (members only).

E144 Twickenham Park

☎(081) 783 1698
Staines Rd, Twickenham, Middx TW2
5JD
On A305 near Hope & Anchor
roundabout.

Municipal parkland course.
9 holes, 3050 yards, S.S.S.69
Designed by Charles Lawrie.
Founded 1977
Visitors: welcome.
Green Fee: £5 (9 holes) WD, £6 WE.
Societies: welcome by arrangement.
Catering: full licensed bar, snacks;
function room.
Driving range.
Hotels: Richmond Gate.

E145 **Upminster**
☎(0708) 222788
114 Hall Lane, Upminster, Essex
A127 towards Southend; M25
junction 29.
Parkland course.
18 holes, 6076 yards, S.S.S.69
Designed by H.A. Colt.
Founded 1927
Visitors: weekdays if member of
recognised club.
Green Fee: on application
Societies: by arrangement.
Catering: meals except Mon.

E146 **Verulam**
☎(0727) 853327, 812201 Fax
London Rd, St Albans, Herts AL1 1JG
A1081 to St Albans, near M25, M10,
M1.
Parkland course.
18 holes, 6457 yards, S.S.S.71
Designed by James Braid.
Founded 1905
Visitors: welcome weekdays, except
Wed.
Green Fee: Mon, £12/round,
£20/day; Tues-Fri, £25/round,
£30/day.
Societies: Tues, Thurs, Fri.
Catering: full facilities except Mon
(bar snacks only).
Hotels: Sopwell House; St Michael's
Manor.

E147 **Wanstead**
☎(081) 989 3938
Overton Drive, Wanstead, London
E11 2LW
Off A12 at Wanstead station, right
into "The Green" into St Mary's Ave,
left at T-junction at St Mary's Church.
Parkland course.
18 holes, 6109 yards, S.S.S.69
Founded 1893
Visitors: welcome on weekdays with
prior arrangement.
Green Fee: £25/day.
Societies: welcome by arrangement
weekdays only.
Catering: bar and restaurant.

Hotels: Sir Alfred Hitchcock
(Leytonstone); Prince Regent
(Woodford Bridge).

E148 **Warley Park**
☎(0277) 224891
Magpie Lane, Little Warley,
Brentwood, Essex CM13 3DX
Off M25 junction 29, A127 Southend,
immediately left Gt Warley, left, 1st
right, right into Magpie Lane (6 mins
from M25).
Undulating parkland course.
27 holes (3 x 9), played 1-2, 1-3,2-3
Designed by R. Plumbridge.
Founded 1975
Visitors: welcome with h/cap cert.
Green Fee: £24/round.
Societies: by arrangement.
Catering: 1st class restaurant.
Large practice ground.
Hotels: Brentwood Post House.

E149 **Warren**
☎(02454) 223258, 223989 Fax
Woodham Walter, Maldon, Essex
CM9 6RW
A414 6 miles E of Chelmsford
towards Maldon.
Undulating parkland course.
18 holes, 6211 yards, S.S.S.70
Founded 1934
Visitors: welcome weekdays,
weekends after 3pm; booking
essential.
Green Fee: on application.
Societies: Mon, Tues, Thurs, Fri.
Catering: full facilities 7 days.
Hotels: Pontlands Park; Blue Boar.

E150 **Weald Hall**
☎(0992) 522118, 522881 Fax
Rayley Lane, North Weald, Essex
CM16 6AR
From M25 exit 27 N on M11 to
junction 7 Harlow turn off, E for 1
mile on A414; course astride A414.
Parkland course.
18 holes, 6239 yards, S.S.S.71
Designed by Peter Aliss & Clive Clark.
Founded Opening spring 1995
Visitors: weekdays only after
9.30am; h/cap certs required.
Green Fee: to be set.
Societies: to be set.
Catering: available on completion of
clubhouse.

E151 **Welwyn Garden City**
☎(0707) 325243
Mannicotts, High Oaks Rd, Welwyn
Garden City, Herts AL8 7BP

Leave A1(M) at junction 4, take B197
Stanborough to Valley Road.
Undulating parkland course.
18 holes, 6074 yards, S.S.S.69
Designed by Hawtree and Son.
Founded 1922
Visitors: welcome weekdays.
Green Fee: £25/round/day.
Societies: Wed and Thur only.
Catering: bar snacks, lunches,
dinners.
Hotels: Clock; Crest; Comet.

E152 **West Essex**
☎(081) 529 7558, 529 4367 Pro,
529 0517 Catering
Bury Rd, Sewardstonebury,
Chingford, London E4 7QL
Off A11, 1.5 miles from Chingford
station; M25 junction 26.
Parkland course.
18 holes, 6289 yards, S.S.S.70
Designed by James Braid.
Founded 1900
Visitors: welcome weekdays; with
member only Thurs pm, Tues after
11am and weekends.
Green Fee: £25/round, £30/day,
(£12.50 with member).
Societies: Mon, Wed, Fri.
Catering: lunches by arrangement.
Hotels: Roebuck; Woodford Moat;
Forest View; Swallow.

E153 **West Herts**
☎(0923) 236484
Cassiobury Park, Watford, Herts WD1
7SL
2 miles from Watford on A412; right
fork at Two Bridges Inn, right into
Linksway, right at end and right into
Rouseborn Lane; entrance 200 yards
on left.
Parkland course.
18 holes, 6488 yards, S.S.S.71
Designed by Tom Morris & Harry
Vardon.
Founded 1890
Visitors: welcome weekdays;
weekends with member only.
Green Fee: £20/round.
Societies: welcome Wed and Fri.
Catering: lunches and teas served.
Hotels: Dean Park; Southern Cross.

E154 **West Middlesex**
☎(081) 574 3450 Sec, 574 1800 Pro
Greenford Rd, Southall, Middx UB1
3EE
A40 from Central London to
Greenford, take left exit off
roundabout, 2 miles straight down
road.

Undulating parkland course.
18 holes, 6242 yards, S.S.S.70
Designed by James Braid.
Founded 1891
Visitors: welcome on weekdays,
Mon and Wed are Public days.
Green Fee: on application.
Societies: can be booked only on
Tues, Thurs and Fri.
Catering: hot and cold snacks
available all week, 3 course meals
should be booked in advance.
Hotels: Carnarvan (Ealing Common).

E155 Whipsnade Park

☎(044 284) 2330
Studham Lane, Dagnall, Herts HP4
1RH.
Off M1 at junction 9 between villages
of Dagnall and Studham.
Parkland course.
18 holes, 6800 yards, S.S.S.72
Founded 1974
Visitors: welcome weekdays.
Green Fee: £21/round, £31/day.
Societies: welcome except Mon and
weekends.
Catering: restaurant and bar snacks,
except Mon.
Hotels: Post House, Hemel
Hempstead.

E156 Whitehill

☎(0920) 438495
Dane End, Ware, Herts SG12 0JS
Turn left at Happy Eater on A10 from
London.

Undulating course.
18 holes, 6636 yards, S.S.S.72
Designed by Golf Landscapes.
Founded May 1990
Visitors: official club h/cap required
or competence certificate from
Whitehill Pros.
Green Fee: £15/round, £20/day WD;
£18/round WE.
Societies: any time by appointment.
Catering: licensed bar, restaurant.
Driving range, practice bunker and
grass practice area; beginners
classes; snooker.

E157 Whitewebbs

☎(081) 363 2951 Club, 363 4454
Booking Office
Beggars Hollow, Clay Hill, Enfield,
Middx EN2 9NJ
1 mile N of Enfield town.
Public parkland course.
18 holes, 5863 yards, S.S.S.68
Founded 1932
Visitors: welcome; very busy
course, queuing for playing times.
Green Fee: £10.60 WD, £12.40 WE.
Societies: applications in writing to
Hon Sec.
Catering: public café on site.
Nature trails and horse riding.
Hotels: West Lodge; Royal Chase.

E158 Woodford

☎(081) 504 0553, 504 3330 Hon Sec
2 Sunset Ave, Woodford Green,
Essex IG8 0ST

A11 to Woodford Green, near
Castle public house; M11 to
junction 4.
Parkland course.
9 holes, 5806 yards, S.S.S.68
Founded 1890
Visitors: welcome weekdays except
Tues and Thurs am, with member
only at weekends.
Green Fee: £15/round.
Societies: by arrangement with Hon
Sec.
Catering: snacks served and meals
by arrangement.
Hotels: Castle; Packfords.

E159 Wyke Green

☎(081) 560 8777 Sec, 847 0685 Pro
Syon Lane, Isleworth, Middx TW7
5PT
From Gillette Corner on A4 Great
West Rd, turn NW into Syon Lane;
club 0.5 mile on right.
Parkland course.
18 holes, 6242 yards, S.S.S.70
Designed by W.H. Tate.
Founded 1928
Visitors: welcome by arrangement,
h/cap cert required.
Green Fee: £28 WD, £42 WE after
3pm.
Societies: welcome Tues and Thurs
by prior arrangement; £49 per head
inclusive.
Catering: full catering facilities
available.
Hotels: Osterley Motel; Master
Robert.

F

BERKSHIRE, BUCKINGHAMSHIRE, OXFORDSHIRE

In men's county golf terms, the amalgamation of Berks, Bucks and Oxon — or BB & O as they are familiarly known — casts a wide net. Twenty years ago, Clubs were thin on the ground but a number of recent developments have boosted the list considerably and, more recently still, Oxfordshire has been inundated with planning applications.

The latest creation is the luxurious Oxfordshire Club, although it does not take green fee payers. It is owned by the Nitto Kogyo Company, owners of Turnberry, in the heart of the countryside near Thame, although some may find the introduction of a contrived landscape a trifle harsh in such a rural setting. It was opened in 1993.

The last few years have seen the Duke's and Duchess courses at Woburn reaching full maturity and taking their place amongst the finest in Britain. Not far away Abbey Hill and Windmill Hill extol the virtues of the more public type of operation, a department in which BB & O are better served than most.

There is Downshire near Bracknell, Farnham Park and Wexham Park near Slough, Hawthorn Hill near Maidenhead and Cherwell Edge near Banbury. More and more such courses are necessary if the demands of the army of new golfers can come close to being met; but many of BB & O's gems remain the longer established Clubs.

There is nothing better than a day's golf over the Red and Blue courses at the Berkshire with a marvellous lunch to rebuild the spirits if the heather has taken its toll. The same goes for Swinley Forest across the road where the Walter Mitty in you imagines it to be your own private course, while the character of heather and birch is echoed by East Berks at Crowthorne, another delightful place to play.

Stoke Poges, Denham and Beacons-field form a convenient triangle for those staying in the area and seeking a change of scene, the clubhouses at Denham and Beaconsfield lending a cosy, rural air unusual so close to London. Out beyond Harewood Downs and Amersham, the Vale of Aylesbury beckons, where Ellesborough near Chequers offers an ideal stopping place for 18 holes with an unmistakable feeling of having got away from it all; and Leighton Buzzard has the new Mentmore Club.

Over in Berkshire again, Maidenhead, Sonning, Temple and Calcot are always worth a visit while Newbury & Crookham is one of the oldest courses in England, and travellers through Pangbourne along the Thames Valley should look out for Goring & Streatley.

Oxfordshire's best known names are Huntercombe and Frilford Heath, the latter now with three courses of great charm and challenge. Frilford has played host to a number of important events including the 1987 English championship for men, its extension from 27 to 36 holes a tribute to the skill of Ken Cotton. The newer part was carved out of the woods that surround the clubhouse, the older version situated looking out on the more open heathland associated with the Club's title.

Since its earliest days, Huntercombe has assumed a more enclosed look, the appearance of the common now liberally laced with trees and bushes. Its distinctive greens bear the hallmark of Willie Park, designer of the Old course at Sunningdale, who use to declare that "a man who can putt is a match for anyone".

One of BB & O's latest recruits is Mill Ride at North Ascot, 11 holes designed on lovely natural land and the rest from the vastness of polo fields. A number of lakes embellish the look of a course whose popularity has grown rapidly.

F1 Abbey Hill

☎(0908) 562408
Monks Way, Two Mile Ash, Stony
Stratford, Milton Keynes MK8 8AA
2 miles S of Stony Stratford.
Public meadowland course.
18 holes, 6193 yards, S.S.S.69
Founded 1975
Visitors: unrestricted.
Green Fee: apply for details.
Societies: on application.
Catering: meals and bar snacks.

F2 Aspect Park

☎(0491) 577562
Remenham Hill, Henley on Thames,
Oxon RG9 3EH
On A423 E of Henley, leave M4 at
junction 8/9.

Parkland course.
9 holes, 5626 yards, S.S.S.66
Visitors: welcome Mon-Fri.
Green Fee: apply for details.
Societies: Mon-Fri by prior
arrangement.
Catering: available; function rooms.
Driving range (12 open bays, green
fee payers only).
Hotels: Red Lion (Henley).

F3 Aylesbury Golf Centre

☎(0296) 393644, 399543 Fax
Hulcott Lane, Bierton, Aylesbury,
Bucks HP22 5GA
Just off A418 1 mile N of Aylesbury.
Public parkland course.
9 holes, S.S.S.68
Designed by A.R. Taylor.

Founded May 1991
Visitors: welcome any day.
Green Fee: £8.50 WD, £9.50 WE.
Societies: Mon-Fri, max 24.
Catering: bar and restaurant.
Driving range
Hotels: Watermead; Forte Crest.

F4 Aylesbury Vale

☎(0525) 240196 Sec, 240197 Pro
Stewkley Rd, Wing, Leighton
Buzzard, Beds LU7 0UJ
Countryside location midway
between Milton Keynes, Aylesbury
and Leighton Buzzard; from village of
Wing on A418 turn N towards
Stewkley; travel for 1.75 miles and
course is on right.
Undulating parkland course.

18 holes, 6622 yards, S.S.S.72
Designed by Don Wright and Mick Robinson.
Founded 1991
Visitors: welcome at all times but please phone in advance; h/cap certs not necessary but no hackers please; normal dress standards – no jeans, T-shirts or trainers.
Green Fee: £12 WD, £18.50 WE & BH.
Societies: welcome weekdays, 36 holes £19; please phone Sec.
Catering: first floor and downstairs bars, light snacks and home-made dishes.
Driving range, indoor golf simulator.
Hotels: Village Green (Northall).

F5 Badgemore Park
☎(0491) 572206 Sec, 573667 Clubhouse, 574175 Pro
Badgemore Park,
Henley-on-Thames, Oxon RG9 4NR
Leave M4 at junction 8/9 on Henley and Oxford spur, over river into Henley, straight through town (leaving Town Hall on right), after 0.75 mile on right hand side.
Parkland course.
18 holes, 6112 yards, S.S.S.69
Designed by Bob Sandow.
Founded July 1972
Visitors: welcome weekdays only.
Green Fee: £27/round/day.
Societies: weekdays only, by arrangement.
Catering: full facilities available.
Hotels: Red Lion; Royal; Little White Hart.

F6 Beaconsfield
☎(0494) 676545
Seer Green, Beaconsfield, Bucks HP9 2UR
Off M40 onto A355 Amersham road, right at Jordans sign, adjacent to Seer Green/Jordans railway halt.
Parkland course.
18 holes, 6469 yards, S.S.S.71
Designed by H.S. Colt.
Founded 1914
Visitors: welcome weekdays.
Green Fee: £34/round, £42/day.
Societies: Tues and Wed.
Catering: full facilities.
Hotels: The Bellhouse.

F7 Bearwood
☎(0734) 760060 Sec, 760156 Pro shop
Mole Rd, Sindlesham, Berks RG11 5DB

On B3030 1.5 miles N of Arborfield Cross.
Parkland course.
9 holes, 5624 yards, S.S.S.68
Founded 1986
Visitors: weekdays only; h/cap cert required.
Green Fee: £8.50 (9 holes), £16 (18 holes).
Catering: meals and bar snacks available.
9-hole Pitch & Putt course.
Hotels: The Moat House.

F8 The Berkshire
☎(0344) 21495
Swinley Rd, Ascot, Berks SL5 8AY
Situated on A332 between Ascot and Bagshot.
Heathland course.
Red course, 18 holes, 6369 yards, S.S.S.70; Blue course, 6260 yards, S.S.S.70
Designed by Herbert Fowler.
Founded 1928
Visitors: on request to Sec.
Green Fee: £50/round, £65/day.
Societies: book with Sec.
Catering: lunch available.
Hotels: Berystede; Cricketers; Royal Foresters.

F9 Bird Hills (Hawthorn Hill)
☎(0628) 75588, 771030, 31023 Fax
Drift Rd, Hawthorn Hill, Nr Maidenhead, Berks SL6 3ST
Leave M4 at exit 8/9; take A330 towards Bracknell for 2.5 miles; course on right at crossroads (Drift Rd).
Public undulating parkland course set around lakes and ponds.
18 holes, 6176 yards, S.S.S.69
Designed by Clive D. Smith.
Founded 1984
Visitors: welcome subject to club competitions; pay-as-you-play.
Green Fee: £12 (18 holes) WD, £15 WE.
Societies: weekdays only; special packages available.
Catering: extensive restaurant and bar facilities; baronial function suite.
Driving range, 1 bunker, snooker.

F10 Blue Mountain Golf Centre
☎(0344) 300200, 360039 Fax
Wood Lane, Binfield, Berks RG12 5EY
Off B3408 Bracknell/Wokingham road.
Public pay-and-play parkland course.

18 holes, 6097 yards, S.S.S.70
Founded 1st April 1993
Visitors: any day, no restrictions.
Green Fee: £14 WD, £18 WE & BH.
Societies: Mon-Fri, must be booked in advance.
Catering: air-conditioned clubhouse with bar, restaurant, conference and banqueting facilities for up to 500.
Driving range, golf academy.
Hotels: Edward Court (Wokingham).

F11 Brailes
☎(0608) 685336
Sutton Lane, Brailes, Banbury, Oxon OX15 5BB
Off B4035, Shipston-on-Stour 4 miles, Banbury 10 miles.
Parkland course.
18 holes, 6270 yards, S.S.S.70
Designed by Brian A. Hull.
Founded 1992
Visitors: welcome.
Green Fee: £18 WD, £22 WE.
Societies: welcome.
Catering: full facilities.

F12 Buckingham
☎(0280) 815566
Tingewick Rd, Buckingham MK18 4AE
2 miles from Buckingham on A421 towards Oxford, 8 miles from M40 junction 9 via A43, B4031 to Finmere then A421.
Undulating parkland course.
18 holes, 6082 yards, S.S.S.69
Founded 1914
Visitors: weekdays; members' guests only at weekend.
Green Fee: £28.
Societies: pre-booking with Sec; Tues and Thurs only.
Catering: lunch, dinner 7 days.
Snooker.
Hotels: Villiers; Buckingham Lodge.

F13 The Buckinghamshire
☎(0895) 835777, 835210 Fax
Denham Court, Denham Court Drive, Denham, Bucks UB9 5BG
Off M40 E of M25, N onto A40; turn into Denham Court Drive at mini-roundabout and sign to club.
Parkland course.
18 holes, 6880 yards, S.S.S.72
Designed by John Jacobs.
Founded 1992
Visitors: by invitation only.
Societies: by invitation only.
Catering: full range of bar snacks, restaurant and private rooms.
Putting green, chipping green.

F14 **Burford**
☎(099 382) 2583
Burford, Oxon OX8 4JG
19 miles W of Oxford at junction of
A40 and A361, at Burford roundabout.
Parkland course.
18 holes, 6405 yards, S.S.S.71
Founded 1936
Visitors: by arrangement.
Green Fee: apply for details.
Societies: limited.
Catering: full facilities available.

F15 **Burnham Beeches**
☎(0628) 661448
Green Lane, Burnham, Bucks SL1
8EG
M40 exit Beaconsfield, follow signs
to Slough, turn right and follow
Burnham signs (not Burnham
Beeches) to Green Lane.
Parkland course.
18 holes, 6463 yards, S.S.S.71
Founded 1891
Visitors: Mon to Fri; weekends guest
of member.
Green Fee: on application
Societies: Wed, Thurs, Fri.
Catering: full facilities except Mon.

F16 **Calcot Park**
☎(0734) 427124, 427797 Pro
Bath Rd, Calcot, Reading, RG3 5RN
From junction 12 on M4 take A4 to
Reading for 1 mile, entrance on left.
Undulating parkland course.
18 holes, 6283 yards, S.S.S.70
Designed by H.S. Colt.
Founded 1930
Visitors: welcome weekdays only,
except Bank Holidays; h/cap cert
required.
Green Fee: on application.
Societies: catered for on Tues, Wed,
Thurs.
Catering: full catering daily.
Hotels: Calcot; Ramada.

F17 **Castle Royle**
☎(0628) 829252, 829299 Fax
Knowl Hill, Reading, Berks RG10 9XA
From M4 junction 8/9 follow signs to
Reading on A4, approx 2.5 miles on
left.
Parkland course.
18 holes, 6785 yards, Par 72
Designed by Neil Coles.
Founded 1992
Visitors: members' guests only.
Green Fee: £25/day (with member
only).
Catering: bar and restaurant.
Hotels: Bird in Hand.

F18 **Chartridge Park**
☎(0494) 791772, 786462 Fax
Chartridge, Chesham, Bucks HP5 2TF
3 miles W of town centre.
Parkland course.
18 holes, 6220 yards, S.S.S.71
Designed by John Jacobs.
Founded 1989
Visitors: always welcome.
Green Fee: £13 WD, £17.50 WE.
Societies: always welcome
Catering: 2 bars, restaurant,
banqueting and function facilities.
Practice ground.
Hotels: accommodation and golf
packages at Chartridge Centre.

F19 **Cherwell Edge**
☎(0295) 711591
Chacombe, Banbury, Oxon
3 miles E of Banbury, A442 to
Northampton; 1.5 miles E of M40
junction 11.
Public parkland course.
18 holes, 5322 metres, S.S.S.68
Designed by Richard Davies.
Founded 1983
Visitors: welcome 7 days.
Green Fee: apply for details.
Societies: Mon to Sat.
Catering: lunches, bar snacks,
evening meals.
Hotels: Whatley Arms; Thatched
House.

F20 **Chesham & Ley Hill**
☎(0494) 784541
Ley Hill, Chesham, Bucks HP5 1UZ
Turn off A41 on to B4505 at
Boxmoor, at Bovingdon follow signs
for Ley Hill.
Wooded heathland course.
9 holes, 5240 yards, S.S.S.66
Founded 1919
Visitors: welcome Mon, Wed (after
12am), Thurs, Fri (after 1pm); Tues,
weekends and Bank Holidays with
member only.
Green Fee: apply for details.
Societies: Thurs by arrangement.
Catering: snacks except Mon.

F21 **Chesterton**
☎(0869) 241204, 242023 Pro
shop/bookings
Chesterton, Bicester, Oxon OX6 8TE
1 mile from M40 exit 9 by A41
towards Bicester, 2nd left, left again
at Red Cow, 500 yards on right; from
Oxford take Northampton road, then
Chesterton sign at Weston-on-the-
Green for 1 mile.

Meadowland course.
18 holes, 6229 yards, S.S.S.71
Designed by R.R. Stagg.
Founded 1973/74
Visitors: no restrictions.
Green Fee: £12-£24.
Societies: weekdays except Tues by
arrangement (£12-£33/head).
Catering: bar daily, full catering by
arrangement.
Snooker

F22 **Chiltern Forest**
☎(0296) 630899 Clubhouse,
631267 Sec, 631817 Pro
Aston Hill, Halton, Aylesbury, Bucks
HP22 5NQ
Off A4011 between Wendover and
Aston Clinton, 5 miles E of Aylesbury.
Hilly woodland course.
18 holes, 5765 yards, S.S.S.70
Visitors: welcome weekdays;
weekends and Bank Holidays with
member only.
Green Fee: £20
Societies: by prior arrangement,
usually Wed.
Catering: limited food Tues, Thurs.
Hotels: Bell Inn; West Lodge.

F23 **Chipping Norton**
☎(0608) 642383
Southcombe, Chipping Norton, Oxon
OX7 5QH
0.5 mile S of town centre on London
road or junction of A3400/A44 on left
driving N.
Parkland course.
18 holes, 6280 yards, S.S.S.70
Founded 1890
Visitors: welcome weekdays; only
with member weekends and Bank
Holidays.
Green Fee: £22 (£10 with member)
WD.
Societies: weekdays.
Catering: full facilities.
Hotels: Crown & Cushion; White
Hart.

F24 **Datchet**
☎(0753) 543887, 541872 Sec,
542755 Pro
Buccleuch Rd, Datchet, Slough,
Berks SL3 9BP
2 miles from Slough and Windsor,
easy access from M4.
Parkland course.
9 holes, 5978 yards, S.S.S.69
Founded 1890
Visitors: welcome weekdays
9am-3pm.
Green Fee: £16/round, £24/day.

Societies: small societies welcome on Tues only.
Catering: bar snacks and lunches.
Hotels: The Manor.

F25 Denham

☎(0895) 832022
Tilehouse Lane, Denham, Bucks UB9 5DE
Just off A412, 4 miles W of Watford; from M40 take Uxbridge/Gerrards cross turn off, take A40 towards Gerrards Cross, turn right onto A412 towards Watford and take 2nd turning left to club.
Parkland course.
18 holes, 6439 yards, S.S.S.71
Designed by H.S. Colt.
Founded 1910
Visitors: welcome Mon to Thurs by prior arrangement.
Green Fee: £48 (36 holes), £32 (18 holes).
Societies: Tues, Wed, Thurs.
Catering: lunches served daily.
Hotels: The Bull (Gerrards Cross).

F26 Donnington Valley Hotel

☎(0635) 32488 Pro shop, 551199 Hotel
Oxford Road, Donnington, Newbury, Berks RG16 9AG
N of Newbury off old Oxford road.
Parkland course.
18 holes, 4215 yards, S.S.S.63
Founded 1985
Visitors: welcome.
Green Fee: apply for details.
Societies: welcome.
Catering: full facilities.
Hotels: Donnington Valley.

F27 Downshire

☎(0344) 302030, 422708
Easthampstead Park, Wokingham, Berks RG11 3DH
Between Bracknell and Wokingham off Nine Mile Ride.
Municipal parkland course.
18 holes, 6382 yards, S.S.S.70
Designed by F. Hawtree.
Founded 1973
Visitors: welcome 7 days, bookings required.
Green Fee: on application.
Societies: welcome by arrangement.
Catering: full bar and restaurant facilities.
9 hole Pitch & Putt, driving range.
Hotels: Ladbroke Mercury; St Annes Manor.

F28 Drayton Park

☎(0235) 550607 Pro shop/bookings, 528989 Clubhouse
Steventon Rd, Drayton, Oxon OX14 2RR
Off A34 2 miles S of Abingdon.
Pay-as-you-Play parkland course.
18 holes, 6000 yards, S.S.S.67; 9 hole Par 3 course
Designed by Hawtree & Co.
Founded 1992
Visitors: welcome, dress rules apply, no jeans/tracksuit bottoms, must wear golf shoes.
Green Fee: £12/round WD, £15/round WE
Societies: very welcome, packages available on request.
Catering: bar, bar snacks, formal and informal dinner facility (seats 120).
Driving range, 9 hole Pitch & Putt, putting green.

F29 East Berkshire

☎(0344) 772041, 777378 Fax
Ravenswood Ave, Crowthorne, Berks RG11 6BD
SW of Bracknell on A3095 and B3348.
Heathland course.
18 holes, 6315 yards, S.S.S.70
Designed by P. Paxton.
Founded 1903
Visitors: welcome weekdays, h/cap essential.
Green Fee: £33.
Societies: Thurs/Fri.
Catering: lunch and snacks daily.
Hotels: Waterloo.

F30 Ellesborough

☎(0296) 622114 Sec/bookings, 623126 Pro
Butlers Cross, Aylesbury, Bucks HP17 0TZ
1 mile W of Wendover on B4010.
Undulating downland course.
18 holes, 6203 yards, S.S.S.70
Designed by James Braid.
Founded 1906
Visitors: weekdays only, h/cap cert required.
Green Fee: on application.
Societies: welcome Wed & Thur only, £50 per day.
Catering: lunches served.
Hotels: Red Lion (Wendover).

F31 Farnham Park (Bucks)

☎(0753) 643332 Pro, 647065 Sec
Park Rd, Stoke Poges, Bucks SL2 4PS

Junction 5 off M4 (Slough Central), A355 signposted Beaconsfield, at Farnham Pump pub 2 mini roundabouts, turn right at 2nd roundabout into Park Road; course 0.5 mile on left.
Municipal parkland course.
18 holes, 5787 yards, S.S.S.69
Designed by Hawtree & Sons.
Founded 1977
Visitors: welcome at any time; municipal course.
Green Fee: £8/round WD, £11 WE; reductions Jnrs and OAPs.
Societies: bookable in advance Tues and Thur.
Catering: grill etc.
Hotels: Burnham Beeches.

F32 Flackwell Heath

☎(0628) 520929 Sec, 520027 Club
Treadaway Rd, Flackwell Heath, Bucks HP10 9PE
From London, exit 3 M40 (1.5 miles); from Oxford, exit 4 M40 (1 mile); turn off A40 High Wycombe-Beaconsfield road at Loudwater roundabout, up Treadaway Hill, on left before apex of hill into Treadaway Rd.
Undulating heathland course.
18 holes, 6207 yards, S.S.S.70
Founded 1905
Visitors: welcome Mon-Fri; h/cap cert required.
Green Fee: £27.
Societies: Wed, Thurs only.
Catering: full facilities Tues-Sun, restricted Mon.
Hotels: Bell House (Beaconsfield); Crest (High Wycombe).

F33 Frilford Heath

☎(0865) 390864/5/6
Frilford Heath, Abingdon, Oxon OX13 5NW
A338 Oxford to Wantage road, 3 miles W of Abingdon.
Wooded heathland course.
18 holes, 6768 yards, S.S.S.73; 18 holes, 6006 yards, S.S.S.69; further 18 holes opening 1994/95
Designed by J.H. Taylor and C.K. Cotton.
Founded 1908
Visitors: welcome but must have h/cap cert; advisable to phone in advance.
Green Fee: £42 WD, £52 WE & BH.
Societies: by previous arrangement Mon, Wed, Fri only.
Catering: cooked meals by prior arrangement, snacks served at any time.
Hotels: Dog House; Crown & Thistle.

F34 **Gerrards Cross**

☎(0753) 883263 Sec, 885300 Pro, (0753) 883593 Fax
Chalfont Park, Gerrards Cross, Bucks SL9 0QA
Leave A40 by A413, continue to 1st roundabout (approx 1 mile) and leave by 3rd exit onto private road.
Parkland course.
18 holes, 6295 yards, S.S.S.70
Designed by Len Holland.
Founded 1922
Visitors: welcome weekdays; phone Pro in advance and bring h/cap cert.
Green Fee: on application
Societies: welcome Wed pm and all day Thur and Fri.
Catering: bar snacks always available; lunches to order.
Hotels: Bull; Greyhound; Bellhouse.

F35 **Goring & Streatley**

☎(0491) 873229
Rectory Rd, Streatley-on-Thames, Berks RG8 9QA
On A417 Wantage road, 0.25 mile from Streatley crossroads.
Parkland course.
18 holes, 6255 yards, S.S.S.70
Founded 1895
Visitors: welcome Mon-Fri; weekend with member only.
Green Fee: £28 (£19 after 4pm).
Societies: apply for details.
Catering: full, à la carte and table d'hôte restaurant.

F36 **Hadden Hill**

☎(0235) 510410
Wallingford Rd, Didcot, Oxon OX11 9BJ
Just E of Didcot on A4130 Wallingford road.
Public parkland course.
18 holes, 6563 yards, S.S.S.71
Designed by Michael V. Morley.
Founded May 1990
Visitors: no restrictions, all starting times bookable by phone.
Green Fee: apply for details.
Societies: welcome weekdays.
Catering: full bar and restaurant facilities all day.
Driving range.
Hotels: George, Springs (Wallingford); George, White Hart (Dorchester).

F37 **Harewood Downs**

☎(0494) 762184, 764102 Pro
Cokes Lane, Chalfont St Giles, Bucks HP8 4TA
Off A413 3 miles E of Amersham.
Parkland course.
18 holes, 5958 yards, S.S.S.69
Founded 1907
Visitors: welcome.
Green Fee: £20/round, £27/day WD; £30 WE.
Societies: weekdays only.
Catering: daily.
Hotels: Crown; Greyhound.

F38 **Hazlemere Golf & Country Club**

☎(0494) 714722, 718298 Pro shop/bookings
Penn Rd, Hazlemere, Bucks HP15 7LR
On B474, 0.5 mile from junction with A404 between High Wycombe and Amersham.
Undulating parkland course
18 holes, 5855 yards, S.S.S.68
Designed by Terry Murray.
Founded 1982
Visitors: weekdays only; no jeans or trainers allowed.
Green Fee: £25/round, £34/day.
Societies: welcome by prior arrangement weekdays only.
Catering: bar and restaurant facilities, bar snacks and full meals.
Hotels: White Hart (Beaconsfield); Crest (High Wycombe); Crown (Amersham); Bellhouse (Gerrards Cross).

F39 **Henley**

☎(0491) 575742
Harpsden, Henley-on-Thames, Oxon RG9 4HG.
M4 to junction 9 Reading, follow A4155 to Caversham/Henley, turn left to Harpsden village 1 mile before reaching Henley, clubhouse on left.
Parkland course.
18 holes, 6130 yards, S.S.S.69
Designed by James Braid.
Founded 1908
Visitors: welcome weekdays, weekends with member.
Green Fee: £30/round/day.
Societies: catered for Wed and Thurs.
Catering: bar snacks daily; other by arrangement.
Hotels: Red Lion; Flohr's.

F40 **Hennerton**

☎(0734) 401000 Sec, 404778 Pro shop, 401042 Fax
Crazies Hill Rd, Wargrave, Reading, Berks RG10 8LT
6 miles from M4 exits 8/9 & 10 and M40 High Wycombe; at Wargrave on A321 take Wargrave Hill turning next to garage, after 0.25 mile take 1st left towards Crazies Hill; course 0.5 mile on left.
Parkland course with extensive views of Thames valley.
9 holes, 5460 yards, S.S.S.67
Designed by Col. Dion Beard.
Founded May 1992
Visitors: welcome, up to 50% of tee times available weekdays, up to 25% at weekends.
Green Fee: £12 (18 holes) WD, £18 WE & BH.
Societies: welcome weekdays, from £24/head; details on application.
Catering: bar and restaurant.
Driving range.
Hotels: Bird in Hand.

F41 **Huntercombe**

☎(0491) 641207
Nuffield, Henley-on-Thames, Oxon RG9 5SL.
A423, 6 miles from Henley towards Oxford.
Woodland/heathland course.
18 holes, 6108 yards, S.S.S.70
Designed by Willie Park Jnr.
Founded 1902
Visitors: weekdays after 10am; no 3 balls or 4 balls; jackets and neckwear required in clubhouse.
Green Fee: apply for details.
Societies: Tues and Thurs only.
Catering: full meals or bar snacks.

F42 **Hurst**

☎(0734) 345143
Sandford Lane, Hurst, Berks RG10 0SQ
Between Reading and Twyford, signposted from Hurst village.
Public parkland course
9 holes, 3113 yards, S.S.S.70
Founded 1977
Visitors: welcome, advisable to book.
Green Fee: apply for details.
Societies: welcome.
Catering: bar facilities.

F43 **Iver**

☎(0753) 655615
Hollow Hill Lane, Langley Park Rd, Iver, Bucks SL0 0JJ
Near Langley Station, Slough.
Parkland course.
9 holes, 6214 yards, S.S.S.70
Designed by David Morgan.
Founded 1984
Visitors: always welcome.
Green Fee: apply for details.

Societies: welcome.
Catering: meals and snacks always available.
Hotels: Holiday Inn (Langley).

F44 Lambourne
☎(0628) 66675, 663301 Fax
Dropmore Rd, Burnham South,
Bucks SL1 8NF
M4 exit 7 or M40 exit 2.
Parkland course.
18 holes, S.S.S.72
Designed by Donald Steel.
Founded 1991
Visitors: by arrangement, h/cap cert required.
Green Fee: £30/day (£20 with member) WD.
Societies: no society meetings.
Catering: full facilities every day, breakfast, lunch and dinner; half-way house refreshments.
Driving range, hairdressing, massage room.
Hotels: Cliveden; Grovefield House.

F45 Lavender Park Golf Centre
☎(0344) 884074 Admin/Fax,
886096 Golf shop
Swinley Rd, Ascot, Berks SL5 8BD
Between Ascot and Bracknell on A329 opposite Royal Foresters Hotel.
Public parkland course.
9 holes Par 3, 1124 yards
Founded 1984
Visitors: welcome any time, no restrictions.
Green Fee: £3.25 (9 holes), £4.50 (18 holes) WD; £4.25 (9 holes), £7 (18 holes) WE.
Societies: welcome.
Catering: lunch 7 days, buffets on request.
Driving range, snooker hall (10 tables), bar.
Hotels: Royal Foresters.

F46 Little Chalfont
☎(0494) 764877
Lodge Lane, Little Chalfont, Bucks
200 yards from A404 at Little Chalfont.
Undulating parkland course.
9 holes, 6800 yards, S.S.S.68
Redesigned by James Dunne.
Founded 1980
Visitors: welcome.
Green Fee: £10 WD, £12 WE & BH.
Societies: welcome weekdays.
Catering: full bar and restaurant facilities.
Hotels: Sportsman (Chorley Wood).

F47 Lyneham
☎(0993) 831841 Sec, 831775 Fax
Lyneham, Chipping Norton, Oxon
OX7 6QQ
4 miles W of Chipping Norton off A361 Chipping Norton-Burford road.
Parkland course.
18 holes, 6669 yards, S.S.S.72
Designed by D. Carpenter, A. Smith.
Founded July 1991
Visitors: unrestricted, can book 3 days in advance including weekends.
Green Fee: £12/round, £19/day WD; £15/round, £26/day WE & BH.
Societies: welcome.
Catering: available. Driving range.
Hotels: Mill (Kingham); White Hart, Crown and Cushion (Chipping Norton); Shaven Crown (Shipton under Wychwood); Hillsborough (Milton under Wychwood).

F48 Maidenhead
☎(0628) 24693 Sec, 20545 Club, 24067 Pro, 35321 Catering
Shoppenhangers Rd, Maidenhead, Berks SL6 2PZ
Off A308, adjacent to Maidenhead railway station.
Parkland course.
18 holes, 6360 yards, S.S.S.70
Founded 1896
Visitors: Mon-Thurs, Fri am only; h/cap cert required.
Green Fee: £28.
Societies: welcome by arrangement.
Catering: snack lunch, tea available; full lunch, dinner by arrangement.
Hotels: Frederick's; Holiday Inn.

F49 Mapledurham
☎(0734) 463353, 463363 Fax
Chazey Heath, Mapledurham, Reading, Berks RG4 7UD
Off A4047 NW of Reading in village of Mapledurham.
Gently undulating parkland course.
18 holes, 5624 yards, Par 69
Designed by MRM Sandow.
Founded 1992
Visitors: welcome.
Green Fee: £13 WD, £16 WE.
Societies: welcome, apply for details.
Catering: bar and restaurant.
Practice ground, Pitch & Putt, practice bunkers, putting green
Hotels: Holiday Inn (Caversham).

F50 Mill Ride
☎(0344) 886777 Pro, 891494 Sec
Mill Ride Estate, Mill Ride, North Ascot, Berkshire SL5 8LT

Turn right into Fernbank Rd at 1st traffic lights on A329 between Ascot and Bracknell. Mill Ride is 0.5 mile on left.
Parkland/inland links course.
18 holes, 6639 yards, S.S.S.72
Designed by Donald Steel.
Founded 1990
Visitors: welcome, but must book in advance.
Green Fee: £35/round WD; £50 WE.
Societies: weekdays, occasional weekends.
Catering: morning coffee, lunch, tea, dinner, bar snacks; private dining room.
Practice ground, saunas, steam bath (men only).
Hotels: Royal Berkshire (Ascot); Berystede (Sunningdale); 4 guest bedrooms on site.

F51 Newbury & Crookham
☎(0635) 40035 Sec, 31201 Pro
Bury's Bank Rd, Greenham, Newbury, Berks RG15 8BZ
2 miles SE of Newbury off A34.
Parkland course.
18 holes, 5880 yards, S.S.S.68
Designed by J.H. Turner.
Founded 1873
Visitors: weekdays members of other clubs; weekends with members only.
Green Fee: £25 (£12.50 with member).
Societies: Wed, Thurs and Fri.
Catering: lunch, snacks and evening meals.
Hotels: Bacon Arms; Chequers; Enborne Grange; Hilton.

F52 North Oxford
☎(0865) 54924, 53977 Pro
Banbury Rd, Oxford OX2 8EZ
Between Kidlington and N Oxford, 2.5 miles N of city centre.
Parkland course.
18 holes, 5805 yards, S.S.S.67
Founded 1907
Visitors: welcome weekdays.
Green Fee: on application.
Societies: book with Sec.
Catering: facilities available.
Hotels: Moat House; Linton Lodge; Randolph.

F53 The Oxfordshire
☎(0844) 278300, 278003 Fax
Rycote Lane, Milton Common, Thame, Oxon OX9 2PU
From M40 northbound, exit 7, turn right for Thame on A329; from M40

southbound, exit 8, 1st right onto A40, then left at A329.
Part parkland, part links style course with American water features.
18 holes, S.S.S.73
Designed by Rees Jones.
Founded July 1993
Visitors: restricted to members and their guests, or by introduction only; h/cap cert required.
Green Fee: £45 WD.
Societies: as for visitors.
Catering: spike bar, lounge bar, restaurant, halfway house.
26-bay driving range, putting greens, practice bunkers, indoor golf school.
Hotels: The Belfry; Hartwell House; Le Manoir au Quat' Saisons; Randolph; Spread Eagle.

F54 Princes Risborough
☎(0844) 346989
Lee Rd, Saunderton Lee, Princes Risborough, Bucks HP27 9NX
M40 to High Wycombe, follow A4010 signposted Aylesbury; 2 miles before Princes Risborough turn left at Rose & Crown inn; club 1 mile on right.
Parkland course.
9 holes, S.S.S.66
Designed by Guy Hunt.
Founded 1991
Visitors: welcome any time.
Green Fee: £12 WD, £16 WE.
Societies: welcome, min 8 players.
Catering: bar, restaurant and lounge.
Hotels: Rose & Crown.

F55 Reading
☎(0734) 472909 Bookings, 476115 Pro
Kidmore End Rd, Emmer Green, Reading, Berks RG4 8SG
2 miles N of Reading off Peppard Rd (B481).
Parkland course.
18 holes, 6212 yards, S.S.S.70
Founded 1910
Visitors: Mon to Thurs (unless with member)
Green Fee: £27/day/round
Societies: Tues, Thurs unlimited; Wed 25 max.
Catering: full facilities except Mon.
Hotels: Ramada; Rainbow Corner (Caversham).

F56 Royal Ascot
☎(0344) 25175, 24656 Pro
Winkfield Rd, Ascot, Berks SL5 7LJ
Ascot Heath (in centre of racecourse) on A329.

Heathland course.
18 holes, 5716 yards, S.S.S.68
Designed by J.H. Taylor.
Founded 1887
Visitors: members' guests only.
Green Fee: on application.
Societies: Wed and Thurs by arrangement.
Catering: available all week by arrangement.
Hotels: Berystede.

F57 Sandmartins
☎(0734) 792711 Sec, 770265 Pro shop, 770282 Fax
Finchhampstead Rd, Wokingham, Berks RG11 3RQ
M4 junction 10 or M3 junction 3; 1 mile S of Wokingham off Nine Mile Ride.
Parkland course.
18 holes, 6235 yards, S.S.S.70
Designed by E.T. Fox.
Founded 15 May, 1993
Visitors: weekdays only.
Green Fee: £25/round, £40/day.
Societies: by arrangement with Sec.
Catering: bar, restaurant, halfway house.
Practice area – driving, bunker, pitching.
Hotels: St Anne's Manor – Stakis (Wokingham).

F58 Silverstone
☎(0280) 850005
Silverstone Rd, Stowe, Buckingham, MK18 5LH
On Silverstone road from Buckingham and Stowe, 1.5 miles beyond racing circuit.
Farmland course.
18 holes, 6164 yards, S.S.S.72
Designed by David Snell.
Founded 1992
Visitors: welcome weekdays and weekends, pay-as-you-play; smart/casual dress required.
Green Fee: £8/round, £12 WE & BH.
Societies: welcome by arrangement.
Catering: full bar and restaurant, lounge, private dining room.
Driving range, 2 × 28 hole putting greens, 9 hole pitching course etc.
Hotels: White Hart (Buckingham); Green Man (Syresham); Forte Travelodge (Towcester).

F59 Sonning
☎(0734) 693332, 692910 Pro, 448409 Fax
Duffield Rd, Sonning-on-Thames, Berks RG4 0GJ

A4 Maidenhead/Reading rd, behind Readingensians Rugby Ground.
Parkland course.
18 holes, 6360 yards, S.S.S.70
Founded 1914
Visitors: weekdays with h/cap cert.
Green Fee: on application
Societies: by prior arrangement.
Catering: full service available.

F60 Southfield
☎(0865) 242158
Hill Top Rd, Oxford OX4 1PF
Cowley Rd, Southfield Rd, then right into Hill Top Rd; between Headington and Cowley.
Undulating parkland course.
18 holes, 6230 yards, S.S.S.70
Designed by James Braid (1875), redesigned H. Colt (1923)
Visitors: welcome weekdays.
Green Fee: on application
Societies: welcome weekdays.
Catering: daily except Mon.

F61 Stoke Poges
☎(0753) 526385, 523609 Pro shop
North Drive, Park Rd, Stoke Poges, Slough, Bucks SL2 4PG
Off M4 or A4 at Slough into Stoke Poges Lane, then 1.5 miles on left.
Parkland course.
18 holes, 6654 yards, S.S.S.72
Designed by H.S. Colt.
Founded 1908
Visitors: weekdays by arrangement with Pro, weekends and Bank Holidays with member only; letter of intro or h/cap cert required.
Green Fee: £35/round, £50/day.
Societies: Mon, Wed, Thurs, Fri.
Catering: full service available.
Hotels: Marriotts, Bull (Gerards Cross); Copthorne (Slough).

F62 Stowe
☎(0280) 813650 Sec
Stowe, Buckingham, MK18 5EH
Parkland course.
9 holes, 4573 yards, S.S.S.63
Founded 1974
Visitors: with member only.
Green Fee: apply for details.
Catering: clubhouse.

F63 Swinley Forest
☎(0344) 20197 Club, 874811 Pro
Coronation Rd, South Ascot, Berks SL5 9LE
1.5 miles from Ascot station, through S Ascot village, right into Coronation Rd and 4th right to club.

Undulating heathland course
18 holes, 5952 yards, S.S.S.69
Designed by H.S. Colt.
Founded 1909
Visitors: welcome only by invitation
of member.
Green Fee: on application.
Societies: apply to Sec.
Catering: lunch served.
Hotels: Berystede; Royal Foresters;
Brockenhurst.

F64 Tadmarton Heath
☎(0608) 737278
Wigginton, Banbury, Oxon OX15 5HL
5 miles W of Banbury off B4035
Shipston-on-Stour road at
Tadmarton village.
Heathland course.
18 holes, 5917 yards, S.S.S.69
Designed by Major C.K. Hutchinson.
Founded 1922
Visitors: weekdays only; must be
members of other clubs with h/cap
certs.
Green Fee: on application.
Societies: Tues, Wed, Fri.
Catering: full facilities.
Hotels: Banbury Moat House; Old
School House (Bloxham).

F65 Temple
☎(0628) 824795 Sec, 824248
Steward, 824254 Pro
Henley Rd, Hurley, Maidenhead,
Berks SL6 5LH
A4130 Maidenhead to Henley from
M4 or A404 from M40.
Undulating parkland course.
18 holes, 6206 yards, S.S.S.70
Designed by Willie Park Jnr.
Founded 1909
Visitors: welcome on weekdays;
must have proof of h/cap.
Green Fee: £40.
Societies: catered for Mon, Tues,
Wed, Fri; max 40.
Catering: full catering.
Squash.
Hotels: Eurocrest (Maidenhead);
Compleat Angler (Marlow).

F66 Thorney Park
☎(0895) 422095 Club, (0753)
686002 Fax
Thorney Mill Lane, Iver, Bucks SL0
9AL
From M4 junction 5 follow signs to
Iver and West Drayton.
Municipal parkland course.
9 holes, 3000 yards, S.S.S.34
Designed by Grundon Leisure Ltd.
Founded Sept 1992

Visitors: welcome.
Green Fee: £5 (9 holes), £8 (18
holes) WD; £8 (9 holes), £12 (18
holes) WE.
Societies: weekdays.
Catering: fully licenced bar and
restaurant.
Practice ground.
Hotels: in Heathrow area (5 mins).

F67 Three Locks
☎(0525) 270050 Pro shop, 270470
Hotel
Great Brickhill, Milton Keynes, Bucks
MK17 9BH
Between Little Brickhill on A5 and
A4146; from Leighton Buzzard
towards Bletchley turn off right just
before The Three Locks public house.
Converted farmland course.
9 holes, 6654 yards, S.S.S.73;
further 9 holes ready for play Oct
1994
Designed by MRM Sandow.
Founded April 1992
Visitors: welcome, no restrictions
except weekend tee times must be
booked.
Green Fee: £5.50 (9 holes), £8.50
(18 holes) WD; £7.50 (9 holes), £10
(18 holes) WE.
Societies: welcome at any time by
arrangement with management; fees
dependent on requirements.
Catering: club bar, bar meals,
lunches and breakfast.
Extensive practice area, snooker
room.
Hotels: B&B executive hotel on site,
free golf for guests.

F68 Waterstock
☎(0844) 338093
Thame Rd, Waterstock, Oxford OX33
1HT
Direct access from M40 junction 8
onto A418 Thame road; less than 5
miles from Oxford and Thame, 30
mins from London and Birmingham.
Public parkland course.
18 holes, 6482 yards, Par 72; further
9 under construction for 1996
Founded April 1994
Visitors: welcome, etiquette and
clothing restrictions only.
Green Fee: £12/round WD,
£16/round WE.
Societies: welcome; attractive fees.
Catering: spike bar, bar and grill; full
meals for societies, catering up to 70.
Driving range, practce bunkering and
putting area.
Hotels: The Belfry (Milton); Country
Inn, Travelodge (Wheatley),

F69 Wavenden Golf Centre
☎(0908) 281811
Lower End Road, Wavendon, Milton
Keynes MK17 8DA
From M1 Junction 13 take A421 to
Milton Keynes, 1st left at roundabout,
1st left into Lower End Rd.
Public parkland course.
18 holes, 5361 yards, S.S.S.67; 9
holes Par 3, 1424 yards, S.S.S.25
Designed by John Drake/Nick Elmer
Founded Nov 1989
Visitors: welcome 7 days.
Green Fee: £9 WD, £12 WE.
Societies: welcome weekdays and
weekends.
Catering: carvery, downstairs bar,
bar meals.
Driving range.
Hotels: The Bell (Woburn); The Bell
(Winslow).

F70 West Berks
☎(0488) 638574
Chaddleworth, Newbury, Berks RG16
0HS
Off M4 at junction 14, follow signs to
RAF Welford.
Downland course.
18 holes, 7059 yards, S.S.S.74
Founded 1978
Visitors: welcome weekdays with
prior reservation.
Green Fee: £24.
Societies: by arrangement.
Catering: full service available.

F71 Weston Turville
☎(0296) 24084, 25949, 395376 Fax
New Rd, Weston Turville, Aylesbury,
Bucks HP22 5QT
A41 or A312, situated 2 miles from
Aylesbury town centre between
Aston Clinton and Wendover.
Parkland course.
18 holes, 6002 yards, S.S.S.69
Founded 1975
Visitors: welcome except Sun am.
Green Fee: on application.
Societies: weekdays, occasional
weekends.
Catering: lunches, evening snacks.

F72 Wexham Park
☎(0753) 663271
Wexham St, Wexham, Slough, Berks
SL3 6ND
2 miles from Slough towards
Gerrards Cross, follow signs to
Wexham Park Hospital and club is
0.5 mile further on.
Parkland courses.

The Duchess takes her Bow

When the idea of golf at Woburn was first conceived, the Dukes and Duchess courses were planned and cleared together. As events finally turned out the Duchess was delayed while the Dukes earned immediate praise, but now the Duchess forms a twin attraction that has very few equals.

In terms of character, the two courses have much in common, arising from the same dense forest in which it was virtually impossible twenty years ago to see more than ten yards ahead. The massive tree felling operation was the biggest ever undertaken on a new golf course in Britain but from the moment in the summer of 1979 when 18 holes on the Duchess were open for play, a remarkable story was complete.

Work only began on its construction in the summer of 1978, and in May 1979, after the severest winter for many years, half of it was not yet sown. Yet by October of that year all 18 holes were being played. Adjustments to the shape and levels of greens were made to mould with the natural contours, thus avoiding regular and artificial patterns.

This was all achieved by the club's own greenkeeping staff who wrought wonders. They were not the only ones who believed that it would have been impossible to have found a finer piece of land for an inland course in Britain; nor in thinking that you could hardly improve upon the arrangement whereby a course is built by those who subsequently have to look after it, but that doesn't lessen their achievement.

Now the courses share a number of professional tournaments and filmed matches as well as hosting the English Amateur strokeplay championship for the Brabazon Trophy, they are both liked and respected.

The Duchess is not as long, nor does it have the spectacular rises and falls that mark the beginning of the Dukes, but it is a supreme test of control, manoeuvrability and varied shotmaking.

The enjoyment of the Duchess lies in an ideal balance of its holes. There is contrast in the par 5s; the short holes vary nicely in length and there is a good mixture of par 4s from a drive and pitch to two full shots. The 1st gives a good first impression, the distant green on an elusive plateau being reached only with a well struck second from a tumbling fairway.

In four holes, in fact, there is all the variation you can have. The 2nd, a par 3 needs a shot through the eye of a needle; the 3rd calls for a straight drive and well judged pitch over a belt of heather and the 4th, a left hand dogleg, is a par 5 where there are many ways of taking six.

The 5th green in its alcove of giant beech is the first on the other side of the lane leading down to Bow Brickhill Church while the 6th, changing direction yet again, rewards positional play more than most par 5s.

It is a rare feature that no two consecutive holes follow the same direction and the short 7th twists back over the ancient earth-works that make an excellent golfing landmark. Next comes the 8th, a classic dogleg to a three level green, and then the turn is reached by way of the 9th green which, like the 10th tee, needed enormous build-up.

Over the brow at the 10th, the chief hazard is the angled green, but the 11th, 12th and 13th all have distinctive markings, the 13th occupying a natural little punchbowl. From there it is over the road again with two spanking two shot holes for the experts and two three shot holes for the rest.

There is no doubt that the finish is demanding but the 16th and 17th offer scenic relief, if nothing else; and by then the 18th is the only obstacle, though a tough one, between you and the other delights which Woburn has to offer. Swimming, tennis and squash await those with the energy to tackle them but a relaxing drink will be the comfort that most seek. In which case, you can survey a sylvan setting and ponder whether golf has anything better to offer.

18 holes, 5890 yards, S.S.S.66; 9 holes, 2851 yards, S.S.S.34; 9 holes, 2283, S.S.S.32
Designed by Emil Lawrence and David Morgan.
Founded 1976
Visitors: welcome.
Green Fee: on application.
Societies: welcome.
Catering: full catering service available.
Hotels: Wexham Park Hall, weekend golfing breaks and midweek packages inc hotel, golf & tuition.

F73 **The White Horse Inn**
☎(0869) 40272
Duns Tew, Oxon OX6 4JS
In centre of Duns Tew.
Hilly parkland course.
18 holes, 6147 yards, Par 72
Designed by Michael Watson-Smyth.
Founded 1986
Visitors: restricted to guests of White Horse Inn; free golf to residents.
Societies: only if resident.

F74 **Whiteleaf**
☎(0844) 274058 Sec
The Clubhouse, Whiteleaf, Aylesbury, Bucks
1.5 miles from Princes Risborough on Aylesbury road, turn 2nd right (The Holloway) for Whiteleaf; at T-junction turn left, then right after 250 yards into private road for club.
Undulating course.
9 holes, 5391 yards, S.S.S.66
Founded 1904

Visitors: not weekends.
Green Fee: £18 (18 holes), £25/day.
Societies: catered for on Thurs only.
Catering: lunch served except Mon.
Hotels: Bernard Arms; Thatchers.

F75 **Windmill Hill**
☎(0908) 378623, 271478 Fax
Tattenhoe Lane, Bletchley, Milton Keynes, Bucks MK3 7RB
M1 exit 13/14, take A421 through Milton Keynes towards Buckingham; 10 mins from M1.
Public parkland course.
18 holes, 6773 yards, S.S.S.72
Designed by Henry Cotton.
Founded 1972
Visitors: welcome at all times.
Green Fee: £6 WD, £8.80 WE.
Societies: welcome any time.
Catering: by prior arrangement.
Driving range.
Hotels: Forte Crest (Milton Keynes); Shenley (Bletchley).

F76 **Winter Hill**
☎(0628) 527613
Grange Lane, Cookham, Maidenhead, Berks SL6 9RP
4 miles from Maidenhead via M4; 6 miles from M40 via Marlow.
Parkland course.
18 holes, 6408 yards, S.S.S.71
Designed by Charles Lawrie.
Founded 1976
Visitors: welcome weekdays only.
Green Fee: £23 WD.
Societies: welcome, main day Wed.
Catering: full service available.
Hotels: Eurocrest.

F77 **Woburn Country Club**
☎(0908) 370756/7/8
Bow Brickhill, Milton Keynes MK17 9LJ
M1 exit 13, into Woburn Sands, turn left for Woburn, after 0.5 mile turn right at sign.
Dukes, 18 holes, 6940 yards, S.S.S.74; Duchess, 18 holes, 6641 yards, S.S.S.72
Designed by Charles Lawrie.
Founded 1976
Visitors: weekdays only by arrangement.
Green Fee: on application.
Societies: company days by prior arrangement.
Catering: meals served.
Hotels: Bedford Arms; Moore Place.

F78 **Wycombe Heights Golf Centre**
☎(0494) 816686, 812862 bookings, 816728 Fax
Rayners Ave, Loudwater, High Wycombe, Bucks HP10 9SW
M40 Junction 3, off A40
Pay-as-you-play parkland course.
18 holes, 6253 yards, S.S.S.72; 18 hole Par 3, 1955 yards
Designed by John Jacobs.
Founded 1991
Visitors: welcome, pay-as-you-play.
Green Fee: £10 WD, £13 WE.
Societies: welcome Tues-Fri, min 18.
Catering: bar, restaurant, family room.
Driving range.
Hotels: Post House Forte; Cressex; Alexandria.

G

BEDFORDSHIRE, NORTHAMPTONSHIRE, CAMBRIDGESHIRE, LEICESTERSHIRE

In the last four or five years, Northampton has gained two new courses on opposite sides of the city. Collingtree is an example of the American style of design and construction while the relocation of the Northampton Golf Club on Lord Spencer's Estate at Althorp epitomises the technique of blending courses harmoniously into a lovely, natural landscape.

Johnny Miller planned Collingtree on the lines of excavating a great lake and using the material to create a series of hills and mounds to balance an area that hitherto was a trifle barren. The lake itself has given rise to a par 5 18th hole with an island green. An impressive part of the development is the extensive teaching and practice facilities.

Harlestone Lake is equally a feature of the new home of the Northampton Golf Club, the 16th and 18th holes playing across it in full view of a delightful clubhouse that enjoys a magnificent position. Close by lies the Northamptonshire County Club at Church Brampton, which upholds a justifiably high reputation as amongst the best inland courses in England. It has the capacity to test all departments of a golfer's game as well as appealing to the aesthetic senses of those who care more about where they play than how they play.

Cold Ashby and Staverton Park are among Northamptonshire's other new courses in the last 20 years but the mantle of seniority belongs to Kettering GC which, in 1991, celebrated its Centenary in spite of the new by-pass running beside one corner of the course.

Gog Magog, east of Cambridge, is the pick of Cambridgeshire's Clubs with its 27 holes but Ramsey, St Ives and St Neots boast a countryside whose largely agricultural character has not been little eroded by the spread of the game. Large, open fen-like fields are not ideal for golf but a word for Ely City and Cambridgeshire Moat House Hotel which meet local needs adequately enough.

Bedfordshire was the birthplace of Henry Longhurst who played most of his early golf at the Bedfordshire GC then known a little less grandly as the Bedford GC. Bedford and County followed in 1912 and nowadays Bedford has a public course called Mowsbury. Memories of Dunstable Downs, South Bedfordshire at Luton and the excellent John O'Gaunt (36 holes) at Biggleswade involve county matches with BB & O in the south-eastern group, but Northamptonshire falls in the Midlands Group along with Leicestershire, where golf revolves much around the county town of Leicester itself.

Rothley Park, Glen Gorse, Leicestershire and Kirby Muxloe are all based on pleasant parkland but, though only 9 holes, one of the most charming courses is Charnwood Forest near the M1 at Loughborough. Hinckley and Market Harborough are established courses, Hinckley starting life as Burbage Common. Humberstone Heights and Kibworth are more recent while Rushcliffe and Willersley Park deserve a visit.

The stock of Leicestershire golf was enhanced considerably by the crowning in 1991 as Amateur champion of Gary Wolstenholme who learned and played all his early golf in the county.

G1 Abbotsley

☎(0480) 215153, 474000, 403280
Fax
Eynesbury Hardwicke, St Neots,
Cambs PE19 4XN
3 miles E of A1(M) through St Neots,
12 miles W of Cambridge on A45;
easy access along A45 from M11
junction 13
Undulating parkland/meadowland
course.
Old course, 18 holes, 6311 yards,
S.S.S.71; New course, 18 holes,
6087 yards, S.S.S.69
Designed by Derek Young, Vivien
Saunders, Jenny Wisson.
Founded 1986
Visitors: welcome every day; no
h/cap necessary.
Green Fee: Old course, £18 WD, £22
WE; New course, £10 WD, £12 WE.
Societies: weekdays and off-peak
weekends.
Catering: snacks, meals served 7
days; restaurant and bar facilities.

Driving range, squash (6 courts),
practise facilities, pool table, Vivien
Saunders residential golf school.
Hotels: 17-bed country Hotel on site.

G2 Aspley Guise & Woburn Sands

☎(0908) 583596 Sec, 582974
West Hill, Aspley Guise, Milton
Keynes MK17 8DX
2 miles W of M1 junction 13,
between Aspley Guise and Woburn
Sands.
Parkland course.
18 holes, 6135 yards, S.S.S.70
Designed by Sandy Herd.
Founded 1914
Visitors: welcome weekdays with
h/cap cert; with members weekends.
Green Fee: £21/round, £26/day.
Societies: Wed and Fri.
Catering: full facilities except Mon.
Hotels: Bedford Arms; Moore Place;
Broughton.

G3 Barkway Park

☎(0954) 50709
Nuthampstead Rd, Barkway, Nr
Royston, Herts SG8 8EN
On B1368 5 miles S of Royston.
Gently undulating woodland course.
18 holes, 7000 yards, Par 74; 9 hole
Par 3
Designed by Vivien Saunders.
Founded 1991
Visitors: welcome; weekend tee
times cannot be booked until Fri pm;
no non h/cap players before 11am.
Green Fee: £12 WD, £19 WE & BH.
Societies: very welcome, terms to
be arranged.
Catering: full facilities.
Practice area, indoor golf school.

G4 Beadlow Manor Hotel, Golf & Country Club

☎(0525) 860800
Beadlow, Nr Shefford, Beds SG17
5PH

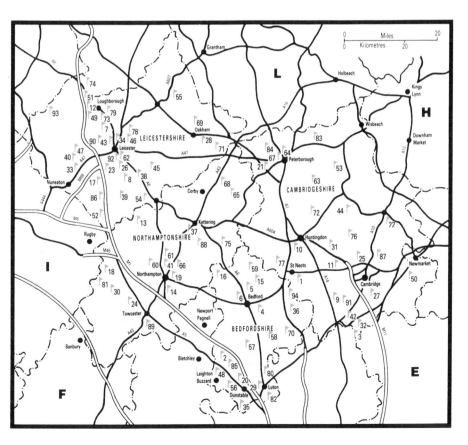

On A507 between Ampthill and Shefford, 1.5 miles W of Shefford.
Parkland course.
Baron Manhatten, 18 holes, 6619 yards, S.S.S.72; Baroness Manhatten, 18 holes, 6072 yards, S.S.S.71
Founded 1973
Visitors: welcome weekdays/weekends with h/cap cert.
Green Fee: approx £14/round WD, £27/round WE.
Societies: welcome anytime, selection of packages available.
Catering: Public bar serving snacks; 2 restaurants; Manor freehouse pub; private golf members bar.
Driving range, health club, 5 conference rooms.
Hotels: 30-bedroom hotel on site.

G5 Bedford & County
☎(0234) 352617, 359189 Pro shop, 357195 Fax
Green Lane, Clapham, Beds MK41 6ET
Off A6 N of Bedford before Clapham village.
Parkland course.
18 holes, 6347 yards, S.S.S.70
Founded 1912
Visitors: welcome weekdays, advisable to phone; with member weekends.
Green Fee: on application
Societies: Mon, Tues, Thurs and Fri.
Catering: available.

G6 Bedfordshire
☎(0234) 261669 Sec, 53241 Members
Bromham Rd, Biddenham, Bedford MK40 4AF
1.5 miles from town centre on A428, NW of town boundary.
Parkland course.
18 holes, 6172 yards, S.S.S.69
Founded 1891
Visitors: welcome weekdays only.
Green Fee: apply for details.
Societies: catered for on weekdays.
Catering: lunch daily.

G7 Birstall
☎(0533) 674322
Station Rd, Birstall, Leicester LE4 3BB
3 miles N of town just off A6.
Parkland course.
18 holes, 6222 yards, S.S.S.70
Founded 1901
Visitors: not weekends.

Green Fee: £25.
Societies: Wed and Fri by prior arrangement; reduction in green fees for parties over 20.
Catering: not Mon.
Billiards.

G8 Blaby
☎(0533) 784804
Lutterworth Rd, Blaby, Leics LE8 3DP
From Leicester, through Blaby village, course on left hand side.
9 holes, 2600 yards, Par 34
Founded 1991
Visitors: welcome, pay-as-you-play.
Green Fee: £4 (9 holes), £6 (18 holes) WD; £6 (9 holes), £8 (18 holes) WE.
Societies: welcome; also specialists in company days.
Catering: bar, bar meals.
Driving range.

G9 Bourn
☎(0954) 718057
Toft Rd, Bourn, Cambridge CB3 7TT
From Cambridge take road to Sandy, branch off on B1046; from M11 junction 12 take A603 to Sandy then B1046.
Parkland course.
18 holes, 6273 yards, S.S.S.70
Designed by J. Hull and S. Bonham.
Founded Sept 1991
Visitors: welcome; dress code applies.
Green Fee: £15/round WD, £25/round WE.
Societies: welcome weekdays.
Catering: bar snacks and restaurant meals.

G10 Brampton Park
☎(0480) 434700 Sec, 434705 Pro
Buckden Rd, Brampton, Huntingdon, Cambs PE18 8NF
0.5 mile E of A1; Northbound take 1st "Huntingdon" turning, Southbound take turning signposted "RAF Brampton".
Picturesque meadowland course by river with wooded lakes section.
18 holes, 6364 yards, S.S.S.73
Designed by Simon Gidman of Hawtree & Sons.
Founded 1990
Visitors: Welcome.
Green Fee: apply for details.
Societies: Welcome by arrangement with Sec except Sat and Sun.
Catering: Members bar; bar snacks and à la carte restaurant for lunch and dinner.

Hotels: Limited overnight accommodation on site; bargain break weekend and single night packages at Lion, Buckden.

G11 Cambridgeshire Moat House Hotel
☎(0954) 780555, 780098 Pro, 780010 Fax
Bar Hill, Cambs CB3 8EU
Adjacent to A604, 4 miles NW of Cambridge.
Undulating parkland course.
18 holes, 6734 yards, S.S.S.72
Founded 1974
Visitors: must be members of a golf club with letter of intro or membership card (unless hotel residents); phone to check course availability.
Green Fee: £19 WD, £25 WE & BH.
Societies: welcome; only resident societies at weekends.
Catering: full facilities.
Leisure facilites for Hotel residents.
Hotels: Cambridgeshire Moat House, bargain breaks/inclusive packages.

G12 Charnwood Forest
☎(0509) 890259
Breakback Rd, Woodhouse Eaves, Loughborough, Leics LE12 8TA
B591 off A6 at Quorndon, follow signs to Woodhouse Eaves; or M1 junction 23.
Undulating heathland course.
9 holes, 5960 yards, S.S.S.69
Founded 1890
Visitors: appointments required.
Green Fee: £17.50 WD, £20.50 WE and BH.
Societies: weekdays.
Catering: full facilities; light catering Mon and Thur.
Hotels: Kings Head; Quorn Country Club; Johnscliffe.

G13 Cold Ashby
☎(0604) 740548, 740099 Pro
Cold Ashby, Northampton NN6 7EP
5 miles E of M1 junction 18, just off A50 Northampton-Leicester road.
Undulating meadowland course.
18 holes, 6007 yards, S.S.S.69; 9 holes, Par 3
Designed by John Day.
Founded 1973
Visitors: welcome weekdays; after 2pm weekends; no h/cap restrictions.
Green Fee: £13.50/round, £20/day WD; £17/round WE.
Societies: welcome weekdays.

Catering: bar and restaurant daily.
Hotels: Post House (Crick); Broomhill (Spratton).

G14 Collingtree Park
☎(0604) 700000, 702600
Windingbrook Lane, Northampton NN4 0XN
From M1 Junction 15, follow A508 to Nottingham.
Parkland course, 18th hole is an Island Green.
18 holes, 6692 yards, S.S.S 72
Designed by Johnny Miller.
Founded 1987
Visitors: welcome, bookings taken 1 week in advance.
Green Fee: £20/round, £30/day WD; £30/round, £40/day WE.
Societies: Mon-Fri by arrangement, please ring for corporate brochure.
Catering: bar snacks at all times; Conservatory Restaurant, à la carte and table d'hôte, banqueting.
Golf Academy; driving range, practice grounds etc.
Hotels: Stakis (adjacent).

G15 Colmworth
☎(0234) 378181
Mill Cottage, Mill Rd, Colmworth, Beds MK44 2NV
5 miles NW of Bedford, off B660.
Undulating farmland course.
18 holes, 6459 yards, S.S.S.71
Designed by John Glasgow.
Founded 1991
Visitors: welcome, ring first; not before 10am or 1-1.30pm weekends.
Green Fee: £10 WD, £18 WE.
Societies: by prior arrangement.
Catering: available.
Practice green.

G16 Colworth
☎(0234) 222221
Unilever Research, Colworth House, Sharnbrook, Bedford MK44 1LQ
10 miles N of Bedford off A6 through village of Sharnbrook.
Parkland course.
9 holes, 2500 yards, S.S.S.32
Founded 1985
Visitors: with member only.
Green Fee: £3 with member only.

G17 Cosby
☎(0533) 864759
Chapel Lane, off Broughton Rd, Cosby, Leics LE9 5RG
A46 or A426 out of Leicester, in Cosby village take Broughton Rd.
Undulating parkland course.
18 holes, 6418 yards, S.S.S.71
Founded 1895
Visitors: welcome weekdays before 4pm; with member only weekends and Bank Holidays.
Green Fee: on application.
Societies: book with Sec in advance.
Catering: bar and meals except Mon; book with Steward.
Snooker.
Hotels: Time Out (Blaby).

G18 Daventry & District
☎(0327) 702829
Norton Rd, Daventry, Northants NN11 5LS
1 mile N of town, next to BBC Station.
Undulating meadowland course.
9 holes, 5812 yards, S.S.S.68
Founded early 1920s
Visitors: welcome, not before 11am Sun.
Green Fee: on application
Societies: contact Pro.
Catering: societies only.

G19 Delapre Park
☎(0604) 764036
Eagle Drive, Nene Valley Way, Northampton NN4 0DU
3 miles from M1 junction 15 on A508.
Public parkland course.
18 holes, 6293 yards, S.S.S.70; 9 holes, 2146 yards, S.S.S.32
Designed by J. Jacobs and J. Corby.
Founded 1976
Visitors: welcome.
Green Fee: on application.
Societies: welcome most days, applications in writing.
Catering: available daily from 9am to 9.30pm.
Driving range.
Hotels: Swallow; Moat House (preferential rates for socs, golf schools).

G20 Dunstable Downs
☎(0582) 604472 Sec, 662806 Pro
Whipsnade Rd, Dunstable, Beds LU6 2NB
2 miles from Dunstable on Whipsnade road B4541; from London via M1 junction 9, then A5 to town centre, left onto A505, left onto B4541; from N via M1 junction 11, A505 and B4541.
Downland course.
18 holes, 6255 yards, S.S.S.70
Designed by James Braid.
Founded 1907

Visitors: welcome weekdays if member of recognised club; h/cap cert required.
Green Fee: £25/round/day.
Societies: Tues and Thurs.
Catering: full facilites except Mon.
Hotels: Old Palace Lodge; Kitts Inn.

G21 Elton Furze
☎(0832) 280189
Bullock Rd, Haddon, Peterborough, Cambs PE7 3TT
From A1 take exit signposted Alwalton/Showground onto old A605; approximately 4 miles W of Peterborough.
Parkland course.
18 holes, S.S.S.70
Designed by Roger Fitton.
Founded April 1993
Visitors: welcome Tues and Thurs; h/cap cert required.
Green Fee: £20/round, £30/day.
Societies: Tues and Thurs, contact Pro shop for details.
Catering: full facilities.
Practice ground.

G22 Ely City
☎(0353) 662751 Sec, 663317 Pro, 668636 Fax
Cambridge Rd, Ely, Cambs CB7 4HX
On A10, on S outskirts of Ely going towards Cambridge.
Parkland course.
18 holes, 6602 yards, S.S.S.72
Designed by Henry Cotton.
Founded 1962
Visitors: h/cap cert required at all times unless playing with member.
Green Fee: £22/day WD, £30 WE & BH.
Societies: welcome Tues-Fri inclusive.
Catering: full facilities; restaurant, bar and bar snacks.
Hotels: Fenland Lodge; Nyton House; Lamb; Highways Motel.

G23 Enderby
☎(0533) 849388
Mill Lane, Enderby, Leics
From M1 junction 21 to Enderby, then follow signposts to Leisure Centre.
Municipal heathland course.
9 holes, 4232 yards, S.S.S.61
Founded 1986
Visitors: no restrictions.
Green Fee: on application
Societies: welcome by arrangement.
Catering: bar and bar snacks.
Leisure Centre.

G24 Farthingstone Hotel Golf & Leisure Club

☎(0327) 36291, 36560, 36566, 36645 Fax
Farthingstone, Towcester, Northants NN12 8HA
Junction 16 off M1, W off A5 between Weedon and Towcester, 3 miles from Weedon.
Undulating parkland course.
18 holes, 6330 yards, S.S.S.71
Designed by M. Gallagher.
Founded 1974
Visitors: welcome at all times.
Green Fee: £10/round, £15/day WD, £20/round, £30/day WE.
Societies: welcome at all times.
Catering: full facilities.
Snooker, squash, aerobics, etc.
Hotels: Farthingstone.

G25 Girton

☎(0223) 276169, 276991 Pro
Dodford Lane, Girton, Cambs CB3 0QE
3 miles N of Cambridge on A604.
Flat open course.
18 holes, 6085 yards, S.S.S.69
Founded 1936
Visitors: welcome weekdays.
Green Fee: £20/day with h/cap cert, £25/day without.
Societies: weekdays.
Catering: lunches, dinners served except Mon.
Hotels: Post House (Impington).

G26 Glen Gorse

☎(0533) 714159 Sec/Manager, 713748 Pro
Glen Rd, Oadby, Leicester LE2 4RF
Follow A6 out of Leicester towards Market Harborough, club on right between Oadby and Great Glen.
Parkland course.
18 holes, 6603 yards, S.S.S.72
Founded 1933
Visitors: welcome weekdays, weekends only with member.
Green Fee: £22/day (£7.50 with member)
Societies: weekdays; snacks or full meals available, green fee £25/day.
Catering: snack meals, sandwiches, full meals served except Mon.
Snooker room.
Hotels: Leicester Moat House.

G27 Gog Magog

☎(0223) 247626, 414990 Fax
Shelford Bottom, Cambridge CB2 4AB
2 miles S of Cambridge on A1307 Colchester road

Undulating course.
18 holes, 6386 yards, S.S.S.70; 9 holes, 5873 yards, S.S.S.68
Designed by Hawtree
Founded 1972
Visitors: weekdays with h/cap cert, weekends with member.
Green Fee: on application to Pro.
Societies: welcome Tues and Thurs by arrangement.
Catering: daily.
Hotels: University Arms; Garden House; Gonville.

G28 Greetham Valley

☎(0780) 460444 Clubhouse, 460666 Pro shop, (0572) 812616 Fax
Wood Lane, Greetham, Nr Oakham, Leics LE15 7RG
1 mile off A1, 8 miles from Oakham on B668; 10 mins from Stamford.
Parkland course.
18 holes, S.S.S.70 (27 holes from spring 1995); 9 holes Par 3
Designed by S.T.R.I.
Founded Oct 1991-April1992
Visitors: welcome any time, no bookings, h/caps rquired.
Green Fee: 18 hole course, £15/round, £25/day; Par 3 course, £3 WD, £4 WE.
Societies: welcome Mon-Fri only; 36 holes plus food for day £36, 36 holes £19, 18 holes £13.
Catering: Clubhouse open to non-members, bar snacks available; Lakeview restaurant open lunchtime and evenings.
Driving range, bowling green (opening 1994).

G29 Griffen

☎(0582) 415573
Caddington, Luton, Beds
From M1 junction 11 head towards Dunstable, left at 1st roundabout (Tesco), left at next roundabout onto A505, turn right to Caddington after 0.75 mile; signposted from Caddington village.
Meadowland course.
9 holes (18 from April 1995), 5516 yards, S.S.S.66
Founded 1982
Visitors: welcome, not before 2pm weekends; half set per person, golf shoes, no jeans.
Green Fee: £10/day (£5 with member) WD and WE after 2pm.
Societies: catered for by arrangement.
Catering: bar and snacks, meals to order.

G30 Hellidon Lakes Hotel and Country Club

☎(0327) 62550
Hellidon, Nr Daventry, Northants NN11 6LN
15 miles from M1 junction 16 by A45 and A361 Banbury road, turn right in village of Charwelton; 15 miles from M40 junction 11 by A361.
Undulating parkland course.
18 holes, 6700 yards, S.S.S.72; additional 9 holes spring 1994.
Designed by David Snell.
Founded Jan 1991
Visitors: welcome but must book through Pro shop; bona fide h/cap certs required at weekends.
Green Fee: £15 WD, £20 WE.
Societies: welcome by arrangement.
Catering: full facilities, restaurant, bar meals, conference and banqueting rooms.
Driving range, fly fishing, horse riding, tennis, snooker, health studio.
Hotels: Own 4-star hotel, inclusive golfing packages.

G31 Hemingford Abbots

☎(0480) 495000
Cambridge Rd, Hemingford Abbots, Cambs PE18 9HQ
Alongside A604 between Huntingdon and St Ives.
Public parkland course.
9 holes, 5468 yards, S.S.S.68
Designed by Advanced Golf Services.
Founded 1991
Visitors: welcome.
Green Fee: on application.
Societies: small meetings welcome.
Catering: bar, snacks etc.
Affiliated driving range.
Hotels: St Ives; The Bridge.

G32 Heydon Grange Golf & Country Club

☎(0763) 208988, 208926 Fax
Heydon, Royston, Herts SG8 7NS
M11 junction 10 onto A505 towards Royston, take 2nd left to Hayden, course signposted.
Downland/parkland course with lakes.
27 holes (3 X 9-hole loops) played in 3 18-hole combinations: A+B, 6512 yards, S.S.S.71; A+C, 6393 yards, S.S.S.70; B+C, 6629 yards, S.S.S.72; 9 holes, Par 3
Designed by Alan Walker.
Founded 1994
Visitors: welcome at all times; book in advance; correct dress required.
Green Fee: c. £15/round WD, £20/round WE.

Societies: and Company Days, welcome; packages available.
Catering: lounge bar, cocktail and wine bar, Grange Restaurant (Indian and SE Asian cuisine), Lakeside Restaurant (à la carte, carvery on Sun); conferences and functions catered for.
Driving range, extensive practice grounds.

G33 Hinckley
☎(0455) 615124
Leicester Rd, Hinckley, Leics LE10 3DR
NE boundary of Hinckley on A47.
Lakeside parkland course.
18 holes, 6517 yards, S.S.S.71
Founded 1894 (as Burbage Common; name changed 1981).
Visitors: Mon, Wed, Thurs and Fri; limited at weekends.
Green Fee: £20/round, £25/day after 9am.
Societies: Mon and Wed only by arrangement.
Catering: daily except Sun evenings. 2 snooker rooms
Hotels: Sketchley Grange; Hinckley Island; Three Pots Inn.

G34 Humberstone Heights
☎(0533) 761905 Office, 764674 Pro shop
Gipsy Lane, Leicester LE5 0TB
Off the Uppingham road opposite Towers Hospital.
Municipal parkland course
18 holes, 6444 yards, S.S.S.71
Designed by Hawtree & Son.
Founded 1978
Visitors: no restrictions.
Green Fee: apply for details.
Societies: weekdays only.
Catering: bar snacks; meals by arrangement.
Pitch & Putt course.

G35 Ivinghoe
☎(0296) 668696
Wellcroft, Ivinghoe, Leighton Buzzard, Beds LU7 9EF
Behind The Kings Head in Ivinghoe village, 4 miles from Tring and 6 miles from Dunstable.
Meadowland course.
9 holes, 4508 yards, S.S.S.62
Designed by R. Garrad & Sons.
Founded 1967
Visitors: after 9am weekdays, after 8am weekends.
Green Fee: £6 (18 holes) WD, £7 (18 holes) WE.

Societies: weekdays.
Catering: lunches except Mon.
Hotels: Rose & Crown (Tring); Stocks (Aldbury).

G36 John O'Gaunt
☎(0767) 260360
Sutton Park, Sandy, Beds SG19 2LY
On B1040 between Potton and Biggleswade.
Undulating parkland courses.
John O'Gaunt, 18 holes, 6513 yards, S.S.S.71; Carthagena, 18 holes, 5869 yards, S.S.S.69
Designed by Hawtree.
Founded 1948
Visitors: welcome, advisable to contact club.
Green Fee: £40/day WD, £50/day WE.
Societies: weekdays only.
Catering: full catering available.
Hotels: Stratton House (Biggleswade); Rose & Crown (Potton).

G37 Kettering
☎(0536) 512074
Headlands, Kettering, Northants NN15 6XA
Headlands joins Bowling Green Rd, on which are the Council Offices; continue along Headlands for c. 0.5 mile, past Fire Station on left, club is over railway bridge on right.
Meadowland course.
18 holes, 6036 yards, S.S.S.69
Designed by Tom Morris.
Founded 1891
Visitors: welcome weekdays; weekends, Bank Holidays with member.
Green Fee: £22, £10 with member.
Societies: Wed and Fri; apply for details.
Catering: lunch and evening meal except Mon.
Hotels: George Hotel; Royal Hotel; Park.

G38 Kibworth
☎(0533) 792301
Weir Rd, Kibworth, Beauchamp, Leics LE8 0LP
8 miles SE of Leicester on A6.
Meadowland course.
18 holes, 6312 yards, S.S.S.70
Founded 1962
Visitors: welcome weekdays.
Green Fee: £21/day (£6 with member)
Societies: catered for Mon, Wed, Thurs.

Catering: full facilities; special all-in package for societies including morning coffee, lunch and dinner.
Driving range, snooker
Hotels: Three Swans (Market Harborough); The Yews (Great Glen); Moat House (Oadby).

G39 Kilworth Springs
☎(0858) 575082
North Kilworth, Lutterworth, Leics LE17 6HJ
5 miles E of M1 junction 20, just off A427 towards Market Harborough.
Font 9 links, back 9 parkland/lake setting.
18 holes Championship course, Par 72
Founded 15th August 1993
Visitors: all welcome when tee times available; members have 7-day booking advantage.
Green Fee: £16/round WD, £20/round WE & BH; members £9 WD, £12 WE & BH.
Societies: welcome any time provided tee times available.
Catering: full catering and bar facilities; function room and board/meeting rooms available.
Hotels: Sun Inn (Marston Trussell); Wharf House (Welford); Denby (Lutterworth).

G40 Kingstand
☎(0533) 387908, 388087 Fax
Beggars Lane, Leicester Forest East, Leicester LE3 3NQ
Off main A47 Hinckley road; 5 mins M1 junction 21.
Parkland course.
9 holes (extending to 18 in 1994), 5380 yards, Par 66
Designed by S. Chenia.
Founded 1991
Visitors: welcome; dress code applies.
Green Fee: £6 (9 holes), £10 (18 holes).
Societies: times to be arranged with Pro; flexible terms.
Catering: bar and restaurant; also excellent Indian restaurant on site.
Driving range, gymnasium.

G41 Kingsthorpe
☎(0604) 710610 Sec, 711173 Clubhouse, 719602 Pro
Kingsley Rd, Northampton NN2 7BU
2 miles from town centre, off A508 to Market Harborough.
Undulating parkland course.
18 holes, 6006 yards, S.S.S.69

Designed by Charles Alison.
Founded 1908
Visitors: welcome weekdays by arrangement, not weekends.
Green Fee: £22/round/day (£10 with member).
Societies: welcome by arrangement, green fees £20 per day/round.
Catering: lunches, dinners served.
Hotels: Moat House; Swallow, Stakis; Holiday Inn.

G42 **Kingsway**
☎(0763) 262727, 263289 Fax
Cambridge Rd, Melbourne, Royston, Herts SG8 6EY
On A10, N of Royston, S of Cambridge.
Pay-and-Play course on landscaped farmland.
9 holes (18 from spring 1995), 2550 yards, Par 33
Founded April 1991
Visitors: welcome any time.
Green Fee: £5/round WD, £6/round WE & BH.
Societies: welcome by arrangement.
Catering: bar and restaurant.
Driving range, 9 hole Pitch & Putt.
Hotels: Cambridge.

G43 **Kirby Muxloe**
☎(0533) 393457 Sec
Station Rd, Kirby Muxloe, Leicester LE9 9EP
On A47 3 miles W of Leicester.
Parkland course.
18 holes, 6303 yards, S.S.S.70
Founded 1893
Visitors: not Tues, must have valid h/cap cert; Captains permission required at weekends.
Green Fee: £20/round, £25/day.
Societies: weekdays except Tues on application.
Catering: full facilities.
Snooker room, banqueting.
Hotels: Post House; Moat House.

G44 **Lakeside Lodge**
☎(0487) 740540 Sec, 741541 Pro/tee reservations
Fen Road, Pidley, Huntingdon, Cambs PE17 3DD
Pidley is on B1040 Ramsey-St Ives road.
Modern, challenging public course; suits all standards of golfer.
18 holes, 6821 yards, S.S.S.73; 9 holes Par 3
Designed by Alistair Headley.
Founded 1991

Visitors: welcome at any time.
Green Fee: 18 holes, £8.50 WD, £14 WE; 9 holes, £5 WD, £8 WE; Par 3 course £2 any time.
Societies: welcome weekdays.
Catering: full facilities available.
Driving range.
Hotels: Slepe Hall (St Ives), George (Ramsey).

G45 **Langton International**
☎(0858) 84374
Langton Hall, Leicester LE16 7TY
11 miles S of Leicester on A6, turn left after Kibworth, course 1.5 miles on left.
Parkland course.
18 holes, 6965 yards, Par 72
Designed by Hawtree & Co.
Founded 1993
Visitors: welcome.
Green Fee: £7round, £12/day WD; £10/round, £18/day WE.
Societies: welcome.
Catering: bar and light snacks.
Practice area.

G46 **Leicestershire**
☎(0533) 738825
Evington Lane, Leicester LE5 6DJ
Evington village in SE district of Leicester, 2 miles from city centre.
Parkland course.
18 holes, 6312 yards, S.S.S.70
Founded 1891
Visitors: welcome.
Green Fee: on application.
Societies: welcome weekdays by prior arrangement.
Catering: lunches and teas served daily.
Hotels: Daval; Rowans; Thornwood; Stanfre House; Gordon Lodge.

G47 **Leicestershire Forest Golf Centre**
☎(0455) 824800
Markfield Lane, Botcheston, Leics LE9 9FJ
2 miles from Botcheston, 3 miles SW of A50; 10 mins from M1 junction 21.
Well-wooded parkland course.
18 holes, 6111 yards, S.S.S.69
Founded March 1991
Visitors: welcome any time, pay-as-you-play; advisable to book tee times.
Green Fee: £10/round WD, £12/round WE.
Societies: welcome any time by arrangement.
Catering: bar, restaurant.
Driving range.

G48 **Leighton Buzzard**
☎(0525) 372143 Pro, 373811 Sec, 373812 Steward
Plantation Rd, Leighton Buzzard, Beds LU7 7JF
1 mile N of Leighton Buzzard off A418, take left fork at Stag Inn; or M1 junction 12 Toddington to Heath and Reach via Hockliffe.
Parkland course.
18 holes, 6101 yards, S.S.S.70
Founded 1925
Visitors: welcome weekdays except Tues with h/cap cert.
Green Fee: £18/round, £25/day, (£10 with member); £14 with member only WE & BH.
Societies: welcome except Tues and weekends, £39.50 full day package.
Catering: available 7 days.
Hotels: Swan; Hunt.

G49 **Lingdale**
☎(0509) 890035 Club, 890703 Sec, 890684 Pro
Joe Moore's Lane, Woodhouse Eaves, Loughborough, Leics LE12 8TF
5 miles S of Loughborough on B5330.
Undulating parkland course.
18 holes 6545 yards, S.S.S.71
Designed by D.W. Tucker & G. Austin.
Founded 1967
Visitors: welcome.
Green Fee: on application.
Societies: Mon to Fri by prior arrangement with Secretary.
Catering: full catering facilities.
Hotels: Kings Head; De Montford.

G50 **Links**
☎(0638) 662708
Cambridge Rd, Newmarket, Suffolk CB8 0TG
1 mile S of Newmarket High St.
Undulating parkland course.
18 holes, 6162 yards, S.S.S.71
Founded 1902
Visitors: not before 11.30am Sun unless with member; h/cap certs required.
Green Fee: £24 WD, £28 WE.
Societies: by arrangement.
Catering: full service except Mon.
Hotels: White Hart.

G51 **Longcliffe**
☎(0509) 239129
Snell's Nook Lane, Nanpantan, Loughborough, Leics LE11 3YA
1 miles from M1 junction 23 off A512 towards Loughborough.

Heathland course.
18 holes, 6551 yards, S.S.S.71
Founded 1904
Visitors: weekdays 8.30am-4.30pm with h/cap cert; weekends with member only.
Green Fee: apply for details.
Societies: Mon-Fri excluding Tues, Ladies day.
Catering: bar, restaurant, bar snacks.
Hotels: Kings Head.

G52 Lutterworth

☎(0455) 552532 Sec, 557199 Pro
Rugby Rd, Lutterworth, Leics LE17 5HN
0.5 mile from M1 exit 20 on A4114.
Undulating course.
18 holes, 5570 yards, S.S.S.67
Designed by D. Snell.
Founded 1904
Visitors: welcome weekdays; weekends with member only.
Green Fee: apply for details.
Societies: Mon to Fri.
Catering: full facilities 7 days.

G53 March

☎(0353) 52364
Frogs Abbey, Grange Rd, March, Cambs PE15 0YH
A141, W off March by-pass, signposted.
Parkland course.
9 holes, 6200 yards, S.S.S.70
Founded 1920
Visitors: weekdays only.
Green Fee: £15 (£7.50 with member)
Societies: welcome Mon to Fri with prior booking.
Catering: bar, normal hours; meals with prior booking.
Pool table.
Hotels: Griffin.

G54 Market Harborough

☎(0858) 463684
Oxendon Rd, Market Harborough, Leics
1 mile S of town on A508 Northampton road.
Parkland course.
9 holes (18 from end 1992), 6168 yards, S.S.S.69
Founded 1898
Visitors: welcome weekdays; with member only weekends.
Green Fee: apply for details.
Societies: welcome by arrangement.
Catering: facilities available.
Hotels: Three Swans.

G55 Melton Mowbray

☎(0664) 62118 Clubhouse/office, 69629 Pro
Thorpe Arnold, Melton Mowbray, Leics LE14 4SD
2 mile NE of Melton Mowbray on A609 Grantham road.
Undulating course.
18 holes, 6222 yards, S.S.S.70
Founded 1925
Visitors: welcome before 3pm.
Green Fee: £18 WD, £25 WE.
Societies: weekdays by arrangement, £27 for 27 holes inc meals etc.
Catering: full bar and restaurant facilities.
Hotels: Grange; George; Harborough; Stapleford Park.

G56 Mentmore

☎(0296) 662020, 662592 Fax
Mentmore, Leighton Buzzard, Beds LU7 0QN
On B489 4 miles SW of Leighton Buzzard.
Rolling parkland course with lakes and trees.
Roseberry, 18 holes, 6864 yards, Par 72; Rothschild, 18 holes, 6896 yards, Par 72
Designed by Bob Sandow.
Founded Oct 1992
Visitors: welcome; apply for details.
Green Fee: £25.
Societies: apply for details.
Catering: bar, restaurant; function suite for 120.
Practice ground, indoor swimming pool, sauna, steamroom, jacuzzi.
Hotels: Peadley Manor (Tring), special arrangements for golfers.

G57 Millbrook

☎(0525) 840252 Office, 402269 Pro shop
Millbrook, Beds MK45 2JB
Just E of M1 between junctions 12 and 13; from S take 12 and proceed to Flitwick, Steppingley and Millbrook: from N take 13, immediately right to Ridgmont and left at main Ampthill-Woburn road; course access opposite Chequers Pub in Millbrook.
Links course.
18 holes, 7100 yards, S.S.S.73
Designed by W. Sutherland.
Founded 1980
Visitors: at 24 hrs notice, weekdays except Thurs, weekends after 10.30am.
Green Fee: £20/half day, £35/day WD; £45day WE.

Societies: weekdays except Thurs; Sun after 12 noon.
Catering: bar and restaurant.
Hotels: White Hart; The Firs GH.

G58 Mount Pleasant

☎(0462) 850999
Station Rd, Lower Stondon, Henlow, Beds SG16 6JL
0.75 mile W of Stondon/Henlow Camp roundabout off A600 Hitchin to Bedford road.
Undulating meadowland course.
9 holes, 6172 yards, S.S.S.69
Designed by Derek Young.
Founded July 1992
Visitors: welcome at all times, booking advisable weekends and also evenings May-Sept.
Green Fee: £5 (9 holes), £9 (18 holes) WD; £7 (9 holes), £13 (18 holes) WE.
Societies: welcome, weekdays preferred.
Catering: bar snacks only, full catering by prior arrangement.
Putting green, pitching green, bunker and undercover nets.
Hotels: Bird in Hand.

G59 Mowsbury

☎(0234) 771041 Sec, 216374 Pro/bookings
Cleat Hill, Kimbolton Rd, Bedford MK41 8DQ
On Kimbolton Rd, from Bedford 2 miles N of city centre.
Municipal parkland course.
18 holes, 6514 yards, S.S.S.71
Designed by Hawtree.
Founded 1975
Visitors: welcome.
Green Fee: £5/round WD, £8/round WE.
Societies: on application to Facilities Manager (0234) 771493.
Catering: snacks, meals, drinks available; functions.
Driving range, squash.

G60 Northampton

☎(0604) 845155, 845102
Harlestone, Northampton NN7 4EF
On A428 Rugby road, approx 4 miles out of Northampton.
Parkland course.
18 holes, 6534 yards, S.S.S.71
Designed by Donald Steel.
Founded 1893
Visitors: currently only playing with member.
Green Fee: £25/day.
Societies: weekdays, not Wed.

Catering: full facilities available.
Snooker, banqueting.
Hotels: Northampton Moat House;
Heyford Manor.

G61 Northamptonshire County

☎(0604) 843025 Sec, 842170 Club,
842226 Pro
Golf Lane, Church Brampton,
Northampton NN6 8AZ
Off A50 Northampton-Leicester road,
4.5 miles from Northampton.
Undulating heathland/parkland
course.
18 holes, 6503 yards, S.S.S.71
Designed by H.S. Colt.
Founded 1909
Visitors: with h/cap by arrangement;
ladies Sat after 3.30pm; Sun after
11.15am.
Green Fee: £35/round/day; £10 with
member.
Societies: normally Wed only.
Catering: 11am-9pm summer;
11am-6pm winter, otherwise by
arrangement.
Hotels: Broomhill (Spratton);
Pytchley (West Haddon); Red Lion
(East Haddon).

G62 Oadby

☎(0533) 709052, 700215 Steward
Leicester Rd, Oadby, Leicester LE2
4AB
On A6 from Leicester, just outside
city limits, inside Leicester Race
Course.
Public meadowland course.
18 holes, 6376 yards, S.S.S.70
Founded 1975
Visitors: welcome.
Green Fee: on application
Societies: on application to Oadby
and Wigston Borough Council.
Catering: apply to Steward.

G63 Old Nene Golf & Country Club

☎(0487) 815622 Clubhouse,
813519 Sec, 710122 Pro shop
Muchwood Lane, Bodsey, Ramsey,
Cambs PE17 1XQ
1 mile N of Ramsey, half way
between Ramsey and Ramsey
Mereside.
Pay-as-you-Play, flat parkland
course with water features.
9 holes, 5524 yards, S.S.S.67
Designed by Richard Edrich.
Founded Aug 1992
Visitors: no restrictions subject to
tee reservations.

Green Fee: £7 (9 holes), £10 (18
holes) WD; £8 (9 holes), £12 (18
holes) WE & BH; reductions
weekdays for OAPs and jnrs.
Societies: welcome by prior booking
with Sec.
Catering: lounge, dining room, bar.
Driving range, snooker table, coarse
fishing.
Hotels: George, Yesteryear GH
(Ramsey); Swallow, Orton Hall
(Peterborough).

G64 Orton Meadows

☎(0733) 237478
Ham Lane, Orton Waterville,
Peterborough, Cambs PE2 0UU
On A625 Peterborough-Oundle road,
2 miles W of Peterborough at
entrance to Ferry Meadows Country
Park.
Municipal parkland course.
18 holes, 5800 yards, S.S.S.68
Designed by Dennis & Roger Fitton.
Founded 1987
Visitors: advance bookings
welcome.
Green Fee: £7.50 WD, £10 WE & BH.
Societies: welcome except before
11am Sun.
Catering: adjoining steakhouse "The
Granary".
Hotels: Moat House (Peterborough).

G65 Oundle

☎(0832) 273267
Benefield Rd, Oundle, Northants PE8
4EZ
On A427 Oundle-Corby road, 1.5
miles from Oundle.
Undulating parkland course.
18 holes, 5600 yards, S.S.S.67
Founded 1893
Visitors: after 10.30am weekends
and Bank Holidays, otherwise no
restriction.
Green Fee: £20/day WD, £30/day
WE.
Societies: welcome except Mon and
weekends.
Catering: full service available,
except Mon.
Hotels: Talbot; Bridge (Thrapston).

G66 Overstone Park

☎(0604) 671471, 671109 Fax
Billing Lane, Northampton NN6 0AP
Take A43 out of N'hampton towards
Kettering, turn off to follow signs for
Overstone; turn right after 200 yards
at signs for Billing/Overstone
Mansion; club clearly signposted off
to left.

Parkland course, set in 800 acre
Victorian walled estate.
18 holes, 6602 yards, S.S.S.72
Designed by Donald Steel.
Founded July 1993
Visitors: guests accompanying
members only.
Catering: bar and brasserie, spike
bar.
Health and leisure club; driving range
for members only.

G67 Peterborough Milton

☎(0733) 380489
Milton Ferry, Peterborough, PE6 7AG
On A47 4 miles W of Peterborough.
Parkland course.
18 holes, 6456 yards, S.S.S.72
Designed by James Braid.
Founded June 1938
Visitors: weekdays only by prior
arrangement with Sec.
Green Fee: on application.
Societies: weekdays only by prior
arrangement with Sec.
Catering: full facilities.
Hotels: Haycock Inn; Moat House.

G68 Priors Hall

☎(0536) 60756
Stamford Rd, Weldon, Northants
A43 Corby to Stamford road, 2 miles
E of Weldon.
Parkland course.
18 holes, 6677 yards, S.S.S.72
Founded 1965
Visitors: unlimited.
Green Fee: apply for details.
Societies: welcome weekdays.
Catering: snacks and meals.
Hotels: Charlon Manor.

G69 RAF Cottesmore

☎(0572) 812241 ext 7760
Oakham, Leicester LE15 7BL
7 miles N of Oakham off B668.
Parkland course,
9 holes, 5622 yards, S.S.S.67
Founded 1980
Visitors: with member only.
Green Fee: £5.

G70 RAF Henlow

☎(0462) 851515 ext 7083
Clubhouse, 7873 Sec
Henlow Camp, Beds SG16 6DN
3 miles SE of Shefford on A505,
follow signs to RAF Henlow.
Meadowland course.
9 holes, 5618 yards, S.S.S.67
Founded 1985
Visitors: only with member.

Northampton

Histories of Golf Clubs show that a great many of them began life on sites different to those which they now enjoy. Some early beginnings are recorded on photographs and plans that adorn clubhouse walls but, though moves have become rarer, one recent exception has been Northampton GC, which forsook their old home in the centre of the city in favour of an exciting future at Harlestone on the edge of Lord Spencer's estate near Althorp.

It came about as a result of intricate negotiations involving the Estate, the Club and a company wishing to develop the city site. Similar deals elsewhere have been discussed, but Northampton is one of the few that have brought hope to life. Having faced the increasing problem of existing within four rigid boundaries, the sense of spaciousness and rural splendour is profound.

However, an equally attractive part of the deal is a fine new clubhouse looking out over Harlestone Lake and three finishing holes which are unusual to say the least. The short 16th and 18th demand shots to carry the water while the 17th is a teasing hole where courage with the drive reaps a telling reward.

As the approach to the clubhouse dips down and up past the church, it is immediately clear that the modern Northampton has a special character that combines challenge with enjoyment — the principle requirements of any good course. There is a pleasant start with a second shot at the 1st to a green below, a short hole over water to a clearing in the wood and a par 5 from a high tee which needs a controlled drive in order to obtain the correct line for a second shot which is compellingly tree lined. This formed part of a clearance operation and the piping of a small stream that supplies the lake on the 2nd.

There are three or four changes of character in the layout which next introduces a dogleg round the perimeter of the wood and then, after another short hole, ventures forth into more open territory where the main features are a few large established trees and the boundary walls of mellow Northamptonshire stone.

Before the turn is reached back near the clubhouse, the 8th has another dropping second shot down a shallow valley while the 9th threads its way between ancient trees that are more trunk than foliage — a haven for owls and insects. The 10th scales a slight crest, leading back to the open ground where several holes run parallel, the par 5 12th carrying the added threat of out of bounds to sliced shots.

Bunkers guard the short 13th but gradually Harlestone Lake looms, the 15th carrying players down a long slope to a green in front of the old boat house reconstructed as a condition of planning approval. The 15th green lies close to the 18th but before the round is complete, there is a searching test of skill, nerve and decision, a climax that will be the centre of much debate, much gnashing of teeth and much jubilation.

Water holes are becoming more common in British golf, although few are more teasing than the par 3 16th with its green that is far wider than it is deep. Clearing the lake is one thing, but there are penalties for being big. Trees and sharp banks surround a sloping putting surface.

Position from the tee is important on the 17th but, in spite of a formidable carry from the 18th and an undulating fairway the other side, the pitch to the green can be quite demanding.

Together with the Collingtree course on the other side of town, the new Northampton has added a powerful dimension to the county's golf.

Green Fee: £6/day/round.
Societies: can be arranged through Sec.
Catering: light refreshment.
Hotels: Bird in Hand.

G71 RAF North Luffenham

☎(0780) 720041 ext 7523 or exchange
North Luffenham, Oakham, Leics LE15 8RL
Follow signposts for RAF North Luffenham from A606, station is close to Rutland Water.
Meadowland course.
9 holes, 6010 yards, S.S.S.70
Founded 1975
Visitors: with member or by appointment through Sec.
Green Fee: £7.
Societies: can be arranged through Sec.
Catering: bar and restaurant facilities.
Hotels: George; Crown.

G72 Ramsey

☎(0487) 812600, 813022 Pro
4 Abbey Terrace, Ramsey, Huntingdon, Cambs PE17 1DD
12 miles SE of Peterborough, off B1040.
Parkland course.
18 holes, 6133 yards, S.S.S.70
Designed by J. Hamilton Stutt.
Founded 1965
Visitors: weekdays only, on production of h/cap cert.
Green Fee: £20/round/day (£10 with member).
Societies: Mon, Tues, Wed.
Catering: full facilities.
6-rink outdoor bowling green.
Hotels: George (Ramsey).

G73 Rothley Park

☎(0533) 302019 Clubhouse, 302809 Sec, 303023 Pro
Westfield Lane, Rothley, Leicester LE7 7LH
6 miles N of Leicester, W of A46.
Parkland course.
18 holes, 6487 yards, S.S.S.71
Founded 1912
Visitors: welcome if member of recognised club with h/cap; members' guests only Tues, weekends and Bank Holidays.
Green Fee: £25/round, £30/day.
Societies: Wed and Thurs.
Catering: full catering except Mon.
Hotels: Rothley Court.

G74 Rushcliffe

☎(0509) 852959
Stocking Lane, East Leake, Loughborough, Leics LE12 5RL
Between Gotham and East Leake 6 miles N of Loughborough; easy reach of M1 junction 24.
Well-wooded heathland course.
18 holes, 6013 yards, S.S.S.69
Founded 1910
Visitors: welcome, properly dressed and preferably club golfers.
Green Fee: £22/day.
Societies: Mon-Fri, April 1 to Oct 31.
Catering: bar and restaurant.

G75 Rushden

☎(0933) 312581
Kimbolton Rd, Chelveston, Wellingborough, Northants NN9 6AN
On A45 2 miles E of Higham Ferrers.
Undulating meadowland course.
10 holes, 6335 yards, S.S.S.70
Founded 1919
Visitors: welcome weekdays except Wed pm; weekends with member only.
Green Fee: £15 (£10 with member).
Societies: bookable in advance.
Catering: any time except Mon.
Hotels: Westwood; Tudor Gate (Finedon).

G76 St Ives

☎(0480) 468392
Westwood Rd, St Ives, Cambs PE17 4RS
B1040 off A45.
Parkland course.
9 holes, 6100 yards, S.S.S.69
Founded 1923
Visitors: welcome weekdays; with member only weekends.
Green Fee: apply for details.
Societies: not weekends.
Catering: not Mon.
Hotels: Slepe Hall.

G77 St Neots

☎(0480) 472363 Sec, 474311 Club
Crosshall Rd, St Neots, Huntingdon, Cambs PE19 4AE
On A45 1.5 miles W of St Neots.
Parkland course with water hazards.
18 holes, 6027 yards, S.S.S.69
Designed by Harry Vardon (original 9).
Founded 1890
Visitors: welcome any day; weekends with member; h/cap cert required.
Green Fee: on application.
Societies: welcome except Sat, Sun, Fri and Mon.

Catering: full service in clubhouse.
Snooker.
Hotels: Eaton Oak; Kings Head.

G78 Scraptoft

☎(0533) 418863
Beeby Rd, Scraptoft, Leicester LE7 9SJ
Turn off A47 main Leicester to Peterborough road to Scraptoft at Thurnby.
Meadowland course.
18 holes, 6146 yards, S.S.S.69
Founded 1928
Visitors: welcome; jacket, collar and tie.
Green Fee: on application.
Societies: Mon-Fri.
Catering: meals served except Mon.
Hotels: White House.

G79 Shelthorpe

☎(0509) 267766
Poplar Road, Loughborough, Leics
From Leicester on A6 turn right at 1st traffic lights, over island, then 2nd left, signposted.
Municipal parkland course.
18 holes Par 3, c. 3000 yards
Visitors: welcome.
Green Fee: apply for details.

G80 South Bedfordshire

☎(0582) 591500 Sec, 591209 Pro
Warden Hill Rd, Luton, LU2 7AA
3 miles N of Luton on A6, signposted (right) into Warden Hill Rd; left at end, slip road to right of School.
Undulating course; some trees, hawthorn hedges; dries well.
Galley course, 18 holes, 6342 yards, S.S.S.71; Warden course, 9 holes, 2490 yards, S.S.S.64
Founded 1892
Visitors: welcome; Galley weekdays only with h/cap cert unless by prior arrangement; Warden any time.
Green Fee: Galley, £17/round, £27/day; Warden, £11 (18 holes).
Societies: mainly Wed, Thurs.
Catering: snacks from 10.30am-9.30pm; set lunch, dinner by arrangement.
Snooker.
Hotels: Culverdene; Chiltern; Strathmore; many small hotels.

G81 Staverton Park

☎(0327) 705911
Staverton, Daventry, Northants NN11 6JT
On A425 Daventry to Leamington

road, 1 mile S of Daventry; near M1 exits 16/18 and M40 exits 11/12. Undulating meadowland course.
18 holes, 6204 yards, S.S.S.70
Designed by Commdr John Harris.
Founded 1978
Visitors: welcome.
Green Fee: apply for details.
Societies: welcome Mon-Fri.
Catering: full facilities at all times.
Snooker, solarium, sauna, trimnasium, banqueting suites.
Hotels: special golf inclusive Badger Breaks, phone for details.

G82 **Stockwood Park**
☎(0582) 413704 Pro
Stockwood Park, London Rd, Luton, Beds LU1 4LX
M1 junction 10, turn left towards town centre, then left at 1st set of traffic lights into Stockwood Park.
Meadowland course.
18 holes, 6049 yards, S.S.S.69
Designed by Charles Lawrie.
Founded 1973
Visitors: welcome at all times.
Green Fee: £7.10 WD, £9.30 WE.
Societies: Mon/Tues/Thurs, contact Pro.
Catering: breakfast and lunch; dinner for societies by arrangement.
Driving range, 9-hole Pitch & Putt.
Hotels: Strathmore.

G83 **Thorney Golf Centre**
☎(0733) 270570
English Drove, Thorney, Peterborough, Cambs PE6 0TJ
A47 E of Peterborough.
Municipal fenland course.
18 holes, S.S.S. 69; 9 holes, Par 3.
Designed by A. Dow.
Founded May 1991
Visitors: unlimited.
Green Fee: 18 hole course, £4.80 WD, £6.80 WE; Par 3, £2.50, unlimited rounds.
Societies: any time.
Catering: bar and restaurant.
Driving range.

G84 **Thorpe Wood**
☎(0733) 267701
Nene Parkway, Peterborough PE3 6SE
On A47 to Leicester 2 miles W of Peterborough, next to Moat House Hotel.
Parkland course.
18 holes, 7086 yards, S.S.S.74
Designed by Peter Alliss & Dave Thomas.

Founded 1975
Visitors: unrestricted.
Green Fee: £8 WD, £11 WE & BH.
Societies: by arrangement up to a year in advance.
Catering: at Greenkeeper.
Hotels: The Moat House.

G85 **Tilsworth**
☎(0525) 210721
Dunstable Rd, Tilsworth, Leighton Buzzard, Beds
On A5, 1 mile N of Dunstable.
Parkland course.
18 holes, 5306 yards, S.S.S.66
Founded 1972
Visitors: welcome all times except Sun 7.30-11.30am.
Green Fee: £8 (18 holes) WD, £10 (18 holes) WE.
Societies: welcome weekdays.
Catering: hot and cold food available lunchtimes Mon-Sat, also Thurs, Fri, Sat evenings.
Driving range.
Hotels: Swan; Crest (Luton).

G86 **Ullesthorpe**
☎(0455) 209023
Frolesworth Rd, Ullesthorpe, Lutterworth, Leics
B577 off A5 to Claybrooke and Ullesthorpe, follow signs to course.
Meadowland course.
18 holes, 6650 yards, S.S.S.72
Visitors: weekdays.
Green Fee: on application
Societies: weekdays.
Catering: bar snacks and restaurant.
Leisure facilities at hotel.
Hotels: 39-bed hotel on site.

G87 **Waterbeach Barracks**
☎(0223) 861048 Sec
39th Engineering Regiment, Waterbeach, Cambs CB5 9PA
Fenland course.
9 holes, 6237 yards, S.S.S.70
Founded 1972
Visitors: HM Forces welcome, civilians must be introduced by and play with member.
Green Fee: apply for details.
Catering: limited bar.

G88 **Wellingborough**
☎(0933) 677234
Harrowden Hall, Great Harrowden, Wellingborough, Northants NN9 5AD
1 mile NE of Wellingborough to right of A509.
Parkland course.

18 holes, 6617 yards, S.S.S.72
Designed by Hawtree & Sons.
Founded 1893
Visitors: welcome weekdays except Tues with h/cap cert.
Green Fee: £22/round, £27/day.
Societies: Wed, Thurs, Fri by prior arrangement; with h/cap certs.
Catering: bar, snacks, restaurant.
Snooker, swimming pool.
Hotels: Hind; Oak House; Tudor Gate.

G89 **West Park Golf & Country Club**
☎(0327) 858092
Whittlebury, Nr Towcester, Northants NN12 8XW
On A413, 15 mins from M1 junction 15a, M40 junction 10.
Parkland/lakeland course.
4 X 9 hole loops, giving 6700 yard, Par 72 combinations.
Designed by Cameron Sinclair.
Founded June 1992
Visitors: welcome; h/cap certs not required but h/cap standard expected.
Green Fee: £20 (18 holes).
Societies: welcome at all times subject to availability.
Catering: bars, bistros and restaurant; function suite.
9 hole indoor course, clay pigeon shoot, archery etc; corporate hospitality.
Hotels: own hotel under construction.

G90 **Western Park**
☎(0533) 872339
Scudamore Rd, Braunstone Frith, Leicester LE3 1UQ
Off A47, 2 miles W of city centre.
Public parkland course.
18 holes.
Designed by F.W. Hawtree.
Founded c. 1900
Visitors: welcome; book at weekends.
Green Fee: on application
Societies: welcome.
Catering: 7 days a week.

G91 **Whaddon Golf Centre**
☎(0223) 207325
Church St, Whaddon, Nr Royston, Cambs SG8 5RX
4 miles N of Royston, 9 miles S of Cambridge off A603.
Public parkland course.
9 holes Par 3, 795 yards

Designed by Richard Green
Founded 1987
Visitors: welcome.
Green Fee: £2.50 (9 holes) WD, £3 WE.
Catering: bar snacks.
Driving range, putting green.

G92 **Whetstone**

☎(0533) 861424
Cambridge Rd, Cosby, Leicester LE9 5SH
4 miles from M1 junction 21, SE of Leicester; take A46 to Narborough, then signposts to Whetstone.
Wooded parkland course with water features.
18 holes, 5795 yards, S.S.S.68
Designed by Nick Leatherland.
Founded 1963
Visitors: welcome; restricted weekends, book in advance.
Green Fee: apply for details.

Societies: by prior arrangement.
Catering: bar and cold snacks.
Driving range.
Hotels: Time Out (Blaby).

G93 **Willesley Park**

☎(0530) 414596
Tamworth Rd, Ashby-de-la-Zouch, Leics LE65 2PF
On B5006 approx 1.5 miles from centre of Ashby-de-la-Zouch S towards Tamworth; from M42 junction 11, 2 miles N towards Ashby-de-la-Zouch on B5006.
Parkland/heathland course.
18 holes, 6304 yards, S.S.S.70
Designed by C.K. Cotton.
Founded 1921
Visitors: with reservation, must be bona fide members of another club.
Green Fee: £25 WD, £30 WE & BH.
Societies: Wed, Thurs, Fri (April-Sept) by arrangement.

Catering: full facilities.
Snooker.
Hotels: Royal; Fallen Knight.

G94 **Wyboston Lakes**

☎(0480) 219200 Sec, 212501 Pro
Wyboston Lakes, Wyboston, Beds MK44 3AL
Off A1 S of St Neots.
Public parkland course round lakes.
18 holes, 5310 yards, S.S.S.69
Designed by Neil Oackden.
Founded 1981
Visitors: welcome; weekend bookings 1 week in advance through Pro.
Green Fee: £10 (18 holes), £5 (9 holes) WD; £14 (18 holes), £7 (9 holes) WE; twighlight ticket £7 after 1pm winter, after 5pm summer.
Societies: welcome.
Catering: full catering
Hotels: motel on site.

H

SUFFOLK, NORFOLK

Suffolk and Norfolk provide all the ingredients for a perfect golfing holiday, any number of excellent courses — seaside and inland — in settings that give golfers a special sense of escape.

Journeys from London have been considerably assisted by new roads plus a bridge over the River Orwell at Ipswich which is spectacular, but East Anglia remains something of a quiet backwater which contributes greatly to its popularity. Felixstowe Ferry, the place where Bernard Darwin learned to play, is the oldest, retaining a measure of its quaintness in spite of many changes since the clubhouse was based around its famous Martello Tower.

The best holes are those nearest the sea, those on the other side of the road filling the flatter land, although perhaps the most unusual hole, the short 12th, straddles the road with the tee shot having to clear a safety net to protect the passers-by — motorised and pedestrian.

Further up the coast lie Aldeburgh and Thorpeness, contrasting Clubs and courses that can, nevertheless, be conveniently taken together. For all the nearness of the sea, neither can be classed as seaside, Thorpeness with a profusion of heather and Aldeburgh weaving its crafty way between the gorse across the common.

Woodbridge is another Suffolk delight in an area around Ipswich which includes Purdis Heath and Rushmere.

Crossing the county boundary into Norfolk, the coastal path heads for Great Yarmouth & Caister, founded in 1882, Sheringham, Brancaster and Hunstanton. Lovers of racing will have identified Great Yarmouth & Caister from the stands, the first and last holes hurdling the rails and several others enclosed by the track.

The best is very good after a slightly mundane start but the focus for the connoisseur is fixed on Hunstanton and the Royal West Norfolk links at Brancaster which occupy as remote a tract as any on which the game is played. Hunstanton, 100 years old in 1991, is a full-blown championship test divided by a central ridge of dunes that gives it a bit of a Jekyll and Hyde character. Brancaster, on the other hand, derives its character more from deep sleepered bunkers, sandy turf, a unique stretch of marshland and a rich variety in the size, angling, shaping and defence of its greens. A year junior to Hunstanton, it rubs shoulders with nature in all its aspects, adverse weather adding a wild, bleak dimension that, for all its ferocity, can add appeal.

On more modern lines are the two courses and varied leisure facilities at Barnham Broom on the outskirts of Norwich, which gain in popularity.

Cambridge University golfers have an understandably soft spot for East Anglia, fixtures, in addition to Hunstanton, including Royal Norwich and, in the old days, a final trial at Thetford which has had a fine new clubhouse and a changed course since then. The changes, dictated by the Thetford-by-pass, necessitated intrusion into the forest — or at least what was forest until the terrible storm of October 1987. Only a few scraggy pines survived the blast but Thetford, ancient and modern, is full of charm that deserves to be sampled.

From Thetford, it is relatively plain sailing to Cambridge either through or round Newmarket but, on the way, there is a port of call at Royal Worlington & Newmarket which you overlook at your peril.

Given the accolade by Bernard Darwin of "the sacred nine", it is a masterpiece of simple design, a triumph in fitting a quart into a pint pot. In winter, it is a veritable haven that offers the ideal of a day of foursomes with the lure of characteristic refreshment to re-fuel the system. Throughout the world, I have enjoyed nothing better.

H1 **Aldeburgh**
☎(0728) 452890, 453309 Pro
Saxmundham Rd, Aldeburgh, Suffolk
IP15 5PE
6 miles E of A12 midway between
Ipswich and Lowestoft.
Heathland course.
18 holes, 6330 yards, S.S.S.71; 9
holes, 4228 yards, S.S.S.64
Designed by John Thompson and
Willie Fernie.
Founded 1884
Visitors: welcome weekdays;
weekends by arrangement with Sec;
h/cap required for 18 hole course; no
3 or 4 ball games permitted on 18
hole course, 2 ball or foursomes only.
Green Fee: on application.
Societies: welcome by arrangement
with Sec.
Catering: lunches served.
Hotels: Wentworth; White Lion;
Brudenell; Uplands.

H2 **Alnesbourne Priory**
☎(0473) 727393
Priory Park, Ipswich, Suffolk IP10
0JT
Leave A45 Ipswich southern by-pass
at exit marked Ransomes Europark,
Nacton; follow signs to Industrial
Estate; take 1st left after 200 yards,
follow single lane road for 1 mile to
reception.
Pretty parkland course fronting
Orwell estuary.
9 holes, 1760 yards, S.S.S.58
Founded 1987
Visitors: always closed Tues,
experienced golfers in correct attire
welcome any other time.
Green Fee: between £9 and £12 for
afternoon or day ticket.
Societies: restricted to Tues only by
arrangement.
Catering: bar and restaurant;
function room.
Tennis, heated outdoor swimming
pool in summer, Adventure
Playground, nature trails.
Hotels: log cabin accommodation on
site; also 50 executive touring sites.

H3 **Barnham Broom Hotel Golf & Country Club**
☎(060 545) 393
Honingham Rd, Barnham Broom,
Norwich, Norfolk NR9 4DD
10 miles SW of Norwich between
A11 and A47.
River valley and parkland courses.
Hill, 18 holes, 6628 yards, S.S.S.72;
Valley, 18 holes, 6470 yards,
S.S.S.71

Designed by Frank Pennink (Valley),
Donald Steel (Hill).
Founded 1977
Visitors: welcome weekdays;
residents 7 days; proof of club
membership required.
Green Fee: £25/round, £30/day.
Societies: welcome, details on
application.
Catering: full restaurant, snack bar.
Leisure centre, squash, tennis,
snooker etc.
Hotels: Barnham Broom, golf
"getaway breaks", details on request.

H4 **Bawburgh**
☎(0603) 746390 Clubhouse,
742323 Pro
Long Lane, Bawburgh, Norfolk NR9
3LX
To S of Royal Norfolk Showground;
take Bawburgh exit off A47 Norwich
southern bypass.
Parkland/heathland course.
18 holes, 6066 yards, S.S.S.70
Designed by S. Manser.
Founded 1978, extended 1992
Visitors: welcome by arrangement.
Green Fee: £14 WD, £20 WE.
Societies: welcome by arrangement
only.
Catering: limited until late 1994; bar
and snack meals.
Driving range.
Hotels: Park Farm.

H5 **Bungay & Waveney Valley**
☎(0986) 892337
Outney Common, Bungay, Suffolk
NR35 1DS
A143 Bury St Edmunds to Great
Yarmouth road, about 0.5 mile from
town centre.
Heathland course.
18 holes, 6063 yards, S.S.S.69
Designed by James Braid.
Founded 1889
Visitors: welcome weekdays only;
with member at weekends.
Green Fee: £18/day/round.
Societies: arranged by writing to
club; weekdays only.
Catering: full (snacks Mon).
Hotels: The Swan; King's Head.

H6 **Bury St Edmunds**
☎(0284) 755979
Tuthill, Bury St Edmunds, Suffolk
IP28 6LG
1st exit eastbound off A45 for Bury,
0.25 mile down B1106 to Brandon on
right.

Parkland course.
18 holes, 6615 yards, S.S.S.72; 9
holes, 4664 yards, S.S.S.62
Designed by Hawtree (9 hole), Ray
(18 hole).
Founded 1924
Visitors: welcome weekdays inc.
Bank Holidays; only with member
weekends.
Green Fee: 18 hole course, £26 (2
rounds); 9 hole course, £11.
Societies: weekdays by
arrangement; not weekends or Bank
Holidays.
Catering: full service available.

H7 **Costessy Park**
☎(0603) 746333
Old Costessy, Norwich, Norfolk NR8
5AL
3 miles W of Norwich, turn off A47 at
Round Well public house.
Parkland/river valley course.
18 holes, 5964 yards, S.S.S.69
Designed by Frank Macdonald.
Founded 1983
Visitors: welcome, not before
11.30am weekends.
Green Fee: apply for details.
Societies: by arrangement.
Catering: full catering and bar
facilities.
Practice area; golf cart hire for
physically handicapped.

H8 **Cretingham**
☎(0728) 685275
Cretingham, Woodbridge, Suffolk
IP13 7BA
2 miles from A1120 at Earl Soham;
10 miles N of Ipswich.
Parkland course.
9 holes, 4024 yards, S.S.S.64
Founded 1984
Visitors: welcome every day from
8am until dusk; h/caps not required.
Green Fee: £7day WD, £10/day WE
& BH.
Societies: by arrangement.
Catering: licensed bar, bar snacks;
catering for groups.
Practice range, 5-hole Pitch & Putt,
snooker, outdoor swimming pool,
tennis, caravan park.

H9 **Dereham**
☎(0362) 695900 Club, 695631 Pro
Quebec Rd, Dereham, Norfolk NR19
2DS
Take B1105 from Dereham.
Parkland course.
9 holes, 6225 yards, S.S.S.70
Founded 1934

Visitors: welcome with h/cap cert; only with member weekends.
Green Fee: £16 WD, £10 WE (with member).
Societies: by arrangement.
Catering: meals and snacks on demand, sandwiches only on Mon.
Hotels: Phoenix; George; Kings Head.

H10 Diss
☎(0379) 642847 Steward/Club, 641025 Sec, 644399 Pro
Stuston Common, Diss, Norfolk IP22 3JB
Half way between Norwich and Ispwich, 2 miles W of A140 (turn at Scole).
Commonland course.
18 holes, 6238 yards, S.S.S.70
Founded 1903
Visitors: welcome, weekends after 4pm in summer; no restrictions Oct-March.
Green Fee: £20/day.
Societies: very welcome weekdays.
Catering: full facilities, excellent restaurant in refurbished clubhouse.
Driving range nearby.

H11 Eagles
☎(0553) 827147
39 School Road, Tilney All-Saints, King's Lynn, Norfolk PE34 4RS
On A47 between King's Lynn and Wisbech, 5 miles from King's Lynn.
Public moorland course.
9 holes, 4284 yards, S.S.S.61; 9 holes Par 3
Designed by David Wilson Horn.
Founded Nov 1990
Visitors: welcome any time.
Green Fee: £5.50 (9 holes) WD, £6.50 WE.
Societies: ring for details.
Catering: bar facilities.
Driving range.
Hotels: Butterfly; Globe.

H12 Eaton
☎(0603) 51686
Newmarket Rd, Norwich NR4 6SF
Off A11 into Sunningdale, signposted; approx 1.5 miles from centre of Norwich.
Undulating course.
18 holes, 6125 yards, S.S.S.69
Founded 1910
Visitors: welcome all week.
Green Fee: £28 (£15 half day) WD; £35 (£20 half day) WE.
Societies: welcome by prior arrangement.

Catering: lunches served weekdays; teas all week.
Hotels: Post House; Hotel Norwich.

H13 Fakenham
☎(0328) 862867 reception, 863534 Pro
Sports Centre, The Race Course, Fakenham, Norfolk
B1146 from Dereham or A1067 from Norwich.
Parkland course.
9 holes, 5992 yards, S.S.S.69
Designed by Charles Lawrie.
Founded 1981
Visitors: welcome.
Green Fee: apply for details.
Societies: by arrangement.
Catering: in Sports Centre.
Hotels: Crown; Limes; The Mill.

H14 Felixstowe Ferry
☎(0394) 286834
Ferry Rd, Felixstowe, Suffolk IP11 9RY
A45 to Felixstowe, avoid turning right off A45; follow signs to Yatching Centre.
Links course.
18 holes, 6042 yards, S.S.S.70
Designed by Henry Cotton & Sir Guy Campbell.
Founded 1880

Visitors: welcome weekdays and after 10.30am weekends and Bank Holidays
Green Fee: £20/day WD, £24 WE & BH.
Societies: Tues, Wed and Fri.
Catering: lunch available 7 days; evening meals by arrangement.
Hotels: Orwell Moat House.

H15 Feltwell
☎(0842) 827644, 827762
Thor Ave, Feltwell, Thetford, Norfolk IP26 9XX
0.5 mile S of Feltwell on B1112; right towards 2 large "Golf balls" (satellite tracking station).
Open heathland course.
9 holes (18 tees), 6260 yards, S.S.S.70
Founded 1972
Visitors: welcome, sometimes restricted at weekends.
Green Fee: £12 WD, £20 WE & BH.
Societies: any weekday.
Catering: bar; catering by arrangement.
Hotels: Brandon House (Brandon).

H16 Flempton
☎(0284) 728291
Flempton, Bury St Edmunds, Suffolk IP28 6EQ.

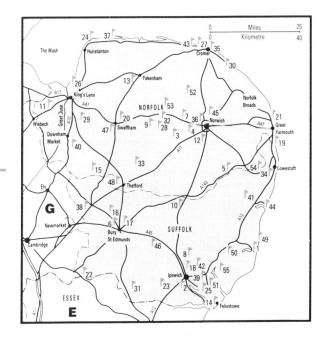

4 miles NE of Bury St Edmunds on A1101 to Mildenhall.
Breckland course.
9 holes, 6240 yards, S.S.S.70
Designed by J. H. Taylor.
Founded 1895
Visitors: with members only at weekends and Bank Holidays; h/cap certs required except when playing with member.
Green Fee: £18.50 (18 holes), £24/day.
Societies: very limited.
Catering: excellent by arrangement.
Hotels: Angel Hotel (Bury St Edmunds); Bell Hotel (Mildenhall).

H17 Fornham Park Golf & Country Club

☎(0284) 706777, 706721 Fax
St John's Hill Plantation, The Street, Fornham All Saints, Bury St Edmunds, Suffolk IP28 6JQ
Off A45 to Bury St Edmunds (2 miles), B1101 to Brandon; or A134 Bury-Thetford road at Fornham St Martin.
Parkland course.
18 holes, 6209 yards, S.S.S.70
Founded 1976
Visitors: welcome, phone Pro; not Tues pm, not before 12am weekends.
Green Fee: £15/round, £20/day WD; E15/round after 12am WE.
Societies: welcome weekdays only.
Catering: bar and meals available.
Hotels: Butterfly, Suffolk, Angel, Priory, Bell (Thetford).

H18 Fynn Valley

☎(0473) 785463, 785632 Fax
Witnesham, Ipswich, Suffolk IP6 9JA
On B1077, 2 miles due N of Ipswich.
Parkland course.
18 holes, 5700 yards, S.S.S.67; 9 holes Par 3, 1000 yards.
Designed by Tony Tyrrell.
Founded April 1991
Visitors: not Sun or Wed am (Ladies); proper golf equipment and clothing on main course.
Green Fee: £7.50 for 9 holes, £13.50 for 18 holes, £15/day; Par 3 course, £3.50/round, £5/day; discounts for jnrs.
Societies: welcome any weekday except Wed.
Catering: bar and light refreshments, full restaurant and lounge.
Driving range, multi-level practice bunkers, chipping and putting greens.

H19 Gorleston

☎(0493) 661911
Warren Rd, Gorleston, Great Yarmouth, Norfolk NR31 6JT
Off A12 Yarmouth to Lowestoft road, Yarmouth end of dual carriageway, follow signs down Links Rd to Squash Club, entrance 200 yards on left.
Seaside course.
18 holes, 6404 yards, S.S.S.71
Founded 1906
Visitors: welcome but phone call advisable; h/cap cert required.
Green Fee: apply for details.
Societies: weekdays by prior arrangement.
Catering: available.
Hotels: Cliff; St Edmunds.

H20 Granary Hotel Golf & Country Club

☎(0328) 701310
Little Dunham, Nr Swaffham, King's Lynn, Norfolk PE32 2DF
Off A47 at Necton/Dunham crossroad.
Parkland course with lakes.
9 holes, 4422 yards, Par 64
Founded 1987
Visitors: welcome.
Green Fee: £10 WD, £14 WE.
Societies: welcome.
Catering: full catering, first class restaurant.
Leisure facilities under development.
Hotels: Granary Hotel.

H21 Great Yarmouth & Caister

☎(0493) 728699
Beach House, Caister-on-Sea, Great Yarmouth, Norfolk NR31 5TD
About 1 mile N of Great Yarmouth on A149 take right turn at roundabout, then right into signposted lane.
Seaside links course.
18 holes, 6235 yards, S.S.S.70
Founded 1882
Visitors: welcome, phone first.
Green Fee: apply for details.
Societies: welcome by arrangement.
Catering: coffee, lunch and evening meals always available.
Hotels: Carlton; Cavendish; Hamilton; Ocean Edge; Sandringham; Windyshore.

H22 Haverhill

☎(0440) 61951, 712628 Pro, 714883 Fax
Coupals Rd, Haverhill, Suffolk CB9 7UW

Leave Haverhill on A604 towards Colchester, pass under railway viaduct, 2nd left into Chalkstone Way, 1st right into Coupals Rd.
Parkland course.
9 holes, 5707 yards, S.S.S.68
Designed by Charles Lawrie.
Founded 1973
Visitors: welcome
Green Fee: £15 (£7.50 with member) WD, £21 (£10.50 with member) WE & BH.
Societies: by arrangement.
Catering: bar facilities; no catering.
Hotels: Woodlands Hotel.

H23 Hintlesham Hall

☎(0473) 652761, 652750 Fax
Hintlesham, Ipswich, Suffolk IP8 3NS
4 miles W of Ipswich, 10 mins from A12, A45.
Parkland course.
18 holes, 6630 yards, S.S.S.72.
Designed by Hawtree & Sons.
Founded Sept, 1991
Visitors: welcome.
Green Fee: £26 WD, £45 WE.
Societies: Mon-Fri by prior booking with Sec.
Catering: Stud bar, lounge bar, restaurant.
Private 10-bay driving range, spa, sauna, steam room, outdoor pool.
Hotels: Hintlesham Hall.

H24 Hunstanton

☎(0485) 532811 Sec/bookings, 532751 Pro
Golf Course Rd, Old Hunstanton, Norfolk PE36 6JQ
Off A149 in Old Hunstanton (club signposted), 1 mile NE of Hunstanton.
Links course.
18 holes, 6670 yards, S.S.S.72
Founded 1891
Visitors: welcome with h/cap cert, except on Bank Holiday weekends; booking advisable; no 3/4 ball play.
Green Fee: £32/day (£15 with member) WD; £38/day (£18 with member) WE; discounted rates in winter season on application.
Societies: welcome by prior arrangement with Sec.
Catering: available, restricted menu on Mon.
Hotels: Le Strange Arms; Lodge; Titchwell Manor.

H25 Ipswich

☎(0473) 728941
Purdis Heath, Bucklesham Rd, Ipswich, Suffolk IP3 8UQ

Comfortable historic hotel with long golfing tradition. Good food and wine served in attractive restaurant overlooking award-winning garden.

Please telephone for brochure.

Victoria Road, Aldeburgh, Suffolk IP15 5DX Tel: (0728) 452420

3 miles E of Ipswich off A45, at roundabout by St Augustine's Church turn into Bucklesham Rd.
Heathland course.
18 holes, 6405 yards, S.S.S.71; 9 holes, 3860 yards, S.S.S.59
Designed by James Braid, Hawtree & Taylor.
Founded 1895
Visitors: only by advance agreement.
Green Fee: £30/day/round WD; £36/day/round WE; 9 hole, £8 WD, £10 WE.
Societies: Mon, Thurs, Fri by advance booking.
Catering: full facilities available.

H26 King's Lynn
☎(0553) 631654 Sec, 631655 Pro, 631656 Steward, 631036 Fax
Castle Rising, King's Lynn, Norfolk PE31 6BD
On A149 from King's Lynn to Hunstanton, at Castle Rising sign turn left, about 0.75 mile on left hand side.
Parkland course.
18 holes, 6646 yards, S.S.S.72
Designed by Alliss & Thomas.
Founded 1923
Visitors: welcome weekdays except Tues.
Green Fee: £30 WD, £38 WE & BH.
Societies: Thurs, Fri only.
Catering: lunches daily weekdays; evening meals by arrangement.
Snooker.
Hotels: Red Cat; Dukes Head; Knights Hill.

H27 Links Country Park
☎(0263) 837691
West Runton, Norfolk NR27 9QH
In West Runton village 2 miles from Sheringham, turn for railway station, over the bridge 100 yards on left.
Undulating downland course.
9 holes, 2407 yards, S.S.S.32

Founded 1978
Visitors: welcome.
Green Fee: apply for details.
Societies: by arrangement.
Catering: full facilities.
Tennis, saunas etc.
Hotels: Links Country Park (free golf for residents).

H28 Mattishall
☎(0362) 850111
South Green, Mattishall, Dereham, Norfolk
B1063 to Mattishall, right at church, 1 mile on left.
Parkland course.
9 holes, 2953 yards, S.S.S.68; 9 hole Pitch & Putt
Founded June 1990
Visitors: all welcome.
Green Fee: apply for details.
Hotels: Phoenix (East Dereham).

H29 Middleton Hall
☎(0553) 841800
Hall Orchards, Middleton, Nr Kings Lynn, Norfolk PE32 1RH
Off A47 4 miles from King's Lynn, between church and station in Middleton then 1st left.
Parkland course.
9 holes, 5570 yards, S.S.S.67
Founded 1989
Visitors: welcome with h/cap cert.
Green Fee: on application.
Societies: welcome by prior booking.
Catering: bar, bar snacks.
Driving range, putting green.

H30 Mundesley
☎(0263) 720095 Sec, 720279 Clubhouse
Links Rd, Mundesley, Norwich, Norfolk NR11 8ES
Turn off the Mundesley-Cromer road by Mundesley Church, signposted as you enter the village.

Undulating course with panoramic views.
9 holes, 5410 yards, S.S.S.66
Designed by Harry Vardon (in part).
Founded 1903
Visitors: welcome except 12.30-3.30pm Wed or until 11.30am Sun; h/cap cert not required but strict dress code.
Green Fee: on application.
Societies: by arrangement.
Catering: available daily.
Pool.

H31 Newton Green
☎(0787) 377217 Sec, 313215 Pro
Newton Green, Sudbury, Suffolk
On A134, 3 miles E of Sudbury.
Moorland course.
9 holes, 5488 yards, S.S.S.67.
Further 9 holes opening Sept 1994.
Founded 1907
Visitors: weekdays; no visitors weekends, Bank Holidays.
Green Fee: £15/round/day approx.
Catering: bar and restaurant.

H32 Reymerston
☎(0362) 850297, 850614 Fax
Hingham Rd, Reymerston, Norwich, Norfolk NR9 4QQ
12 miles W of Norwich off B1135 Dereham to Wymondham road.
Farmland course.
18 holes, S.S.S.72
Designed by ADAS
Founded June 1993
Visitors: welcome any time, h/cap certs required.
Green Fee: £20/round, £30/2 rounds WD; £25/round, £35/2 rounds WE.
Societies: welcome any day, min 12; various options available.
Catering: bar and snacks, Fairway restaurant, function room for 120.
9 hole Pitch & Putt with own catering facilities.
Hotels: Hotel Norwich; Phoenix (Dereham).

H33 **Richmond Park**

☎(0953) 881803
Saham Road, Watton, Thetford,
Norfolk IP25 6EA
A11 to Thetford, then A1075 to
Watton, turn left at top of High St,
Saham Rd at bottom.
Parkland/meadowland course.
18 holes, c. 6300 yards, S.S.S.70
Designed by R. Jessup, R. Scott.
Founded July 1990
Visitors: welcome; h/cap cert
weekends to 11am.
Green Fee: £15/round, £20/day WD,
£20/day/round WE.
Societies: welcome, bookings only
Catering: bar meals 7 days, à la
carte restaurant Tues-Sat.
Putting green, practice
ground/driving range, mini gym.

H34 **Rookery Park**

☎(0502) 560380
Carlton Colville, Lowestoft, Suffolk
NR33 8HJ
2 miles W of Lowestoft on A146.
Parkland course.
18 holes, 6650 yards, S.S.S.72
Designed by Charles Lawrie.
Founded 1975
Visitors: welcome all year.
Green Fee: apply for details.
Societies: any weekday except Tues
am.
Catering: full facilities 7 days.
9-hole Par 3 course, snooker.
Hotels: Hedley House; Broadlands.

H35 **Royal Cromer**

☎(0263) 512884
145 Overstrand Rd, Cromer, Norfolk
NR27 0JH
1 mile E of Cromer on B1159 coast
road, adjoins Cromer lighthouse.
Undulating seaside course.
18 holes, 6508 yards, S.S.S.71
Designed by James Braid.
Founded 1888
Visitors: accepted weekdays and
after 11am most weekends; booking
essential 1st April-31st Oct.
Green Fee: £25 WD, £30 WE & BH.
Societies: accepted weekdays.
Catering: daily.
Hotels: Cliftonville; Cliff House;
Anglia Court; Red Lion.

H36 **Royal Norwich**

☎(0603) 49928
Drayton High Rd, Hellesdon, Norwich
NR6 5AH
500 yards down A1067 Fakenham
road from ring road.

Parkland course.
18 holes, 6603 yards, S.S.S.72
Founded 1893
Visitors: must have h/cap.
Green Fee: on application.
Societies: book in advance.
Catering: restaurant facilities.

H37 **Royal West Norfolk**

☎(0485) 210223, 210087 Sec and
Fax
Brancaster, King's Lynn, Norfolk
PE31 8AX
7 miles E of Hunstanton on A149,
take Beach Rd from Brancaster
village to club.
Seaside links course.
18 holes, 6428 yards, S.S.S.71
Designed by Holcombe Ingleby.
Founded 1892
Visitors: must be members of
recognised golf club, hold official
h/cap cert and make prior
arrangements with Sec; no visitors,
unless with member, from start of
last week in July to end 1st week Sept.
Green Fee: £32 WD, £42.50 WE.
Societies: small societies by
arrangement; no new visiting
societies at weekends.
Catering: snacks daily; lunches by
arrangement.
Hotels: The Manor (Titchwell); Hoste
Arms (Burnham Market).

H38 **Royal Worlington & Newmarket**

☎(0638) 712216
Golf Links Rd, Worlington, Bury St
Edmunds, Suffolk IP28 8SD
6 miles NE of Newmarket, A45 then
A11 towards Thetford; follow signs to
Worlington.
Inland links course.
9 holes, 3105 yards, S.S.S.70
Designed by H.S. Colt.
Founded 1893
Visitors: weekdays only, phone first;
h/cap cert required.
Green Fee: £30 WD.
Societies: Tues, Thurs by
appointment; limited 24 players.
Catering: lunch and tea only.
Hotels: Bull Inn (Barton Mills);
Worlington Hall (Worlington);
Riverside (Mildenhall).

H39 **Rushmere**

☎(0473) 725648 Sec, 728076 Pro
Rushmere Heath, Ipswich, Suffolk
IP4 5QQ
3 miles E of Ipswich off Woodbridge
road A1214.

Heathland/common land course.
18 holes, 6263 yards, S.S.S.70
Founded 1927
Visitors: weekdays only; h/cap cert
or bona fide member of golf club.
Green Fee: £18/round/day.
Societies: when dates available.
Catering: full facilities.

H40 **Ryston Park**

☎(0366) 383834 Sec, 382133
Steward
Denver, Downham Market, Norfolk
PE38 0HH
On A10 just before turning to village
of Denver, 1 mile S of Downham
Market.
Parkland course.
9 holes, 6292 yards, S.S.S.70
Founded 1933
Visitors: weekdays.
Green Fee: on application.
Societies: weekdays.
Catering: full facilities except Mon.

H41 **St Helena**

☎(0986) 875567, 874565 Fax
Bramfield Rd, Halesworth, Suffolk
IP19 9XA
1 mile from Halesworth off A144
Bramfield road.
Parkland course, pay-as-you-play.
18 holes, 6580 yards, S.S.S.72; 9
holes, 3059 yards, S.S.S.36
Designed by J.W. Johnson
Founded 1990
Visitors: welcome, no restrictions.
Green Fee: 18 holes: £14.20/round,
£18/day WD; £17/round, £20/day
WE: 9 holes, £7.10/round
Societies: welcome.
Catering: full facilities.
Driving range.

H42 **Seckford**

☎(0394) 388000, 382818 Fax
Seckford Hall Rd, Great Bealings,
Woodbridge, Suffolk IP13 6NT
Adjacent main A12 and next door to
Seckford Hall Hotel.
Pay-and-Play, parkland course.
18 holes, S.S.S.67
Designed by Johnny Johnson.
Founded Aug 1991
Visitors: experienced golfers only,
h/caps not required.
Green Fee: £12/round.
Societies: always welcome; play all
day inc lunch £20.
Catering: superb facilities at
adjacent hotel.
Driving range, Pitch & Putt.
Hotels: Seckford Hall.

Royal Worlington & Newmarket

Royal Worlington, like the Old Course at St Andrews, has always struck me as a freak of nature. No one seems to know who designed it but since 1892, when the golf course and Club came into being, it has grown up on its own and today has the reputation of being the greatest 9-hole course in the world. I have never heard anyone beg to differ since no one playing over what Bernard Darwin described as "The Sacred Nine" has ever claimed to have played a better.

It has other similarities with the Old Course at St Andrews, having been laid out for the gutty ball and yet, with scarcely any modifications, it remains a great test with the rubber core ball and the steel shaft. Like St Andrews, too, it may not quite measure up at first sight to all the tributes paid to it but the more familiar it becomes the more the special quality of the golf becomes evident. Not for a moment is one deterred by the prospect of playing the same holes eight times in a weekend. Rather the opposite.

For generations, Cambridge golfers have been blessed by being allowed to adopt it as their golfing home and, for this reason, they are one up on Oxford every March before they start. In early days the undergraduates' journey ended with the guard producing a special pair of steps for their descent from the train at Worlington Halt close to the 4th green but even before the line was declared unplayable by Dr Beeching, the fashionable means of transport was a varied assortment of cars which, depending on their vintage, took between 17 and 35 minutes for the 23 odd miles.

The course has been well described as seaside links inland, a characteristic that has been religiously preserved by wise committees along with greens, managed with the minimum of artificial aids, which are unbelievably fast and true.

The short game, is vital, to low scoring at Worlington but there is one other similarity with the Old Course at St Andrews. Nobody would describe Worlington as a narrow course and yet it is essentially a great driver's course since, owing to the pace of the greens, it is necessary to place the tee shot at every hole in order to get a shot at the flag; and, again owing to the pace of the greens, good iron play is rewarded almost more than anywhere else.

For a course laid out on an unbelievably small acreage, it is a wonderfully complete test but each hole offers something different rather, it is said, like Beethoven's Symphonies. The 9 begins with a splendid par 5 with the threat of the road on the right adding menace to the drive and is followed by a long, short hole whose green is about as hard to stay on as a policeman's helmet. It is guarded by a deep bunker, and slopes to the left towards some grassy pimples.

Then comes the glorious hole that in the days of the gutty ball must have held even more challenge than it does today; then, with two more short holes in between, come the 4th, 6th and 8th sometimes in range of 2 shots and sometimes not.

The 6th offers a superb second to a green set into the gap at the end of the majestic line of pine trees that dominates the course; and the 8th, another over a row of good, old-fashioned cross bunkers, offers a testing second shot before the 9th turns for home with one of the best short par 4's in the country. There is the temptation to bite off more than is wise with the drive although the drive must be bold if there is any hope of pitching close to the flag.

The scratch man is expected to be out in about 35 but it is doubtful whether he will be and, though one of the beauties of a 9-hole course is that scores should not vary much in view of knowing what to expect the second time round, this seldom applies at Worlington. Each round is joyously different.

The celebrated short 5th with its long glassy hog's back green, where tee shots can be in sight of a 2 one minute and doomed for a 5 the next, is no respecter of the law of averages; indeed, one of the favourite local stories is of the golfer who was once on the green in one and off in 10; and the 5th has no bunkers to bolster its defences.

H43 Sheringham
☎(0263) 823488, 822980 Pro,
825189 Fax
Weybourne Rd, Sheringham, Norfolk
NR26 8HG
0.5 mile from Sheringham on A149.
Clifftop course.
18 holes, 6464 yards, S.S.S.71
Designed by Tom Dunn.
Founded 1891
Visitors: welcome with h/cap; phone
first.
Green Fee: £25 WD, £30 WE & BH.
Societies: by arrangement with Sec
weekdays.
Catering: available all week.
Hotels: Beaumaris, Southlands
(Sheringham); The Links (West
Runton).

H44 Southwold
☎(0502) 723234 Clubhouse,
723790 Pro
The Common, Southwold, Suffolk
IP18 6TB
From A12 follow A1095 signposted
Southwold, turn right at Kings Head
Hotel, proceed across Common, golf
club about 0.5 mile on right hand
side.
Common land course.
9 holes, 6050 yards, S.S.S.69
Founded 1884
Visitors: welcome except on
competition days; phone in advance.
Green Fee: £14 WD, £18 WE.
Societies: welcome by prior
arrangement.
Catering: full bar and catering
facilities.

H45 Sprowston Park
☎(0603) 410657 Sec, 417264 Pro,
788884 Fax
Wroxham Rd, Sprowston, Norwich,
Norfolk NR7 8RP
1.5 miles from ring road on A1151
Wroxham road; follow Sprowston
Park signs.
Parkland course
18 holes, 5985 yards, S.S.S.69
Founded Oct 1980
Visitors: welcome.
Green Fee: £12/round WD, £15 WE
& BH.
Societies: welcome 7 days.
Catering: snacks, meals, dinners,
Sun lunch; spacious dining room,
daily specialities.
East Anglian Academy of Golf; driving
range, 18-hole putting green.
Hotels: Sprowston Manor; bargain
breaks and golf breaks on application
(0603) 410871.

H46 Stowmarket
☎(0449) 736473 Sec, 736392 Pro
Lower Rd, Onehouse, Stowmarket,
Suffolk IP14 3DA
2.5 miles SW of Stowmarket, off
B1115 Stowmarket-Bidlestone road;
look for Shepherd & Dog public
house at junction with Lower Rd.
Parkland course.
18 holes, 6101 yards, S.S.S.69
Reformed in 1962
Visitors: welcome weekdays;
weekends must have h/cap cert.
Green Fee: £19/round, £24/day WD;
£25/round, £33/day WE.
Societies: Thurs and Fri.
Catering: meals usually available at
all times.
Hotels: Cedars (Stowmarket).

H47 Swaffham
☎(0760) 721611
Cley Rd, Swaffham, Norfolk PE37
8AE
1 mile out of town on Cockley Cley
road, signposted in market place.
Heathland course.
9 holes, 6252 yards, S.S.S.70
Founded 1922
Visitors: welcome weekdays,
weekends only with member.
Green Fee: £18/round/day.
Societies: welcome by arrangement.
Catering: snacks 7 days, full
catering except Mon and Tues.
Hotels: George.

H48 Thetford
☎(0842) 752169 Sec, 752258 Club,
752662 Pro
Brandon Rd, Thetford, Norfolk IP24
3NE
Take B1107 signposted Brandon
from roundabout on A11 Thetford
by-pass, course 0.5 mile on left.
Wooded, heathland course.
18 holes, 6879 yards, S.S.S.73
Designed by C.H. Mayo, Donald Steel.
Founded 1912
Visitors: welcome weekdays with
current h/cap cert; weekends and
Bank Holidays with member only.
Green Fee: £26 WD.
Societies: Wed, Thurs, Fri only.
Catering: available daily.
Hotels: Bell; Thomas Paine;
Wereham House.

H49 Thorpeness
☎(0728) 452176
Thorpeness, Suffolk IP16 4NH
Leave A12 at Saxmundham, on to
B119, then B1353.

Moorland course.
18 holes, 6241 yards, S.S.S.71
Designed by James Braid.
Founded 1923
Visitors: welcome weekdays.
Green Fee: apply for details.
Societies: catered for weekdays
only.
Catering: full catering service.
Hotels: Thorpeness Golf Club.

H50 Ufford Park Hotel
☎(0394) 383555
Yarmouth Road, Ufford, Woodbridge,
Suffolk IP12 1QW
Approx 2 miles N of Woodbridge on
B1438.
Parkland course in Deben valley.
18 holes, 6300 yards, S.S.S.70
Designed by Phil Pilgrem.
Founded Oct 1991
Visitors: welcome at any time.
Green Fee: £12/round, £18/day WD,
£15/round, £24/day WE & BH.
Societies: welcome at any time.
Catering: bar, bar snacks,
restaurant.
Driving nets, indoor swimming pool,
sauna, health, fitness and beauty
facilities; conferences, banqueting.
Hotels: Own hotel and Leisure
Centre, weekend breaks and golfing
packages available.

H51 Waldringfield Heath
☎(0473) 736768 Sec/Manager,
736417 Pro
Newbourne Road, Waldringfield,
Woodbridge, Suffolk IP12 4PT
3 miles NE of Ipswich.
Heathland course
18 holes, 6153 yards, S.S.S.69
Designed by P. Pilgrim.
Founded 1 April 1983
Visitors: welcome weekdays, after
12am weekends.
Green Fee: on application.
Societies: weekdays.
Catering: full catering facilities
available.
Hotels: Marlborough (Ipswich).

H52 Wensum Valley
☎(0603) 261012
Beech Avenue, Taverham, Norwich,
Norfolk NR8 6HP
4 miles NW of Norwich on A1067.
Parkland course.
18 holes, 6000 yards, S.S.S.69; 9
holes, 2953 yards, S.S.S.68
Designed by B.C. Todd.
Founded July 1989
Visitors: welcome.

Green Fee: £12/day WD, £15/day WE.
Societies: welcome at all times.
Catering: full bar and catering.
Driving range, snooker, bowls.
Hotels: Accommodation at club; golf breaks arranged; phone for details.

H53 **Weston Park**

☎(0603) 871842 Bar, 872998 Pro
Weston Longville, Norwich, Norfolk NR9 5JW
Off Norwich-Fakenham road; 8 miles from Norwich turn left to Weston Longville then 1st right into Morton Lane, course 500 yards on right.
Parkland course.
9 holes (18 from mid-1995), 3132 yards, S.S.S.70
Founded June 1993
Visitors: welcome at any time, h/cap certs required.
Green Fee: £17 WD, £22 WE.
Societies: welcome.

Catering: full facilities.
Putting green, practice area, snooker.
Hotels: Lenwade House.

H54 **Wood Valley (Beccles)**

☎(0502) 712244
The Common, Beccles, Suffolk NR34 9BX
1 mile off A146, 18 miles Norwich, 10 miles Lowestoft.
Heathland course.
9 holes, 2781 yards, S.S.S.67
Founded 1899
Visitors: welcome, weekdays unrestricted, weekends with member or phone.
Green Fee: £10 (18 holes) WD, £12 WE & BH.
Societies: welcome, not Sunday.
Catering: bar and bar snacks; meals to order.
Hotels: Kings Head; Waveney House; Broadland.

H55 **Woodbridge**

☎(0394) 382038
Bromeswell Heath, Woodbridge, Suffolk IP12 2PF
Leave A12 N of Woodbridge on road signposted to Melton; after traffic lights follow road to Orford (B1084); course 2.5 miles E of Woodbridge.
Heathland course.
18 holes, 6314 yards, S.S.S.70; 9 holes, S.S.S.31
Designed by F. Hawtree.
Founded 1893
Visitors: weekdays only, h/cap certs required, advance phone call advisable; 9 hole course open all week, no restrictions, no h/cap cert required.
Green Fee: £25/round/day.
Societies: by advance booking only, Mon-Fri.
Catering: full bar and dining room facilities.
Hotels: Melton Grange; Seckford Hall.

I

GLOUCESTERSHIRE, WARWICKSHIRE, HEREFORD & WORCESTER

The Three Choirs Festival, the province of the cathedrals of Hereford, Worcester and Gloucester, would have been close to the heart of Sir Edward Elgar, the most English of all composers. Less well known was his love of golf and, in particular, his connections with the Worcestershire Golf Club at Malvern Wells, although how much inspiration his musical scores owed to the latter is not clear.

Judging by the excellent centenary history of the Club, it can be assumed that his game was based more on hope than glory — perhaps even enigmatic and variable — but the beauty of the Malvern Hills has been solace to many and it is appropriate therefore to head an introduction to this section with mention of the most senior Club in the area. Almost 20 years later came the Alister Mackenzie designed Worcester Golf and Country Club in more parkland surroundings, but one of Worcestershire's most attractive courses is undoubtedly Blackwell near Bromsgrove.

Far more modern is Abbey Park at Redditch which is a valuable addition to the county's facilities but, as an example of true dedication and private enterprise, there is nothing in the entire country, to match the tale of Ross-on-Wye. Having existed for almost 60 years as a nine-hole course, they built themselves a new 18-hole home in pleasant woodland in the 1960s. What is more, the cost of course and clubhouse did not exceed £50,000 although the sacrifices and contributions of the original course committee, a gallant and cheerful band, never featured in the calculations.

In those days, golf in Herefordshire was confined to Kington, the highest golf course in the land, one at Raven's Causeway and the 9 holes at Ross but Ross emerged from a wilderness of roots, scrub, thickets, marsh and typical red earth that, at first, Ken Cotton believed to be unsuitable; but his skill, allied to the faith, patience and determination of the small committee, worked a minor miracle in a corner of England still blessed with meadows, orchards and green hills.

Ross is a short drive from Gloucester, a county not as well populated with courses as its size — or the playing strength of its men's county team in recent years — might suggest. From Tewkesbury Park and the new Puckrup Hall in the north to Cotswold Edge and Westonbirt in the south, the setting is generally one of pasture and park, with the exception of the higher reaches of Gloucester itself and the ancient elevated common at Minchinhampton.

Two Ryder Cup matches at the Belfry have done a lot to publicise golf in the Birmingham area in recent years, but Warwickshire, particularly in the area around Birmingham, is full of variety. Some of the older clubs include Handsworth, Edgbaston, Harborne, Moseley, Kidderminster, Robin Hood and Sandwell Park, a stone's throw from the home of West Bromwich Albion Football Club.

Olton and Copt Heath are the pride of Solihull, both ideal as enjoyable, if stiff, tests but, besides the Belfry, there is a fine new hotel complex at Forest of Arden. The Arden course was bought by Country Club Hotels who added both hotel and a second course, the Arden, dramatically upgraded in 1992 to host the Murphy's English Open in 1993.

With the Belfry, it is the only 36-hole complex in the area, although Kings Norton has an honourable 27.

I1 Abbey Park Golf & Country Club

☎(0527) 63918
Dagnell End Rd, Redditch, Worcs B98 7BD
Off A441 Redditch to Birmingham road.
Parkland course.
18 holes, 6411 yards, S.S.S.71
Designed by Donald Steel.
Founded 1985
Visitors: welcome subject to available tee times.
Green Fee: £10 WD, £12.50 WE.
Societies: welcome by prior arrangement.
Catering: 3 bars, restaurant; meals served all day.
Snooker, swimming pool, gym, sauna etc.
Hotels: Abbey Park (32 beds), bargain breaks available.

I2 Ansty Golf Centre

☎(0203) 621341 Pro shop, 602671
24-hr ans service & Fax
Brinklow Rd, Ansty, Coventry CV7 9JH
From M6 junction 2 take B4065 parallel to M69 and signposted to Ansty; go through village of Ansty, take 1st right into B4029 Brinklow road; Golf Centre is 500 yards on left.
Pay-and-Play parkland course.
18 holes, 5793 yards, Par 71
Designed by D. Morgan.
Founded August 1990
Visitors: always welcome.
Green Fee: £4.50 (9 holes), £9 (18 holes); members £3.75 and £7.
Societies: welcome any time, 24 hrs notice required.
Catering: full bar and catering 7 days a week. Driving range.
Hotels: Ansty Hall; Hilton National.

I3 Atherstone

☎(0827) 713110
The Outwoods, Atherstone, Warwicks CV9 2RL
Coleshill Rd out of Atherstone, 0.5 mile on left approached by private road.
Undulating parkland course.
11 holes (18 tees), 6239 yards, S.S.S.70
Founded 1894
Visitors: welcome weekdays; Sat with member only, Sun after 5pm only.
Green Fee: £17 (£8 with member), BH £22 (£7 with member), Sun after 5pm £7.
Societies: weekdays by prior arrangement.
Catering: full catering facilities available.
Hotels: Old Red Lion; Three Tuns.

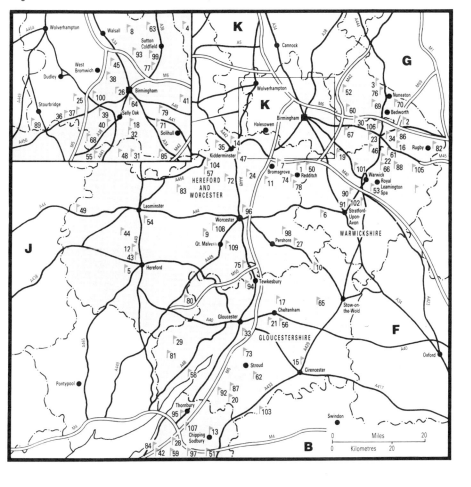

BIDFORD GRANGE GOLF CLUB

Stratford Road, Bidford on Avon, Warks B50 4LY Tel: (0789) 490319 Fax: (0789) 778184

Location B439 5 miles west of Stratford on Avon

18 holes 7,233 yds SSS 74 Par 72 Full USGA spec. All sand greens. Designed by Howard Swan and Paul Tillman

Green Fees £12 W/D £14 W/E £20 per day

Societies catered for on weekdays. Catering refreshment available

I4 The Belfry
☎(0675) 470301
Lichfield Rd, Wishaw, N Warwicks
B76 9PR
M6 junction 4, follow signs to
Lichfield along A446, sited at the
apex of A4091 to Tamworth and
A446 to Lichfield; or exit 9 from M42.
Parkland course, Championship
courses.
Brabazon, 18 holes, 6975 yards,
S.S.S.72; Derby, 18 holes, 6077
yards, S.S.S.70
Designed by Peter Alliss & Dave
Thomas.
Founded 1977
Visitors: welcome at all times.
Green Fee: apply for details.
Societies: welcome at all times.
Catering: full facilities available
within Hotel.

I5 Belmont Lodge and Golf Course
☎(0432) 352666
Belmont House, Belmont, Hereford
HR2 9SA
2 miles S of Hereford on
Abergavenny road, A465.
Undulating meadowland course.
18 holes, 6490 yards, S.S.S.71
Designed by R. Sandow.
Founded 1983
Visitors: welcome.
Green Fee: on application.
Societies: welcome.
Catering: restaurant, bar and bar
snacks.
Fishing, tennis, bowls, snooker.
Hotels: hotel on course.

I6 Bidford Grange
☎(0789) 490319, 778184 Fax
Stratford Rd, Bidford on Avon,
Warwicks B50 4LY
B439 5 miles W of Stratford on Avon.
Full USGA spec, all sand greens.
18 holes, 7233 yards, S.S.S.74
Designed by Howard Swan and Paul
Tillman.
Visitors: welcome.
Green Fee: £12 WD, £14 WE,
£20/day.
Societies: welcome, catered for on
weekdays.
Catering: refreshment available.

I7 Blackwell
☎(021) 445 1994 Sec, 445 1781
Steward, 445 3113 Pro
Blackwell, Bromsgrove, Worcs B60
1PY
3 miles E of Bromsgrove; from
Blackwell village centre, along
Station Rd and under railway bridge,
club entrance on left after 40 yards.
Parkland course.
18 holes, 6212 yards, S.S.S.71
Designed by H. Fowler and T.
Simpson
Founded 1983
Visitors: unrestricted weekdays;
with member only weekends and
Bank Holidays.
Green Fee: £36/day, parties over 16
£30
Societies: Wed, Thurs, Fri by
arrangement with Sec.
Catering: full by prior arrangement.

I8 Boldmere
☎(021) 354 3379
Monmouth Drive, Sutton Coldfield, W
Midlands
A452 Chester road, 6 miles NE of
Birmingham City centre.
Municipal parkland course.
18 holes, 4463 yards, S.S.S.62
Founded 1936
Visitors: welcome any time.
Green Fee: apply for details.
Catering: light snacks only.
Hotels: Parson & Clerk.

I9 Bransford (Pine Lakes)
☎(0886) 833551 Sec, 833621 Pro,
832461 Fax
Bank House Hotel, Bransford,
Worcester WR6 5JD
M5 junction 7 to Worcester; take
A4103 Hereford road out of
Worcester for 3.5 miles, hotel is on
left off roundabout.
'Florida' style course.
18 holes (from April 1994), S.S.S.70
Designed by Bob Sandow.
Founded April 1993
Visitors: welcome.
Green Fee: £20
Societies: welcome all week;
residential availability at hotel.
Catering: 3 bars, restaurant, bar
meals.

Driving range, flat green, 9-lane
championship bowling green
(outdoor); fitness centre.
Hotels: Bank House (70 beds).

I10 Broadway
☎(0386) 853683 Sec, 853275 Pro
Willersey Hill, Broadway, Worcs
WR12 7LG
1.25 miles E of Broadway off A44.
Undulating parkland course.
18 holes, 6216 yards, S.S.S.70
Designed by James Braid.
Founded 1896
Visitors: must book, h/cap cert
required; not before 3pm Sat; some
restrictions Sun & BH for club
competitions.
Green Fee: £23/round, £28 (36
holes) WD; £27/round, £32 (36
holes) WE & BH.
Societies: Wed, Thur, Fri; max
number 40.
Catering: bar and restaurant, not
Mon.
Hotels: Dormy House; Noel Arms
(Chipping Campden).

I11 Bromsgrove Golf Centre
☎(0527) 575886, 570505 Bookings
Stratford Road, Bromsgrove,
Worcestershire B60 1LD
At junction of A38 Bromsgrove
eastern by-pass and A448 Redditch
road; take A38 from M5 Junction 4 or
5, or M42 Junction 1.
Public, pay-as-you-play, course;
grade 2 undulating farmland.
9 holes, 3250 yards, S.S.S.36
Designed by Hawtree & Sons.
Founded 1992
Visitors: welcome.
Green Fee: £6 (9 holes), £10 (18
holes).
Societies: weekdays, with plenty of
notice. Driving range.

I12 Burghill Valley
☎(0432) 760456
Tillington Road, Burghill, Hereford
HR4 7RW
A4110 from Hereford, at Three Elms
Inn take Tillington road for 2 miles,
club on left.

Parkland course.
9 holes (further 9 from 1993), 3073 yards, S.S.S. applied for.
Founded July 1991
Visitors: welcome any time.
Green Fee: apply for details.
Societies: by arrangement.
Catering: bar and light meals all day.
Hotels: Priory (Stretton Sugwas) golfing packages available.

I13 Chipping Sodbury
☎(0454) 319042 Sec, 318047 Pro
Chipping Sodbury, Bristol BS17 6PU
Leave M4 at exit 18 and M5 at exit 14; from Chipping Sodbury take Wickwar road, first turn on right.
Parkland course.
18 holes, 6912 yards, S.S.S.73; 9 holes, 3076 yards
Designed by Fred Hawtree.
Visitors: welcome, but after 12 noon at weekends.
Green Fee: on application.
Societies: welcome by arrangement on weekdays.
Catering: meals served.
Practice ground.
Hotels: Moda; Cross Hands.

I14 Churchill & Blackdown
☎(0562) 700018, 700454 Pro
Churchill Lane, Blakedown, Kidderminster, Worcs DY10 3NB
Off A456 3 miles NE of Kidderminster, turn under railway viaduct in village of Blakedown.
Undulating parkland course.
9 holes, 6472 yards, S.S.S.71
Founded 1926
Visitors: welcome weekdays; weekends and Bank Holidays with member only.
Green Fee: £17.50 (£7.50 with member) WD; £10 with member WE.
Societies: apply to Sec.
Catering: lunch, evening meals except Mon.
Hotels: Cedars, Gainsborough House (Kidderminster); Granary (Shenstone); Travel Inn (Hagley).

I15 Cirencester
☎(0285) 652465 Sec/bookings, 653939 Members, 659987 Catering, 656124 Pro, 650665 Fax
Cheltenham Rd, Bagendon, Cirencester, Glos GL7 7BH
Adjoins A435
Cirencester-Cheltenham road, 1.5 miles from Cirencester.
Undulating course.

18 holes, 6002 yards, S.S.S.69
Designed by James Braid.
Founded 1893
Visitors: welcome at all times; h/cap certs required.
Green Fee: £20 (£10 with member) WD, £25 (£13 with member) WE & BH.
Societies: Tues, Wed, Fri.
Catering: lunch and evening meals.
Hotels: Kings Head; Stratton House; Fleece.

I16 City of Coventry (Brandon Wood)
☎(0203) 543141
Brandon Lane, Brandon, Coventry
On A45 6 miles S of Coventry, 120 yards S of London Rd roundabout.
Public parkland course.
18 holes, 6530 yards, S.S.S.71
Designed by Frank Pennink.
Visitors: welcome.
Green Fee: on application.
Societies: welcome but must book.
Catering: meals served every day.
Driving range.
Hotels: Brandon Hall.

I17 Cleeve Hill
☎(0242) 672025 club, 672592 Pro shop
Cheltenham, Glos GL52 3PW
Approx 6 miles N from M5, 4 miles N of Cheltenham off A46.
Municipal heathland course.
18 holes, 6217 yards, S.S.S.71
Founded 1891
Visitors: welcome anytime weekday; 8-11am and 3pm onwards on Sat, 11.30am onwards Sun.
Green Fee: £7/round WD, £8/round WE.
Societies: any day by arrangement, package to include 2 course meal.
Catering: full bar and restaurant daily.
Skittles, pool table.
Hotels: Malvern View; De La Bere; Cleeve Hill.

I18 Cocks Moor Woods
☎(021) 444 3584
Alcester Rd South, Kings Heath, Birmingham B14 6ER
On A435, near city boundary.
Public parkland course.
18 holes, 5819 yards, S.S.S.68
Founded 1924
Visitors: welcome.
Green Fee: £4.50 (9 holes), £6.60 (18 holes).
Societies: by arrangement.
Catering: snacks served.

I19 Copt Heath
☎(0564) 772650
1220 Warwick Rd, Knowle, Solihull, W Midlands B93 9LN
On A4141 0.25 mile S of M42 junction 5.
Parkland course.
18 holes, 6500 yards, S.S.S.71
Designed by H. Vardon.
Founded 1910
Visitors: members of recognised club with official club h/cap welcome, intro by member at weekend.
Green Fee: £30/round/day.
Societies: Mon, Wed and Thurs by arrangement with Sec.
Catering: full facilities except Mon.
Hotels: Greswolde.

I20 Cotswold Edge
☎(0453) 844167 Sec, 844398 Pro
Upper Rushmire, Wotton-under-Edge, Gloucestershire GL12 7PT
On B4058 Wotton-Tetbury road, 8 miles from M5 junction 14.
Meadowland course.
18 holes, 5816 yards, S.S.S.68
Founded 1980
Visitors: welcome weekdays, phone in advance; with member only weekends.
Green Fee: £15/day.
Societies: by prior arrangement with Sec.
Catering: full facilities available.
Hotels: Hare & Hounds; Amberley Inn; Calcot Manor; Thornbury Castle.

I21 Cotswold Hills
☎(0242) 515264 Sec, 515263 Pro
Ullenwood, Cheltenham, Glos GL53 9QT
3 miles S of Cheltenham, between A436 and B4070.
Undulating course.
18 holes, 6716 yards, S.S.S.72
Designed by M.D. Little.
Founded 1902
Visitors: members of recognised clubs welcome.
Green Fee: £21/round, £26/day.
Societies: Wed and Thurs.
Catering: bar snacks, lunches and dinners except Mon when sandwiches available.
Hotels: Royal George (Birdlip).

I22 Coventry
☎(0203) 414152, 411298 Pro
St Martin's Rd, Finham Park, Coventry, Warwicks CV3 6PJ

2 miles S of Coventry off A45 on A444 Stoneleigh-Leamington Spa road.
Parkland course.
18 holes, 6613 yards, S.S.S.72
Founded 1887
Visitors: welcome weekdays only.
Green Fee: £30.
Societies: Wed and Thurs, May-Sept only.
Catering: full facilities.
Hotels: Leofric; Trust House Forte; Windmill Farm.

I23 Coventry Hearsall
☎(0203) 713470 Sec, 713156 Pro
Beechwood Ave, Earlsdon, Coventry CV5 6DF
Just off A45 on Kenilworth-Coventry road.
Parkland course.
18 holes, 5983 yards, S.S.S.69
Founded 1894
Visitors: welcome Mon-Fri, Sat, Sun with member only.
Green Fee: on application.
Societies: Tues or Thurs by prior arrangement.
Catering: lunches, sandwiches available lunchtime, evening meals by prior arrangement.
Hotels: Leofric; De Vere; Hylands; Post House (Allesley).

I24 Droitwich Golf & Country Club
☎(0905) 774344
Westford House, Ford Lane, Droitwich WR9 0BQ
Junction 5 off M5, off A38 1 mile N of town.
Undulating meadowland course.
18 holes, 6040 yards, S.S.S.69
Founded 1897
Visitors: welcome Mon to Fri with h/cap cert; weekends with member only.
Green Fee: £24/day.
Societies: Wed and Fri.
Catering: bar, bar meals, restaurant. Snooker.
Hotels: Raven; St Andrews.

I25 Dudley
☎(0384) 254020 Pro, 233877 Sec
Turners Hill, Rowley Regis, Warley, W Midlands B65 9DP
1 mile S of town centre.
Undulating parkland course.
18 holes, 5704 yards, S.S.S.68
Founded 1893
Visitors: weekdays only.
Green Fee: £18/day.

Societies: by arrangement.
Catering: lunch and evening meals available.
Hotels: Station; Ward Arms.

I26 Edgbaston
☎(021) 454 1736 Sec, 454 3226 Pro, 454 8295 Fax
Church Rd, Edgbaston, Birmingham B15 3TB
From Birmingham City centre take A38 (Bristol road), after 1 mile and at 3rd set of lights turn right into Priory Rd, then left at end into Church Rd; Club entrance 100 yards on left.
Parkland course.
18 holes, 6118 yards, S.S.S.69
Designed by H.S. Colt.
Founded 1896
Visitors: h/cap cert required; members only before 9.30am and 12.30-1.30pm daily.
Green Fee: £32/day WD, £42 WE.
Societies: weekdays only by prior arrangement.
Catering: bar and bar lunches, other meals by arrangement; catering for business meetings, seminars etc. Snooker.

I27 Evesham
☎(0386) 860395 Club, 861144 Pro
Craycombe Links, Old Worcester Rd, Fladbury, Pershore, Worcs WR10 2QS
3 miles from Evesham on B4084, 4 miles from Pershore on A4538.
Parkland course.
9 holes (18 tees), 6415 yards, S.S.S.71
Founded 1894
Visitors: welcome weekdays; weekends only with member; avoid Tues (Ladies Day).
Green Fee: £15/round/day (£7 with member).
Societies: by arrangement, max 24.
Catering: bar snacks always available; special meals by arrangement.
Hotels: Waterside, Northwick (Evesham); Star (Pershore).

I28 Filton
☎(0272) 694169
Golf Course Lane, Filton, Bristol BS12 7QS
From Almondsbury interchange (M4/M5) take A38 towards Bristol; after 2 miles turn right at roundabout (Southmead Rd) and right at lights (Golf Course Lane).
Parkland course.

18 holes, 6042 yards, S.S.S.69
Designed by F. Hawtree & Son.
Founded 1909
Visitors: welcome on weekdays; weekends with member only.
Green Fee: £20/round, £25/day WD (£12 with member).
Societies: catered for on weekdays.
Catering: available all day.
Hotels: Crest Hotel; Hambrook.

I29 Forest Hills
☎(0594) 562899
Mile End Road, Coleford, Gloucestershire
On road from Coleford centre to Mile End on left hand side.
Parkland course.
18 holes, 5900 yards, S.S.S.68
Designed by Adrian Stiff.
Founded 1992
Visitors: welcome.
Green Fee: apply for details.
Societies: by arrangement.
Catering: full facilities.
Hotels: Wyndham Arms; Angel; Speech House; Lambsquay.

I30 Forest of Arden Hotel Golf & Country Club
☎(0676) 22335, 23721
Maxstoke Lane, Meriden, Coventry, Warwicks CV7 7HR
Off A45 10 miles NW of Coventry, 2.5 miles E of Birmingham International Airport; take Maxstoke turn off from A45 and follow lane for 2 miles.
Parkland course.
Aylesford, 18 holes, 6525 yards, S.S.S.69; Arden, 6915 yards, S.S.S.71
Designed by Donald Steel.
Founded 1970
Visitors: welcome with h/cap cert except Sat, Sun am.
Green Fee: apply for details.
Societies: welcome weekdays by prior arrangement with golf co-ordinator (weekends residential only).
Catering: restaurant 10am-10pm, bar and lounge; private facilities available.
Tennis (3 floodlit), snooker, swimming pool, squash (2), health and beauty facilities.
Hotels: Forest of Arden (153 beds), golf breaks details on request.

I31 Fulford Heath
☎(0564) 822806, 824758
Tanners Green Lane, Wythall, Birmingham B47 6BH

1 mile from main Alcester Rd, signposted to Tanners Green.
Parkland course.
18 holes, 6216 yards, S.S.S.70
Founded 1933
Visitors: welcome weekdays.
Green Fee: £25.
Societies: Tues or Thurs.
Catering: lunches and evening meals served except Mon.
Hotels: George; Regency.

I32 Gay Hill
☎(021) 430 6523/8544/7077, 474 6001, 436 7796 Fax
Hollywood Lane, Hollywood, Birmingham B47 5PP
On A435, 7 miles from city centre, 3 miles from M42 junction 3.
Meadowland course.
18 holes, 6532 yards, S.S.S.71
Founded 1913 (1921 on present course).
Visitors: unaccompanied weekdays; with member only weekends and not before 12.30pm Sunday.
Green Fee: £28.50
Societies: Thurs only.
Catering: meals available.
Hotels: George (Solihull); Robin Hood Motel (Hall Green).

I33 Gloucester
☎(0452) 411331
Robinswood Hill, Matson Lane, Gloucester GL4 9EA
2 miles S of Gloucester city centre on B4073 to Painswick.
Parkland course.
18 holes, 6100 yards, S.S.S.69; 9 holes Par 3, 990 yards
Designed by Donald Steel.
Founded 1976
Visitors: welcome any time; phone for tee times.
Green Fee: apply for details.
Societies: weekdays only, £37.25 includes 36 holes, coffee, lunch and dinner.
Catering: full facilities available.
Driving range, snooker.
Hotels: Gloucester Hotel at course, special weekend and weekday golfing breaks.

I34 Grange (GPT Golf Club)
☎(0203) 451465
Copsewood, Coventry, W Midlands CV3 1HS
2.5 miles from Coventry centre on Binley Rd, A428.
Meadowland course.

9 holes, 6002 yards, S.S.S.69
Re-designed by T.J. McAuley.
Founded 1924
Visitors: welcome weekdays before 2pm; Sun after 11am; not Sat.
Green Fee: on application.
Societies: by arrangement with Sec.
Catering: none; may arrange for Societies.

I35 Habberley
☎(0562) 745756
Habberley, Kidderminster, Worcs DY11 5RG
3 miles N of Kidderminster on Trimpley road.
Hilly parkland course.
9 holes, 5104 yards, S.S.S.69
Founded 1924
Visitors: welcome weekdays if member of recognised club.
Green Fee: on application.
Societies: by arrangement.
Catering: by prior notice.
Hotels: Gainsborough, Kidderminster; Swan, Stourport.

I36 Hagley Country Club
☎(0562) 883701 Clubhouse, 883852 Pro shop
Wassell Grove, Hagley, W Midlands DY9 9JW
4 miles S of Birmingham on A456, turn right into Wassell Grove, 0.5 mile.
Undulating parkland course.
18 holes, 6353 yards, S.S.S.72
Founded 1979
Visitors: welcome weekdays; weekends with member only, after 10am.
Green Fee: £20/round, £25/day.
Societies: welcome weekdays; prior arrangement essential through Club Manager.
Catering: bar and full restaurant facilities.
Squash.

I37 Halesowen
☎(021) 501 3606
The Leasowes, Halesowen, W Midlands B62 8QF
M5 junction 3 to Kidderminster, then to Halesowen.
Parkland course.
18 holes, 5486 yards, S.S.C.67
Founded 1902
Visitors: not weekends; Bank Holidays by arrangement.
Green Fee: £16/round, £23/day.
Societies: by arrangement.
Catering: not Mon.

I38 Handsworth
☎(021) 554 0599 Clubhouse, 554 3387 Office, 523 3594 Pro
11 Sunningdale Close, Handsworth Wood, Handsworth, Birmingham B20 1NP
M5 junction 1 towards Birmingham, left at lights into Island Rd, Oxhill Rd, left at lights into Friary Rd, 2nd left Greystone Ave, 2nd left Sunningdale Close; M6 junction 7, take A34 through lights, 1st right Old Walsall Rd, up Hamstead Hill, right into Vernon Ave, right into Craythorne Ave, 1st left Sunningdale Close.
Parkland course.
18 holes, 6312 yards, S.S.S.70
Founded 1895
Visitors: welcome weekdays; h/cap certs required.
Green Fee: £25/day (£7 with member).
Societies: weekdays by arrangement; special packages available.
Catering: lunch and dinner served except Mon.
Squash.
Hotels: Villa Nova; Post House; Moat House.

I39 Harborne
☎(021) 427 3058
40 Tennal Rd, Birmingham B32 2JE
Via Harborne village and War Lane, SW of Birmingham.
Undulating parkland/moorland course.
18 holes, 6235 yards, S.S.S.70
Designed by H.S. Colt.
Founded 1893
Visitors: welcome weekdays; Bank Holidays and weekends with member only.
Green Fee: £29 WD, £10 with member WE.
Societies: welcome Mon, Wed, Thurs, Fri.
Catering: available 7 days.
Hotels: Claremont; Apollo.

I40 Harborne Church Farm
☎(021) 427 1204 Phone/Fax
Vicarage Rd, Harborne, Birmingham B17 0SN
From Birmingham, via Broad St, Harborne Rd and War Lane to Vicarage Rd.
Municipal parkland course.
9 holes, 4914 yards, S.S.S.62
Founded 1926
Visitors: welcome.
Green Fee: on application.
Catering: snacks and meals in café.

I41 Hatchford Brook

☎(021) 743 9821
Coventry Rd, Sheldon, Birmingham
B26 3PY
Almost on city boundary adjacent to
Airport, on main A45 Coventry road.
Public parkland course.
18 holes, 6164 yards, S.S.S.69
Founded 1969
Visitors: all welcome.
Green Fee: apply for details.
Catering: canteen facilities while
course open.

I42 Henbury

☎(0272) 500044
Henbury Hill, Westbury-on-Trym,
Bristol BS10 7BQ
M5 junction 17, 2nd exit from
roundabout, right at 3rd roundabout
into Crow Lane, left at T-junction,
course at top of hill on right.
Parkland course.
18 holes, 6039 yards, S.S.S.70
Founded 1891
Visitors: welcome weekdays with
h/cap cert.
Green Fee: on application.
Societies: catered for on Tues and
Fri by arrangement.
Catering: full range available.
Hotels: Henbury Lodge; Ship
(Bristol).

I43 Hereford Municipal

☎(0432) 278178, 266281 Fax
Holmer Road, Hereford HR4 9UD
A49 through Hereford towards
Leominster.
Public course in middle of race
course.
9 holes, 2898 yards, S.S.S.68
Founded 1983
Visitors: welcome, closed on race
days.
Green Fee: £3.20 (9 holes), £5.20
(18 holes) WD; £4.40 (9 holes), £7
(18 holes) WE.
Societies: welcome with advance
booking.
Catering: bar and restaurant.
Practice ground, adjacent leisure
centre.
Hotels: Beefeater Starting Gate
Travel Inn.

I44 Herefordshire

☎(0432) 830219 Sec/bookings
Ravens Causeway, Wormsley,
Hereford HR4 8LY
6 miles NW of Hereford on road to
Weobley; turn left off B4110 at Three
Elms Inn.
Undulating parkland course.
18 holes, 6200 yards, S.S.S.69
Designed by Major Hutchison.
Founded 1898 (at Wormsley from
1932)
Visitors: welcome weekdays;
limited at weekends.
Green Fee: £14/round, £20/day WD;
£18/round, £26/day WE
Societies: all weekdays except Wed,
some weekends; package available
on application to Sec.
Catering: restaurant meals, bar and
bar snacks.
Hotels: Pilgrim; Green Dragon
(Hereford).

I45 Hill Top

☎(021) 554 4463
Park Lane, Handsworth Wood,
Birmingham B21 8JP
Public parkland course.
18 holes, 6200 yards, S.S.S.69
Founded 1980
Visitors: welcome.
Green Fee: apply for details.
Societies: welcome.
Catering: available.

I46 Kenilworth

☎(0926) 58517, 512732 Pro, 54038
Catering
Crew Lane, Kenilworth, Warwicks
CV8 2EA
A429 Kenilworth road, then via
Common Lane, Knowle Hill and Crew
Lane to clubhouse.
Undulating course.
18 holes, 6413 yards, S.S.S.71
Founded 1889
Visitors: welcome daily; advisable to
ring Pro beforehand.
Green Fee: on application.
Societies: apply in writing; society
days Weds.
Catering: full facilities daily,
advisable to contact Caterer.
Hotels: De Montfort; Avonside;
Chesford Grange.

I47 Kidderminster

☎(0562) 822303
Russell Rd, Kidderminster, Worcs
DY10 3HT
Course signposted off A449, within 1
mile of town centre.
Parkland course.
18 holes, 6223 yards, S.S.S.71
Founded 1909
Visitors: welcome weekdays only;
proof of membership of recognised
golf club must be provided.
Green Fee: £22.

Societies: welcome by prior
arrangement Thurs only.
Catering: full facilities except Mon.
Snooker
Hotels: The Collingdale;
Gordonhouse.

I48 Kings Norton

☎(0564) 826789
Brockhill Lane, Weatheroak,
Alvechurch, Birmingham B48 7ED
8 miles from centre of Birmingham
between A435 and A441; from M42
junction 3 turn towards Birmingham,
signs to club on left after 200 yards.
Parkland course
27 holes (3 loops of 9); Blue 9 holes,
3567 yards; Red 9 holes, 3294
yards; Yellow 9 holes, 3283 yards;
S.S.S.72; also 12 hole Par 3 course.
Designed by F. Hawtree & Son.
Founded 1892
Visitors: weekdays only, with
member only at weekends;
accredited h/cap required.
Green Fee: £27 (18 holes),
£29.50/day.
Societies: weekdays only.
Catering: full facilities; conferences
and banqueting.
Hotels: St Johns (Solihull).

I49 Kington

☎(0544) 230340, 231320 Pro
Bradnor, Kington, Herefordshire HR5
3RE
Take B4355 from A44 Kington
by-pass, turn left after 150 yards.
Moorland course; highest 18 hole
course in England.
18 holes, 5820 yards, S.S.S.68
Designed by C.K. Hutchinson.
Founded 1925
Visitors: welcome.
Green Fee: £11/round, £14/day WD;
£16/round, £20/day WE & BH.
Societies: welcome especially
weekdays.
Catering: lunches and dinners;
snacks only Mon.
Hotels: Burton; Oxford Arms.

I50 Ladbrook Park

☎(05644) 2264 Sec, 2581 Pro Shop
Poolhead Lane, Tanworth-in-Arden,
Warwicks B94 5ED
M42 junction 3; S on A435 forking
left after 500 yards to Tanworth/Penn
Lane, continue to T-junction, turn left
into Broad Lane, then 1st left into
Poolhead Lane; clubhouse 50 yards
on left; approx 2.5 mile from M42.
Undulating parkland course.

18 holes, 6427 yards, S.S.S.71
Designed by H.S. Colt.
Founded 1908
Visitors: welcome by prior
arrangement, contact Pro shop.
Green Fee: on application.
Societies: by prior arrangement,
contact Sec.
Catering: daily except Mon by prior
arrangement.
Hotels: George, St Johns Swallow
(Solihull); Aylesbury House (Hockley
Heath).

I51 Lansdown
☎(0225) 422138 Sec, 425007 Club/
Steward, 420242 Pro, 339252 Fax
Lansdown, Bath, Avon BA1 9BT
From M4 junction 18 take A46
towards Bath; at roundabout take
A420 towards Bristol, take 1st left
and club is approx 2 miles on right by
Bath Racecourse.
Elevated parkland course.
18 holes; White Course, 6316 yards,
S.S.S.70; Yellow Course, 6007
yards, S.S.S.69
Designed by Harry Colt.
Founded 1894/5
Visitors: welcome weekdays, with
h/cap weekends; not competition
days.
Green Fee: £18/round, £24/day WD;
£30 WE & BH.
Societies: welcome by prior
arrangement.
Catering: full range of snacks and
meals available.
Hotels: Lansdowne Grove; Francis;
Hilton.

I52 Lea Marston Hotel & Leisure Complex
☎(0675) 470468
Haunch Lane, Lea Marston,
Warwickshire B76 0BY
1 mile from M42 Junction 9 on
A4097 Kingsbury road; 2 miles from
Belfry golf course.
Public parkland course.
9 holes Par 3
Designed by J.R. Blake
Founded 1983
Visitors: smart casual dress.
Green Fee: £3.50 (9 holes), £4.25
(18 holes).
Societies: any time.
Catering: 6 bars, 100 place
restaurant.
Driving range, tennis, crown green
bowls, pool etc, health club, indoor
swimming pool.
Hotels: Lea Marston on site; special
golfing breaks.

I53 Leamington & County
☎(0926) 425961
Golf Lane, Whitnash, Leamington
Spa, Warwicks CV31 2QA
2 miles S of town centre, off A452.
Undulating parkland course.
18 holes, 6425 yards, S.S.S.71
Designed by H.S. Colt.
Founded 1908
Visitors: welcome.
Green Fee: on application.
Societies: welcome Wed, Thurs.
Catering: lunch and evening meal
served except Mon.
Snooker.
Hotels: Regent; Ladbroke Mercury.

I54 Leominster
☎(0568) 612863 Clubhouse,
611402 Pro, (0432) 880493 Sec
Ford Bridge, Leominster, Hereford
HR6 0LE
On A49 Leominster bypass 3 miles S
of Leominster, clearly signposted.
Undulating meadowland course.
18 holes, 6104 yards, S.S.S.69
Designed by Bob Sandow.
Founded 1967
Visitors: welcome weekdays;
weekends by prior arrangement.
Green Fee: £17/day WD, £21/day
WE & BH.
Societies: weekdays except Mon,
some weekends; by prior
arrangement.
Catering: bar facilities daily;
restaurant and snacks except Mon.
Driving range adjacent to course,
coarse fishing on River Lugg.
Hotels: Talbot; Green Dragon
(Hereford).

I55 Lickey Hills (Rose Hill)
☎(021) 453 3159
Lickey Hills, Rednal, Birmingham
M5 exit 4, on city boundary.
Public parkland course.
18 holes, 6010 yards, S.S.S.69
Designed by Carl Bretherton.
Founded 1927
Visitors: welcome.
Green Fee: £6.60/round,
£4.50/9holes.
Societies: by arrangement.
Catering: snacks served.

I56 Lilley Brook
☎(0242) 526785
Cirencester Rd, Charlton Kings,
Cheltenham, Glos GL53 8EG
3 miles from centre of Cheltenham
on Cheltenham-Cirencester road,
A435.

Parkland course.
18 holes, 6226 yards, S.S.S.70
Founded 1922
Visitors: bona fide members of golf
club with official h/cap.
Green Fee: £20 WD.
Societies: weekdays.
Catering: lunches, dinners served.
Hotels: Queens; Carlton.

I57 Little Lakes
☎(0299) 266385
Lye Head, Rock, Bewdley, Worcs
DY12 2UU
A456 2 miles W of Bewdley, turn left
at Greenhouse and Garden Centre,
proceed for 0.5 mile.
Undulating parkland course.
9 holes (18 from June 1994), 6247
yards, S.S.S.72
Designed by Michael Cooksey.
Founded 1975
Visitors: welcome weekdays; not
weekends or Bank Holidays.
Green Fee: £12/round, £15/day WD.
Societies: weekdays by
arrangement.
Catering: lunches served.
Hotels: Heath; George; Black Boy.

I58 Lydney
☎(0594) 842614, 841561 Sec
Lakeside Ave, Lydney, Glos GL15 5QA
Entering Lydney on A48 from
Gloucester, turn left at bottom of
Highfield Hill and look for Lakeside
Ave, 7th turning on left.
Parkland course.
9 holes, 5329 yards, S.S.S.66
Founded 1909
Visitors: welcome; weekends and
Bank Holidays with member only.
Green Fee: £12/day.
Societies: small societies welcome,
full facilities available, lunch, dinner
but not morning coffee.
Catering: light snacks only.
Hotels: Wyndham Arms (Clearwell).

I59 Mangotsfield
☎(0272) 565501
Carson's Rd, Mangotsfield, Bristol
BS17 3LW
M32, leave at junction Filton/
Downend, follow sign for Downend
and Mangotsfield.
Hilly meadowland course.
18 holes, 5300 yards, S.S.S.66
Founded 1975
Visitors: welcome.
Green Fee: £9 WD, £11 WE.
Societies: apply to Manager.
Catering: meals served.

I60 Maxstoke Park

☎(0675) 464915, 466743 Fax
Castle Lane, Coleshill, Warwicks B46
2RD
3 miles NE of Coleshill, M6 junction 4.
Parkland course.
18 holes, 6442 yards, S.S.S.71
Founded 1898
Visitors: welcome weekdays; with
member only weekends and Bank
Holidays.
Green Fee: £25/round, £35 more
than 18 holes.
Societies: Tues and Thurs.
Catering: full bar and restaurant
facilities.
Hotels: Lea Marston.

I61 Memorial Park

☎(0203) 675415
Memorial Park Golf Office,
Leamington Road, Coventry, W
Midlands
About 5 miles from city centre;
access from Leamington Rd car park
at Memorial Park.
18 hole Par 3 municipal course.
Visitors: 8.30am-2pm (last round)
winter; 9am-9pm summer.
Green Fee: £2.95; reductions for
OAPs and jnrs (under 16).
Catering: café in park in summer.
Bowling greens, 10 tennis courts,
playground, aviary.

I62 Minchinhampton

☎(0453) 833840 New, 836382 Old
New Course, Minchinhampton,
Stroud, Glos GL6 9BE; Old Course,
Minchinhampton, Stroud, Glos GL6
9AQ
Leave M5 at junction 13; New
Course, 3 miles E of Minchinhampton
on Avening road; Old Course, 1 mile
W of Minchinhampton on
Minchinhampton Common.
Parkland course (New), common
land course (Old).
New, 18 holes, 6675 yards, S.S.S.72;
Old, 18 holes, 6295 yards, S.S.S.71
Designed by F.W. Hawtree (New),
Robert Wilson (Old)
Founded 1889
Visitors: welcome at all times with
prior notice; h/cap certs required for
New Course.
Green Fee: New, £24 WD, £30 WE &
BH; Old, £10 WD, £13 WE & BH.
Societies: by prior arrangement.
Catering: available most times;
limited hours in winter.
Hotels: Bear at Rodborough;
Burleigh Court; Amberley Inn; Hare
and Hounds (Tetbury).

I63 Moor Hall

☎(021) 308 6130 Sec, 308 5106 Pro
Moor Hall Park, Sutton Coldfield, W
Midlands B75 6LN
From M42 take A446 to Bassets Pole
roundabout, follow Sutton Coldfield
road to 1st traffic lights, entrance
200 yards on left.
Parkland course.
18 holes, 6249 yards, S.S.S.70
Founded 1932
Visitors: welcome weekdays only.
Green Fee: £25/round, £32/day.
Societies: Tues and Wed only.
Catering: full service except Mon.
Hotels: Moor Hall; Penns Hall.

I64 Moseley

☎(021) 444 4957 Sec (10am-
4.30pm), 444 2115 Club, 441 4662
Fax
Springfield Rd, Kings Heath,
Birmingham B14 7DX
On Birmingham ring road, 0.5 mile E
of Alcester Rd.
Parkland course.
18 holes, 6285 yards, S.S.S.70
Founded 1892
Visitors: reference to Sec, letter of
intro, official (Club) h/cap cert.
Green Fee: £34.
Societies: Wed, Thurs, bookings via
Sec
Catering: available.

I65 Naunton Downs

☎(0451) 850090, 850092 Pro,
850093 Bar/restaurant, 850091 Fax
Naunton, Cheltenham,
Gloucestershire GL54 3AE
Off B4068 Stow-on-the-Wold/
Cheltenham road adjacent to the
village of Naunton.
Downland course.
18 holes, S.S.S.69
Designed by Jacob Pot.
Founded July 1993
Visitors: on application.
Green Fee: £19.95; guests £12.95.
Societies: on application.
Catering: lounge bar, spike bar,
drawing room, restaurant.
Hotels: Lords of the Manor (Lower
Slaughter); Grapevine
(Stow-on-the-Wold).

I66 Newbold Comyn

☎(0926) 421157
Newbold Terrace East, Leamington
Spa, Warwicks
Off B4099 Willes Rd, centrally
located.
Parkland course.

18 holes, 6259 yards, S.S.S.70
Founded 1972
Visitors: welcome.
Green Fee: apply for details.
Societies: apply to Pro.
Catering: bar and restaurant.

I67 North Warwickshire

☎(0676) 22259 Pro, 22915 Sec
Hampton Lane, Meriden, W Midlands
CV7 7LL
6 miles N of Coventry on A45.
Parkland course.
9 holes, 3195 yards, S.S.S.70
Founded 1894
Visitors: weekdays except Thur
(Ladies Day); weekends with
member only.
Green Fee: £20 WD, £15 WE with
member only.
Societies: welcome by prior
arrangement.
Catering: bar snacks.
Snooker.
Hotels: Manor Hotel (Meriden); Post
House (Coventry).

I68 North Worcestershire

☎(021) 475 1047 Sec, 475 5721 Pro
Frankley Beeches Rd, Northfield,
Birmingham B31 5LP
7 miles S of Birmingham City centre,
just off A38, approx 4 miles from M5
junction 4.
Meadowland course.
18 holes, 5919 yards, S.S.S.69
Designed by James Braid.
Founded 1907
Visitors: welcome weekdays; no
visitors weekends.
Green Fee: £19.50/round (£8.50
with member), £29.50/day WD.
Societies: catered for Tues and
Thurs.
Catering: full facilities.

I69 Nuneaton

☎(0203) 347810
Golf Drive, Whitestone, Nuneaton,
Warwicks CV11 6QF
Leave M6 at junction 3 on A444, 2
miles S of Nuneaton.
Wooded undulating meadowland
course.
18 holes, 6429 yards, S.S.S.71
Founded 1906
Visitors: welcome weekdays, with
member only weekends.
Green Fee: on application.
Societies: Wed, Fri only.
Catering: full catering facilities
except Mon.
Hotels: Long Shoot; Chase.

I70 Oakridge

☎(0676) 41389 Sec, 40542 Pro
Arley Lane, Ansley Village, Nuneaton,
Warwicks CV10 9PH
Off B4112, 3 miles W of Nuneaton.
Parkland course.
18 holes, 6200 yards, S.S.S.71
Founded 1993
Visitors: welcome weekdays, h/cap
cert required.
Green Fee: £15/round.
Societies: welcome Mon-Thurs by
arrangement.
Catering: full à la carte, set meals,
snacks.
Practice range, snooker.

I71 Olton

☎(021) 705 1083, 711 2010 Fax
Mirfield Rd, Solihull, W Midlands B91
1JH
2 miles off junction 5 M42 – A41 to
Birmingham.
Parkland course.
18 holes, 6229 yards, S.S.S.71
Founded 1893
Visitors: welcome weekdays except
Wed; not weekends unless with
member.
Green Fee: £30 (£10 with member)
WD.
Societies: weekdays by
arrangement, not Wed.
Catering: available.
Snooker.
Hotels: St Johns; George.

I72 Ombersley

☎(0905) 620747, 620047 Fax
Bishops Wood Road, Lineholt,
Ombersley, Droitwich, Worcs WR9
0LE
Off A449 between Worcester and
Kidderminster; at Mitre Oak pub
roundabout take A4025 to Stourport,
after 400 yards turn 1st left.
Parkland course with views over
Severn Valley.
18 holes, 6139 yards, Par 72
Designed by On Course Design
(David Morgan).
Founded Sept 1991
Visitors: welcome at any time, no
restrictions.
Green Fee: £9.60/round WD, £12.80
WE; reductions for jnrs and OAPs.
Societies: welcome by arrangement,
not weekends.
Catering: full catering facilities
available.
Driving range, putting green, practice
bunker; disabled facilities.
Hotels: Stourport Moat House; Mitre
Oak.

I73 Painswick

☎(0452) 812180
Painswick Beacon, Painswick,
Stroud, Glos GL6 6TL
1 mile N of Painswick village on A46.
Commonland course.
18 holes, 4780 yards, S.S.S.64
Founded 1891
Visitors: welcome weekdays; Sat,
Sun with member only.
Green Fee: apply for details.
Societies: by arrangement with Sec.
Catering: by arrangement with
Steward; snacks normally available.
Hotels: Hatton Court; Painswick.

I74 Pitcheroak

☎(0527) 541054
Plymouth Rd, Redditch, Worcs B97
4PB
In centre of Redditch, signposted.
Municipal parkland course
9 holes (18 tees), 4500-5000 yards,
S.S.S.62
Founded 1973
Visitors: welcome any time.
Green Fee: apply for details.
Catering: bar and restaurant.

I75 Puckrup Hall Hotel

☎(0684) 296200, 850788 Fax
Puckrup, Tewkesbury, Glos GL20 6EL
4 miles N of Tewkesbury on A38, 0.5
mile from M50 junction 1.
Parkland course.
18 holes, S.S.S.71
Designed by Simon Gidman.
Founded Oct 1992
Visitors: welcome subject to
availability and golfing ability.
Green Fee: £19.50 WD, £25 WE.
Societies: non-residential Tues and
Thurs, min 12.
Catering: available all day every day
in Hotel; brasserie restaurant.
Hotel Leisure Club.
Hotels: Puckrup Hall.

I76 Purley Chase Golf & Country Club

☎(0203) 393118 office, 397468
club, 395348 Pro shop
Ridge Lane, Nr Nuneaton, CV10 0RB
4 miles W of Nuneaton, 2 miles SW of
Atherstone, signposted.
Parkland course.
18 holes, 6734 yards, S.S.S.71
Designed by B. Tomlinson.
Founded 1976
Visitors: welcome weekdays, at
weekends subject to availability.
Green Fee: apply for details.
Societies: welcome weekdays.

Catering: full facilities.
Driving range.
Hotels: Mancetter Manor; Lea
Marston.

I77 Pype Hayes

☎(021) 351 1014
Eachelhurst Rd, Walmley, Sutton
Coldfield, W Midlands B76 8EP
Off M6 at Spaghetti Junction, onto
Tyburn Rd, 1 mile to Eachelhurst Rd.
Public parkland course.
18 holes, 5811 yards, S.S.S.68
Founded 1932
Visitors: welcome.
Green Fee: apply for details.
Societies: welcome.
Catering: full facilities; no bar.

I78 Redditch

☎(0527) 543309
Lower Grinsty Lane, Callow Hill,
Redditch, Worcs B97 5JP
3 miles W of town centre; take
Heathfield road off A448 Redditch-
Bromsgrove road, turn left into Green
Lane.
Parkland (1st 9), woodland (2nd 9)
course.
18 holes, 6671 yards, S.S.S.72
Designed by F. Pennink.
Founded 1913
Visitors: members of recognised
golf club welcome weekdays; with
member weekends.
Green Fee: £27.50/day (£8 with
member).
Societies: weekdays by
arrangement.
Catering: full service except Mon.
Snooker.
Hotels: Southcrest; Hotel Montville.

I79 Robin Hood

☎(021) 706 0061 Sec, 706 0806 Pro
St Bernards Rd, Solihull, W Midlands
B92 7DJ
From Olton station (6 miles S of
Birmingham on A41) travel NE up St
Bernards Rd for 1 mile, drive to
clubhouse on right.
Parkland course.
18 holes, 6635 yards, S.S.S.72
Designed by H.S. Colt.
Founded 1893
Visitors: welcome weekdays except
official holidays, Tues am, Wed pm.
Green Fee: £29/round, £35/day.
Societies: Tues pm, Thurs and Fri.
Catering: bar snacks Tues to Fri;
evening meals by arrangement.
Hotels: St Johns Swallow; George;
Flemings.

Ross-on-Wye

In the summer of 1961, Ken Cotton was busy building two new courses, one in the stately old deer park of St Pierre by the Newport Road out of Cheptstow and the other in rather damp woodland on the outskirts of Ross-on-Wye. Both were adventurous, new ventures at a time when golf course building had only just begun to revive after the War.

It was a happy day therefore when Cotton phoned to extend an invitation to see the construction work, but not the least remarkable part of a remarkable tale is that it very nearly did not happen at all.

At the behest of a small group of men who had formed a special committee of the existing 9-hole Ross-on-Wye Club close to the race course, he inspected the land in question only to report that he felt it unsuitable. It was only when the committee drove to Cotton's house near Pangbourne to plead with him to give it a try that he relented.

The committee had been searching high and low for a suitable site and saw this as their last chance. The decision to start was an act of faith by all concerned because the first steps involved a comprehensive clearance operation unsurpassed even with the making of Woburn a dozen or so years later.

My first memory was the sight of the head woodsman, then in his eighties, fuelling a woodland fire with fresh scrub and branches and cooking a lunch of bacon and eggs on the back of a carefully cleaned shovel. Even after working on many, many new courses, it is still something of a marvel that it all took shape as, indeed, was the speed with which Cotton conceived his layout.

After walking round the perimeter in pouring rain, and cogitating later in his bath, he presented the committee with a plan that needed virtually no change, although the patience needed to implement it requires almost as much praise as the initial inspiration.

Without the enormous personal contribution and sacrifice of the committee it would undoubtedly have failed and neither before nor since has there been such a shining example of unselfish enterprise. They had only the aim in mind of assuring the future of Ross-on-Wye Golf Club, an aspiration they achieved with flying colours.

The new course was more than just a notable addition in an area virtually devoid of golf, it now ranks as one of the best inland courses in Britain. It has a handful of blind shots and there is a high demand on control from the tee, but from an enclosed, dark woodland, has emerged a beautiful setting for the game, one in which the distant beauty enhances the aesthetic pleasures of trees and pretty flowers.

It is hard nowadays to believe the problems faced at the outset but it needs a realisation of them to judge the success achieved and to pay tribute to the vision and skill which brought it about.

It made the official opening on May 7th, 1967 an auspicious occasion. For one thing, new courses were rare in those days and, for another, the opening ceremony was performed by one of Cotton's partners, Frank Pennink, in his capacity as President of the English Golf Union.

It was a happy gathering that followed the exhibition game, marvelling how the course had been so patiently moulded from the forest and how the whole operation, including purchase of the land and the building of the clubhouse, had cost only £41,000. Twenty-five years later, that would have provided no more than a couple of holes — on some expensive enterprises, not even one.

180 Ross-on-Wye

☎(0989 82) 267 Sec, 439 Pro, 660 Steward/stewardess
Two Park, Gorsley, Ross-on-Wye, Hereford HR9 7UT
Adjacent M50 junction 3, 5 miles N of Ross.
Parkland course.
18 holes, 6500 yards, S.S.S.73
Designed by C.K. Cotton.
Founded 1903
Visitors: must be members of recognised club.
Green Fee: on application.
Societies: welcome Wed, Thurs, Fri, 16 min.
Catering: full bar and restaurant facilities; bar snacks only Mon. 2 snooker tables.
Hotels: Chase; Royal.

181 Royal Forest of Dean

☎(0594) 832583, 833689 Pro
Lords Hill, Coleford, Glos GL16 8BD
Between M4, M5 and M50; from M5, M50 4 miles Monmouth, 8 miles Ross, from M4 8 miles Chepstow.
Parkland/meadowland course.
18 holes, 5535 yards, S.S.S.69
Designed by John Day of Alphagreen Ltd.
Founded 1973
Visitors: welcome.
Green Fee: £10 WD, £12 WE.
Societies: Mon-Thurs; lunch, 3-course evening meal, 36 holes, £24 per person (10-35 persons).
Catering: bar open all day; restaurant serving table d'hôte, à la carte meals and snacks all year round; banqueting for up to 170. Outdoor swimming pool, tennis, bowls.
Hotels: own 32 bedroom hotel in centre of course, sporting weekends inc free golf £92; midweek breaks £39.50/day.

182 Rugby

☎(0788) 542306
Clifton Rd, Rugby, CV21 3RD
On Rugby-Market Harborough road, on right just past railway bridge as leaving town.
Parkland course.
18 holes, 5457 yards, S.S.S.67
Founded 1891
Visitors: welcome weekdays; weekends and Bank Holidays with member.
Green Fee: on application
Societies: weekdays by arrangement.
Catering: meals daily except Tues.

183 Sapey Golf

☎(0886) 853288, 853567, 853485 Fax
Upper Sapey, Nr Worcester, Worcs WR6 6XT
Midway between Bromyard and Stourport on B4203.
Open parkland course.
18 holes, 5,900 yards, S.S.S.69
Founded July 1990
Visitors: welcome with 24 hours notice.
Green Fee: £12/round, £19/day WD; £19/round, £25/day WE & BH.
Societies: welcome at all times; 14 days notice required.
Catering: bar facilities all week; restaurant open from Wed to Sun inclusive.
Driving range.
Hotels: The Granary (Collington).

184 Shirehampton Park

☎(0272) 822083 Sec, 823059 Club, 822488 Pro
Park Hill, Shirehampton, Bristol BS11 0UL
1.5 miles from M5 junction 18, B4018 through village of Shirehampton; course at top of hill overlooking River Avon.
Undulating parkland course.
18 holes, 5521 yards, S.S.S.67
Founded 1907
Visitors: weekdays welcome, weekends only if accompanied by member.
Green Fee: £18/round, £25 weekends by arrangement only
Societies: Mon only by arrangement with Sec.
Catering: snacks, lunch always available; evening meals by arrangement.
Swallow Royal.

185 Shirley

☎(021) 744 6001
Stratford Rd, Monkspath, Shirley, Solihull, W Midlands B90 4EW
From M42 junction 4, 500 yards on left towards Birmingham.
Parkland course.
18 holes, 6510 yards, S.S.S.71
Founded 1953
Visitors: welcome weekdays, h/cap cert required.
Green Fee: apply for details.
Societies: welcome Mon-Fri by arrangement.
Catering: meals and snacks daily.
Snooker.
Hotels: St John's (Solihull); Regency (Shirley).

186 Sphinx

☎(0203) 458890, 451361 after 7pm
Siddeley Ave, Coventry, W Midlands CV3 1FZ
Approx 4 miles S of centre of Coventry, close to main Binley Rd.
Parkland course
9 holes, 2101 yards, Par 60.
Founded 1940s (as Rolls Royce Sports Club).
Visitors: welcome; with member only weekends.
Green Fee: £8 WD, £10 WE.
Societies: recognised societies welcome.
Catering: bar and bar meals.

187 Stinchcombe Hill

☎(0453) 542015
Stinchcombe Hill, Dursley, Glos GL11 6AQ
1 mile along narrow lane (signposted) off A4135 Tetbury-Dursley road; or approach direct from Dursley town centre, 0.5 mile up hill past bus station.
Meadowland/downland course.
18 holes, 5723 yards, S.S.S.68
Founded 1889
Visitors: welcome any day; restricted weekends and Bank Holidays except with member.
Green Fee: apply for details.
Societies: by arrangement.
Catering: full facilities available.
Hotels: Hare & Hounds; Prince of Wales.

188 Stoneleigh Deer Park

☎(0203) 639991/639912 tee times, 511533 Fax
The Old Deer Park, Coventry Rd, Stoneleigh, Warwicks CV8 3DR
A46 Stoneleigh exit, course 1 mile S of village.
Parkland course beside River Avon.
Tantara, 18 holes, 6083 yards, S.S.S.68; Avon, 9 holes, 1251 yards, Par 3
Designed by K. Harrison.
Founded 1991
Visitors: welcome; book starting times through shop.
Green Fee: £12 WD, £15 WE.
Societies: Mon-Fri by booking.
Catering: bar, restaurant.

189 Stourbridge

☎(0384) 395566
Worcester Lane, Stourbridge DY8 2RB
2 miles from Stourbridge town centre on Worcester road.

Parkland course.
18 holes, 6178 yards, S.S.S.70
Founded 1892
Visitors: welcome weekdays; with member only weekends.
Green Fee: £22.
Societies: restricted to Tues and Fri.
Catering: available except Mon.
Hotels: Pedmore House.

I90 Stratford Oaks
☎(0789) 731571, 731700
Bearley Road, Snitterfield,
Stratford-upon-Avon, Warwicks
CV37 0EZ
5 miles M40 junction 15, or A34 to Stratford and follow signs for Snitterfield.
Parkland course.
18 holes, 6100 yards, S.S.S.71
Designed by Howard Swan.
Founded 1989
Visitors: welcome any time.
Green Fee: £15 WD, £22.50 WE.
Societies: Mon-Fri.
Catering: bar and restaurant facilities.
Driving range, putting greens, practice chipping area, practice grass area.
Hotels: Arden Valley; Alveston Manor.

I91 Stratford-upon-Avon
☎(0789) 205749
Tiddington Rd, Stratford-upon-Avon,
Warwicks CV37 7BA
0.5 mile from river bridge on B4089.
Parkland course.
18 holes, 6309 yards, S.S.S.70
Founded 1894 (1928 on present site)
Visitors: weekdays by arrangement.
Green Fee: £25/round, £28/day WD; £35/round WE & BH.
Societies: Tues and Thurs by arrangement.
Catering: snacks and meals.

I92 Streamleaze
☎(0453) 843128
Canons Court Farm, Bradley,
Wotton-under-Edge, Glos GL12 7PN
Turn left off B4058 3 miles from M5 junction 14.
Farmland course.
9 holes, 2291 yards
Founded 1982
Visitors: welcome.
Green Fee: apply for details.
Catering: bar and bar snacks available.
Hotels: caravan site adjacent to course.

I93 Sutton Coldfield
☎(021) 353 9633, (Sutton Coldfield Ladies GC (021) 353 1682)
110 Thornhill Rd, Streetly, Sutton Coldfield B74 3ER
Located in Sutton Park, 9 miles NE of Birmingham on B4138; nearest motorway access is M6 junction 6; car park entrance on pposite side of Thornhill Rd to course.
Heathland course.
18 holes, 6248 yards, S.S.S.71
Re-designed by Dr Mackenzie.
Founded 1889
Visitors: welcome weekdays except Tues am.
Green Fee: £30/day (£6 with member).
Societies: not accepted on Tues, weekends or Bank Holidays; written applications required.
Catering: lunches, snacks daily.
Snooker.
Hotels: Parson & Clerk; Fairlawns; Sutton Court.

I94 Tewkesbury Park Hotel
☎(0684) 295405
Lincoln Green Lane, Tewkesbury,
GL20 7DN
0.5 mile S of town on A38, 3 miles from junction 9 off M5.
Parkland course.
18 holes, 6533/6197 yards, S.S.S.71/69
Designed by Frank Pennink.
Founded 1976
Visitors: welcome with h/cap cert.
Green Fee: apply for details.
Societies: welcome; weekends residential only.
Catering: snacks and meals available.
Hotels: Tewkesbury Park.

I95 Thornbury Golf Centre
☎(0454) 281144, 281177 Fax
Bristol Rd, Thornbury, Avon
On S side of Thornbury from A38.
Newly landscaped parkland course.
18 holes, c. 6500 yards, Par 72; 18 holes Par 3, c.2800 yards.
Designed by Hawtree.
Founded 1992
Visitors: welcome.
Green Fee: Main course, £12/round; Par 3 course, £6.50/round.
Societies: Mon-Fri, min 12.
Catering: full facilities.
Driving range.
Hotels: 11 bedrooms in farmhouse on site.

I96 Tolladine
☎(0905) 21074, 726180 Pro shop
Tolladine Rd, Worcester WR4 9BA
Leave M5 at junction 6 Warndon, about 1 mile from city centre opposite Virgin Tavern.
Meadowland course.
9 holes, 5134 yards, S.S.S.67
Founded 1898
Visitors: welcome weekdays, weekends with member only.
Green Fee: £15 WD (£7.50 with member), £7.50 WE & BH with member.
Societies: by appointment weekdays.
Catering: available at Virgin Tavern opposite.
Hotels: Fownes; The Star; Gifford.

I97 Tracy Park Country Club
☎(0275) 372251
Bath Rd, Wick, Bristol BS15 5RN
Junction 18 off M4, S on A46 for 4 miles, right on A420 for 2 miles.
Parkland course.
27 holes offering 3 × 18-hole combinations; Avon, 6834 yards, S.S.S.73; Bristol, 6861 yards, S.S.S.73; Cotswold, 6203 yards, S.S.S.70
Designed by Grant Aitken.
Founded 1975
Visitors: welcome, telephone ahead.
Green Fee: apply for details.
Societies: welcome 7 days by arrangement.
Catering: lunch, dinner, bar snacks.
Squash, tennis, swimming, croquet, snooker.
Hotels: Lansdown Grove; Linden; Manor House.

I98 The Vale Golf & Country Club
☎(038 682) 781, 520 Pro shop, 660 Fax
Hill Furze Rd, Bishampton, Pershore,
Worcs WR10 2LZ
Off B4084 near Bishampton village, 7 miles M5 junction 6, 6 miles Evesham, 5 miles Pershore.
Parkland/downland course.
International, 18 holes, 6519-7779 yards, S.S.S.73-76; Lenches, 9 holes, 5836 yards, S.S.S.68
Founded June 1991
Visitors: welcome, phone Pro to book.
Green Fee: apply for details.
Societies: society/company days welcome any day, 2 courses available.

Recently converted 16th Century half timbered barn situated midway between Ross-on-Wye and Lebury. ¼ mile off A449. Over 20 courses within easy reach. Brochure with course locations on request.

Rocks Place, Yatton, Ross-on-Wye, Herefordshire. HR9 7RD Tel: 053 184 218

Catering: Vale bar, Spikes bar, snacks and brunch, full à la carte restaurant and carvery; function room (140), conference room. Driving range.
Hotels: Chequers (Fladbury), golf packages available.

I99 Walmley
☎(021) 373 0029 Club, 373 7103 Pro shop
Brooks Rd, Wylde Green, Sutton Coldfield, W Midlands B72 1HR
6 miles N of Birmingham, turn off Birmingham to Sutton Coldfield road 0.25 mile N of Chester Rd (Yenton Pub), right into Greenhill Rd, Brooks Rd continues from this.
Parkland course.
18 holes, 6537 yards, S.S.S.72
Founded 1902
Visitors: welcome weekdays.
Green Fee: £25/round, £30/day, (£10 with member).
Societies: weekdays.
Catering: not Mondays.
Hotels: Penns Hall (Wylde Green), New Hall.

I100 Warley
☎(021) 429 2440
Lightwoods Hill, Smethwick, Warley, W Midlands
Off A456 4.5 miles W of centre of Birmingham, behind Dog public house.
Municipal parkland course.
9 holes, 2606 yards, S.S.S.64
Founded 1921
Visitors: welcome at all times, phone bookings in operation.
Green Fee: £6.
Societies: not advised.
Catering: available.

I101 Warwick
☎(0926) 494316
The Racecourse, Warwick, CV34 6HW

Centre of Warwick Racecourse.
Public meadowland course.
9 holes, 2682 yards, S.S.S.66
Designed by D.G. Dunkley.
Founded 1886
Visitors: welcome except race days.
Green Fee: £3.80 (9 holes) WD, £5.50 (9 holes) WE.
Catering: bar only.
Driving range.
Hotels: Tudor House; Fourpenny Shop; Hilton International.

I102 Welcombe Hotel
☎(0789) 295252, 299012
Clubhouse, 414666 Fax
Warwick Rd, Stratford-upon-Avon, Warwicks CV37 0NR
5 miles from M40 junction 15, 1.5 miles from Stratford on A439.
Parkland course.
18 holes, 6217 yards, S.S.S.70
Designed by T.J. McCauley.
Founded 1980
Visitors: phone booking essential.
Green Fee: £35 WD, £40 WE.
Societies: weekdays only on request.
Catering: Pub style food and bar.
Driving range, floodlit tennis, snooker, buggies.
Hotels: Welcombe, golf breaks available.

I103 Westonbirt
☎(0666) 880242
Tetbury, Glos GL8 8QG
Turn off A433 3 miles SW of Tetbury, through Westonbirt village, take turning opposite Westonbirt Arboretum entrance.
Parkland course.
9 holes, 4504 yards, S.S.S.62
Designed by Monty Hearn.
Visitors: welcome.
Green Fee: £7/day WD (£4.50 jnrs), £7/round WE & BH (£4.50 jnrs).
Societies: welcome by prior arrangement.

Catering: available at Holford Arms, teas and snacks on course.
Hotels: Hare & Hounds.

I104 Wharton Park
☎(0299) 405222, 405163 Pro shop, 405121 Fax
Long Bank, Bewdley, Worcs
On A456 at W end of Bewdley by-pass.
Undulating parkland course in Wyre Forest.
18 holes, c. 6500 yards, Par 73
Founded 1992
Visitors: welcome.
Green Fee: £10-£12.50, £18 day ticket.
Societies: by booking, no limit.
Catering: full facilities, conferences, function room.
Snooker, driving range.

I105 Whitefields
☎(0788) 521800, 521695 Fax
Coventry Rd, Thurlaston, Nr Rugby, Warwicks CV23 9JR
Just off M45 on A45 to Coventry; easy reach from M6, M40, M69, M1.
Parkland course.
18 holes
Founded Aug 1992
Visitors: welcome.
Green Fee: £15 WD, £18 WE.
Societies: welcome Mon-Fri.
Catering: bars, spike bar, restaurant, catering for over 100.
Driving range (opening 1994).
Hotels: own 15 room hotel.

I106 Windmill Village Hotel
☎(0203) 407241
Birmingham Road, Allesley, Coventry, W Midlands CV5 9AL
Off A45 westbound
Coventry-Birmingham road.
Part flat, part hilly course.
18 holes, 4778 yards, S.S.S.64

Designed by Robert Hunter & John Harrhy.
Founded 1990
Visitors: welcome except Sun am.
Green Fee: apply for details.
Societies: welcome weekdays only.
Catering: 2 bars, 2 restaurants.
Swimming pool, 8 snooker tables, fitness gym, sauna, conference facilities.
Hotels: Windmill Village (90 beds).

I107 Woodlands

☎(0454) 773361
Woodlands Lane, Almondsbury, Bristol BS12 4JZ
M5 exit 16 to large roundabout, left exit signed Woodlands Lane.
Public parkland course.
18 holes, 6068 yards, Par 70
Founded 1989
Visitors: pay-as-you-play.
Green Fee: apply for details.

Societies: by arrangement.
Catering: full facilities.
Hotels: The Grange, Starkeys, Aztec West (Bradley Stoke).

I108 Worcester G & CC

☎(0905) 422555 Sec, 422044 Pro, 421132 Catering
Boughton Park, Worcester WR2 4EZ
1.5 miles from town centre on Bransford Rd (A4103); from M5 junction 7 follow signs for Hereford.
Parkland course.
18 holes, 6154 yards, S.S.S.69
Designed by Dr A. Mackenzie.
Founded 1898
Visitors: welcome with h/cap cert; with member only at weekends; phone Pro.
Green Fee: £23.
Societies: weekdays.
Catering: every day.
Tennis, squash, snooker.

I109 Worcestershire

☎(0684) 575992, 573905
Wood Farm, Malvern Wells, Worcs WR14 4PP
2 miles S of Great Malvern, turn off A449 on to B4209, follow signs to course.
Meadowland/parkland course.
18 holes, 6449 yards, S.S.S.71
Designed by Colt, Mackenzie, Braid and later Jiggins and Hawtree.
Founded 1879/1880
Visitors: members of recognised club with h/cap certs, no play before 10am weekends.
Green Fee: £25 WD, £30 WE.
Societies: welcome by arrangement Thurs and Fri.
Catering: max 70 seating; full facilities except Mon.
Snooker.
Hotels: Abbey; Foley Arms; Cottage in the Wood; Mount Pleasant; Royal Malvern.

J

WALES

Golf in Wales can be divided very clearly into North and South with one or two notable exceptions in the central region like Borth & Ynyslas, which is well worth a break in any journey.

Road access to the Principality is usually by way of the Severn Bridge, the coast road from Chester to Bangor or into the mountain heart by way of Shrewsbury, Llangollen or Dolgellau. Bernard Darwin, who always favoured the train, made the latter a much publicised route, and was able to recite at will the stations that came between Shrewsbury and his beloved Aberdovey where he spent an annual holiday.

The station at Aberdovey itself is right beside the clubhouse and little time need be lost in launching a round across an historic piece of land, which Darwin described with sentimental love and warmth. It is among a host of Clubs celebrating their centenary in 1992. Although two years' Aberdovey's junior, Royal St David's enjoys an even more resplendent setting, under the historic shadow of Harlech Castle, with more distant views of Snowdonia. It is a well trodden favourite for the staging of Welsh championships.

The north coast is well served by Conwy (Caernarvonshire) and by Prestatyn which, after a somewhat flat beginning, blossoms into ideal duneland territory. Llandudno GC at Maesdu and North Wales GC next door are familiar names.

For an instant introduction to Welsh golf in the south, nothing beats the convenience of St Pierre, which was one of the first new courses to be built in the wake of World War II and undoubtedly one of the best. It weaves a most pleasant path through stately trees of ancient origin, providing a sheltered home for the game that contrasts sharply with the exposed reaches of Royal Porthcawl, Southerndown, Pyle & Kenfig, Ashburnham and Tenby.

Temptation to reach Porthcawl may make travellers overlook the charms of Newport at Rogerstone, but Porthcawl is rightly hailed the most noble of the Welsh championship links, every hole commanding sight of the ocean and the first three rubbing shoulders with it. There is greater change of level at Porthcawl than on any other seaside course in England and Wales. For a lofty perch, however, Southerndown is a distinguished example — enjoying a bird's eye view of Porthcawl into the bargain.

The drive to the Club scales the side of a mountain while the first hole climbs what is left. Pyle & Kenfig, on the other side of Porthcawl, returns to sea level, the course split in two by a road which also acts as a division of character.

Pennard beyond Swansea is a lovely, remote links that never attracts the praise it warrants but this is more the province of West Wales, with the attractions of Ashburnham and Tenby which combine a stern challenge with scenic blessings.

Ashburnham is as well known for golf as the neighbouring town of Llanelli is for rugby, but Tenby beckons for those who look upon themselves as connoisseurs of glorious places to play. Host to countless championships, it is a seaside links of unrivalled joy and beauty and, for the historically minded, it has an important additional qualification – it is the oldest constituted Club in the Principality.

It is golf on the grand scale, frequently influenced by the wind and calling for an ability to flight the ball low and indulge in the art of the chip and run which many in other parts of the world regard as a relic of a lost age.

This section has been dominated by north and south but Cradoc at Brecon, Knighton and Llandrindod Wells are some contrasting courses in contrasting settings for those desirous of exploring more central parts.

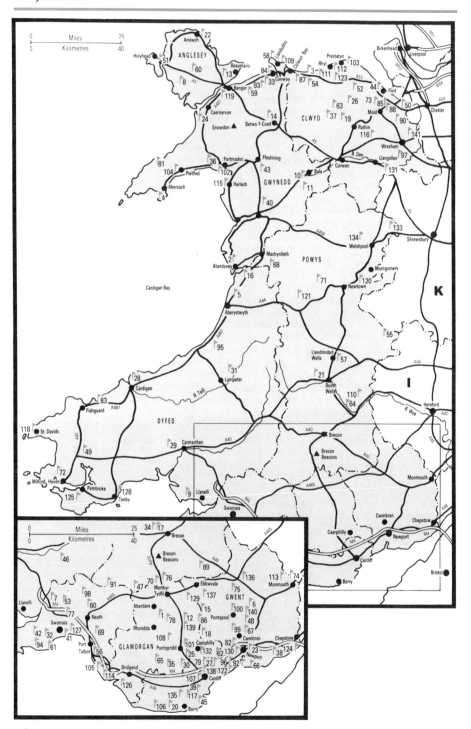

J1 Aberdare

☎(0685) 871188 club, 872797 Sec, 878735 Pro
Abernant, Aberdare, Mid-Glam CF44 0RY
0.5 mile from town centre (A4059), past General Hospital.
Mountain course with parkland features.
18 holes, 5875 yards, S.S.S.69
Founded 1921
Visitors: welcome weekdays; Sat with member only; Sun and Bank Holidays by advance notice to Sec.
Green Fee: £14 WD, £18 WE & BH.
Societies: welcome on application to Sec.
Catering: full range of bar snacks and meals; not Mon.
Snooker.
Hotels: Baverstock; Ty Newydd.

J2 Aberdovey

☎(0654) 767210, 767493 Sec
Aberdovey, Gwynedd LL35 0RT
On main A493 immediately W of Aberdovey.
Seaside links course.
18 holes, 6445 yards, S.S.S.71
Amendments by James Braid.
Founded 1892
Visitors: welcome; h/cap certs required.
Green Fee: from £20/round to £36/day.
Societies: weekdays only.
Catering: daily 10.30am-8.30pm; bar 11am-11pm. Snooker.
Hotels: list available from Sec.

J3 Abergele & Pensarn

☎(0745) 824034
Tan-y-Gopa Rd, Abergele, Clwyd LL28 8DS
Through Abergele from A55, turn left in direction of Llanddulas; course below Gwrych Castle.
Parkland course.
18 holes, 6450 yards, S.S.S.71
Designed by Hawtree & Sons.
Founded 1910
Visitors: welcome.
Green Fee: £22 WD, £28 WE & BH.
Societies: by prior arrangement.
Catering: restaurant except Mon.
Snooker.

J4 Abersoch

☎(0758) 812622
Golf Rd, Abersoch, Gwynedd LL53 7EY
6 miles from Pwllhelli; 1st left through village.

Seaside links course.
18 holes, 5819 yards, S.S.S.68
Designed by Harry Vardon.
Founded 1910
Visitors: welcome with h/cap cert; booking required.
Green Fee: £15.
Societies: by arrangement.
Catering: meals served.
Hotels: Egryn; Wylfa; Riverside; Neigwl; Deugoch.

J5 Aberystwyth

☎(0970) 615104, 625301 Pro
Bryn y-Mor, Aberystwyth, Dyfed SY23 3QD
N end of promenade immediately behind sea front hotels, access road adjacent to Cliff Railway, 1 mile from town centre.
Undulating meadowland course.
18 holes, 6109 yards, S.S.S.71
Designed by Harry Vardon.
Founded 1911
Visitors: limited at weekends.
Green Fee: £15.
Societies: by appointment.
Catering: bar and restaurant.
Hotels: apply to Sec for details.

J6 Alice Springs

☎(0873) 880772
Bettws Newydd, Usk, Gwent NP5 1JY
A449 into Usk, N on B4598, 1.5 miles take right to Bettws Newydd, course (Queens) 1.5 miles on left; for Kings course take same B4598, do not turn off, course 3 miles N on right.
Parkland course.
Queens, 18 holes, 6041 yards, S.S.S.69; Kings, 6868 yards, S.S.S.71
Designed by Keith R. Morgan.
Founded Aug 1989
Visitors: phone for tee time weekends and Bank Holidays.
Green Fee: £12.50/round.
Societies: Mon-Fri; weekends by arrangement.
Catering: bar and snacks all day, restaurant with phone booking.

J7 Allt-y-Graban

☎(0792) 885757, 883279
Allt-y-Graban Rd, Pontlliw, Swansea, West Glam SA4 1DT
From M4 exit 47 follow A48 through Penllergaer and Pontlliw; take 1st turning left after Glamorgan Arms onto Allt-y-Graban Rd; course opposite garden centre.
Parkland course.

9 holes, 6 Par 4, 3 Par 3
Designed by F.G. Thomas.
Founded August 1993
Visitors: welcome 9.30am to 1 hour before dusk.
Green Fee: £6 (9 holes), £9 (18 holes).
Societies: weekdays; contact club for terms.
Catering: clubhouse open spring 1994 with refreshment and changing facilities.
Hotels: Fforest Motel (Fforestfach); Diplomat (Llanelli).

J8 Anglesey

☎(0407) 810930 Manager, 810219 Steward, 811202 Pro
Station Rd, Rhosneigr, Gwynedd LL64 5QT
S off A5 about 8 miles from Holyhead onto A4080, in 3 miles turn right at Llanfaelog church, under railway bridge, about 1 mile to course.
Seaside links course.
18 holes, 5773 yards, S.S.S.68
Founded 1914
Visitors: h/cap cert required, preferable to phone.
Green Fee: £15 WD, £20 WE & BH.
Societies: by arrangement, reduction for 10+.
Catering: meals served.
Hotels: Maelog Lake (Rhosneigr).

J9 Ashburnham

☎(055 46) 2269 Sec
Cliffe Terrace, Burry Port, Dyfed SA16 0HN
9 miles from Llanelli exit on M4, 4 miles from Llanelli on A484.
Championship links course.
18 holes, 6916 yards, S.S.S.73; 18 holes, 6627 yards, S.S.S.72
Founded 1894
Visitors: weekdays; some weekends.
Green Fee: apply for details.
Societies: welcome weekdays.
Catering: full facilities.

J10 Bala

☎(0678) 520359 (9am-3pm April-Sept, 9am-10am Oct-March, evenings all year)
Penlan, Bala, Gwynedd LL23 7YD
Take A494 out of Bala to Dolgellau, turn 1st right on leaving Bala.
Upland course.
10 holes, 4962 yards, S.S.S.64
Founded 1973
Visitors: welcome, some restrictions Sat and Sun pm.

Green Fee: on application.
Societies: welcome by prior arrangement.
Catering: bar; catering by prior arrangement.
Snooker, pool.
Hotels: Plas Goch; White Lion; Pale Hall.

J11 Bala Lake Hotel
☎(0678) 520344
Bala, Gwynned, LL23 7YF
Off B4403 1.5 miles from Bala.
Public parkland course.
9 holes, 4281 yards, S.S.S.61
Founded 1960
Visitors: welcome.
Green Fee: apply for details.
Societies: welcome.
Catering: full catering facilities available.
Open air swimming pool.
Hotels: Bala Lake Hotel.

J12 Bargoed
☎(0443) 830143
Heolddu, Bargoes, Mid-Glam
20 miles from Cardiff on A469 to town centre; moorland road.
Moorland course.
18 holes, 6213 yards, S.S.S.70
Founded c. 1921
Visitors: welcome weekdays; weekends with member only.
Green Fee: £15 WD (£10 with member).
Societies: by arrangement.
Catering: bar snacks and evening meals served.
Hotels: Park Hotel; Maes Manor.

J13 Baron Hill
☎(0248) 810231
Beaumaris, Anglesey, Gwynedd LL58 8YN
Follow A545 Menai Bridge-Beaumaris, course is signposted on left when approaching Beaumaris.
Undulating moorland.
9 holes, 5564 yards, S.S.S.67
Founded 1895
Visitors: welcome, h/cap cert preferred, parties contact Sec; Tues Ladies day, Sun competitions until mid-afternoon).
Green Fee: £14/day, £60/week (reduced with member).
Societies: booking necessary, not Sun.
Catering: clubhouse fire damaged, rebuilding planned 1994.
Hotels: Bulkeley Arms; Bishopsgate; Bull.

J14 Betws-y-Coed
☎(0690) 710556
Betws-y-Coed, Gwynedd
Just off main A5 road in the middle of village of Betws-y-Coed.
Parkland course.
9 holes, 4996 yards, S.S.S.64
Founded 1977
Visitors: welcome.
Green Fee: £12.50 WD, £17.50 WE.
Societies: arrangements to be made in writing to Sec or phone (0492) 641663 after 6pm..
Catering: everyday except Mon.
Hotels: Royal Oak; Plas Hall.

J15 Blackwood
☎(0495) 223152
Cwmgelli, Blackwood, Gwent NP2 1EL
0.75 mile N of Blackwood on A4048, Tredegar road.
Meadowland course.
9 holes, 5304 yards, S.S.S.66
Founded 1914
Visitors: welcome weekdays, weekends by arrangement.
Green Fee: £12 WD, £15 WE & BH.
Societies: weekdays by arrangement.
Catering: golf societies only by arrangement.
Hotels: Maes Manor; Plas Inn.

J16 Borth & Ynyslas
☎(0970) 871202 Sec, 871557 Pro
Borth, Dyfed SY24 5JS
8 miles N of Aberystwyth; travel N from Aberystwyth to Machynlleth and turn left N side of village of Bow Street.
Traditional links course (oldest in Wales).
18 holes, 6110 yards, S.S.S.70
Founded 1885
Visitors: members of a golf club with club h/cap.
Green Fee: £16 WD, £22 WE (winter £12 WD, £15 WE).
Societies: and properly constituted parties catered for after consultation with Sec; 7 days, but weekends may be difficult.
Catering: full facilities, prior booking necessary.
Hotels: Cliff Haven; Railway; Glanmor (Borth); Ynyshir Country House (Eglwysfach); Black Lion (Talybont).

J17 Brecon
☎(0874) 622004, 625547 Sec
Newton Park, Llanfaer, Brecon, Powys LD3 8PA

300 yards from roundabout on bypass S of town.
Meadowland course.
9 holes, 5218 yards, S.S.S.66
Founded 1902
Visitors: welcome.
Green Fee: £10/day.
Societies: welcome by prior arrangement.
Hotels: Castle of Brecon; Bishops Meadow; several guest houses.

J18 Bryn Meadows Golf & Country Club
☎(0495) 225590 or 227276
The Bryn, Hengoed, Mid-Glam CF8 7SM
A469 15 miles from Cardiff, turn up lane opposite filling station near Crown Hotel.
Parkland course.
18 holes, 6132 yards, S.S.S.69
Designed by E. Jefferies & B. Mayo.
Founded 1973
Visitors: welcome weekdays, weekends by arrangement.
Green Fee: £17.50 (£12.50 with member) WD, £22.50 (£17.50 with member) WE.
Societies: welcome weekdays by arrangement.
Catering: full facilties except Sun; banqueting.
Indoor heated pool, jacuzzi, pool table, full leisure facilities.
Hotels: Bryn Meadows, special 2-day packages.

J19 Bryn Morfydd Hotel
☎(0745) 78280 Hotel/Sec, 78556 Reservations/golf shop
The Duchess Course, Llanrhaeadr, Nr Denbigh LL16 4NP
2.5 miles E of Denbigh on A525.
Mature parkland course.
Dukes Course, 18 holes, 5601 yards, S.S.S.68, Par 71; Duchess, 9 holes, 1200 yards, Par 27
Designed by Allis & Thomas (Duchess Course); Muirhead & Henderson (Dukes Course).
Founded 1982 (Duchess); 1993 (Dukes)
Visitors: welcome, no h/cap cert required.
Green Fee: Duchess Course £5; Dukes Course £10 WD, £13 WE & BH.
Societies: welcome, rates on application.
Catering: full hotel facilities, separate golf clubhouse
British School of Golf, practice ground, tennis, swimming pool.
Hotels: Bryn Morfydd (on site).

20 Brynhill

☎(0446) 720277 Sec, 735061
Clubhouse
Port Rd, Barry, S Glam CF6 7PH
M4 junct 33, follow signs to Barry
and Cardiff (Wales) Airport; golf club
on Port Rd near Colcot Arms Hotel.
Undulating meadowland course.
18 holes, 5949 yards, S.S.S.68
Designed by C.K. Cotton.
Founded 1921
Visitors: welcome Mon-Sat,
membership or h/cap cert required;
no visitors Sun.
Green Fee: £20 (£9 with member)
WD, £25 Sat (£9 with member).
Societies: catered for weekdays.
Catering: lunches, dinners served
except Mon.
Hotels: Mount Sorrel; International;
Copthorne (Culverhouse Cross).

J21 Builth Wells

☎(0982) 553296
Golf Club Rd, Builth Wells, Powys
LD2 3NF
A483 immediately W of Builth Wells.
Parkland course.
18 holes, 5376 yards, S.S.S.67
Founded 1923
Visitors: welcome anytime.
Green Fee: £15 WD, £20 WE & BH.
Societies: any time by arrangement.
Catering: available, societies by
arrangement.
Hotels: send for brochure.

J22 Bull Bay

☎(0407) 830960, 831188 Pro
Bull Bay Rd, Amlwch, Anglesey LL68
9RY
A5025 18 miles from Menai Bridge.
Undulating coastal heathland course
– Wales's northernmost golf course.
18 holes, 6217 yards, S.S.S.70
Designed by Herbert Fowler and
Walton Heath.
Founded 1913
Visitors: welcome, h/cap cert
required.
Green Fee: £15 WD, £20 WE.
Societies: by arrangement with Sec;
discount for parties over 12.
Catering: full facilities available;
new clubhouse planned for
completion summer 1994.
Hotels: Bull Bay; Dinorben; Gadlys;
Lastra Farm; Trecastell.

J23 Caerleon

☎(0633) 420342
Broadway, Caerleon, Newport,
Gwent NP6 1AY
3 miles from M4 junction 25.
Public parkland course.
9 holes, 3092 yards, S.S.S.34
Designed by D. Steel.
Founded 1974
Visitors: welcome.
Green Fee: £3 (9 holes) WD, £3.75
WE.
Catering: snack bar.
Driving range, pool.

J24 Caernarfon

☎(0286) 678359 Manager
Aberforeshore, Llanfaglan,
Caernarfon LL54 5RP
2 miles S of town off
Caernarfon-Pwllheli road.
Parkland course.
18 holes, 5870 yards, S.S.S.68
Founded 1905
Visitors: welcome.
Green Fee: £18 WD, £22 WE.
Societies: by arrangement.
Catering: full facilities.
Hotels: Bryn Eisteddfod; Erw Fair;
Caeau Capel; Black Boy; Deugoch;
Seiont Manor.

J25 Caerphilly

☎(0222) 883481 Club, 863441 Sec,
869104 Pro
Pencapel, Mountain Rd, Caerphilly,
Mid-Glam CF8 2SY
7 miles from Cardiff centre on A469;
12 miles from Newport; 6 miles from
M4 on A470 N; 250 yards from
bus/rail station.
Mountain/parkland course; 2 holes
on steep gradient.
14 holes (further 4 under
construction), 6253 yards, S.S.S.71
Designed by Fernie (original 9).
Founded 1905
Visitors: welcome weekdays with
proof of club membership and h/cap
cert; not Sun or Bank Holidays unless
with member.
Green Fee: £20/day, (£10 with
member); jnrs £6.
Societies: Mon-Fri only.
Catering: bar; restaurant meals by
arrangement.
Snooker.
Hotels: Mount; Greenhill; Moat
House; Cedar Tree.

J26 Caerwys Nine Of Clubs

☎(0352) 720692
Caerwys, Mold, Clwyd CH7 5AQ
1.5 miles S of A55 expressway
midway between Holywell and St
Asaph.
Undulating parkland course.
9 holes, 3088 yards, Par 60
Designed by Eleanor Barlow.
Founded May 1988
Visitors: welcome; pay-as-you-play.
Green Fee: £4.50 (18 holes) WD,
£5.50 WE & BH; £2.50 WD, £4.50 WE
& BH jnrs; day tickets £7 WD, £8 WE
& BH.
Societies: by booking only.
Catering: light refreshments.
Putting green, snooker, table tennis.
Hotels: Holywell; also self-catering
accomodation (4-6 persons) on site.

J27 Cardiff

☎(0222) 753320 Sec, 753067
Clubhouse, 754772 Pro
Sherborne Ave, Cyncoed, Cardiff, S
Glam CF2 6SJ
Take A48M off the M4, 3 miles to
Pentwyn exit, take industrial road for
2 miles to village, turn left at
roundabout and again left at Spar
shop, club 150 yards.
Undulating parkland course.
18 holes, 6016 yards, S.S.S.70
Founded 1921
Visitors: welcome weekdays
arranged in advance, restricted Tues
am (Ladies Day); with member only
at weekends.
Green Fee: on application.
Societies: Thurs by advance
booking.
Catering: full facilities available.
Hotels: Post House; Stakis Inn. ·

J28 Cardigan

☎(0293) 612035
Gwbert-on-Sea, Cardigan, Dyfed
SA43 1PR
3 miles NW of Cardigan, take left fork
at Cardigan Cenotaph at N end of
town.
Seaside meadowland course.
18 holes, 6641 yards, S.S.S.72
Founded 1928
Visitors: unrestricted.
Green Fee: £15/day WD, £20/day
WE & BH.
Societies: welcome any day with
previous arrangement.
Catering: full facilities.
Squash, pool.
Hotels: Cliff; Castell Malgwyn
(Llechryd); Gwbert.

J29 Carmarthen

☎(0267) 87588
Blaenycoed Rd, Carmarthen, Dyfed
SA33 6EH
4 miles NW of Carmarthen.

Undulating parkland course.
18 holes, 6212 yards, S.S.S.71
Founded 1929
Visitors: welcome, Tues ladies day
(tee reserved 12am-2.30pm).
Green Fee: £15 WD, £20 WE.
Societies: by arrangement.
Catering: full bar 12am-11pm; no
catering Wed otherwise 12am-2pm
and 4pm-10pm.
Hotels: Falcon; Ivy Bush.

J30 Castell Heights
☎(0222) 886666 Bookings, 886686
Club
Blaengwynlais, Caerphilly,
Mid-Glamorgan CF8 1NG
4 miles from M4 junction 32 on
Tongwynlais-Caerphilly road, by
Mountain Lakes Golf Club.
Public, mountainside course.
9 holes, 2688 yards, S.S.S.66
Founded 1982
Visitors: welcome, pay-as-you-play.
Green Fee: apply for details.
Societies: by arrangement.
Catering: bar and bar snacks.
Mountain Lakes Driving Range.

J31 Cilgwyn
☎(057 045) 286
Llangybi, Lampeter, Dyfed SA48 8NN
5 miles NE of Lampeter on A485 in
village of Llangybi.
Parkland course.
9 holes, 5327 yards, S.S.S.67
Founded 1905
Visitors: welcome.
Green Fee: £10 WD, £15 WE & BH,
£60/week.
Societies: catered for all year.
Catering: restaurant and bar meals.
available Tues to Sun.
Pool table
Hotels: Black Lion; Falcondale.

J32 Clyne
☎(0792) 401989
120 Owls Lodge Lane, Mayals, Black
Pill, Swansea SA3 5DP
Coast road from Swansea to Blackpyl
(3 miles); turn right into Mayals Rd.
Moorland course.
18 holes, 6312 yards, S.S.S.71
Designed by H.S. Colt.
Founded 1921
Visitors: welcome.
Green Fee: £20 WD, £25 WE
Societies: not weekends; £17 per
head 1-20, £15 per head 21+.
Catering: full facilities except Mon.
Hotels: Osborne; Forte Crest;
Swansea Marriott.

J33 Conwy
(Caernarvonshire)
☎(0492) 593400, 593225 Pro,
592423 Sec
Morfa, Conwy, Gwynedd LL32 8ER
Follow signs for Conwy Marina off
A55 Chester-Bangor expressway;
course adjacent to Marina.
Championship links course.
18 holes, 6901 yards, S.S.S.73
Founded 1890
Visitors: times restricted, contact Pro
Green Fee: £22/day WD, £27 WE &
BH.
Societies: on application to Sec.
Catering: available except Mon
evening and Tues all day.
Hotels: Castle Bank; Bryn Cregin;
Caerlyr.

J34 Cradoc
☎(0874) 623658 Sec, 625524 Pro
Penoyre Park, Cradoc, Brecon,
Powys LD3 9LP
2 miles N of Brecon on B4520.
Parkland course.
18 holes, 6318 yards, S.S.S.71
Designed by C.K. Cotton.
Founded 1974
Visitors: welcome; not Sun.
Green Fee: £17 WD, £20 WE & BH.
Societies: welcome with prior
arrangement; not Sun.
Catering: full facilities daily except
Mon by special arrangement.
Snooker, practice ground.
Hotels: Wellington; Castle of Brecon;
George; Bishops Meadow; Lake
(Llangammarch Wells).

J35 Creigiau
☎(0222) 890263
Creigiau, Cardiff, S Glam CF4 8NN
4 miles NW of Cardiff towards
Llantrisant.
Parkland course.
18 holes, 5979 yards, S.S.S.69
Founded 1926
Visitors: welcome weekdays; Tues
Ladies Day.
Green Fee: £22.
Societies: welcome weekdays by
arrangement.
Catering: lunch, dinner.
Hotels: Miskin Manor; Park; Royal;
Angel.

J36 Criccieth
☎(0766) 522154
Ednyfed Hill, Criccieth, Gwynedd
A497, 4 miles from Portmadoc, turn
right past Memorial Hall, 0.5 mile up
hill.

Undulating hilltop course.
18 holes, 5787 yards, S.S.S.68
Founded around 1904
Visitors: welcome.
Green Fee: on application.
Societies: welcome.
Catering: meals and snacks served
by arrangement with Steward.
Hotels: George IV; Bron Eifion;
Marine; Lion.

J37 Denbigh
☎(0745) 816669 Sec, 814159 Pro,
816664 Caterer
Henllan Rd, Denbigh, Clwyd
B5382 Denbigh to Henllan road, 1
mile out of Denbigh.
Undulating parkland course.
18 holes, 5650 yards, S.S.S.67
Designed by John Stockton.
Founded 1922
Visitors: welcome; phone Pro shop
for reservation.
Green Fee: £15/round WD,
£20/round, WE & BH.
Societies: daily except Thurs.
Catering: full facilities 7 days,
licenced bar.
Snooker.
Hotels: Oriel House (St Asaph); Tan y
Gyrt Hall (Nantglyn).

J38 Dewstow
☎(0291) 430444, (0291) 425816
Fax
Caerwent, Newport, Gwent NP6 4AH
On A48 between Newport and
Chepstow, turn off at Caerwent,
course signposted; 4 miles W of
Chepstow.
Parkland course.
Park Course: 18 holes, 6100 yards,
S.S.S.69. Valley Course: 6100 yards,
S.S.S.70.
Founded 1988
Visitors: welcome any time, normal
dress standards, no h/cap cert
required.
Green Fee: £12 WD, £16 WE.
Societies: anytime but weekends
limited; from £16.50 inc 1 course
meal.
Catering: lounge, bar, restaurant
(full menu), bar snacks
Driving range.

J39 Dinas Powis
☎(0222) 512727 Sec, 512157 Club
Golf House, Old Highwalls, Dinas
Powis, S Glam CF6 4AJ
M4 junction 33, on A4055 to Dinas
Powis via Barry (Cardiff Airport).
Parkland course.

The Mill at Glynhir

Llandybie, Nr Ammanford, Dyfed SA18 2TE
Telephone: (0269) 850672

Originally a XVIIth-century mill, now converted to a small secluded luxury hotel. Extensive views over River Loughor valley and adjacent **18-hole golf course – free to residents.** Indoor swimming pool, practice area within grounds and free fishing. All rooms with private spa bath and colour TV. Terms include unlimited golf and our highly recommended 4 course dinners. Bargain breaks (min 2 nights) from **£39.75 pppn D, B&B.** Ideal for touring Brecons and SW Wales as well as walking and pony trekking.
Alas no under elevens.

---

18 holes, 5377 yards, S.S.S.66
Founded 1914
Visitors: welcome with h/cap cert and proof of club membership.
Green Fee: £20 WD, £25 WE.
Societies: limited to 40.
Catering: bar and restaurant.
Hotels: Star.

J40 Dolgellau
☎(0341) 422603
Pencefn, Golf Rd, Dolgellau, Gwynedd LL40 1SL
Off town by-pass onto old A494, turn right just after main bridge, then signposted; course 0.5 mile from town centre.
Parkland course.
9 holes (18 tees), 4671 yards, S.S.S.63
Founded 1911
Visitors: welcome weekdays; ring Sat.
Green Fee: £12/day, £15 WE & BH.
Societies: by arrangement.
Catering: available through year.
Hotels: Royal Ship; Bontoon Hall; Dolserau Hall.

J41 Earlswood
☎(0792) 321578
Earlswood Golf Course, Jersey Marine, Neath SA10 6JP
Turn off A483 Neath-Swansea road onto B4920, proceed towards Jersey Marine village, then 1st right; course signposted.
Public course.
18 holes, S.S.S.68
Founded May 1993
Visitors: welcome. no restrictions.
Green Fee: £8.
Societies: welcome.

J42 Fairwood Park
☎(0792) 203648, 299194 Pro
Blackhills Lane, Upper Killay, Swansea SA2 7JN

From central Swansea follow signs for Sketty and Killay then Swansea Airport; take left turn opposite Airport entrance; course 0.5 mile up Blackhills Lane on left.
Parkland championship course.
18 holes, 6741 yards, S.S.S.72
Founded 1969
Visitors: welcome with h/cap cert; advisable to phone in advance.
Green Fee: £25 WD, £30 WE & BH.
Societies: welcome weekdays and weekends by prior arrangement.
Catering: breakfast, lunch, dinner, tea, coffee, snacks; licensed bar. Snooker, pool, darts.
Hotels: In Swansea.

J43 Ffestiniog
☎(0766 76) 2637
Clwb Golff Ffestiniog, Y Cefn, Ffestiniog, Gwynned
1 mile from Ffestiniog on Bala road.
Scenic mountain course.
9 holes, 5032 metres, S.S.S.66
Founded 1893
Visitors: hardly any restrictions.
Green Fee: £8 daily.
Societies: by arrangement only.
Catering: bar only.
Hotels: Abbey Arms.

J44 Flint
☎(0352) 732327, 733461, 732186 Sec (home)
Cornist Park, Flint, Clwyd CH6 5HJ
A548 coast road, or M56/A55; course is 1 mile from town centre; from Town Hall, follow signs to Cornist Park.
Parkland course.
9 holes, 5953 yards, S.S.S.69
Founded 1966
Visitors: welcome weekdays.
Green Fee: £12/day.
Societies: Mon-Fri.
Catering: prior arrangement for catering and bar. Snooker.
Hotels: Chequers; Northop Hall; Springfield; Pentre; Halkyn.

J45 Glamorganshire
☎(0222) 701185 Sec, 707/048 Members, 707401 Pro
Lavernock Rd, Penarth, S Glam CF6 2UP
Take junction 33 off M4, join A4232 and then A4267 which passes club.
Parkland course.
18 holes, 6150 yards, S.S.S.70
Founded 1890
Visitors: welcome except on competition days, Bank Holidays and when Societies on course; must have bona fide h/cap cert from own club.
Green Fee: £24 WD, £30 WE & BH.
Societies: on application to Sec.
Catering: first class facilities, à la carte menus, bar snacks; lunches every day.
Snooker, practice area.
Hotels: Walton House.

J46 Glynhir
☎(0269) 850472
Glynhir Rd, Llandybie, Ammanford, Dyfed SA18 2TF
1.25 miles from Ammanford on A483 Llandybie road, turn right up Glynhir Rd and continue for almost 2 miles to club.
Undulating parkland/meadowland course.
18 holes, 5952 yards, S.S.S.69
Designed by F.W. Hawtree.
Founded 1964 – moved from previous course at Llandeilo.
Visitors: bona fide members of recognised golf clubs with current membership and h/cap certs welcome weekdays and by permission weekends and holidays in summer.
Green Fee: apply for details.
Societies: weekdays welcome, Sat only on occasions, not Sun or holidays; all by prior appointment.
Catering: restaurant, bar meals daily.
Hotels: The Mill at Glynhir; Glynhir Golf Clubhouse; Cawdor, White Hart (Llandeilo); Red Lion (Llandybie).

J47 Glynneath
☎(0639) 720452
Pen-y-craig, Pontneathvaughan
(Powys), Nr Glynneath, W Glam SA11
5UH
11 miles N of Neath, 2 miles NE of
Glynneath on B4242.
Picturesque woodland course
overlooking Vale of Neath.
18 holes, 5533 yards, S.S.S.67
Designed by Cotton, Pennink, Lawrie
& Partners.
Founded 1931
Visitors: no restrictions.
Green Fee: £12/round, £15/day WD;
£18 WE.
Societies: weekdays by
arrangement.
Catering: by arrangement; bar from
12am.
Snooker.
Hotels: Plas-y-Felin.

J48 Greenmeadow
☎(06333) 69321, 62626 Pro
Treherbert Road, Croesyceiliog,
Cwmbran, Gwent NP44 2BZ
Off A4042.
Parkland course.
14 holes, 5597 yards, S.S.S.67
Founded 1978
Visitors: welcome.
Green Fee: apply for details.
Societies: welcome.
Catering: full facilities.
Hotels: Parkway; Commodore.

J49 Haverfordwest
☎(0437) 764523 Sec, 768409 Pro,
763565 Clubhouse/Steward
Arnolds Down, Haverfordwest, Dyfed
SA61 2XQ
1 mile E of town on A40.
Parkland course.
18 holes, 6005 yards, S.S.S.69
Founded 1904
Visitors: bona fide golfers welcome.
Green Fee: £17/day WD, £24/day
WE.
Societies: by arrangement.
Catering: restaurant; hot and cold
bar snacks; licensed bars.
Hotels: Hotel Mariners; St Brides(
Saundersfoot); County.

J50 Hawarden
☎(0244) 531447
Groomsdale Lane, Hawarden,
Deeside, Clwyd CH5 3EH
A55 9 miles W of Chester, 1st left
after Hawarden station.
Parkland course.
9 holes, 5620 yards, S.S.S.67

Founded 1911
Visitors: with member only.
Green Fee: £15.
Societies: by arrangement with Sec.
Catering: full facilities.
Hotels: St Davids (Ewloe).

J51 Holyhead
☎(0407) 763279 Sec, 762119 Bar,
762022 Pro
Trearddur Bay, Holyhead, Gwynedd
LL65 2YG
Follow A5 from Bangor, left at Valley
traffic lights, approx 4 miles on left.
Undulating heathland course.
18 holes, 6058 yards, S.S.S.70
Designed by James Braid.
Founded 1912
Visitors: welcome, particularly
weekdays and residential; h/cap cert
required.
Green Fee: £20/day WD, £25/day
WE & BH.
Societies: recognised societies
welcome subject to prior
arrangement with Sec.
Catering: lunchtime bar snacks;
evening meals by arrangement.
Hotels: Beach; Trearddur Bay;
Dormie residence on site.

J52 Holywell
☎(0352) 710040 Pro, 713937
Sec/Fax
Brynford, Nr Holywell, Clwyd CH8
8LQ
Turn off A55 onto A5026, turn left at
traffic lights, 1 mile to crossroads,
turn right.
Undulating moorland/parkland
links-type course.
18 holes, 6005 yards, S.S.S.70
Founded 1906
Visitors: welcome except on
competition days, weekends with a
member or by prior arrangement.
Green Fee: £12 WD, £18 WE.
Societies: by prior arrangement with
Sec.
Catering: lunch and evening meals,
bar facilities.
Snooker.
Hotels: Fielding Arms; Victoria;
Stamford Gate; Springfield.

J53 Inco
☎(0792) 844216, 843336 Sec
Clydach, Swansea, W Glamorgan
2 miles N of M4 junction 45.
Flat parkland course with river and
trees.
12 holes, 6273 yards, S.S.S.70
Founded 1965

Visitors: welcome.
Green Fee: apply for details.
Societies: welcome by prior
arrangement.
Catering: bar and snacks (evenings
only).

J54 Kinmel Park Golf Complex
☎(0745) 833548
Bodelwyddan, Clwyd, N Wales LL18
5SR
Just off main A55 expressway at
Bodelwyddan between Abergele and
St Asaph.
9 hole Par 3 course, transformed at
dusk into Britain's first night-time
course – 'lightsticks' and luminous
balls.
Designed by Peter Stebbings.
Founded 1988
Visitors: welcome; booking
essential for night-time through
Peter Stebbings Golf.
Green Fee: from £3/round.
Societies: welcome by prior
arrangement.
Catering: bar and restaurant.
Driving range.
Hotels: Kinmel Manor (Abergele).

J55 Knighton
☎(0547) 528646
The Ffrydd, Knighton, Powys LD7
1EF
0.5 mile S of Knighton.
Undulating course.
9 holes, 5320 yards, S.S.S.66
Designed by Harry Vardon.
Founded 1913
Visitors: welcome.
Green Fee: £8 WD, £10 WE.
Societies: by prior arrangement with
Sec.
Catering: snacks available
weekends, other by prior
arrangement.
Hotels: Red Lion; Knighton Hotel.

J56 Lakeside
☎(0639) 883486, 899959
Water St, Margam, Port Talbot, West
Glam SA13 2PA
Just off M4 junction 38.
Parkland course.
9 holes, approx 1900 yards.
Designed by D.T. Thomas.
Founded May 1992
Visitors: all welcome; good dress
sense, golf shoes or trainers only.
Green Fee: £5 WD, £6 WE.
Catering: bar and restaurant,
disabled facilities.

J57 Llandrindod Wells

☎(0597) 823873 Sec/manager,
2010 Club
Llandrindod Wells, Powys LD1 5NY
Signposted from A483, 0.5 mile E of
town, above lake.
Mountain course.
18 holes, 5759 yards, S.S.S.68
Designed by Harry Vardon.
Founded 1905
Visitors: welcome at all times.
Green Fee: £12 WD, £18 WE.
Societies: welcome by prior
arrangement.
Catering: bar and restaurant
facilities; closd Tues.
Hotels: Severn Arms; Metropole;
Commodore; Glen Usk; Llanerch,;
Bell Inn; Pencerrig; Guidfa House.

J58 Llandudno (Maesdu)

☎(0492) 876450, 871570 Fax
Hospital Rd, Llandudno, Gwynedd
LL30 1HU
Alongside main Llandudno Hospital,
approx 1 mile from town centre.
Seaside parkland course.
18 holes, 6513 yards, S.S.S.72
Designed by Tom Jones.
Founded 1915
Visitors: members of recognised
clubs.
Green Fee: £22 WD, £30 WE.
Societies: accepted any day; max
30 players weekends.
Catering: prior booking.
Snooker
Hotels: Royal; Bryn Cregin; Imperial.

J59 Llanfairfechan

☎(0248) 680144, 680524 Sec
Llannerch Road, Llanfairfechan,
Gwynedd LL33 0EB
In Llanfairfechan between Conwy
and Bangor.
Parkland course.
9 holes, 3119 yards, S.S.S.57
Founded 1972
Visitors: welcome any time except
during competitions (mostly Sun).
Green Fee: £6 WD, £10 WE & BH.
Societies: write to Sec.
Catering: bar open all evenings, and
11.30am-2pm weekends.
Hotels: Split Willow.

J60 Llangefni (Public)

☎(0248) 722193
Llangefni, Anglesey, N Wales
A5 to Llangefni.
Parkland course.
9 holes, 1467 yards, S.S.S.28
Designed by Hawtree & Sons.

Founded 1983
Visitors: welcome.
Green Fee: apply for details.

J61 Llangland Bay

☎(0792) 366023
Llangland Bay, Swansea, W Glam
SA3 4QR
M4 to Swansea, 6 miles W.
Seaside parkland course.
18 holes, 5827 yards, S.S.S.69
Founded 1904
Visitors: welcome if member of
recognised club.
Green Fee: apply for details.
Societies: welcome if booked in
advance, max 36.
Catering: bar meals; cooked meals
to order before playing.
Hotels: Osborne.

J62 Llanishen

☎(0222) 755078
Cwm, Lisvane, Cardiff CF4 5UD
5 miles to N of Cardiff city centre, 1.5
miles N of Llanishen church via Heol
Hir.
Parkland course.
18 holes, 5296 yards, S.S.S.66
Founded 1905
Visitors: weekdays unlimited;
weekends and Bank Holidays with
member only; h/cap cert required.
Green Fee: £22.
Societies: Thurs only by previous
arrangement.
Catering: full facilities except Mon.
Hotels: Phoenix (Cardiff).

J63 Llannerch Park

☎(0745) 730805
North Wales Golf Range and Course,
Llannerch Park, St Asaph, Clwyd
LL17 0BD
On A525 Denbigh-St Asaph road,
Tourist Board signposted.
Parkland course.
9 holes, 1587 yards, Par 30
Founded 1988
Visitors: welcome 10am until dusk;
pay-as-you-play.
Green Fee: £2/9 holes (£1.50 jnrs).
Societies: by prior arrangement,
start before 10am.
Catering: light refreshments.
Driving range.

J64 Llanstephan

☎(0267) 83526
Llanstephan, Carmarthen, Dyfed
SA33 5LU
2 miles SW of Llanstephan – through

Llanstephan, past church on left,
bear left at top of hill and keep
straight on for 2 miles.
Pay-and-play, coastal downland
course, views of sea from every tee.
9 holes, over 2000 yards, Par 30
Designed by A.M. Fry.
Founded 1991
Visitors: welcome.
Green Fee: £3 (9 holes), £5 (18
holes), £2 jnrs.
Societies: welcome.
Catering: available shortly.
Putting green and practice net.
Hotels: The Mansion House.

J65 Llantrisant & Pontyclun

☎(0443) 222148, 224601, 228169
Pro
Lanlay Rd, Talbot Green, Mid-Glam
CF7 8HZ
M4 junction 34, then A4119 to Talbot
Green.
Parkland course.
12 holes, 5712 yards, S.S.S.68
Founded 1927
Visitors: welcome weekdays.
Green Fee: £20 (£10 with member).
Societies: weekdays, max 25.
Catering: by prior arrangement with
Steward.
Hotels: Heronstone; New Inn; City
Inn.

J66 Llanwern

☎(0633) 412029
Tennyson Ave, Llanwern, Newport,
Gwent NP6 2DY
1 mile from M4 junction 24.
Parkland course.
18 holes, 6115 yards, S.S.S.69; 9
holes, 5237 yards, S.S.S.67
Founded 1928
Visitors: with proof of h/cap and
membership of recognised club.
Green Fee: apply for details.
Societies: Wed and Thurs by
arrangement.
Catering: full bar and restaurant
facilities.
Snooker table.
Hotels: Stakis County Court.

J67 Llanyrafon Golf Course

☎(0633) 874636
Llanfrechfa Way, Cwmbran, Gwent
M4 junction 26, head N to Pontypool,
turn left into Llanfrechfa Way.
Municipal parkland course.
9 holes Par 3
Founded 1981

Visitors: no restrictions.
Green Fee: £2.05/round WD,
£3.10/round WE; reductions for jnrs
and OAPs.
Hotels: Commodore; Park Way;
Central.

J68 Machynlleth
☎(0654) 702000
Ffordd, Drenewydd, Machynlleth,
Powys SY20 8UH
Approaching Machynlleth on A489,
left before speed restriction signs.
Undulating course.
9 holes, 5726 yards, S.S.S.67
Designed by James Braid.
Founded 1907
Visitors: welcome apart from
competition days; welcome Sun.
Green Fee: £12 WD, £15 WE.
Societies: by arrangement.
Catering: by arrangement.
Hotels: Wynnstay; White Lion.

J69 Maesteg
☎(0656) 734106 Sec, 732037
Clubhouse, 735742 Pro
Mount Pleasant, Neath Rd, Maesteg,
Mid-Glam CF34 9PR
Adjacent to main Maestag to Port
Talbot road; 0.5 mile from Measteg
town centre on B4282.
Moorland course.
18 holes, 5900 yards, S.S.S.69
Designed by James Braid (1945).
Founded 1912
Visitors: no restrictions; over 12
visitors in group by arrangement.
Green Fee: £15 WD, £20 WE & BH.
Societies: by arrangement.
Catering: bar meals available daily.

J70 Merthyr Tydfil
☎(0685) 723308
Cloth Hall Lane, Cefn Coed, Merthyr
Tydfil, Mid-Glam CF48 2NU
Take turning to Pontsticill off A470 at
Cefn Coed, then 1st left.
Mountain course in Brecon Beacons
National Park.
11 holes, 5957 yards, S.S.S.69
Founded 1908
Visitors: welcome except Sun.
Green Fee: £12 WD, £16 WE
Societies: apply in writing.
Catering: evenings only.

J71 Mid-Wales Golf Centre
☎(0686) 688303
Maesmawr, Caersws, Nr Newtown,
Powys

38 miles W of Shrewsbury, 6 miles W
of Newtown; 0.75 mile off main road
clearly signposted.
Public farmland course.
9 holes Par 3, 1277 yards.
Designed by Jim Walters.
Founded July 1992
Visitors: no restrictions unless
competition being played; advisable
to ring beforehand; reasonable
standard of dress and etiquette.
Green Fee: £6 WD, £8 WE.
Societies: by arrangement.
Catering: light refreshments.
Driving range, children's play area.
Hotels: Maesmawr Hall.

J72 Milford Haven
☎(0646) 692368
Woodbine House, Hubberston,
Milford Haven
Follow road to Dale 0.75 mile to W of
town.
Meadowland course.
18 holes, 6071 yards, S.S.S.71
Designed by David Snell.
Founded 1913
Visitors: welcome at all times.
Green Fee: £13 WD, £18 WE & BH.
Societies: welcome at most times;
fees negotiable on numbers.
Catering: full facilities available.
Hotels: Lord Nelson; Sir Benfro;
Little Haven.

J73 Mold
☎(0352) 740318, 741513
Cilcain Rd, Pantymwyn, Mold, Clwyd
3 miles from Mold; leave on Denbigh
road, turn left 100 yards before
Drovers and club is 2.5 miles on left.
Undulating parkland course.
18 holes, 5521 yards, S.S.S.67
Designed by Hawtree.
Founded 1909
Visitors: welcome.
Green Fee: on application.
Societies: welcome.
Catering: bar snacks, full facilities.
Hotels: Bryn Awel; Chequers.

J74 Monmouth
☎(0600) 712212, 712941 Sec
Leasebrook Lane, Monmouth, Gwent
1 mile along A40 Monmouth to Ross
road.
Parkland course.
18 holes, 5698 yards, S.S.S.69
Founded 1896
Visitors: welcome weekdays and
weekends.
Green Fee: £15/day.
Societies: by arrangement with Sec.

Catering: every day.
Hotels: King's Head; Pilgrim (Much
Birch).

J75 Monmouthshire
☎(0873) 852606 Sec, 852532 Pro
Llanfoist, Abergavenny, Gwent NP7
9HE
M4 to Newport then A4042, take
road to Llanfoist at Llanellen.
Meadowland course.
18 holes, 6054 yards, S.S.S.70.
Designed by James Braid.
Founded 1892
Visitors: must have proof of
membership of recognised club and
h/cap cert.
Green Fee: on application.
Societies: Mon and Fri only, apply
before Dec preceding year.
Catering: full catering facilities
except Tues.
Hotels: Angel; Llanwenarth Arms.

J76 Morlais Castle
☎(0685) 722822
Pant, Dowlais, Merthyr Tydfil,
Mid-Glam CF48 2UY
Follow signs for Brecon Mountain
Railway.
Moorland course.
18 holes, 6320 yards, S.S.S.71
Founded 1900
Visitors: welcome except Sat pm
and Sun am.
Green Fee: £14/day (£8 with
member) WD; £16 (£10 with
member) WE.
Societies: welcome on application
to Sec.
Catering: bar/snacks; lunches and
evening meals served to order.
Hotels: Tregenna Castle;
Baverstocks.

J77 Morriston
☎(0792) 771079
160 Clasemont Rd, Morriston,
Swansea, W Glam SA6 6AJ
3 miles N of Swansea city centre on
A4067, then 0.5 mile W along A48;
from M4 junction 45, E on A48.
Parkland course.
18 holes, 5734 yards, S.S.S.68
Founded 1919
Visitors: welcome at all times.
Green Fee: £18 WD, £25 WE & BH;
one-third reduction with member.
Societies: on application.
Catering: lunches served daily
except Mon.
Hotels: Dragon; Dolphin; Forest
Motel; Hilton; Holiday Inn.

DRIVE OFF TO NORTH WALES

and let us take all the hassle of organizing your golf break for you.
All you need to do is let us know where you want to play and we will do the rest, from booking your
teeing off times to serving your 5 course evening meal. All inclusive price from £52.00 per day.

CAEAU CAPEL HOTEL, NEFYN, GWYNEDD 0758 720 240

Welsh Tourist Board 3 Crowns Highly Commended.

J78 Mountain Ash
☎(0443) 479459
Cefnpennar, Mountain Ash,
Mid-Glam CF45 4DT
A470 Cardiff to Abercynon, then
A4059 to Mountain Ash.
Mountain course.
18 holes, 5553 yards, S.S.S.68
Founded 1908
Visitors: welcome; with member
only weekends.
Green Fee: £18 (£10 with member)
WD.
Societies: welcome.
Catering: full facilities except Mon.
Hotels: Baverstock.

J79 Mountain Lakes
☎(0222) 861128, 869030 Fax
Blaengwynlais, Nr Caerphilly,
Mid-Glam CF8 1NG
4 miles from M4 junction 32 on
Tongwynlais-Caerphilly road, by
Castell Heights golf course.
Moorland/parkland course with
water hazards.
18 holes, 6800 yards, S.S.S.74
Designed by Bob Sandow.
Founded 1988
Visitors: must ring in advance to
check availability; h/cap certs
required.
Green Fee: £15/round, £20/day.
Societies: brochure on request.
Catering: day restaurant and bar;
banqueting, conferences, functions.
Driving range
Hotels: list available on request.

J80 Neath
☎(0639) 643615 Clubhouse/Pro
shop, 632759 Sec
Cadoxton, Neath, W Glam SA10 8AH
2 miles from Neath town centre,
opposite Cadoxton Church.
Mountain course.
18 holes, 6465 yards, S.S.S.72
Designed by James Braid.
Founded 1934
Visitors: welcome. With member
only weekends and Bank Holidays.
Green Fee: £17 (£12 with member).
Societies: reduced terms for 20+,
Wed-Fri h/cap certs required.
Catering: full except Mon.
Snooker.

J81 Nefyn & District
☎(0758) 720996 Sec, 720218
Steward, 720102 Pro, 720476 Fax
Morfa Nefyn, Pwllheli, Gwynedd
LL53 6DA
1 mile W of Nefyn, 20 miles W of
Caernarfon on B4417.
Seaside clifftop course.
18 holes, 6537 yards, S.S.S.71; 9
holes, 2979 yards, S.S.S. 34
Founded 1907
Visitors: h/cap certs required
April-Oct incl.
Green Fee: £20/round, £25/day WD,
£24/round, £35/day WE.
Societies: by prior arrangement with
Sec, limited weekends.
Catering: full facilities. Snooker.
Hotels: Caeau Capel; Linksway;
Woodlands Hall; Nanhoran Arms;
Llys Olwen GH.

J82 Newport
☎(0633) 892643, 896794
Great Oak, Rogerstone, Newport,
Gwent NP1 9FX
From M4 junction 27 take B4591 for
1 mile, across roundabout then right
at Bosch services.
Parkland course.
18 holes, 6431 yards, S.S.S.71
Founded 1903
Visitors: welcome weekdays,
members of recognised club only.
Green Fee: £30 (£40 WE & BH).
Societies: Wed, Thurs, Fri.
Catering: bar (men's), mixed lounge,
dining room.
Hotels: Country Court; Lodge; Harris;
Celtic Manor.

J83 Newport (Pembs)
☎(0239) 820244
Newport, Dyfed SA42 0NR
Follow signs to Newport Sands from
Newport.
Seaside course.
9 holes, 5815 yards, S.S.S.68
Designed by James Braid
Founded 1925
Visitors: welcome.
Green Fee: £12.50
Societies: by arrangement.
Catering: full bar and restaurant.
Hotels: self-catering holiday flats
adjacent clubhouse; Golden Lion.

J84 North Wales
☎(0492) 875325
72 Bryniau Rd, West Shore,
Llandudno, Gwynedd LL30 2DZ
On A496, 1 mile from Llandudno
town centre overlooking Conway
Bay
Seaside links course.
18 holes, 6132 yards, S.S.S.69
Founded 1894
Visitors: welcome by prior
reservation.
Green Fee: £22/day WD, £28 WE &
BH.
Societies: welcome by prior
reservation.
Catering: full facilities available.
Snooker.
Hotels: Bryn Cregin; Royal.

J85 Northop Country Park
☎(0352) 840440, 840445 Fax
Northop, Nr Chester, Clwyd CH7
6WA
Parkland course.
18 holes, 6680 yards, S.S.S.72
Designed by John Jacobs.
Opening 1st June 1994
Visitors: welcome, prior booking
required.
Green Fee: approx £25 WD, £35 WE.
Societies: welcome weekdays by
arrangement.
Catering: bar and restaurant
facilities.
Tennis, gym, sauna, snooker.
Hotels: St David's Park.

J86 Oakdale
☎(0495) 220044
Llwynon Lane, Oakdale, Gwent NP2
0NF
M4 junction 28, A467 to Crumlin,
then B4251 to Oakdale.
Public parkland course.
9 holes, 1235 yards, S.S.S.28
Designed by Ian Goodenough.
Founded 1990
Visitors: welcome
Green Fee: £3.50/9 holes any day,
£2.50 jnrs.
Societies: welcome, bookings only.
Catering: snacks in clubhouse (no
license).
Driving range.
Hotels: The Old Forge.

J87 Old Colwyn

☎(0492) 515581
Woodland Ave, Old Colwyn, Clwyd
LL29 9NL
200 yards off A55 in Old Colwyn, turn
into Boddelwyddan Ave between
chapel and M & K Garage.
Undulating meadowland course.
9 holes, 5243 yards, S.S.S.66
Founded 1907
Visitors: welcome except Sat pm
and Tues and Wed evenings.
Green Fee: £10 WD, £15 WE
Societies: by arrangement except
Sat.
Catering: by arrangement.

J88 Old Padeswood

☎(0244) 547401
Station Rd, Padeswood, Mold, Clwyd
CH7 4JL
2.5 miles S of Mold, 8 miles W of
Chester on A5118.
Meadowland course.
18 holes, 6728 yards, S.S.S.72; 9
holes, Par 3
Designed by Arthur Joseph.
Founded 1933
Visitors: welcome except
Competition Days.
Green Fee: £16 WD, £20 WE & BH;
Par 3, £2 (£1 jnr).
Societies: weekdays only by
appointment; phone (0244) 550414.
Catering: bar and restaurant
facilities at all times.
Hotels: Bryn Awel; St David's Park.

J89 Old Rectory Hotel

☎(0873) 810373
Llangattock, Crickhowell, Powys NP8
1PH
Off A40 to Crickhowell between
Abergavenny and Brecon.
Parkland course.
9 holes, 2360 yards, S.S.S.54
Founded 1979
Visitors: welcome.
Green Fee: £10/day.
Societies: welcome.
Catering: bar, restaurant, function
suites.
Outdoor swimming pool, pool table.
Hotels: Old Rectory.

J90 Padeswood & Buckley

☎(0244) 550537 Office, 543636 Pro
and Members
The Caia, Station Lane, Padeswood,
Mold, Clwyd CH7 4JD
Off A5118, 3 miles E of Mold, 2 miles
S of Buckley, 2nd club on right.
Parkland/meadowland course.

18 holes, 5823 yards, S.S.S.68
Founded 1933
Visitors: welcome weekdays
9.30am-4.30pm; permission of Sec
or Captain required on Sun.
Green Fee: apply for details.
Societies: weekdays.
Catering: snacks, lunches and
evening meals.
Hotels: The Druid; Chequers;
Beaufort Palace.

J91 Palleg

☎(0639) 842193
Palleg Rd, Lower Cwmtwrch,
Swansea, W Glam
15 miles N of Swansea on Brecon
road A4067, left at Aubrey Arms
roundabout, 1 mile.
Meadowland/moorland course.
9 holes, 3260 yards, S.S.S.72
Designed by C.K. Cotton.
Founded 1930
Visitors: welcome.
Green Fee: apply for details.
Societies: not Bank Holidays.
Catering: by arrangement except
Mon.

J92 Parc Golf

☎(0633) 680933
Church Lane, Coedkernew, Newport,
Gwent NP1 9TU
M4 junction 28, onto A48 towards
Cardiff for 1.5 miles, then
signposted.
Parkland course.
18 holes, 5600 yards, S.S.S.67
Designed by B. Thomas & T. Hicks.
Founded 1989
Visitors: welcome weekdays and by
prior arrangement weekends.
Green Fee: £10/round WD,
£12/round WE.
Societies: by prior arrangement.
Catering: full facilities.
Driving range
Hotels: Coach & Horses (Castleton).

J93 Penmaenmawr

☎(0492) 623330
Conway Rd, Penmaenmawr,
Gwynedd LL34 6RD
Main A55 expressway from Colwyn
Bay taking Bangor signs; at 1st
roundabout after tunnels take left
exit and sharp left again; 1st right
thereafter to top of hill (crossing
intersection); turn left, clubhouse
within 20 yards of corner.
Undulating parkland course.
9 holes, 5031 yards, S.S.S.65
Founded 1910

Visitors: welcome.
Green Fee: £15/day WD, £18/day
WE.
Societies: welcome; fees by
arrangement.
Catering: by prior arrangement.
Hotels: Caerlyr; Sychnant Pass
(Conway); Split Willow
(Llanfairfechan).

J94 Pennard

☎(0792) 233131 Club, 233451 Pro
2 Southgate Rd, Southgate,
Swansea, W Glam SA3 2BT
8 miles W of Swansea, on A4067 and
B4436 to Pennard Church, then
unclassified to club.
Undulating seaside course.
18 holes, 6289 yards, S.S.S.71
Founded 1896
Visitors: welcome at all times.
Green Fee: £18/day (£12 with
member) WD; £22 (£15 with
member) WE & BH; jnrs £9 WD, £11
WE.
Societies: Weekdays only, h/cap
cert required, 12 or more, £14 each.
Catering: bar snacks; lunches and
evening meals by prior arrangement.
Snooker, squash.
Hotels: Osborne; Winston;
Nicholaston; Cefn Goleua Park; Fairy
Hill.

J95 Penrhos Golf & Country Club

☎(0974) 202999
Llanrhystud, Nr Aberystwyth, Dyfed,
SY23 5AY
Between Aberystwyth and
Aberaeron, just off A487 on B4337.
Parkland course.
18 holes, 6641 yards, S.S.S.72
Designed by Jim Walters.
Founded July 1991
Visitors: welcome; booking advised.
Green Fee: £12 WD, £18 WE
Societies: welcome by
arrangement, Sat included.
Catering: full facilities.
Leisure complex, tennis, driving
range.
Hotels: Conrah County; Marine
(Aberystwyth); self catering
available-please ring for details.

J96 Peterstone Golf & Country Club

☎(0633) 680009
Peterstone, Wentlooge, Cardiff CF3
8TM
Off A48, turning to Marshfield.
Seaside parkland course.

18 holes, 6497 yards, S.S.S.71
Designed by Bob Sandow.
Founded May 1990
Visitors: welcome.
Green Fee: apply for details.
Societies: welcome.
Catering: bar, à la carte restaurant,
conference room.
Driving range.
Hotels: accommodation (7 rooms) in
Country Club.

J97 Plassey
☎(0978) 780020
The Plassey Golf Course, Eyton,
Wrexham, Clwyd LL13 0SP
From Wrexham take Bangor-on-Dee
exit off A483 Chester-Ruabon
bypass, follow tourist board anvil
signs to 'The Plassey'.
Public parkland course.
10 holes, extending to 18, 1994/5
Founded April 1992
Visitors: welcome, no restrictions.
Green Fee: £4 (9 holes), £6 (18
holes) WD; £5 (9 holes), £8 (18 holes)
WE.
Societies: welcome by
arrangement, 8-20 players; from
£10 for 18 holes and 3-course lunch.
Catering: Ham Bank Inn offering
special golfers' lunches, dinner,
parties; Plassey real ale brewed on
site.
Leisure facilities at caravan park on
complex.

J98 Pontardawe
☎(0792) 863118, 830041 Sec,
830977 Pro
Cefn Llan, Pontardawe, Swansea, W
Glam SA8 4SH
4 miles N of M4 on A4067.
Meadowland course.
18 holes, 6097 yards, S.S.S.70
Founded 1924
Visitors: welcome weekdays, h/cap
cert required
Green Fee: £18 WD
Societies: on application.
Catering: full except Mon
(bookable).
Snooker.
Hotels: Pen-yr-Allt; Pink Geranium.

J99 Pontnewydd
☎(06333) 2170
West Pontnewydd, Cwmbran, Gwent
NP4 4AR
Follow signs for West Pontnewydd or
Upper Cwmbran, W slopes of
Cwmbran.
Meadowland course.

10 holes, 5353 yards, S.S.S.67
Founded 1875
Visitors: welcome weekdays,
weekends only with member.
Green Fee: apply for details.
Catering: available.
Hotels: Parkway; Commodore.

J100 Pontypool
☎(0495) 763655
Lasgarn Lane, Trevethin, Pontypool,
Gwent NP4 8TR
1 mile N of Pontypool.
Heathland/parkland course.
18 holes, 6046 yards, S.S.S.69
Founded 1903
Visitors: welcome; h/cap certs
required
Green Fee: £16.50 WD, £22.50 WE.
Societies: welcome; h/cap certs
required.
Catering: available daily.
Hotels: Commodore; Parkway.

J101 Pontypridd
☎(0443) 402359 Club, 409904 Sec,
491210 Pro
Ty-Gwyn, The Common, Pontypridd,
Mid-Glam CF37 4DJ
9 miles from Cardiff, take A470 N to
Pontypridd and Merthyr.
Wooded undulating mountain course.
18 holes, 5721 yards, S.S.S.68
Designed by Bradbeer.
Founded 1905
Visitors: welcome weekdays if bona
fide member of another club; only
with member weekends and Bank
Holidays, h/cap certs required.
Green Fee: £17 (£10 with member)
WD; £17 WE & BH.
Societies: weekdays only, prior
arrangement with Sec.
Catering: bar, lounge, dining room,
meals/bar snacks; no meals Thurs.
Snooker.

J102 Porthmadog
☎(0766) 512037, 514638, 513828
Pro shop, 514124 Sec
Morfa Bychan, Porthmadog,
Gwynedd LL49 9UU
2 miles W of Porthmadog, take road
to Morfa Bychan and Black Rock
Sands; turn at Woolworths in High St.
Seaside heathland course.
18 holes, 6320 yards, S.S.S.70
Founded 1900
Visitors: welcome.
Green Fee: on application to Match
Sec.
Societies: by arrangement with
Match Sec.

Catering: meals and snacks served.
Newly extended clubhouse, snooker.
Hotels: Royal Sportsman; Tyddyn
Lywyn; Plas Gwyn.

J103 Prestatyn
☎(0745) 854320
Marine Rd East, Prestatyn, Clwyd
LL19 7HS
Follow A548 coast road to Prestatyn,
cross railway bridge and turn right at
Pontins, Prestatyn Sands.
Links championship course.
18 holes, 6764 yards, S.S.S.73
Designed by S. Collins.
Founded 1905
Visitors: welcome, except Sat and
Tues mornings.
Green Fee: £18 WD, £25 WE & BH.
Societies: by arrangement with Sec
only; no Sats or Tues.
Catering: full facilities.
Hotels: Bryn Gwalia; Nant Hall;
Kinmel Manor (Abergele); Royal
(Llandudno).

J104 Pwllheli
☎(0758) 612520, 701633, 701644
Sec
Golf Rd, Pwllheli, Gwynedd LL53 5PS
Turn into Cardiff Rd in town centre,
right at 1st fork, course signposted.
Parkland/links course.
18 holes, 6091 yards, S.S.S.69
Designed by Tom Morris extended by
James Braid
Founded 1900
Visitors: welcome.
Green Fee: £18/day WD, £25 WE &
BH.
Societies: any day by prior
arrangement with Sec.
Catering: full facilities.
Snooker table.
Hotels: Caeau Capel (Nefyn);
Woodlands Hall (Edern); Bryn
Eisteddfod (Clynnnogfawr).

J105 Pyle & Kenfig
☎(0656) 783093 Sec, 772446 Pro
Waun-y-Mer, Kenfig, Mid-Glam
CF33 4PU
Leave M4 at junction 37, follow
Porthcawl signs; 1st right after 3rd
roundabout.
Seaside links and downland course.
18 holes, 6650 yards, S.S.S.73
Designed by H. Colt.
Founded 1922
Visitors: welcome weekdays,
advisable to phone in advance; with
member only weekends and Bank
Holidays.

Green Fee: £25/round, £30/day (£15 with member).
Societies: by arrangement with Sec.
Catering: full facilities available.
Hotels: Seabank; Rose and Crown; Fairways; Atlantic.

J106 RAF St Athan
☎(0446) 751043, 797186 Manager
St Athan, Barry, S Glam
1st right after St Athan village on the Cowbridge road.
Public parkland course.
9 holes, 6452 yards, S.S.S.71
Founded 1982
Visitors: any time except Sun am.
Green Fee: £10 WD, £15 WE.
Societies: apply to Sec.
Catering: available.

J107 Radyr
☎(0222) 842408 Manager, 842442 Members
Drysgol Rd, Radyr, Cardiff CF4 8BS
M4 junction 32, off A470 at Taffs Well.
Parkland course.
18 holes, 6015 yards, S.S.S.70
Founded 1902
Visitors: weekdays with h/cap cert; weekends with member only.
Green Fee: £25/day.
Societies: Wed, Thur and Fri.
Catering: full facilities 7 days.
Snooker.

J108 Rhondda
☎(0443) 433208
Golf House, Penrhys, Rhondda CF43 3PW
On Cardiff to Rhondda road 3 miles from Porth.
Mountain-top course.
18 holes, 6246 yards, S.S.S.70
Founded 1904/1910
Visitors: welcome weekdays, weekends with member.
Green Fee: £15 WD, £20 WE.
Societies: weekdays by arrangement.
Catering: meals, bar snacks except Mon.
Snooker.
Hotels: Dunraven; Heritage.

J109 Rhos-on-Sea
☎(0492) 549641, 549100
Penrhyn Bay, Llandudno, Gwynedd LL30 3PU
A55 to Old Colwyn, follow coast road to Penrhyn Bay, course by sea.
Parkland course without trees.

18 holes, 6064 yards, S.S.S.69
Founded 1899
Visitors: welcome anytime, pre-booking required for large parties and weekends.
Green Fee: £15 WD, £20 WE.
Societies: welcome any day by booking.
Catering: lounge bar daily, bar snacks, breakfast, restaurant meals. Snooker tables.
Hotels: Dormy House Hotel on site.

J110 Rhosgoch
☎(0497) 851251
Rhosgoch, Builth Wells, Powys LD2 3JY
5 miles N of Hay-on-Wye.
Parkland course.
9 holes, 4842 yards, S.S.S.64
Designed by Herbie Poore.
Founded 1984
Visitors: welcome.
Green Fee: £7/day WD, £10/day WE.
Societies: welcome.
Catering: bar, snacks; dinner by arrangement.
Hotels: 2 holiday appartments.

J111 Rhuddlan
☎(0745) 590217, 590898 Pro
Meliden Rd, Rhuddlan, Clwyd LL18 6LB
Off A55 3 miles N of St Asaph.
Parkland course.
18 holes, 6482 yards, S.S.S.71
Designed by Hawtree & Co.
Founded 1930
Visitors: welcome; guests of members only on Sun.
Green Fee: £20 WD, £25 Sat and BH.
Societies: welcome Mon-Fri.
Catering: lunch and dinner daily. Snooker.
Hotels: Talardy Park (St Asaph); Kinnel Manor (Abergele).

J112 Rhyl
☎(0745) 353171, 338204 Sec
Coast Rd, Rhyl, Clwyd LL18 3RE
1 mile from station on A548 road to Prestatyn.
Seaside links course.
9 holes, 6153 yards, S.S.S.70
Redesigned by James Braid.
Founded 1890
Visitors: welcome except competition days.
Green Fee: £12 WD, £15 WE & BH.
Societies: by arrangement with Sec.
Catering: bar snacks, meals all day. Snooker.
Hotels: Grange; Marina.

J113 The Rolls of Monmouth
☎(0600) 715353, 713115 Fax
The Hendre, Monmouth, Gwent NP5 4HG
3.25 miles W of Monmouth on B4233 (Abergavenny road).
Undulating parkland course.
18 holes, 6723 yards, S.S.S.72
Designed by Urbis Planning.
Founded 1982
Visitors: no restrictions
Green Fee: £30 WD, £35 WE & BH (approx).
Societies: welcome weekdays and weekends.
Catering: full catering facilities 7 days.
Hotels: Kings Head; Priory Motel; Pilgrim.

J114 Royal Porthcawl
☎(0656) 782251, 773702 Pro
Rest Bay, Porthcawl, Mid-Glam CF36 3UW
Leave M4 at junction 37 to Porthcawl seafront, turn right, follow to Locks Common and bear left.
Links course.
Championship course 18 holes, 6691 yards, S.S.S.74
Designed by Charles Gibson.
Founded 1891
Visitors: welcome, h/cap cert required.
Green Fee: on application.
Societies: by arrangement (no weekends).
Catering: lunches, teas and dinner by arrangement.
Hotels: Atlantic; Seabank; Fairways.

J115 Royal St David's
☎(0766) 780857 Pro, 780361 Sec/Manager and tee bookings
Harlech, Gwynedd LL46 2UB
Between Barmouth and Porthmadog on A496.
Links championship seaside course.
18 holes, 6427 yards, S.S.S.71
Founded 1894
Visitors: welcome weekdays and weekends, prior arrangement advisable; must have regular h/cap cert.
Green Fee: £23/day WD, £30/day WE & BH.
Societies: catered for by prior arrangement.
Catering: full catering facilities available.
Hotels: St David's; Maes y Newydd; Talsarnau; Noddfa; Rum Hole; Castle; Castle Cottage; Byrdir GH.

St Pierre

In the summer of 1987, St Pierre celebrated its 25th anniversary. In a game which goes back centuries, that might not seem much of a landmark but St Pierre earned itself pride of place by being the first post-war championship course to be built in Britain — the herald of a new era.

When it comes to personal sentiment, it was the first new course I saw under construction. In the winter of 1961-2, Ken Cotton was invited to design two courses in the border country of England and Wales, one in the old deer park alongside the main road to Newport and Cardiff and the other in unpromising woodland at Ross-on-Wye. He thought a visit to see how it was done would be a good experience for a young writer — and how right he was.

The two courses could not possibly have been more of a contrast. St Pierre was largely ready-made in terms of fairways whereas Ross-on-Wye, a miracle of enterprise by a devoted band, had to be stripped root by root before the holes took shape.

That Cotton succeeded in both instances showed that he was a master of his craft. You can only judge the results if you knew the original terrain, the difficulties encountered and the budgets available. Both St Pierre and Ross-on-Wye were built on the thinnest of shoestrings. Bill Graham, who had dreamed of a course in the lovely park in St Pierre, drove past one day, and discovering that it was on the market, proved himself a man of action by buying it.

The land, the ancient manor house where the Crown Jewels were stored during the Battle of Agincourt, and the cost of construction of the course came to something under £30,000. However absurdly modest that seems nowadays, one or two sacrifices had to be made but

Graham's reasons for purchasing had to be commercially based and here he showed how valid his instincts were. Floodlit golf proved to be one of his few ideas to misfire. When St Pierre was built, the motorway systems were already well launched, and the opening of the Severn Bridge only a few years away. St Pierre was, and is, wonderfully accessible from London, Birmingham and Bristol, as well as South Wales.

It wasn't given long to settle down before it was much in demand. Dunlop made it a frequent home for their much lamented Masters and in 1980 the Ladies Golf Union paid it the ultimate compliment by holding the Curtis Cup there. Regular calls have been made upon it by organisers of small tournaments and company days, all of whom flock to take advantage of its residential amenities and a host of other sporting facilities.

The addition of the second course brought alteration to Cotton's orgiginal design, and more land was purchased on higher ground. However, nothing destroyed Cotton's first impression that, for Club golfers at large, it is a delightful place to play.

Stately ancient trees feature strongly. After a mild introduction to them at the 1st, the 2nd is dominated by them, although there follows a break on the loftier reaches of the 3rd to the 6th. At the 6th, the eye is caught by the distant sights but with the 7th, the trees return and, from then on, there is no let-up.

Several recent changes and a few new back tees have made the professionals flex their muscles a little more. However, one hole where no change is contemplated, and certainly none required, is the 18th across the lake. One of golf's oldest clichés is that nothing is certain until the last putt is holed: nowhere is this more apt than at St Pierre.

J116 Ruthin Pwllglas

☎(0824) 703427
Ruthin Pwllglas, Ruthin, Clwyd
2.5 miles S of Ruthin in A494, right
fork before Pwllglas village.
Parkland/moorland course.
9 holes, 5418 yards, S.S.S.66
Designed by David Lloyd Rees.
Founded 1906
Visitors: welcome.
Green Fee: apply for details.
Societies: by arrangement.
Catering: parties catered for by
arrangement.
Hotels: Ruthin Castle.

J117 St Andrews Major

☎(0446) 722227
Coldbrook Rd East, Nr Cadoxton,
Barry, S Glam CF6 3BB
From M4 exit 33 follow signs to Barry
and Rhoose Airport, take left turn to
Sully just after Wenvoe Golf Club,
turn left on Coldbrook Rd East.
Pay-as-you-Play, parkland course.
9 holes, 5862 yards, S.S.S.68
(provisional)
Designed by MRM Leisure.
Founded 1993
Visitors: no restrictions, but usually
very busy at weekends and public
holidays.
Green Fee: £7 (9 holes), £12 (18
holes).
Societies: welcome, no restrictions.
Catering: bar and restaurant (from
spring 1994).
Hotels: Copthorne.

J118 St Davids City

☎(0437) 721751 Clubhoue, 720312
Sec/bookings
Whitesands, St Davids,
Pembrokeshire
2 miles W of St Davids, follow signs
for Whitesands Bay.
Links course with views of
Whitesands Bay and St Davids Head,
most westerly course in Wales.
9 holes (18 tees), 6121 yards,
S.S.S.70
Founded 1902
Visitors: welcome, no restrictions
but Ladies day Fri pm and club
competitions Sat.
Green Fee: £13/day.
Societies: welcome by prior
arrangement with Sec.
Catering: at Whitesands Bay Hotel,
adjacent to Course.
Hotels: Whitesands Bay; Old Cross;
St Nons; Warpool Court; numerous
guest houses and self-catering
cottages.

J119 St Deiniol

☎(0248) 353098
Bangor, Gwynedd LL57 1PX
Off A5/A55 junction on to A5122 for 1
mile into Bangor; on E outskirts of
town, golf club signposted.
Undulating parkland course.
18 holes, 5068 yards, S.S.S.67
Designed by James Braid.
Founded 1905
Visitors: welcome at any time;
parties by arrangement.
Green Fee: £12/day WD, £16/day
WE & BH.
Societies: welcome by prior
arrangement.
Catering: full catering service.
Snooker.
Hotels: British Hotel; Eryl Mor.

J120 St Giles

☎(0686) 625844, 622223 Sec
Pool Rd, Newtown, Powys SY16 3AJ
0.5 mile E of Newtown on main
Welshpool to Newtown road, A483.
Parkland course.
9 holes, 5936 yards, S.S.S.68
Founded 1910
Visitors: welcome weekdays, some
weekends.
Green Fee: on application.
Societies: must write to Sec for
booking.
Catering: meals except Mon.

J121 St Idloes

☎(0686 41) 2559
Penrallt, Llanidloes, Powys SY18 6LG
Off A470 at Llanidloes, 1 mile B4569.
Slightly undulating course on hill
plateau with superb views.
9 holes, 5320 yards, S.S.S.66
Designed by the members.
Founded 1920
Visitors: welcome with club h/cap
cert.
Green Fee: £12/round/day,
£50/week.
Societies: very welcome by
appointment with Sec.
Catering: available on request;
banqueting, functions.
Hotels: Unicorn; Trewythen Arms;
Lion; Mount Inn.

J122 St Mellons

☎(0633) 680408 Sec, 680101 Pro,
680401 Club
St Mellons, Cardiff, S Glam CF3 8XS
On A48 between Newport and Cardiff
on left, follow yellow sign for St
Mellons Country Club.
Parkland course.

18 holes, 6275 yards, S.S.S.70
Founded 1964
Visitors: welcome.
Green Fee: £25.
Societies: weekdays only by
arrangement.
Catering: available.
Hotels: St Mellons Country Club.

J123 St Melyd

☎(0745) 854405 Club, 888858 Club
shop, 853574 Sec (Home)
The Paddock, Prestatyn, Clwyd LL19
9NB
Between Prestatyn and Meliden
village on main road A547.
Undulating parkland course.
9 holes, 6017 yards, S.S.S.68
Founded 1922
Visitors: welcome any time.
Green Fee: £15 WD, £19 WE & BH.
Societies: welcome except Sat.
Catering: faciltities available any
time
Hotels: Pontins Holiday Village; Nant
Hall; Bryn Gwalia; Graig Park.

J124 St Pierre Hotel Golf & Country Club

☎(0291) 625261
St Pierre Park, Chepstow, Gwent NP6
6YA
On A48 Chepstow-Newport road, 2
miles from Chepstow.
Old course parkland, New course
meadowland.
Old, 18 holes, 6700 yards, S.S.S.73;
New, 18 holes, 5762 yards, S.S.S.68
Old course designed by C.K. Cotton,
New by Bill Cox.
Founded 1962
Visitors: h/cap cert required;
booking advised.
Green Fee: on application
Societies: Mon to Fri; weekends
residential only.
Catering: full facilities.
Conferences (up to 220 delegates),
extensive sports and leisure
facilities.
Hotels: St Pierre.

J125 South Pembrokeshire

☎(0646) 683817
Defensible Barracks, Pembroke
Dock, Dyfed
1.5 miles S of Hobbs Point at W end
of A477, 0.5 mile from Pembroke
Dock.
Seaside parkland course.
9 holes, 5804 yards, S.S.S.69
Founded 1970
Visitors: welcome.

ST. PIERRE HOTEL
GOLF & COUNTRY CLUB

St. Pierre Park, Chepstow, Gwent NP6 6YA Tel: Chepstow (0291) 625261 Fax: (0291) 629975

St Pierre, the premier golf, leisure and conference resort in Wales, is set in 400 acres of beautiful parkland overlooking the Severn estuary.

St Pierre has two golf courses. The world famous championship 'Old' Course, playing host to decades of top PGA events, such as the Epson Grand Prix, the Dunlop Masters, the Silk Cut Masters and the Gary Player Classic, and the Mathern course, known locally as 'The Wee Nastie'.

Getting There
Junction 22 off the M4 Motorway, follow signs toward Chepstow and turn left onto the A48 towards Newport. St Pierre is two and a half miles on the left.

The Course	Old Course	Mathern Course
Yards	6748	5713
Par	71	68
SSS	73	68
Green Fees		
Per weekday round	£35	£25
Per weekend or Bank Holiday round	£45	£25

One round per course, per weekday   £50
Per weekend day or Bank Holiday   £65
Note: There are no reduced fees for children, and no weekly rates.
Methods of Payment: Cash/Cheque (with valid banker's card) American Express/Diners Club/Visa/Access/Mastercard

Handicap requirements
A handicap Certificate is required by all visiting players, a maximum 28 for men and 36 for women.

How to contact the club
Contact the Professional shop through the main switchboard to book a star time.

The leisure complex includes an indoor swimming pool, sauna, solarium, jacuzzi and steamroom, and facilities for squash, badminton, tennis, snooker and croquet.

St Pierre is a 4 star, 146 bedroom hotel, opening its doors for 1994 after a multi-million pound renovation programme, including all bedrooms, conference rooms and public areas.

Green Fee: apply for details.
Societies: apply to Sec.
Catering: bar except Mon, meals by arrangement.

J126 Southerndown
☎(0656) 880476 Club, 880326 Pro
Ewenny, Bridgend, Mid-Glam CF32 0QP
4 miles from Bridgend on the coast road to Ogmore-by-Sea; turn off at Pelican Inn opposite Ogmore Castle.
Links/downland course.
18 holes, 6417 yards, S.S.S.72
Designed by W. Herbert Fowler, Willie Park, H.S. Colt.
Founded Feb 1906
Visitors: weekdays; weekends with member; h/cap certs required.
Green Fee: £24 WD, £30 WE.
Societies: weekdays only by arrangement with Sec.
Catering: facilities daily. Snooker.
Hotels: Sea Lawns; Sea Bank; Heronston.

J127 Swansea Bay
☎(0792) 814153, 812198, 816159 Pro
Jersey Marine, Neath, W Glam SA10 6JP

Off B4290, Jersey Marine turning off A483 dual carriageway between Neath and Swansea.
Links course.
18 holes, 6605 yards, S.S.S.72
Founded 1892
Visitors: welcome.
Green Fee: £16 WD, £22 WE & BH.
Societies: catered for.
Catering: meals served.
Hotels: Castle.

J128 Tenby
☎(0834) 812978 Sec, 814447 Pro
The Burrows, Tenby, Dyfed SA70 7NP
A40 from Carmarthen to St Clears, then A477 on W of Tenby town centre.
Seaside links course.
18 holes, 6232 yards, S.S.S.71
Founded 1888 (oldest in Wales)
Visitors: welcome must be member of recognised club with h/cap cert.
Green Fee: £18 WD, £22.50 WE & BH.
Societies: welcome with prior booking.
Catering: full catering facilities, bar snacks; restaurant meals to be pre-booked.
Hotels: Kinloch Court; Imperial.

J129 Tredegar & Rhymney
☎(0685) 840743
Cwmtysswg, Rhymney, Mid-Glam
B4256 1.5 miles from Rhymney.
Undulating mountain course.
9 holes, 2788 yards, S.S.S.67
Founded 1921
Visitors: welcome.
Green Fee: £12 (£8 with member) WD, £15 (£11 with member) WE.
Societies: weekdays only.
Catering: no catering daytime; evenings by arrangement.
Hotels: Red Lion Inn (Tredegar).

J130 Tredegar Park
☎(0633) 894433 Sec, 895219 Club, 894517 Pro
Bassaleg Rd, Newport, Gwent NP9 3PX
M4 junction 27, to Newport, 1st right in Western Ave and right at end.
Parkland course.
18 holes, 6097 yards, S.S.S.70
Designed by James Braid.
Founded 1923
Visitors: must provide evidence of membership of affiliated club.
Green Fee: £25 WD, £30 WE & BH.
Societies: by arrangement.
Catering: members and visitors only.
Hotels: The Kings; Celtic Manor.

J131 Vale of Llangollen
☎(0978) 86096 Sec, 860040 Pro
Llangollen, Clwyd LL20 7PR
On A5, 1 mile S of Llangollen.
Parkland course.
18 holes, 6661 yards, S.S.S.72
Founded 1908
Visitors: welcome weekdays and some weekends.
Green Fee: £20 WD, £25 WE.
Societies: weekdays by prior arrangement with Sec.
Catering: full catering.
Hotels: Royal; The Hand; Tyn y Wern; Bryn Howel.

J132 Virginia Park
☎(0222) 863919, 863113 Fax
Virginia Park, Caerphilly, Mid Glam CF8 3SW
In centre of town.
Municipal parkland course.
9 holes, S.S.S.66
Founded Aug 1992
Visitors: welcome, h/cap cert required.
Green Fee: £6 (9 holes), £11 (18 holes).
Societies: welcome.
Catering: bars, full refreshments.
Driving range.

J133 Welsh Border Golf Complex
☎(0743) 884247
Bulthy Farm, Bulthy, Middletown, Nr Welshpool, Powys SY21 8ER
Via A458 Shrewsbury/Welshpool road, turn off to club signposted in Middletown.
Parkland course.
9 holes, 3006 yards, S.S.S.69; 9 holes Par 3, 1614 yards
Designed by Andrew Griffiths.
Founded 1991
Visitors: proper dress, h/cap certs not required; no restrictions for Par 3 course.
Green Fee: £7 (9 holes), £10 (18 holes), £18/day; Par 3 course, £4 (9 holes), £6 (18 holes).
Societies: welcome any time by arrangement with Sec.
Catering: bar and restarant.
Driving range.
Hotels: Rowlon Castle; Bulthy Farm GH.

J134 Welshpool
☎(0938) 83249
Golfa Hill, Welshpool, Powys
4 miles from Welshpool on A458.
Mountain course.

18 holes, 5708 yards, S.S.S.69
Designed by James Braid.
Founded 1929
Visitors: welcome.
Green Fee: apply for details.
Societies: by arrangement.
Catering: facilities available.
Hotels: Golfa Hall; Royal Oak.

J135 Wenvoe Castle
☎(0222) 594371 Sec, 593649 Pro
Wenvoe, Cardiff CF5 6BE
A48 W from Cardiff, left after 3 miles onto A4050, course 2 miles on right.
Parkland course.
18 holes, 6411 yards, S.S.S.71
Founded 1936
Visitors: Mon-Fri with h/cap cert; Sat/Sun with member only.
Green Fee: £22.
Societies: Mon-Fri by prior application; reduction for 16 plus.
Catering: bars, lunches, dinner, snacks.
Snooker.
Hotels: Copthorne (Culverhouse Cross).

J136 Wernddu Golf Centre
☎(0873) 856223
Abergavenny, Gwent NP7 8NG
1.5 miles E of Abergavenny on B4521 off A465.
Public parkland course.
9 holes, Par 31
Designed by G. Watkins.
Founded 1992
Visitors: 8am to dusk every day; correct dress required.
Green Fee: £6 (9 holes), £9 (18 holes).
Societies: by arrangement weekdays.
Catering: bar, light refreshments available.
Driving range, 9-hole Pitch & Putt, practice putting area.
Hotels: self-catering holiday cottages available.

J137 West Monmouthshire
☎(0495) 310233, 312746 Sec
Pond Rd, Nantyglo, Gwent NP3 4QT
Heads of Valley road A465, western valley A467 to Semtex roundabout, follow Winchestown signs.
Heathland course (14th tee highest in England and Wales, 1450ft).
18 holes, 6118 yards, S.S.S.69
Founded 1906
Visitors: welcome, Mon-Sat; Sun guests only.

Green Fee: £15 WD (£10 with member).
Societies: by appointment Mon-Fri.
Catering: bar and restaurant.

J138 Whitchurch (Cardiff)
☎(0222) 620985 Sec, 620125 Club, 529860 Fax
Pantmawr Rd, Whitchurch, Cardiff, S Glam CF4 6XD
Off M4 at exit 32, 0.5 mile on A470 to Cardiff.
Parkland course.
18 holes, 6319 yards S.S.S.70
Re-designed by James Braid.
Founded 1915
Visitors: welcome, h/cap cert required.
Green Fee: £26 WD, £26 WE & BH.
Societies: Thurs only.
Catering: facilities available every day.
Hotels: Travelodge; Masons Arms.

J139 Whitehall
☎(0443) 740245
The Pavilion, Nelson, Treharris, Mid-Glam CF46 6ST
Take Treharris and Nelson exit at roundabout on A470, turn right and head S for 0.25 mile, take 1st left turning up Mountain Rd.
Mountain course.
9 holes, 5666 yards, S.S.S.68
Founded 1922
Visitors: welcome weekdays; with member at weekends.
Green Fee: on application
Societies: welcome by arrangement with Sec.
Catering: available by prior arrangement.
Hotels: Llechwen Hall (Pontypridd).

J140 Woodlake Park Golf & Country Club
☎(0291) 673933, 673811 Fax
Glascoed, Pontypool, Gwent NP4 0TE
Situated on eastern bank of Llandegfedd Reservoir 3 miles from Usk; 10 miles M4 junction 24, 8 miles junction 26.
Parkland course.
18 holes, S.S.S.70
Designed by M.J. Wood and H.N. Wood.
Founded August 1993
Visitors: welcome at any time; must be member of bona fide club.
Green Fee: £20/round, £25/day.
Societies: packages from £20 per person; weekends available; booking essential.

Catering: spikes bar, function room/ restaurant for 120.
Indoor Golf Academy; extensive practice facilities; pitching/chipping and bunkers; 9-hole putting green; driving into nets.
Hotels: 3 Salmons (Usk); Parkway (Cwmbran); Cwrt Bleddyn (Llangibie).

J141 Wrexham
☎(0978) 364268, 261033, 351476
Holt Rd, Wrexham, Clwyd LL13 9SB
Situated on A534 2 miles E of Wrexham.
Undulating sandy course.
18 holes, 6139 yards, S.S.S.69
Designed by James Braid.

Founded 1906 (present location 1923)
Visitors: welcome.
Green Fee: on application.
Societies: Mon, Thurs, Fri.
Catering: full facilities.
Snooker.
Hotels: Holt Lodge.

K

SHROPSHIRE, STAFFORDSHIRE, CHESHIRE

In the last few years, Staffordshire and Shropshire have made the headlines on account of their golfing sons and daughters. Diane Bailey and Geoffrey Marks became the first to captain victorious Curtis and Walker Cup teams on American soil. David Gilford, a member of Trentham Park, won a place in the Ryder Cup team in 1991 along with Ian Woosnam, whose county golf as an amateur was played for Shropshire in company with Sandy Lyle who was raised at Hawkstone Park.

Hawkstone is part of a hotel complex that provides popular golfing facilities about 14 miles north of Shrewsbury in an area that is full of largely rural delights. It has recently seen significant change.

In Shropshire, Bridgenorth is a delight, with several holes along the river. But, while Shropshire's courses are relatively few and far between, Staffordshire enjoys quantity as well as quality. It includes Little Aston, Penn, home of the late and great Charlie Stowe, and South Staffordshire at Wolverhampton, as well as the delights of Beau Desert, Drayton Park, Leek, Trentham, Trentham Park, Enville, Uttoxeter (which the locals pronounce Uttcheter) and Patshull Park.

Enville was the home course as a girl of Diane Bailey (neé Robb) while Geoffrey Marks has remained loyal all his playing days to Trentham — to the south of Stoke-on-Trent. Enville's two contrasting courses are very good, while Trentham is a parkland course with nice changes of level, very much like its neighbour Trentham Park.

Newcastle Municipal is a relatively recent public course that is now much used, but probably the best courses in this section are Whittington Barracks, a slightly forbidding name for a moorland retreat that has championship status, and Little Ashton which epitomises the very best of parkland golf, the main hazards taking the form of characteristically large bunkers a couple of lakes, some majestic trees and a degree of undulation which tests one's judgment of distance

South of the Mersey the first ports of call after emerging from the tunnel are the celebrated links of Wallasey and Royal Liverpool. Wallasey is less well known in spite of its association in bygone days with Dr Frank Stableford, mastermind of the excellent scoring system that bears his name — a system less cruel than the rigours of undiluted medal play.

Maybe he devised the idea from his battles with Wallasey's glorious seaside links and the winds that plague golfers even more. The latest version of the course incorporates rather more of the flat, plain land than it used to, but flatness is also a feature of Royal Liverpool at Hoylake, which few have seen fit to criticise in an area that has changed hardly at all in character since the Club was founded in 1869.

As the second oldest seaside course in England, Royal Liverpool wears the local crown but Caldy and Heswall are other Wirral landmarks not far off the road back to Chester, where most of the best golfing country lies to the east and the south-east.

Sandiway, Delamere Forest and Mere are all redoubtable courses in beautiful settings but nothing could match the splendour of the setting of Portal at Tarporley, which opened its doors for the first time in 1991, although an even more recent creation is Carden Park at Malpas.

K1 **Alderley Edge**
☎(0625) 585583
Brook Lane, Alderley Edge, Cheshire
SK9 7RU
From Alderley Edge, turn left off A34
opposite Tower Garage towards
Mobberley/Knutsford, B5085.
Undulating parkland course.
9 holes, 5839 yards, S.S.S.68
Designed by T. G. Renouf.
Founded 1907
Visitors: welcome subject to proof of
h/cap; restricted Tues, Wed,
weekends.
Green Fee: apply for details.
Societies: catered for I hurs.
Catering: full catering facilities
except Mon.
Hotels: De Trafford Arms.

K2 **Alsager G & CC**
☎(0270) 875700, 882207 Fax
Audley Rd, Alsager, Stoke-on-Trent
ST7 2UR
Leave M6 at junction 16, take A500
towards Stoke-on-Trent for 1 mile,
leave at 1st turn left for Alsager;
course 2 miles.
Parkland course.
18 holes, 6206 yards, S.S.S.70
Founded 1976
Visitors: correct dress required, no
jeans, ties and jackets after 7pm.
Green Fee: on application
Societies: Mon, Wed, Thurs.
Catering: available.
Banqueting, snooker, bowls.

K3 **Altrincham**
☎(061) 928 0761
Stockport Rd, Timperley, Altrincham,
Cheshire WA15
On a560 1 mile W of Altrincham.
Public undulating parkland course.
18 holes, 6162 yards, S.S.S.69
Founded 1935
Visitors: welcome; advance
bookings at all times.
Green Fee: apply for details.
Catering: no facilities at club;
Beefeater restaurant next door.
Hotels: Cresta Court; Woodlands
Park.

K4 **Arrowe Park**
☎(051) 677 1527 Pro
Arrowe Park, Woodchurch,
Birkenhead, Merseyside L49 5LW
3 miles from town centre, take
Borough Rd, Woodchurch Rd and
then opposite Landicon Cemetery;
M53 junction 3, 1 mile.
Municipal parkland course.

18 holes, 6377 yards, S.S.S.70
Founded 1932
Visitors: welcome, phone first.
Green Fee: £6.
Societies: arrange with Pro.
Catering: restaurant.

K5 **Arscott**
☎(0743) 860114, 860881 Pro
Arscott, Pontesbury, Shropshire SY5
0XP
4 miles SW of Shrewsbury on A488,
midway between Hanwood and
Pontesbury.
Elevaled parkland course with
extensive views.
18 holes, 6025 yards, S.S.S.69
Designed by Martin Hamer.
Founded 1992
Visitors: welcome at all times;
bookings required, Mar-Oct.
Green Fee: £14/day WD, £18/day
WE.
Societies: weekdays and some
weekends, bookings advised; rates
on request.
Catering: full bar and restaurant
facilities at all times.
Hotels: Boar's Head (Bishops
Castle); Sandford House, Rowton
Castle (Shrewsbury).

K6 **Ashton on Mersey**
☎(061) 973 3220
Church Lane, Sale, Cheshire M33
5QQ
2 miles from Sale station.
Parkland course.
9 holes, 6202 yards, S.S.S.69
Founded 1897
Visitors: welcome, except Tues after
3pm (Ladies Day).
Green Fee: apply for details.
Societies: by arrangement.
Catering: snacks, lunches, evening
meals.
Hotels: Cresta Court.

K7 **Astbury**
☎(0260) 272772, 279139 Office,
298663 Pro
Peel Lane, Astbury, Nr Congleton,
Cheshire CW12 4RE
On outskirts of Congleton; leave A34
Congleton-Newcastle road at
Astbury village.
Parkland/meadowland course.
18 holes, 6269 yards, S.S.S.70
Founded 1922
Visitors: members of recognised
golf clubs welcome; must be
accompanied by member at
weekends.

Green Fee: £25/day (£8 with
member).
Societies: Thurs only, by
arrangement; £20 per person per
day.
Catering: by prior arrangement only.
Hotels: Bulls Head; Lion and Swan.

K8 **Barlaston**
☎(0782) 372867 Sec, 372795 Pro
shop
Meaford Rd, Stone, Staffs ST15 8UX
From M6 junction 14 take A34
towards Stoke-on-Trent; over
Warton roundabout at Stone, past
Wayfarers public house on left and
turn right 0.25 mile after traffic
lights; club is 300 yards beyond
power station.
Moorland course.
18 holes, 5800 yards, S.S.S.68
Designed by Peter Alliss.
Founded 1977
Visitors: welcome weekdays, not
before 10am weekends.
Green Fee: £18 WD, £22.50 WE.
Societies: weekdays only.
Catering: bar daily, meals by
arrangement.
Hotels: Stonehouse.

K9 **Beau Desert**
☎(0543) 422626
Hazel Slade, Cannock, Staffs WS12
5PJ
Take A460 from Cannock through
Hednesford, right at signpost to
Hazel Slade, and next left.
Moorland course.
18 holes, 6300 yards, S.S.S.71
Designed by H. Fowler.
Founded 1921
Visitors: welcome weekdays; Sat
and Sun phone Pro.
Green Fee: £30/day.
Societies: welcome.
Catering: available.
Hotels: Cedar Tree (Rugeley);
Roman Way (on A5 Cannock).

K10 **Bidston**
☎(051) 638 3412, 630 6650 Pro
Scoresby Rd, Leasowe, Wirral,
Merseyside L46 1QQ
A551 from Wallasey, 0.75 mile.
Parkland course.
18 holes, 6207 yards, S.S.S.70
Founded 1913
Visitors: welcome weekdays.
Green Fee: on application
Societies: weekdays only.
Catering: full facilities.
Hotels: Leasowe Castle (Moreton).

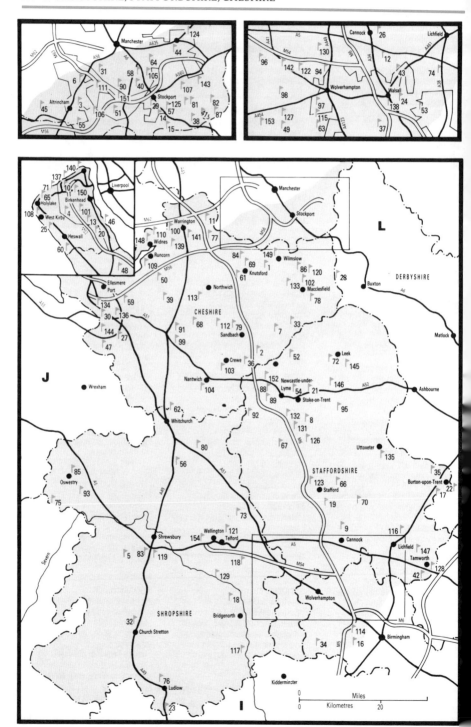

K11 Birchwood

☎(0925) 818819
Kelvin Close, Risley, Warrington,
Cheshire WA3 7PB
M62 junction 11; follow A574 for
Risley/Birchwood (opposite Digital).
Parkland course.
18 holes, 6850 yards, S.S.S.73
Designed by T. J. McAuley.
Founded 1979
Visitors: welcome weekdays.
Green Fee: £24-£32.
Societies: Mon, Wed, Thurs; send
for brochure.
Catering: à la carte, bar snacks,
carvery, 7 days.
Banqueting, snooker.
Hotels: Lord Daresbury; Garden
Court.

K12 Bloxwich

☎(0922) 476593 Sec, 476889 Pro,
405724 club
136 Stafford Rd, Bloxwich, Walsall,
W Midlands WS3 3PQ
Off main Walsall-Cannock road
(A34), 4 miles N of Walsall centre.
Semi-parkland course.
18 holes, 6286 yards, S.S.S.70
Designed by J. Sixsmith.
Founded 1924
Visitors: welcome except weekends
and Bank Holidays.
Green Fee: £20/round, £25/day (£5
with member).
Societies: catered for, preferably
weekdays; reduced rates over 20.
Catering: bar, restaurant (not Mon);
lunch by arrangement. Snooker.
Hotels: Barons Court; County;
Beverley; Royal.

K13 Brackenwood

☎(051) 608 5394
Bracken Lane, Bebington, Wirral,
Merseyside L63 2LY
M53 junction 7, to Clatterbridge and
Bebington.
Public parkland course.
18 holes, 6285 yards, S.S.S.70
Founded 1933
Visitors: on application to Pro.
Green Fee: apply for details.
Societies: by arrangement.
Catering: at Pro's shop.
Hotels: Thornton Hall; Village,
Dibinsdale (Bromborough).

K14 Bramhall

☎(061) 439 4057, 439 6092 Sec,
439 1171 Pro
Ladythorn Rd, Bramhall, Stockport,
Cheshire SK7 2EY
Near Bramhall station, 8 miles S of
Manchester on A5102.
Parkland course.
18 holes, 6280 yards, S.S.S.70
Founded 1905
Visitors: welcome, subject to
members competitions, book with
Pro.
Green Fee: Mon-Thurs £25 (£8 with
member), £35 WE & BH (£10 with
member).
Societies: catered for Wed, book
with Sec.
Catering: à la carte, bar snacks.
Hotels: Moat House; Oakley Manor;
Etrop Grange.

K15 Bramhall Park

☎(061) 485 3119
20 Manor Rd, Bramhall, Stockport
SK7 3LY
8 miles S of Manchester, A6 to
Bramhall Lane, then A5102 to
Carrwood Rd.
Parkland course.
18 holes, 6214 yards, S.S.S.70
Founded 1894
Visitors: not Fri (no catering).
Green Fee: on application.
Societies: Tues up to 60 players;
Thurs small parties up to 25.
Catering: full except Fri.
Hotels: Oakley Manor (Cheadle
Hulme); Alma Lodge.

K16 Brand Hall

☎(021) 552 2195
Heron Road, Oldbury, Warley, W
Midlands B68 8AQ
6 miles NW of Birmingham, 1.5 miles
from M5 junction 2.
Public parkland course.
18 holes, 5734 yards, S.S.S.68
Visitors: welcome.
Green Fee: apply for details.
Societies: welcome.
Catering: café, clubhouse, bar.
Putting green.

K17 Branston

☎(0283) 43207
Burton Rd, Branston,
Burton-on-Trent DE14 3DP
Take A5121 off the A38 towards
Burton-on-Trent, past church on
right, over railway bridge, past petrol
station on right, entrance to club 200
yards on right.
Parkland course.
18 holes, 6408 yards, S.S.S.71
Founded 1976
Visitors: welcome on weekdays.
Green Fee: apply for details.

Societies: weekdays.
Catering: full catering, except Mon.
Hotels: Riverside; Dog & Partridge.

K18 Bridgnorth

☎(0746) 763315
Stanley Lane, Bridgnorth, Shropshire
WV16 4SF
Through High St, along Broseley Rd
for 400 yards, right into Stanley
Lane.
Parkland course.
18 holes, 6668 yards, S.S.S.72
Founded 1889
Visitors: welcome daily except Mon
and Wed.
Green Fee: £16.50/day WD, £25 WE
& BH, (half price with member).
Societies: catered for weekdays by
arrangement with Sec.
Catering: full catering facilities
except Mon.
Hotels: Falcon; Kings Head; Croft;
Whitburn Grange.

K19 Brocton Hall

☎(0785) 662627, 661901 Manager
Brocton, Stafford ST17 0TH
4 miles S of Stafford on A34, turn left
at crossroads signposted Brocton,
club entrance 300 yards on left.
Parkland course.
18 holes, 6095 yards, S.S.S.69
Designed by Harry Vardon.
Founded 1894
Visitors: accepted.
Green Fee: £25 WD, £30 WE & BH.
Societies: bookings accepted on
Tues and Thurs.
Catering: by arrangement with the
caterer.
Hotels: Tillington Hall.

K20 Bromborough

☎(051) 334 2155, 334 4499 Pro
Raby Hall Rd, Bromborough, Wirral,
Merseyside L63 0NW
0.5 mile from Bromborough station,
0.75 mile from A41
Birkenhead-Chester road; M53
junction 5.
Parkland course.
18 holes, 6650 yards, S.S.S.73
Founded 1904
Visitors: welcome weekdays; check
with Pro
Green Fee: £26 (£9 with member)
WD, £30 (£9 with member) WE & BH.
Societies: Wed; early booking
essential.
Catering: extensive snack menu,
meals by arrangement.
Hotels: Dibbinsdale; Thornton Hall.

K21 **Burslem**
☎(0782) 837006
Wood Farm, High Lane, Tunstall,
Stoke-on-Trent ST6 7JT
2 miles N of Hanley, situated on High
Lane.
Moorland course.
11 holes, 5527 yards, S.S.S.67
Founded 1907
Visitors: welcome weekdays; not
weekends.
Green Fee: apply for details.
Societies: weekdays.
Catering: apply to Steward.

K22 **Burton-on-Trent**
☎(0283) 44551
43 Ashby Rd East, Burton-on-Trent
DE15 0PS
3 miles E of Burton-on-Trent on A50.
Undulating wooded parkland course.
18 holes, 6555 yards, S.S.S.71
Designed by H.S. Colt.
Founded 1894
Visitors: welcome, letter of intro,
h/cap cert required; phone
reservation advisable.
Green Fee: £20/round WD,
£25/round WE & BH.
Societies: weekdays except Mon.
Catering: full facilities except Mon.
Snooker.
Hotels: Stanhope Arms (Bretby);
Newton Park (Newton Solney).

K23 **Cadmore Lodge**
☎(0584) 810044
Berrington Green, Tenbury Wells,
Worcester WR15 8TQ
Off A456 12 miles W of
Kidderminster.
Parkland course with lakes.
9 holes, 5129 yards, S.S.S.65
Designed by John Weston.
Founded 1990
Visitors: welcome, no restrictions.
Green Fee: £7/day WD, £10/day WE.
Societies: welcome, book in
advance.
Catering: full facilities.
Bowls.

K24 **Calderfields**
☎(0922) 640540 Manageress,
32243 Pro shop
Aldridge Rd, Walsall, W Midlands
WS4 2JS
From M6 junction 7, take A454
Aldridge-Walsall road; entrance by
Dilke Arms public house.
Parkland course.
18 holes, 6700 yards, S.S.S.72
Designed by Roy Winter.

Founded 1983
Visitors: welcome any time, no
restriction except weekends am.
Green Fee: apply for details.
Societies: phone manageress.
Catering: full bar and restaurant.
Pool tables, darts.
Hotels: Crest; Post House; Barons
Court.

K25 **Caldy**
☎(051) 625 5660
Links Hey Rd, Caldy, Wirral,
Merseyside, L48 1NB
A540 from Chester turn left at Caldy
crossroads.
Seaside/parkland course.
18 holes, 6665 yards, S.S.S.73
Designed by James Braid, John
Salvesen.
Founded 1907
Visitors: welcome weekdays; Tues
Ladies Day; weekends with member.
Green Fee: on application
Societies: Thurs main day; not Wed.
Catering: lunch; dinner by
arrangement.

K26 **Cannock Park**
☎(0543) 578850 Phone/Fax
Stafford Rd, Cannock, Staffs WS11
2AL
On A46 Stafford road, 0.5 mile from
Cannock centre on left hand side
situated behind Leisure Centre.
Municipal parkland course playing
over Cannock Chase.
18 holes, 5048 yards, S.S.S.65
Designed by John Mainland.
Founded 1988
Visitors: welcome; busy course,
phone bookings on the day or by
letter for societies.
Green Fee: £6 WD, £7.50 WE.
Societies: welcome; write to Sec.
Catering: full facilities.
Putting green, swimming,
badminton, gym etc.

K27 **Carden Park**
☎(0829) 731000, 250539 Fax
Carden Park, Chester, Cheshire CH3
9DQ
On A534 towards Wrexham, 1.5
miles from junction with A41.
Park and woodland course.
18 holes, 6828 yards, S.S.S.73; 9
hole Par 3 short course
Designed by Alan Higgins
Founded Aug 1993
Visitors: welcome, h/cap certs
required for 18 hole course, please
ring for reservations.

Green Fee: £25/round, £35/day WD;
weekend fees on application.
Societies: details on application.
Catering: 2 restaurants and full bar
facilities.
Driving range, country pursuits and
leisure activities within estate.
Hotels: Birches Hotel at Carden Park
(84 suites).

K28 **Chapel-en-le-Frith**
☎(0298) 812118 Club, 813943 Sec
The Cockyard, Manchester Rd,
Chapel-en-le-Frith, Stockport,
Cheshire SK12 6UH
1 mile N of Chapel-en-le-Frith on
B5470 almost opposite Hanging Gate
public house.
Meadowland course.
18 holes, 6119 yards, S.S.S.69
Founded 1906
Visitors: welcome, small numbers
without reservation.
Green Fee: £20 WD, £30 WE & BH.
Societies: by arrangement.
Catering: all meals daily except
Mon.
Hotels: Kings Arms.

K29 **Cheadle**
☎(061) 491 4452 Sec, 428 2160
Club, 491 3878 Steward, 428 9878
Pro
Shiers Drive, Cheadle, Cheshire SK8
1HW
1.5 miles from junction 11 M63,
follow signs for Cheadle; 1 mile S of
Cheadle village, 1.5 miles from
Cheadle Hulme railway station.
Undulating parkland course.
9 holes, 5006 yards, S.S.S.65
Designed by R. Renouf.
Founded 1885
Visitors: members of golf club with
official h/cap; not Tues or Sat.
Green Fee: on application.
Societies: by written application to
Sec; no parties Sat, Sun or Tues.
Catering: bar and lunches daily
except Thur, at other times by
arrangement with Steward.
Snooker.
Hotels: The Village; Alma Lodge.

K30 **Chester**
☎(0244) 677760
Curzon Park North, Chester CH4 8AR
1 mile from centre of Chester, off
A55, course located behind Chester
Racecourse.
Parkland course.
18 holes, 6508 yards, S.S.S.71
Founded 1901

Visitors: welcome by arrangement.
Green Fee: £21 WD, £26 WE.
Societies: by arrangement.
Catering: full facilities.

K31 **Chorlton cum Hardy**
☎(061) 881 3139, 881 5830 Sec,
881 9911 Pro
Barlow Hall Rd, Chorlton,
Manchester M21 7JJ
3 miles from city centre, off A5103,
near Southern Cemetery.
Meadowland course.
18 holes, 6004 yards, S.S.S.69
Founded 1903
Visitors: telephone Pro.
Green Fee: £20 WD, £25 WE.
Societies: Thurs.
Catering: snacks and meals
available every day (limited hours)
except Mon (sandwiches etc only);
evening meals to order.
Hotels: Longford Park; Trust House;
Post House; Northenden.

K32 **Church Stretton**
☎(0694) 722281, 722633
Sec/bookings
Hunters Moon, Trevor Hill, Church
Stretton, Shropshire SY6 6JH
0.25 mile W of town centre, off
Cardingmill Valley Rd, up the winding
Trevor Hill.
Hillside course on lower slopes of
Longmynd.
18 holes, 5020 yards, S.S.S.65
Designed by James Braid.
Founded 1898
Visitors: welcome weekdays; Sat
not 9-10.30am or 1.30-2.30pm; Sun
not before 10.30am or
12.30-3.30pm.
Green Fee: £12 WD, £18 WE & BH.
Societies: by arrangement, not Sun.
Catering: bar and catering.
Hotels: Denehurst; Longmynd.

K33 **Congleton**
☎(0260) 273540
Biddulph Rd, Congleton, Cheshire
SW12 3LZ
1 mile SE of Congleton station on
main Congleton-Biddulph road A527.
Parkland course.
9 holes, 5080 yards, S.S.S.65
Founded 1898
Visitors: welcome daily.
Green Fee: £14 WD, £20 WE & BH
(half price with member).
Societies: welcome Mon and Thurs
by arrangement.
Catering: snacks; phone for full
meals; not Mon.

K34 **Corngreaves**
☎(0384) 67880
Corngreaves Road, Cradley Heath, W
Midlands
2 miles E of Dudley.
Public parkland course.
18 holes Par 3
Founded 1985
Visitors: welcome.
Green Fee: apply for details.

K35 **Craythorne Golf Centre**
☎(0283) 64329, 37992, 33745 Pro
shop, 511908 Fax
Craythorne Rd, Stretton,
Burton-on-Trent, Staffs DE13 0AZ
Take N exit for Burton-on-Trent from
A38, into Stretton village, turn right at
church.
Parkland course.
18 holes, 5230 yards, S.S.S.66; 9
holes, Par 3
Designed by Cyril Johnson.
Founded 1972
Visitors: welcome any time; booking
at weekends.
Green Fee: £12/round, £18/day WD;
£15/round, £21/day Sat; £18/round,
£23/day Sun.
Societies: weekdays only by
arrangement.
Catering: full bar and restaurant.
Driving range.
Hotels: Craythorne Farm (special
golfing breaks available).

K36 **Crewe**
☎(0270) 584099 Sec, 585032 Pro,
584227 Steward
Fields Rd, Haslington, Crewe,
Cheshire CW1 1TB
1 mile SW of A534 at Haslington,
between Crewe and Sandbach.
Parkland course.
18 holes, 6229 yards, S.S.S.70
Founded 1911
Visitors: weekdays only unless with
member.
Green Fee: £27, £22 after 1pm (£12
with member).
Societies: Tues only by prior
arrangement.
Catering: bar snacks, lunches,
dinners. Snooker.
Hotels: Crewe Arms; Saxon Cross
Motel; Lamb (Nantwich).

K37 **Dartmouth**
☎(021) 588 2131
Vale St, West Bromwich, W Midlands
B71 4DW
1.5 miles from M5/6 junction 1.

Undulating meadowland/parkland
course.
9 holes (16 tees), 6060 yards,
S.S.S.70
Founded 1910
Visitors: welcome weekdays, h/cap
cert preferred; with member only
some weekends.
Green Fee: approx £16.50/day
(£8/day with member).
Societies: by prior arrangement any
weekday.
Catering: by arrangement.
Snooker.
Hotels: Moat House; Albion.

K38 **Davenport**
☎(0625) 877321 Clubhouse,
877319 Pro, 876951 Sec
Worth Hall, Middlewood Rd, Poynton,
Stockport, Cheshire SK12 1TS
From Stockport take A6 to Rising Sun
at Hazel Grove, then A523
Macclesfield road, at Poynton traffic
lights turn left into Park Lane, club is
approx 1.5 miles.
Undulating parkland course.
18 holes, 6066 yards, S.S.S.69
Designed by Fraser Middleton.
Founded 1913
Visitors: welcome most days other
than Sat, phone Pro to check.
Green Fee: £24 WD, £30 WE; one
-third price with member.
Societies: Tues and Thurs,
£30/person.
Catering: by arrangement with
Steward; fixed hours for snacks.
Hotels: Belfry; Belgrade.

K39 **Delamere Forest**
☎(0606) 882807 Steward, 883264
Sec, 883307 Pro
Station Rd, Delamere, Northwich,
Cheshire CW8 2JE
From A556 Manchester-Chester
road take B5152 towards Frodsum;
lane to club is on right, approx 1 mile
from A556, immediately by
Delamere station.
Undulating heathland course.
18 holes, 6305 yards, S.S.S.70
Designed by Herbert Fowler.
Founded 1910
Visitors: welcome; 2 balls only
weekends and Bank Holidays.
Green Fee: £25/round, £35/day WD;
£30/round WE & BH; £10 if playing
with member.
Societies: Tues and Thurs.
Catering: bar snacks; restaurant if
booked in advance.
Hotels: Hartford Hall; Swan;
Willington Hall.

K40 **Didsbury**

☎(061) 998 9278 Sec, 998 2811 Pro
Ford Lane, Northenden, Manchester
M22 4NQ
Off M63 junction 9, near Northenden
Church, club sign on wall.
Parkland course.
18 holes, 6273 yards, S.S.S.70
Founded 1891
Visitors: welcome; Ladies day Tues;
weekends by arrangement.
Green Fee: £22 (£9 with member)
WD, £25 (£10 with member) WE.
Societies: Thurs and Fri.
Catering: restaurant and snacks.
Hotels: Post House; Britannia.

K41 **Disley**

☎(0663) 762071
Stanley Hall Lane, Jackson's Edge,
Disley, Cheshire SK12 2JX
A6, 6 miles S of Stockport.
Moorland/meadowland course.
18 holes, 6015 yards, S.S.S.69
Designed by James Braid.
Founded 1889
Visitors: Mon, Tues and Wed.
Green Fee: apply for details.
Societies: Tues and Wed.
Catering: bar; catering all days
except Mon.
Hotels: Moorside (Stockport).

K42 **Drayton Park**

☎(0827) 251139, 284035 Fax
Drayton Park, Tamworth, Staffs B78
3TN
2 miles S of Tamworth on A4091.
Parkland course.
18 holes, 6214 yards, S.S.S.71
Designed by James Braid.
Founded 1897
Visitors: by arrangement weekdays.
Green Fee: £27/day/round.
Societies: Tues and Thurs.
Catering: full facilities from
10.30am. Snooker.
Hotels: Gungate; Castle; Beafeater.

K43 **Druids Heath**

☎(0922) 55595
Stonnall Rd, Aldridge, W Midlands
WS9 8JZ
Off A452 6 miles NW of Sutton
Coldfield.
Undulating course.
18 holes, 6914 yards, S.S.S.73
Founded 1973
Visitors: welcome weekdays.
Green Fee: on application.
Societies: weekdays.
Catering: by prior arrangement.
Hotels: Barons Court; Fairlawns.

K44 **Dukinfield**

☎(061) 338 2340
Yew Tree Lane, Dukinfield, Cheshire
SK16 5DF
From Ashton Rd 1 mile then right into
Yew Tree Lane, club 1 mile on right,
on hill behind Senior Service factory.
Hillside course.
18 holes, 5303 yards, S.S.S.66
Founded 1913
Visitors: weekdays except Wed pm.
Green Fee: on application.
Societies: by arrangement with Sec.
Catering: meals by arrangement.
Hotels: York House.

K45 **Dunham Forest Golf & Country Club**

☎(061) 928 2605
Oldfield Lane, Altrincham, Cheshire
WA14 4TY
2 miles N of M56 junction 7, proceed
in direction of Manchester, course is
on left of main road.
Parkland course.
18 holes, 6800 yards, S.S.S.72
Founded 1961
Visitors: welcome.
Green Fee: on application.
Societies: weekdays except Wed.
Catering: bar and restaurant.
Hotels: Bowdon; Cresta Court.

K46 **Eastham Lodge**

☎(051) 327 3008 Pro, 327 3003
Sec, 327 1483 Club
117 Ferry Rd, Eastham, Wirral L62
0AP
Off A41 Birkenhead-Chester road,
follow signs for Eastham Country
Park, club on left of Ferry Rd
approaching Country Park.
Parkland course.
15 holes, 5864 yards, S.S.S.68
Designed by Hawtree & Sons.
Founded 1975
Visitors: welcome on weekdays, at
weekends only with member.
Green Fee: £22/day/round, £9 with
member.
Societies: Tues only.
Catering: bar snacks or full meal
pre-ordered.
Snooker.
Hotels: Village Hotel & Leisure
Centre (Bromborough).

K47 **Eaton**

☎(0244) 335885, 335782 Fax
Guy Lane, Waverton, Chester, CH3
7PH
3 miles SE of Chester off the A41.
Parkland course.

18 holes, S.S.S.71
Designed by Donald Steel.
Founded 1965 (Club), 1993 (Course)
Visitors: h/caps required; weekdays
only.
Green Fee: on request.
Societies: weekdays only.
Catering: full catering available.

K48 **Ellesmere Port**

☎(051) 339 7689
Chester Rd, Childer Thornton, S
Wirral, Cheshire L66 1QF
W on M53, take A41 turning S
towards Chester for 2 miles, club at
rear of St Paul's Church, Hooton.
Municipal parkland/meadowland
course.
18 holes, 6432 yards, S.S.S.71
Designed by Cotton, Pennink, Lawrie
& Partners.
Founded 1971
Visitors: welcome.
Green Fee: £5.30/round WD,
£6.10/round WE & BH.
Societies: weekdays and weekends,
booking fee £1.15 per head.
Catering: full facilities, bar and
restaurant all day.
Squash centre.
Hotels: Brook Meadow; Chimney
(Hooton); Village Hotel and Leisure
Club (Bromborough).

K49 **Enville**

☎(0384) 872074 Sec and Manager,
872551 Club, 872585 Pro
Highgate Common, Enville,
Stourbridge, W Midlands DY7 5BN
5 miles W of Stourbridge; from A449
follow A458 Bridgenorth road for 1.8
miles; club signposted.
Heathland/woodland course.
Highgate, 18 holes, 6556 yards,
S.S.S.72; Lodge, 18 holes, 6217
yards, S.S.S.70
Founded 1935
Visitors: welcome weekdays and
with member at weekends.
Green Fee: £22 (18 holes), £26.50
(27 holes), £32 (36 holes).
Societies: by arrangement a year in
advance if possible; weekdays only.
Catering: full facilities except Mon
evening.
Hotels: Anchor (Kinver).

K50 **Frodsham**

☎(0928) 732159
Office/Sec/Manager, 739442 Pro
shop
Simons Lane, Frodsham, Cheshire
WA6 6HE

Delights of Enville and Bridgenorth

Enville and Bridgnorth lie to the west of Wolverhampton and Stourbridge — marking the start of the rural tapestry which continues its spread across the border counties with Wales. Enville is closer to the industrial pulse of the West Midlands but its two courses, the Highgate and Lodge, are unexpectedly remote, a woodland setting not so very far removed from the famous courses of Surrey and Berkshire.

Of the two, the Highgate might be termed the old and the Lodge the new. The extension to 36-holes is relatively recent, long after, in fact, Diane Bailey (née Robb) developed her skills there in the 1950s. The Highgate is also my favourite, largely because of the quality and beauty of the holes on either side of the turn.

The seventh and eighth, two relatively short par 4s, are sandwiched between the difficult par 4 sixth and the magnificent dogleg par 5 ninth where some majestic trees make bunkers redundant. Another of the par 5s is the tenth which curves the opposite way to the ninth; but the pleasant part of both courses is the contrast in character between the more open, heathland holes and those dominated by trees.

The latter typify the new holes on the Lodge on the other side of the road, but many prefer the less inhibited start and finish although the demands are almost as exacting.

Bridgnorth is also a combination of old and new, the Club existing for most of its life on the edge of the attractive town as nine holes, starting and finishing (as they still do) with a couple of holes memorable for their eccentricity.

Both are dominated by the same prominent ridge or hill over which the drive at the first and the second shot at the eighteenth are played, opinion of them ranging from praise to condemnation.

Perhaps modern machinery would have sculpted them differently, the long slopes down to both greens calling for a nice mixture of luck and judgement. The 18th is the longer and more demanding, a tough finish in any context, but, variety being the spice of life, both add an unusual note in a golfing world that is often dully predictable. Something of the same theme surrounds the second, although the second shot to the elevated green has to be truly struck and judged to the inch, the opening triangle of three holes then completed by an inviting downhill par 3.

The next fourteen holes occupy the flatter land between the road and the river, the best part of the outward half being the sixth, seventh and eighth, the eighth a most challenging hole with a raised green that is stoutly defended. Its nomination as Stroke Index 1 tells its own story.

The sixth and seventh are flanked on the right by the river but on the thirteenth the river awaits the hook, the second of three par 5s in four holes. A long tee shot is required to find the green on the fourteenth but the toughest drive is perhaps the fifteenth between the road on the left and the trees that characterise the right hand side. The fairway is emphatically the place to be.

After that, the drive at the seventeenth enjoys considerably greater latitude but it is really a second shot hole, calling for a high iron over a horseshoe bunker around the front of the green.

Then, it is back over the road for a climax that, whatever its critics may say, rewards the art of positional play: the better placed the drive the greater the chance of attacking the flag, even if a proper assessment of its success has to await scaling the central rise.

10 minutes from M56 junction 12; turn left at lights in Frodsham centre onto B5152, 0.75 mile turn right after pedestrian crossing, 0.5 mile up hill turn right, club is 1st on left.
Parkland course.
18 holes, 6289 yards, Par 70
Designed by John Day.
Founded July 1990
Visitors: welcome all days except competition days; tee times booked through shop.
Green Fee: £18/day WD, £25/day WE & BH.
Societies: welcome weekdays only, contact office for details.
Catering: full bar and wide selection of food served throughout the day.
Hotels: self-catering accommodation close to clubhouse; favourable rates for inclusive packages; contact office.

K51 **Gatley**

☎(061) 437 2091 or 436 2830 Pro
Waterfall Farm, off Styal Rd, Heald Green, Cheadle, Cheshire SK8 3TW
Off Yew Tree Grove and Styal Rd 2 miles from Cheadle, 1 mile from Manchester Airport.
Parkland course.
9 holes, 5934 yards, S.S.S.68
Founded 1912
Visitors: welcome weekdays except Tues.
Green Fee: on application
Societies: apply to Sec.
Catering: full facilities.

K52 **Goldenhill**

☎(0782) 784715
Mobberley Rd, Goldenhill, Stoke-on-Trent, Staffs ST6 55S
On A50 between Tunstall and Kidsgrove.
Public parkland/meadowland course (in old open-cast mine basin).
18 holes, 5957 yards, S.S.S.68
Founded 1983
Visitors: welcome; booking system at weekends.
Green Fee: £6/round WD, £7/round WE.
Societies: welcome by arrangement.
Catering: bar and restaurant.
Practice ground, putting green.

K53 **Great Barr**

☎(021) 358 4376
Chapel Lane, Great Barr, Birmingham B43 7BA
Adjacent to exit 7, off M6, 6 miles NW of Birmingham.

Meadowland course.
18 holes, 6545 yards, S.S.S.72
Designed by J. Hamilton Stutt.
Founded 1961
Visitors: weekdays.
Green Fee: apply for details.
Societies: small societies Tues, Thurs.
Catering: by arrangement.
Hotels: Post House.

K54 **Greenway Hall**

☎(0782) 503158
Stockton Brook, Stoke-on-Trent ST9 9LI
Off A53 Stoke to Leek road, approx 5 miles from Stoke.
Meadowland course.
18 holes, 5676 yards, S.S.S.67
Founded 1908
Visitors: with member only. not weekends.
Green Fee: £14/day.
Societies: by appointment only.
Catering: by prior arrangement.

K55 **Hale**

☎(061) 980 4225, 904 0835 Pro
Rappax Rd, Hale, Altrincham, Cheshire WA15 0NU
2 miles SE of Altrincham.
Undulating parkland course.
9 holes, 5780 yards, S.S.S.68
Founded 1903
Visitors: weekdays except Thurs; weekends and Bank Holidays only with member.
Green Fee: £20 WD.
Societies: by arrangement with Hon Sec.
Catering: lunch except Tues and Thurs by arrangement with Steward.
Hotels: Bowdon; Ashley.

K56 **Hawkstone Park Hotel**

☎(0939) 200611, 200311 Fax
Weston-under-Redcastle, Shrewsbury, Shropshire SY4 5UY
Off A49, 12 miles N of Shewsbury; off A442, 12 miles N of Telford (M54 junction 6); off A53, 12 miles SW of Newcastle-under-Lyme (M56 junction 15).
Parkland course
Hawkstone, 18 holes, 6174 yards, S.S.S.70
Founded 1935 (additional 18 hole course opens 1995)
Visitors: h/cap cert required, must book.
Green Fee: from £20/round
Societies: book through golf centre.

Catering: terrace restaurant/bar.
Golf centre, practice range, putting and pitching green, 5 hole/Par 3 Academy course.
Hotels: own hotel on site, residential golf breaks from £59.95 per person.

K57 **Hazel Grove**

☎(061) 483 3978 Manager/Sec, 483 7272 Pro, 483 3217 Steward
Buxton Rd, Hazel Grove, Stockport, Cheshire SK7 6LU
Buxton Rd is on A6.
Parkland course.
18 holes, 6310 yards, S.S.S.71
Founded 1913
Visitors: welcome weekdays.
Green Fee: on application
Societies: Thurs and Fri.
Catering: daily.

K58 **Heaton Moor**

☎(061) 432 2134, 432 0846 Pro
Heaton Mersey, Stockport, Cheshire SK4 3NX
2 miles from Stockport.
Parkland course.
18 holes, 5876 yards, S.S.S.68
Founded 1892
Visitors: welcome except Tues, Wed.
Green Fee: apply for details.
Societies: by arrangement.
Catering: meals served.

K59 **Helsby**

☎(0928) 722021 Sec
Towers Lane, Helsby, Cheshire WA6 0JB
M56 junction 14 to Helsby; through traffic lights, take 1st right into Primrose Lane; 1st right into Towers Lane.
Parkland course.
18 holes, 6262 yards, S.S.S.70
Designed by James Braid.
Founded 1902
Visitors: welcome weekdays.
Green Fee: £20/round, £27.50/day.
Societies: catered for Tues and Thurs only.
Catering: full service except Mon.
Hotels: Chester Grosvenor; Queens.

K60 **Heswall**

☎(051) 342 1237, 342 7431
Cottage Lane, Gayton, Heswall, The Wirral, Cheshire L60 8PB
M53 exit 4; at roundabout turn into Well Lane, leads into Cottage Lane.
Parkland course.
18 holes, 6472 yards, S.S.S.72

Founded 1901
Visitors: not Tues and Thurs; phone call advisable.
Green Fee: £30 WD, £35 WE & BH, winter package available.
Societies: Wed and Fri only; full catering min 24.
Catering: bar snacks every day. Large practice area, snooker.
Hotels: Craxton Wood; Crabwell Manor; Mollington Banastre; Thornton Hall; Woodhey; Victoria.

K61 **Heyrose**
☎(0565) 733664 Sec, /34267 Pro, 733623 Bar
Budworth Rd, Tabley, Knutsford, Cheshire WA16 0HY
4 miles W of Knutsford, 0.5 mile along Budworth Rd, off Pickmere Lane; M6 junction 19 1 mile.
Wooded converted farmland with water features.
18 holes, 6510 yards, S.S.S.73
Designed by E.L.C.N. Bridge.
Founded June 1990
Visitors: welcome except before 2pm Sat.
Green Fee: £18/round WD, £23/round WE.
Societies: weekdays only by arrangement.
Catering: bar and restaurant. Practice ground, practice bunker, putting green, snooker.
Hotels: Cottons (Knutsford); Swan (Bucklow Hill); The Old Vicarage (Tabley).

K62 **Hill Valley Golf & Country Club**
☎(0948) 663584, 665927 Fax
Terrick Rd, Whitchurch, Shropshire SY13 4JZ
Off A49/A41 bypass, 1 mile from centre of Whitchurch.
Undulating parkland course.
West course: 18 holes, 6050 yards, S.S.S.69; East course: 18 holes, 5306 yards, S.S.S.66; 9 holes, Par 3
Designed by P. Alliss & D. Thomas.
Founded 1975
Visitors: welcome at all times.
Green Fee: West course: £19 WD, £25 WE; East course: £6 WD, £9 WE
Societies: at all times.
Catering: open 8am-11pm; lunch breakfast, dinner daily; conferences, wedding receptions up to 200. Health & beauty centre, snooker, tennis courts.
Hotels: Terrick Hall; Dodington Lodge; motel accommodation within clubhouse.

K63 **Himley Hall Golf Centre**
☎(0902) 895207
Log Cabin, Himley Hall Park, Dudley, W Midlands DY3 4DF
From A449 Wolverhampton to Kidderminster road turn at lights signposted Dudley onto B4176, then turn into Himley Hall Park on left.
Public parkland course.
9 holes, 6180 yards, S.S.S.70
Designed by D.A. Baker.
Founded 1980
Visitors: welcome.
Green Fee: £3.80 (9 holes) £5.50 (18 holes) WD; £4.20, £6 WE.
Societies: by prior arrangement.
Catering: café, snacks only.
Hotels: Himley House; Park Hall.

K64 **Houldsworth**
☎(061) 442 9611/1714/1712
Houldsworth Park, Reddish, Stockport SK5 6BN
M63 to Stockport, left onto A6 Stockport-Manchester road, right at lights at Barlow Rd.
Parkland course.
18 holes, 6078 yards, S.S.S.69
Designed by T.G. Renouf.
Founded 1911
Visitors: welcome weekdays (Ladies Day Tues 1.30-3.30pm).
Green Fee: on application
Societies: advance booking only.
Catering: full facilities.

K65 **Hoylake Municipal**
☎(051) 632 2956 or 632 4883
Carr Lane, Hoylake, Merseyside L47 4BG
Off M53 10 miles SW of Liverpool, follow signs for Hoylake, 100 yards from Hoylake station.
Municipal parkland course.
18 holes, 6313 yards, S.S.S.70
Designed by James Braid.
Founded 1933
Visitors: unrestricted; phone for weekends 1 week in advance; Sat from 8.30am.
Green Fee: on application
Societies: welcome, after 1.30pm weekends; phone Pro.
Catering: hot snacks, meals, bar meals.

K66 **Ingestre Park**
☎(0889) 270845
Ingestre, Stafford ST18 0RE
6 miles E of Stafford off A51 via Great Haywood and Tixall Rd; M6 junctions 13 and 14.

Undulating parkland course in former estate of Earl of Shrewsbury.
18 holes, 6334 yards, S.S.S.70
Designed by Hawtree & Son.
Founded 1977
Visitors: welcome with h/cap cert weekdays; only with member weekends and Bank Holidays.
Green Fee: £20/round, £25/day WD (£8 with member); £10 with member WE.
Societies: Mon, Tues, Thurs, Fri by arrangement with Manager.
Catering: snacks and meals daily. Snooker.
Hotels: Garth; Tillington Hall; Happy Eater Motel.

K67 **Izaak Walton**
☎(0785) 760900
Eccleshall Rd, Cold Norton, Stone, Staffs ST15 0NS
M6 junction 14, A34 to Stone, B5206 towards Eccleshall for 2 miles.
Meadowland course.
18 holes, S.S.S.72
Designed by Mike Lowe.
Founded May 1993
Visitors: welcome weekdays, h/cap certs required.
Green Fee: £15/round WD, £20/round WE.
Societies: welcome weekdays.
Catering: bar and restaurant. Practice facilities.
Hotels: Stone House (Stone); St George's (Eccleshall).

K68 **Knights Grange**
☎(0606) 552780
Grange Lane, Winsford, Cheshire
In centre of Winsford.
Public meadowland course
9 holes, 2995 metres, S.S.S.71; new layout spring 1994.
Founded 1983
Visitors: no restrictions.
Green Fee: £2.55, £3.80 (9 holes); £3.40, £5.10 (18 holes).
Societies: apply in writing to the Manager.
Catering: bar and bar snacks. Tennis, bowls, practice area, caravan site etc.

K69 **Knutsford**
☎(0565) 633355
Mereheath Lane, Knutsford, Cheshire
2 miles from junction 19 on M6, make for Knutsford entrance to Tatton Park, club a few yards on right down Mereheath Lane.

Parkland course.
10 holes, 6288 yards, S.S.S.70
Founded 1891
Visitors: welcome weekdays except Wed by arrangement with Sec.
Green Fee: on application.
Societies: catered for on Thurs by arrangement.
Catering: by arrangement with Steward.
Hotels: George; Angel; Cottons; Rose & Crown; Swan.

K70 **Lakeside (Rugeley)**
☎(0889) 575667, 584472 Sec
Rugeley Power Station, Armitage Rd, Rugeley, Staffs WS15 1PR
Between Lichfield and Stafford.
Parkland course.
18 holes, 5534 yards, S.S.S.67
Founded 1969
Visitors: only with member.
Green Fee: £7.
Societies: by arrangement.
Catering: evening only.

K71 **Leasowe**
☎(051) 677 5852
Leasowe Rd, Moreton, Wirral L46 3RD
Take Wallasey turn off M53 1 mile after Queensway tunnel, 1 mile W of Wallasey village.
Links course.
18 holes, 6227 yards, S.S.S.71
Designed by John Ball Jnr.
Founded 1891
Visitors: welcome weekdays, weekends by arrangement.
Green Fee: £18 WD, £22 WE & BH.
Societies: welcome by arrangement any day except Mon and Sat, min 16 players.
Catering: restaurant, bar, snacks. 2 snooker tables, large practice area.
Hotels: Leasowe Castle.

K72 **Leek**
☎(0538) 384779 Sec, 385899 Club
Cheddleton Rd, Leek, Staffs ST13 5RE
0.75 mile S of Leek on A520.
Semi-moorland course.
18 holes, 6240 yards, S.S.S.70
Founded 1892
Visitors: welcome weekdays before 3pm.
Green Fee: £24 WD, £30 WE.
Societies: Wed only.
Catering: lunches except Sun; evening meals except Sun and Mon. Snooker.
Hotels: Abbey Inn; Three Horseshoes; Jester.

K73 **Lilleshall Hall**
☎(0952) 604776, 603840
Lilleshall, Newport, Shropshire TF10 9AS
5 miles from Newport turn off A41 into Sheriffhales Rd, after 2 miles right into Abbey Rd, course is to N..
Parkland course.
18 holes, 5906 yards, S.S.S.68
Designed by H.S. Colt.
Founded 1937
Visitors: weekdays unaccompanied; weekends with members only.
Green Fee: apply for details.
Societies: by prior arrangement.
Catering: 9am-6.30pm daily.
Hotels: Royal Victoria; White House (Donnington).

K74 **Little Aston**
☎(021) 353 2066 Clubhouse, 353 2942 Sec/Pro
Streetly, Sutton Coldfield B74 3AN
Off A454, 3 miles N of Sutton Coldfield in Little Aston Park.
Parkland course.
18 holes, 6670 yards, S.S.S.73
Designed by Harry Vardon.
Founded 1908
Visitors: welcome weekdays.
Green Fee: on application.
Societies: weekdays only.
Catering: lunches served to order except Mon.
Hotels: Fairlawns.

K75 **Llanymynech**
☎(0691) 830542 Club, 830983 Sec, 830879 Pro
Pant, Oswestry, Shropshire SY10 8LB
1 mile W of A483 Welshpool to Oswestry road and 6 miles S of Oswestry, turn by Cross Guns Inn, signposted to club in village of Pant.
Upland course; holes 4,5,6 in England, remainder in Wales.
18 holes, 6114 yards, S.S.S.69
Founded 1933
Visitors: welcome.
Green Fee: on application
Societies: apply to Sec.
Catering: lunch, dinner except Mon.

K76 **Ludlow**
☎(0584 77) 285, 366 Pro
Bromfield, Ludlow, Shropshire SY8 2BT
Take A49 Shrewsbury road, turn right 2 miles N of Ludlow, signposted.
Parkland course.
18 holes, 6239 yards, S.S.S.70
Founded 1889

Visitors: welcome, ring Pro in advance.
Green Fee: £18/day WD, £24/day WE.
Societies: weekdays April-Oct by arrangement.
Catering: bar and restaurant facilities.

K77 **Lymm**
☎(092 575) 5020 Sec, 2177 Clubhouse, 5054 Pro
Whitbarrow Rd, Lymm, Cheshire WA13 9AN
5 miles SE of Warrington.
Parkland course.
18 holes, 6319 yards, S.S.S.70
Founded 1907
Visitors: welcome weekdays; Thurs Ladies Day, no visitors before 2.30pm; only with member weekends and Bank Holidays.
Green Fee: £20.
Societies: catered for, usually on Wed.
Catering: meals available.
Hotels: Lymm; Statham Lodge; Dingle.

K78 **Macclesfield**
☎(0625) 615845 Sec, 423227 Club
Hollins Rd, Macclesfield, Cheshire SK11 7EA
Turn into Windmill St at traffic island in Leek Rd (A527).
Hilly course.
18 holes, 5625 yards, S.S.S.69
Designed by Hawtree & Son.
Founded 1889
Visitors: welcome most days.
Green Fee: £17 WD, £20 WE.
Societies: welcome by prior arrangement.
Catering: bar and restaurant, not Tues.
Hotels: Sutton Hall.

K79 **Malkins Bank**
☎(0270) 765931
Betchton Rd, Sandbach, Cheshire
1.5 miles from M6 junction 17.
Municipal parkland course.
18 holes, 6071 yards, S.S.S.69
Designed by Hawtree & Son.
Founded 1980
Visitors: welcome 7 days; booking system in operation 7 days.
Green Fee: on application.
Societies: catered for daily.
Catering: bar and catering facilities daily.
Hotels: Old Hall (Sandbach); Saxon Cross Motel (M6 junction 17).

K80 **Market Drayton**
☎(0630) 652266
Sutton, Market Drayton, Shropshire
1.5 miles S of town.
Undulating meadowland course.
18 holes, 6230 yards, S.S.S.70
Founded 1911
Visitors: welcome except Sun and
Bank Holidays.
Green Fee: £20.
Societies: welcome on application
to Sec.
Catering: available all day.
Hotels: Corbet Arms; Bear Inn;
bungalow (sleeps 6) available for
rent.

K81 **Marple**
☎(061) 427 2311
Hawk Green, Marple, Stockport,
Cheshire SK6 7EL
Off A6 at High Lane for 2 miles, left at
Hawk Green.
Parkland/meadowland course.
18 holes, 5700 yards, S.S.S.67
Founded 1892
Visitors: welcome excluding
competition days.
Green Fee: apply for details.
Societies: Tues and Wed only;
special inclusive package for
societies of 12 or more.
Catering: full facilities.
Hotels: West Towers.

K82 **Mellor & Townscliffe**
☎(061) 427 2208, 427 5759 Pro
Tarden, Gibb Lane, Mellor, Stockport,
Cheshire SK6 5NA
Off A626 opposite Devonshire Arms
on Longhurst Lane, Mellor.
Parkland/moorland course.
18 holes, 5925 yards, S.S.S.69
Founded 1894
Visitors: welcome, except Sat when
must be with member.
Green Fee: £20/day (£8 with
member) WD; £27.50 (£10 with
member) WE & BH.
Societies: welcome
Catering: full facilities, except Tues.
Hotels: Pack Horse Inn (New Mills).

K83 **Meole Brace**
☎(0743) 364050
Meole Brace, Shrewsbury,
Shropshire SY2 6QQ
S of Shrewsbury at junction of
A5/A49.
Municipal parkland course with
water features.
9 holes, 2915 yards, S.S.S.68
Founded 1976

Visitors: welcome.
Green Fee: apply for details.
Societies: welcome, booking
weekends.

K84 **Mere Golf & Country Club**
☎(0565) 830155, 830518 Fax
Chester Rd, Mere, Knutsford,
Cheshire WA16 6LJ
From M6 junction 19 take A556 for 1
mile; from M56 junction 7 take A556
past Swan at Bucklow Hill.
Parkland course.
18 holes, 6817 yards, S.S.S.73
Designed by Duncan and Braid.
Founded 1934
Visitors: by prior arrangement Mon,
Tues and Thurs.
Green Fee: £50.
Societies: Mon, Tues, Thurs.
Catering: very extensive; breakfast,
lunch and dinner 7 days.
Driving range with floating golf balls
(only open to golfing visitors).
Hotels: Swan (Bucklow Hill), discount
rates; Kilton Inn; Lord Daresbury..

K85 **Mile End**
☎(0691) 670580 Sec, 671246 Pro
Mile End, Oswestry, Shropshire SY11
4JE
1 mile SE of Oswestry, just off A5,
well signposted.
Parkland course, converted farmland.
9 holes, 3065 yards, S.S.S.69
Designed by Michael Price.
Founded June 1992
Visitors: welcome with h/cap cert or
proof of membership of recognised
club; restrictions when members
competitions in progress; please ring.
Green Fee: £10 (18 holes), £14/day
WD; £14/£18 WE.
Societies: on application; discounts
available.
Catering: lunchtime bar and meals
except Wed.
Driving range, putting green.

K86 **Mottram Hall Hotel**
☎(0625) 820064, 828135 bookings
Wilmslow Road, Mottram St Andrew,
Prestbury, Cheshire SK10 4QT
From M56 junction 6 follow A538
through Wilmslow into Prestbury.
Parkland/woodland course.
18 holes, 6905 yards, S.S.S.72
Designed by David Thomas.
Founded May 1991
Visitors: welcome with h/cap cert.
Green Fee: apply for details.
Societies: welcome.

Catering: bar and restaurant.
Putting green, practice facilities.
Hotels: Mottram Hall (133 beds).

K87 **New Mills**
☎(0663) 43485
Shaw Marsh, New Mills, Stockport,
Cheshire
Take St Mary Rd from centre of New
Mills, about 0.75 miles.
Moorland course.
9 holes, 5707 yards, S.S.S.68
Founded 1907
Visitors: welcome weekdays and
Sat am except competition days.
Green Fee: apply for details.
Societies: welcome weekdays by
arrangement with Sec.
Catering: snacks and meals served.
Hotels: Pack Horse and Sportsman;
Moorside.

K88 **Newcastle Municipal**
☎(0782) 627596
Newcastle Rd, Keele, Staffs ST5 2QB.
M6 junction 15 onto A525 for 2 miles.
Public parkland course.
18 holes, 6256 yards, S.S.S.70
Founded 1975
Visitors: rounds bookable any time.
Green Fee: £6.75 WD, £8.20 WE.
Societies: on application to
Newcastle B.C. (0782) 717717.
Catering: bar/bar meals.
Driving range.
Hotels: Keele University Hospitality
(opposite), golf packages.

K89 **Newcastle-under-Lyme**
☎(0782) 618526 Pro, 616583
Steward
Whitmore Rd, Newcastle under
Lyme, Staffs ST5 2QB
1.5 miles SW of Newcastle under
Lyme on A53.
Parkland course.
18 holes, 6229 yards, S.S.S.70
Founded 1908
Visitors: weekdays with h/cap cert.
Green Fee: apply for details.
Societies: Mon, Thurs pm.
Catering: bar and restaurant.
Snooker.
Hotels: Post House; Borough Arms.

K90 **Northenden**
☎(061) 998 4738 Sec, 998 2934
Steward/Members, 998 4079 Pro,
945 5592 Fax
Palatine Rd, Northenden,
Manchester M22 4FR
M63 exit 9, 1 mile into Northenden.

Parkland course.
18 holes, 6469 yards, S.S.S.71
Founded 1913
Visitors: no restrictions, phone
beforehand.
Green Fee: £25 (£12 with member)
WD, £27.50 (£12 with member) WE.
Societies: Tues and Fri.
Catering: bar and restaurant.
Snooker.
Hotels: Britannia; Post House.

K91 Oaklands Golf and Country Club
☎(0829) 733884, 733703 Pro shop,
733666 Fax
Forest Rd, Tarporley, Cheshire CW6
0JA
Approx 15 miles S of Warrington on
main A49, 0.5 mile N of Tarporley
village.
Undulating parkland course.
18 holes, 6473 yards, S.S.S.71.
Designed by Tim Rouse of Golf
Corporation (UK) Ltd.
Founded May 1990
Visitors: welcome Mon-Fri.
Green Fee: £16/round WD, £21 WE,
£30/day
Societies: Mon-Fri by arrangement.
Catering: full restaurant and bar
facilities.
Sauna, snooker; function room,
banqueting for up to 200.
Hotels: Swan (Tarporley); Wild Boar
(Beeston).

K92 Onneley
☎(0782) 750577
Onneley, Crewe, Cheshire CW3 5QF
1 mile from Woore on A51 to
Newcastle.
Undulating meadowland course.
9 holes, 5584 yards, S.S.S.67
Founded 1968
Visitors: welcome Mon, Wed, Thur,
Fri; Sat only with member.
Green Fee: £15/round (£8 with
member)
Societies: welcome by prior booking
with Sec; £18/day including meal.
Catering: by arrangement with
Stewardess (0782) 751227.
Hotels: Wheatsheaf Inn.

K93 Oswestry
☎(0691) 610221, 610535
Aston Park, Oswestry, Shropshire
SY11 4JJ
NW of Shrewsbury, just off A5, 2
miles from Oswestry.
Parkland course.
18 holes, 6038 yards, S.S.S.69

Designed by James Braid.
Founded 1930
Visitors: welcome, must be member
of club and hold h/cap cert or play
with member.
Green Fee: £18 WD, £25 WE;
reduction if playing with member.
Societies: Wed and Fri only.
Catering: every day.
Hotels: Wynstay; Sweeney Hall;
Ashfield Country.

K94 Oxley Park
☎(0902) 25892 Sec
Bushbury, Wolverhampton WV10 6DE
Off A449, 1 mile N of Wolverhampton.
Parkland course.
18 holes, 6168 yards, S.S.S.69
Founded 1913
Visitors: welcome, booking
advisable at weekends.
Green Fee: £18/round, £22/day WD.
Societies: Wed by arrangement.
Catering: breakfast, lunch, dinner.
Snooker.
Hotels: Mount; Goldthorn; Park Hall.

K95 Parkhall
☎(0782) 599584 Course Manager,
(0831) 456409
Hulme Road, Weston Coyney,
Stoke-on-Trent, Staffs ST3 5BH
1 mile outside Longton on main A50.
Public moorland course.
18 holes, 2335 yards, Par 54
Founded Nov 1989
Visitors: welcome.
Green Fee: apply for details.
Societies: booking times: weekends
and Bank Holidays only.

K96 Patshull Park Hotel Golf and Country Club
☎(0902) 700100 Golf administrator,
700874 Fax
Pattingham, Wolverhampton, WV6
7HR
M54 junction 3 onto A41 (W'hampton)
right into Albrighton, right at Crown
Inn cross-road, 1 mile to A464; right
(Shifnal), 1st left to Patshull and
Pattingham (via Burnhill Green): or
A41 from W'hampton/Whitchurch
road, left to Pattingham.
Lakeside, parkland course.
18 holes, 6460 yards, S.S.S.71
Designed by John Jacobs.
Founded 1979
Visitors: welcome, telephone for tee
reservation, h/cap preferred.
Green Fee: £20 WD, £25 WE; 2 day
golf breaks £120 (3 rounds, B&B,
lunch and dinner).

Societies: full range of golf
packages available from £30/head.
Catering: restaurant, coffee shop,
golfers bar, banqueting/conferences.
Snooker, practice ground,
swimming, leisure club, gymnasium,
trout & coarse fishing.
Hotels: own hotel group, residential
bargain breaks.

K97 Penn
☎(0902) 341142
Penn Common, Penn,
Wolverhampton, W Midlands WV4
5JN
2 miles SW of W'hampton off A449.
Heathland course.
18 holes, 6465 yards, S.S.S.71
Founded 1908
Visitors: welcome weekdays.
Green Fee: £20.
Societies: weekdays.
Catering: lunch weekdays except
Mon; dinner weekdays except Mon
and Wed.
Hotels: Goldthorn; Park Hall.

K98 Perton Park Golf Centre
☎(0902) 380073
Wrottesley Park Road, Perton,
Wolverhampton, W Midlands WV6
7HL
6 miles from W'hampton, just off
A454 Bridgnorth to W'hampton road:
or A41 W'hampton to Newport road 4
miles from W'hampton.
Flat meadowland course in open
countryside.
18 holes, 7007 yards, S.S.S.72
Founded 1990
Visitors: welcome.
Green Fee: £5/round Mon-Thurs, £7
Fri, £12 WE & BH.
Societies: welcome by arrangement.
Catering: new club house with fully
licensed bar and restaurant.
Driving range, snooker.

K99 Portal
☎(0829) 733933
Cobblers Cross, Tarporley, Cheshire
CW6 0DJ
0.5 mile N of Tarporley village on
A49, 10 miles N of Chester.
Public parkland course.
18 holes, 7145 yards, S.S.S.73.
Designed by Donald Steel.
Founded May 1991
Visitors: welcome, no restrictions.
Green Fee: on application.
Societies: and corporate business
days, catered for 7 days a week.

Catering: full facilities 7 days a week; 3 banqueting suites.
Hotels: Nunsmere Hall (Tarporley); Wild Boar (Beeston).

K100 Poulton Park
☎(0925) 812034, 825220
Dig Lane, Cinnamon Brow, Warrington
Off A574, turn into Crab Lane, 3 miles from Warrington.
Meadowland course.
9 holes, 4937 metres, S.S.S.66
Founded 1978
Visitors: welcome weekdays, restricted weekends.
Green Fee: £16 (£8 with member) WD; £18 (£9 with member) WE.
Societies: weekdays.
Catering: meals served except Mon.
Hotels: Paddington House; Garden Court.

K101 Prenton
☎(051) 608 1053, 608 1461, 608 1636 Pro
Golf Links Rd, Prenton, Birkenhead, Wirral L42 8LW
2 miles W of Birkenhead off A552; M53 junction 3.
Flat parkland course.
18 holes, 6411 yards, S.S.S.71
Designed by Colt Mackenzie & Co.
Founded 1905
Visitors: welcome any day except competition days (Sat in summer).
Green Fee: £23 (£8 with member) WD, £25 WE & BH.
Societies: Wed, Fri by arrangement.
Catering: full service available.
Snooker.
Hotels: Leasowe Castle; Crabwell Manor; Riverhill; Bowler Hat.

K102 Prestbury
☎(0625) 828241
Macclesfield Rd, Prestbury, Cheshire SK10 4BJ
2 miles NW of Macclesfield on Macclesfield Rd leaving Prestbury village.
Undulating parkland course.
18 holes, 6359 yards, S.S.S.71
Designed by Colt & Morrison.
Founded 1920
Visitors: welcome weekdays, with member at weekends; advisable to phone in advance.
Green Fee: apply for details.
Societies: Thurs only.
Catering: lunch, dinner, bar snacks except Mon. Snooker.
Hotels: Edge; Mottram Hall.

K103 Queen's Park
☎(0270) 666724
Queen's Park Gardens, Crewe, Cheshire
Just off Victoria Ave to S of Crewe centre.
Public meadowland course
9 holes, 2460 yards, S.S.S.64
Founded 1985
Visitors: welcome except Sun before 10.30am.
Green Fee: on application
Societies: welcome by arrangment.
Catering: bar and bar meals.
Bowls, tennis.
Hotels: Crewe Arms; Hunter's Lodge.

K104 Reaseheath
☎(0270) 625131
Reaseheath College, Nantwich, Cheshire
Research course, approved centre for greenkeeper training.
9 holes 3332 yards, S.S.S.54
Designed by D. Mortram
Founded 1987
Visitors: small parties and societies only, min 8; by prior arrangement; April-Oct preferred
Green Fee: £3 (18 holes).
Catering: at local hostelry.

K105 Reddish Vale
☎(061) 480 2359, 480 3824 Pro
Southcliffe Rd, Reddish, Stockport, Cheshire SK5 7EE
1.5 miles N of Stockport, off Reddish road B6167.
Undulating course in valley.
18 holes, 6086 yards, S.S.S.69
Designed by Dr A. Mackenzie.
Founded 1912
Visitors: welcome weekdays (not 12.30-1.30pm), with member only at weekends.
Green Fee: £22.
Societies: weekdays by prior arrangement.
Catering: generally available during normal bar opening hours.
Hotels: Belgrade; Old Rectory, Haughton Green.

K106 Ringway
☎(061) 980 8432 Pro, 980 2630 Sec, 904 0940 catering
Hale Rd, Hale Barns, Altrincham, Cheshire WA15 8SW
8 miles S of Manchester, off M56 junction 6 (A538), follow signs for Hale and Altrincham, just through Hale Barns village.
Parkland course.
18 holes, 6494 yards, S.S.S.71
Designed by James Colt and James Braid.
Founded 1909
Visitors: welcome, not Friday; Tues and Sat are Club competition days.
Green Fee: £28 WD, £34 WE.
Societies: Thur only, May-Sep.
Catering: full, by arrangement with Catering Manageress.
Snooker.
Hotels: Cresta Court; Four Seasons; Unicorn.

K107 Romiley
☎(061) 430 2392
Goosehouse Green, Romiley, Stockport SK6 4LJ
On B6104 off A560, 0.75 mile from Romiley station.
Undulating parkland course.
18 holes, 6335 yards, S.S.S.70
Founded 1897
Visitors: welcome except Thurs (Ladies Day).
Green Fee: apply for details.
Societies: apply to Sec.
Catering: full service except Mon.

K108 Royal Liverpool
☎(051) 632 3101 Sec, 632 6757 starter, 632 5868 Pro, (051) 632 6737 Fax
Meols Drive, Hoylake, Wirral, Merseyside L47 4AL
On A553 from M53 junction 2.
Championship links course.
18 holes, 6804 yards, S.S.S.74
Founded 1869
Visitors: welcome by prior arrangement with Sec or Starter. Members priority to 9.30am and 1-2pm; Thurs am Ladies.
Green Fee: £40/round, £55/day WD; £55/round, £80/day WE.
Societies: Tue-Fri (not Thurs am).
Catering: soup/sandwiches available daily, dining room (jacket and tie) for lunches or dinners by prior arrangement.
Snooker, practice range.
Hotels: Crabwall Manor (Chester); Thornton Hall (Thornton Hough); Bowler Hat (Oxton).

K109 Runcorn
☎(0928) 572093, 574214 Sec
Clifton Rd, Runcorn, Cheshire WA7 4SU
Signposted The Heath off A557.
High parkland course.
18 holes, 6035 yards, S.S.S.69
Founded 1909

Visitors: welcome weekdays except Tues; bona fide h/cap cert required.
Green Fee: £16/day WD, £20/day WE & BH.
Societies: Mon and Fri.
Catering: bar and dining room, meals by arrangement.
Snooker.
Hotels: Crest.

K110 St Michael Jubilee

☎(051) 424 6230, 423 6461
Dundalk Rd, Widnes, Cheshire
Close to Widnes centre.
Public parkland course
18 holes, 5638 yards, S.S.S.67
Founded 1977
Visitors: welcome weekdays, with booking at weekends.
Green Fee: apply for details.
Societies: welcome by arrangement; full catering facilities.
Catering: full facilities.
Practice area.
Hotels: Hillcrest.

K111 Sale

☎(061) 973 3404 Catering, 973 1638 Manager, 973 1730 Visitors
Sale Lodge, Golf Rd, Sale, Cheshire M33 2LU
Edge of Sale, 1 mile from station, half mile from M63 junction 8.
Parkland course.
18 holes, 6346 yards, S.S.S.70
Founded 1913
Visitors: welcome any day, phone for confirmation.
Green Fee: £23 WD, £30 WE and BH.
Societies: by arrangement with Manager.
Catering: bar and catering 7 days.
Snooker.
Hotels: Post House; Normanhurst; Lennox Lea.

K112 Sandbach

☎(0270) 762117
117 Middlewich Rd, Sandbach, Cheshire CW11 9EA
1 mile N of town centre on A533 Middlewich Rd. off M6 junction 17.
Meadowland course.
9 holes, 5614 yards, S.S.S.67
Founded 1921
Visitors: welcome weekdays; weekends and Bank Holidays by invitation only.
Green Fee: £16/round/day.
Societies: limited to a few each year.
Catering: available except Mon and Thurs.
Hotels: Saxon Cross Motel; Old Hall.

K113 Sandiway

☎(0606) 883247 Sec, 883180 Pro, 888548 Fax
Chester Rd, Sandiway, Northwich, Cheshire CW8 2DJ
On A556 14 miles E of Chester, 4 miles from Northwich.
Undulating parkland course.
18 holes, 6435 yards, S.S.S.72
Designed by Ted Ray.
Founded 1921
Visitors: weekdays and certain weekends with letter of intro.
Green Fee: £30 WD, £35 WE & BH.
Societies: catered for Tues.
Catering: meals daily by arrangement.
Hotels: Hartford Hall; Oaklands.

K114 Sandwell Park

☎(021) 553 4637 Sec, 553 4384 Pro
Birmingham Rd, West Bromwich, W Midlands B71 4JJ
M5 junction 1, 0.25 mile from West Bromwich Albion Football Ground.
Parkland/heathland course.
18 holes, 6422 yards, S.S.S.72
Founded 1897
Visitors: weekdays unlimited; weekends with member.
Green Fee: £32.50/day/round.
Societies: any weekday, societies over 20 £27.50.
Catering: full facilities except Mon.
Hotels: Moat House.

K115 Sedgley Golf Centre

☎(0902) 880503
Sandyfields Rd, Sedgeley, Dudley, W Midlands DY3 3DL
0.5 mile from Sedgley town centre near Cotwall End Nature Centre, just off A463.
Pay-as-you-play course; wooded, undulating with extensive views.
9 holes, 3147 yards, Par 37.
Designed by W.G. Cox.
Founded Sept 1989
Visitors: book at weekends.
Green Fee: £4 (9 holes), £6 (18 holes).
Societies: weekdays preferred by prior arrangement.
Catering: meals available for societies by arrangement; all day breakfasts Sat, am only Sun.
Driving range.
Hotels: Park Hall (Wolverhampton); Station, Ward Arms (Dudley).

K116 Seedy Mill

☎(0543) 417333
Elm Hurst, Lichfield, Staffs WS13 8HE
1.5 miles N of Lichfield off A515.
Undulating parkland course.
18 holes, 6247 yards, S.S.S.70
Designed by Hawtree & Sons.
Founded 1991
Visitors: welcome; pay-as-you-play.
Green Fee: £13/round WD, £20/round WE.
Societies: welcome Mon-Fri.
Catering: full facilities.
Hotels: Cedar Tree (Rugeley).

K117 Severn Meadows

☎(0746) 862212
Highley, Nr Bridgnorth, Shropshire WV16 6HZ
10 miles N of Bewdley via B4194, B4363, B4555; 8 miles S of Bridgenorth.
Hilly parkland course in Severn Valley.
9 holes, 2521 yards, S.S.S.65
Founded 1989
Visitors: welcome weekdays, pay-as-you-play, must book at weekends.
Green Fee: apply for details.
Societies: booking only.
Catering: clubhouse and bar, meals to order.
Putting green, practice nets.
Hotels: Bull (Chelmarsh).

K118 Shifnal

☎(0952) 460330
Decker Hill, Shifnal, Shropshire TF11 8QL
On B4379 1 mile from Shifnal; from M54 junction 4 turn left, left again, travel with motorway for 2 miles, left again, 500 yards left again.
Parkland course.
18 holes, 6422 yards, S.S.S.71
Designed by Frank Pennink.
Founded 1929
Visitors: weekdays; weekends only with member.
Green Fee: £22/round, £30/day WD.
Societies: Tues, Wed or Fri.
Catering: lunch and evening meals.
Hotels: Park House; Jerningham Arms.

K119 Shrewsbury

☎(0743) 872976 club, 872977 Sec, 873751 Pro
Condover, Shropshire SY5 7BL
4 miles SW of Shrewsbury, follow signs for Condover and golf club.
Parkland course.
18 holes, 6212 yards, S.S.S.70
Designed by C.K. Cotton, Pennink, Lawrie & Partners.
Founded 1890

Visitors: must have h/cap certs.
Green Fee: £15/round WD,
£20/round/day WE & BH.
Societies: apply to Pro.
Catering: full catering facilities
available.
Snooker.
Hotels: Deanhurst.

K120 **Shrigley Hall Hotel**
☎(0625) 575757, 573323 Fax
Shrigley Park, Pott Shrigley,
Macclesfield, Cheshire SK10 5SH.
From M63 Stockport take A6 towards
Hazel Grove and Buxton, then A523
towards Macclesfield; turn left at Lee
Arms in Adlington, signposted Pott
Shrigley, 2 miles.
Parkland course.
18 holes; 6305 yards, S.S.S.71
Designed by Donald Steel.
Founded 2 May 1989
Visitors: welcome.
Green Fee: £22/round, £35/day WD;
£28/round WE.
Societies: welcome.
Catering: bars and restaurants.
Pitch & Putt, swimming, tennis,
squash, fishing and other leisure
facilities.
Hotels: Shrigley Hall (weekend
golfing packages available).

K121 **The Shropshire**
☎(0952) 677866 Bookings,
677800, 677622 Fax
Muxton Grange, Muxton, Telford,
Shropshire TF2 8PQ
5 miles NE of Telford; 5 mins M54
junction 4 on B5060, signposted off
Granville roundabout and located
next to Granville Country Park.
Pay-as-you-Play, variable undulating
course.
27 holes, 3 loops of 9 (Blue, Silver,
Gold), Par 70-71
Designed by Martin Hawtree.
Founded July 1992
Visitors: open 7 days a week,
booking up to 7 days in advance; golf
shoes required.
Green Fee: 9 holes, £6 WD, £8.50
WE; 18 holes, £10 WD, £15 WE; 27
holes, £15 WD, £23 WE; reductions
for jnrs.
Societies: 7 days a week with prior
booking.
Catering: 2 traditional bars, snack
bar, 80-seat restaurant, 3 function
rooms, 240-seat permanent
marquee.
Driving range, 12 hole Pitch & Putt,
18-hole and 9-hole putting greens.
Hotels: details on request.

K122 **South Staffordshire**
☎(0902) 751065
Sec/Manager/bookings, 754816 Pro
Danescourt Rd, Tettenhall,
Wolverhampton WV6 9BQ
A41 from Wolverhampton to
Tettenhall, clubhouse and course
behind cricket club.
Parkland course.
18 holes, 6513 yards, S.S.S.71
Designed by Harry Vardon (original);
H.S. Colt.
Founded 1892
Visitors: weekdays except Tues am.
Green Fee: £27.50/round, £30/day.
Societies: welcome except Tues am
and weekends.
Catering: snacks, lunches, dinners.
Hotels: Mount; Connaught
(Wolverhampton).

K123 **Stafford Castle**
☎(0785) 223821
Newport Rd, Stafford
0.5 mile from Stafford main street.
Meadowland course.
9 holes, 6347 yards, S.S.S.70
Founded 1907
Visitors: welcome weekdays.
Green Fee: £14
Societies: by prior arrangement.
Catering: bar meals daily, others by
arrangement except Mon.
Hotels: Swan; Tillington Hall; Vine.

K124 **Stamford**
☎(0457) 832126, 834829 Pro
Oakfield House, Huddersfield Rd,
Heyheads, Stalybridge, Cheshire
SK15 3PY
On B6175 Huddersfield Rd, 3 miles
from Ashton-under-Lyne off A6108.
Undulating moorland course.
18 holes, 5619 yards, S.S.S.67
Founded 1900
Visitors: welcome weekdays (Ladies
Day Tues afternoon).
Green Fee: apply for details.
Societies: weekdays except Mon
and Tues.
Catering: meals served except Mon.
Hotels: York House (Ashton-u-Lyne).

K125 **Stockport**
☎(061) 427 2001 Tel /Fax, 427
8369 Sec, 427 2421 Pro
Offerton Rd, Offerton, Stockport SK2
5HL
1 mile along A627 from Hazel Grove
to Marple.
Parkland course.
18 holes, 6326 yards, S.S.S.71
Founded 1906

Visitors: members of other clubs
welcome.
Green Fee: on application
Societies: welcome. catered for
Wed and Thur.
Catering: restaurant (closed Mon).

K126 **Stone**
☎(0785) 813103
Filleybrooks, Stone, Staffs ST15 0NB
0.5 mile N of Stone on A34 next to
Wayfarer Hotel.
Meadowland course.
9 holes, 6299 yards, S.S.S.70
Founded 1896
Visitors: welcome weekdays.
Green Fee: £15/round, £20/day.
Societies: welcome weekdays.
Catering: lunch and evening meal
except Mon.
Hotels: Stonehouse (on A34); Crown.

K127 **Swindon**
☎(0902) 897031
Bridgnorth Road, Swindon, Dudley,
West Midlands DY3 4PU
On B4176 Bridgnorth road, 5 miles
from Wolverhampton; just off A449
Stourbridge to Wolverhampton road.
Woodland/parkland course;
exceptional views.
18 holes, 6042 yards, S.S.S.69; 9
holes Par-3, 1135 yards.
Founded 1974
Visitors: welcome, booking not
required.
Green Fee: £15/round, £25/day WD;
£25/round, £40/day WE & BH.
Societies: by arrangement
weekdays only.
Catering: fully licensed bar and
restaurant.
Driving range, snooker tables.

K128 **Tamworth Municipal**
☎(0827) 53850
Eagle Drive, Amington, Tamworth,
Staffs B77 4EG
M42 junction 10, proced towards
Tamworth, signposted round town;
off B5000 Polesworth road.
Municipal parkland course.
18 holes, 6083 metres, S.S.S.72
Founded 1975
Visitors: welcome 7 days.
Green Fee: £7.70 adult, £3.85
jnrs/OAPs.
Societies: Mon to Fri.
Catering: bar and daily catering;
special functions by arrangement.
Practice area, snooker (club
members).
Hotels: Canada Lodge (M42).

THE TYTHERINGTON CLUB
Macclesfield, Cheshire SK10 2JP
Telephone (0625) 434562   Fax (0625) 611076

Magnificent 6780 yard par 72 championship golf course in beautiful parkland setting
Headquarters of the Womens Professional Golfers European Tour and venue for the Ladies English Open.
Private dining and bar facilities, superb society dining, gourmet restaurant, all day bar and golfers snacks.
Visitors very welcome. Society and Company days.
Country club facilities include pool, sauna & steam, tennis, bowls and squash. Clay shoot arrangement.
Company & Sportsman Dinners – speakers, discos & bands arranged.
Society packages £37.50–£58.00   Green fees £25.00–£35.00

K129 **Telford Hotel Golf & Country Club**
☎(0952) 585642, 586602 Fax
Great Hay, Telford, Shropshire TF7 4DT
Off A442 at Sutton Hill, S of Telford.
Undulating meadowland course.
18 holes, 6274 yards, S.S.S.70
Designed by John Harris.
Founded 1981
Visitors: welcome with h/cap cert.
Green Fee: apply for details.
Societies: by arrangement.
Catering: meals served every day.
Driving range, squash, swimming pool, snooker, sauna etc.
Hotels: Telford Hotel Country Club.

K130 **Three Hammers Golf Complex**
☎(0902) 790428
Old Stafford Rd, Coven, Staffordshire WV10 7PP
M54 junction 2, N on A449, course 1 mile on right.
Public 18 hole Par 3 short course.
Designed by Henry Cotton.
Visitors: welcome.
Green Fee: on application.
Societies: welcome weekdays and Sat.
Catering: bar and bistro, à la carte restaurant, private dining facilities.
Driving range.

K131 **Trentham**
☎(0782) 658109
14 Barlaston Old Rd, Trentham, Stoke-on-Trent ST4 8HB
Off M6 junction 15 towards Stoke, follow A34 to Trentham Gardens, turn left, 1st right.
Parkland course.
18 holes, 6644 yards, S.S.S.72
Founded 1894
Visitors: welcome with h/cap cert; not Sat or Sun am.
Green Fee: £30.
Societies: Wed, Thurs, max 40.

Catering: bar and restaurant facilities.
Squash, snooker.
Hotels: Post House; Clayton Lodge; Stonehouse (Stone).

K132 **Trentham Park**
☎(0782) 658800
Trentham Park, Trentham, Stoke-on-Trent ST4 8AE
4 miles S of Newcastle under Lyme on A34, 1 mile from M6 junction 15.
Parkland course.
18 holes, 6422 yards, S.S.S.71
Founded 1936
Visitors: h/cap cert and club membership required.
Green Fee: £22.50/round, £25/day WD, £30 WE & BH.
Societies: welcome Wed and Fri by arrangement.
Catering: full catering facilities available.
Snooker.
Hotels: Clayton Lodge; Post House.

K133 **The Tytherington**
☎(0625) 434562
Macclesfield, Cheshire, SK10 2JB
Approx 2 miles from Macclesfield on A523 Stockport road.
Modern championship parkland course.
18 holes, 6767 yards, S.S.S.73 (Ladies 5592 yards, S.S.S.75).
Designed by Dave Thomas, Patrick Dawson.
Founded Oct 1986
Visitors: h/cap certs required.
Green Fee: £25 WD, £30 WE
Societies: weekdays, £22 (18 holes), £33 (36 holes), all-day catering.
Catering: bar, conservatory, restaurant, private rooms available.
Tennis, snooker, pool, health club, bowls, clay shoot.
Hotels: special arrangements with local hotels.

K134 **Upton-by-Chester**
☎(0244) 381183 Sec, 381333 Pro
Upton Lane, Chester CH2 1EE
Off A41 Liverpool-Chester road, near Upton zoo.
Parkland course.
18 holes, 5808 yards, S.S.S.68
Founded 1934
Visitors: unlimited except competition days.
Green Fee: £20/day WD, £25 WE 1 round only.
Societies: Wed, Thurs, Fri.
Catering: full restaurant facilities.
Hotels: Mollington Banastre; Dene; Euro Hotel.

K135 **Uttoxeter**
☎(0889) 565108, 564884 Pro, 566552 Sec
Wood Lane, Uttoxeter, Staffs ST14 8JR
Off B5017 Uttoxeter-Marchington road, about 0.5 mile along Wood Lane, just past race course.
Moorland course
18 holes, 5456 yards, S.S.S.68
Founded 1972
Visitors: welcome except invitation days etc; subject to availability.
Green Fee: £13 WD, £17 WE; half price with member and jnrs.
Societies: all year by arrangement; £27.50 per person, min 4.
Catering: available except Mon. Pool.
Hotels: White Hart; Bank.

K136 **Vicars Cross**
☎(0244) 335174
Tarvin Rd, Great Barrow, Chester CH3 7HN
A51 3 miles E of Chester.
Undulating parkland course.
18 holes, 6243 yards, S.S.S.70
Designed by E. Parr.
Founded 1939
Visitors: welcome Mon-Thurs all day; any day after 4pm; course

closed for major competitions, advisable to ring beforehand for availability.
Green Fee: £20/day, £14 after 4pm.
Societies: Tues, Thurs only Apr-Oct.
Catering: full facilities.
Hotels: Oaklands; Hoole Hall.

K137 **Wallasey**
☎(051) 691 1024
Bayswater Rd, Wallasey, Merseyside L45 8LA
From Liverpool through Wallasey Tunnel to junction 1; follow signs to New Brighton.
Seaside links course.
18 holes, 6607 yards, S.S.S.73
Designed by Tom Morris Snr.
Founded 1891
Visitors: welcome weekdays, limited weekends.
Green Fee: £25/day WD, £30/day WE & BH; £10 with member.
Societies: Mon-Fri by arrangement.
Catering: full facilities.
Snooker.
Hotels: Leasowe Castle; Grove House.

K138 **Walsall**
☎(0922) 613512
The Broadway, Walsall, W Midlands WS1 3EY
1 mile S of Walsall centre, 400 yards from the Crest Motel; take A34 from M6 junction 7.
Parkland/meadowland course.
18 holes, 6232 yards, S.S.S.70
Founded 1907
Visitors: welcome weekdays, with member weekends.
Green Fee: on application
Societies: welcome.
Catering: full service.

K139 **Walton Hall**
☎(0925) 266775 Club, 263061 Pro shop/bookings
Warrington Rd, Higher Walton, Warrington WA4 5LU
1 mile from M56 junction 11; turn right at 2nd set of traffic lights.
Municipal, scenic parkland course.
18 holes, 6801 yards, S.S.S.73
Designed by Dave Thomas.
Founded 1972
Visitors: welcome unrestricted; from 6am in summer, 8am in winter.
Green Fee: £6 WD, £7 WE.n.
Societies: by arrangement through Pro shop.
Catering: full service available 1st April to 31st Oct.

K140 **Warren**
☎(051) 639 5730
The Grange, Grove Rd, Wallasey, Merseyside
500 yards up Grove Rd, beyond Grove Rd station.
Municipal links course.
9 holes, 2700 yards, S.S.S.34(68)
Founded 1911
Visitors: welcome weekdays; phone first at weekends.
Green Fee: apply for details.
Catering: lunch and tea in café.
Hotels: Grove House.

K141 **Warrington**
☎(0925) 265431 Pro, 261775 Sec
London Rd, Appleton, Warrington, Cheshire WA4 5HR
On A49 from M56 or S on A49 through town, 3 miles S of Warrington.
Undulating parkland course.
18 holes, 6217 yards, S.S.S.70
Designed by James Braid.
Founded 1902
Visitors: welcome.
Green Fee: on application
Societies: apply to Sec.
Catering: available except Mon.

K142 **Wergs**
☎(0902) 742225
Keepers Lane, Tettenhall, Wolverhampton WV6 8UA
Follow A41 Telford road out of Wolverhampton for approx 2.5 miles; turn right (course signposted) into Keepers Lane, 0.5 mile on right.
Public parkland course.
18 holes, 6949 yards, S.S.S.73
Designed by C.W. Moseley.
Founded June 1990
Visitors: pay-as-you-play.
Green Fee: £12.50 WD, £15 WE & BH.
Societies: at all times.
Catering: lounge/spike bar and restaurant.
Large practice area.
Hotels: Novotel (W'hampton).

K143 **Werneth Low**
☎(061) 368 2503
Werneth Low Rd, Hyde, Cheshire SK14 3AF
2 miles from Hyde town centre via Gee Cross and Joel Lane.
Moorland course.
11 holes, 5888 yards, S.S.S.69
Designed by Peter Campbell.
Founded 1912
Visitors: welcome except Sun.

Green Fee: on application
Societies: weekdays by arrangement.
Catering: daily, except Wed.

K144 **Westminster Park**
☎(0244) 680231
Hough Green, Chester, Cheshire CH4 8JQ
In Saltney on SW outskirts of Chester.
Public parkland course
9 holes Par 3, 900 yards, S.S.S.27
Visitors: welcome.
Green Fee: apply for details.

K145 **Westwood (Leek)**
☎(0583) 398385
Wallbridge, Newcastle Rd, Leek, Staffs ST13 7AA
0.5 mile S of Leek on A53.
Moorland/parkland course.
18 holes, 6156 yards, S.S.S.69
Founded 1923
Visitors: welcome weekdays, with member Sat; not Sun.
Green Fee: £18 (£7 with member).
Societies: Mon and Thurs or by arrangement, contact Mrs J. Mitchell.
Catering: available.
Snooker, pool.

K146 **Whiston Hall**
☎(0538) 266260, (0850) 903815
Whiston, Nr Cheadle, Staffs ST10 2HZ
A52 midway between Stoke-on-Trent and Ashbourne, 3 miles from Alton Towers.
Challenging course set in beautiful countryside.
18 holes, 5675 yards, S.S.S.71
Designed by Thomas Cooper.
Founded 1971
Visitors: welcome, please avoid 8.15-10am Sun, 11.45-1.30pm Sat.
Green Fee: £8 WD, £12 WE & BH.
Societies: welcome any time by prior arrangement.
Catering: bar and catering at weekends all year, some weekdays in summer.
Snooker, fly fishing lakes.
Hotels: Stakis Grand (Stoke-on-Trent).

K147 **Whittington Barracks**
☎(0543) 432317 Clubhouse, 432261 Pro, 432317 Sec
Tamworth Rd, Lichfield, WS14 9PW
On A51 2.5 miles from Lichfield station.

Heathland course.
18 holes, 6448 yards, S.S.S.71
Founded 1886
Visitors: welcome weekdays with
h/cap cert or letter of intro.
Green Fee: £32/day/round.
Societies: catered for Wed and
Thurs, max 40.
Catering: snack lunches, evening
meals available except Mon.
Hotels: George; Little Barrow; Swan.

K148 **Widnes**
☎(051) 424 2995
Highfield Rd, Widnes, Cheshire
Near town centre.
Parkland course.
18 holes, 5688 yards, S.S.S.67
Founded 1923/4
Visitors: welcome weekdays.
Green Fee: apply for details.
Societies: welcome weekdays,
except Tues.
Catering: meals served by
arrangement.

K149 **Wilmslow**
☎(0565) 872148 Sec, 873620 Pro
Great Warford, Mobberley,
Knutsford, Cheshire WA16 7AY
2 miles from Wilmslow on B5085
Knutsford road, turn at Warford Lane.
Parkland course.
18 holes, 6607 yards, S.S.S.72
Founded 1889
Visitors: welcome Mon-Fri;
restricted weekends, Wed after 2pm.
Green Fee: £30/round, £40/day WD;
£40/round, £50/day WE.
Societies: welcome Tues and Thurs
by arrangement.
Catering: full facilities.
Hotels: Edge; The Belfry.

K150 **Wirral Ladies**
☎(051) 652 1255
93 Bidston Rd, Oxton, Birkenhead,
Merseyside L43 6TS
On A41 adjacent to M53 exit 3.
Moorland course.
18 holes, 4539 yards, S.S.S.70
Designed by H. Hilton.
Founded 1894
Visitors: welcome anytime.
Green Fee: £20/round.
Societies: apply to Sec.
Catering: meals at all times.

K151 **Withington**
☎(061) 445 9544, 434 8716
Catering
243 Palatine Rd, West Didsbury,
Manchester M20 8UD
From Manchester S on A5103 then
B5166 through Northenden.
Parkland course.
18 holes, 6411 yards, S.S.S.71
Founded 1892
Visitors: welcome weekdays.
Green Fee: apply for details.
Societies: catered for weekdays
except Thurs.
Catering: full; phone caterer.

K152 **Wolstanton**
☎(0782) 622413 Sec, 616995
Clubhouse, 622718 Pro
Dimsdale Old Hall, Hassam Parade,
Newcastle under Lyme, Staffs ST5
9DR
1.5 miles NW of Newcastle under
Lyme on A34, turn at The Sportsman
Hotel into Dimsdale Parade, then 1st
right into Hassam Parade.
Meadowland/parkland course.
18 holes, 5807 yards, S.S.S.68
Founded 1904

Visitors: welcome weekdays.
Green Fee: on application.
Societies: welcome Mon, Wed,
Thurs and Fri.
Catering: lunches served Mon-Sat
(not Fri).
Hotels: The Friendly Hotel

K153 **Worfield**
☎(07464) 372
Roughton, Nr Bridgnorth, Shropshire
WV15 5HE
On A454 Bridgenorth to
Wolverhampton road.
Parkland course.
18 holes, 6798 yards, S.S.S.73
Designed by T. Williams.
Founded Sept 1987
Visitors: welcome Mon-Fri, after
10am Sat/Sun; h/cap cert required.
Green Fee: £15/round, £20/day WD;
£20/round, £25/day WE.
Societies: welcome at all times.
Catering: bars and restaurant, all
catering available.
Practice area.
Hotels: Vicarage (Worfield);
Pengwern (Shrewsbury).

K154 **Wrekin**
☎(0952) 44032
Ercall Woods, Wellington, Telford TF6
5BX
Off M54 back along B5061 to Golf
Links Lane.
Parkland course.
18 holes, 5699 yards, S.S.S.67
Founded 1905
Visitors: welcome weekdays.
Green Fee: apply for details.
Societies: catered for weekdays
except Mon.
Catering: booked in advance.

DERBYSHIRE, NOTTINGHAMSHIRE, LINCOLNSHIRE

Seacroft at Skegness may not be the most accessible of golf courses. Nevertheless, there is a strong argument to make that that is the key to its appeal. On the other hand, there is nothing like a rave notice to start the queues forming and the ensuing disturbance of the peace will not be to the liking of the locals.

Golfers place a high premium on tranquillity, particularly when seeking a leisurely round, and Seacroft fits that bill admirably. Its true seaside qualities may be slow to blossom as the opening holes are flanked on the right by trim avenues and typically large Lincolnshire fields. Out of bounds, in fact, is an obvious threat most of the way to the turn but, from the moment that the short 10th turns back, diagonally to the line of play hitherto, there are inspiring sights of the sea and many memorable holes.

Seacroft lies on the opposite side of The Wash from Hunstanton, on the edge of the Gibraltar Point wildlife sanctuary, which epitomises its joyous remoteness. It is the only true seaside links between Hunstanton and Seaton Carew, a pick of the Eastern seaboard, but Lincolnshire has another gem in Woodhall Spa, again a peaceful retreat though widely contrasting in character. It highlights the best of British inland golf, a stout championship challenge revolving around glorious heathland, deep bunkers and handsome trees. A word too, for Luffenham Heath near Stamford which is almost as good.

Seacroft and Woodhall Spa are the perfect foil for each other but the Notts Golf Club at Hollinwell is a rival to Woodhall Spa in its severity as a test and in a pleasant setting that largely obscures evidence of the mining community that surrounds it. It lies in a gentle valley fringed by pine trees and boasts a collection of par 4s which are notably good. There is also a little climbing to be done which tends to be enlightening rather than exhausting.

Hollinwell has distinguished neighbours in Sherwood Forest and Coxmoor, courses that enjoy similarly appealing golfing terrain with problems to match.

Part of Lindrick falls in Nottinghamshire, although I am inclined to think the bulk of it is in Yorkshire — or used to be. However, wherever its loyalties are directed, it is a superb course that has rightly attracted its share of big events including victory in the 1957 Ryder Cup at a time when Great Britain and Ireland were not used to winning.

Newark is worthy of recommendation and Wollaton Park in Nottingham has also housed professional events but, if Derbyshire, the third county in this particular trinity, lacks the outstanding courses of the other two, some of them bear the signature of famous architects. Cavendish at Buxton is the work of Alister Mackenzie while James Braid and John Morrison had a hand in Kedleston Park. To Harry Colt goes credit for Chesterfield and Frank Pennink made changes at Mickleover. Since the last edition of this guide, a second course has been added to Breadsall Priory Hotel Golf and Country Club which is part of the Country Club Hotels chain that includes St Pierre and Dalmahoy.

The first course, opened in 1977, indulges in a good deal of up and down but the second course, which opened in 1992, commands marvellous views from nicely rolling moorland with exactly the same feeling of escape that can be experienced on the distant coast at Seacroft.

L1 **Alfreton**
☎(0773) 832070
Highfields, Wingfield Rd, Oakthorpe,
Derbys DE5 7DH
Take Matlock road out of Alfreton,
about 0.75 mile.
Parkland course.
9 holes, 5074 yards, S.S.S.65
Founded 1892
Visitors: welcome; Sat, Sun and
Mon with member only.
Green Fee: £13/round, £17/day.
Societies: catered for weekdays on
consultation with Sec.
Catering: full facilities except Mon.
Hotels: Swallow (S Normanton);
Granada (Swanwick).

L2 **Allestree Park**
☎(0332) 550616
Allestree Hall, Allestree, Derbys
Leave Derby on A6, 4 miles from city
centre, signposted Allestree Park.
Undulating parkland course.
18 holes, 5661 yards, S.S.S.67
Founded 1940
Visitors: welcome at all times,
except for competition days or Sun
mornings.

Green Fee: £10.
Societies: welcome.
Catering: by prior arrangement;
(0332) 552971.
Hotels: Clovelly (Derby).

L3 **Ashbourne**
☎(0335) 42078
Clifton, Nr Ashbourne, Derbys DE6
4BN
1 mile S of Ashbourne on A515 to
Sudbury and Lichfield.
Undulating parkland course.
9 holes, 5359 yards, S.S.S.66
Designed by Frank Pennink.
Founded 1910
Visitors: welcome.
Green Fee: apply for details.
Societies: small.
Catering: by arrangement, not
Thurs.

L4 **Bakewell**
☎(0629) 812307
Station Rd, Bakewell, Derbys DE45
1GB
0.75 mile from Bakewell Square,
cross bridge over River Wye on A619

Sheffield-Chesterfield road, right up
Station Rd, right before Industrial
Estate.
Hilly parkland course.
9 holes, 5240 yards, S.S.S.66
Designed by George Low.
Founded 1899
Visitors: welcome weekdays;
Ladies' Day Thurs.
Green Fee: £12.
Societies: welcome by arrangement.
Catering: meals and bar service
except Mon.
Hotels: Rutland Arms.

L5 **Beeston Fields**
☎(0602) 257062
Beeston Fields, Nottingham NG9 3DD
Off A52 4 miles W of Nottingham, 4
miles from M1 exit 25.
Parkland course.
18 holes, 6414 yards, S.S.S.71
Designed by Tom Williamson.
Founded 1922
Visitors: daily by arrangement.
Green Fee: on application.
Societies: catered for Mon and Wed.
Catering: meals served every day.
Hotels: The Priory; Novotel.

L6 Belton Park

☎(0476) 67399
Belton Lane, Londonthorpe Rd,
Grantham, Lincs NG31 9SH
A607 from Grantham signposted to
Sleaford and Lincoln, turn right at
traffic lights at Park signposted
Londonthorpe, club is 1 mile on left.
Parkland courses.
Brownlow, 9 holes, 6420 yards,
S.S.S.71; Belmont, 9 holes, 6016
yards, S.S.S.69; Ancaster, 9 holes,
6252 yards, S.S.S.70
Designed by Thomas & Alliss.
Founded 1890
Visitors: welcome, preferably with
h/cap cert; proper dress.
Green Fee: apply for details.
Societies: not Tues or weekends.
Catering: full facilities at all times.
2 practice fairways.
Hotels: Angel & Royal; King's; Lodge
(Marston); Travel Lodge.

L7 Belton Woods Hotel & Country Club

☎(0476) 593200, 74547 Fax
Belton, Nr Grantham, Lincolnshire
NG32 2LN
2 miles E of A1 via Gonerby Moor
services; 2 miles N of Grantham on
A607 to Lincoln.
Rolling parkland courses with mature
trees and adjacent woodland.
Lancaster, 18 holes, 7021 yards,
S.S.S.74; Wellington, 18 holes, 6875
yards, S.S.S.73; Spitfire, 9 holes Par
3, 1184 yards
Founded Jan 1991
Visitors: welcome any day; 10 days
advance booking only.
Green Fee: summer (1st April-31st
Oct), £19.50 (18 holes), £10 (9
holes); special winter rates and
reductions for residents.
Societies: Mon-Fri by prior
arrangement; special Company and
Society Golf Days.
Catering: leisure restaurant
7am-10pm, bar snacks 11am-10pm;
à la carte restaurant, banqueting for
240; health, sports, leisure and
conference facilities.
Driving range, putting green.
Hotels: Belton Woods, golfing breaks
for individuals and groups; golf
tuition holidays.

L8 Birch Hall

☎(0246) 291979, 291934 Manager
Sheffield Rd, Unstone, Sheffield S18
5DH
3 miles from Chesterfield, 7 miles
from Sheffield on old A61 road.

Parkland course.
18 holes, S.S.S.74
Designed by David Tucker.
Founded Oct 1992
Visitors: welcome except Sat and
Sun am.
Green Fee: £14/round.
Societies: welcome 7 days with
prior arrangement.
Catering: bar and restaurant; bar
has public house license, named The
Inn on the Green.
Hotels: Sandpiper Motel adjoining
course; Sheffield Moat House.

L9 Blankney

☎(0526) 320263 Sec, 320202 Pro,
322521 Fax
Blankney, Lincoln, Lincs LN4 3AZ
10 miles from Lincoln, 1 mile past
Metheringham on B1188.
Parkland course.
18 holes, 6378 yards, S.S.S.71
Designed by Cameron Sinclair
(updated design).
Founded 1903
Visitors: phone General
Manager/Pro in advance.
Green Fee: £15/round, £20/day WD;
£20/round, £30/day WE.
Societies: weekdays and weekends.
Catering: full facilities.
Snooker.
Hotels: Self-catering bungalow for
up to 6 available; £30 per double
room.

L10 Bondhay Golf & Country Club

☎(0909) 723608
Bondhay Lane, Whitwell, Worksop,
Notts S80 3EH
Just off A619, 5 mins from M1
junction 30.
Parkland course.
18 holes, 6800 yards, Par 72; 9 hole
family course.
Designed by Donald Steel.
Founded 1991
Visitors: welcome, no restrictions;
book in advance.
Green Fee: £14.95; family course
£3.95 (9 holes).
Societies: book in advance.
Catering: full facilities.
Driving range, Health club.
Hotels: Vandykes (Worksop);
Beeches (Rotherham).

L11 Boston

☎(0205) 362306 Club, 350589 Sec
Cowbridge, Horncastle Rd, Boston,
Lincs PE22 7EL

2 miles N of Boston on B1183, look
for sign on right crossing 1st bridge.
Parkland course; water on 10 holes.
18 holes, 5795 yards, S.S.S.68
Designed by B.S. Cooper, extended
by Donald Steel.
Founded 1962
Visitors: welcome.
Green Fee: apply for details.
Societies: welcome weekdays.
Catering: full facilities except Wed
when only bar snacks available.
Hotels: White Hart; Bridge Foot; New
England; Wide Bargate; Boston.

L12 Bramcote Hills Golf Course

☎(0602) 281880
Thoresby Rd, off Derby Rd,
Bramcote, Nottingham
M1 junction 25, take A52 towards
Nottingham, past Bramcote Leisure
Centre, turn left 0.25 mile further on.
Parkland course.
18 holes Par 3, 1501 yards
Founded 1981
Visitors: pay-as-you-play.
Green Fee: £4.30 WD, £4.80 WE &
BH, reductions for jnrs.
Societies: bookings welcomed.
Catering: refreshments only.

L13 Breadsall Priory Hotel Golf & Country Club

☎(0332) 832235, 833509 Fax
Moor Rd, Morley, Derbys DE7 6DL
3 miles NE of Derby off A61, towards
Breadsall, turn left into Rectory Lane
and right onto Moor Rd.
Priory course, parkland; Moorland
course, moorland.
Priory, 18 holes, 5871 yards,
S.S.S.70; Moorland, 18 holes, 5820
yards, S.S.S.69
Founded 1977 (Priory), 1992
(Moorland)
Visitors: welcome weekdays; by
prior arrangement weekends.
Green Fee: £23/round, £32/day WD;
£26/round WE.
Societies: weekdays only;
residential societies at weekends.
Catering: 5 bars, 2 restaurants;
breakfast, lunch and dinner.
Tennis, squash, pool, snooker, etc.
Hotels: Breadsall Priory.

L14 Breedon Priory

☎(0332) 863081
The Clubhouse, Wilson, Nr Derby,
DE7 1AT
1 mile E of A 453 between E Midlands
Airport and Ashby-de-la-Zouche.

Parkland course.
18 holes, 5512 yards, S.S.S.66
Founded 1990
Visitors: Welcome Mon-Fri;
weekends pm only and by
arrangement.
Green Fee: £12.
Societies: weekdays by
arrangement; also catering for
Corporate Days.
Catering: bar, bar snacks, à la carte
restaurant.
Hotels: Park Farmhouse (Nr Castle
Donnington).

L15 **Bulwell Forest**
☎(0602) 770576
Hucknall Rd, Bulwell, Nottingham
NG5 9LQ
4 miles N of city centre, follow signs
for Bulwell or Hucknall, 3 miles from
M1 junction 26.
Moorland course.
18 holes, 5572 yards, S.S.S.67
Founded 1902
Visitors: welcome.
Green Fee: £8.60 WD, £10 WE.
Societies: by arrangement.
Catering: by arrangement.

L16 **Burghley Park**
☎(0780) 53789, 54222 Pro
St Martins Without, Stamford, Lincs
PE9 3JX
Leave A1 at roundabout S of town,
course entrance is 1st gateway on
the right, 1 mile S of Stamford.
Parkland course.
18 holes, 6236 yards, S.S.S.70
Designed by the Rev J.D. Day.
Founded 1890
Visitors: welcome weekdays only;
h/cap certs essential.
Green Fee: £20.
Societies: welcome weekdays.
Catering: lunches and teas, dinner
for Societies and by arrangement.
Hotels: George of Stamford; Crown;
Cavalier, Collyweston; Lady Anne's;
Garden House.

L17 **Buxton & High Peak**
☎(0298) 23453, 26263
Waterswallows Rd, Fairfield, Buxton,
Derbys
1 mile N from Buxton station on A6.
Meadowland course.
18 holes, 5954 yards, S.S.S.69
Founded 1887
Visitors: welcome.
Green Fee: £20 WD, £25 WE & BH.
Societies: by arrangement with
House Manageress; full and half-day

packages, Mon-Fri full day inc lunch
and dinner, 36 holes £33.
Catering: full facilities and supper
licence.
Hotels: Buckingham; Palace;
Portland; Egerton; Grovesnor House;
Givenchy GH; Barms Farm; Hawthorn
Farm.

L18 **Canwick Park**
☎(0522) 522166
Canwick Park, Washingborough
Road, Lincoln LN4 1EF
2 miles E of city centre.
Parkland course.
18 holes, 6237 yards, S.S.S.70
Designed by Hawtree & Partners.
Founded 1973
Visitors: welcome weekdays.
Green Fee: £15/round, £22/day WD;
£19/round £26/day WE.
Societies: weekdays.
Catering: lunches and evening
meals except Mon.
Hotels: Eastgate; Brierley House.

L19 **Carholme**
☎(0522) 523725 Sec, 536811 Pro
Carholme Rd, Lincoln LN1 1SE
On A57, 1 mile from city centre.
Parkland course.
18 holes, 6114 yards, S.S.S.69
Founded 1906
Visitors: welcome weekdays, with
member weekends.
Green Fee: on application.
Societies: weekdays only.
Catering: lunches served except
Mon.

L20 **Cavendish**
☎(0298) 23494, 25052
Pro/bookings, 23256 Sec
Gadley Lane, Buxton, Derbys SK17
6XD
0.75 mile from town centre going W
on A53 Leek road, right on Carlisle
Rd, then left on Watford Rd
signposted.
Parkland/downland course.
18 holes, 5833 yards, S.S.S.68
Designed by Dr Alistair Mackenzie.
Founded 1925
Visitors: welcome.
Green Fee: £22/day WD, £33/round
WE; half price with member.
Societies: catered for weekdays by
arrangement with Pro.
Catering: snacks available at all
times and meals by arrangement.
Snooker table.
Hotels: Lee Wood; Buckingham;
Portland; Egerton.

L21 **Chatsworth**
☎(0246) 582204
Chatsworth Park, Bakewell, Derbys
Parkland course.
9 holes (18 tees), 5248 yards,
S.S.S.66
Visitors: none; members and guests
only.

L22 **Chesterfield**
☎(0246) 279256
Walton, Chesterfield, Derbys S42 7LA
2 miles from town centre on Matlock
road A632.
Parkland course.
18 holes, 6326 yards, S.S.S.70
Designed by H. Colt.
Founded 1897
Visitors: welcome weekdays.
Green Fee: apply for details.
Societies: catered for on weekdays
if booked in advance.
Catering: lunch, dinner every day.
Hotels: Chesterfield; Portland.

L23 **Chesterfield Municipal**
☎(0246) 273887, 239500 bookings
Murray House, Crow Lane,
Chesterfield, Derbys S41 0EQ
Near centre of Chesterfield,
signposted.
Municipal parkland course.
18 holes, 6013 yards, S.S.S.69; 9
holes, 2700 yards, Par 34
Founded 1934
Visitors: welcome any time; booking
system all week, up to 6 days in
advance.
Green Fee: apply for details.
Societies: welcome by prior
arrangement.
Catering: bar and restaurant
facilities.
Pitch & Putt.

L24 **Chevin**
☎(0332) 841864
Golf Lane, Duffield, Derbys DE6 4EE
5 miles N of Derby on A6, just outside
Duffield.
Hilly parkland course.
18 holes, 6043 yards, S.S.S.69
Founded 1894
Visitors: welcome weekdays, not
before 9.30am nor 12am-2pm; with
member at weekends.
Green Fee: apply for details.
Societies: not weekends; no meals
Mon.
Catering: meals served except Mon.
Snooker.
Hotels: Strutt Arms adjacent.

L25 Chilwell Manor
☎(0602) 258958
Meadow Lane, Chilwell, Nottingham
NG9 5AE
4 miles W of Nottingham, near
Beeston, on A6005.
Parkland course.
18 holes, 6379 yards, S.S.S.69
Founded 1906
Visitors: welcome weekdays,
restricted to 4 per hour.
Green Fee: £13/round/day.
Societies: catered for Mon, Wed, Fri.
Catering: lunches served weekdays;
evening meals by arrangement.
Hotels: Post House; Novotel.

L26 Cleethorpes
☎(0472) 812059, 814060
Kings Rd, Cleethorpes, S Humberside
DN35 0PN
Off A1031 1 mile S of Cleethorpes.
Meadowland course; considerably
altered after April 1994.
18 holes, 6360 yards, S.S.S.69
Designed by Harry Vardon (now
vastly altered).
Founded 1894
Visitors: must be members of
recognised club (Ladies only,
Wed pm).
Green Fee: £15 (£10 with member)
WD, £20 (£15 with member) WE.
Societies: by arrangement.
Catering: full facilities available by
arrangement with Steward.
Hotels: Kingsway; Wellow.

L27 Cotgrave Place Golf & Country Club
☎(0602) 333349 Office, 334686 Pro
Stragglethorpe, Nottingham NG12
3HB
Approx 3.5 miles from Nottingham on
A52 Grantham road, take right turn to
Cotgrave.
Parkland course, lake bestrewn.
3 x 9 holes, c. 6500 yards,
S.S.S.71-72
Founded 1992
Visitors: apply for details.
Green Fee: apply for details.
Societies: apply for details;
Catering: full facilities.
Driving range.

L28 Coxmoor
☎(0623) 559878 Club, 557359
Office, 559906 Pro shop
Coxmoor Rd, Sutton-in-Ashfield,
Notts NG17 5LF.
On A611 5 miles from M1 junction
27, 2 miles SW of Mansfield.
Heathland course.
18 holes, 6251 yards, S.S.S.70
Founded 1913
Visitors: weekdays except Tues
(Ladies' Day); must book in advance.
Green Fee: £27/day.
Societies: Mon, Wed, Thurs, Fri.
Catering: full facilities.
Hotels: Pine Lodge; Carr Bank
Manor; Dalestorth GH; Hole in the
Wall; Swallow.

L29 Derby
☎(0332) 766462 Pro shop, 766323
Catering
Shakespeare St, Sinfin, Derby DE24
9HD
1 mile off A5111 at Sinfin, vehicle
access via Wilmore Rd.
Municipal parkland course.
18 holes, 6183 yards, S.S.S.69
Founded 1923
Visitors: welcome.
Green Fee: on application.
Societies: weekdays by prior
arrangement.
Catering: bar and catering daily.

L30 Edwalton Municipal
☎(0602) 234775
Edwalton Village, Nottingham
Left at A606 from Nottingham at
Edwalton Hall Hotel.
Parkland course.
Main, 9 holes, 3336 yards, S.S.S.36;
Par 3, 9 holes, 1592 yards, S.S.S.27
Designed by Frank Pennink.
Founded 1981
Visitors: welcome.
Green Fee: on application.
Societies: weekdays.
Catering: lunches, evening meals.
Hotels: Edwalton Hall.

L31 Elsham
☎(0652) 680291 Manager, 680432
Pro
Barton Rd, Elsham, Brigg, S
Humberside DN20 0LS
Situated on E side of Brigg to Barton
road, B1206, 3 miles N of Brigg.
Parkland course.
18 holes, 6411 yards, S.S.S.71
Founded 1901
Visitors: welcome weekdays.
Green Fee: on application.
Societies: weekdays except Thurs.
Catering: full bar all day.

L32 Erewash Valley
☎(0602) 323258
Stanton-by-Dale, Ilkeston, Derbys
From M1 junction 25 follow signs to
Stanton Ironworks Co Ltd, through
Sandiacre.
Meadowland/parkland course.
18 holes, 6487 yards, S.S.S.71
Founded 1905
Visitors: welcome weekdays.
Green Fee: £22/round, £27/day WD;
£27/round/day WE & BH.
Societies: catered for weekdays.
Catering: lunches, evening meals by
arrangement.
Snooker, bowling green.
Hotels: Post House; Novotel.

L33 Gainsborough
☎(0427) 613088
Thonock, Gainsborough, Lincs DN21
1PZ
1 mile NE of Gainsborough.
Parkland course.
18 holes, 6515 yards, S.S.S.71
Founded 1985
Visitors: welcome weekdays.
Green Fee: £25/round, £30/day (inc
lunch).
Societies: Mon-Fri, book in advance.
Catering: bar, restaurant, coffee
shop all day.
Driving range, putting green, snooker.
Hotels: Hemswell Cliff; Hickman Hill.

L34 Gedney Hill
☎(0406) 330922 Pro
West Drove, Gedney Hill, Nr
Holbeach, Lincs PE12 0NT
6 miles from Crowland on B1166, 6
miles from Thorney by A47 and
B1167.
Public links type course, reasonably
flat, small greens.
18 holes, 5357 yards, S.S.S.66
Designed by C. Britton.
Founded 1988
Visitors: welcome; smart dress on
and off course.
Green Fee: £5.75 WD, £8.75 WE;
reductions for Jnrs and OAPs.
Societies: welcome weekdays.
Catering: casual bar, bar snacks;
restaurant for meals and functions.
Driving range, snooker, heated
swimming pool.

L35 Glossop & District
☎(0457) 853117
Hurst Lane, off Sheffield Rd, Glossop,
Derbys SK13 8RH
1 mile out of town on A57 Sheffield
road.
Moorland course.
11 holes, 5726 yards, S.S.S.68
Founded 1895

Visitors: welcome.
Green Fee: apply for details.
Societies: welcome.
Catering: meals served by arrangement.
Hotels: Hurst Lee GH.

L36 Grange Park

☎(0724) 762945
Butterwick Rd, Messingham, Scunthorpe, S Humberside DN17 3PP
Signposted from Messingham.
Public parkland course.
9 holes, 2970 yards, Par 35; 9 holes Par 3.
Designed by Ray Price.
Founded July 1991
Visitors: welcome, no restrictions.
Green Fee: £4 WD, £6 WE; jnrs half price.
Catering: coffee bar.
Driving range.

L37 Grassmoor Golf Centre

☎(0246) 856044, 856200 Fax
North Wingfield Rd, Grassmoor, Chesterfield, Derbys S42 5EA
M1 junction 29; 2 miles S of Chesterfield.
Moorland course.
18 holes, S.S.S.69
Designed by Michael Shattock.
Founded Nov 1992
Visitors: all welcome, phone to reserve time.
Green Fee: £6-10.
Societies: welcome weekdays and weekends.
Catering: bar and restaurant facilities.
Driving range, sauna.

L38 Grimsby

☎(0472) 342630 Sec, 342823
Clubhouse, 356981 Pro
Littlecoates Rd, Grimsby, S Humberside DN34 4LU
1 mile W of town centre; turn left off A18 at 1st roundabout, 0.75 mile on left, next to Forte Post House.
Undulating parkland course.
18 holes, 6058 yards, S.S.S.69
Founded 1922
Visitors: members of golf clubs only; Ladies Day Tues.
Green Fee: £18 WD, £23 WE.
Societies: catered for Mon and Fri only.
Catering: available; full meals by arrangement, except Wed.
Bowls, bridge.
Hotels: Forte Posthouse.

L39 Holme Hall

☎(0724) 862078 Sec/bookings, 840909 Club
Holme Lane, Bottesford, Scunthorpe, S Humberside DN16 3RF
2 miles SE of Scunthorpe near M180 exit 4.
Parkland course.
18 holes, 6475 yards, S.S.S.71
Founded 1908
Visitors: welcome weekdays, not weekends or Bank Holidays.
Green Fee: £20/round/day.
Societies: not Mon.
Catering: meals by arrangement, bar snacks daily except Mon.
Hotels: Royal; Wortley; Beverley; Briggate Lodge.

L40 Horncastle

☎(0507) 526800
West Ashby, Horncastle, Lincs LN9 5PP
Just off A158 between Lincoln and Skegness; down hill at Edlington, follow AA signs.
Heathland course with trees and water features.
18 holes, 5717 yards, S.S.S.70
Designed by Ernie Wright.
Founded July 1990
Visitors: welcome.
Green Fee: £10/round, £15/day.
Societies: 7 days a week.
Catering: bars and restaurant; conferences, ballroom.
Driving range, coarse fishing.
Hotels: Petwood, Golf (Woodhall Spa); Bull, Admiral Rodney (Horncastle).

L41 Horsley Lodge

☎(0332) 780838 Clubhouse, 781400 Proshop, 781118 Fax
Horsley Lodge, Smalley Mill Road, Horsley, Derbys DE21 5BL.
4 miles from Derby on A608
Derby-Heanor road turn left at Rose & Crown then 2nd left.
Undulating parkland course.
18 holes, 6443 yards, S.S.S.71
Designed by George 'Bill' White.
Founded 1990
Visitors: welcome, not during weekend competitions.
Green Fee: £17/round, £25/day.
Societies: welcome any week day or non-competition Sat.
Catering: 2 bars, à la carte restaurant, function room, banqueting.
Driving range, tennis, sauna etc.
Hotels: Own luxury hotel on site; free golf for residents, bargain breaks.

L42 Humberston Park

☎(0472) 210404
Humberston Ave, Humberston, S Humberside
Humberstone Avenue at back of Cherry Garth Scouts Field.
Parkland course.
9 holes, Par 30
Founded 1970
Visitors: welcome, not before 12am weekends.
Green Fee: £8 (18 holes) WD, £12 (18 holes) WE.
Societies: welcome by arrangement.
Catering: bar and snacks.

L43 Ilkeston Borough (Pewit)

☎(0602) 307704
West End Drive, Ilkeston, Derbyshire DE7 5GH
0.5 mile E of Ilkeston town centre.
Municipal meadowland course.
9 holes, 4002 yards, S.S.S.60
Founded 1920
Visitors: welcome.
Green Fee: £6 (18 holes)
Societies: welcome, weekdays only.

L44 Immingham

☎(0469) 575298, 575493
Church Lane, Immingham, Grimsby, S Humberside DN40 2EU
A180 Immingham exits, Pelham Rd; Bluestone Lane or Washdyke Lane both lead into Church Lane.
Parkland course.
18 holes, 6161 yards, S.S.S.69
Designed by Hawtree & Son (1st 9), F. Pennink (2nd 9).
Founded 1974
Visitors: welcome weekdays, restrictions at weekends.
Green Fee: £14/round WD.
Societies: weekdays by prior arrangement.
Catering: snacks, bar meals, arranged with Steward.

L45 Kedleston Park

☎(0332) 840035
Kedleston, Quarndon, Derby DE6 4JD
Off A38 follow signs to Kedleston Hall.
Parkland course.
18 holes, 6611 yards, S.S.S.71
Designed by James Braid and Morrison & Co.
Founded 1947
Visitors: weekdays only by appointment.
Green Fee: £25/round.
Societies: weekdays only by appointment.

Catering: restaurant and bar. Snooker.
Hotels: Kedleston; Midland; Mundy Arms.

L46 Kenwick Park
☎(0507) 605134
Kenwick, Nr Louth, Lincs LN11 8NY
On Mablethorpe road out of Louth.
Woodland/parkland course.
18 holes, 6815 yards, S.S.S.73
Designed by Patrick Tallack.
Founded 1992
Visitors: members and guests only unless resident at Kenwick Hall.
Catering: bar and restaurant. Practice ground.
Hotels: Kenwick Hall.

L47 Kilton Forest
☎(0909) 486563 Pro
Blyth Rd, Worksop, Notts S81 0TL
2 miles NE of town centre on B6045; on by-pass follow signs for Blyth.
Public parkland course
18 holes, 6444 yards, S.S.S.71
Founded 1978
Visitors: welcome, booking system in operation weekends and Bank Holidays.
Green Fee: £6.40 WD, £8.60 WE & BH.
Societies: welcome by arrangement, Club competitions weekends and some Bank Holidays.
Catering: bar meals; not Sun. Bowling green adjacent.
Hotels: Regancy.

L48 Kingsway
☎(0724) 840945
Kingsway, Scunthorpe, S Humberside DN15 7ER
S of A18 between Berkeley and Queensway roundabouts.
Undulating parkland course.
9 holes, 1915 yards, S.S.S.59
Designed by R.D. Highfield.
Founded 1971
Visitors: welcome every day.
Green Fee: £2.75 WD, £3.25 WE.
Catering: snacks available.

L49 Kirton Holme
☎(0205) 290669
Holme Rd, Nr Boston, Lincs PE20 1SY
2 miles W of Boston off A52.
Parkland course.
9 holes, 2884 yards, Par 35
Designed by D.W. Welberry.
Founded 1992
Visitors: welcome, no restrictions.

Green Fee: £4/round (9 holes), £7/day WD; £5/round, £8/day WE & BH.
Societies: by arrangement.
Catering: light snacks; bar and bar meals from summer 1994.
Hotels: Poachers Inn.

L50 Lincoln
☎(042 771) 210
Torksey, Lincoln LN1 2EG
Off A156, 12 miles NW of Lincoln.
Undulating meadowland course.
18 holes, 6438 yards, S.S.S.71
Founded 1891
Visitors: welcome with reservation weekdays only.
Green Fee: apply for details.
Societies: weekdays by arrangement.
Catering: meals by arrangement.
Hotels: White Hart; Grand; Crest.

L51 Lindrick
☎(0909) 475282
Lindrick, Worksop, Notts S81 8BH
On A57, 4 miles W of Worksop.
Heathland course.
18 holes, 6612 yards, S.S.S.72
Designed by Tom Dunn, Willie Park and N.H. Fowler.
Founded 1891
Visitors: weekdays with prior notice.
Green Fee: Nov-Mar £25/round/day WD; Apr-Oct £40/round/day WD, £45/round WE.
Societies: weekdays except Tues.
Catering: lunches served most days; evening meals for visiting societies or parties, prior notice required.
Hotels: Red Lion (Todwick); Fourways, Charnwood (Blyth); Olde Bell (Barnby Moor).

L52 Louth Golf & Squash Club
☎(0507) 603681 Tel/Fax
Crowtree Lane, Louth, Lincs LN11 9LJ
W of Louth in triangle between A157 Louth by-pass and A153.
Undulating parkland course in AONB.
18 holes, 6477 yards, S.S.S.71
Founded 1965
Visitors: welcome.
Green Fee: £16/round, £20/day WD; £20/round, £25/day WE & BH.
Societies: weekdays; £5 deposit when booking.
Catering: full catering provided. Squash courts.
Hotels: Priory; Kings Head; Masons Arms; Brakenborough Arms.

L53 Luffenham Heath
☎(0780) 720205 Sec, 720298 Pro, 721095 Catering
Ketton, Stamford, Lincs PE9 3UU
6 miles SW of Stamford on A6121 by Fosters Bridge, off A47 at Morcott onto A6121.
Undulating heathland course.
18 holes, 6253 yards, S.S.S.71
Designed by James Braid.
Founded 1911
Visitors: by prior arrangement; h/cap certs required.
Green Fee: £30 WD, £35 WE.
Societies: Wed, Thurs, Fri, bookings through Sec.
Catering: by arrangement.
Hotels: George (Stamford); Cavalier (Collyweston).

L54 The Manor Golf Course
☎(0472) 873468
Laceby Manor, Laceby, Grimsby, S Humberside DN37 7EA
1 mile from Laceby roundabout on A18, on left; large green and white sign.
Parkland course.
9 holes, S.S.S.70 (extending to 18 holes by summer 1995)
Designed by Sir Charles Nicholson and Rushton.
Founded June 1992
Visitors: welcome any time when competitions not being played; restricted play 1st and 3rd Tues am each month (Ladies' Mornings), 2nd and 4th Tues (over 55s).
Green Fee: £6 (9 holes), £9 (18 holes) WD; £7 (9 holes), £11 (18 holes) WE & BH.
Societies: phone Sec to discuss.
Catering: bar, coffee etc.
Hotels: Oaklands (0.75 mile).

L55 Mansfield Woodhouse
☎(0623) 23521
Leeming Lane North, Mansfield Woodhouse, Notts NG19 9EU
On A60 Mansfield-Worksop road, 2 miles N of Mansfield.
Public parkland course
9 holes, 2411 yards, S.S.S.65
Founded 1973
Visitors: not Sat before 11am.
Green Fee: apply for details.
Catering: full facilities.

L56 Mapperley
☎(0602) 265611
Central Ave, Mapperley Plains, Nottingham NG3 5RH

From Nottingham take B684 Woodborough Rd, Central Ave is about 4 miles NE of Nottingham, turn right at Speeds (Volvo) Garage.
Hilly meadowland course.
18 holes, 6224 yards, S.S.S.70
Founded c. 1905
Visitors: welcome.
Green Fee: £15.50/round, £18.50/day WD; £17.50/round, £20.50/day WE.
Societies: weekdays.
Catering: lunch and evening meals served except Wed, when only snacks available.

L57 Market Rasen & District
☎(0673) 842416
Legsby Rd, Market Rasen, Lincs LN8 3DZ
B1202 off A46, 1 mile S of racecourse.
Moorland course.
18 holes, 6043 yards, S.S.S.69
Founded 1922
Visitors: welcome weekdays; with member weekends.
Green Fee: £15/round, £20/day.
Societies: Tues and Fri by arrangement with Sec.
Catering: lunch except Mon.

L58 Market Rasen Race Course
☎(0673) 843434
Market Rasen Race Course, Legsby Rd, Market Rasen, Lincs LN8 3EA
Off A631.
Public pay-as-you-play course.
9 holes, 2532 yards, Par 33
Founded May 1989
Visitors: welcome, not race days.
Green Fee: £4 (9 holes), £6 (18 holes) WD; £5 (9 holes), £8 (18 holes) WE; reductions for jnrs and OAPs.
Societies: welcome.
Catering: available on race course. Children's playground.
Hotels: The Limes.

L59 Matlock
☎(0629) 582191
Chesterfield Rd, Matlock, Derbys DE4 5LF
On A632 Matlock-Chesterfield road, 1.5 miles out of Matlock.
Moorland/parkland course.
18 holes, 5801 yards, S.S.S.68 (yellow tees)
Founded 1907
Visitors: welcome weekdays, weekends with member only.

Green Fee: £25 WD, £12.50 WE & BH with member only.
Societies: catered for weekdays by arrangement.
Catering: snacks available, meals to order except Mon.
Hotels: Peacock; New Bath.

L60 Maywood
☎(0602) 392306
Rushy Lane, Risley, Draycott, Derbys DE72 3ST
Off M1 junction 25; then off A52 to Risley by Post House Hotel.
Wooded course with water features.
9 holes, 2883 yards, Par 68; 18 holes, S.S.S.71
Founded 1990
Visitors: welcome
Green Fee: £15 WD, £20 WE
Societies: by arrangement.
Catering: bar, snacks.
Hotels: Post House; Novotel.

L61 Mickleover
☎(0332) 513339 Clubhouse, 518662 Pro
Uttoxeter Rd, Mickleover, Derby
3 miles W of Derby; take A516 out of Derby, join B5020 to Mickleover.
Meadowland course.
18 holes, 5708 yards, S.S.S.68
Founded 1923
Visitors: welcome.
Green Fee: £20 WD, £25 WE & BH.
Societies: Tues, Thurs, £19.
Catering: full catering facilities available.
Hotels: Crest; International.

L62 Millfield
☎(042 771) 255, 8473 Phone/Fax
Laughterton, Torksey, Nr Lincoln, Lincs LN1 2LB
8 miles E of Lincoln between A57 and A158 on A113, 10 miles from Gainsborough.
Inland links course.
18 holes, 5986 yards, S.S.S.69; 9 holes Par 3, 1500 yards; further 15 hole intermediate course, 4100 yards, from summer 1992.
Founded 1984
Visitors: no restrictions, pay-as-you-play.
Green Fee: £7 (18 hole course), £4 (15 hole course).
Societies: weekdays by arrangement.
Catering: light refreshments. Driving range, tennis, bowls.
Hotels: self-catering apartments in complex.

L63 Newark
☎(0636) 626282 Sec/Manager, 626241 Club
Kelwick, Coddington, Newark, Notts NG24 2QX
On A17 between Newark and Sleaford, just past Coddington roundabout.
Parkland course.
18 holes, 6482 yards, S.S.S.71
Founded 1901
Visitors: welcome any time; h/cap cert required; Tues Ladies' Day.
Green Fee: £20/round; £25/day WE.
Societies: welcome except Tues and weekends; catering with booking.
Catering: bar and meals all day. Snooker, pool.
Hotels: Robin Hood; George Inn (Leadenham).

L64 Normanby Hall
☎(0724) 720252 Clubhouse, 844303 Sec, 720226 Pro shop
Normanby Park, Normanby, Scunthorpe, S Humberside DN15 9HU
5 miles N of Scunthorpe adjacent to Normanby Hall.
Parkland course.
18 holes, 6548 yards, S.S.S.71
Designed by Jiggens, Hawtree & Sons.
Founded 1978
Visitors: welcome, ring Pro for times.
Green Fee: £9.50/round, £15/day WD; £12/round WE & BH.
Societies: not after 2.30pm Fri, weekends or Bank Holidays; book on (0724) 280444 Ext 852.
Catering: full facilities; banqueting etc at Normanby Hall and Country Park adjacent to course.
Hotels: Royal; Wortley House.

L65 North Shore
☎(0754) 763298, 761902 Fax
North Shore Rd, Skegness, Lincs PE25 1DN
1 mile N of town on seaward side of Ingoldmells Rd.
Links/parkland course.
18 holes, 6134 yards, S.S.S.71
Designed by James Braid.
Founded 1910
Visitors: welcome if member of recognised club with h/cap cert.
Green Fee: £15/round, £20/day WD; £20/round, £26/day WE & BH.
Societies: as for visitors, special package available.
Catering: normal hotel services. Snooker, tenpin bowls, banqueting.
Hotels: North Shore, golf breaks.

L66 **Nottingham City**
☎(0602) 278021, 272767
Pro/individual bookings, 276916
Sec/party bookings (am only)
Lawton Drive, Bulwell, Nottingham
NG6 8BL
2 miles off M1 at junction 26.
Municipal parkland course.
18 holes, 6120 yards, S.S.S.70
Founded 1910
Visitors: welcome weekdays and by
booking at weekends.
Green Fee: £8/day WD, £10/day WE.
Societies: welcome.
Catering: meals served.

L67 **Notts (Hollinwell)**
☎(0623) 753225, 753655 Fax
Hollinwell, Derby Rd,
Kirkby-in-Ashfield, Notts NG17 7QR
Leave M1 at junction 27, then 2 miles
N on A611.
Undulating heathland course.
18 holes Championship, 7020 yards,
S.S.S.74
Designed by Willie Park Jnr.
Founded 1887
Visitors: reserved for members
12am-1pm Mon/Tues, 12am-2pm
Wed/Thurs, and until 12.30pm Fri.
Green Fee: £33/round, £42/day.
Societies: by arrangement.
Catering: full facilities every day.
Hotels: Swallow; Pine Lodge.

L68 **Oakmere Park (Oxton)**
☎(0602) 653545, 655628 Fax
Oaks Lane, Oxton, Notts NG25 0RH
On A614 and A6097 8 miles NE of
Nottingham.
Parkland course.
18 holes, 6046 metres, S.S.S.72; 9
holes, 3193 metres, Par 37.
Designed by F. Pennink.
Founded 1974
Visitors: welcome but should make
reservation at weekends.
Green Fee: 18 hole course approx
£16 WD, £20 WE & BH; 9 hole course
£6 WD, £8 WE.
Societies: welcome 7 days; max
possible notice for weekends.
Catering: clubhouse bar, spike bar,
restaurant (resident chef).
Driving range.

L69 **Ormonde Fields
Country Club**
☎(0773) 742987 Pro, 570043 Sec
Nottingham Rd, Codnor, Ripley,
Derbys DE5 9RG
Off M1 at junction 26, take A610
towards Ripley for about 2 miles.

Undulating course.
18 holes, 6007 yards, S.S.S.69
Founded 1906
Visitors: welcome weekdays; by
arrangement with Sec weekends.
Green Fee: £10/round WD.
Societies: by arrangement.
Catering: full facilities.

L70 **Pastures**
☎(0332) 513921 extn 348
Pastures Hospital, Mickleover, Derby
DE3 5DQ
On A516 4 miles W of Derby.
Undulating meadowland course.
9 holes, 5005 yards, S.S.S.64
Designed by Frank Pennink.
Founded 1969
Visitors: with member only.
Green Fee: on application.
Societies: weekdays by special
arrangement.
Catering: for societies only.

L71 **RAF Waddington**
☎(0522) 720271 ext 955
Waddington, Lincoln, LN5 9NB
Airfield course.
18 holes, 5223 yards, S.S.S.69
Founded 1973
Visitors: only introduced by member.
Green Fee: apply for details.
Catering: limited bar facility.

L72 **Radcliffe-on-Trent**
☎(0602) 333000 Sec/Manager,
332396 Pro, 335771 Steward
Dewberry Lane, Cropwell Rd,
Radcliffe on Trent, Notts NG12 2JH
From Nottingham take A52 to
Grantham, right at 1st set of lights
after dual carriageway ends, 400
yards up Cropwell Rd on left.
Undulating parkland course.
18 holes, 6434 yards, S.S.S.71
Designed by F. Pennink.
Founded 1909
Visitors: weekdays except Tues,
h/cap cert must be produced.
Green Fee: £21 WD, £26 WE.
Societies: apply in writing or phone
Sec; Wed only.
Catering: bar, restaurant, snacks.
Hotels: Bridgford Lodge,
Nottingham.

L73 **Ramsdale Park Golf
Centre**
☎(0602) 655600, 654105 Fax
Oxton Rd, Calverton, Notts NG14 6NU.
NE Nottingham on the B6386 Oxton
to Calverton road.

Pay-as-you-Play parkland course.
18 holes, 6546 yards, S.S.S.71; 18
holes, 2844 yards, Par 3
Designed by Hawtree & Co.
Founded May 1992
Visitors: welcome
Green Fee: £11.50 (main course), £6
(Par 3 course).
Societies: Mon to Fri only
Catering: full facilities.
Driving range.

L74 **Retford**
☎(0777) 703733
Ordsall, Retford, Notts DN22 7VA
S off A620.
Woodland course.
18 holes, 5829 yards, S.S.S.70
Visitors: welcome weekdays, with
member at weekends.
Green Fee: £16/round, £20/day,
(£10 with member).
Catering: full meal facilities.

L75 **Ruddington Grange**
☎(0602) 846141, 24139 Club
Wilford Road, Ruddington,
Nottingham NG11 6NB
S of Nottingham via M1 junction 24,
A453, A52 Grantham road.
Parkland course.
18 holes, 6496 yards, S.S.S.71
Designed by Eddie McCausland,
David Johnson.
Founded 1988
Visitors: welcome with h/cap certs;
not Sat.
Green Fee: £20/round, £22/day WD,
£24/round, £26/day WE.
Societies: welcome, advance
bookings only.
Catering: bars, restaurant, function
rooms.
Practice ground, putting green.

L76 **Sandilands**
☎(0507) 441432, 441617
Sea Lane, Sandilands,
Sutton-on-Sea, Mablethorpe, Lincs
LN12 2RJ
4 miles S of Mablethorpe on A52
coast road, course runs next to sea
wall.
Seaside links course.
18 holes, 5995 yards, S.S.S.69
Founded 1901
Visitors: welcome any time.
Green Fee: £12/round, £18/day WD;
£18/round WE & BH.
Societies: on application.
Catering: bar meals at all times.
Hotels: Grange & Links, 3-day golf
breaks, societies welcome.

THE SHERWOOD FOREST GOLF CLUB LTD

EAKRING ROAD, MANSFIELD, NOTTS. NG18 3EW
Club House Telephone No. 23327

Secretary:	K. Hall	Tel: 0623 26689
Professional:	K. Hall	Tel: 0623 27403
Catering Manageress D. McCart		Tel: 0623 23327

Full catering service available with dining for up to 70 persons at one sitting. Course is heathland, set in the very heart of Robin Hood country, and was designed by James Braid. Yellow markers distance is 6,294 yds. SSS 71. White markers distance is 6,714 yds. SSS 73.

The Course is the venue for the
Midland region Qualifying Round for the Open Championship 1990 – 1996
Green Fees on application.
All applications to be made with the secretary.
Within a few miles of places of interest – such as the Major Oak (Robin Hood's Larder), Newstead Abbey, Thoresby Hall, Clumber Park, and 14 miles from the centre of Nottingham.

L77 Scunthorpe
☎(0724) 866561, 868972 Pro
Burringham Rd, Scunthorpe, S
Humberside DN17 2AB
On B1450, adjoining Mallard Hotel.
Parkland course.
18 holes, 6281 yards, S.S.S.71
Founded 1936
Visitors: Mon to Fri.
Green Fee: £20/round, £24/day.
Societies: Mon to Fri.
Catering: full facilities Mon to Fri.
Hotels: Royal.

L78 Seacroft
☎(0754) 763020
Drummond Rd, Skegness, Lincs
PE25 3AU
1 mile S of Skegness alongside road
to Gibraltar Road Bird Sanctuary.
Undulating seaside links course.
18 holes, 6490 yards, S.S.S.71
Founded 1895
Visitors: welcome from bona fide
club with h/cap.
Green Fee: £20/round, £28/day WD;
£25/round, £35/day WE.
Societies: as for visitors.
Catering: available daily except
Tues.
Hotels: Vine; Crown.

L79 Sherwood Forest
☎(0623) 26689 Sec, 27403 Pro,
23327 Club, 27403 Fax
Eakring Rd, Mansfield, Notts NG18
3EW
M1 junction 27, take Mansfield exit
from roundabout, left at T-junction,
left at next T-junction (5 miles), right
at next T-junction, right at next lights,
left at lights, right at 3rd
mini-roundabout, course two-thirds
mile on left.
Heathland course, Championship
standard.
18 holes, 6714 yards, S.S.S.73
Designed by H.S. Colt, redesigned by
James Braid.
Founded 1895
Visitors: must be members of golf
club with h/cap.
Green Fee: £30/round, £35/day WD;
£35/round WE.
Societies: Mon, Thurs, Fri.
Catering: full facilities daily.
Hotels: Pine Lodge; Midland;
Swallows.

L80 Shirland
☎(0773) 834935 Pro
Lower Delves, Shirland, Derbys DE5
6AU

1 mile N of Alfreton off A61; 3 miles
from M1 junction 28 via A38.
Tree-lined rolling parkland course
18 holes, 6072 yards, S.S.S.69
Founded 1976
Visitors: no restrictions weekdays,
book through Pro at weekends.
Green Fee: £15/round, £25/day WD;
£20/round WE.
Societies: welcome weekdays, book
through Pro.
Catering: full catering facilities
available.
Practice grounds, county standard
bowling green.

L81 Sickleholme
☎(0433) 651306
Saltergate Lane, Bamford, Sheffield
S30 2BH
On A625, 14 miles W of Sheffield,
near Marquis of Granby.
Hillside meadowland course.
18 holes, 6064 yards, S.S.S.69
Founded 1898
Visitors: welcome but not Wed am;
preferably phoned in advance.
Green Fee: on application
Societies: catered for on weekdays
by arrangement.
Catering: by arrangement.

Seacroft

For years, the temptation to get to Woodhall Spa blinded me to some of the other attractions of Lincolnshire's golf, notably the links of Seacroft which lie between Skegness and the nature reserve at Gibraltar Point. The British coastline is dotted with a profusion of courses with many qualities, although settings that are off the beaten track are denied the championship recognition of the Birkdales, Formbys and Muirfields.

However, remoteness is a characteristic to be cherished and at Seacroft it adds to the appeal of a course that typifies the virtues of seaside links.

From the clubhouse, doubts may be gained by the road and row of houses that line the opening holes, but very soon a firm impression is formed that the threat of out of bounds cannot be shirked by cowardly play to the left. Limiting factors make their appearance there, too.

A central spine of dunes divides the course at two levels and there is the added feature, one unique in my experience, of a huge host of thorn bushes that are punishing in more senses than one. The 3rd, blind from the back tee, is a short par 4 with a little pitch to an elevated green that it is unwise to miss on the right. But the 4th introduces us to a series of short holes that are first class, the 4th involving another elevated green and a tee shot that needs to be solidly hit to negotiate the hint of a valley in between.

After the 5th, where there is little fruitful option to hitting the fairway, the 6th offers the first significant change of direction but the 7th, 8th and 9th continue the journey to the furthest point from the clubhouse with sandhills offering the main hazards and providing a series of interesting shots. The second half begins with another beautifully, simple short hole, but it is the 225 yard 12th which heads towards the sea and introduces a stretch of 4 or 5 holes that are quite delightful both in the challenge and enjoyment they present and in giving us views of the sea. On a clear day, the outline of Hunstanton can be detected across the Wash, but the 13th demands the closest attention, a hole that can be approached in a number of different ways.

The green stands on a small plateau and is guarded by a big bunker in the face of the hill. It needs two of the best to get home and discretion is often the better part of valour. The more conservative way is to hit over a prominent ridge and launch a high pitch at the green.

Beyond the green is a marshy lagoon separating the course from the beach but the genuine seaside nature of the links is maintained by the 3rd par 3 in five holes and a drive over a hill at the 15th followed by a nasty second in a cross wind to a green standing back to back with the 3rd. All the attributes of a good dogleg are embraced by the 16th and the need for proper control is highlighted by the 17th and 18th which become more and more overlooked by houses.

It is no wonder that those who know Seacroft are lost in admiration of a challenge that has everything, including the essential power of enjoyment.

However, the last word must belong to Bernard Darwin who, writing in his famous book *The Golf Courses of the British Isles* reminded readers of the posters, familiar in the early years of the century, which proclaimed with more accuracy than is usual in such circumstances, "Skegness is so bracing".

In closing his chapter on East Anglia with a description of Seacroft, he lauded the fact that there was good turf and plenty of sand and the sea itself, although he added "we do not often see it. Neither do we see — and this is an unmixed blessing — the teeming swarms of trippers that come to Skegness to be braced".

L82 Sleaford

☎(0529) 488273
Willoughby Rd, South Rauceby,
Sleaford, Lincs NG34 8PL
Signposted off A153 Sleaford to
Grantham road, 2 miles W of
Sleaford.
Heathland course.
18 holes, 6443 yards, S.S.S.71
Designed by Tom Williamson.
Founded 1905
Visitors: welcome except winter
Sun.
Green Fee: £19 WD, £27 WE & BH;
reductions when playing with
member.
Societies: Mon-Fri by prior
arrangement.
Catering: full bar; meals and snacks
except Mon.
Hotels: Carre Arms.

L83 South Kyme

☎(0526) 861113
Skinners Lane, South Kyme, Lincoln
LN4 4AT
On B1395 off A17 and A153.
Fenland course.
18 holes, S.S.S.71
Designed by Graham Bradley.
Founded July 1990
Visitors: welcome.
Green Fee: £10 WD, £12 WE.
Societies: welcome booked in
advance.
Catering: bar and bar menu, hot
drinks and snacks all day; lunch and
dinner for larger parties by prior
arrangement.
Hotels: Golf, Petwood (Woodhall
Spa).

L84 Spalding

☎(0775) 680386 Sec, 680234 Club,
680474 Pro
Surfleet, Spalding, Lincs PE11 4EA
4 miles N of Spalding off A16; course
is approx 1 mile off A16, well
signposted.
Meadowland course.
18 holes, 6432 yards, S.S.S.71
Founded 1908
Visitors: welcome if members of
recognised clubs; h/cap cert
required unless accompanied by
member.
Green Fee: £20 WD (£10 with
member), £25 WE (£12 with
member).
Societies: welcome, Thurs only on
application.
Catering: full catering facilities
except Tues.
Extensive practice area.

L85 Stanedge

☎(0246) 566156
Walton Hay Farm, Stanedge,
Chesterfield, Derbys S45 0LW
5 miles SW of Chesterfield, at top
of long hill on A632, turn on to
B5057; club 300 yards W of Red
Lion Inn.
Undulating moorland course.
9 holes, 4867 yards, S.S.S.64
Founded 1931
Visitors: welcome weekdays am;
with member only afternoons,
weekends and Bank Holidays.
Green Fee: £15 (£7.50 with
member) WD; £15 WE & BH with
member only.
Societies: by prior arrangement
only.
Catering: provided for parties by
prior arrangement.
Hotels: The Chesterfield; Portland;
Glen Stuart; Olde House.

L86 Stanton-on-the-Wolds

☎(0602) 372044 Club, 372390 Pro,
372264 Steward
Stanton-on-the-Wolds, Keyworth,
Notts NG12 5BH
Off A606 at Blue Star Garage 8 miles
SE of Nottingham.
Meadowland course.
18 holes, 6437 yards, S.S.S.71
Designed by Tom Williamson.
Founded 1906
Visitors: weekdays if no
competitions in progress; weekends
and Bank Holidays with member
only.
Green Fee: £20/round/day; societies
£25/round/day.
Societies: welcome, write to Sec,
H.G. Gray FCA, 2 Golf Rd,
Stanton-on-the-Wolds, Notts NG12
5BH, or phone (0602) 372006.
Catering: available, ring Steward in
advance.
Hotels: Edwalton, Nottingham.

L87 Stoke Rochford

☎(047 683) 275
Stoke Rochford, Grantham, Lincs
Off A1 northbound carriageway 5
miles S of Grantham, entrance at
A.J.S. Service area.
Parkland course.
18 holes, 6251 yards, S.S.S.70
Designed by C. Turner.
Founded 1926
Visitors: welcome, not before
10.30am Sat or Sun unless
accompanied by member; contact
Pro before visiting.
Green Fee: on application.

Societies: catered for Mon, Tues and
Fri only.
Catering: lunches and evening
meals served upon request.
Snooker, pool.

L88 Sudbrook Moor

☎(0400) 50796 Pro, 50876
Catering/Enquiries
Carlton Scroop, Nr Grantham, Lincs
NG32 3AT
On A607 8 miles N of Grantham.
Parkland course.
9 holes, 4712 yards, S.S.S.63
Designed by Tim Hutton.
Founded 1986
Visitors: welcome.
Green Fee: £5/day WD, £7 WE & BH.
Societies: by arrangement.
Catering: coffee shop.
Practice ground.
Hotels: phone for details.

L89 Sutton Bridge

☎(0406) 350323, 351080 Pro
New Rd, Sutton Bridge, Spalding,
Lincs
On A17 10 miles W of Kings Lynn.
Parkland course.
9 holes, 5820 yards, S.S.S.68
Founded 1914
Visitors: weekdays only.
Green Fee: £15.
Catering: meals, sandwiches; not
Mon.

L90 Toft Hotel

☎(0778) 33616
Toft, Nr Bourne, Lincs PE10 0XX
6 miles N of Stamford on A6121.
Undulating parkland course with
water features.
18 holes, 6486 yards, S.S.S.71
Designed by Derek and Roger Fitton.
Founded 1988
Visitors: welcome; standard dress
etiquette; tees bookable 14 days in
advance.
Green Fee: on application.
Societies: welcome by arrangement.
Catering: full bar, bar snack and
restaurant facilities in adjacent hotel;
function room (120).
Hotels: Toft, weekend/bargain
breaks, reduced green fees for
residents.

L91 Trent Lock Golf Centre

☎(0602) 464398
Lock Lane, Sawley, Long Eaton,
Notts NG10 3DD

2 miles off M1 junction 25.
Parkland course.
9 holes, 2878 yards, S.S.S.68
Designed by E.W. McCausland.
Founded 1991
Visitors: welcome any day, must book at weekends.
Green Fee: £4.50 (9 holes), £8.50 (18 holes) WD; £8.50 (9 or 18 holes) WE.
Societies: welcome by prior arrangement.
Catering: bar snacks and restaurant, 11am to 10pm; private function room.
Driving range.

L92 **Wollaton Park**

☎(0602) 787574
Wollaton Park, Nottingham NG8 1BT
Parkland course.
18 holes, 6494 yards, S.S.S.71
Designed by T. Williamson.
Founded 1927
Visitors: welcome weekdays.
Green Fee: apply for details.
Societies: welcome Tues and Fri by arrangement.
Catering: daily except Mon.

L93 **Woodhall Spa**

☎(0526) 352511
The Broadway, Woodhall Spa, Lincs LN10 6PU
On B1191 6 miles SW of Horncastle, 18 miles SE of Lincoln, 18 miles NE of Sleaford.
Heathland course.
18 holes, 6907 yards, S.S.S.73
Designed by Col S.V. Hotchkin.
Founded 1905
Visitors: welcome all week by prior arrangement with Sec, max h/cap 20, ladies 30.
Green Fee: £24/round, £35/day WD; £28/round, £40/day WE & BH.
Societies: as for visitors.
Catering: full facilities 7 days.
Hotels: Golf; Petwood; Dower House; Eagle Lodge; Village Limits.

L94 **Woodthorpe Hall**

☎(0507) 450294
Woodthorpe, Alford, Lincs LN13 0DD
3.5 miles from Alford off B1371.
Parkland course.
18 holes, 4659 yards, S.S.S.63
Founded 1986
Visitors: welcome.

Green Fee: £9/round.
Societies: by prior arrangement with Sec on (0507) 463276.
Catering: available.
Fishing, snooker, bowls.
Hotels: self-catering accommodation at Woodthorpe Leisure Park.

L95 **Worksop**

☎(0909) 477731 Sec, 477732 Pro, 472696 Members
Windmill Lane, Worksop, Notts S80 2SQ
On SE of town, from new by-pass (A57) take A6005, follow local signposts for Sherwood Forest, turn immediately left into Windmill Lane.
Sandy heathland course.
18 holes, 6651 yards, S.S.S.73
Founded 1904
Visitors: welcome, telephone first.
Green Fee: £18.50/round, £26/day WD; £26/round WE & BH.
Societies: by arrangement, not weekends, Bank Holidays.
Catering: full, with notice.
Hotels: Van Dyk; Regancy; Aston Hall; Red Lion; Clumber Park.

M

LANCASHIRE, ISLE OF MAN, CUMBRIA

Lancashire encompasses the great chain of coastal courses between Liverpool and Southport that, for the championship status many possess, is as prolific a stretch as any in the world. West Lancashire is the most senior, the modern clubhouse conveniently served by Hall Road Station on the electric railway line that also gets a good view of Formby, Southport & Ainsdale, and Hillside. West Lancashire is noble seaside terrain although the rugged dimensions of the dunes grow a cubit or two as they approach Southport.

Royal Birkdale, scene of seven Opens, provides a succession of avenues between sandhills, its fairways possessing few of the eccentric humps and hollows which golfers either love or hate. Royal Birkdale's fame is very much post-war, its reputation fairly galloping after it had staged its first Open in 1954, but its neighbour, Hillside, has come even more recently to the distinction of hosting championships.

Jack Nicklaus made his professional debut in Britain there in 1962, but the course has undergone major change since then, the alterations enabling it to graduate to higher realms. It needs no stressing that Birkdale and Hillside constitute mighty days' golf and that Formby, more secluded, keeps them company. Hesketh and Southport & Ainsdale should also be included in select itineraries of the Southport area, the latter having staged two pre-war Ryder Cup matches — that in 1933 resulting in a rare home victory.

Of the Lancashire courses north of Southport, Royal Lytham & St Annes is a pillar of strength, a championship links renowned for the severity of its challenge. Although its visitors invariably retire battered and bruised, it does not stop them coming. Royal Lytham is a relentless test but the Lytham area has other notable attractions.

St Annes Old Links, next to Blackpool Airport, and Fairhaven, are demanding enough to have played host to qualifying rounds for the Open but there is plenty of variety in a part of the world where golf is as popular as black pudding. Knott End, near Fleetwood, Blackpool North Shore and Lytham Green Drive offer enjoyable detours, while Ormskirk and Pleasington stand out in Lancashire's heartland.

Castletown in the Isle of Man is only a short hop from Blackpool Airport, and the links and their lovely hotel only a short taxi ride from the terminal buildings at Ronaldsway, which are remarkably free of the unattractive bustle of bigger airports.

But the Isle of Man has other golfing temptations that may be more to the liking of those less anxious to grapple with such a stern task. Not the least of the scenic delights of the island are the distant views of the lakeland hills, conjuring up thoughts of fell walkers, poets, climbers and relaxation on a boat.

Golf is secondary in the minds of the majority of Cumbria's visitors but Seascale and Silloth occupy an important place as fine seaside courses both locally and nationally. Seascale is the more remote, a small town south of Whitehaven and Workington just off the road that makes a grand coastal sweep round the Lake District. Furness and Grange over Sands are worthy of a short detour, but Seascale is true links with more undulation than some.

Then it is on up past St Bees Head to the edge of the Solway Firth and Silloth on Solway which is an authentic championship setting in a town well known for its flour mill and the little harbour that serves it.

M1 Accrington & District
☎(0254) 232734
New Barn Farm, Devon Ave, West
End, Oswaldtwistle, Accrington,
Lancs BB5 4LS
On A679 5 miles from Blackburn.
Moorland course.
18 holes, 5954 yards, S.S.S.69
Designed by James Braid.
Founded 1893
Visitors: welcome at any time.
Green Fee: on application.
Societies: by arrangement.
Catering: full facilities.
Hotels: Kendal; Moat House.

M2 Allerton Municipal
☎(051) 428 1046
Allerton, Liverpool 18
From city centre on Allerton Rd.
Undulating parkland course.
9 holes, 1845 yards, S.S.S.34; 18
holes, 5494 yards, S.S.S.67
Visitors: welcome; times can be
booked for 18 hole course by phone
or in person.
Green Fee: on application.
Societies: on application.
Catering: snacks served.

M3 Alston Moor
☎(0434) 381675
The Hermitage, Alston, Cumbria CA9
3DB
1.75 miles from Alston on B6277 to
Middleton in Teesdale.
Parkland course.
10 holes, 6450 yards, S.S.S.66
Founded 1906
Visitors: welcome anytime.
Green Fee: £7 WD, £10 WE & BH.
Societies: any time by arrangement.
Catering: by prior arrangement.
Hotels: George & Dragon; Hillcrest;
Bluebell Inn; Nenthall.

M4 Appleby
☎(07683) 51432
Brackenber Moor, Appleby-in-
Westmorland, Cumbria CA16 6LP
2 miles E of Appleby on A66.
Moorland course.
18 holes, 5913 yards, S.S.S.68
Designed by Willie Fernie of Troon.
Founded 1903
Visitors: welcome at any time.
Green Fee: £12 WD, £16 WE & BH.
Societies: welcome at any time
subject to prior arrangement.
Catering: by arrangement.
Snooker.
Hotels: Tufton Arms; Royal Oak;
Appleby Manor; The Gate.

M5 Ashton & Lea
☎(0772) 726480, 735282
Tudor Ave, off Blackpool Rd, Lea,
Preston PR4 0XA
3 miles from Preston centre on
Blackpool road, turn opposite Pig and
Whistle.
Parkland course.
18 holes, 6289 yards, S.S.S.70
Designed by J. Steer.
Founded 1913
Visitors: phone (0772) 720374 for
tee reservations.
Green Fee: £20 WD, £24 WE & BH.
Societies: weekdays on application
to Sec.
Catering: full facilities daily.
Snooker.
Hotels: Crest; Tickled Trout; Travel
Inn.

M6 Ashton-in-Makerfield
☎(0942) 719330, 727267
Garswood Park, Liverpool Rd,
Ashton-in-Makerfield WN4 0YT
On A58, off M6 0.5 mile to course.
Parkland course.
18 holes, 6205 yards, S.S.S.70
Designed by F.W. Hawtree.
Founded 1902
Visitors: welcome weekdays except
Wed; with member at weekends.
Green Fee: on application.
Societies: Tues and Thurs.
Catering: meals except Mon.
Hotels: Cranberry.

M7 Ashton-under-Lyne
☎(061) 330 1537
Gorsey Way, Ashton-under-Lyne,
Lancs OL6 9HT
From Ashton take Mossley Rd, left at
Queens Rd, right at St Christophers
Rd.
Moorland course.
18 holes, 6209 yards, S.S.S.70
Founded 1913
Visitors: welcome if member of golf
club; Sat and Sun only with member.
Green Fee: apply for details.
Societies: by arrangement, not Wed
or weekends.
Catering: full facilities except Mon.
Snooker.
Hotels: York House; Birch Hall
(Oldham).

M8 Bacup
☎(0706) 873170
Maden Rd, Bacup, Lancs OL13 8HOff
A671, 7 miles N of Rochdale, 0.5 mile
from Bacup centre.
Meadowland course.

9 holes, 5652 yards, S.S.S.67
Founded 1911
Visitors: welcome weekdays, except
Mon, Tues, and at weekends after
competitions.
Green Fee: apply for details.
Societies: welcome weekdays
except Mon and Tues.
Catering: full facilities.
Snooker.

M9 Barrow
☎(0229) 825444, 832121 Pro
Rakesmoor Lane, Hawcoat,
Barrow-in-Furness, Cumbria LA14
4QB
Turn left to Hawcoat off Dalton
by-pass (opposite Scotts Paper Mill)
on entering boundary of Barrow.
Undulating meadowland course.
18 holes, 6209 yards, S.S.S.70
Founded 1922
Visitors: welcome, ladies day Fri.
Green Fee: £15 WD, £25 WE.
Societies: by arrangement.
Catering: by arrangement.
Hotels: Abbey House, Glen Garth;
Lisdoonie.

M10 Baxenden & District
☎(0254) 234555
Top-o'-the Meadow, Wooley Lane,
Baxenden, Nr Accrington, Lancs
Take Accrington exit from M65,
follow signs for Baxenden, course
signposted in village.
Moorland course.
9 holes, 5702 yards, S.S.S.68
Founded 1913
Visitors: welcome weekdays, with
member only weekends.
Green Fee: apply for details.
Societies: welcome weekdays by
arrangement.
Catering: bar and bar snacks, meals
if ordered in advance.

M11 Beacon Park
☎(0695) 622700
Beacon Lane, Dalton, Up Holland,
Wigan, Lancs WN8 7RU
Signposted from centre of Up Holland
on A577 and from A5209 near Parbold
– located on side of Ashurst Beacon
Hill overlooking Skelmersdale.
Public hilly parkland course.
18 holes, 5996 yards, S.S.S.69
Designed by Donald Steel.
Founded 1982
Visitors: welcome at any time.
Green Fee: apply for details.
Societies: welcome weekdays, by
arrangement weekends.

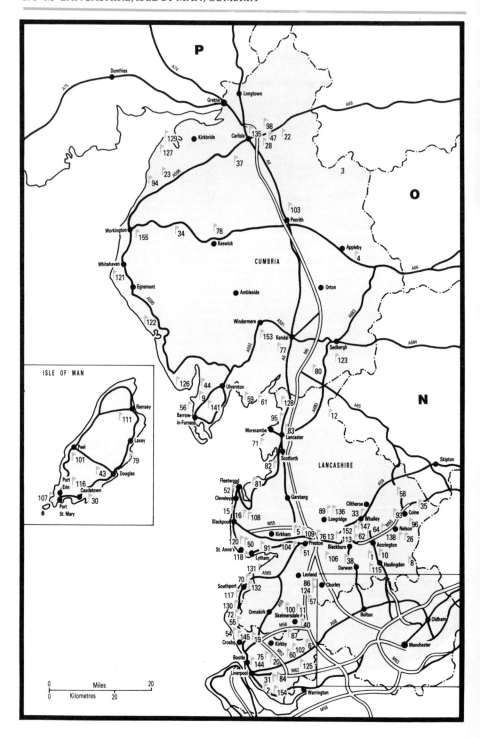

Catering: bar meals during bar hours; other meals by arrangement. Driving range.
Hotels: Balcony Farm, Skelmersdale.

M12 **Bentham**
☎(05242) 61018, 62455 Sec
Robin Lane, Bentham, Lancaster LA2 7AG
Half way between Lancaster and Settle on B6480, 13 miles E of M6 junction 34.
Undulating meadowland course.
9 holes, 5760 yards, S.S.S.69
Founded 1922
Visitors: welcome.
Green Fee: apply for details.
Societies: by arrangement.
Catering: snacks.
Hotels: Bridge Hotel (Ingleton); Post House (Lancaster).

M13 **Blackburn**
☎(0254) 51122 Sec/Club, 55942 Pro
Beardwood Brow, Blackburn, Lancs BB2 7AX
Easy access from M6, M61, M65; in W end of town off Revidge Rd, from Moat House Hotel on A677 turn left at lights, left at Dog Hotel.
Undulating meadowland course.
18 holes, 6140 yards, S.S.S.70
Founded 1894
Visitors: welcome weekdays (restricted Tues).
Green Fee: £19 (£7 with member) WD, £22 (£8 with member) WE & BH.

Societies: welcome; contact Sec for special terms.
Catering: daily except Mon.
Snooker.
Hotels: Moat House (Blackburn); Dunkenhalgh (Clayton-le-Moors).

M14 **Blackley**
☎(061) 654 7770 Sec, 643 2980 Club
Victoria Ave East, Blackley, Manchester M9 6HW
5 miles N of city centre.
Parkland course.
18 holes, 6237 yards, S.S.S.70
Founded 1907
Visitors: Mon, Tues, Wed, Fri; Thurs, weekends and Bank Holidays with member only.
Green Fee: £19.
Societies: Mon-Fri, special all-in fee inc bar lunch and evening meal £29.
Catering: all types available.
Hotels: Bower (Chadderton).

M15 **Blackpool North Shore**
☎(0253) 52054 Sec, 54640 Pro, 51017 bar/catering
Devonshire Rd, Blackpool FY2 0RD
N of town centre 0.5 mile from Promenade.
Undulating parkland course.
18 holes, 6400 yards, S.S.S.71
Founded 1906
Visitors: restricted Thurs and Sun; not Sat.
Green Fee: £21.

Societies: Mon, Tues, Wed, Fri; special package rates.
Catering: bar and full catering.
Snooker.
Hotels: Sheraton; Doric.

M16 **Blackpool Stanley Park**
☎(0253) 33960
North Park Drive, Blackpool, Lancs FY3 8LS
1.5 miles E of centre of Blackpool.
Parkland course.
18 holes, 6060 yards, S.S.S.69
Designed by Dr Mackenzie.
Founded 1926
Visitors: welcome anytime.
Green Fee: apply for details.
Societies: welcome weekdays.
Catering: everyday except Tues.

M17 **Bolton**
☎(0204) 843067
Lostock Park, Chorley New Rd, Bolton BL6 4AJ
Leave M61 at exit 6, off main road midway between Bolton and Horwich.
Parkland course.
18 holes, 6215 yards, S.S.S.70
Founded 1891
Visitors: weekdays except Tues.
Green Fee: £26 Mon, Thurs, Fri; £30 Wed, Sat, Sun, BH.
Societies: Thurs.
Catering: all day.
Hotels: Crest.

M18 **Bolton Old Links**
☎(0204) 842307 Office am, 840050 Club, 843089 Pro
Chorley Old Rd, Bolton BL1 5SU
On B6226 just N of A58 from M61 junction 5.
Moorland course.
18 holes, 6406 yards, S.S.S.72
Designed by Dr A. Mackenzie.
Founded 1891
Visitors: welcome except competition days.
Green Fee: £25 WD, £30 WE & BH.
Societies: by prior arrangement on weekdays.
Catering: daily except Mon.
Snooker.
Hotels: Crest; Pack Horse; Last Drop; Bolton Moat House.

M19 **Bootle**
☎(051) 928 6196, 928 1371 Bookings
Dunnings Bridge Rd, Bootle, Merseyside L30 2PP

A565, 5 miles from Liverpool. Municipal seaside links course. 18 holes, 6362 yards, S.S.S.70 Designed by F. Stephens. Founded 1934
Visitors: welcome.
Green Fee: on application.
Societies: by arrangement.
Catering: meals served.
Hotels: Park.

M20 **Bowring**
☎(051) 489 1901
Bowring Park Golf Course, Roby Rd, Huyton, Liverpool L36 4HD
6 miles N of Liverpool city centre. Municipal parkland course.
9 holes, 5651 yards, S.S.S.66
Founded c. 1911
Visitors: welcome, 8am-5pm winter, 8am-9.30pm summer.
Green Fee: £4/round.
Societies: book in advance.
Catering: snacks.

M21 **Brackley**
☎(061) 790 6076
Bullows Rd, Little Hulton, Worsley, Manchester M38 9TR
9 miles from Manchester on A6, turn right at White Lion Hotel into Highfield Rd, left into Captain Fold Rd, left into Bullows Rd.
Parkland course.
9 holes, 3003 yards, S.S.S.69
Founded 1976
Visitors: welcome.
Green Fee: £3/round.

M22 **Brampton**
☎(06977) 2255 Clubhouse, 2000 Pro
Brampton, Cumbria CA8 1HN
1.75 miles from Brampton on B6413 Castle Carrock road.
Moorland course.
18 holes, 6420 yards, S.S.S.71
Designed by James Braid.
Founded 1907
Visitors: welcome; standard tee bookings 9.30-10.30am Mon, Wed and Thurs.
Green Fee: £16 WD, £20 WE & BH.
Societies: by arrangement weekdays; limited at weekends.

Catering: full bar and catering. Snooker.
Hotels: reduced green fees offered by numerous local hotels and guest houses; details available on request.

M23 **Brayton Park Golf Course**
☎(069 73) 20840
Brayton, Aspatria, Carlisle, Cumbria CA5 3TD
Off A596, W of Carlisle.
Parkland course.
9 holes, 2521 yards, Par 32
Founded 1978
Visitors: welcome, no restrictions.
Green Fee: £5 (9 holes), £7 (18 holes) WD; £6/£8 WE.
Societies: by prior booking.
Catering: full facilities.
Driving range.
Hotels: Kelsey (Mealsgate); Wheyrigg (Abbeytown).

M24 **Breightmet**
☎(0204) 27381 Sec
Red Bridge, Ainsworth, Bolton, Lancs BL2 5PA
From Bolton 3 miles on main road to Bury and turn left to Red Bridge.
Parkland course.
9 holes, 6448 yards, S.S.S.71
Designed by Alliss & Thomas.
Founded 1911
Visitors: weekdays except Wed.
Green Fee: £15 WD, £18 WE & BH (£8 with member WD, £10 WE & BH).
Societies: welcome Tues, Thurs, Fri.
Catering: every day except Mon. Snooker.
Hotels: Pack Horse.

M25 **Brookdale**
☎(061) 681 4534 or 681 2655
Ashbridge", Woodhouses, Failsworth, Manchester M35 9W5
miles N of Manchester.
Parkland, meadowland course.
18 holes, 6040 yards, S.S.S.68
Founded 1962
Visitors: welcome.
Green Fee: apply for details.
Societies: welcome by arrangement with Sec; packages can be arranged.
Catering: daily except Mon.

M26 **Burnley**
☎(0282) 421045
Glen View, Burnley BB11 3RW
Off A56 to Glen View Rd, after 300 yards turn right.
Moorland/meadowland course.
18 holes, 5900 yards, S.S.S.69
Founded 1905
Visitors: weekdays and Sun; limited Sat.
Green Fee: £18/day WD, £25/day WE & BH.
Societies: weekdays, Sun.
Catering: snacks and full meals except Mon and Wed pm.
Hotels: Kierby; Rosehill House; Oaks.

M27 **Bury**
☎(061) 766 4897, 766 2213 Pro shop
Unsworth Hall, Blackford Bridge, Bury BL9 9TJ
On A56 7 miles N of Manchester.
Undulating moorland course.
18 holes, 5961 yards, S.S.S.69
Founded 1890
Visitors: welcome with reservation; h/cap cert required.
Green Fee: £20 WD.
Societies: catered for Wed, Thurs and Fri.
Catering: available daily except Mon.
Hotels: Red Hall; Village Leisure.

M28 **Carlisle**
☎(0228) 513303
Aglionby, Carlisle CA4 8AG
2 miles E of Carlisle, leave M6 at exit 43 and take A69 for about 0.75 mile.
Parkland course.
18 holes, 6278 yards, S.S.S.70
Designed by Tom Simpson, Mackenzie Ross and (latterly) Frank Pennink.
Founded 1909
Visitors: welcome, advisable to check availability.
Green Fee: £20/round, £27.50/day.
Societies: Mon, Wed and Fri; party rates for 12 or more.
Catering: meals and snacks served daily.
Hotels: Queens Arms; Bridge; Kilorran; Cumbria Park.

THE EDEN GOLF COURSE
Near Crosby-on-Eden, Carlisle, Cumbria
Telephone (0228) 573003 Fax (0228) 818435

Situated alongside the River Eden and with magnificent views of the Pennines this 18 hole championship course offers a wonderful challenge to the most discerning golfer.

The Golf Professional Phil Harrison offers advice on equipment as well as coaching for all standards in the 16 bay floodlit Driving Range.

Catering of the highest standard is available in our new Clubhouse and Golf societies are welcome. Residential packages can easily be arranged to suit your requirements at two or three excellent local country hotels.

Please call for further details or to make reservations.

M29 Castle Hawk
☎(0706) 40841
Heywood Rd, Castledon, Rochdale
Leave Rochdale on Castledon road, in Castledon turn right directly before railway station, follow until reach Heywood Rd (dirt track).
Undulating parkland/meadowland course.
18 holes, 3158 yards, S.S.S.65; 9 holes, 5398 yards, S.S.S.68
Designed by T. Wilson.
Founded 1965
Visitors: welcome.
Green Fee: on application.
Societies: welcome.
Catering: snacks and lunches available; evening meals by arrangement.

M30 Castletown
☎(0624) 822201
Fort Island, Castletown, Isle of Man
1.5 miles E of Castletown.
Seaside course.
18 holes, 6804 yards, S.S.S.73
Designed by Mackenzie Ross.
Founded 1 June 1892
Visitors: welcome.
Green Fee: apply for details.
Societies: by arrangement.
Catering: bar snacks served all day; full à la carte lunch and dinner.
Snooker, indoor swimming pool, sauna, solarium.
Hotels: Castletown Golf Links; DBB/Golf & flight packages available.

M31 Childwall
☎(051) 487 0654
Naylor's Rd, Liverpool L27 2YB
2 miles M62 exit 6, 5 miles from Liverpool city centre.
Parkland course.
18 holes, 6025 yards, S.S.S.71
Designed by James Braid.
Founded 1922
Visitors: 9.45am and 2pm, Mon, Wed, Thurs, Fri.

Green Fee: £25 WD, £35 WE (approx).
Societies: as for visitors (not weekends).
Catering: bars and restaurant. Snooker.
Hotels: Logwood Mill; Derby Lodge.

M32 Chorley
☎(0257) 480263
Hall o' th'Hill, Heath Charnock, Nr Chorley, Lancs PR6 9HX
On A673 100 yards S of junction with A6 at Skew Bridge traffic lights.
Heathland course.
18 holes, 6277 yards, S.S.S.70
Designed by J.A. Steer.
Founded 1898
Visitors: welcome by prior arrangement with Sec, Tues-Fri only (not Bank Holidays).
Green Fee: £25.
Societies: as for visitors.
Catering: full bar and restaurant facilities; societies by arrangement.
Snooker, pool.
Hotels: Parkville; Hartwood Hall; Gladmar.

M33 Clitheroe
☎(0200) 22618 Club, 22292 Sec, 24242 Pro
Whalley Rd, Pendleton, Clitheroe BB7 1PP
Off A59 2 miles S of Clitheroe.
Undulating parkland course.
18 holes, 6311 yards, S.S.S.71
Designed by James Braid.
Founded 1891
Visitors: welcome subject to competition days on Sat and Thurs.
Green Fee: £25 WD, £30 WE & BH.
Societies: welcome by arrangement; max 48 Mon, Tues, Wed; max 24 Thurs, Fri, Sun (not Sat).
Catering: bar and restaurant facilities.
Hotels: Post House; Swan and Royal; Brooklyn GH; Stirk House.

M34 Cockermouth
☎(07687) 76223, (0900) 822650 Sec (Home)
Embleton, Cockermouth, Cumbria CA13 9SG
4 miles E of Cockermouth.
Fell land course.
18 holes, 5496 yards, S.S.S.67
Designed by James Braid.
Founded 1896
Visitors: weekdays unrestricted before 5pm except Wed; not Sun before 11am and 2-3.15pm.
Green Fee: £9/day WD, £15 WE & BH.
Societies: apply to Sec.
Catering: snacks and meals by arrangement with Stewardess.
Snooker.
Hotels: Armathwaite Hall; Globe.

M35 Colne
☎(0282) 863391
Law Farm, Skipton Old Rd, Colne, Lancs BB8 7EB
Leave end of M65, straight on 0.75 mile to roundabout, take small road in left hand corner signposted Lothersdale; club at top of hill.
Moorland course.
9 holes, 5961 yards, S.S.S.69
Founded 1901
Visitors: welcome except competition days; 2 balls only Thurs; no parties weekends April-Oct; normal dress and equipment requirements.
Green Fee: £12 WD, £16 WE.
Societies: by appointment.
Catering: snacks or full meals; parties (to 100) by negotiation with Steward.
Snooker tables.

M36 Crompton & Royton
☎(061) 624 2154
Highbarn, Royton, Oldham, Lancs OL2 6RW
Off A627 at Royton centre.

Castletown, Isle of Man

When the weather is fine, the greens holding and there is no wind, seaside links often present fewer problems than other types of course; but the moment the wind stirs it is another matter.

Tales of the 1979 P.G.A. Cup match at Castletown in the Isle of Man centred largely on days of sunshine, the ball running a mile, and agreement that it was an idyllic spot. My baptism was a little more severe, a near gale springing up overnight and rain slanting in from the Irish Sea. The clear outline of mountain peaks disappeared and there was a remoteness, almost a loneliness, on the little peninsula. But not even a princely soaking could dampen my admiration. Castletown's position as one of the great courses of the British Isles is undoubted.

Its modern version owes everything to Mackenzie Ross whose restoration after the war was similar to the miracle he wrought at Turnberry. Good driving is essential. On such as the 7th and 8th, the fairway is the only place to be; yet the line from the championship tees involves quite a carry.

Castletown's hazards are all natural — gorse, bracken, rough, rocks and a beach which gives the course more coastal frontage than perhaps any other in the world. Apart from a clump of forlorn palms behind the 8th green, and some planting to mask the wall behind the 4th there isn't a tree to be seen. Though the golfer has nothing to shield him, there is nothing to obscure the magnificent array of views either; the sea, two great sweeps of bay, the landmark of the castle and, on a good day, the Cumbrian Hills.

In days gone by, it was the residence of the Earl of Derby who, as Lord of Man, started the Derby at Castletown prior to taking it to Epsom. The 10th was the actual site, the hole not surprisingly assuming the name 'Racecourse'.

Castletown deserves undivided attention, although the start is no indication of what lies ahead. The 1st is a short, uphill par 4, one yard, in fact, over the par 3 limit, and the 2nd a somewhat plain two

shotter. It is when you turn away down the long 5th, a dogleg round the corner of a stone wall, with a second shot (or third or fourth) between a large mound and an old pill box, that the course really begins.

The 5th, not quite such a good par 5 as the 3rd, sandwiches the 4th where the drive must be left to obtain the correct angle to negotiate the slope of the green and to miss the guardian bunkers on the right. Castletown's short holes make a wonderful set, the 6th, the shortest of them, providing an inviting shot even if the green is encircled by trouble. The same applies to the drive at the 7th and the second shot to a green typical of Mackenzie Ross's imaginative designs.

The 8th is no easier. The fairway may present a nice target at a lower level but it is also alarmingly narrow and the road is only a thin strip separating errant drives from the beach on which balls, pebbles and boulders are indistinguishable. The drive at the 9th must be aimed on the outline of King William's College, a fortress of Manx stone. And at what may have been the home turn in the first Derby down by the 10th green, Castletown Bay hoves in sight. There is no let-up.

At the delightful short 11th and the next two par 4s, it is all too simple to let a tee shot drift to the right and, if the 14th is a shade less of a threat in this regard, the tee marker tells the bad news that it is 468 yards. On the 15th, a stone wall denotes out of bounds and the contouring of the greens foil those playing too safe to the left; but the best is yet to come — notably the 17th with its gaping gorge in front of the tee and resplendent rocks to the right. The 18th is a challenging finish, set against the square form of the welcoming Links Hotel.

Those who originally spied out the land knew what they were doing; but a question must be asked of the island's emblem of the Three Legs of Man and its motto 'whichever way you throw me, I shall stand'. Did they ever experiment on the championship tee at the 17th with a gale off the sea?

Moorland course.
18 holes, 6222 yards, S.S.S.70
Founded 1908
Visitors: welcome.
Green Fee: £24 (£10 with member)
WD, £30 (£10 with member) WE &
BH.
Societies: welcome by arrangement,
package deals available.
Hotels: Avant, Periquito (Oldham).

M37 **Dalston Hall**
☎(0228) 710165
Dalston, Nr Carlisle, Cumbria CA5
7JX
From M6 junction 42 follow signs for
Dalston, through village, course 0.5
mile on right.
Parkland course.
9 holes, 5294 yards, S.S.S.67
Designed by David Pearson.
Founded May 1990
Visitors: tee booking required at
weekends and after 4pm weekdays.
Green Fee: £5 (9 holes), £8 (18
holes) WD; £6 (9 holes), £10 (18
holes) WE.
Societies: throughout the season,
booking required.
Catering: bar and restaurant.
Fly fishing.
Hotels: Dalston Hall caravan park,
tourers and tents welcome.

M38 **Darwen**
☎(0254) 704367 Sec, 701287 Club,
776370 Pro
Winter Hill, Darwen, Lancs BB3 0LB
1.5 miles from Darwen town centre,
off A666 Bolton-Blackburn road.
Moorland course.
18 holes, 5752 yards, S.S.S.68
Founded Sept 1893
Visitors: welcome weekdays and
with advance bookings at weekends.
Green Fee: £14 (£7 with member)
WD, £20 (£10 with member) WE.
Societies: catered for except Mon,
Tues, Sat.
Catering: full, except Mon.
Hotels: Red House Motel; Whitehall
Country Club.

M39 **Davyhulme Park**
☎(061) 748 2856 Club, 748 2260
Sec/bookings, 748 3931 Pro
Gleneagles Rd, Davyhulme, Urmston,
Manchester M41 8SA
8 miles S of Manchester, adjacent to
Trafford Hospital, Moorside Rd,
Davyhulme.
Parkland course.
18 holes, 6237 yards, S.S.S.70

Founded 1910
Visitors: welcome except
competition days.
Green Fee: on application.
Societies: Mon, Tues, Thurs.
Catering: all week.
Snooker.

M40 **Dean Wood**
☎(0695) 622219
Lafford Lane, Up Holland,
Skelmersdale, Lancs WN8 0QZ
M6 exit 26, 1.5 miles on A577 to Up
Holland.
Undulating parkland course.
18 holes, 6137 yards, S.S.S.70
Designed by James Braid.
Founded 1922
Visitors: welcome weekdays,
preferably by arrangement;
weekends by introduction.
Green Fee: £24 WD, £30 WE & BH.
Societies: weekdays only by
arrangement.
Catering: daily. Snooker.
Hotels: Holland Hall.

M41 **Deane**
☎(0204) 651808 Sec, 61944 Club
and Pro
Broadford Rd, Bolton, Lancs BL3 4NB
M61 exit 5, 1 mile towards town
centre, Dealey Rd on left leads
directly to club.
Undulating parkland course.
18 holes, 5595 yards, S.S.S.67
Founded 1906
Visitors: members of other clubs
only unless playing with member.
Green Fee: £18/day WD, £22.50/day
WE & BH.
Societies: Tues, Wed, Fri.
Catering: full facilities except Mon.
Hotels: Crest; Pack Horse; Moat
House.

M42 **Denton**
☎(061) 336 3218 Hon Sec, 336
2070 Pro
Manchester Rd, Denton, Manchester
M34 2NU
A57, 5 miles SE of Manchester; also
M66 Denton roundabout from
Stockport.
Parkland course.
18 holes, 6541 yards, S.S.S.71
Founded May 1909
Visitors: welcome weekdays and at
weekends with member.
Green Fee: on application.
Societies: catered for Mon, Wed,
Thurs and Fri; book through Sec.
Catering: lunch served except Mon.

M43 **Douglas**
☎(0624) 675952
Pulrose Rd, Douglas, Isle of Man
1 mile from Douglas town centre,
clubhouse situated near to large
cooling tower for Electricity Dept
Power Station.
Municipal parkland course.
18 holes, 6080 yards, S.S.S.69
Designed by Dr Mackenzie.
Founded 1927
Visitors: welcome.
Green Fee: on application.
Societies: welcome.
Catering: meals and snacks served
11am-11pm from May to end Sept.

M44 **Dunnerholme**
☎(0229) 62675
Duddon Rd, Askam-in-Furness,
Cumbria LA16 7AW
A590 to Askam, turn left over railway
line into Duddin Rd, down towards
seashore over cattle grid on right.
Links course.
10 holes, 6181 yards, S.S.S.69
Founded 1905
Visitors: welcome but not Sun until
after 4.30pm.
Green Fee: apply for details.
Societies: welcome almost any time
if telephoned in advance.
Catering: facilities available.
Pool.
Hotels: Railway; White Water;
Clarence; Wellington; Abbey House.

M45 **Dunscar**
☎(0204) 303321 Club, 301090 Sec,
592992 Pro
Longworth Lane, Bromley Cross,
Bolton BL7 9QY
N of Bolton about 2 miles off A666
Blackburn road, course signed to left
at Dunscar Bridge.
Parkland/moorland course.
18 holes, 6085 yards, S.S.S.70
Founded 1908
Visitors: welcome, steward's day off
Mon; weekends by special
arrangement.
Green Fee: £20 WD, £30 WE; (£10
with member).
Societies: details from Sec.
Catering: lunch, dinner except Mon.
Hotels: Last Drop; Egerton House;
Moat House.

M46 **Duxbury Park**
☎(0257) 268 5380
Duxbury Park, Chorley, Lancs
1.5 miles S of Chorley off A6, 200
yards along A5106 Chorley-Wigan rd.

Municipal parkland course.
18 holes, 6390 yards, S.S.S.70
Founded 1970
Visitors: municipal course, booking accepted by phone.
Green Fee: £6.25 WD, £8.50 WE.
Societies: booked in writing, not Sat or Sun.
Catering: separate facilities from club.
Hotels: Hartwood Hall; Kilhey Court.

M47 **Eden**
☎(0228) 573003, 818435 Fax
Crosby-on-Eden, Carlisle, Cumbria CA6 4RA
2 miles E of Carlisle, 3 miles from M6; full directions from Pro shop.
Parkland course.
18 holes, 6973 yards, S.S.S.72
Designed by E. MacCauslin.
Founded June 1992
Visitors: welcome.
Green Fee: £15 WD, £20 WE.
Societies: welcome.
Catering: full facilities.
Driving range.

M48 **Ellesmere**
☎(061) 790 2122 Club, 790 8591 Pro
Old Clough Lane, Worsley, Manchester M28 5HZ
5 miles W of Manchester, on A580, adjacent to junction 14 on M62.
Undulating parkland course.
18 holes, 5954 yards, S.S.S.69
Founded 1913
Visitors: members of recognised club welcome by arrangement with Pro, except during club competitions and Bank Holidays.
Green Fee: apply for details.
Societies: catered for weekdays by prior arrangement; apply in writing to Hon Sec.
Catering: available at all times by prior arrangement with Steward's wife.

M49 **Fairfield Golf & Sailing Club**
☎(061) 370 1641, 370 2292 Pro
Booth Rd, Audenshaw, Manchester M34 5GA
A635 6 miles from city centre.
Parkland course.
18 holes, 5654 yards, S.S.S.68
Founded 1892
Visitors: welcome weekdays; club competitions Wed pm, Thurs and weekends am.
Green Fee: £16 WD, £22 WE.

Societies: by arrangement, Tues preferred; not Wed, Thurs, weekends.
Catering: full, by arrangement.
Hotels: Village (Hyde).

M50 **Fairhaven**
☎(0253) 736976
Lytham Hall Park, Ansdell, Lytham-St-Annes FY8 4JU
On B5261 2 miles from Lytham, next to Fylde Rugby Ground.
Semi-links course.
18 holes, 6883 yards, S.S.S.73
Designed by James Steer & James Braid.
Founded 1895
Visitors: welcome by arrangement.
Green Fee: on application.
Societies: by arrangement.
Catering: meals served except Mon (sandwiches available from bar).
Snooker, card room, banqueting.
Hotels: Clifton Arms; Grand; Dalmeney; Fearnlea.

M51 **Fishwick Hall**
☎(0772) 798300, 795870 Pro shop
Glenluce Drive, Farringdon Park, Preston, Lancs PR1 5TD
From M6 junction 31 take A59 towards Preston, past Tickled Trout, Glenluce Drive is 1st left at top of hill.
Meadowland/parkland course.
18 holes, 6092 yards, S.S.S.69
Founded 1912
Visitors: welcome.
Green Fee: £20 WD, £25 WE & BH; reduction Nov-Feb and with member.
Societies: by arrangement weekdays; also some weekends.
Catering: full facilities.
Hotels: Tickled Trout Motel; Crest.

M52 **Fleetwood**
☎(0253) 873661 Pro and Catering, 773573 Sec
Princes Way, Fleetwood, Lancs FY7 8AF
On A587, 7 miles N of Blackpool.
Links course alongside beach.
18 holes, 6723 yards, S.S.S.71
Designed by Edwin Steer.
Founded 1932
Visitors: welcome any day, h/cap cert required.
Green Fee: £20 WD, £25 WE.
Societies: weekdays; weekends by special arrangement.
Catering: bar 11.30am-11pm (restricted Sun), catering 7 days.
Snooker.
Hotels: Boston; North Euston; Briar Dene (Thornton Cleveleys).

M53 **Flixton**
☎(061) 748 2116 Club, 746 7160 Pro, 748 7545 Catering/Soc bookings
Church Rd, Flixton, Urmston, Manchester M41 6EP
0.5 mile from Flixton village on B5213.
Meadowland course.
9 holes, 6410 yards, S.S.S.71
Founded 1896
Visitors: welcome weekdays except Wed, weekends with member only.
Green Fee: £17.50/day.
Societies: by arrangement weekdays except Wed.
Catering: bar snacks available; full meals by arrangement.
Snooker.

M54 **Formby**
☎(07048) 72164
Golf Rd, Formby, Liverpool L37 1LQ
1 mile W of A565, adjacent to Freshfield station.
Links course.
18 holes, 6701 yards, S.S.S.73
Designed by Willie Park.
Founded 1884
Visitors: visitors by arrangement with Sec; not before 9.30am; some extra restrictions on Wed/Sat/Sun.
Green Fee: £45.
Societies: Tues, Thurs, Fri.
Catering: lunches except Mon.
Hotels: Tree Tops.

M55 **Formby Ladies**
☎(07048) 874127 club, 873493 Sec
Golf Rd, Formby, Liverpool L37 1YH
6 miles S of Southport off A565.
Seaside course.
18 holes, 5374 yards, S.S.S.71
Founded 1896
Visitors: welcome, ring first.
Green Fee: £25 WD, £31 WE.
Societies: by arrangement.
Catering: bar snacks and salads.
Hotels: Prince of Wales; Royal Clifton; Scarisbrick; Bold.

M56 **Furness**
☎(0229) 471232
Central Drive, Walney Island, Barrow-in-Furness, Cumbria LA14 3LN
A590 to Barrow, towards Walney Island, over bridge, through lights, 0.5 mile on right.
Seaside links course.
18 holes, 6363 yards, S.S.S.71
Founded 1872
Visitors: welcome, h/cap cert required; parties booked in advance.

Green Fee: £15/day (£10 with member).
Societies: advance booking; not competition days.
Catering: bar meals available, Sun lunch and evening dinner.
Snooker, darts.
Hotels: White House; Abbey House.

M57 Gathurst

☎(025 75) 2861
Miles Lane, Shevington, Wigan WN6 8EW
1 mile S of M6 junction 27, 0.25 mile W of Shevington village centre.
Meadowland course.
9 holes, 6308 yards, S.S.S.70
Founded 1913
Visitors: Mon, Tues, Thurs and Fri.
Green Fee: £20/day.
Societies: by arrangement.
Catering: lunch served daily except Mon, Tues.
Hotels: Lindley (Parbold); The Beeches (Standish).

M58 Ghyll

☎(0282) 842466 (no booking necessary unless more than 8 people)
Ghyll Brow, Barnoldswick, Colne, Lancs BB8 6JQ
M65 then A56 to Thornton-in-Craven, turn left on B6252, 1 mile on left.
Scenic parkland course.
9 holes (11 from 1994), 5796 yards, S.S.S.68
Founded 1907
Visitors: not Tues am, not Fri after 4.30pm, not Sun; h/cap certificates not required.
Green Fee: £14 (£7 with member) WD & BH, £16 (£12 with member) WE.
Societies: welcome at same times as visitors, £14/day per person; parties above 8 ring Sec.
Catering: bar (evenings only), catering by arrangement.
Hotels: Stirk House (Gisburn); Tempest (Elslack).

M59 Grange Fell

☎(05395) 32536
Fell Rd, Grange-over-Sands, Cumbria LA11 6HB
On main road to Cartmel from Grange at top of the hill.
Hillside course with panoramic Lakeland views.
9 holes, 4826 metres, S.S.S.66
Founded 1952

Visitors: welcome; closed most Sun in the season.
Green Fee: £10 WD, £15 WE & BH.
Hotels: Grange; Netherwood; Cumbria Grand.

M60 Grange Park

☎(0744) 26318
Prescot Rd, St Helens, Merseyside WA10 3AD
On A58 1 mile from town centre towards Prescot.
Parkland course.
18 holes, 6429 yards, S.S.S.71
Founded 1891
Visitors: welcome weekdays (Ladies Day Tues), by arrangement weekends.
Green Fee: £21 WD, £26 WE.
Societies: Mon, Wed, Thur, Fri.
Catering: full restaurant facilities.
Hotels: Post House; Chalon Court; Haydock Thistle.

M61 Grange-over-Sands

☎(05395) 33180, 33754 Sec, 35937 Pro
Meathop Rd, Grange-over-Sands, Cumbria LA11 6QX
Leave A590 at roundabout signposted Grange, course on left just before entering Grange.
Flat parkland course.
18 holes, 5938 yards, S.S.S.69
Founded 1921
Visitors: welcome at any time (Thurs Ladies day).
Green Fee: £15/round, £20/day WD; £20/round, £25/day WE & BH.
Societies: by arrangement weekdays and weekends.
Catering: except Tues.
Hotels: Grange; Cumbria Grand; Berners Close; Netherwood.

M62 Great Harwood

☎(0254) 884391
Harwood Bar, Great Harwood, Lancs BB6 7TE
Between Blackburn and Burnley, off A680 Accrington-Whalley road.
Parkland course.
9 holes, 6140 yards, S.S.S.71
Founded 1896 (1928 present site)
Visitors: welcome any time except competition days; must be member of recognised club.
Green Fee: apply for details.
Societies: on application.
Catering: bar and restaurant facilities except Mon.
Snooker.
Hotels: Duncan House.

M63 Great Lever & Farnworth

☎(0204) 656137 Sec, 656650 Pro
Lever Edge Lane, Bolton BL3 3EN
1.5 miles from town centre.
Meadowland course.
18 holes, 5958 yards, S.S.S.69
Founded 1917
Visitors: welcome weekdays.
Green Fee: £15 (£6 with member) WD; £25 (£10 with member) WE & BH.
Societies: weekdays by prior arrangement.
Catering: lunch except Mon.
Hotels: Crest (Bolton).

M64 Green Haworth

☎(0254) 237580
Green Haworth, Accrington, Lancs BB5 3SL
From Accrington town centre take main road to Blackburn, turn left on Willows Lane, follow road for 2 to 3 miles, sign just past Red Lion Hotel.
Moorland course.
9 holes, 5470 yards, S.S.S.67
Founded 1914
Visitors: welcome weekdays; Sat with reservation.
Green Fee: apply for details.
Societies: catered for.
Catering: by arrangement.
Hotels: Moat House (Blackburn).

M65 Greenmount

☎(0204 88) 3712
Greenhalgh Fold Farm, Greenmount, Bury BL8 4LH
Exit M66 Bury, follow signs for Ramsbottom, at lights in Holcombe village turn left, 0.25 mile turn left into Holcombe Rd, 1 mile turn right into Holhouse Lane, over speed bumps, turn right approaching Convent into Clubhouse.
Undulating parkland course.
9 holes, 4920 yards, S.S.S.64
Founded 1920
Visitors: welcome weekdays and with member at weekends.
Green Fee: £14 (£7 with member).
Societies: Thurs, Fri only, book in advance.
Catering: full service except Mon.
Snooker.
Hotels: Red Hall; Old Mill; Red Lion.

M66 Haigh Hall

☎(0942) 833337, 831107 Pro
Haigh Country Park, Aspull, Wigan, Lancs WN2 1PE
M6 exit 27, B5239 to Standish, 6 miles NE of Wigan.

Municipal parkland course.
18 holes, 6423 yards, S.S.S.71
Founded 1973
Visitors: welcome any time;
telephone bookings via Pro.
Green Fee: apply for details.
Societies: contact Pro.
Catering: cafeteria.
Hotels: Brocket; Oak; Almond Brook
Moathouse.

M67 Harwood

☎(0204) 22878
Springfield, Roading Brook Rd,
Harwood, Bolton BL2 4JD
On B6391 off A666 4 miles NE of
Bolton town centre.
Undulating parkland course.
9 holes, 5958 yards, S.S.S.69
Founded 1926
Visitors: welcome weekdays, must
be members of recognised club.
Green Fee: £15 (£6 with member).
Societies: on application.
Catering: on request.
Snooker.
Hotels: Last Drop (Bromley Cross);
Grants Arms (Ramsbottom).

M68 Haydock Park

☎(0925) 228525 Sec, 224389 Bar
manager
Golborne Park, Newton-le-Willows,
Merseyside WA12 0HX
M6 to A580, then 1 mile E.
Parkland course.
18 holes, 6043 yards, S.S.S.69
Founded 1877
Visitors: weekdays except Tues.
Green Fee: £24/round/day.
Societies: weekdays except Tues.
Catering: on request.
Hotels: Kirkfield.

M69 Heaton Park

☎(061) 798 0295
Prestwich, Manchester
Leave M62 at exit 19, right at A576,
200 yards on right.
Public undulating parkland course.
18 holes, 5849 yards, S.S.S.68
Designed by C.H. Taylor.
Founded 1912
Visitors: welcome, advance booking
weekend only.
Green Fee: £5.50 WD, £6.50 WE.
Societies: by arrangement.

M70 Hesketh

☎(0704) 536897 Sec, 530050 Pro
Cockle Dick's Lane, off Cambridge
Rd, Southport, Merseyside PR9 9QQ

1 mile N of Southport town centre on
main Preston road, A565.
Links course.
18 holes, 6407 yards, S.S.S.72
Designed by J.O.F. (Jamie) Morris.
Founded 1885
Visitors: welcome weekdays,
occasionally weekends; advance
booking for societies.
Green Fee: £25/round, £35/day WD;
£40 WE.
Societies: catered for weekdays.
Catering: bar snacks and dining
room facilities always available.
Hotels: details on application.

M71 The Heysham

☎(0524) 851011 Sec/Manager,
852000 Pro
Trumacar Park, Middleton Rd,
Heysham, Lancs LA3 3JH
3 miles from M6, 2 mile S of
Morecambe on right of road to
Middleton.
Parkland course.
18 holes, 6258 yards, S.S.S.70
Designed by H. Vardon.
Founded 1910
Visitors: welcome.
Green Fee: £18/round, £23/day WD;
£28 WE & BH; half price with member.
Societies: by arrangement with
Sec/Manager.
Catering: full facilities daily.
Snooker.
Hotels: Midland; Clarendon;
Strathmore; Post House.

M72 Hillside

☎(0704) 67169 Sec, 68360 Pro,
(0704) 63192 Fax
Hastings Rd, Hillside, Southport PR8
2LU
Take A565 Southport-Liverpool road,
turn right before Hillside railway
station, club at end of Hastings Rd.
Championship links course.
18 holes, 6850 yards, S.S.S.74
Designed by Fred Hawtree.
Founded 1909 (1923 on present site)
Visitors: welcome weekday,
advance booking recommended,
limited times Sun.
Green Fee: £35/round, £45/day.
Societies: by appointment.
Catering: all day, 50 seat restaurant.
Snooker.
Hotels: Prince of Wales; Scarisbrick.

M73 Hindley Hall

☎(0942) 55131, 55991 Pro
Hall Lane, Hindley, Wigan, Lancs
WN2 2SQ

M61 junction 6 onto A6, take
Dicconson Lane, then after 1 mile left
at church into Hall Lane, club just
after lake.
Moorland course.
18 holes, 5875 yards, S.S.S.68
Founded 1895
Visitors: welcome if member of
recognised club, advisable to check
with Sec in advance.
Green Fee: £20 WD, £27 WE & BH.
Societies: by arrangement.
Catering: meals by served
arrangement with chef, call
(0942) 525552.
Hotels: Brockett Arms (Wigan).

M74 Horwich

☎(0204) 696980
Victoria Rd, Horwich, Bolton BL6 5PH
1.5 miles from M61.
Parkland course.
9 holes, 5800 yards, S.S.S.67
Founded 1895
Visitors: with member only.
Green Fee: on application.
Societies: catered for weekdays
only by application.
Catering: full facilities.

M75 Huyton & Prescot

☎(051) 489 3948
Hurst Park, Huyton Lane, Huyton,
Liverpool L36 1UA
Approx 10 miles from Liverpool city
centre, just off M57.
Parkland course.
18 holes, 5738 yards, S.S.S.68
Founded 1905
Visitors: must be members of
recognised golf clubs.
Green Fee: on application.
Societies: by arrangement
weekdays only.
Catering: every day.
Hotels: Derby Lodge; Hillcrest.

M76 Ingol Golf & Squash Club

☎(0772) 734556
Tanterton Hall Rd, Ingol, Preston,
Lancs PR2 7BY
Leave M6 junction 32, turn left
towards Preston, follow signpost on
left marked Ingol.
Parkland course.
18 holes, 5868 yards, S.S.S.68
Designed by Cotton, Pennink, Lawrie
& Partners.
Founded 1980
Visitors: welcome any day.
Green Fee: on application.
Societies: by arrangement.

Catering: full facilities.
Squash, snooker, banqueting.
Hotels: Barton Grange; Broughton
Park; Fulwood Park.

M77 Kendal

☎(0539) 724079 Clubhouse,
733708 Office, 723499 Pro
The Heights, Kendal, LA9 4PQ
To Kendal on A6 signposted in town.
Moorland course.
18 holes, 5515 yards, S.S.S.67
Founded 1891
Visitors: welcome any time but prior
application suggested.
Green Fee: on application.
Societies: catered for any time
subject to availability.
Catering: full facilities except Mon.
Hotels: County; Woolpack.

M78 Keswick

☎(07687) 79324 Sec, 79010
Pro/tee bookings
Threlkeld Hall, Threlkeld, Keswick,
Cumbria CA12 4SX
Off A66 4 miles E of Keswick.
Moorland/parkland course.
18 holes, 6225 yards, S.S.S.72
Designed by Eric Brown.
Founded 1975
Visitors: welcome even at most
weekends and Bank Holidays.
Green Fee: £15 WD, £20 WE.
Societies: apply to sec; some
weekends and Bank Holidays.
Catering: bar and dining facilities.
Hotels: Lodore Swiss; Keswick;
Borrowdale; Wordsworth; all have
free midweek golf.

M79 King Edward Bay (Howstrake)

☎(0624) 620430, 676794
Groudle Rd, Onchan, Isle of Man
On A11, 2 miles NE of Douglas.
Moorland/seaside course.
18 holes, 5457 yards, S.S.S.66
Founded 1893
Visitors: welcome Mon-Sat; Sun by
arrangement; h/cap cert required.
Green Fee: £12 WD, £14 WE & BH.
Societies: weekdays; weekends by
arrangement.
Catering: 10am-10pm daily.
Putting greens, driving nets,
snooker, sauna, sunbed.

M80 Kirkby Lonsdale

☎(046 836) 365, 366
Scalebar Lane, Barbon, Carnforth,
Cumbria LA6 2LE

2.5 miles N of Kirkby Lonsdale on
A368 to Sedbergh; Clubhouse on
Backfoot Lane.
Parkland course next to River Lune.
18 holes, 6286 yards, S.S.S.70
Moved to new course 1991
Visitors: no restrictions.
Green Fee: apply for details.
Societies: Tues and Thurs.
Catering: available.

M81 Knott End

☎(0253) 810576 Sec, 811365 Pro
Wyreside, Knott End on Sea,
Blackpool FY6 0AA
Take A585 Fleetwood road off M55,
and then B2588 to Knott End.
Meadowland course.
18 holes, 5852 yards, S.S.S.68
Designed by James Braid.
Founded 1911
Visitors: welcome weekdays, not
before 9.30am or 12.30-1.30pm.
Green Fee: £20 WD, £24 WE & BH.
Societies: by arrangement.
Catering: every day.
Hotels: Bourne Arms; Seven Stars.

M82 Lancaster

☎(0524) 751247, 751105 Caterer,
751802 Pro
Ashton Hall, Ashton-with-Stodday,
Lancaster LA2 0AJ
On A588 2.5 miles SW of Lancaster.
Undulating parkland course.
18 holes, 6282 yards, S.S.S.71
Designed by James Braid.
Founded 1933
Visitors: welcome weekdays only.
Green Fee: on application.
Societies: welcome by arrangement.
Catering: meals served.
Hotels: Post House; residential
dormy house (18 persons).

M83 Lansil

☎(0524) 39269 Club
Caton Rd, Lancaster, Lancs LA1 3PE
2 miles E of Lancaster on A683.
Parkland/meadowland course.
9 Holes, 5608 yards, S.S.S.67
Founded 1947
Visitors: welcome; after 1pm Sun.
Green Fee: apply for details.
Societies: weekdays.
Catering: light refreshments only.
Hotels: Farmers Arms; Post House.

M84 Lee Park

☎(051) 487 3882 Sec
Childwall Valley Rd, Gateacre,
Liverpool L27 3YA

On B5171 off A562, next to Lee
Manor High School.
Parkland course.
18 holes, 6024 yards, S.S.S.69
Designed by Frank Pennink.
Founded 1950
Visitors: welcome with reservation.
Green Fee: £18.50 WD, £25.50 WE.
Societies: Mon, Thur, Fri (not 12.15
to 2.15pm) by arrangement with Sec.
Catering: bar snacks; meals by
arrangement on (051) 487 9861.
Hotels: Gateacre Hall.

M85 Leigh

☎(0925) 763130, 762013 Pro,
762943 Sec
Kenyon Hall, Broseley Lane,
Culcheth, Warrington WA3 4BG
2 mins from Culcheth centre; from
A580 (E Lancs road) A574 or B5207.
Parkland course.
18 holes, 5861 yards, S.S.S.68
Founded 1906
Visitors: any time except during club
competitions.
Green Fee: £25 WD, £32 WE & BH.
Societies: Mon, Tues on application.
Catering: bar snacks/full catering.
Snooker.
Hotels: Greyhound Motel (Leigh);
Thistle (Haydock).

M86 Leyland

☎(0772) 436457
Wigan Rd, Leyland, Lancs PR5 2UD
On A49, 0.25 mile from M6 exit 28.
Meadowland course.
18 holes, 6123 yards, S.S.S.69
Founded 1923
Visitors: weekdays unrestricted,
weekends with member.
Green Fee: £24.
Societies: apply to Sec.
Catering: daily except Mon.
Hotels: Ladbroke Mercury.

M87 Liverpool Municipal

☎(051) 546 5435
Ingoe Lane, Kirkby, Liverpool L32 4SS
M57 junction 6, 300 yards on right of
B5192.
Municipal meadowland course.
18 holes, 6706 yards, S.S.S.72
Founded 1966 (1967 Kirkby GC).
Visitors: welcome every day, tee
booking at weekends.
Green Fee: £5.50
Societies: welcome, tee booking at
weekends 1 week in advance.
Catering: bar and cafeteria.
Practice ground.
Hotels: Golden Eagle (Kirkby).

M88 Lobden

☎(0706) 343228
Lobden Moor, Whitworth, Nr
Rochdale OL12 8XJ
A671 4 miles from Rochdale, 0.5
mile from centre of village.
Moorland course.
9 holes, 5750 yards, S.S.S.68
Founded 1888
Visitors: weekdays and Sun.
Green Fee: apply for details.
Catering: by arrangement with
Steward. Snooker.

M89 Longridge

☎(0772) 783291
Fell Barn, Jeffery Hill, Longridge,
Preston, Lancs PR3 2TU
Off B6243 8 miles NE of Preston,
follow signs to Jeffery Hill.
Moorland course, panoramic views.
18 holes, 5800 yards, S.S.S.68
Founded 1877
Visitors: welcome; check by phone
or letter.
Green Fee: £18/day Mon-Thurs, £21
Fri, Sat, Sun and BH.
Societies: apply in writing to Sec.
Catering: bar and meals at
reasonable times.
Snooker.
Hotels: Shireburn Arms (Hurst
Green); Gibbon Bridge (Chipping);
Black Moss GH.

M90 Lowes Park

☎(061) 764 1231, (0706) 367331
Sec
Hill Top, Bury, Lancs BL9 6SU
A56 Walmersley Rd, right into Lowes
Rd, follow signs to club; approx 1.5
miles from Bury centre, right at
General Hospital.
Moorland course (usually windy).
9 holes, 6009 yards, S.S.S.69
Founded 1914
Visitors: welcome weekdays, except
Wed (Ladies Day), Sat and
competition days; Sun by
appointment only.
Green Fee: £13.50 WD, £20 Sun.
Societies: contact Sec.
Catering: full facilities except Mon.
Hotels: Woolfield House (Wash
Lane).

M91 Lytham Green Drive

☎(0253) 737390, 731350 Fax
Ballam Rd, Lytham, Lancs FY8 4LE
0.75 mile from Lytham centre.
Parkland course.
18 holes, 6175 yards, S.S.S.69
Founded 1922
Visitors: weekdays only, h/cap cert
required.
Green Fee: £26.
Societies: by arrangement with Sec.
Catering: full service daily.
Hotels: Clifton Arms.

M92 Manchester

☎(061) 643 3202
Hopwood Cottage, Rochdale Rd,
Middleton, Manchester M24 2QP
7 miles N of city on A664, 2 miles
from exits 19 and 20 off M62.
Undulating moorland course.
18 holes, 6540 yards, S.S.S.72
Designed by H.S. Colt
Founded 1882
Visitors: weekdays only, h/cap certs
required.
Green Fee: £25/day.
Societies: weekdays.
Catering: full facilities available.
Driving range (for green fee payers
only), snooker, banqueting.
Hotels: Norton Grange; Midway.

M93 Marsden Park

☎(0253) 67525
Downhouse Rd, Belson, Lancs BB9
8GD
Off A56, 8 miles N of Burnley.
Undulating meadowland course.
18 holes, 5806 yards, S.S.S.68
Designed by C.K. Cotton & Partners.
Founded 1968
Visitors: welcome.
Green Fee: apply for details.
Societies: by arrangement.
Catering: snacks evenings and
weekends.

M94 Maryport

☎(0900) 812605
Bank End, Maryport, Cumbria CA15
6PA
N of Maryport, turn left off A596 onto
B5300 (Silloth), course 1 mile.
Seaside links course.
18 holes, 6088 yards, S.S.S.70
Founded 1905
Visitors: welcome at any time.
Green Fee: £15/day WD, £20 WE.
Societies: catered for.
Catering: by prior arrangement.
Hotels: Ellenbank; The Waverley.

M95 Morecambe

☎(0524) 412841 Sec, 418050
Members, 415596 Pro
Bare, Morecambe, Lancs LA4 6AJ
5 miles from M6 at Carnforth, follow
signs to Morecambe.
Seaside/parkland course.
18 holes, 5766 yards, S.S.S.68
Designed by Dr Clegg.
Founded 1922
Visitors: welcome at all times except
before 9.30am or 12am-1.30pm
Mon-Sat and before 1.30pm Sun;
h/cap certs required.
Green Fee: £16/round, £21/day WD;
£21/round, £26/day WE & BH.
Societies: welcome by arrangement
with Sec, if members of recognised
golf clubs.
Catering: full catering available
except Mon when bar snacks only.
Hotels: Elms; Strathmore.

M96 Nelson

☎(0282) 64583
King's Causeway, Brierfield, Belson,
Lancs BB9 0EU
Off A682 2 miles E of Brierfield.
Moorland course.
18 holes, 5967 yards, S.S.S.69
Founded 1902
Visitors: welcome weekdays except
Thurs afternoons; weekends and
Bank Holidays by application.
Green Fee: apply for details.
Societies: by arrangement.
Catering: lunches except Mon,
evening meals except Mon or Fri.
Hotels: Kierby; Oaks.

M97 New North Manchester

☎(061) 643 2941 Clubhouse, 643
9033 Sec, 643 7094 Pro Shop
Rhodes House, Manchester Old Rd,
Middleton, Manchester M24 4PE
5 miles N of Manchester, M62 exit 18.
Moorland/parkland course.
18 holes, 6527 yards, S.S.S.72
Founded 1894
Visitors: welcome weekdays and by
arrangement at weekends.
Green Fee: on application.
Societies: weekdays.
Catering: full service 7 days.
Hotels: Bower (Oldham); Birch
(Heywood).

M98 Newby Grange Hotel & Golf Course

☎(0228) 573645
Newby Grange, Carlisle, Cumbria
A69 to Newcastle, turn left to Little
Corby, through village, take road to
Carlisle, course on right.
Riverbank parkland course.
18 holes, 6973 yards, S.S.S.75
Designed by Eddie MacCauslin.
Founded 1992

Visitors: welcome.
Green Fee: apply for details.
Societies: welcome.
Catering: full bar and restaurant facilities.
Driving range.
Hotels: Newby Grange.

M99 Oldham

☎(061) 624 4986 or 626 8346
Lees New Rd, Oldham OL4 5EN
Just off minor road between Oldham and Ashton-under-Lyne or on A669 turn right at Lees.
Moorland/parkland course.
18 holes, 5045 yards, S.S.S.65
Founded registered 1891
Visitors: unlimited, but phone for arrangements on competitions.
Green Fee: apply for details.
Societies: by arrangement.
Catering: full facilities.

M100 Ormskirk

☎(0695) 572112
Cranes Lane, Lathom, Ormskirk, Lancs L40 5UJ
2 miles E of Ormskirk.
Parkland course.
18 holes, 6358 yards, S.S.S.70
Founded 1899
Visitors: advanced booking advised.
Green Fee: apply for details.
Societies: book in advance.
Catering: daily except Mon.

M101 Peel

☎(0624) 843456 (Mon-Fri am)
Rheast Lane, Peel, Isle of Man
On A1, signposted on outskirts of Peel, coming from Douglas.
Moorland course.
18 holes, 5914 yards, S.S.S.68
Designed by A. Herd.
Founded 1895
Visitors: welcome weekdays; by arrangement weekends (after 10.30am).
Green Fee: £14/day WD, £18/day WE & BH.
Societies: apply to Sec.
Catering: meals and snacks to order by arrangement with Steward.

M102 Pennigton

☎(0942) 607278
Pennigton Country Park, St Helen's Road, Leigh, Greater Manchester
Off A572 to S of town centre; M6 junctions 22/23.
Public parkland course.
9 holes, 2929 yards, S.S.S.34

Visitors: welcome.
Green Fee: apply for details.
Catering: snack bar.
Fishing, bird watching.

M103 Penrith

☎(0768) 62217, 891915
Salkeld Rd, Penrith, Cumbria CA11 8SG
0.5 mile NE of Penrith, M6 junction 41.
Parkland course.
18 holes, 6026 yards, S.S.S.69
Founded 1890
Visitors: must be member of golf club with h/cap.
Green Fee: £20/round £25/2 rounds WD; £25/round, £30/2 rounds WE.
Societies: by arrangement.
Catering: all day 7 days.
Snooker.
Hotels: George; Edenhall.

M104 Penwortham

☎(0772) 744630
Blundell Lane, Penwortham, Preston, Lancs PR1 0AX
Off A59 at Penwortham traffic lights, 1 mile from Preston.
Parkland course.
18 holes, 5915 yards, S.S.S.68
Founded 1908
Visitors: weekdays (not Tues).
Green Fee: £22 (£8 with member) WD, £28 (£10 with member) WE & BH.
Societies: weekdays (not Tues).
Catering: lunches, evening meals.
Hotels: Crest.

M105 Pike Fold

☎(061) 740 1136
Cooper Lane, Victoria Ave, Blackley, Manchester M9 2QQ
4 miles N of city centre off Rochdale road; off Victoria Ave from M62 junction 18.
Undulating meadowland course.
9 holes, 5789 yards, S.S.S.68
Founded 1909
Visitors: welcome weekdays.
Green Fee: £12/round/day WD (£5 with member), £7/round WE with member only.
Societies: welcome by appointment.
Catering: full facilities by prior arrangement with Steward. Snooker.
Hotels: Piccadilly; Midland.

M106 Pleasington

☎(0254) 202177, 201630 Pro
Pleasington, Blackburn, Lancs BB2 5JF
3 miles from Blackburn off A674.

Undulating parkland course.
18 holes, 6417 yards, S.S.S.71
Founded 1891
Visitors: Mon, Wed, Fri by prior arrangement; h/cap cert required.
Green Fee: £26 WD, £30 WE & BH.
Societies: Mon, Wed, Fri.
Catering: full facilities.
Hotels: Moat House Motel.

M107 Port St Mary Golf Pavilion

☎(0624) 834932
Port St Mary, Isle of Man
Just outside Port St Mary towards the sea, signposted.
Public seaside links course.
9 holes, 5454 yards, S.S.S.66
Designed by George Duncan.
Founded 1936
Visitors: welcome any time.
Green Fee: on application.
Societies: welcome, discount for 10 or more.
Catering: bar, cafeteria (closed Mon and Tues until May).
Putting green, outdoor chessboard.
Hotels: Point; Bay View.

M108 Poulton-le-Fylde.

☎(0253) 893150/892444
Myrtle Farm, Breck Rd, Poulton-le-Fylde, Lancs
0.5 mile N of Poulton town centre.
Municipal meadowland course.
9 holes, 2779 yards, S.S.S.69
Founded 1974
Visitors: welcome, no restrictions.
Green Fee: apply for details.
Societies: by arrangement.
Catering: bar, snacks, lunches daily.
Snooker, games room.

M109 Preston

☎(0772) 700011, 700022 Pro Shop
Fulwood Hall Lane, Fulwood, Preston, Lancs PR2 4DD
From M6 junction 31 take Blackpool Rd, turn right at Deepdale Rd, turn left at Watling St Rd, turn right at Fulwood Hall Lane.
Undulating course.
18 holes, 6233 yards, S.S.S.70
Designed by James Braid.
Founded 1892
Visitors: welcome weekdays.
Green Fee: £22/round, £27/day.
Societies: Mon, Wed, Fri (max 48); Tues, (max 16); Thurs (max 32); no parties weekends or Bank Holidays.
Catering: lunches, breakfast, dinner, snacks.
Hotels: Broughton Park.

METROPOLE HOTEL, SOUTHPORT

Portland Street, Southport PR8 1LL   Tel 0704 536836   Fax 0704 549041

RAC/AA 2-star hotel. Centrally situated and close to Royal Birkdale and 5 other championship courses.
Fully licensed with late bar facilities for residents. Full sized snooker table.
Golfing proprieters will assist with tee reservations.

M110 **Prestwich**
☎(061) 773 4578
Hilton Lane, Prestwich, Manchester
M25 8SB
On A4066 0.25 mile W of junction
with A56.
Parkland course.
18 holes, 4712 yards, S.S.S.63
Founded 1908
Visitors: h/cap certs required.
Green Fee: apply for details.
Societies: welcome except Tues
(Ladies Day).
Catering: by arrangement with
Steward, except Mon.
Hotels: Village Squash; Hazel Dean.

M111 **Ramsey**
☎(0624) 812244
Brookfield, Ramsey, Isle of Man
12 miles N of Douglas, 5 minutes
walk from town centre.
Parkland course.
18 holes, 6019 yards, S.S.S.69
Designed by James Braid.
Founded 1890
Visitors: welcome; phone in
advance.
Green Fee: £15/day WD, £18/day
WE.
Societies: apply to Sec.
Catering: lunches daily; dinner
Thurs, Fri, Sat (bookings).
Hotels: Grand Island.

M112 **Regent Park (Bolton)**
☎(0204) 844170 Club, 842336 Pro
shop
Links Rd, Lostock, Bolton, Lancs BL6
4AF
M61 exit 6 to Bolton, entrance on
right after 1 mile approx.
Municipal parkland course.
18 holes, 6250 yards, S.S.S.71
Founded 1932
Visitors: welcome 7 days;
restrictions every alternate time
on Sat.
Green Fee: £4.75 WD, £6.75 WE &
BH.
Societies: welcome Mon-Fri by
arrangement.
Catering: bar, take-away,
restaurant.
Practice fairway.
Hotels: Forte-Crest; Swallowfield.

M113 **Rishton**
☎(0254) 884442
Eachill Links, Hawthorne Drive,
Rishton, Blackburn, Lancs BB1 4HG
3 miles E of Blackburn, signposted
from church in village.
Meadowland course.
9 holes, 6094 yards, S.S.S.69
Founded 1928
Visitors: welcome weekdays;
weekends and Bank Holidays with
member; restricted Wed (Ladies day).
Green Fee: £12.
Societies: welcome with prior
arrangement, letter to Sec.
Catering: lunch and evening meals,
closed Mon. Snooker.
Hotels: Dunkenhalgh.

M114 **Rochdale**
☎(0706) 43818 Sec, 46024 Club,
522104 Pro
Edenfield Rd, Bagslate, Rochdale
OL11 5YR
3 miles from M62 exit 20 on A680.
Parkland course.
18 holes, 6002 yards, S.S.S.69
Founded 1888
Visitors: welcome but restricted.
Green Fee: on application.
Societies: Wed and Fri.
Catering: coffee, lunch and evening
meals served except Mon. Snooker.
Hotels: Crimble; Midway.

M115 **Rossendale**
☎(0706) 831339 Sec
Ewood Lane Head, Haslingden,
Rossendale, Lancs BB4 6LH
16 miles from Manchester off M66.
Moorland/meadowland course.
18 holes, 6267 yards, S.S.S.70
Founded 1903
Visitors: welcome except Sat.
Green Fee: £22.50 WD, £27.50 Sun
& BH.
Societies: welcome.
Catering: full facilities except Mon.
Snooker, banqueting.
Hotels: Queen's; Royal.

M116 **Rowany**
☎(0624) 834072 Manager, 834108
Steward
Rowany Drive, Port Erin, Isle of Man

4 miles W of Castletown, located at
end of Port Erin promenade.
Parkland/seaside course.
18 holes, 5840 yards, S.S.S.69
Founded 1895
Visitors: welcome, no restrictions.
Green Fee: £12 WD £17 WE & BH,
groups of 20+ 25% discount.
Societies: always welcome;
arrangements to be made with
Manager (9am-1pm weekdays).
Catering: bar, bar snacks, lunches,
evening meals.
Hotels: Port Erin Royal; Cherry
Orchard.

M117 **Royal Birkdale**
☎(0704) 69913, 67920 Sec
Waterloo Rd, Birkdale, Southport,
Merseyside PR8 2LX
1.5 miles S of Southport on A565.
Seaside course.
18 holes, 6703 yards, S.S.S.73
Designed by Hawtree & Taylor.
Founded 1889
Visitors: letter of intro required from
home club with confirmation of h/cap.
Green Fee: winter, £35 WD;
summer, £50/round, £70/day.
Societies: welcome weekdays by
arrangement.
Catering: light lunches and
afternoon teas, full lunches and
dinners by arrangement for societies.

M118 **Royal Lytham & St Annes**
☎(0253) 724206
Links Gate, St Annes on Sea, Lancs
FY8 3LQ
1 mile from centre of St Annes.
Links course.
18 holes, 6673 yards, S.S.S.73
Founded 1886
Visitors: weekdays by arrangement;
weekends, dormy visitors only.
Green Fee: apply for details.
Societies: by arrangement.
Catering: full catering and bar
facilities. Snooker.

M119 **Saddleworth**
☎(0457) 873653
Mountain Ash, Ladcastle Rd,
Uppermill, Oldham OL3 6LT

5 miles from Oldham, signposted off A670 Ashton-Huddersfield road at bend where road crosses railway bridge.
Scenic moorland course.
18 holes, 5976 yards, S.S.S.69
Designed by Dr Mackenzie.
Founded 1904
Visitors: welcome.
Green Fee: apply for details.
Societies: catered for weekdays.
Catering: facilities daily.

M120 St Annes Old Links
☎(0253) 723597 Sec, 722432 Pro
Highbury Rd, St Annes, Lytham St Annes, Lancs FY8 2LD
M6 to junction 32; M55 to junction 4, follow signs to Blackpool Airport; past airport, left at A584 coast road to St Annes; 1 mile to lights, left into Highbury Rd, course immediately over railway bridge.
Championship links course.
18 holes, 6616 yards, S.S.S.72
Designed by James Herd.
Founded 1901
Visitors: welcome weekdays; restricted Tues and weekends.
Green Fee: £25 WD, £30 WE & BH.
Societies: apply to Sec.
Catering: lunches, teas, dinner daily.
Men's bar, snooker, practice ground.
Hotels: St Ives; Warwick (Blackpool).

M121 St Bees
☎(0946) 824300
Station Rd, St Bees, Cumbria
On B5345, 4 miles S of Whitehaven.
Seaside course.
9 holes, 5097 yards, S.S.S.65
Founded 1942/43
Visitors: welcome except on competition days in summer.
Green Fee: apply for details.

M122 Seascale
☎(09467) 28202 Phone/Fax
The Banks, Seascale, Cumbria CA20 1QL
On coast to N of village; clubhouse at top of hill.
Seaside links course.
18 holes, 6416 yards, S.S.S.71
Founded 1893
Visitors: unrestricted.
Green Fee: £19 WD, £23 WE & BH.
Societies: apply to Sec, terms for parties of 12 or more.
Catering: full facilities except Mon, Tues (by arrangement).
Hotels: Scawfell; Calder House; 3-day bargain breaks available.

M123 Sedbergh
☎(05396) 20993 Hon Sec, 21551 Club
Catholes-Abbot Holme, Dent Rd, Sedbergh, Cumbria LA10 5SS
1.5 miles S of Sedbergh on road to Dent; 5 miles from M6 junction 37.
Scenic undulating parkland course, easy walking.
9 holes, 5588 yards, S.S.S.68
Designed by W.G. Squires
Founded 1896 (new site 1991)
Visitors: welcome except Sun am; advisable to phone; h/cap certificate may be requested.
Green Fee: £12/round, £18/day WD; £15/round, £21/day WE and BH.
Societies: welcome by arrangement, company days available.
Catering: good facilities, licenced bar.
Hotels: bargain breaks arranged, ring Sec for details.

M124 Shaw Hill Hotel Golf & Country Club
☎(0257) 269221, 261223 Fax
Preston Rd, Whittle-le-Woods, Nr Chorley, Lancs PR6 7PP
From M6 exit 28, just off A6 towards Chorley; from M61 exit 8, just off A6 towards Preston.
Parkland course.
18 holes, 6467 yards, S.S.S.71
Designed by T. McCauley.
Founded 1925
Visitors: welcome with proof of h/cap.
Green Fee: apply for details.
Societies: weekdays only.
Catering: bar, full à la carte restaurant and function rooms.
Sauna, solarium, snooker room.
Hotels: own 3 star hotel.

M125 Sherdley Park
☎(0744) 815518 Club, 813149 Pro
Sherdley Park, St Helens, Merseyside
2 miles S of town centre on Warrington road.
Public undulating parkland course.
18 holes, 5941 yards, S.S.S.69
Designed by P.R. Parkinson.
Founded 1973
Visitors: welcome.
Green Fee: apply for details.
Societies: by arrangement.
Catering: bar and cafeteria.
Hotels: Post House, Thistle

M126 Silecroft
☎(0229) 774250
Silecroft, Cumbria LA18 4NX
On A5093 3 miles N of Millom, through Silecroft towards shore.
Seaside course.
9 holes (18 tees), 5712 yards, S.S.S.68
Founded 1903
Visitors: normally unrestricted weekdays; weekends and Bank Holidays often restricted 12am-5.30pm.
Green Fee: £10/round/day WD or WE.
Societies: by arrangement.
Catering: by prior arrangement for visiting groups.
Hotels: Bankfield; Miners Arms; John Bull.

M127 Silloth on Solway
☎(06973) 31304
Silloth on Solway, Carlisle, Cumbria CA5 4BL
B5302 at A596 at Wigton, 18 miles W of Carlisle.
Undulating seaside course.
18 holes, 6445 yards, S.S.S.72
Designed by Dr Leitch and Willie Park jnr.
Founded 1892
Visitors: welcome any time.
Green Fee: £22/day WD, £27/round WE & BH.
Societies: welcome.
Catering: full facilities except Mon.
Hotels: Golf; Queens; Skinburness.

M128 Silverdale
☎(0524) 701300
Redbridge Lane, Silverdale, Carnforth, Lancs LA5 0SP
Off M6 at Carnforth, course opposite Silverdale railway station via Carnforth and Warton.
Hilly heathland course.
12 holes, 5417 yards, S.S.S.67
Founded 1906
Visitors: welcome, not competition days (Sun Men, Wed Ladies).
Green Fee: £12 WD, £17 WE & BH (£6 with member).
Societies: by arrangement.
Catering: usually, by special arrangement.
Hotels: Wheatsheaf; Silverdale.

M129 Solway Village Golf Centre
☎(06973) 31236
Solway Village, Silloth-on-Solway, Cumbria CA5 4QQ
Easily located in village of Silloth.
Scenic parkland course.
9 holes, 2000 yards, Par 3 course
Founded 1988

Visitors: welcome any time.
Green Fee: £5/day, £15/week.
Catering: bar and restaurant.
Driving range, swimming pool,
indoor bowls.
Hotels: Skinburness; Golf.

M130 Southport & Ainsdale

☎(0704) 578000, 570896 Fax
Bradshaws Lane, Ainsdale,
Southport, Merseyside PR8 3LG
3 miles S of Southport on A565, 0.5
mile from Ainsdale station.
Championship links course.
18 holes, 6612 yards, S.S.S.73
Designed by James Braid.
Founded 1907
Visitors: weekdays only, must be
members of a golf club; advance
booking recommended.
Green Fee: £30/round, £40/day.
Societies: weekdays only, must be
members of a golf club; advance
booking essential.
Catering: full facilities.
Snooker.
Hotels: Prince of Wales; Scarisbrick;
Royal Clifton.

M131 Southport Municipal

☎(0704) 535286, (530133 Park Golf
Club)
Park Rd West, Southport, Merseyside
PR9 0JS
N end of Promenade.
Public seaside course.
18 holes, 5953 yards, S.S.S.69
Founded 1914 (Park Golf Club)
Visitors: welcome.
Green Fee: apply for details.
Societies: by arrangement.
Catering: meals served.

M132 Southport Old Links

☎(0704) 28207
Moss Lane, Southport, Merseyside
PR9 7QS
From town centre take Lord St to
roundabout at Law Courts, turn right
into Manchester Rd, into Roe Lane
and into Moss Lane.
Seaside course.
9 holes, 6486 yards, S.S.S.72
Founded 1920
Visitors: preferably not Wed or
weekends.
Green Fee: apply for details.
Societies: by arrangement if party of
12 or more.
Catering: snacks or light cooked
meals as arranged with Steward.
Hotels: Bold.

M133 Springfield Park

☎(0707) 56401 (weekends only)
Springfield Park, Bolton Rd,
Rochdale, Lancs
3 miles from M62.
Parkland course.
18 holes, 5337 yards, S.S.S.66
Founded 1927
Visitors: welcome anytime.
Green Fee: on application.
Hotels: Midway (Castleton).

M134 Stand

☎(061) 766 3197 Sec, 766 2388
Club
The Dales, Ashbourne Grove,
Whitefield, Manchester M25 7NL
1 mile N of M62, exit 17.
Undulating parkland course.
18 holes, 6426 yards, S.S.S.71
Designed by Alex Herd.
Founded 1904
Visitors: welcome weekdays,
weekends by arrangement.
Green Fee: £25 (£10 with member)
WD, £30 (£13 with member) WE &
BH.
Societies: weekdays; Mon, Wed and
Fri preferred.
Catering: lunches/snacks served
except Mon.

M135 Stonyholme Municipal

☎(0228) 34856 Pro, 33208 Club
St Aidans Rd, Carlisle, Cumbria
Off A69, 1 mile W of M6, junction 43.
Flat meadowland course.
18 holes, 5773 yards, S.S.S.68
Designed by Frank Pennink.
Founded 1974
Visitors: welcome.
Green Fee: apply for details.
Societies: welcome.
Catering: meals served.

M136 Stonyhurst Park

☎(0200) 23089 Hon Sec, (0254)
826478 The Bayley Arms
c/o The Bayley Arms, Hurst Green,
Blackburn BB6 9QB
On B6243 Clitheroe-Longridge road.
Parkland course.
9 holes, 5529 yards, S.S.S.66
Founded 1979
Visitors: welcome except
weekends; phone Bayley Arms.
Green Fee: £12.
Societies: welcome by prior
arrangement; letter to Sec.
Catering: at Bayley Arms; snacks, à
la carte always available.
Hotels: Bayley Arms.

M137 Swinton Park

☎(061) 794 1785
East Lancashire Rd, Swinton,
Manchester M27 5LX
On A580 Manchester-Liverpool road,
about 4 miles from Manchester.
Parkland course.
18 holes, 6726 yards, S.S.S.72
Designed by Braid & Taylor.
Founded 1926
Visitors: welcome weekdays only.
Green Fee: on application.
Societies: by arrangement Tues,
Wed and Fri.
Catering: bar snacks, meals
throughout day (excluding Mon).
Snooker.

M138 Towneley

☎(0282) 38473 bookings, 451636
bar and catering
Todmorden Rd, Burnley, Lancs BB11
3ED
Off Todmorden Rd approx 2 miles
from town centre.
Public parkland course.
18 holes, 5900 yards, S.S.S.68; 9
holes Par 3
Designed by Burnley Council.
Founded 1932
Visitors: welcome anytime; normal
dress rules; booking required.
Green Fee: £5 WD, £6 WE & BH.
Societies: any weekday by
arrangement with Burnley Borough
Council.
Catering: bar 12am-4pm,
7.30-11pm; restaurant 12am-2pm
daily or by arrangement with
Steward.
Snooker table.

M139 Tunshill

☎(0706) 342095
Kiln Lane, Milnrow, Lancs
M62 junction 21 to Milnrow; follow
Kiln Lane out of Milnrow town centre,
continue along narrow lane to club.
Moorland course.
9 holes, 2902 yards, S.S.S.68
Founded 1943
Visitors: welcome weekdays except
Tues evening; with special
permission at weekends.
Green Fee: apply for details.
Societies: welcome weekdays.
Catering: by prior arrangement.
Snooker, pool.

M140 Turton

☎(0204) 852235
Wood End Farm, Chapeltown Rd,
Bromley Cross, Bolton BL7 9QH

4 miles NW of Bolton, use Hospital Rd, Bromley Cross, Bolton; near Last Drop Hotel.
Moorland course.
9 holes (18 from summer 1994), 5894 yards, S.S.S.68
Designed by James Braid.
Founded 1908
Visitors: welcome except Wed 11.30-3pm, Sat, Sun and special competition days.
Green Fee: £15/day WD.
Societies: by arrangement.
Catering: every day except Mon, resident Steward and Stewardess.
Hotels: Last Drop; Egerton House.

M141 Ulverston
☎(0229) 52824
The Club House, Bardsea Park, Ulverston, Cumbria LA12 9QJ
From Ulverston town centre to Bardsea on B5087.
Parkland course.
18 holes, 6142 yards, S.S.S.70
Designed by W.H. Colt.
Founded 1895 (present course 1910)
Visitors: welcome; introduction card or h/cap cert preferred; Tues Ladies Day; not Sat if Men's Competition.
Green Fee: £20 WD, £25 WE & BH Mar-Oct incl; £15 WD, £18 WE Nov-Feb.
Societies: by arrangement.
Catering: full meals, bar snacks daily; full time Steward.
Hotels: Virginia House; Sefton House; White Water (Backbarrow).

M142 Walmersley
☎(061) 764 1429 Club, 764 5057 Sec
Garretts Close, Walmersley, Bury
On A56 about 2.5 miles N of Bury; M66 junction 1, then 0.5 mile S; turn into Old Rd at Walmersley PO.
Moorland course.
9 holes, 3057 yards, S.S.S.70
Founded 1906
Visitors: Mon, Wed and Fri; Sun with member.
Green Fee: £15/day.
Societies: by arrangement Wed-Fri.
Catering: available except Mon. Snooker.
Hotels: Old Mill; Red Hall.

M143 Werneth (Oldham)
☎(061) 624 1190
Green Lane, Garden Suburb, Oldham, Lancs OL8 3AZ
5 miles from Manchester, take A62 to Hollinwood and then A6104.

Moorland course.
18 holes, 5363 yards, S.S.S.66
Founded 1908
Visitors: welcome weekdays only.
Green Fee: £16.50 WD.
Societies: weekdays.
Catering: lunch and evening meals served except Mon. Snooker.
Hotels: Periquito (Oldham).

M144 West Derby
☎(051) 254 1034 Sec, 220 5478 Pro
Yew Tree Lane, Liverpool L12 9HQ
4 miles E of Liverpool centre, 1 mile S of West Derby village.
Parkland course.
18 holes, 6346 yards, S.S.S.70
Founded 1896
Visitors: welcome weekdays.
Green Fee: on application.
Societies: by arrangement.
Catering: facilities.
Hotels: Derby Lodge.

M145 West Lancashire
☎(051) 924 1076
Hall Rd West, Blundellsands, Liverpool L23 8SZ
M57 to Aintree, A5036 to Seaforth, then A565 to Crosby, follow signs to club, by Hall Rd station.
Seaside links course.
18 holes, 6756 yards, S.S.S.73
Designed by C.K. Cotton.
Founded 1873
Visitors: welcome with h/cap cert except competition days.
Green Fee: £22/round, £33/day WD, £40 WE.
Societies: Mon, Wed, Thurs, Fri.
Catering: lunch daily, other by arrangement.
Hotels: Blundellsands.

M146 Westhoughton
☎(0942) 811085
Long Island, Westhoughton, Bolton, Lancs BL5 2BR
4 miles SW of Bolton on A58.
Meadowland course.
9 holes, 5834 yards, S.S.S.68
Founded 1929
Visitors: welcome weekdays, with member only at weekends.
Green Fee: apply for details.
Societies: by arrangement.
Catering: snacks, meals except Mon.

M147 Whalley
☎(0254) 822236
Portfield Lane, Whalley, Blackburn, Lancs BB6 9DR

A59 to Whalley, course on left of road to Accrington.
Parkland course.
9 holes, 6258 yards, S.S.S.70
Founded 1912
Visitors: welcome except Thurs 12.30-4pm (Ladies Day) and Sat during April-Sept.
Green Fee: £15 (£8 with member) WD, £20 (£8 with member) WE & BH.
Societies: by arrangement.
Catering: lunches, teas and dinners except Mon. Snooker.
Hotels: Moat House; Dunkenhalgh.

M148 Whitefield
☎(061) 766 2904
81/83 Higher Lane, Whitefield, Manchester M25 7EZ
Leave M62 at exit 17 onto A56, club is 200 yards on left in Higher Lane.
Parkland course.
18 holes, 5714 yards, S.S.S.68
Founded 1932
Visitors: welcome.
Green Fee: apply for details.
Societies: Tues-Fri, special rates on application.
Catering: meals served.
Hotels: Bolton Crest; Hazeldean.

M149 Whittaker
☎(0706) 378310
Shore Lane, Littleborough, Lancs OL15 0LH
1.5 miles from town centre.
Moorland course.
9 holes, 5576 yards, S.S.S.67
Founded 1906
Visitors: welcome except Sun and Tues pm.
Green Fee: £10 (£5 with member) WD, £12 (£5 with member) WE.
Societies: apply to Sec.
Catering: none, bar can be arranged.

M150 Wigan
☎(0257) 421360
Arley Hall, Haigh, Wigan WN1 2UH
Leave M6 at exit 27, through Standish on B5239, turn left at traffic lights at Canal Bridge, opposite Crawford Arms public house.
Parkland course.
9 holes, 6058 yards, S.S.S.69
Founded 1898
Visitors: welcome any day except Tues and Sat.
Green Fee: £25 WD, £30 WE (reduced for parties of 12+).
Societies: on application, special package available.

Catering: available.
Hotels: Bellingham; Brockett Arms; Kilhey Court.

M151 **William Wroe**
☎(061) 748 8680
Pennybridge Lane, Flixton, Manchester M31 3DL
M63 exit 4, B5124, then B5158 to Flixton road; 12 miles N of Manchester centre.
Municipal parkland course.
18 holes, 4395 yards, S.S.S.61
Visitors: welcome, 8am-4.30pm.
Green Fee: £5/round WD, £7/round WE & BH.
Societies: welcome, book 7 days in advance.

M152 **Wilpshire**
☎(0254) 248260
72 Whalley Rd, Wilpshire, Blackburn, Lancs BB1 9LF
On A666 4 miles N of Blackburn.
Moorland course.
18 holes, 5911 yards, S.S.S.69
Founded 1890
Visitors: welcome weekdays.
Green Fee: on application.
Societies: welcome, catered for weekdays.
Catering: lunches served daily, except Mon.
Hotels: Moat House; Trafalgar (Salmesbury).

M153 **Windermere**
☎(05394) 43123
Cleabarrow, Windermere, Cumbria LA23 3NB
1.25 miles from Bowness on Kendal road B5284.
Undulating parkland course.
18 holes, 5006 yards, S.S.S.65
Designed by George Low.
Founded 1891
Visitors: welcome; must be members of recognised golf club and have official handicaps.
Green Fee: £20/day WD, £25/day WE & BH.
Societies: welcome by prior arrangement, numbers 12-60 catered for.
Catering: bar daily, bar meals 12am-2pm, 6.30-9pm except Mon. Snooker.
Hotels: Wild Boar (Crook).

M154 **Woolton**
☎(051) 486 2298 Sec, 486 1298 Pro
Doe Park, Speke Rd, Woolton, Liverpool L25 7TZ
6 miles from City centre.
Parkland course.
18 holes, 5706 yards, S.S.S.68
Founded 1901
Visitors: welcome.
Green Fee: £20 WD, £28 WE.
Societies: catered for weekdays; not Tues.
Catering: by arrangement.

M155 **Workington**
☎(0900) 603460 Steward, 67828 Pro
Branthwaite Rd, Workington, Cumbria CA14 4SS
Off A595 2 miles SE of town centre.
Undulating meadowland course.
18 holes, 6217 yards, S.S.S.70
Designed by James Braid.
Founded 1893
Visitors: welcome, must be members of golf club and hold current h/cap cert.
Green Fee: £17 WD, £22 WE & BH.
Societies: apply to Sec.
Catering: except Mon and Thurs pm.
Hotels: Westlands; Trout; Moota; Hunday Manor; Workington; Cockermouth.

M156 **Worsley**
☎(061) 789 4202
Stableford Ave, Monton, Eccles, Manchester M30 8AP
1 mile from junction of M62/M63.
Parkland course.
18 holes, 6217 yards, S.S.S.70
Designed by James Braid.
Founded 1894
Visitors: welcome if member of golf club with official h/cap.
Green Fee: £20/day.
Societies: Mon, Wed and Thurs.
Catering: available from 12am. Snooker.
Hotels: Wendover.

YORKSHIRE

Crossing the Pennines and approaching Yorkshire on the M62 gives a perfect impression of the wild loneliness of the countryside, an impression that can only be reinforced as you travel north.

Nevertheless, the area around Leeds is the one most blessed with the quality of its golf and its courses. Few courses, if any, are as much dominated by a river as Ilkley, particularly the opening holes which have a habit of destroying a score before it has taken shape. For all its modest length, Ilkley is quite a handful.

Alwoodley, Moor Allerton, Moortown and Sand Moor formed a distinguished cluster until Moor Allerton sold up and moved out towards Wike. The development of houses on the old course and on part of Sand Moor meant that Moortown became so surrounded that a redesign of their layout was essential. Sand Moor relocated their clubhouse on the other side of Alwoodley Lane and added several new holes but both Moortown and Sand Moor have preserved their considerable reputations.

Alwoodley, handiwork of the legendary Alister Mackenzie, is undoubtedly one of his finest, an elegant, demanding course in a wonderful setting that is not as well known as it should be. The latest version of Moor Allerton lies close by, the creation of Robert Trent Jones, while the outlying areas of Yorkshire's county town have pleasant golfing attractions, notably Headingley, Scarcroft, Garforth and the new Lees Golf Centre between Moor Allerton and Alwoodly.

Neighbouring Bradford boasts West Bowling and the Bradford Club while Halifax is well served and Huddersfield claims Crosland Heath, Woodsome Hall and the Huddersfield GC at Fixby which is probably the pick. Bradley Park, on the edge of the M62 is a well used public course. Moving south-east, the Sheffield district is full of good things. Hallamshire, Hallowes, Dore & Totley, Abbeydale, Lees Hall and Phoenix constitute the pick; nor must one forget Doncaster Town Moor, Wheatley and the Doncaster Club as thoughts move to the East Riding. Doncaster Town Moor is close to the racecourse and Doncaster Rovers FC, a real sporting cocktail.

Of the old North Riding courses, Ganton surely wears the crown. Lying in the midst of the lovely Vale of Pickering, it is without doubt one of the finest inland courses in Britain and the only one to have housed the British Amateur championship, which it did for the first time in 1964. Michael Bonallack's "impertinence" in going round in 61 in the final of the 1968 English Championship should not deceive anyone into thinking that it is short or straightforward.

A round at Ganton is always a boost to the spirits, but Pannal at Harrogate and Fulford, York, are other courses that have welcomed their share of professional tournaments. From a clubhouse position close to the Leeds/Harrogate road, Pannal rises onto higher ground but Fulford is almost entirely flat, the stiffest climb being over the bridge that crosses the York by-pass. It splits the course virtually in two, a layout more on the lines of ancient seaside links which take the golfer straight out for six holes, then, after a pleasant loop, straight back.

Scarborough has both North Cliff and South Cliff, the one designed by James Braid, the other by Alister Mackenzie. North Cliff is the sterner but Braid also had a hand in Bridlington, while Filey is a course of which I retain happy memories of a pleasant round many years ago.

Further south, Beverley & East Riding and Driffield form convenient stopping-off spots for travellers to the area of Hull which has a municipal course at Springhead Park, plus the Hull GC and Hessle. Boothferry is another municipal course while up in the north of the county Catterick Garrison and Richmond stand out along with Bedale and, just to the south, the pleasant 9 holes of Ripon City.

N1 **Abbeydale**
☎(0742) 360763
Twentywell Lane, Dore, Sheffield
S17 4QA
Off A621 5 miles S of Sheffield.
Parkland course.
18 holes, 6419 yards, S.S.S.71
Founded 1895
Visitors: welcome by arrangement;
not before 9.30am, or
12am-1.30pm.
Green Fee: £27 WD, £32 WE & BH.
Societies: Tues and Fri by
arrangement.
Catering: bar snacks and restaurant
throughout the day. Snooker.
Hotels: Beauchief; Sheffield Moat
House.

N2 **Aldwark Manor**
☎(0347) 838353, 838867 Fax
Aldwark, Alne, York YO6 2NF
12 miles N of York in village of
Aldwark off A19; 5 miles SE of
Boroughbridge off A1.
Parkland course, easy walking.
18 holes, 6171 yards, S.S.S.69
Founded 1978
Visitors: welcome weekdays,
weekends by arrangement.

Green Fee: £16/round, £20/day WD;
£20/round, £24/day WE & BH.
Societies: by arrangement.
Catering: snacks and full restaurant;
banqueting and private parties.
Hotels: Aldwark Manor on course.

N3 **Alwoodley**
☎(0532) 681680
Wigton Lane, Alwoodley, Leeds LS17
8SA
5 miles N of Leeds on A61
Leeds-Harrogate road.
Heathland/moorland course.
18 holes, 6686 yards, S.S.S.72
Designed by Dr A. Mackenzie/H. Colt.
Founded 1907
Visitors: weekdays only by
arrangement.
Green Fee: apply for details.
Societies: welcome by arrangement.
Catering: bar and restaurant
facilities by arrangement.
Hotels: Harewood Arms.

N4 **Ampleforth College**
☎(0439) 70678
c/o Sec, Beckdale Cottage, 56 High
St, Helmsley, York YO6 5AE

In village of Gilling East, 20 miles N of
York on Helmsley road B1363.
Parkland course.
10 holes, 4018 yards, S.S.S.63
Designed by Ampleforth College.
Founded 1962
Visitors: welcome except visitors
must give way to College pupils
2-4pm during term time; apply for
play and pay green fees at Fairfax
Arms in Gilling East.
Green Fee: £6/day WD, £12/day WE
& BH.
Societies: apply to Sec.
Catering: at Fairfax Arms in village.

N5 **Austerfield Park**
☎ and Fax; (0302) 710841, 710850
Cross Lane, Austerfield, Doncaster, S
Yorks DN10 6RF
On roundabout, A614 2 miles N of
Bawtry.
Parkland course.
18 holes, 6828 yards, S.S.S.73
Designed by E. and M. Baker Ltd.
Founded 1974
Visitors: welcome any day.
Green Fee: £13, £8 Eurogolf and
guest WD; £17, £9 Eurogolf and
guest WE.

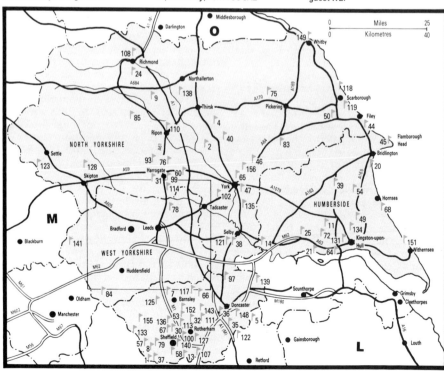

Societies: welcome, packages from £14.
Catering: full bar and restaurant. Driving range, Pitch & Putt Par 3, flat green bowls.
Hotels: Crown; Mount Pleasant; Punches; Three Counties.

N6 **Baildon**
☎(0274) 584266
Moorgate, Baildon, Shipley, W Yorks BD17 5PP
5 miles N of Bradford, A6037 to Shipley, 0.75 mile NE on A6038, left at Junction Hotel.
Moorland course.
18 holes, 6278 yards, S.S.S.70
Founded 1896
Visitors: welcome weekdays and at weekends by arrangement.
Green Fee: on application.
Societies: welcome.
Catering: lunches except Mon.
Hotels: Bankfield (Cottingley).

N7 **Barnsley**
☎(0226) 382856
Wakefield Rd, Staincross, Nr Barnsley, S Yorks S75 6JZ
On A61 3 miles from Barnsley.
Public meadowland course.
18 holes, 6048 yards, S.S.S.69
Founded 1928
Visitors: welcome.
Green Fee: apply for details.
Societies: arrange with Pro.
Catering: bar meals.
Hotels: Queens; Ardley Moat House.

N8 **Beauchief**
☎(0742) 620040, 367274
Abbey Lane, Sheffield S8 0DB
5 miles from city centre, Abbeydale Rd is on A625 to Baslow.
Municipal meadowland course.
18 holes, 5452 yards, S.S.S.66
Founded 1925
Visitors: welcome.
Green Fee: £7.50/round; day tickets not available.
Societies: weekdays only, by arrangement with City of Sheffield Recreation Dept, Meersbrook Park, Sheffield S8 9FL.
Catering: meals served daily.
Hotels: Beauchief adjacent to course.

N9 **Bedale**
☎(0677) 422568
Leyburn Rd, Bedale, N Yorks DL8 1EZ
On A684 immediately on leaving Bedale.
Parkland course.
18 holes, 6565 yards, S.S.S.71
Founded 1894
Visitors: welcome.
Green Fee: £16 WD, £24 WE.
Societies: weekdays only.
Catering: served daily except Mon.
Hotels: Leeming Motel (N'allerton); Old Vicarage (Bedale).

N10 **Ben Rhydding**
☎(0943) 608759
High Wood, Ben Rhydding, Ilkley, W Yorks LS29 8SB

Keep left after passing Wheatley Hotel to top of hill, then left to golf course.
Moorland course.
9 holes, 4711 yards, S.S.S.64
Founded 1947
Visitors: welcome; not weekends.
Green Fee: £10 WD, £15 WE.
Hotels: Wheatley; Craiglands.

N11 **Beverley & East Riding**
☎(0482) 868757
Anti Mill, Westwood, Beverley HU17 8RG
On Beverley-Walkington road.
Undulating course.
18 holes, 5937 yards, S.S.S.69
Designed by Dr J.J. Fraser.
Founded 1889
Visitors: welcome weekdays.
Green Fee: £11 WD, £15 WE & BH.
Societies: weekdays.
Catering: lunch and evening meals served.
Hotels: Beverley Arms; Lairgate.

N12 **Bingley St Ives**
☎(0274) 562436, 562506 Pro
The Mansion, St Ives Estate, Bingley, W Yorks BD16 1AT
Turn off A650, Bingley town centre on Harden-Cullingworth road; 0.5 mile on right, turn right into St Ives Estate.
Wooded parkland/moorland course.
18 holes, 6480 yards, S.S.S.71
Designed by Alistair Mackenzie.
Founded 1931
Visitors: welcome weekdays.
Green Fee: on application.
Societies: weekdays.
Catering: meals served daily except Mon.
Hotels: Bankfield.

N13 **Birley Wood**
☎(0742) 647262, 471258 Captain
Birley Lane, Sheffield S12 3BP
4 miles S of Sheffield off A616 towards Mosborough; M1 junctions 30 or 33.
Public open course.
18 holes, 5100 yards, S.S.S.64
Founded 1974
Visitors: no restrictions.
Green Fee: £4 (9 holes), £6.95 (18 holes) WD; £7.50 WE.
Societies: welcome, phone Sheffield Recreation Dept (500500).
Catering: meals at Fairways Inn adjoining course.
Hotels: Grosvenor (Sheffield).

N14 Boothferry

☎(0430) 430364
Spaldington, Howden, Goole DN14 7NG
A63 towards Howden then B1228 to Bubwith for 3 miles.
Public meadowland course.
18 holes, 6651 yards, S.S.S.72
Designed by Donald Steel.
Founded 1982
Visitors: welcome weekdays, weekends and Bank Holidays except Christmas Day.
Green Fee: on application.
Societies: catered for any day except certain club competitions days; reduced rates for societies of 12 players or more.
Catering: meals and snacks served all lunchtimes except Christmas Day, and summer season evenings except Mon.

N15 Bradford

☎(0943) 875570 Sec, 873719 Pro
Hawksworth Lane, Guiseley, Leeds LS20 8NP
From Shipley 3.5 miles NE on A6038, left to Hawksworth Lane.
Moorland/parkland course.
18 holes, 6303 yards, S.S.S.71
Founded 1891
Visitors: weekdays unlimited; weekends not before noon.
Green Fee: £20/round £25/day WD, £32/round/day WE.
Societies: weekdays.
Catering: full facilities; functions. Snooker.
Hotels: Chevin Lodge; Hollins Hall.

N16 Bradford Moor

☎(0274) 638313
Scarr Hall, Pollard Lane, Bradford BD2 4RW
2 miles from Bradford city centre.
Undulating meadowland course.
9 holes, 5900 yards, S.S.S.68
Founded 1907
Visitors: welcome; after 4pm Fri and WE & BH visitors must play with member.
Green Fee: £12/round/day (£6 with member) WD; £8 with member Fri after 4pm, WE & BH.
Societies: welcome weekdays.
Catering: meals served. Snooker.

N17 Bradley Park

☎(0484) 539988
Bradley Rd, Huddersfield, W Yorks HD2 1PZ

M62 runs alongside course between junctions 24 and 25, boundary borders on A6107 Bradley Rd, entrance to course signposted midway along Bradley Rd.
Public undulating parkland course.
18 holes, 6220 yards, S.S.S.70; 9 holes Par 3
Designed by Donald Steel.
Founded 1977
Visitors: welcome anytime.
Green Fee: £8.75/round WD, £12.75 WE.
Societies: Mon-Fri, not weekends; contact Pro.
Catering: full facilities. Driving range.
Hotels: Ladbroke; George; Golf House.

N18 Brandon

☎(0532) 737471
Holywell Lane, Shadwell, Leeds, W Yorks LS17 8EZ
NW of Leeds, 1 mile from N Leeds ring road at Roundhay Park.
Parkland course.
18 holes, 3650 yards, S.S.S.62
Designed by George Eric Allamby.
Founded 1967
Visitors: 8am-dusk 7 days, must have set of clubs each and appropriate footwear.
Green Fee: £7 WD, £7.50 WE & BH; reduced rates for jnrs and OAPs.
Societies: weekdays, 10 days notice.
Catering: snacks available all day.
Hotels: White House; Rydal Bank.

N19 Branshaw

☎(0535) 647441 Bookings, 643235 Clubhouse
Branshaw Moor, Oakworth, Keighley, W Yorks BD22 7ES
B6143 2 miles SW of Keighley.
Moorland course.
18 holes, 5858 yards, S.S.S.69
Designed by James Braid, Alastair McKenzie.
Founded 1912
Visitors: welcome any time but must phone Pro for time; h/cap cert required.
Green Fee: £16 WD, £21 WE & BH.
Societies: weekdays, package available from Pro.
Catering: every day except Mon.
Hotels: Old Hall; White Lion.

N20 Bridlington

☎(0262) 672092, 606367
Belvedere Rd, Bridlington, E Yorkshire YO15 3NA

1.5 miles S of Bridlington station, off A165 from Hull.
Seaside course.
18 holes, 6491 yards, S.S.S.71
Designed by James Braid.
Founded 1905
Visitors: welcome.
Green Fee: £15 WD, £20 WE & BH.
Societies: welcome by arrangement with Hon Sec.
Catering: full facilities.
Hotels: Marine; The Spa; Monarch.

N21 Brough

☎(0482) 667291 Sec, 667374 Club, 667483 Pro
Cave Rd, Brough, N Humberside HU15 1HB
10 miles W of Hull off A63.
Parkland course.
18 holes, 6159 yards, S.S.S.69
Founded 1893
Visitors: weekdays only; Wed after 2.30pm only.
Green Fee: on application.
Societies: Tues and Fri.
Catering: available.
Hotels: Cave Castle; Crest (Hull).

N22 Calverley

☎(0532) 569244 Pro, 564362 Club
Woodhall Lane, Pudsey, Leeds LS28 5QY
7 miles from Leeds centre, 4 miles from Bradford centre.
Parkland course, 18 holes private, 9 holes public.
18 holes, 5527 yards, S.S.S.67; 9 holes, 2581 yards, Par 34
Founded 1983
Visitors: welcome; h/cap cert required for 18 hole course; 9 hole course unrestricted.
Green Fee: £10 WD, £15 WE; 9 hole course, £6 any day (for 18 holes).
Societies: any time by arrangement.
Catering: bar and restaurant.

N23 Castle Fields

☎(0484) 712108
Rastrick Common, Rastrick, Brighouse, W Yorks
Parkland course.
6 holes, 2406 yards, S.S.S.50
Founded 1903
Visitors: only with member.
Green Fee: apply for details.

N24 Catterick Garrison

☎(0748) 833268 Sec, 833271 Pro
Leyburn Rd, Catterick Garrison, N Yorks DL9 3QE

Alwoodley

Alwoodley is a course of unsuspected beauty. It lies a shortish bus ride from the centre of Leeds suggesting a setting within sight and sound of urban outline and bustle, but those familiar with the glorious Dales country to the north will know how quickly it can be reached and that the Club's attractive name is remarkably descriptive and apt.

For much of its existence, Alwoodley has been one of the most private clubs in the country where a round for the visitor was very much a privilege. There was no wish or need for the club to seek attention and nobody could blame them for that. But in 1965, they acted as host to the Yorkshire Amateur Championship for what, according to *The Golfers Handbook*, was the first time and in 1966 the English Women had the pleasure of holding their Championship there.

Alwoodley is a close neighbour of Moortown and Sand Moor, Alwoodley's first secretary being the eminent golf course architect, Dr Alister Mackenzie who had a hand in the present layout.

Golf at Alwoodley, on part of Lord Harewood's Estate, had, before my first visit, been described to me in enthusiastic terms but, even so, I confess surprise at finding what must surely rank as one of the finest inland courses in Britain. Its admirers had not done it justice.

It was my good luck to have Rodney Foster, winner of the 1965 Yorkshire Amateur at Alwoodley, as my guide and we were fortunate in having a glorious day for our round but the immediate impression was of the number of challenging strokes to be met. From the back tees in any sort of wind, a scratch man could be delighted with a score of 75.

In appearance, the course is a little like Woodhall Spa with an added hint of Walton Heath. Its character is moorland with plenty of heather, gorse, bushes, trees and consuming undergrowth and there is a constant feeling of escape from the city. There is even a fair chance of completing a premature introduction to agricultural surroundings by driving over the hedge on the left of the first tee which is an alarmingly full view of the charming clubhouse but, for all the excellence of the drive and pitch 2nd hole, the course really starts after crossing the road to the 3rd.

This is a five for most people's money and, by the time the first short hole is reached at the 7th, other fives at the 4th, 5th and 6th may also have to be marked down. However, nobody need ever be ashamed of a five at the 8th (543 yards), a magnificent hole curving around a wood into which it is so easy to hook. Not that one's troubles end with the drive. The second shot must make a formidable carry or else find a narrow elbow of fairway.

After such a severe beginning, there are mercifully three short ones among five holes around the turn but the 10th is another of Alwoodley's classic doglegs where nobody is quite happy until he has left it behind. This a sharp left-hander where a long drive is needed to negotiate what can be a full second shot to a green in a hidden dell.

The other is the 15th, with danger this time awaiting the slicer, and a superb approach to an unusually shaped green awaiting everyone; but in between, are two grand fours and the longest short hole (211 yards), a testing stroke in a cross wind. These holes provide perfect balance to the round which ends with three more par 4s, the shortest of which is 435 yards.

No matter how one plays them, or has scored as a whole, three strong impressions remain. Enjoyment will have been increased by the excellence of the lies on springy turf. There will undoubtedly be an urge to return and the completeness of the examination faced is confirmed by the fact that you will probably have used, at sometime, every club in the bag. Not many courses can make claims such as these but an interesting tailpiece is contained in Mackenzie's book on Golf Architecture which informs the reader that at Alwoodley and Moortown "practically every green and every hummock has been artificially made, and yet it is difficult to convince the stranger that this is so".

6 miles SW of Scotch Corner, turn off A1 at Catterick Garrison and follow signs (2.5 miles).
Undulating moorland/parkland course.
18 holes, 6332 yards, S.S.S.70
Designed by Arthur Day.
Founded 1932
Visitors: welcome.
Green Fee: £17.50 WD, £25 WE & BH.
Societies: on application.
Catering: restaurant and bar snacks.
Hotels: Bridge House (Catterick Bridge); Golden Lion (Leyburn).

N25 Cave Castle Hotel
☎(0430) 421286 Golf, 422245 Hotel
South Cave, Brough, E Yorks HU15 2EU
10 miles from city of Kingston upon Hull, junction of A63/M62 East.
Parkland course.
18 holes, 6900 yards, S.S.S.73
Founded July 1989
Visitors: welcome weekdays and weekends.
Green Fee: apply for details.
Societies: weekdays and weekends, special rates by arrangement.
Catering: full facilities; conference and banqueting up to 300, à la carte.
Hotels: Cave Castle, weekday and weekend golfing breaks.

N26 City of Wakefield
☎(0924) 360282 Pro shop
Lupset Park, Horbury Rd, Wakefield, W Yorks WF2 8QS
Approx 2 miles from M1 junctions 39 or 40, course situated on A642 Huddersfield road, turn at Empire Mail Order Stores.
Public parkland course.
18 holes, 6299 yards, S.S.S.70
Founded 1936
Visitors: welcome.
Green Fee: on application.
Societies: apply to Stewardess (0924) 367242.
Catering: meals and snacks for groups, arrange with Stewardess.
Hotels: Swallow; Post House; Cedar Court.

N27 Clayton
☎(0274) 880047
Thornton View Rd, Clayton, Bradford, W Yorks BD14 6JX
On A647 from Bradford, then turn right and follow signs to Clayton.
Moorland course.
9 holes, 5407 yards, S.S.S.67
Founded 1906

Visitors: welcome weekdays and Sat unless tee closed for competition.
Green Fee: £8 WD, £10 Sun (not before 4pm) and Bank Holidays.
Societies: welcome by arrangement; apply to Sec.
Catering: bar and bar snacks except Mon; other by arrangement.
Snooker.
Hotels: Guide Post.

N28 Cleckheaton & District
☎(0274) 874118, 851266 Sec, 851267 Pro
Bradford Rd, Cleckheaton, W Yorks BD19 6BU
M62 exit 26 onto A638 towards Bradford.
Parkland course.
18 holes, 5847 yards, S.S.S.69
Founded 1900
Visitors: welcome.
Green Fee: £22 WD, £28 WE (if available).
Societies: catered for weekdays.
Catering: full facilities available; morning coffee, lunches, afternoon teas, dinner every day except Mon.
Hotels: Novotel (Bradford).

N29 Cocksford
☎(0937) 834253, 530344
Stutton, Tadcaster, N Yorkshire LS24 9NG
1.5 miles S of Tadcaster near village of Stutton.
Parkland course.
18 holes, 5566 yards, S.S.S.69
Designed by Townend and Brodigan.
Founded 1991
Visitors: welcome, correct dress, tee times from Pro shop.
Green Fee: £16/round, £20/day WD, £21/round, £25/day WE & BH.
Societies: welcome weekdays by prior arrangement, £15/round, £20/day, phone for details.
Catering: lounge bar, bar snacks, Sparrows Restaurant, open to non-members.
Hotels: 4 luxury holiday cottages on site; phone as for societies.

N30 Concord Park
☎(0742) 456806 Sec
Shiregreen Lane, Sheffield, S Yorks
Off A6135, 3.5 miles N of Sheffield, next to Concord Sports Centre.
Public undulating parkland course.
18 holes, 4321 yards, S.S.S.62
Founded 1952

Visitors: welcome.
Green Fee: £5.20.
Catering: in adjacent sports centre.

N31 Crimple Valley
☎(0423) 883485
Hookstone Wood Rd, Harrogate, N Yorks HG2 8PN
1 miles S of town centre; turn off A61 at crossroads at Appleyards Garage, after 0.75 mile signposted to right.
Gently sloping fairways in rural setting.
9 holes, 2500 yards, S.S.S.33
Founded 1976
Visitors: welcome at all times.
Green Fee: on application.
Catering: licensed bar, lunches weekdays, breakfasts at weekends.

N32 Crookhill Park
☎(0709) 862979 Pro/Manager, 862974 Clubhouse
Conisbrough, Nr Doncaster, S Yorks DN12 2AH
Between Conisbrough and Edlington; turn off A630 Doncaster-Rotherham road onto B6094, signposted.
Public parkland course.
18 holes, 5839 yards, S.S.S.68
Founded 1975
Visitors: welcome, no restrictions.
Green Fee: £7.50/round all week.
Societies: welcome by arrangement; written confirmation required.
Catering: bar and bar snacks.
Hotels: Consort Suite (Thurcroft); Moat House (Doncaster).

N33 Crosland Heath
☎(0484) 653216, 653262 Sec
Felk Stile Rd, Crosland Heath, Huddersfield HD4 7AF
Take A62 Huddersfield-Oldham road for 3 miles, then follow signs for Goodalls Caravans.
Moorland course.
18 holes, 5962 yards, S.S.S.70
Founded 1913
Visitors: welcome by arrangement; h/cap cert required.
Green Fee: on application.
Societies: welcome except Sat; contact Sec.
Catering: full facilites except Mon.
Hotels: Dryclough (Crosland Moor); Durker Roods (Meltham).

N34 Dewsbury District
☎(0924) 492399, 496030 Pro
The Pinnacle, Sands Lane, Mirfield, W Yorks WF14 8HJ

Off A644, 2.5 miles from Dewsbury, at Swan Hotel turn left into Steanard Lane, sign at Sands Lane.
Undulating meadowland/moorland course.
18 holes, 6256 yards, S.S.S.71
Re-designed by Peter Allis & Dave Thomas (1970).
Founded 1891
Visitors: welcome weekdays by prior arrangement, also weekends after 4pm.
Green Fee: on application.
Societies: welcome.
Catering: full facilites except Mon.
Hotels: Flowerpot Motel; Woolpack.

N35 **Doncaster**
☎(0302) 865632 Office, (0302) 865994 Fax
278 Bawtry Rd, Bessacarr, Doncaster, S Yorks DN4 7PD
Easy to locate between Doncaster and Bawtry on A638.
Undulating heathland course.
18 holes, 6015 yards, S.S.S.69
Founded 1894
Visitors: welcome with or without member, not weekends.
Green Fee: on application.
Societies: welcome weekdays except Wed by prior arrangement with Sec.
Catering: main meals available by prior arrangement daily.
Hotels: Punch's; Danum.

N36 **Doncaster Town Moor**
☎(0302) 535286 Pro, 533167 Clubhouse/Sec
Bawtry Rd, Belle Vue, Doncaster, S Yorks DN4 5HU
400 yards S of racecourse roundabout on A638 travelling towards Bawtry; entrance as for Doncaster Rovers Football Ground.
Parkland course.
18 holes, 6094 yards, S.S.S.69
Founded 1895
Visitors: welcome except Sun before 11.30am.
Green Fee: £13/round, £15/day WD; £15/round, £17/day WE & BH.
Societies: apply to Competition Sec.
Catering: available; contact Steward (0302) 533167.
Hotels: Danum; Earl of Doncaster; Punches; Rockingham; Grand St Leger.

N37 **Dore & Totley**
☎(0742) 360492, 366844 Pro, 369872 Sec

Bradway Rd, Sheffield, S Yorks S17 4QR
Off A61 Sheffield-Chesterfield road on Holmesfield Rd.
Parkland course.
18 holes, 6301 yards, S.S.S.70
Founded 1913
Visitors: welcome by prior arrangement.
Green Fee: £28.
Societies: welcome weekdays except Wed.
Catering: full facilities except Mon. Snooker.
Hotels: Beauchief.

N38 **Drax**
☎(0405) 860533 Sec
Drax, Nr Selby, N Yorks, N Yorks YO8 8PQ
Off A1041 6 miles S of Selby, opposite Drax Power Station.
Parkland course with many trees.
9 holes, 5510 yards, S.S.S.67
Founded 1989
Visitors: only if introduced by member.
Green Fee: on application.
Catering: at Drax Sports and Social Club.

N39 **Driffield**
☎(0377) 253116 Clubhouse, 240599 Office/Fax, 240448 Pro
Sunderlandwick, Driffield, N Humberside YO25 9AD
1 mile from Driffield town centre towards Hull on A164.
Parkland course.
18 holes, 6199 yards, S.S.S.70
Founded 1935
Visitors: welcome, h/cap certs required.
Green Fee: £18/round/day WD, £28 WE.
Societies: catered for weekdays.
Catering: not Mon, except parties by arrangement.
Hotels: Bell.

N40 **Easingwold**
☎(0347) 821486, 821964 Pro
Stillington Rd, Easingwold, N Yorks YO6 3ET
0.75 mile off A19, entering Easingwold from York turn right immediately past garage.
Parkland course.
18 holes, 6262 yards, S.S.S.70
Founded 1930
Visitors: welcome.
Green Fee: £23/day WD, £28/day WE & BH.

Societies: by arrangement (not weekends or Bank Holidays).
Catering: bar lunches, lunches, dinners except Mon.
Hotels: George.

N41 **East Bierley**
☎(0274) 681023
South View Rd, Bierley, Bradford, W Yorks
3 miles SE of Bradford on Wakefield-Heckmondwike Rd.
Undulating moorland course.
9 holes, 4692 yards, S.S.S.62
Founded 1909
Visitors: no restrictions except Mon evening and Sun.
Green Fee: apply for details.
Societies: welcome by arrangement, write for details.
Catering: bar and restaurant daily. Snooker.

N42 **Elland**
☎(0422) 372505
Hammerstones, Leach Lane, Elland, W Yorks HX5 0TA
Leave M62 at junction 24, look for Blackley sign, approx 1 mile.
Parkland course.
18 holes, 5630 yards, S.S.S.66
Founded 1912
Visitors: welcome weekdays.
Green Fee: apply for details.
Societies: by arrangement.
Catering: meals, bar snacks except Mon.
Hotels: Hilton National; The Rock.

N43 **Ferrybridge 'C'**
☎(0977) 674188 extn 2852
Ferrybridge 'C' P.S. Golf Club, P.O. Box 39, Strangland Lane, Knottingley, W Yorks WF11 8SQ
400 yards to W side of A1, on Castleford-Knottingley road.
9 holes, 5138 yards, S.S.S.65
Designed by N.E. Pugh.
Founded 1976
Visitors: with member only.
Green Fee: £5/day WD, £6/day WE & BH.
Societies: by arrangement.

N44 **Filey**
☎(0723) 513293 Sec
West Ave, Filey, N Yorks YO14 9BQ
Private road off end of West Ave in S end of town.
Seaside course.
18 holes, 6104 yards, S.S.S.69
Founded 1897

Visitors: unaccompanied with proof of membership of a golf club and/or h/cap cert.
Green Fee: winter, £16 WD, £20 WE; summer, £20 WD, £25 WE.
Societies: by arrangement, not Bank Holidays.
Catering: all year. Snooker.
Hotels: White Lodge.

N45 Flamborough Head
☎(0262) 850333
Lighthouse Rd, Flamborough, Bridlington, N Humberside YO15 1AR
5 miles NE of Bridlington on B1255, near lighthouse on headland at Flamborough.
Undulating course.
18 holes, 5438 yards, S.S.S.66
Founded 1932
Visitors: welcome; restricted Sun am, Wed 10.30am-1.30pm.
Green Fee: £12 WD, £16 WE & BH.
Societies: apply to Sec.
Catering: full facilities except Mon. Snooker table.
Hotels: Flaneburg; Timoneer.

N46 Forest Park
☎(0904) 400425
Stockton on Forest, York, N Yorks YO3 9UW
2 miles from E end of York by-pass, in village of Stockton on Forest.
Parkland course.
18 holes, 6211yards, S.S.S.71; 9 holes, S.S.S.70
Founded 1991
Visitors: welcome, phone for tee times.
Green Fee: £15/round, £20/day WD; £20/round WE & BH.
Societies: welcome by arrangement.
Catering: bar, dining room; snacks and full catering.
Driving range.

N47 Fulford
☎(0904) 413579 Sec, 412882 Pro
Heslington Lane, Heslington, York YO1 5DY
Off A19 from York, follow signs to University.
Parkland course.
18 holes, 6779 yards, S.S.S.72
Designed by Dr A. Mackenzie.
Founded 1906
Visitors: by prior arrangement.
Green Fee: on application.
Societies: contact Sec.
Catering: morning coffee, lunch and evening meal.
Hotels: Alfreda.

N48 Fulneck
☎(0532) 565191
The Clubhouse, Fulneck, Pudsey, W Yorks LS28 8NT
Between Leeds and Bradford.
Undulating wooded parkland course.
9 holes, 5432 yards, S.S.S.67
Founded 1892
Visitors: welcome weekdays, with member only weekends.
Green Fee: £12 (£6 with member).
Societies: by arrangement.
Catering: by arrangement.

N49 Ganstead Park
☎(0482) 811280 Sec, 811121 Pro
Longdales Lane, Coniston, Hull HU11 4LB
On A165 E of Hull, 2 miles from city boundary.
Parkland course.
18 holes, 6801 yards, S.S.S.73
Designed by Peter Green.
Founded 1976
Visitors: any day except Sun am.
Green Fee: £15/round, £20/day (£10 with member) WD; £20 (£12 with member) WE.
Societies: by arrangement.
Catering: lunches, evening meals.
Hotels: Hull Marina; Beverley Arms.

N50 Ganton
☎(0944) 710329
Ganton, Scarborough, N Yorks YO12 4PA
11 miles from Scarborough on A64.
Heathland course.
18 holes, 6720 yards, S.S.S.74
Designed by Dunn, Vardon, Colt, C.K. Cotton.
Founded 1891
Visitors: by prior arrangement.
Green Fee: on application.
Societies: welcome by prior arrangement.
Catering: available.
Hotels: Hackness Grange; Crown; Crescent (Scarborough).

N51 Garforth
☎(0532) 862021
Long Lane, Garforth, Leeds LS25 2DS
6.5 miles E of Leeds on A63, then left onto A642.
Parkland course.
18 holes, 6296 yards, S.S.S.70
Founded 1913
Visitors: welcome weekdays.
Green Fee: apply for details.
Societies: during the week.
Catering: all days except Tues.

N52 Gott's Park
☎(0532) 310492
Armley Ridge Rd, Leeds LS12 2QX
About 3 miles W of city centre.
Public parkland course.
18 holes, 4960 yards, S.S.S.64
Founded 1933
Visitors: welcome.
Green Fee: on application.
Societies: on application to Leeds Council.
Catering: meals served.
Hotels: Queens; Dragonara.

N53 Grange Park
☎(0709) 559497 Pro
Upper Wortley Rd, Rotherham S61 2SJ
2 miles W of town on A629.
Municipal parkland course.
18 holes, 6461 yards, S.S.S.71
Founded 1971
Visitors: no restrictions.
Green Fee: £7 WD, £8 WE.
Catering: available on request (private clubhouse).

N54 Hainsworth Park
☎(0964) 542362
Brandesburton, Driffield, E Yorks YO25 8RT
On A165 8 miles N of Beverley.
Parkland course.
18 holes, 5950 yards, S.S.S.69
Founded 1983
Visitors: some restrictions. phone beforehand.
Green Fee: £10 WD, £15 WE & BH.
Societies: any time.
Catering: bar and restaurant facilities.
Hotels: Burton Lodge on course.

N55 Halifax
☎(0422) 244171
Union Lane, Ogden, Halifax HX2 8XR
4 miles from town centre on A629 Halifax-Keighley road.
Moorland course.
18 holes, 6037 yards, S.S.S.70
Designed by W.H. Fowler, James Braid.
Founded 1895
Visitors: welcome weekdays.
Green Fee: £20/day WD, £30/day WE & BH.
Societies: weekdays and limited weekends.
Catering: full range of catering facilites, à la carte and table d'hôte, except Mon.
Hotels: Holdsworth House (Holmfield); Princess (Halifax).

N56 Halifax Bradley Hall

☎(0422) 374108
Stainland Rd, Holywell Green,
Halifax, W Yorks HX4 9AN
Half-way between Halifax and
Huddersfield on B6112.
Moorland course.
18 holes, 6213 yards, S.S.S.70
Founded 1924
Visitors: welcome.
Green Fee: £18 WD, £24 WE & BH.
Societies: on application.
Catering: full except Mon and Tues.
Snooker.
Hotels: Old Golf House (Outlane).

N57 Hallamshire

☎(0742) 302153 Sec, 301007
Clubhouse, 305222 Pro
The Clubhouse, Sandygate, Sheffield
S10 4LA
A57 from centre of Sheffield, left fork
at Crosspool (3 miles from centre), 1
mile to course.
Moorland course.
18 holes, 6396 yards, S.S.S.71
Founded 1897
Visitors: weekdays and limited
weekends.
Green Fee: £27 WD, £33 WE & BH,
fees negotiable for large parties.
Societies: weekdays except Tues.
Catering: full facilities.
Snooker.
Hotels: Hallam Tower; Rutland.

N58 Hallowes

☎(0246) 413734 Sec, 411196 Pro
Hallowes Lane, Dronfield, Sheffield
S18 6UA
Take A61 Sheffield-Chesterfield road
into Dronfield (do not take by-pass),
turn sharp right under railway bridge,
club signposted.
Undulating moorland course.
18 holes, 6342 yards, S.S.S.70
Founded 1892
Visitors: weekdays only, unless with
member.
Green Fee: £20/round, £27/day.
Societies: limited.
Catering: by arrangement with the
Stewardess.

N59 Hanging Heaton

☎(0924) 461606, 467077 Pro shop,
430100 Sec's office
White Cross Rd, Bennett Lane,
Dewsbury, W Yorks WF12 7DT
On A653 1 mile from Dewsbury
centre.
Parkland course.
9 holes, 5874 yards, S.S.S.67
Founded 1922
Visitors: welcome weekdays.
Green Fee: on application.
Societies: welcome weekdays.
Catering: lunch except Mon.

N60 Harrogate

☎(0423) 862999 Sec, 862547 Pro,
863158 Steward, 860278
Chef/caterer
Forest Lane Head, Harrogate, N
Yorks HG2 7TF
On right of A59, 2.5 miles from
Harrogate towards Knaresborough.
Undulating parkland course.
18 holes, 6241 yards, S.S.S.70
Designed by Sandy Herd.
Founded 1892
Visitors: welcome.
Green Fee: £26 WD, £40 WE & BH.
Societies: weekdays only by
arrangement, parties over 12.
Catering: bar and restaurant, chef
catering. Snooker.
Hotels: Dower House; Newton House
(Knaresborough).

N61 Headingley

☎(0532) 679573 Sec, 675100 Pro
Back Church Lane, Adel, Leeds LS16
8DW
At roundabout on Leeds ring road
take A660 towards Otley, turn right
after 1 mile at lights, then left, course
is just past Adel Church.
Undulating parkland course.
18 holes, 6298 yards, S.S.S.70
Founded 1892
Visitors: members of other clubs
welcome, prior reservation preferred.
Green Fee: £24/round, £30/day WD;
£36/round/day WE & BH.
Societies: recognised societies
welcome if previous arrangements
made with Sec.
Catering: full facilities (not Fri).
2 snooker tables.
Hotels: Post House; Parkway.

N62 Headley

☎(0274) 833481
Headley Lane, Thornton, Bradford, W
Yorks BD13 3AJ
4 miles W of Bradford, on B6145
Thornton road, in village of Thornton.
Moorland course.
9 holes, 2457 yards, S.S.S.64
Founded 1906
Visitors: unlimited, not Sat.
Green Fee: £6/day, £10 WE.
Societies: by arrangement.
Catering: by arrangement.
Hotels: Norfolk Gardens.

N63 Hebden Bridge

☎(0422) 842896
Wadsworth, Hebden Bridge, W
Yorkshire HX7 8PH
1 mile N of Hebden Bridge past
Birchcliffe Centre.
Moorland course.
9 holes, 5114 yards, S.S.S.65
Founded 1930
Visitors: weekdays no restrictions,
weekends check first.
Green Fee: £10 WD, £15 WE; 50%
reduction with member.
Societies: welcome by arrangement.
Catering: meals and bar snacks
except Mon.
Hotels: Carlton (reduced green fees),
Hebden Lodge, Old Civic Hall; White
Lion.

N64 Hessle

☎(0482) 650171
Westfield Rd, Cottingham, Hull, N
Humberside HU16 5YL
3 miles SW of Cottingham, off A164.
Undulating meadowland course.
18 holes, 6638 yards, S.S.S.72; 18
holes, 6290 yards, S.S.S.70
Designed by Peter Allis & Dave
Thomas.
Founded 1906; new course opened
June 1975
Visitors: not Tues. 9.15am-1pm.
Green Fee: apply for details.
Societies: recognised golfing
societies welcome by prior
arrangement with Sec.
Catering: all days during summer
months.

N65 Heworth

☎(0904) 422389 Pro
Muncaster House, Muncastergate,
York YO3 9JX
1.5 miles from city centre, on A1036
York-Scarborough road.
Meadowland/parkland course.
11 holes, 6078 yards, S.S.S.69
Founded 1911
Visitors: weekdays, weekends
restricted availability.
Green Fee: on application.
Societies: weekdays.
Catering: full except Mon.

N66 Hickleton

☎(0709) 896081 Sec, 892496 Club,
895170 Pro.
Hickleton, Nr Doncaster, S Yorks DN5
7BE
7 miles out of Doncaster on B6411,
off A635 to Barnsley.
Undulating parkland course.

THE CARLTON LODGE

Set in the North Yorkshire Moors National Park, within easy reach of courses at Kirkbymoorside, Malton, Easingwold, York (5) & Scarborough (4 inc championship Ganton), THE CARLTON LODGE offers 2, 3 & 5 day golfing breaks. Award winning cuisine, en suite accommodation and genuine hospitality from convivial hosts.

Bondgate, Helmsley, North Yorkshire, YO6 5EY Tel: (0439) 770557 Fax: (0439) 770623

---

18 holes, 6403 yards, S.S.S.71
Designed by Huggett, Coles & Dyer.
Founded 1909
Visitors: welcome if members of recognised club; after 2.30pm weekends and Bank Holidays.
Green Fee: apply for details.
Societies: weekdays; annual society open day.
Catering: available except Mon.

N67 Hillsborough

☎(0742) 349151 Sec, 332666 Pro
Worrall Rd, Sheffield S6 4BE
Moorland/parkland course.
18 holes, 5518 metres, S.S.S.69
Founded 1920
Visitors: welcome weekdays.
Green Fee: £28/round/day WD, £35 WE & BH.
Societies: by arrangement.
Catering: soup/sandwiches any lunch time except Fri; full meals by prior arrangement.
Snooker.
Hotels: Grosvenor; Rutland.

N68 Hornsea

☎(0964) 532020 Sec, 534989 Pro, 535488 Clubhouse.
Rolston Rd, Hornsea, N Humberside HU18 1XG
Follow sign for Hornsea Pottery in Hornsea, clubhouse is approx 600 yards further on road to Withernsea.
Parkland/moorland course.
18 holes, 6450 yards, S.S.S.71
Designed by Sandy Herd.
Founded 1898
Visitors: every day; after 3pm Sat and Sun, after 2pm Tues.
Green Fee: £18/round, £25/day, £30 WE.
Societies: by arrangement with Sec, not weekends.
Catering: Steward's day off Mon, catering available by arrangement.
Snooker.
Hotels: Tickton Grange; Burton Lodge.

N69 Horsforth

☎(0532) 586819, 585200 Pro
Layton Rd, Horsforth, Leeds, W Yorks LS18 5EX

On A65 Leeds-Ilkley road, Layton Rd is on right after crossing A6120
Leeds ring road, and after passing Rawdon Crematorium on left.
Undulating pastureland course.
18 holes, 6243 yards, S.S.S.70
Founded 1905
Visitors: welcome, not weekends.
Green Fee: £24/day, £30 WE.
Societies: weekdays and Sun.
Catering: full service available.
Hotels: Post House (Bramhope).

N70 Howley Hall

☎(0924) 472432
Scotchman Lane, Morley, Leeds LS27 0NX
From A650 Bradford-Wakefield road, take B6123, situated in Morley.
Parkland course.
18 holes, 6346 yards, S.S.S.71
Founded 1900
Visitors: welcome except Sat.
Green Fee: £19/round, £23/day WD; £26/round/day WE.
Societies: weekdays.
Catering: daily except Mon. Snooker.
Hotels: Post House (Ossett).

N71 Huddersfield (Fixby)

☎(0484) 426203 Sec, 420110
Clubhouse, 426463 Pro.
Fixby Hall, Lightridge Rd, Huddersfield HD2 2EP
M62 exit 24 to Huddersfield, 3rd exit A643 at roundabout, signposted Brighouse, 1 mile to traffic lights (Sun Inn), turn right, after 0.75 mile turn right on Lightridge Rd, entrance to club 500 yards on right.
Heathland course.
18 holes, 6402 yards, S.S.S.71
Designed by Herbert Fowler, amendments by Hawtree.
Founded 1891
Visitors: welcome; societies and companies must book in advance; starting sheets operate; tee reservation recommended.
Green Fee: £25/round, £35/day WD; £35/round, £45/day WE.
Societies: Mon, Wed, Thurs, Fri only.
Catering: lunch, à la carte restaurant by prior arrangement. Snooker.
Hotels: Pennine Hilton; Forte; Clifton; Brighouse.

N72 Hull

☎(0482) 658919
The Hall, 27 Packman Lane, Kirkella, Hull HU10 7TJ
5 miles W of Hull, off A164.
Parkland course.
18 holes, 6242 yards, S.S.S.70
Designed by James Braid.
Founded 1921
Visitors: Mon to Fri only.
Green Fee: £20/round, £25/day.
Societies: Tues and Thurs by prior arrangement.
Catering: prior arrangement if possible, lunches served Mon to Fri.
Snooker.
Hotels: Willerby Manor; Grange Park.

N73 Ilkley

☎(0943) 600214 Sec, 607277
Steward, 607463 Pro
Myddleton, Ilkley, W Yorks LS29 0BE
On A65 18 miles NW of Leeds.
Parkland course.
18 holes, 6262 yards, S.S.S.70
Founded 1890
Visitors: welcome by arrangement.
Green Fee: £30 WD, £35 WE & BH.
Societies: by arrangement weekdays only.
Catering: full facilities.
Hotels: Rombalds; Grove.

N74 Keighley

☎(0535) 604778 Manager, 603179
Clubhouse; 665370 Pro
Howden Park, Utley, Keighley, W Yorks BD20 6DH
1 mile W of Keighley on old Keighley/Skipton road.
Parkland course.
18 holes, 6139 yards, S.S.S.70
Founded 1904
Visitors: not before 9am or 12.30-1.30pm weekdays; Ladies' Day Tues; no visitors Sat, by arrangement Sun.
Green Fee: £21/round £25/day WD; £23/round, £27/day Sun.
Societies: welcome by arrangement with Manager.
Catering: bar and catering 12-2pm and 4.30-10.30pm every day except Mon.
Hotels: Dalesway; Beeches.

N75 Kirkbymoorside

☎(0751) 31525
Manor Vale, Kirkbymoorside, N Yorks
YO6 6EG
On A170 Thirsk to Scarborough road;
Helmsley 7 miles, Pickering 7 miles.
Undulating moorland course.
18 holes, 6027 yards, S.S.S.69
Founded 1905
Visitors: welcome, advisable to
telephone first.
Green Fee: £17 (£7.50 with
member) WD; £20 WE & BH.
Societies: by arrangement with Mrs
Rivis.
Catering: meals and snacks daily
except Mon. Snooker.
Hotels: George & Dragon; Feversham
Arms; Feathers (Helmsley); Worsley
Arms (Hovingham).

N76 Knaresborough

☎(0423) 862690, 863219
Butterhills, Boroughbridge Rd,
Knaresborough HG5 0QQ
1.5 miles N of Knaresborough off
main Boroughbridge road.
Parkland course.
18 holes, 6232 yards, S.S.S.70
Designed by Hawtree & Son.
Founded 1920
Visitors: welcome, few restrictions.
Green Fee: £18/round, £24/day WD
(all year); £24/round, £29/day WE
(available Apr-Oct only).
Societies: catered for.
Catering: every day except Mon.
Hotels: Dower House; Newton House.

N77 Leeds (Cobble Hall)

☎(0532) 658775, 659203 Sec,
658786 Pro
Elmete Lane, Leeds LS8 2LJ
Off A58 Wetherby road, 4 miles from
Leeds.
Parkland course.
18 holes 6097 yards, S.S.S.69
Founded 1896
Visitors: weekdays with prior
booking, weekends only with
member.
Green Fee: £19/round, £25/day.
Societies: by advance booking only,
weekdays.
Catering: full catering and bar
facilities. Snooker.
Hotels: Queens; Hotel Metropole;
Bromhope Post House.

N78 Leeds Golf Centre

☎(0532) 886186
Wike Ridge Lane, Shadwell, Leeds
LS17 9JW

Follow Harrogate signs on A61, turn
right at Wigton Lane, left at T junction
into Wike Ridge Lane.
Heathland course.
18 holes, 6780 yards, Par 72; 9
holes, 1350 yards, Par 3
Designed by Donald Steel.
Founded 1993
Visitors: welcome 7 days, no
restrictions.
Green Fee: £15 WD, £20 WE.
Societies: welcome weekdays.
Catering: full catering all day.
Driving range.
Hotels: Marriott (Leeds).

N79 Lees Hall

☎(0742) 554402 Club, 552900 Sec,
551526 Steward
Hemsworth Rd, Norton, Sheffield S8
8LL
3 miles S of Sheffield, A61 then
A6054 towards Gleadless, 1st exit at
roundabout, follow road to next
roundabout passing water tower on
left, take 1st exit, course 300 yards
on right.
Parkland course.
18 holes, 6137 yards, S.S.S.69
Founded 1907
Visitors: always welcome.
Green Fee: £20/round, £27/day WD;
£30 WE & BH.
Societies: weekdays subject to prior
booking.
Catering: no catering on Tues.
Snooker.
Hotels: Grosvenor House; Hallam
Towers; Sheffield Moat House.

N80 Lightcliffe

☎(0422) 202459
Knowle Top Rd, Lightcliffe, Halifax
On A58 Leeds-Halifax road, on left
entering Lightcliffe/Hipperholme
village 4 miles E of Halifax.
Parkland course.
9 holes, 5388 yards, S.S.S.68
Founded 1907
Visitors: welcome apart from Wed
and Sat.
Green Fee: on application.
Societies: catered for on weekdays
except Wed.
Catering: lunch and evening meals
except Mon.
Hotels: Clifton Trust House.

N81 Longley Park

☎(0484) 422304
Maple St, off Somerset Rd,
Huddersfield HD5 9AX
0.5 mile from town centre.

Parkland course.
9 holes, 5269 yards, S.S.S.66
Founded 1911
Visitors: welcome weekdays except
Wed and Thurs; restricted
weekends.
Green Fee: £11 WD, £13.50 WE.
Societies: by arrangement except
Wed, Thurs and Sat.
Catering: except Mon by
arrangement.

N82 Low Laithes

☎(0924) 273275 Club, 274667 Pro
Parkmill Lane, Flushdyke, Ossett, W
Yorks WF5 9AP
Leave M1 at exit 40, signposted on
Dewsbury road, 1st turning from
northbound exit M1.
Parkland course.
18 holes, 6463 yards, S.S.S.71
Designed by McKenzie.
Founded 1925
Visitors: dress rules and reasonable
golfers.
Green Fee: £22 WD, £30 WE & BH.
Societies: by prior arrangement, not
weekends.
Catering: full facilities daily.
Hotels: Post House; Mews; Swallow.

N83 Malton & Norton

☎(0653) 692959 Clubhouse,
697912 Sec, 693882 Pro
Welham Park, Malton, N Yorks YO17
9QE
From Malton and Norton level
crossing, S on Welham road for 0.75
mile, turn right.
Parkland course.
27 holes: Welham course, 6456
yards, S.S.S.71; Park course, 6231
yards, S.S.S.70; Derwent course,
6267 yards, S.S.S.70
Designed by Hawtree & Son.
Founded 1910
Visitors: welcome, restricted on club
competition days.
Green Fee: £20 WD, £25 WE & BH.
Societies: apply to Sec.
Catering: full facilities, breakfast by
arrangement.
Hotels: Talbot; The Mount;
Burythorpe House; Oakdene Country
House.

N84 Marsden

☎(0484) 844253
Mount Rd, Hemplow, Marsden,
Huddersfield HD7 6NN
Off A62 8 miles out of Huddersfield
towards Manchester.
Moorland course.

9 holes, 5702 yards, S.S.S.68
Designed by Dr Mackenzie.
Founded 1920
Visitors: welcome weekdays.
Green Fee: on application.
Societies: catered for by
arrangement weekdays.
Catering: lunches except Tues,
evening meals by arrangement.
Hotels: Durker Roods (Meltham).

N85 **Masham**
☎(0765) 689379, 689491 Sec
Swinton Rd, Masham, Ripon, N Yorks
HG4 4HT
9 miles N of Ripon on A6108.
Parkland course.
9 holes, 5308 yards, S.S.S.66
Founded 1895
Visitors: welcome weekdays,
weekends and Bank Holidays with
member only.
Green Fee: £15/day.
Societies: apply to Sec.
Catering: bar all day, catering
daytime only.
Hotels: Kings Head.

N86 **Meltham**
☎(0484) 850227, 851521
Pro/bookings
Thick Hollins, Meltham, Huddersfield
HD7 3DQ
5 miles from Huddersfield on B6108,
in Meltham take B6107; from
Holmfirth take A635 and turn right at
Ford Inn.
Moorland/parkland course.
18 holes, 6145 yards, S.S.S.70
Founded 1908
Visitors: any day except Wed, Sat.
Green Fee: £20 WD, £25 WE & BH.
Societies: welcome weekdays, Sun.
Catering: available every day.
Hotels: Durker Roods (Meltham); Old
Bridge (Holmfirth).

N87 **Mid Yorkshire**
☎(0977) 704522, 600823 Fax
Havercroft Lane, Darrngton, Nr
Pontefract, Yorks
400 yards on A1 S from M62/A1
intersection.
Parkland course.
18 holes, S.S.S.71
Designed by Steve Marnoch.
Founded May 1993
Visitors: welcome weekdays;
weekends with member only.
Green Fee: £15 Mon-Tues, £20
Wed-Fri, £15 (with member only) WE.
Societies: unrestricted weekdays by
prio booking; weekends 1-4.30pm.

Catering: public bar, lounge bar,
function suite for up to 200.
Driving range, golf clinic.
Hotels: Darrington.

N88 **Middleton Park**
☎(0532) 700449
Ring Rd, Beeston, Leeds 10, LS10
3TN
3 miles S of city centre.
Public parkland course.
18 holes, 5233 yards, S.S.S.66
Designed by Leeds City Council.
Founded 1932
Visitors: welcome weekdays.
Green Fee: on application.
Societies: can be booked.

N89 **Moor Allerton**
☎(0532) 661154 Administrator,
665209 Pro
Coal Rd, Wike, Leeds LS17 9NH
Take A61 Harrogate Rd, about 1 mile
past intersection with A6120 ring
road turn right onto Wigton Lane, at
T-junction take 1st left, then 1st right
then signposted.
Championship undulating parkland
course.
1-18 The Lakes, 6045 yards,
S.S.S.71; 10-27 Blackmoor, 6222
yards, S.S.S.72; 1-9/19-27 High
Course, 6930 yards, S.S.S.75
Designed by Robert Trent Jones.
Founded 1923
Visitors: welcome weekdays and Sat
Green Fee: on application.
Societies: weekdays, small groups
accepted Sat with prior booking.
Catering: lunches every day; dinner
Tues, Wed, Thurs, unlimited
numbers; Mon, Fri min 40 required;
banqueting for up to 250.

N90 **Moortown**
☎(0532) 686521 Sec, 681682 Club,
683636 Pro, 686521 Fax
Harrogate Rd, Leeds LS17 7DB
A61 approx 5 miles N of Leeds.
Moorland course.
18 holes, 6544 yards, S.S.S.72
Designed by Dr Mackenzie.
Founded 1909
Visitors: welcome weekdays, apply
to Sec/Pro weekends.
Green Fee: £35/round, £40/day WD;
£40/round, £45/day WE.
Societies: weekdays by
arrangement with Sec.
Catering: lunches served except
Mon; other meals by arrangement.
Snooker.
Hotels: Harewood Arms; Post House.

N91 **Normanton**
☎(0924) 892943
Syndale Rd, Normanton, Wakefield,
W Yorks WF6 1PA
Off M62 at junction 31, 0.5 mile from
Normanton centre.
Flat meadowland course.
9 holes, 5184 yards, S.S.S.66
Founded 1903
Visitors: weekdays and Sat,
members only Sun.
Green Fee: apply for details.
Societies: weekdays only.
Catering: full facilities.

N92 **Northcliffe**
☎(0274) 584085
Steward/Clubhouse, 596731
Sec/ans phone, 587193 Pro
High Bank Lane, Shipley, W Yorks
BD18 4LJ
Take A650 Bradford-Keighley road to
Saltaire roundabout, turn up
Moorhead Lane, leading to High Bank
Lane, club 0.5 mile on left.
Parkland course.
18 holes, 6104 yards, S.S.S.69
Designed by James Braid and Harry
Vardon.
Founded 1920
Visitors: welcome except Sat and
Sun; (Tues Ladies Day).
Green Fee: £20 WD, £25 WE & BH.
Societies: welcome Wed-Fri.
Catering: bar, snacks except Mon;
dinner by arrangement with Steward.
Hotels: Bankfield; Regency.

N93 **Oakdale**
☎(0423) 567162
Oakdale, Harrogate HG1 2LN
From Ripon Rd, Harrogate, turn into
Kent Rd, follow signs.
Undulating parkland course with
panoramic views.
18 holes, 6456 yards, S.S.S.71
Designed by Dr Mackenzie.
Founded 1914
Visitors: welcome.
Green Fee: £22/round, £29.50/day
WD; £27.50/round WE.
Societies: weekdays.
Catering: full dining facilities except
Mon lunchtime, dinner by
arrangement.
Hotels: Crown; Fern; Majestic;
Studley; Old Swan; Balmoral.

N94 **Otley**
☎(0943) 465329 Sec, 461015 Club,
463403 Pro
West Busk Lane, Otley, W Yorks LS21
3NG

On Otley-Bradford road 1.5 miles from Otley.
Parkland course.
18 holes, 6225 yards, S.S.S.70
Founded 1906
Visitors: welcome.
Green Fee: apply for details.
Societies: by arrangement.
Catering: full facilities available except Mon.
Hotels: Post House; Devonshire Arms.

N95 **Oulton Park**
☎(0532) 823152
Rothwell, Leeds LS26 8EX
M62 junction 30, A642 to Rothwell, over 1st roundabout (1 mile), immediately left at 2nd roundabout.
Municipal parkland course.
18 holes, 6550 yards, S.S.S.70; 9 holes, 3299 yards, S.S.S.35
Designed by Peter Allis & Dave Thomas.
Founded 1990
Visitors: no restrictions, pay-and-play course, must book at weekends.
Green Fee: 18 hole course, £6.20/round WD, £6.75/round WE; 9 hole course, £4 WD and WE.
Societies: any time during week, after 1pm weekends.
Catering: bar and bar meals all day; restaurant 9am-6pm.
Driving range, pool table.
Hotels: Oulton Park (adjacent).

N96 **Outlane**
☎(0422) 374762
Slack Lane, Outlane, Huddersfield, W Yorks HD3 3YL.
Off A640 Rochdale road, 4 miles out of Huddersfield, through village of Outlane, turn left under motorway.
Semi-moorland course.
18 holes, 6000 yards, S.S.S.68
Founded 1906
Visitors: welcome.
Green Fee: £18 (£9 with member) WD; £25 (£13 with member) WE & BH; reduced rates for jns (18 yrs and under).
Societies: by arrangement with Mrs C. Hirst (on above number).
Catering: meals daily except Mon.
Hotels: Old Golf House; Ladbroke Mercury.

N97 **Owston Park**
☎(0302) 330821
Owston Hall, Owston, Nr Carcroft, Doncaster, S Yorks DN6 9JF

Off A19, 10 mins N of Doncaster.
Parkland course.
9 holes, 3042 yards, S.S.S.71
Designed by Michael Parker.
Founded 1988
Visitors: welcome, pay-as-you-play.
Green Fee: apply for details.
Societies: welcome.

N98 **Painthorpe House Golf & Country Club**
☎(0924) 255083
Painthorpe Lane, Crigglestone, Wakefield, W Yorks WF4 3HE
2 mins from M1 junction 39.
Parkland course.
9 holes, 4250 yards, S.S.S.62
Founded 1961
Visitors: welcome Mon-Fri only.
Green Fee: apply for details.
Societies: by arrangement.
Catering: 4 bars, dining room, 2 ball rooms; conferences, etc.
Hotels: Cedar Court (Durkar).

N99 **Pannal**
☎(0423) 872628 Sec/reservations, 870043 Fax
Follifoot Rd, Pannal, Harrogate HG3 1ES
Just off A61 Leeds-Harrogate road at Pannal.
Parkland/moorland championship course.
18 holes, 6659 yards, S.S.S.72
Designed by Sandy Herd.
Founded 1906
Visitors: welcome weekdays, limited time at weekends.
Green Fee: £29/round, £35/day WD, £35/round WE & BH.
Societies: weekdays by arrangement with Sec.
Catering: meals, bar snacks daily.

N100 **Phoenix**
☎(0709) 382624
Pavilion Lane, Brinsworth, Rotherham, W Yorks
1 mile along Bawtry turning from Tinsley roundabout on M1.
Undulating meadowland course.
18 holes, 6145 yards, S.S.S.69
Founded 1932
Visitors: welcome if member of recognised golf club.
Green Fee: £21/day (£8 with member) WD; £28 (£12 with member) WE & BH.
Societies: welcome.
Catering: full on request.
Hotels: Fairways; Brinsworth; Moat House; Brecon.

N101 **Phoenix Park**
☎(0274) 667573, 610335 Fax.
Phoenix Park, Dick Lane, Thornbury, Bradford, W Yorks
From Bradford take Leeds road (A647) for 2.5 miles to Thornbury roundabout, course situated at side of roundabout.
Undulating parkland course.
9 holes, 4776 yards, S.S.S.63
Visitors: welcome weekdays only.
Green Fee: £8.
Societies: by prior arrangement with Sec.
Catering: by arrangement with Steward prior to visit.

N102 **Pike Hills**
☎(0904) 706566
Tadcaster Rd, Askham Bryan, York YO2 3UW
Turn left towards York off A64 Leeds-Scarborough road immediately after by-pass flyover.
Parkland course.
18 holes, 6121 yards, S.S.S.69
Founded 1920
Visitors: weekdays before 4.30pm; weekends and Bank Holidays only with member.
Green Fee: £15/round, £20/day Summer; £12/round, £15/day Winter (Oct-Mar).
Societies: parties of 12+ welcome if previously booked, correct dress essential, each member must have recognised h/cap.
Catering: full facilities except Mon.

N103 **Pontefract & District**
☎(0977) 792241
Park Lane, Pontefract, W Yorks WF8 4QS
M62 exit 32, situated on B6134.
Parkland course.
18 holes, 6227 yards, S.S.S.70
Founded 1900
Visitors: welcome weekdays.
Green Fee: £25 Wd, £32 WE & BH.
Societies: weekdays except Wed.
Catering: daily, except Mon.
Hotels: Red Lion; Wentbridge House; Park Side Inne.

N104 **Pontefract Park**
☎(0977) 702799
Park Road, Pontefract, W Yorkshire
0.5 mile from M62 towards Pontefract beside race course.
Public parkland course.
9 holes, 2034 yards, Par 31
Visitors: welcome.
Green Fee: apply for details.

N105 **Queensbury**
☎(0274) 882155
Brighouse Rd, Queensbury, Bradford,
W Yorks BD13 1QF
4 miles from Bradford on A647.
Undulating parkland course.
9 holes, 5102 yards, S.S.S.65
Founded 1923
Visitors: bona fide golfers welcome.
Green Fee: apply for details.
Societies: by arrangement.
Catering: during normal licensing
hours.

N106 **Rawdon**
☎(0532) 506040
Buckstone Drive, Rawdon, Leeds
LS19 6BD
On A65 6 miles from Leeds.
Undulating parkland course.
9 holes, 5964 yards, S.S.S.69
Founded 1896
Visitors: welcome weekdays.
Green Fee: on application.
Societies: welcome weekdays by
arrangement.
Catering: lunch except Mon.
3 all-weather tennis courts, 4 grass
(summer).
Hotels: Peas Hill; Robin Hood.

N107 **Renishaw Park**
☎(0246) 432044
Station Rd, Renishaw, Sheffield S31
9UZ
M1 junction 30, take the sign for
Eckington, club 1.5 miles on right.
Parkland course.
18 holes, 6253 yards, S.S.S.70
Designed by R. Sitwell.
Founded 1911
Visitors: welcome weekdays; ring
club for dress rule.
Green Fee: on application.
Societies: by arrangement.
Catering: full bar and restaurant.
Hotels: Sitwell Arms; Mosborough
Hall.

N108 **Richmond**
☎(0748) 822457 Pro, 825319 Sec
Bend Hagg, Richmond, N Yorks DL10
5EX
A6108 from Scotch Corner, turn right
at traffic lights after 4 miles.
Parkland course.
18 holes, 5769 yards, S.S.S.68
Designed by Frank Pennink.
Founded 1892
Visitors: welcome; not before
11.30am on Sun.
Green Fee: £16 WD, £25 WE.
Societies: catered for

Catering: daily.
Hotels: Frenchgate; holiday cottage
on course (for up to 8 people).

N109 **Riddlesden**
☎(0535) 602148
Howden Rough, Riddlesden,
Keighley, W Yorks
A650 Keighley-Bradford road, left
into Bar Lane, left into Scott Lane for
2 miles.
Moorland course.
18 holes, 4185 yards, S.S.S.61
Founded 1927
Visitors: unlimited weekdays; after
2pm Sat and Sun.
Green Fee: £10/round/day (£6 with
member) WD, £15 (£10) WE.
Catering: 12-2pm and 6-10pm
weekdays, 12-5.30pm weekends.
Hotels: Dalesway.

N110 **Ripon City**
☎(0765) 603640
Palace Rd, Ripon, N Yorks HG4 3HH
1 mile NW on A6108 towards
Masham/Leyburn.
Undulating parkland course.
18 holes, 6067 yards, S.S.S.69
Designed by ADAS.
Founded 1905
Visitors: Sat very busy, Tues and
Sun starting sheet in operation.
Green Fee: £18 WD, £25 WE & BH.
Societies: package deals available
by prior arrangement.
Catering: luchtime Tues-Sun; other
times by prior arrangement.
Hotels: Ripon Spa; Nags Head
(Pickhill).

N111 **Rotherham**
☎(0709) 850812 Sec, 850466
Clubhouse, 854612 Course
Manager, 850480 Pro
Thrybergh Park, Thrybergh,
Rotherham S65 4NU
On A631 Doncaster-Rotherham road,
from A1M; 3 miles from M18 at
Bramley; 7 miles from M1 junction 35.
Parkland course.
18 holes, 6324 yards, S.S.S.70
Founded 1903
Visitors: by arrangement with Pro.
Green Fee: £26.50/round/day.
Societies: parties of 16+ to book
with Sec; not Wed, weekends or
Bank Holidays; reductions for
societies over 16.
Catering: full facilities every day.
Snooker.
Hotels: Swallow; Moat House;
Limes; Brecon.

N112 **Roundhay**
☎(0532) 662695, 661686 Pro shop
Park Lane, Leeds LS8 2EJ
A58 to Oakwood Clock, then Princes
Ave, Street Lane, right at Park Lane,
4 miles from city centre.
Municipal parkland course.
9 holes, 5322 yards, S.S.S.65
Founded 1921
Visitors: unrestricted.
Green Fee: £6.60 WD, £6.75 WE
Societies: by arrangement with Pro.
Catering: restaurant Tues-Sun
evenings; snacks available daily.
Hotels: Beech Wood.

N113 **Roundwood**
☎(0709) 523471
Off Green Lane, Rawmarsh,
Rotherham, S Yorks S62 6LA
2.5 miles N of Rotherham on A633.
Parkland course.
9 holes, 5600 yards, S.S.S.67
Founded 1977
Visitors: welcome, not Sat or Sun am.
Green Fee: £12/day (£5 with
member); £15 WE & BH (£8 with
member).
Societies: welcome.
Catering: bar and snacks, not Sun,
Mon, Tues.
Practice putting green.
Hotels: Marquis; Guest House.

N114 **Rudding Park**
☎(0423) 872100
Follifoot, Harrogate, N Yorks HG3 1DJ
Off A658 Harrogate southern
by-pass, signposted.
Parkland course.
18 holes, 6800 yards, S.S.S.72
Designed by Hawtree.
Visitors: welcome at all times,
advisable to phone.
Green Fee: on application.
Societies: welcome by arrangement.
Catering: full facilities.
Driving range.
Hotels: Majestic.

N115 **Ryburn**
☎(0422) 831355
The Shaw, Norland, Sowerby Bridge,
W Yorkshire
3 miles S of Halifax.
Moorland course.
9 holes, 5002 yards, S.S.S.65
Founded 1910
Visitors: welcome, no restrictions.
Green Fee: £20 (£14 with member).
Societies: by application only.
Catering: available.
Hotels: The Hobbit.

N116 Sand Moor

☎(0532) 685180
Alwoodley Lane, Leeds LS17 7DJ
A61 N from Leeds city centre 6 miles,
turn left into Alwoodley Lane, 0.5
mile on right.
Undulating parkland/moorland
course.
18 holes, 6429 yards, S.S.S.71
Designed by N. Barnes.
Founded 1926
Visitors: welcome weekdays;
members reserved times
12am-1.30pm; Tues 9.30-10.30am;
Thurs 8.30-12am.
Green Fee: £28/round WD; WE & BH
by arrangement with Sec.
Societies: weekdays.
Catering: full facilities weekdays
except Mon (lunches and snacks
only, unless by prior arrangement).
Hotels: Harewood Arms; Parkway;
Forte Crest.

N117 Sandhill

☎(0226) 753444
C/o Colliery Farm, Little Houghton,
Barnsley, S Yorks
Off A635 1 mile E of Darfield, 6 miles
E of Barnsley.
Meadowland course.
18 holes, 6214 yards, S.S.S.70
Designed by John Royston.
Founded Oct 1991
Visitors: welcome, unlimited; ring to
book tee times.
Green Fee: £8 WD, £10 WE.
Societies: by arrangement.
Catering: not yet available.
Driving range.

N118 Scarborough North Cliff

☎(0723) 360786
North Cliff Ave, Burniston Rd,
Scarborough YO12 6PP
2 miles N of town centre on coast
road (Burniston Rd), turn right along
North Cliff Ave.
Seaside/parkland course.
18 holes, 6425 yards, S.S.S.71
Designed by James Braid.
Founded 1928
Visitors: no restrictions except
before 10am Sun; must be
recognised golfers.
Green Fee: £23/day WD; £28/day
WE & BH.
Societies: mainly weekdays by prior
arrangement with Sec, parties 8 to 36.
Catering: soup, sandwiches to
5.30pm; bar snacks lunchtime and
7-10pm; not Sun, Mon evening.
Hotels: Clifton; Majestic; Overdale.

N119 Scarborough South Cliff

☎(0723) 374737
Deepdale Ave, Scarborough YO11
2UE
1 mile S of Scarborough on main
Filey road.
Parkland/seaside course.
18 holes, 6085 yards, S.S.S.69
Designed by Dr Mackenzie.
Founded 1903
Visitors: welcome.
Green Fee: £20/round, £30/day WD;
£27.50/round, £35/day WE.
Societies: catered for on weekdays
and weekends.
Catering: full catering facilities.
Hotels: Crown; St Nicholas;
Southlands; Mount House.

N120 Scarcroft

☎(0532) 892311
Syke Lane, Leeds LS14 3BQ
On A58 NE of Leeds in Scarcroft
village, immediately after the New
Inn on the left is Syke Lane.
Parkland course.
18 holes, 6426 yards, S.S.S.71
Designed by Major C. Mackenzie.
Founded 1937
Visitors: welcome weekdays,
weekends by prior arrangement only.
Green Fee: £25/round, £30/day WD;
£35/round WE by prior arrangement
with Sec.
Societies: welcome Tues-Fri by
arrangement, all-in rates for 20+.
Catering: meals daily except Mon.
Hotels: Harewood Arms; Swan &
Talbot (Wetherby).

N121 Selby

☎(0757) 228622
Mill Lane, Brayton, Selby, N Yorks
YO8 9LD
3 miles SW of Selby, 1 mile E of A19
at Brayton village; from M62 junction
34, A19 (Selby-Doncaster) for 5
miles N towards Selby, 1st left in
Brayton into Mill Lane, club 1 mile on
right.
Links style course.
18 holes, 6246 yards, S.S.S.70
Designed by Taylor & Hawtree.
Founded 1907
Visitors: welcome weekdays with
h/cap certs; members and guests
only at weekends.
Green Fee: £22/round, £24/day.
Societies: Wed, Thurs and Fri.
Catering: every day.
Snooker, large practice ground.
Hotels: Londesbro; Selby Fork
Motel; The Owl (Hambleton).

N122 Serlby Park

☎(0777) 818268 Club, (0302)
536336 Hon Sec
Serlby, Doncaster, S Yorkshire DN10
6BA
3 miles S of Bawtry.
Parkland course on Galway Estate.
9 holes, 5370 yards, S.S.S.66
Designed by Viscount Galway.
Founded 1895
Visitors: must be accompanied by
member.
Green Fee: £8 WD, £11 WE.
Societies: selected few.
Catering: available.
Hotels: Crown (Bawtry); Mount
Pleasant, Olde Bell (Barnby Moor).

N123 Settle

☎(0729) 825288
Buckhaw Brow, Settle, N Yorks BD24
Main A65 Settle-Kendal road,
opposite Giggleswick Quarry.
Parkland/moorland course.
9 holes, 4600 yards, S.S.S.62
Designed by Tom Vardon.
Founded 1891
Visitors: welcome, restricted Sun.
Green Fee: £10/day.
Hotels: Falcon Manor.

N124 Shipley

☎(0274) 563212 Clubhouse,
563674 Pro, 568652 Sec
Beckfoot Lane, Cottingley Bridge,
Bingley, W Yorks BD16 1LX
Situated on A650 Bradford-Keighley
road at Cottingley Bridge, Bingley.
Parkland course.
18 holes, 6218 yards, S.S.S.70
Designed by Colt, Alison and
Mackenzie assisted by James Braid.
Founded 1896
Visitors: welcome except Tues
before 2pm, Sat before 4pm.
Green Fee: £26/day WD, £35/day
WE & BH, (£13 with member).
Societies: by arrangement with Sec.
Catering: except Mon, bar snacks
and evening meals by arrangement
with Steward. Snooker.
Hotels: Bankfield; Oakwood Hall;
Hall Bank.

N125 Silkstone

☎(0226) 790328, 790128 Pro
Field Head, Silkstone, Barnsley, S
Yorks S75 4OD
1 mile from M1 on A628 towards
Manchester.
Undulating meadowland course.
18 holes, 6045 yards, S.S.S.70
Founded 1893

Visitors: welcome weekdays.
Green Fee: on application.
Societies: catered for weekdays.
Catering: full facilities except Mon.
Hotels: Ardsley Moat House;
Brooklands Motel.

N126 Silsden
☎(0525) 652998
High Brunthwaite, Silsden, Keighley
BD20 0NH
A629, 4 miles from Keighley, on to
A6034 to Silsden town centre, turn E
at canal.
Moorland/meadowland course.
14 holes, 4870 yards, S.S.S.64
Founded 1913
Visitors: welcome; restrictions Sat
pm and Sun am.
Green Fee: apply for details.
Hotels: Steeton Hall.

N127 Sitwell Park
☎(0709) 541046 Sec/office,
540961 Pro, 700799 Stewardess
Shrogswood Rd, Rotherham, S Yorks
S60 4BY
From M1 exit 31, take A630 and
A631 to Bawtry; from M18 exit 1,
follow A631 Sheffield road; club 2
miles SE of Rotherham.
Undulating parkland course.
18 holes, 6203 yards, S.S.S.70
Designed by Dr Mackenzie.
Founded 1913
Visitors: welcome.
Green Fee: £20/round, £24/day WD;
£24/round, £28/day WE & BH.
Societies: welcome weekdays; book
through Sec.
Catering: meals booked through
Stewardess. Snooker.
Hotels: Moat House; Brecon;
Brentwood; Limes.

N128 Skipton
☎(0756) 795657
North-West By-Pass, Skipton, N
Yorks BD23 1LL
Off NW by-pass (A59 and A65) 1 mile
from town centre.
Undulating course with panoramic
views.
18 holes, 6191 yards, S.S.S.70
Founded 1905
Visitors: welcome; phone Pro
beforehand.
Green Fee: winter (Nov-Mar) £12
WD, £20 WE & BH; summer
(April-Oct) £20 WD, £26 WE & BH.
Societies: welcome, special terms
for parties of 12 or more; contact
general manager.

Catering: available every day
except Mon.
Hotels: Randell's; Herriot's;
Devonshire Arms (Bolton Abbey).

N129 South Bradford
☎(0274) 679195 Club, 673346 Pro
Pearson Rd, Odsal, Bradford BD6
1BH
From Odsal roundabout take Stadium
Rd (1st road left down Cleckheaton
Rd) then Pearson Rd to club.
Undulating meadowland course.
9 holes, 6004 yards, S.S.S.69
Founded 1906
Visitors: welcome weekdays.
Green Fee: £13 (£6 with member)
WD, £20 (£8 with member) WE.
Societies: weekdays.
Catering: lunches and evening
meals served except Mon.
Hotels: Guide Post.

N130 South Leeds
☎(0532) 700479
Gypsy Lane, off Middleton Ring Rd,
Leeds LS11 5TU
From M62 junction 28 take
Leeds-Dewsbury road to lights at
Tommy Wass Hotel, turn right, follow
ring road for 100 yards then left into
Gypsy Lane; approx 2 miles.
Parkland course.
18 holes, 5890 yards, S.S.S.68
Founded 1914
Visitors: welcome any time (reduced
green fees if playing with member).
Green Fee: £18/day/round WD, £22
WE & BH.
Societies: apply to Sec.
Catering: every day except Mon.
Snooker.
Hotels: Dragonara; Queens; Red
Lion.

N131 Springhead Park
☎(0482) 656309
Willerby Rd, Hull, Yorks HU5 5JE
4 miles W of Hull centre.
Municipal parkland course.
18 holes, 6402 yards, S.S.S.71
Founded 1930
Visitors: welcome, no restrictions.
Green Fee: £5/round WD,
£6.50/round WE, reductions for jnrs
and OAPs, no phone bookings, queue
to play.
Societies: on application to Hull City
Council.
Catering: light snacks; bar for
members and guests only.
Hotels: Willerby Manor; Grange
Park.

N132 Springmill
☎(0924) 272515
Queens Drive, Osset, W Yorks
M1 junction 40, 1 mile out of Osset
towards Wakefield.
Public parkland course.
9 holes Par 3, 1165 yards.
Visitors: welcome.
Green Fee: apply for details.
Societies: welcome.

N133 Stocksbridge & District
☎(0742) 882003
30 Royd Lane, Townend, Deepcar,
Sheffield S30 5RZ
A616 into Deepcar, 1st left into Carr
Rd, course 1 mile on left.
Moorland course.
18 holes, 5221 yards, S.S.S.66
Designed by Peter Allis, Dave
Thomas (extension).
Founded 1924
Visitors: welcome any time.
Green Fee: £15/day WD, £24/day
WE.
Societies: on request, not
weekends.
Catering: on request except Mon.
Hotels: Grosvenor; Hallam Towers.

N134 Sutton Park
☎(0482) 74242
Saltshouse Rd, Holderness Rd, Hull,
N Humberside HU8 9HF
4 miles E of city centre on A165
(B1237).
Municipal parkland course.
18 holes, 6251 yards, S.S.S.70
Founded 1935
Visitors: unlimited.
Green Fee: £4.50/round WD,
£6.50/round WE.
Societies: on application to Hull City
Council Leisure Services.
Catering: bar snacks lunchtime, full
meals by arrangement.
Snooker.
Hotels: Royal Station.

N135 Swallow Hall
☎(0904) 448219, 448889
Swallow Hall, Crockey Hill, York YO1
4SG
A64 York ring road, take A19 S for
Selby, after 1.5 miles left in Crockey
Hill signposted Wheldrake; course 2
miles on left.
Public parkland course.
18 holes, 3092 yards, Par 3
Founded May 1991
Visitors: welcome, dawn to dusk.
Green Fee: £3.50 (9 holes), £7 (18).

Societies: welcome any time.
Catering: coffee machine and cold drinks. Driving range.

N136 Tankersley Park
☎(0742) 468247
High Green, Sheffield S30 4LG
Close to M1 between junctions 35a (northbound only) or 36, on A616.
Parkland course.
18 holes, 6212 yards, S.S.S.70
Designed by Hawtree.
Founded 1907
Visitors: weekdays unlimited, after 3pm weekends; must have h/cap.
Green Fee: £17/round (£7 with member), £22/day.
Societies: Mon-Fri only.
Catering: bar and restaurant.
Snooker.

N137 Temple Newsam
☎(0532) 645624
Temple Newsam Rd, Leeds LS15
On A63 Selby road, 5 miles from Leeds centre, follow signs for Temple Newsam House.
Public undulating parkland course.
18 holes, 6448 yards, S.S.S.71; 18 holes, 6029 yards, S.S.S.70
Founded 1923
Visitors: welcome.
Green Fee: municipal rates.
Societies: by arrangement.
Catering: bar daily, carvery Sat, Sun.
Hotels: Windmill; Mercury.

N138 Thirsk & Northallerton
☎(0845) 522170 Club, 525115 Sec, 526216 Pro
Thornton-le-Street, Thirsk, N Yorks YO7 4AB
2 miles N of Thirsk on A168, the Northallerton spur 0.5 mile from the dual carriageway A19.
Meadowland course.
9 holes, 6257 yards, S.S.S.70
Founded 1914
Visitors: welcome.
Green Fee: on application.
Societies: weekdays except Tues and Wed pm; must be members of recognised golf club; book in writing well in advance.
Catering: full facilites except Tues.
Hotels: Golden Fleece; Three Tuns.

N139 Thorne
☎(0405) 812084
Kirton Lane, Thorne, Doncaster, S Yorks DN8 5RJ

Follow signposts to Thorne from M18 junction 6 or M180 junction 1.
Public parkland course.
18 holes, 5500 yards, S.S.S.65
Designed by Richard Highfield.
Founded 1980
Visitors: welcome, no restrictions.
Green Fee: £7.60/round WD, £8.60/round WE & BH.
Societies: book in advance.
Catering: full facilities.
Hotels: Belton.

N140 Tinsley Park
☎(0742) 560237
High Hazel Park, Darnall, Sheffield S9
Take A57 off M1 at junction 33, at traffic lights turn right on Greenland Rd and right by bus depot.
Parkland course.
18 holes, 6064 yards, S.S.S.69
Founded 1921
Visitors: unrestricted.
Green Fee: £7.50 approx.
Societies: by arrangement with Sheffield City Council Recreation Dept.
Catering: any day except Tues.
Hotels: Royal Victoria.

N141 Todmorden
☎(0706) 812986
Rive Rocks, Cross Stone Rd, Todmorden OL14 7RD
From town centre proceed approx 1.5 miles along Halifax road, turn right.
Moorland course.
9 holes, 5858 yards, S.S.S.68
Founded 1895
Visitors: Tues-Fri no restrictions (Thurs Ladies' Day); weekends by prior arrangement.
Green Fee: apply for details.
Societies: Tues-Fri.
Catering: full facilities except Mon.
Hotels: Scaitliffe Hall; Brandschatter Berghoff.

N142 Wakefield
☎(0924) 255104 Club, 255380 Pro, 258778 Sec
Woodthorpe Lane, Sandal, Wakefield WF2 6JH
3 miles S of Wakefield on A61, from M1 exit 39.
Parkland course.
18 holes, 6611 yards, S.S.S.72
Designed by Alex (Sandy) Herd.
Founded 1891
Visitors: by arrangement.
Green Fee: £25 WD, £27 WE.
Societies: apply to Sec.

Catering: except Mon.
Snooker.
Hotels: Cedar Court; Swallow.

N143 Wath
☎(0709) 878677
Abdy, Blackamoor, Rotherham, S Yorks S62 7SJ
Off A633 in Wath, 7 miles N of Rotherham.
Meadowland course.
18 holes, 5857 yards, S.S.S.68
Founded 1904
Visitors: welcome weekdays, with member at weekends.
Green Fee: apply for details.
Societies: welcome by arrangement; special package.
Catering: snacks and bar food.
Hotels: Marquis Hotel.

N144 West Bowling
☎(0274) 724449 Clubhouse, 393207 Sec, 728036 Pro
Newall Hall, Rooley Lane, Bradford, W Yorks BD5 8LB
Corner of M606 and Bradford ring road East.
Parkland course.
18 holes, 5570 yards, S.S.S.67
Founded 1898
Visitors: welcome weekdays, restricted weekends.
Green Fee: £22/round/day WD, £28 WE.
Societies: not weekends; apply to manager.
Catering: full facilities except Mon Oct-Mar. Snooker.
Hotels: Novotel; Norfolk Gardens; Guide Post; Tong Village; Victoria.

N145 West Bradford
☎(0274) 542767
Chellow Grange, Haworth Rd, Bradford, W Yorks BD9 6NP
B6144 3 miles from Bradford on Haworth Rd.
Meadowland course.
18 holes, 5752 yards, S.S.S.68
Founded 1900
Visitors: welcome weekdays.
Green Fee: apply for details.
Societies: weekdays.
Catering: meals served except Mon.
Hotels: Norfolk Gardens.

N146 West End (Halifax)
☎(0422) 353608 Clubhouse, 363293 Pro, 341878 Sec
Paddock Lane, Highroad Well, Halifax, W Yorks HX2 0NT

Leave Halifax on Burnley/Rochdale road, turn right at 1st lights by People's Park (Parkinson Lane), over lights to T-junction, turn right to next T-junction and turn left, take 2nd on right (Court Lane) to junction, turn left into Paddock Lane.
Parkland course.
18 holes, 5951 yards, S.S.S.69
Designed by members.
Founded 1906
Visitors: welcome.
Green Fee: £15/round, £20/day WD; £18/round, £25/day WE.
Societies: to be booked through Sec; not Sat.
Catering: full facilities except Mon. Snooker.
Hotels: Tower House; Holdsworth House; Crown Imperial.

N147 **Wetherby**
☎(0937) 583375 Pro, 580089 Sec/Manager
Linton Lane, Wetherby, LS22 4JF
Off A1 at Wetherby, then travel SW; course in village of Linton, 1 mile from Wetherby centre.
Parkland course.
18 holes, 6235 yards, S.S.S.70
Founded 1910
Visitors: subject to 12.15-1.15pm reservation for members, welcome at all times.
Green Fee: on application.
Societies: welcome Mon, Wed, Thurs, Fri, 9.30am and 2pm starting times.
Catering: full catering service, 7 days.
Hotels: Wetherby Resort.

N148 **Wheatley**
☎(0302) 831655
Armthorpe Rd, Doncaster, S Yorks DN2 5QB
Follow S ring road from old A1 E along boundary of St Leger racecourse to next crossroads, clubhouse is on right opposite large water tower.
Undulating parkland course.
18 holes, 6209 yards, S.S.S.70
Designed by George Duncan.
Founded 1913 (relocated 1933)
Visitors: welcome.
Green Fee: £21/round, £25/day WD; £26/round WE & BH.
Societies: welcome weekdays only by arrangement, phone (0302) 831655.
Catering: restaurant facilities.
Hotels: Balmoral; Earl of Doncaster; Punches.

N149 **Whitby**
☎(0947) 602768 Club, 600660 Sec, 602719 Pro shop
Sandsend Rd, Low Straggleton, Whitby, N Yorks YO21 3SR
On A174 main coast road between Whitby and Sandsend.
Seaside course.
18 holes, 6134 yards, S.S.S.69
Founded 1892.
Visitors: welcome, ring Pro shop.
Green Fee: on application.
Societies: parties over 12 (experienced golfers); ring Sec.
Catering: available except Mon.
Hotels: Saxonville; White House; Royal.

N150 **Whitwood**
☎(0977) 512835
Altofts Lane, Whitwood, Castleford, W Yorkshire WF10 5PZ
M62 junction 31, 0.5 mile towards Castleford.
Public parkland course.
9 holes, 6282 yards, S.S.S.70
Designed by Steve Wells.
Founded April 1986
Visitors: welcome at all times, booking system at weekends.
Green Fee: municipal rates.
Societies: address requests to A.Conway, King Charles II House, Pontefract, W Yorks.
Catering: local inn.
Hotels: Bridge Inn.

N151 **Withernsea**
☎(0964) 612258 Clubhouse, 612978 Sec/office
Chestnut Ave, Withernsea, N Humberside HU19 2PG
20 miles NE of Hull at S end of town.
Seaside course.
9 holes, 5112 yards, S.S.S.64
Founded 1907
Visitors: welcome; not before 3pm weekends and Bank Holidays unless with member.
Green Fee: £10/round/day (£5 with member).
Societies: on application to Sec.
Catering: evening meals weekdays; breakfast, lunch, evening meal weekends; private functions.
Hotels: St Hilda GH; Vista Mar GH.

N152 **Wombwell (Hillies)**
☎(0226) 754433
Wentworth View, Wombwell, Barnsley, S Yorkshire S73 0LA
4 miles SE of Barnsley, 3 miles M1 junction 36.
Municipal meadowland course.
9 holes, 2095 yards, S.S.S.60
Founded 1981
Visitors: no restrictions.
Green Fee: £3 (9 holes), £5.75 (18 holes) WD; £3.70, £7.30 WE;
Societies: by arrangement.
Catering: evening and weekend bar service.
Hotels: Tankersley Manor; Churchill.

N153 **Woodhall Hills**
☎(0532) 554594 Sec, 562857 Pro
Woodhall Rd, Calverley, Pudsey, W Yorks
Turn off A647 Leeds-Bradford road to Calverley, 1 mile.
Moorland course.
18 holes, 6102 yards, S.S.S.69
Founded 1905
Visitors: after 9.30am weekdays and 10.30am Sun; no visitors Sat.
Green Fee: on application; reduced rates ater 4.30pm Sat, 3.30pm Sun.
Societies: contact Sec.
Catering: dining room service. Snooker.

N154 **Woodsome Hall**
☎(0484) 602971, 602739 Sec, 602034 Pro
Fenay Bridge, Huddersfield, W Yorks HD8 0LQ
5 miles SE of Huddersfield off A629 Sheffield-Penistone road.
Parkland course.
18 holes, 6080 yards, S.S.S.69
Founded 1922
Visitors: welcome weekdays with h/cap cert, jackets and ties; not before 4pm Tues; limited weekends.
Green Fee: £25 WD, £30 WE & BH.
Societies: weekdays.
Catering: full facilities except Mon.
Hotels: George; Ladbroke Mercury.

N155 **Wortley**
☎(0742) 885294 Sec, 882139 Steward, 886490 Pro
Hermit Hill Lane, Wortley, Sheffield S30 4DF
Off M1 at junction 35A (from S) or 36 (from N), take A629 through Wortley village, course 1st right.
Undulating wooded parkland course.
18 holes, 6033 yards, S.S.S.69
Founded 1894
Visitors: no restrictions.
Green Fee: £21 WD, £25 WE & BH.
Societies: Wed, Fri by arrangement.
Catering: by arrangement.
Hotels: Hallam Towers (Sheffield); Brooklands (Barnsley).

N156 **York**
☎(0904) 490304 Pro, 491840 Sec,
491852 Fax
Lords Moor Lane, Strensall, York
YO3 5XF

2 miles N of A1234 (ring road), exit at
Earswick/Strensall roundabout.
Woodland course.
18 holes, 6285 yards, S.S.S.70
Designed by J.H. Taylor (1904).

Founded 1890
Visitors: ring beforehand.
Green Fee: £25 WD, £28 Sun.
Societies: catered for except Sat.
Catering: full facilities except Fri.

O

NORTHUMBERLAND, DURHAM, CLEVELAND, TYNE & WEAR

Northumberland is one of the most lovely counties, a rich tapestry of seascape, woodland, lonely moor and fertile farmland. A welcome addition to the golfing map has been the extravagant development at Slaley Hall near Hexham, a comfortable drive west of Newcastle. A man-sized course is an attractive adjunct to housing plans although the long stretch of Northumberland's coastline, running parallel to the A1, makes it an obvious target for those who like sea air in their nostrils and golf that can be described, in the most complimentary of veins, as off the beaten track.

The best is Berwick-upon-Tweed at Goswick, a true links approached along a quiet lane that crosses the main railway line and goes no further when the entrance to the Club is reached. The course divides itself neatly into two, the best and most enchanting being the few holes that nestle between the dunes and open up views of the hallowed, ancient ground of Holy Island.

It is the second oldest place in the county where golf is played, the distinction of being the oldest belonging to the little village 9-hole course at Alnmouth. For the golfer travelling along the coast, there are several pleasant stopping-off spots, notably at Bamburgh Castle, Dunstanburgh, Warkworth, Newbiggin-by-the-Sea and Seahouses. I have particularly happy memories of a game at Dunstanburgh, a course that is certainly great fun in an ancient setting.

The northern outskirts of Newcastle boast Ponteland, Gosforth and the Northumberland Club in High Gosforth Park, much of which is confined within the white rails of the racecourse. It is a Club that has housed both the men's English amateur championship and the Women's Commonwealth tournament, testimony to its quality as a test of golf and to its convenience as a location.

Crossing the Tyne into Durham marks a distinct change of scenery although there are two outstanding courses in Seaton Carew, a magnificent links even if its backcloth is industrial, and Brancepeth Castle south west of Durham, designed by the master, Harry Colt, and of which Leonard Crawley was inordinately fond. That is enough of a recommendation, ideally situated as it is for anyone intent on breaking the journey to Scotland. Crook and Bishop Auckland, both great names in the heyday of amateur football, are close by and Durham City was founded in 1887.

Again, however, there is a natural inclination to head from Durham towards the sea and sample the coastal chain of courses starting with Hartlepool, the handiwork of James Braid, and then sandwiching Seaton Carew between Hartlepool and the ancient Cleveland Club at Redcar.

Seaton Carew, host to a variety of national championships, is one of the very few seaside links on the East of England coast north of Norfolk but there are other good ports of call.

Eaglescliffe and Middlesborough are two more courses out of the Braid stable. Moving west towards Darlington, there are Teeside, Billingham, Dinsdale Spa, and in or near Darlington itself are Stressholme and Blackwell Grange.

Somewhat more remote are Barnard Castle and Allendale; but a final word for Hexham, just north of Allendale. Designed in 1907 by Harry Vardon, it occupies pleasant, undulating parkland.

O1 Allendale

☎(091) 267 5875 Sec
High Studdon, Allenheads Rd,
Allendale, Hexham, Northumberland
N47 9DQ
1.5 miles south of Allendale on
B6295.
Moorland/parkland course.
9 holes, 5044 yards, S.S.S.65
Designed by members with advice
from EGU and Sports Council.
Founded 1907 (relocated Sept 1992)
Visitors: any time except Sun am,
August Bank Holiday and some Sat;
h/cap cert not required, competitions
have priority at all times.
Green Fee: £5 WD, £7 WE & BH (£3
and £4 for jnrs).
Societies: weekdays and most Sat
by arrangement.
Catering: coffee & tea making
facility.
Hotels: Kings Head; Hotspur.

O2 Alnmouth

☎(0665) 830231, 830922 Fax
Foxton Hall, Lesbury, Alnwick,
Northumberland NE66 3BE
Alnmouth road from Alnwick, left at
Alnmouth, Foxton 1 mile on right.
Seaside meadowland course.
18 holes, 6484 yards, S.S.S.71
Founded 1869
Visitors: welcome Mon, Tues and
Thurs; h/cap cert required.
Green Fee: £25/day.
Societies: by arrangement; max 30.
Catering: available at all times.
Hotels: Marine House; Schooner;
Dormy House, golf inclusive
packages.

O3 Alnmouth Village

☎(0665) 830370
Marine Rd, Alnmouth,
Northumberland
From Alnwick on A1 to Alnmouth on
A1068.
Undulating seaside course.
9 holes, 6078 yards, S.S.S.70
Founded 1869
Visitors: welcome.
Green Fee: £15 WD, £20 WE & BH.
Societies: welcome; official golf
club h/caps required.
Catering: by arrangement.
Hotels: Marine.

O4 Alnwick

☎(0665) 602632, 602499 Sec
Swansfield Park, Alnwick,
Northumberland
From S, 1st left off A1, into

Willowburn Ave, 3rd left into
Swansfield Park Rd, carry on to top of
hill, follow signs Alnwick Golf Club.
Parkland course.
9 holes (extending to 18 in 1994/5),
5387 yards, S.S.S.66
Founded 1907
Visitors: welcome except on
competition days; allowed most Suns
11.30am-12.30pm in 3 balls, should
contact Sec.
Green Fee: £10/round, £15/day WD;
£15/round, £20/day WE & BH.
Societies: apply to Sec.
Catering: limited catering service.
Hotels: White Swan; The Oaks;
Plough.

O5 Arcot Hall

☎(091) 236 2794
Dudley, Cramlington,
Northumberland NE23 7QP
1 mile E of A1 off A1068 near Holiday
Inn.
Parkland course.
18 holes, 6389 yards, S.S.S.70
Designed by James Braid.
Founded 1910
Visitors: weekdays and
non-competition weekends.
Green Fee: £25 WD, £28 WE.
Societies: not weekends.
Catering: full facilities all day.
Hotels: Holiday Inn; Gosforth Park;
Metro Park.

O6 Backworth

☎(091) 268 1048
Backworth Welfare, The Hall,
Backworth, Shiremoor, Tyne and
Wear NE27 0AH
Off Tyne Tunnel link road at
Holystone roundabout.
Parkland course.
9 holes, 5930 yards, S.S.S.69
Founded 1937
Visitors: welcome with restrictions,
ring for details.
Green Fee: apply for details.
Catering: bar, snacks; catering by
arrangement.
Pool, bowls, banqueting.

O7 Bamburgh Castle

☎(0668) 214378
Steward/bookings, 214321 Sec
The Wynding, Bamburgh,
Northumberland NE69 7DE
Turn off A1 between Alnwick and
Berwick on B1341 or B1342 and
proceed to Bamburgh village, turn
left opposite Lord Crewe Arms and
travel along The Wynding.

Seaside course.
18 holes, 5621 yards, S.S.S.67
Designed by George Rochester.
Founded 1896
Visitors: welcome, restricted Bank
Holidays, weekends and competition
days; h/cap certs required.
Green Fee: April-Oct, £23/day/round
WD, £35/day, £30/round WE & BH;
Oct-Mar £23/day/round WD,
£30/day/round WE & BH; jnrs (under
18) £9 all year; 5 day weekday ticket
£60 (jnrs £20).
Societies: by arrangement.
Catering: lunches, teas and evening
meal except Tues.
Hotels: Sunningdale; Mizen Head;
Victoria; Lord Crewe Arms.

O8 Barnard Castle

☎(0833) 38355, 31980 Pro
Harmire Rd, Barnard Castle, Co
Durham DL12 8QN
On N boundary of town on B6278
Barnard Castle-Eggleston road.
Undulating parkland course.
18 holes, 5838 yards, S.S.S.68; new
holes coming into play summer 1994.
Visitors: welcome except on
competition days.
Green Fee: £18 WD, £24 WE & BH.
Societies: welcome, max 40.
Catering: meals and bar snacks.
Snooker.
Hotels: Rose and Crown (Romaldkirk)
Jersey Farm Hotel; Montalbo.

O9 Beamish Park

☎(091) 370 1382
The Clubhouse, Beamish, Stanley,
Co Durham DH9 0RH
Take Chester-le-Street turn-off from
A1(M), follow signs for Beamish
Museum.
Parkland course.
18 holes, 6205 yards, S.S.S.70
Designed by Henry Cotton (part).
Founded c. 1925
Visitors: not Sun, not before 9am on
any day.
Green Fee: £16/round, £20/day.
Societies: not sat, Sun.
Catering: bar and restaurant;
banqueting.

O10 Bedlingtonshire

☎(0670) 822457 Sec, 822087 Pro
Acorn Bank, Bedlington,
Northumberland
0.5 mile W of Bedlington on A1068.
Public meadowland/parkland
course.
18 holes, 6224 metres, S.S.S.73

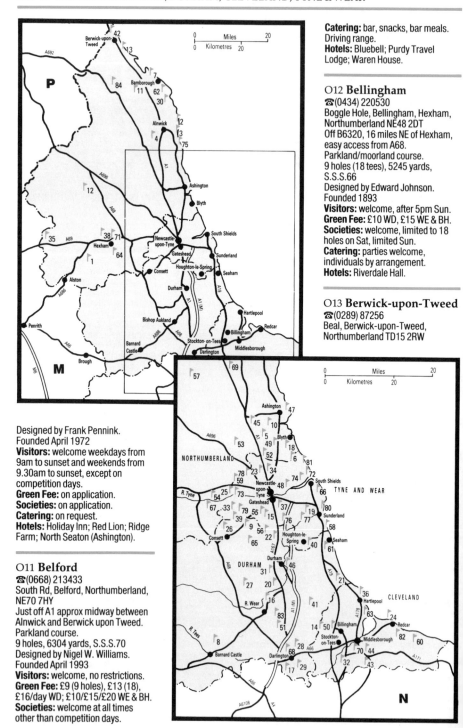

Catering: bar, snacks, bar meals. Driving range.
Hotels: Bluebell; Purdy Travel Lodge; Waren House.

O12 Bellingham
☎(0434) 220530
Boggle Hole, Bellingham, Hexham, Northumberland NE48 2DT
Off B6320, 16 miles NE of Hexham, easy access from A68.
Parkland/moorland course.
9 holes (18 tees), 5245 yards, S.S.S.66
Designed by Edward Johnson.
Founded 1893
Visitors: welcome, after 5pm Sun.
Green Fee: £10 WD, £15 WE & BH.
Societies: welcome, limited to 18 holes on Sat, limited Sun.
Catering: parties welcome, individuals by arrangement.
Hotels: Riverdale Hall.

O13 Berwick-upon-Tweed
☎(0289) 87256
Beal, Berwick-upon-Tweed, Northumberland TD15 2RW

Designed by Frank Pennink.
Founded April 1972
Visitors: welcome weekdays from 9am to sunset and weekends from 9.30am to sunset, except on competition days.
Green Fee: on application.
Societies: on application.
Catering: on request.
Hotels: Holiday Inn; Red Lion; Ridge Farm; North Seaton (Ashington).

O11 Belford
☎(0668) 213433
South Rd, Belford, Northumberland, NE70 7HY
Just off A1 approx midway between Alnwick and Berwick upon Tweed.
Parkland course.
9 holes, 6304 yards, S.S.S.70
Designed by Nigel W. Williams.
Founded April 1993
Visitors: welcome, no restrictions.
Green Fee: £9 (9 holes), £13 (18), £16/day WD; £10/£15/£20 WE & BH.
Societies: welcome at all times other than competition days.

Off A1 approx 3 miles S of
Berwick-upon-Tweed.
Links course.
18 holes, 6425 yards, S.S.S.71
Designed by James Braid.
Founded 1890
Visitors: welcome from 9.30am
weekdays, from 10am to 12am and
after 2pm weekends.
Green Fee: £18/round, £24/day WD;
£24/round, £32/day WE & BH.
Societies: special rate for parties
and societies, Mon-Fri only, £25/day
including catering.
Catering: all week; evening meals
available except Mon, soup and
sandwiches available all day.
Hotels: Blue Bell, Purdy Lodge
(Belford).

O14 Billingham
☎(0642) 554494, 533816
Sandy Lane, Billingham, Cleveland
TS22 5NA
E of A19 Billingham by-pass, near
town centre.
Undulating parkland course.
18 holes, 6334 yards, S.S.S.71
Designed by Frank Pennink.
Founded 1967
Visitors: weekdays not before 9am
or between 12am and 1.30pm;
weekends not before 10am.
Green Fee: £20/day WD, £33/day
WE.
Societies: weekdays only after
9.30am and 1.30pm by prior
arrangement.
Catering: daily except Mon.
Hotels: Billingham Arms.

O15 Birtley
☎(091) 410 2207
Portobello Rd, Birtley, Co Durham
A6127 off A1, 6 miles S of
Newcastle.
Parkland course.
9 holes, 5154 yards, S.S.S.67
Founded 1921
Visitors: welcome weekdays only
unless accompanied by member.
Green Fee: apply for details.
Societies: by arrangement.
Catering: bar facilities, evenings.

O16 Bishop Auckland
☎(0388) 602198 Club, 663648 Sec,
661618 Pro
High Plains, Durham Rd, Bishop
Auckland, Co Durham DL14 8DL
Leave Market Place, up Durham Rd
towards Spennymoor and Durham;
course on left half-way up the bank.

From Spennymoor or Rushyford,
take Canney Hill turn off, course
entrance on right half way down
bank.
Parkland course.
18 holes, 6420 yards, S.S.S.71
Founded 1894
Visitors: welcome, no visiting
parties Sat or Sun.
Green Fee: £20/round WD
(£24/round for parties over 20),
£26/round WE.
Societies: best days Wed, Thurs, Fri
(Ladies Day Tues).
Catering: full facilities except Mon.
2 snooker tables.
Hotels: Park Head; Old Manor House
(West Auckland).

O17 Blackwell Grange
☎(0325) 464464 Clubhouse,
464458 Sec, 462088 Pro
Briar Close, Blackwell, Darlington, Co
Durham DL3 8QX
1 mile S of Darlington, 0.25 mile W
off A66.
Undulating parkland course.
18 holes, 5621 yards, S.S.S.67
Designed by Frank Pennink.
Founded 1930
Visitors: welcome except Wed
afternoon (Ladies Day).
Green Fee: £18/day WD, £20/round
WE & BH.
Societies: by arrangement on
weekdays.
Catering: full service Tues-Sat.
Hotels: Blackwell Grange Moat
House.

O18 Blyth
☎(0670) 367728
New Delaval & Newsham, Blyth,
Northumberland NE24 4DB
11 miles N of Newcastle, 6 miles N of
Whitley Bay.
Parkland course.
18 holes, 6533 yards, S.S.S.72
Designed by Hamilton Stutt & Co.
Founded 1905
Visitors: weekdays only before 3pm,
unless with member.
Green Fee: £16/round, £18/day (£6
with playing member).
Societies: welcome by arrangement
(28 days in advance).
Catering: full facilities.

O19 Boldon
☎(091) 536 5360 Sec/Office, 536
4182 Clubhouse, 536 5385 Pro
Dipe Lane, East Boldon, Tyne & Wear
NE36 0PQ

On A184, 1 mile E of A19/A1 junction.
Parkland course.
18 holes, 6362 yards, S.S.S.70
Founded 1912
Visitors: welcome weekdays,
weekends and Bank Holidays
restricted.
Green Fee: apply for details.
Societies: by arrangement.
Catering: bar snacks all day; meals
by arrangement. Snooker table.
Hotels: George Washington;
Friendly.

O20 Brancepeth Castle
☎(091) 378 0075, 378 3835 Fax
Brancepeth Village, Durham DH7
8EA
4 miles W of Durham city on A690 to
Crook; turn left at crossroads in
village of Brancepeth and take slip
road to left immediately before Castle
gates.
Parkland course.
18 holes, 6415 yards, S.S.S.71
Designed by H.S. Colt.
Founded 1924
Visitors: weekdays only for parties,
individuals at weekends.
Green Fee: casual £24 WD, £30 WE
& BH.
Societies: weekdays, reduced green
fees dependent on numbers in party.
Catering: lunches and bar snacks
pm, dinners by prior booking.
Hotels: Bridge (Croxdale).

O21 Castle Eden & Peterlee
☎(0429) 836220, 836510 Sec.
Castle Eden, Hartlepool, Cleveland
TS27 4SS
Durham-Hartlepool road off A19,
follow signs to Castle Eden, course
opposite Whitbread Brewery.
Parkland course.
18 holes, 6262 yards, S.S.S.70
Designed by Henry Cotton (2nd 9).
Founded 1927
Visitors: welcome at all times.
Green Fee: £20/day WD, £30/day
WE (£10 with member).
Societies: weekdays.
Catering: every day.
Hotels: Crossways; Peterlee Lodge;
Hardwick Manor.

O22 Chester-le-Street
☎(091) 388 3218, 389 0157 Pro
Lumley Park, Chester-le-Street, Co
Durham DH3 4NS
Leave A1(M) to Chester-le-Street,
follow A167 signposted Durham,

course 0.25 mile E of Chester-le-Street, beside Lumley Castle.
Parkland course.
18 holes, 6054 yards, S.S.S.69
Designed by J.H. Taylor (original 9).
Founded 1909
Visitors: welcome weekdays, not before 9.30am or 12am-2pm weekends; must have letter of intro/h/cap cert.
Green Fee: £20 WD, £25 WE & BH.
Societies: welcome; not weekends.
Catering: bar 11am-11pm Mon-Sat; snacks, lunches and evening meals.
Snooker.
Hotels: Lumley Castle; Lambton Arms.

O23 City of Newcastle
☎(091) 285 1775
Three Mile Bridge, Gosforth, Newcastle upon Tyne NE3 2DR
3 miles N of Newcastle city centre on left hand side of B1318 road heading N, opposite Three Mile Inn.
Parkland course.
18 holes, 6508 yards, S.S.S.71
Designed by Harry Vardon.
Founded 1892
Visitors: welcome (on men's competition days only at quiet times).
Green Fee: £19 (£8 with member) WD, £21 (£9 with member) WE & BH.
Societies: Mon, Tues, Wed, Thurs and exceptionally other days.
Catering: lunches, bar snacks, sandwiches every day.
Snooker, pool.
Hotels: Gosforth Park.

O24 Cleveland
☎(0642) 483693 Clubhouse, 471798 Sec
Queen St, Redcar, Cleveland TS10 1BT
From A174 to A1042 to Coatham.
Championship links course.
18 holes, 6707 yards, S.S.S.72
Founded 1887
Visitors: welcome.
Green Fee: £16 WD, £25 WE & BH.
Societies: welcome weekdays, brochure from Sec.
Catering: excellent.
Hotels: The Park; The Royal.

O25 Close House
☎(0661) 852953
Close House, Heddon-on-the-Wall, Newcastle-upon-Tyne NE15 0HT
9 miles W of Newcastle off A69.
Parkland course.
18 holes, 5506 yards, S.S.S.67

Founded 1968
Visitors: societies only accepted, by prior arrangement with Sec.
Green Fee: apply for details.

O26 Consett & District
☎(0207) 502186, 580210 Pro, 562261 Sec
Elmfield Rd, Consett, Co Durham DH8 5NN
Off A68 2 miles from Castleside or Allensford; 12 miles from Durham (A691) and Newcastle (A694).
Undulating parkland course.
18 holes, 6013 yards, S.S.S.69
Designed by Harry Vardon.
Founded 1911
Visitors: welcome; prior confirmation at weekends advisable.
Green Fee: £15 WD, £22 WE & BH.
Societies: welcome by arrangement, max 40.
Catering: full catering by arrangement, limited Mon.
Snooker.

O27 Crook
☎(0388) 762429
Low Jobs Hill, Crook, Co Durham DL15 9AA
On A689 6 miles W of Durham city between Willington and Crook.
Moorland/parkland course.
18 holes, 6089 yards, S.S.S.69
Founded 1919
Visitors: welcome all times.
Green Fee: £15 WD (£8 with member), £20 WE (£15 with member).
Societies: by appointment.
Catering: daily except Thurs.
Hotels: Kensington Hall; Uplands; Matthews Motel.

O28 Darlington
☎(0325) 463936, 355324
Haughton Grange, Darlington, Co Durham DL1 3JD
From A1M follow A167 S then A66, 1 mile on left.
Parkland course.
18 holes, 6032 yards, S.S.S.70
Designed by Mackenzie.
Founded 1908
Visitors: welcome.
Green Fee: £22/day.
Societies: welcome, max 40, not weekends, 10-12am, 2-4pm.
Catering: excellent bar and restaurant facilities except Mon.
Snooker.
Hotels: Kings Head; White Horse; Blackwell Grange.

O29 Dinsdale Spa
☎(0325) 332297 Sec, 332515 Pro, 332222 Clubhouse
Middleton-St-George, Darlington, Co Durham DL2 1DW
From A66 or A19 follow signs for Teeside Airport until Middleton-St-George, club is 1.5 miles from village on Neasham road.
Parkland course.
18 holes, 6090 yards, S.S.S.69
Founded 1906
Visitors: welcome weekdays.
Green Fee: £20/day, £16/round.
Societies: by arrangement.
Catering: facilities available.
Hotels: Devenport; Croft Spa.

O30 Dunstanburgh Castle
☎(0665) 576562
Embleton, Alnwick, Northumberland NE66 3XQ
Off A1, 7 miles NE of Alnwick (follow signs to Embleton not Dunstanburgh Castle).
Seaside links course in AONB.
18 holes, 6298 yards, S.S.S.70
Designed by James Braid.
Founded 1900
Visitors: welcome every day (after 10am Sun). No 4 balls on Sat/Sun am.
Green Fee: £12.50/day WD; £16/round, £18.50/day WE & BH.
Societies: welcome every day (after 10am Sun).
Catering: meals and snacks available all day, licenced bar.
Hotels: Dunstanburgh Castle.

O31 Durham City
☎(091) 378 0069, 378 0029 Pro, 386 0200 Sec
Littleburn Farm, Langley Moor, Durham DH7 8HL
Off A690 2 miles SW of Durham City.
Meadowland course.
18 holes, 6326 yards, S.S.S.70
Designed by C.C. Stanton.
Founded 1887
Visitors: welcome weekdays.
Green Fee: £18 WD, £20 WE.
Societies: weekdays.
Catering: daily except Mon.
Hotels: Royal County; Three Tuns; Duke of Wellington.

O32 Eaglescliffe
☎(0642) 780098
Yarm Rd, Eaglescliffe, Stockton-on-Tees, Cleveland TS16 0DQ
On the left of A135 from Stockton-on-Tees to Yarm.

Undulating parkland course.
18 holes, 6045 yards, S.S.S.69
Designed by James Braid,
modification by H. Cotton.
Founded 1914
Visitors: welcome weekdays,
restricted Tues and Fri (Ladies Days).
Green Fee: £20 WD, £26 WE.
Societies: catered for weekdays.
Catering: full except Mon.
Hotels: Parkmore (Eaglescliffe);
Swallow (Stockton).

O33 Garesfield
☎(0207) 561278, 561309
Chopwell, Tyne & Wear NE17 7AP
A694 Newcastle-Consett road to
Rowlands Gill, take B6315 to High
Spen, then take Chopwell road 1 mile
on left.
Parkland course.
18 holes, 6603 yards, S.S.S.72
Designed by William Woodend.
Founded 1922
Visitors: weekdays unrestricted,
weekends and Bank Holidays not
before 4.30pm unless with member.
Green Fee: apply for details.
Societies: by arrangement.
Catering: full facilities during
licensing hours.

O34 Gosforth (Bridlepath)
☎(091) 285 3495
Broadway East, Gosforth, Newcastle
upon Tyne NE3 5ER
3 miles N of city centre; turn right at
1st main roundabout after Regent
Centre metro station.
Meadowland course.
18 holes, 6043 yards, S.S.S.69
Founded 1905
Visitors: welcome weekdays;
members' guests only before 4pm
weekends and Bank Holidays.
Green Fee: apply for details.
Societies: weekdays.
Catering: full facilities except Mon.
Hotels: Gosforth Park.

O35 Haltwhistle
☎(06977) 47367
Banktop, Greenhead, Via Carlisle,
Northumberland
3 miles W of Haltwhistle, 0.25 mile
off A69 on road to Gilsland.
Undulating parkland course.
12 holes, 5968 yards, S.S.S.69
Founded 1968
Visitors: welcome any day except
Sun am.
Green Fee: £10/day May-Oct,
£5/day Nov-April.

Societies: welcome except Sun;
contact W.E. Barnes, Secretary,
Croftlynn, Haltwhistle NE49 9JR,
(0434) 320337
Catering: bar; catering by prior
arrangement.
Hotels: beneficial arrangements for
golfers at Greenhead Hotel and
Gilsland Spa.

O36 Hartlepool
☎(0429) 274398, 267473 Pro
Hart Warren, Hartlepool, Cleveland
TS24 9QF
N boundary of Hartlepool off A1086,
well signposted.
Seaside links course.
18 holes, 6255 yards, S.S.S.70
Designed by James Braid (in part).
Founded 1906
Visitors: weekdays unrestricted,
weekends limited.
Green Fee: £17 WD, £22 WE.
Societies: weekdays.
Catering: available by arrangement
with Steward.
Snooker.
Hotels: Grand; Staincliffe; Marine.

O37 Heworth
☎(091) 469 2137
Gingling Gate, Heworth, Tyne & Wear
NE10 8XY
Parkland course.
18 holes, 6437 yards, S.S.S.71
Founded 1912
Visitors: not before 10am weekends.
Green Fee: £13 WD, £16 WE.
Societies: by arrangement.
Catering: bar and restaurant.

O38 Hexham
☎(0434) 603072
Spital Park, Hexham,
Northumberland NE46 3RZ
On A69, 1 mile W of Hexham centre.
Undulating parkland course.
18 holes, 6026 yards, S.S.S.68
Designed by Harry Vardon.
Founded 1907
Visitors: welcome any day.
Green Fee: £20/round, £26/day.
Societies: by arrangement, not Sat
or Sun.
Catering: full facilities every day.
Hotels: Beaumont; Royal.

O39 Hobson Municipal
☎(0207) 570189 Sec, 70941
catering, 71605 Pro
Burnopfield, Newcastle-upon-Tyne,
Tyne & Wear

On main Newcastle-Consett road.
Municipal parkland course.
18 holes, 6582 yards, S.S.S.71
Founded 1980
Visitors: restricted Sat (Club
competitions).
Green Fee: on application.
Societies: apply to Pro.
Catering: bar, lounge and
restaurant.
Hotels: Harperley.

O40 Houghton-le-Spring
☎(091) 584 1198
Copt Hill, Houghton-le-Spring DH5
8LU
On A1085 Houghton-le-Spring to
Seaham Harbour road, 0.5 mile from
Houghton-le-Spring.
Undulating hillside course.
18 holes, 6450 yards, S.S.S.71
Founded 1908
Visitors: welcome any day,
restrictions at weekends and
competition days.
Green Fee: on application.
Societies: welcome, prior
arrangement for meals.
Catering: available most days.
Hotels: White Lion; Ramside Hall;
Rainton Lodge.

O41 Knotty Hill Golf Centre
☎(0740) 620320
Sedgefield, Stockton-on-Tees,
Cleveland TS21 2BB
A1(M) junction 60, A689; 1 mile N of
Sedgefield A177.
Undulating parkand course,
Pay-as-you-Play.
North course, 18 holes, 6700 yards,
S.S.S.72; South course (from 1995),
18 holes, S.S.S.72
Designed by C. Stanton.
Founded Sept 1992
Visitors: welcome at all times.
Green Fee: £7 (9 holes), £12 (18
holes).
Societies: any day except Sun,
information available on request.
Catering: restaurant and bar.
Driving range.
Hotels: Hardwick Hall adjoining
course.

O42 Magdalene Fields
☎(0289) 306384, 330700
Greenranger
Berwick-upon-Tweed
5 minutes walk from town centre.
Seaside course (parkland fairways).
18 holes, 6551 yards, S.S.S.71

Visitors: welcome, limited weekend tee-offs available; contact Greenranger.
Green Fee: £14/round, £18/day WD; £16/round, £20/day WE.
Societies: by arrangement, ring Sec.
Catering: meals during summer, at other times by arrangement.
Hotels: Berwick Walls; Kings Arms; Cat Inn.

O43 Middlesbrough
☎(0642) 311515, 316430
Brass Castle Lane, Marton, Middlesbrough, Cleveland TS8 9EE
5 miles S of Middlesbrough, 1 mile W of A172.
Parkland course.
18 holes, 6167 yards, S.S.S.69
Designed by James Braid.
Founded 1908
Visitors: weekdays except Tues/Sat.
Green Fee: £25 (£10 with member) WD; £30 (£15 with member) WE & BH.
Societies: Wed, Thurs and Fri.
Catering: full facilities except Mon.
Hotels: Marton Hotel & Country Club; Blue Bell Inn (Acklam).

O44 Middlesbrough Municipal
☎(0642) 315533
Ladgate Lane, Middlesbrough, Cleveland TS5 7YZ
Access from A19 via A174 to Acklam.
Undulating parkland course.
18 holes, 6314 yards, S.S.S.70
Designed by Middlesborough Borough Council Planning Dept.
Founded 1977
Visitors: welcome but need a starting time.
Green Fee: apply for details.
Catering: lunches and evening meals, open to the public.
Driving range.
Hotels: Blue Bell.

O45 Morpeth
☎(0670) 504942 Sec, 519980 Club, 515675 Pro
The Common, Morpeth, NE61 2BT
On A197 1 mile S of Morpeth.
Parkland course.
18 holes, 6215 yards, S.S.S.70
Designed by Harry Vardon (1922).
Founded 1906
Visitors: welcome.
Green Fee: on application.
Societies: weekdays, apply to Sec.
Catering: snacks, bar lunches, dinners; booking advisable.
Hotels: Waterford Lodge.

O46 Mount Oswald
☎(091) 386 7527, 386 0975 Fax
Mount Oswald Manor, South Rd, Durham DH1 3TQ
SW of Durham on A1050.
Parkland (part wooded) course.
18 holes, 6162 yards, S.S.S.69
Founded c.1924
Visitors: welcome any time; members only until 10am Sun.
Green Fee: £10 WD, £12 WE.
Societies: welcome any time; special rates for 12 or more inc weekends.
Catering: meals 9.30am-9.30pm; Sun lunch; function room (75-80), smaller rooms for other parties. Pool table.
Hotels: Royal County; Bridge; Three Tuns.

O47 Newbiggin-by-the-Sea
☎(0670) 817344
Clubhouse, Newbiggin-by-the-Sea, Northumberland NE64 6DW
Off A197 16 miles N of Newcastle, 8 miles E of Morpeth; at easternmost point of village adjacent Church Point Caravan Park.
Seaside links course.
18 holes, 6423 yards, S.S.S.71
Founded 17 July 1884
Visitors: welcome after 10am; not competition days.
Green Fee: on application.
Societies: apply to Sec.
Catering: bar meals, lunch, dinner except Tues. Snooker.

O48 Newcastle United
☎(0632) 864693
Ponteland Rd, Cowgate, Newcastle-upon-Tyne, Northumberland NE5 3JW
1 mile W of city centre.
Moorland course.
18 holes, 6498 yards, S.S.S.71
Founded 1892
Visitors: welcome weekdays.
Green Fee: £12.50.
Societies: by arrangement.
Catering: meals by arrangement. Snooker.

O49 Northumberland
☎(091) 236 2009 Steward, 236 2498 Sec
High Gosforth Park, Newcastle-upon-Tyne NE3 5HT
Situated off A6125 4 miles N of Newcastle-upon-Tyne city centre.
Undulating parkland course.

18 holes, 6629 yards, S.S.S.72
Designed by H.S. Colt & James Braid.
Founded 1898
Visitors: welcome weekdays by reservation with Sec and letter of intro.
Green Fee: on application.
Societies: catered for Tues, Thurs and Fri only.
Catering: luncheon served except Mon.
Hotels: Gosforth Park; Holiday Inn.

O50 Norton Golf Course
☎(0642) 676385
Junction Rd, Stockton-on-Tees, Cleveland TS20 1SU
Parkland course.
18 holes, 6100 yards, Par 71
Founded 1989
Visitors: no jeans, correct footwear, half set of clubs each player.
Green Fee: apply for details.
Societies: welcome by arrangement.
Catering: bar and bar meals.

O51 Oak Leaf Golf Complex (Aycliffe)
☎(0325) 310820
School Aycliffe Lane, Newton Aycliffe, Co Durham DL5 6QZ
Take A68 from A1(M), turn right to Newton Aycliffe; course on left, illuminated sign at end of road.
Municipal parkland course.
18 holes, 5334 yards, S.S.S.66
Visitors: welcome, no restrictions.
Green Fee: £6.50 (18 holes) WD, £7.50 WE & BH; reductions OAPs, jnrs.
Societies: off peak tee times, £25 deposit on booking; min 9 or 3 X 3 balls.
Catering: bar at sports complex. Driving range; sports and leisure complex.
Hotels: Redworth Hall (Redworth); Eden Arms (Rushyford).

O52 Parklands
☎(091) 236 4480, 417 2626
High Gosforth Park, Newcastle-upon-Tyne NE3 5HQ
N of Newcastle on A1.
Parkland course.
18 holes, 6060 yards, S.S.S.69
Founded 1971
Visitors: no restrictions.
Green Fee: apply for details.
Societies: welcome.
Catering: bar and restaurant. Driving range, 9-hole Pitch & Putt.
Hotels: Gosforth Park.

O53 Ponteland
☎(0661) 822689
53 Bell Villas, Ponteland,
Newcastle-upon-Tyne NE20 9BD
On A696 road to Jedburgh, 1.5 miles
N of Newcastle Airport.
Parkland course.
18 holes, 6524 yards, S.S.S.71
Designed by Harry Ferney.
Founded 1927
Visitors: Mon to Thurs.
Green Fee: £22.50/day/round.
Societies: catered for Tues and
Thurs.
Catering: full in bar hours, by prior
arrangement at other times.

O54 Prudhoe
☎(0661) 32466
Eastwood Park, Prudhoe,
Northumberland NE42 5DX
12 miles W of Newcastle on A695.
Parkland course.
18 holes, 5812 yards, S.S.S.68
Founded 1930
Visitors: welcome weekdays.
Green Fee: apply for details.
Societies: welcome weekdays.
Catering: bar snacks and meals
served.

O55 Ravensworth
☎(091) 487 6014, 491 3475 Pro,
488 7549 Sec
Moss Heaps, Wrekenton, Gateshead,
Tyne & Wear NE9 7UU
Off A1, 2 miles S of Gateshead.
Moorland/parkland course.
18 holes, 5872 yards, S.S.S.68
Founded 1906
Visitors: welcome.
Green Fee: £17/round (£8 with
member) WD; £25/round (£12 with
member) WE & BH.
Societies: weekdays.
Catering: any day but Mon.
Hotels: Springfield.

O56 Roseberry Grange
☎(091) 370 2047 office, 370 0660
Pro, 370 0670 Club
Grange Villa, Chester-le-Street,
Durham DH2 3NF
Off A693 from Chester-le-Street to
Stanley, turn left before Beamish
Museum.
Parkland course.
18 holes, 5892 yards, S.S.S.68
Founded 1986
Visitors: welcome.
Green Fee: £7.50/round WD,
£10.30/round WE; reductions for
jnrs, OAPs and unemployed.

Societies: welcome, book in writing
via District Council.
Catering: bar, snacks daily.
Driving range, putting green.

O57 Rothbury
☎(0669) 21271 Clubhouse, 20718
Sec
Old Race Course, Rothbury, Morpeth,
Northumberland NE65 7UB
Off A697, 15 miles NE of Morpeth.
Meadowland course.
9 holes, 5560 yards, S.S.S.67
Founded 1891
Visitors: weekdays except Tues pm;
some weekends by arrangement
only.
Green Fee: £11/day WD, £16/day
WE & BH.
Societies: as for visitors.
Catering: bar, bar meals, snacks,
open weekdays 11am-3pm.
Pool table.
Hotels: Coquetvale; Queens Head;
Newcastle; Railway.

O58 Ryhope
☎(091) 523 7333
c/o Mr Winfield, 30 Rosslyn Avenue,
Ryhope, Sunderland, Durham SR2
0SB
Turn off A19 at Ryhope village
towards Hollycarrside.
Municipal parkland course.
9 holes, 5510 yards, S.S.S.69
Designed by Sunderland Borough
Council.
Founded March 1991
Visitors: unrestricted.
Green Fee: apply for details.
Catering: temporary club house.

O59 Ryton
☎(091) 413 3737
Dr Stanners, Clara Vale, Ryton, Tyne
& Wear NE40 3TD
Off A695 8 miles from Newcastle,
follow signs from Ryton to Wylam
then Clara Vale.
Moorland/parkland course.
18 holes, 6034 yards, S.S.S.69
Founded 1891
Visitors: welcome weekdays, by
arrangement weekends.
Green Fee: apply for details.
Societies: welcome by arrangement.
Catering: full facilities every day.

O60 Saltburn-by-the-Sea
☎(0287) 622812 Sec, 624653 Pro
Hob Hill, Saltburn-by-Sea, Cleveland
TS12 1NJ

1 mile from Saltburn on A1268
Guisborough road on left.
Parkland course.
18 holes, 5846 yards, S.S.S.68
Founded 1894
Visitors: welcome; h/cap cert
preferred.
Green Fee: £19 WD, £22 WE.
Societies: by arrangement, not
Thurs or Sat.
Catering: full facilities except Mon.
Snooker.
Hotels: Royal York; Park.

O61 Seaham
☎(091) 581 2354, 513 0837 Pro
Dawdon, Seaham, Co Durham SR7
7RD
Off A19, 6 miles S of Sunderland,
take road to Seaham.
Heathland course.
18 holes, 5972 yards, S.S.S.69
Designed by Dr A. Mackenzie.
Founded May 1911
Visitors: welcome.
Green Fee: £15/day WD, £18/day
WE.
Societies: to be booked through Sec.
Catering: meals to be booked.
Snooker.

O62 Seahouses
☎(0665) 720794
Beadnell Rd, Seahouses,
Northumberland NE68 7XT
Off A1 5 miles N of Alnwick; B1340.
Seaside course.
18 holes, 5462 yards, S.S.S.67
Founded 1913
Visitors: welcome at all times; at
weekends contact club beforehand
for availability of starting times.
Green Fee: on application.
Societies: weekdays and most
weekends.
Catering: lunches, bar meals and full
à la carte.
Hotels: Bamburgh Castle; Beach
House; Sunningdale.

O63 Seaton Carew
☎(0429) 266249
Tees Rd, Seaton Carew, Hartlepool,
Cleveland TS25 1DE
Off A178 3 miles S of Hartlepool.
Championship seaside links course.
Old, 18 holes, 6604 yards, S.S.S.72;
Brabazon, 18 holes, 6849 yards,
S.S.S.73
Designed by Duncan McCuaig.
Founded 1874
Visitors: on application to Hon Sec.
Green Fee: apply for details.

Seaton Carew

One of the great joys of golf in the West of Ireland is the feeling of spaciousness and the fact that the views from the links are dominated by natural beauty. For those who never venture further from Donegal than Rosses Point, it might be thought such beauty is an integral part of all courses but one of the game's great strengths is the number of contrasting settings in which it is played.

It seems to me, therefore, that the citizens of Hartlepool are every bit as justified in their ardent counting of their blessings over Seaton Carew as the Irish are in their admiration for Tralee or Lahinch.

Modern Seaton Carew is set in surroundings of industrial chimneys and chemical production plants but that has never been, and never will be, a deterrent to golfers. It is something to which you get used in the same way that, by the end of a round at Royal Mid-Surrey, you never notice the aeroplanes or, at West Hill, the trains.

Courses are judged by the challenge and enjoyment they provide and both are high on the list at Seaton Carew, whose distinction is heightened by being one of the few outstanding links on the seaboard of eastern England. Its championship qualities have been recognised by the staging of the English Amateur strokeplay and British Boys' championships, events that enhanced the course's admirable and deserved reputation.

All the same, one view from the course is of the swings and roundabouts of the amusement park, a reminder that Seaton Carew's attractions are not all confined to golf. Nevertheless, Seaton Carew, founded in 1874 as the Durham and Yorkshire GC, is the oldest in either county and its seniority undoubtedly adds to its eminence.

The current course is one of 22 holes, a convenient method of giving members playing options rather than an attempt to set new fashions, although the Old Course at St Andrews started as 22 holes. Some prefer Seaton Carew's old course which plays more or less out and back although with more variation in direction than on many seaside links, but Frank Pennink's design of four new holes gave rise to the championship version of the course, as well as making it significantly more formidable.

An opening hole named "Rocket" calls to mind that Seaton Carew is very much in railway country but the tempo rises with the long 2nd and the short 3rd which turns back towards the clubhouse. The short 6th also follows the line of the 3rd but the new 10th is the only hole that runs east, a timely signal that the flavour of the golf gains a piquant touch as it nears the sea.

The 10th is a straight par 4 but the dogleg 11th leads on to another fine par 4 aptly named "Beach" on account of its proximity to the fence guarding the shore.

By now, the sea buckthorn has begun to dominate and the 13th and 14th, both par 5s, are flanked on the right by a hazard that is statistically punishing and physically painful. There is relief from it at the 208 yard 15th but there is no escaping the buckthorn on the last three holes, which constitute quite a finish. It is particularly easy to become engulfed by it on the right of the 18th, a hole with an unusually contoured fairway, but the most renowned hole is the 17th, its title of "Snag" carrying more than a hint of understatement. It is the second shot and, more especially, the distinctive green which make demands on our cunning, although the drive can become entangled with the same central spine of hillocks encountered on the way out; and the drive can err a little too safely the other way. However, a correct angle for the second shot is essential to hold a green shaped like a scallop shell, bunkered all around and contoured ingeniously on several levels.

It wouldn't do if all greens presented such problems but golf would be duller without its teasers and the 17th green at Seaton Carew is as notable an instrument of torture as man can devise.

Societies: apply to Hon Sec.
Catering: full facilities. Snooker.
Hotels: Grand; Staincliffe Marine.

O64 Slaley Hall

☎(0434) 673691, 673350 club
Slaley, Hexham, Northumberland
NE47 0BY
Off A68 near Corbridge.
Mainly heathland course with lakes
and woods.
18 holes, 7038 yards, S.S.S.73
Designed by Dave Thomas.
Founded 1989
Visitors: welcome with h/cap cert;
bookings only.
Green Fee: apply for details.
Societies: welcome by appointment.
Catering: full facilities.
Driving range, practice ground,
leisure complex.
Hotels: hotel on site

O65 South Moor

☎(0207) 232848 Club, 283525 Pro
The Middles, Craghead, Stanley, Co
Durham DH9 6AG
2 miles from Stanley on B6313; 8
miles NW of Durham.
Moorland course.
18 holes, 6445 yards, S.S.S.71
Designed by Dr A. Mackenzie.
Founded 1923
Visitors: welcome.
Green Fee: £14/round, £21/day WD
(£10 and £15 with member);
£25/day WE & BH (£12/round,
£18/day with member).
Societies: welcome, not Sun.
Catering: lunches and evening
meals served all week. Snooker.
Hotels: Post House; Lumley Castle;
Imperial; Beamish Park; Royal
County.

O66 South Shields

☎(091) 456 0475 Club, 456 8942
Office
Cleadon Hills, South Shields, Tyne &
Wear NE34 8EG
Near Cleadon Chimney, prominent
landmark.
Seaside course.
18 holes, 6264 yards, S.S.S.70
Founded 1893
Visitors: welcome at all times.
Green Fee: apply for details.
Societies: by arrangement.
Catering: meals any time; bar
11am-11pm weekdays, 12am-2pm
and 7pm-10.30pm Sun.
Hotels: New Crown; Marsden Inn;
Sea Hotel.

O67 Stocksfield

☎(0661) 843041
New Ridley, Stocksfield,
Northumberland NE43 7RE
On A695 between Corbridge and
Prudhoe.
Parkland/wooded course.
18 holes, 5594 yards, S.S.S.68
Designed by Pennink Associates.
Founded 1912
Visitors: welcome any time
weekdays, after 4.30pm weekends.
Green Fee: on application.
Societies: by arrangement.
Catering: sandwiches, meals by
prior booking.
Hotels: Broomhaugh (Riding Mill).

O68 Stressholme Golf Centre

☎(0325) 461002
Snipe Lane, Darlington, Co Durham
DL2 2SA
About 8 miles N of Scotch Corner, 2
miles N of Darlington centre.
Municipal parkland course.
18 holes, 6382 yards, S.S.S.69
Founded 1976
Visitors: welcome, 8am-5.30pm.
Green Fee: £7.30/round WD,
£8.50/round WE.
Societies: by arrangement with Pro.
Catering: drinks, snacks, meals.

O69 Swarland Hall

☎(0670) 787010 Sec, 602016 Reg
Office, 787940 Caterer
Coast View, Swarland, Morpeth,
Northumberland NE65 9JG
In village of Swarland approx 1 mile
W of A1 trunk road some 9 miles S of
Alnwick.
Parkland course.
9 holes (extending to 18 summer
1994), S.S.S.68
Founded 1993
Visitors: welcome Mon-Fri;
members may bring guests at
weekends.
Green Fee: £10/round.
Societies: will be welcome when
course extended to 18 holes.
Catering: bar, bar meals, dining
room.

O70 Teesside

☎(0642) 676249 Club, 616516 Sec
Acklam Rd, Thornaby, Cleveland
TS17 7JS
Off A19 take A1130 to Stockton,
course 0.5 mile from A19 on right.
Meadowland course, flat and
treelined.

18 holes, 6505 yards, S.S.S.71
Founded 1901
Visitors: welcome weekdays before
4.30pm, Bank Holidays after 11am,
unless with member.
Green Fee: on application.
Societies: weekdays.
Catering: full facilities except Mon.
Hotels: Post House; Golden Eagle.

O71 Tynedale

☎(0434) 608154
Tyne Green, Hexham,
Northumberland
From A69 take road into Hexham,
turn right into Countryside Park,
course 500 yards on S of River Tyne.
Public parkland course.
9 holes, 5643 yards, S.S.S.67
Founded 1907
Visitors: welcome; not Sun am.
Green Fee: £10/day WD, £12/day
WE.
Societies: welcome, bookings only.
Catering: full catering.
Hotels: Beaumont; County; Royal.

O72 Tynemouth

☎(091) 257 4578
Spital Dene, Tynemouth, North
Shields, Tyne & Wear NE30 2ER
On A695.
Parkland course.
18 holes, 6403 yards, S.S.S.71
Designed by Willie Park.
Founded 1913
Visitors: welcome weekdays.
Green Fee: £20/day WD, £8 with
member only WE.
Societies: weekdays.
Catering: lunches, teas and snacks
served except Mon.
Hotels: Moat House; Park.

O73 Tyneside

☎(091) 413 2742 Sec, 413 2177
Clubhouse
Westfield Lane, Ryton, Tyne & Wear
NE40 3QE
7 miles W of Newcastle upon Tyne on
S side of Tyne, on A695, turn N at
Ryton down to Old Ryton village, turn
left, past Cross Inn, and then right at
end of row of old houses on right.
Parkland course.
18 holes, 6055 yards, S.S.S.69
Designed by H.S. Colt (1910).
Founded 1879
Visitors: welcome.
Green Fee: £21/day WD, £26/round
WE.
Societies: weekdays only by prior
arrangement with Sec.

INTERNATIONAL HOTELIERS

WASHINGTON MOAT HOUSE
STONE CELLAR ROAD, HIGH USWORTH,
DISTRICT 12, WASHINGTON,
TYNE & WEAR, NE37 1PH
Telephone Tyneside (091) 417 2626
Telex 537143 WSHMH

The **WASHINGTON MOAT HOUSE** extends a stylish welcome, with a warmth that's special to the North East, and offers a combination of first class business and leisure facilites.

★ 18 hole Championship Golf Coures
★ 9 hole Par 3 ★ Floodlit Driving Range
★ Snooker Table ★ Squash ★ Sauna
★ Solarium ★ Indoor Pool ★ Spa Bath
★ Gym ★ Restaurant ★ Bars
★ Conference Facilities

For further details, telephone Reservations:
091 417 2626

Catering: bar, tea/coffee, bar snacks, lunch, high tea, dinner (service 10.30am-9pm).
Hotels: Ryton Park Country House.

O74 Wallsend
☎(091) 262 1973
Bigges Main, Wallsend-on-Tyne, Northumberland NE28 8SX
E of Newcastle on coast road to Whitley Bay.
Public parkland course.
18 holes, 6608 yards, S.S.S.72
Founded 1905
Visitors: no visitors before 12.30pm weekends.
Green Fee: £10.50 WD, £12.50 WE.
Societies: on written request.
Catering: hot or cold snacks.
Driving range.

O75 Warkworth
☎(0665) 711596
The Links, Warkworth, Morpeth, Northumberland NE65 0SW
Off A1068 to Warkworth, 10 miles N of Morpeth, 7 miles SE of Alnwick.
Seaside course.
9 holes, 5856 yards, S.S.S.68
Designed by Tom Morris.
Founded 1891
Visitors: welcome except Tues and Sat (competitions).
Green Fee: on application.
Societies: apply to Sec.
Catering: by arrangement with Stewardess.
Hotels: Sun; Warkworth House.

O76 Washington Moat House
☎(091) 417 2626
Stone Cellar Rd, High Usworth, District 12, Washington, Tyne & Wear NE37 1PH

A1M/A194M, well signposted.
Parkland course.
18 holes, 6267 yards, S.S.S.72
Founded 1990
Visitors: by appointment.
Green Fee: £16 WD, £25 WE.
Societies: by appointment.
Catering: full facilities.
Driving range, Pitch & Putt, snooker.
Hotels: Washington Moat House.

O77 Wearside
☎(091) 534 2518 Clubhouse, 534 2518 Sec, 534 4269 Pro
Coxgreen, Sunderland, Tyne & Wear SR4 9JT
Take A183 direction Chester-le-Street from A19, after 100 yards turn right at Coxgreen sign, left at small T-junction, follow road down hill to clubhouse, (2 mins from A19).
Meadowland/parkland course.
18 holes, 6343 yards, S.S.S.70
Founded 1892
Visitors: welcome; unaccompanied visitors must show h/cap cert.
Green Fee: on application.
Societies: on application to Sec.
Catering: full facilities, except Mon during winter.
Par 3 course and practice field.
Hotels: George Washington Sports Centre; Seaburn; Ramside Hall; Rainton Motel; The Wessington Travel Inn.

O78 Westerhope
☎(091) 286 9125 Club, 286 7636 Sec/bookings), 286 0594 Pro
Whorlton Grange, Westerhope, Newcastle-upon-Tyne NE5 1PP
5 miles W of Newcastle; Airport Rd for 3 miles then follow signs to Westerhope.
Parkland course.

18 holes, 6468 yards, S.S.S.71
Designed by Alexander "Sandy" Herd.
Founded 1941
Visitors: Mon to Fri.
Green Fee: £16/round, £22/day.
Societies: catered for Mon to Fri.
Catering: available.
Hotels: Moat House (Newcastle Airport); Novotel.

O79 Whickham
☎(091) 488 7309 Club, 488 1576 Sec/Manager
Hollinside Park, Whickham, Newcastle-upon-Tyne NE16 5BA
5 miles W of Newcastle.
Undulating parkland course.
18 holes, 6129 yards, S.S.S.68
Founded 1911
Visitors: unrestricted weekdays, by arrangement weekends.
Green Fee: on application.
Societies: weekdays only.
Catering: snacks, cooked meals by arrangement. Snooker.
Hotels: Gibside (Whickham).

O80 Whitburn
☎(091) 529 2144, 529 4210 Pro, 529 4944 Sec
Lizard Lane, South Shields, Tyne & Wear NE34 7AH
Half-way between Sunderland and South Shields off coast road.
Parkland course.
18 holes, 5773 yards, S.S.S.68
Founded 1932
Visitors: welcome weekdays (restricted Tues); at weekends phone Pro beforehand.
Green Fee: £15/round/day WD, £20/round/day WE.
Societies: weekdays except Tues.
Catering: full facilities.
Hotels: Seaburn; Roker; Sea Hotel.

O81 **Whitley Bay**

☎(091) 252 0180
Claremont Rd, Whitley Bay, Tyne &
Wear NE26 3UF
On A183, 10 miles NE of Newcastle;
at N end of town.
Links/parkland course.
18 holes, 6617 yards, S.S.S.72
Founded 1890
Visitors: not weekends.
Green Fee: £18/round, £25/day.
Societies: weekdays by
arrangement.
Catering: full bar and restaurant
facilities except Mon.
Hotels: Gosforth Park; Holiday Inn;
Windsor.

O82 **Wilton**

☎(0642) 465265 Sec, 454626
Members
Wilton, Redcar, Cleveland TS10 4QY
8 miles E of Middlesborough and 4
miles W of Redcar on A174; follow
signs to Wilton Castle.
Parkland course.
18 holes, 6145 yards, S.S.S.69

Founded 1952
Visitors: wlcome after 10am; no
visitors Sat.
Green Fee: £18 WD, £24 Sun & BH.
Societies: Mon, Wed, Fri, occasional
Thurs and Sun, by arrangement with
Sec.
Catering: bars, dining area.
Practice ground, snooker.
Hotels: Park (Redcar); Post House
(Thornaby).

O83 **Woodham Golf & Country Club**

☎(0325) 318346, 301551 Catering
Burnhill Way, Newton Aycliffe,
Durham DL5 4PN
2 miles A1(M), 1 mile N of Newton
Aycliffe.
Parkland course with lakes.
18 holes, 6727 yards, S.S.S.72
Designed by J. Hamilton Stutt.
Founded 1983
Visitors: unlimited weekdays, by
appointment weekends.
Green Fee: £15/round, £20/day WD;
£20/round, £25/day WE & BH.

Societies: by appointment.
Catering: à la carte restaurant.
Hotels: Redworth Hall.

O84 **Wooler**

☎(0668) 281956 Sec
Dod Law, Doddington, Wooler,
Northumberland NE71 6EA
Signposted from B6525 Wooler-
Berwick road.
Moorland course with heather and
bracken and panoramic views.
9 holes (18 tees), 6358 yards,
S.S.S.70
Designed by club members.
Founded 1970 (present course 1976)
Visitors: usually no restrictions.
Green Fee: £10/round/day WD,
£15/round/day WE & BH.
Societies: apply to Sec (23 Ryecroft
Crescent, Wooler, NE71 6EA).
Catering: bar every night 8-11pm;
catering by arrangement May-Sept.
Hotels: Ryecroft; Tankerville Arms;
Black Bull; Angel Inn; Red Lion;
Anchor Inn; Wheatsheaf; Loretto GH;
St Leonards B&B.

P

LOTHIAN, BORDERS, DUMFRIES & GALLOWAY

This is an area embracing the south-west of Scotland, the Borders (more famous for rugby than golf), and the part of central Scotland which incorporates East Lothian, one of the oldest and most famous regions in the expanding world of golf.

Until Muirfield was opened in 1892, Musselburgh was a regular home of the Open championship between 1874 and 1889, while North Berwick staged a number of challenge matches that are part of the game's folklore.

Today, you could stay for a week and play a different East Lothian course of championship standard each day without having to drive for more than twenty minutes. The old Musselburgh course, enveloped by Edinburgh racecourse, is the place to start on historical grounds, although Royal Musselburgh has a more sheltered parkland home a mile or two down the road to North Berwick which bristles with golfing retreats.

Longniddry, and the shorter Kilspindie at Aberlady, provide contrasting pleasures but the true heart of East Lothian lies around Gullane Hill and the incomparable stretch of natural terrain that houses Luffness New and Gullane Nos 1, 2 and 3. From a distance, they are indistinguishable the one from the other, green ribbons of fairway lined by taller grass running down to the edge of Aberlady Bay — a bird sanctuary and nature reserve that profits rather than suffers from its proximity to golf.

Luffness is enchanting, neither stern nor straightforward with magnificently true, small greens, but Gullane Hill is a dominant feature of all three Gullane courses, hiding the road from the holes bordering the Firth of Forth and a series of resplendent views. Everyone has courses for which he feels unreasoning affection, and Luffness and Gullane No. 1 are two particular favourites.

The incomparable stretch of country on which they stand was introduced to me by a kind cousin during my time at school in Edinburgh, when a day at Luffness really was an escape from Plato and Pythagoras; apart from the greens, my memories are of a blind short hole across a quarry — and a magnificent and very welcome lunch.

On the other side of the hill lies Muirfield, third home of the Honourable Company of Edinburgh Golfers and invariably placed top in polls on British courses. It has no enemies, a noble combination of ancient and modern that never disappoints. North Berwick, on the other hand, has changed very little through the years in spite of the advance in manufacture of equipment which has softened some of its terrors. The last of the coastal courses is Dunbar which, too, has many admirers.

As well as East Lothian, there are Midlothian and West Lothian which, though full of good courses, are less remarkable. Boyhood memories compel me to single out Bruntsfield, Dalmahoy and the Royal Burgess at Barnton, a mile or two from the Forth Bridge.

The Border country has several 9-hole courses in scenic settings and two or three of grander dimensions. However, the county of Dumfries & Galloway deserves greater recognition than it invariably receives, particularly around the countryside fringing the Solway Firth. Southerness is the flagship, a championship test which Mackenzie Ross designed and built at about the time he was resurrecting Turnberry after the war, and where heather and gorse put a heavy onus on fine driving.

Other recommendations must include Powfoot, Thornhill and, working a path westward, the courses of Wigtownshire County, Stranraer and, last but not least, Portpatrick (Dunskey).

P1 Baberton

☎(031) 453 4911
Baberton Ave, Juniper Green,
Edinburgh EH14 5DU
5 miles W of Edinburgh on A70
Lanark road.
Parkland course.
18 holes, 6098 yards, S.S.S.69
Designed by Willie Park.
Founded 1893
Visitors: on introduction by a
member.
Green Fee: £17/round, £25/day.
Societies: Mon-Fri only by
arrangement with Sec.
Catering: full facilities.

P2 Bathgate

☎(0506) 52232 Club, 630553 Pro,
630505 Sec, 636775 Fax
Edinburgh Rd, Bathgate, W Lothian
EH48 1BA
400 yards E from town centre.

Parkland course.
18 holes, 6328 yards, S.S.S.70
Designed by Willie Park.
Founded 1892
Visitors: unrestricted weekdays,
limited at weekends.
Green Fee: on application.
Societies: welcome by prior
arrangement with Sec.
Catering: coffee, lunch, high tea.
Hotels: Golden Circle; Dreadnought;
Fairway.

P3 Braid Hills

☎(031) 452 9408, 445 2044 Sec
(Braids United), 447 6666 starter
Braid Hills Approach Rd, Edinburgh
EH10 6JY
A702 from city centre S.
Public hillside courses.
18 holes, 5731 yards, S.S.S.68; 18
holes, 4832 yards, S.S.S.64
Founded 1897

Visitors: unrestricted.
Green Fee: apply for details.
Societies: by prior arrangement.
Catering: by prior arrangement.

P4 Broomieknowe

☎(031) 663 9317
36 Golf Course Rd, Bonnyrigg,
Midlothian EH19 2HZ
About 0.5 mile into Bonnyrigg from
Eskbank Rd roundabout on A7.
Gently undulating parkland course.
18 holes, 5754 yards, S.S.S.68
(6200 yards, Par 70 from June 1994)
Designed by James Braid; alterations
by Hawtree and Son.
Founded 1906
Visitors: welcome weekdays.
Green Fee: £15/round, £25/day.
Societies: Mon-Fri.
Catering: bar lunches, evening
meals by arrangement with Steward.
Hotels: Dalhousie Castle.

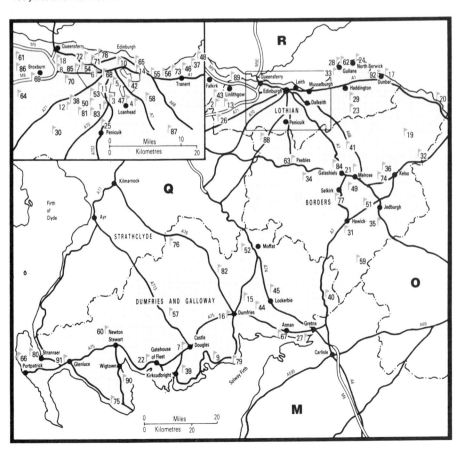

P5 **Bruntsfield Links**
☎(031) 336 1479 Sec, 2006
Clubhouse, 4050 Pro
32 Barnton Ave, Davidsons Mains,
Edinburgh EH4 6JH
Off A90 in Davidsons Mains 2 to 3
miles W of Edinburgh city centre.
Parkland course.
18 holes, 6407 yards, S.S.S.71
Designed by Willie Park.
Founded 1761
Visitors: welcome weekdays by
appointment.
Green Fee: on application.
Societies: by appointment.
Catering: luncheon daily, evening
meals during playing season.
Hotels: Barnton.

P6 **Carrickknowe**
☎(031) 337 1096
Glendevon Park, Edinburgh EH12
5VZ
Opposite the Post House Hotel, down
Balgreen Rd.
Public meadowland course.
18 holes, 6299 yards, S.S.S.70
Founded 1933
Visitors: welcome.
Green Fee: apply for details.
Societies: by arrangement.
Catering: by arrangement with Sec.
Hotels: Post House.

P7 **Castle Douglas**
☎(0556) 502801, 502099 Sec
Abercromby Rd, Castle Douglas,
Kirkcudbrightshire
400 yards on Ayr road A713 from
town clock.
Parkland course.
9 holes, 5408 yards, S.S.S.66
Visitors: welcome.
Green Fee: £10.
Societies: welcome.
Catering: bar facilities during
summer months.
Hotels: Imperial; Douglas Arms.

P8 **Cogarburn**
☎(031) 333 4718 Starter, 333 4110
Clubhouse
Hanley Lodge, Newbridge,
Midlothian EH28 8NN
Westbound A8 Glasgow road, turn
sharp left at commencement of
airport slip road, left again at
T-junction.
Parkland course.
12 holes, 5070 yards, S.S.S.65
Founded 1975
Visitors: welcome, not after 5pm.
Green Fee: £8/round.

Societies: by arrangement with Sec.
Catering: usually available;
licensed. Pool table.
Hotels: Barnton; Royal Scot.

P9 **Colvend**
☎(055 663) 398, (0556) 610878
Sec
Sandyhills, by Dalbeattie,
Kirkcudbrightshire DG5 4PY
6 miles from Dalbeattie on A710
Solway coast road.
Undulating meadowland course.
9 holes, 2322 yards, S.S.S.63
Designed by Willie Fernie (Troon)
1905; extended 1982 with advice
from Dave Thomas.
Founded 1905
Visitors: welcome; course closed
April-Sept at 2pm Tues and 5.30pm
Thurs.
Green Fee: £10/day; under 18
half-price except Sat and Sun.
Societies: apply to Sec.
Catering: April-Oct full lunch and
dinner facilities; winter restricted to
weekends.
Hotels: Clonyard House.

P10 **Craigentinny**
☎(031) 554 7501 Starter
143 Craigentinny Ave, Edinburgh,
Scotland
1 mile from Meadowbank Stadium,
2.5 miles E of city centre.
Public links course.
18 holes, 5418 yards, S.S.S.66
Founded 1891
Visitors: welcome.
Green Fee: apply for details.
Societies: welcome by appointment.

P11 **Craigmillar Park**
☎(031) 667 2837 Clubhouse, 667
0047 Office
1 Observatory Rd, Edinburgh EH9
3HG
Approx 3 miles from city centre close
to Royal Observatory, Blackford Hill.
Parkland course.
18 holes, 5859 yards, S.S.S.68
Designed by James Braid.
Founded 1895
Visitors: non-introduced visitors
must produce h/cap cert, letter of
intro or proof of club membership; off
first tee by 3.30pm weekdays; not
weekends or Bank Holidays.
Green Fee: £15/round, £23/day WD.
Societies: on application.
Catering: bar lunches, high teas on
request.
Hotels: Iona.

P12 **Dalmahoy**
☎(031) 333 4105, 335 3203 Fax
Kirknewton, Midlothian EH27 8EB
7 miles W of Edinburgh centre on A71.
Rolling parkland course.
East, 18 holes, 6677 yards, S.S.S.72;
West, 18 holes, 5185 yards, S.S.S.66
Designed by James Braid.
Founded 1922
Visitors: welcome weekdays,
weekends by application.
Green Fee: East £34 WD, West £24
WD.
Societies: welcome weekdays.
Catering: extensive facilities in
country club.
Tennis, squash, swimming pool,
snooker, health and beauty facilities.
Hotels: Dalmahoy; golf and leisure
breaks available.

P13 **Deer Park Golf & Country Club**
☎(0506) 31037, 35608 Fax
Golf Course Rd, Knightsbridge,
Livingston, W Lothian EH54 8PG
Leave M8 at junction 3, Livingston
exit follow signs to Knightsbridge,
club signposted from there.
Parkland course.
18 holes, 6775 yards, S.S.S.72
Designed by Charles Lawrie.
Founded 1978
Visitors: welcome 7 days.
Green Fee: £15/round, £20.50/day
WD; £25/round, £35/day WE.
Societies: welcome 7 days.
Catering: full facilities 7 days.
Swimming pool, squash, snooker,
pool, 10-pin bowling, saunas etc.
Hotels: Hilton; Houston House.

P14 **Duddingston**
☎(031) 661 7688 or 661 4301 Pro
Duddingston Rd, W Edinburgh EH15
3QD
3 miles from city centre E of A1.
Parkland course.
18 holes, 6647 yards, S.S.S.72
Designed by Capability Brown.
Founded 1895
Visitors: Mon-Fri only.
Green Fee: £21/round, £27.50/day.
Societies: Tues, Thurs only;
£18/round, £24/day.
Catering: lunches, high teas, bar
every day.
Hotels: Lady Nairne; King's Manor;
Duddingston Mansion House.

P15 **Dumfries & County**
☎(0387) 53585
Edinburgh Rd, Dumfries DG1 1JX

1 mile N of Dumfries town centre on A701.
Parkland course.
18 holes, 5928 yards, S.S.S.68
Designed by Willie Fernie.
Founded 1912
Visitors: welcome except Sat.
Green Fee: £21 WD, £25 WE.
Societies: apply to Sec.
Catering: full facilities every day.
Hotels: Station; Moreig; Cairndale.

P16 Dumfries & Galloway
☎(0387) 53582, 63848 Sec
Laurieston Ave, Dumfries DG2 7NY
On A75 W of Dumfries.
Parkland course.
18 holes, 5782 yards, S.S.S.68
Founded 1880
Visitors: welcome without reservation except competition days.
Green Fee: on application.
Societies: catered for.
Catering: full facilities except Mon.

P17 Dunbar
☎(0368) 862317
East Links, Dunbar EH42 1LT
0.5 mile from Dunbar centre.
Seaside course.
18 holes, 6426 yards, S.S.S.71
Founded 1794
Visitors: unrestricted except Thurs.
Green Fee: £25/day WD, £40/day WE.
Societies: by arrangement with Sec in writing.
Catering: full facilities 7 days.
Hotels: Royal Mackintosh; Battleblent; Hillside; Goldenstones; Craig en Gelt.

P18 Dundas Park
☎(031) 331 5603
3 Loch Place, South Queensferry, W Lothian EH30 9NG
1 mile S of Queensferry, on right of A8000.
Parkland course (good practice course).
9 holes, 6024 yards, S.S.S.69
Founded 1957
Visitors: with member only.
Green Fee: apply for details.
Societies: welcome, written request to Sec.
Catering: self-catering snacks in clubhouse.

P19 Duns
☎(0361) 82717 Sec
Hardens Rd, Duns, Berwicks

1 mile W of Duns off A6105.
Undulating meadowland course.
9 holes, 5826 yards, S.S.S.68
Founded 1894
Visitors: unrestricted.
Green Fee: £10/round/day.
Societies: welcome if previously arranged with Sec.
Catering: limited bar facilities, mainly at weekends.
Hotels: "Freedom of the Fairways" package from Scottish Borders Tourist Board.

P20 Eyemouth
☎(08907) 50551
Gunsgreen House, Eyemouth TD14 5DY
2.5 miles E of Burmouth, off A1, signposted on A1107.
Seaside course.
9 holes, 5446 yards, S.S.S.66
Founded 1884
Visitors: unrestricted weekdays, after 10.30am Sat, 12am Sun.
Green Fee: £10/day (£4 jnrs), £35/week (£16 jnrs).
Societies: by arrangement.
Catering: bar open evenings and lunchtime weekends.
Snooker, pool.
Hotels: Home Arms; Contented Sole; Ship; Whale.

P21 Galashiels
☎(0896) 3724 Clubhouse, 55307 Sec
Ladhope Recreation Ground, Galashiels, Selkirkshire TD1 2NJ
At N end of town off A7.
Hilly course.
18 holes, 5309 yards, S.S.S.66
Designed by James Braid.
Founded 1884
Visitors: weekends by arrangement.
Green Fee: £10/round, £14/day WD; £14/round, £18/day WE (approx).
Societies: welcome by arrangement.
Catering: by arrangement only via Sec. Pool table.
Hotels: Kingsknowes; Kings; Abbotsford Arms.

P22 Gatehouse
☎(0557 814734 Sec
Laurieston Rd, Gatehouse-of-Fleet
Turn right at War Memorial on entering town from E.
Public, undulating course with gorse in places.
9 holes, 4796 yards, S.S.S.63
Founded 1921
Visitors: welcome any time.

Green Fee: on application.
Societies: apply to Sec.
Hotels: Cally; Murray Arms; both offer free golf.

P23 Gifford
☎(062 081) 267, 591 Clubhouse
c/o Sec, Calroust, Tweddale Ave, Gifford, E Lothian, EH41 4QN
4.5 miles S of Haddington off A6137.
Meadowland/woodland course.
9 holes, 6138 yards, S.S.S.69
Designed by Willie Wood.
Founded 1904
Visitors: welcome, except Tues/Wed from 4pm or Sat/Sun from 12 noon.
Green Fee: £10/day WD, £10/round (18 holes) WE.
Hotels: Goblin Ha'; Tweeddale Arms.

P24 Glen
☎(0620) 5288
East Links, Tantallon Terrace, North Berwick EH39 4LE
22 miles NE of Edinburgh on A198, follow road along E beach, clubhouse is last building on right.
Seaside/parkland course.
18 holes, 6098 yards, S.S.S.69
Designed by Mackenzie Ross.
Founded 1906
Visitors: no restrictions.
Green Fee: £11.50/round, £17/day WD; £14.50/round, £21/day WE.
Societies: welcome at all times, advance booking recommended.
Catering: bar lunches, high teas, coffee.
Hotels: Royal; Blenheim House; Nether Abbey.

P25 Glencorse
☎(0968) 77189
Milton Bridge, Pencuik, Midlothian EH26 0RD
On A701, 9 miles S of Edinburgh.
Parkland course, burns on 10 holes.
18 holes, 5205 yards, S.S.S.66
Designed by Willie Park Jnr.
Founded 1890
Visitors: welcome most weekdays and weekends if no competitions.
Green Fee: apply for details.
Societies: most weekdays.
Catering: full facilities.
Hotels: Inveravon House (Loanhead); Original, Royal (Roslin).

P26 Greenburn
☎(0501) 70292
6 Greenburn Rd, Fauldhouse, W Lothian EH47 9HG

Midway between Edinburgh and Glasgow, off M8 at Whitburn, 3 miles.
Moorland course.
18 holes, 6210 yards, S.S.S.70
Founded 1953
Visitors: weekdays.
Green Fee: on application.
Societies: welcome by prior booking.
Catering: weekends and midweek when societies are booked in.
Hotels: Hillcroft (Whitburn).

P27 Gretna

☎(0461) 338464
'Kirtle View', Gretna, Dumfriesshire DG16 5HD
0.5 mile W of Gretna on S side of A75, 1 mile from M74/A75 junction.
Parkland course.
9 holes, 3215 yards, S.S.S.71
Designed by Nigel Williams; Bothwell
Founded 1991
Visitors: welcome 7 days, no restrictions unless competition being played.
Green Fee: £5 (9 holes), £10/day.
Societies: welcome by prior arrangement, terms on application.
Catering: bar meals and refreshments available at most times.
Driving range.
Hotels: 7 recommended hotels within 1 mile.

P28 Gullane

☎(0620) 842255, 842327 Fax
Gullane, East Lothian EH31 2BB
Off A1, on A198 to Gullane.
Links courses.
No. 1, 18 holes, 6466 yards, S.S.S.71; No. 2, 18 holes, 6244 yards, S.S.S.70; No. 3, 18 holes, 5166 yards, S.S.S.65
Founded 1882
Visitors: welcome on No. 1 course Mon-Fri and on Nos 2 & 3 at all times.
Green Fee: No. 1 course £37/round, £53/day WD; £47/round WE: No. 2 course £17/round, £25/day WD; £21/round, £32/day WE: No. 3 £11/round, £16/day WD; £13/round, £19/day WE.
Societies: by arrangement (except No. 1 at weekends).
Catering: bar meals any day, dining room lunches daily except Mon; dinners by arrangement.
New visitors clubhouse now open.
Hotels: Grey Walls; Golf Inn; Mallard; Queens; Marine (N Berwick); Open Arms (Dirleton).

P29 Haddington

☎(062 082) 3627
Amisfield Park, Whittinghame Dr, Haddington, E Lothian
17 miles E of Edinburgh on A1, cross Victoria Bridge on E edge of town, golf course is 500 yards on left.
Public parkland course.
18 holes, 6280 yards, S.S.S.70
Founded 1865
Visitors: welcome with pre-booking, Sat and Sun 7-10am, 12am-2pm.
Green Fee: £10/round, £13.50/day
Societies: welcome.
Catering: lunches, bar snacks, bar meals, high tea, except Tues.
Hotels: Mercat; Railway; Browns; Maitland Field.

P30 Harburn

☎(0506) 871131 Sec, 871256 members, 871582 Pro
West Calder, West Lothian EH55 8RS
Turn S at West Calder off A71 Kilmarnock-Edinburgh road.
Parkland course.
18 holes, 5853 yards, S.S.S.68
Founded 1933
Visitors: welcome.
Green Fee: £12.50/round, £18.50/day WD; £18.50/round, £25/day WE.
Societies: by arrangement.
Catering: bar snacks; full facilities by arrangement.
Hotels: Harburn House; West End.

P31 Hawick

☎(0450) 72293 Clubhouse, 75594 Sec
Vertish Hill, Hawick, Roxburgh TD9 0NY
SE of Edinburgh on A7.
Parkland course.
18 holes, 5927 yards, S.S.S.69
Founded 1877
Visitors: welcome, phone to arrange, not Sat.
Green Fee: £15/round, £21/day (approx).
Societies: phone Sec, limited to 24, one round only on Sun.
Catering: full facilities.
Hotels: Kirklands; Elm House; Mansfield Park.

P32 Hirsel

☎(0890) 882678
Kelso Rd, Coldstream, Berwickshire TS12 4LG
W end of Coldstream on A697, Edinburgh-Newcastle road.
Parkland course.

18 holes, 6092 yards, S.S.S.69
Founded 1948
Visitors: any time.
Green Fee: on application.
Societies: by arrangement.
Catering: Apr-Sept or by arrangement.
Hotels: Tillmouth Park; Newcastle Arms.

P33 Honourable Company of Edinburgh Golfers

☎(0620) 842123
Muirfield, Gullane, East Lothian EH31 2EG
Last road on left leaving Gullane for North Berwick on A198, approx 18 miles from Edinburgh.
Links course.
Medal, 18 holes, 6941 yards, S.S.S.73
Designed by Tom Morris.
Founded 1744
Visitors: Tues and Thurs; must be members of recognised golf club and have h/cap of 18 or better if gentlemen, 24 if Ladies.
Green Fee: £50/round, £70/day.
Societies: no reduced rates or packages; same as for visitors.
Catering: morning coffee (50p) lunch (£12), afternoon tea (£1); there are limited changing facilities for Ladies, but they are not allowed to eat in the Clubhouse.
Hotels: Greywalls; Open Arms (Dirleton).

P34 Innerleithen

☎(0896) 830951, 830071 Sec
Leithen Water, Leithen Road, Innerleithen EH44 6NL
1 mile from Innerleithen on Heriot road.
Heathland course.
9 holes, 5984 yards, S.S.S.69
Designed by Willie Park.
Founded 1886
Visitors: no restrictions except Medal days.
Green Fee: £8 WD, £11 WE, day ticket only.
Societies: by arrangement.
Catering: by arrangement.

P35 Jedburgh

☎(0835) 63587
Dunion Rd, Jedburgh, Roxburghshire TD8 6DQ
0.75 mile W of Jedburgh.
Undulating parkland course.
9 holes, 5555 yards, S.S.S.67
Founded 1892

Visitors: welcome except competition days at weekends.
Green Fee: apply for details.
Societies: booked at least 2 weeks in advance.
Catering: bar and meals April-Oct.
Hotels: Royal; Jedforest.

P36 Kelso
☎(0573) 23009, 23259 Sec.
Racecourse Rd, Kelso, Roxburgh TD5 7SL
1 mile N of town centre within National Hunt Racecourse.
Flat parkland course.
18 holes, 6066 yards, S.S.S.69
Designed by James Braid.
Founded 1887
Visitors: welcome.
Green Fee: apply for details.
Societies: by arrangement.
Catering: available except Mon and Tues; societies on these days by prior arrangement.

P37 Kilspindie
☎(0875) 358, 216
Aberlady, East Lothian EH32 0QD
Immediately E of Aberlady village, private road to left leading to club.
Seaside course.
18 holes, 5410 yards, S.S.S.66
Designed by Ross & Sayers, extended by Willie Park.
Founded 1867
Visitors: welcome subject to members' demands; advisable to enquire in advance.
Green Fee: apply for details.
Societies: welcome weekdays if booked in advance.
Catering: full facilities except Fri.
Hotels: Kilspindie House (Aberlady).

P38 Kingsknowe
☎(031) 441 4030 Pro, 441 1145 Sec
326 Lanark Rd, Edinburgh EH14 2JD
W of Edinburgh on A71.
Parkland course.
18 holes, 5979 yards, S.S.S.69
Designed by Alex Herd, James Braid, J.C. Stutt.
Founded 1908
Visitors: welcome weekdays.
Green Fee: £16/round, £20/day WD.

Societies: welcome weekdays on application to Sec.
Catering: bar, lunch, high tea except Mon. Snooker.
Hotels: Capital Moat House; Orwell Lodge.

P39 Kirkcudbright
☎(0557) 330314
Stirling Crescent, Kirkcudbright
Turn left off A75 into town from Castle Douglas.
Hilly parkland course.
18 holes, 5598 yards, S.S.S.67
Founded 1893
Visitors: welcome except on competition days.
Green Fee: £15/day.
Societies: by arrangement.
Catering: available.
Hotels: Arden House; Royal; Selkirk; Gordon House.

P40 Langholm
☎(03873) 80265 Visitor enquiries, 80395 Sec
Whitaside, Langholm, Dumfriesshire DG13 0JR
Between Carlisle and Hawick on A7, 400 yards E of Market Place.
Hillside course.
9 holes, 5744 yards, S.S.S.68
Founded 1892
Visitors: welcome weekdays and weekends except competitions.
Green Fee: £10/round/day.
Societies: apply to Sec.
Catering: can be arranged.

P41 Lauder
☎(05782) 526
Galashiels Rd, Lauder, Berwickshire
Off A68, 0.5 mile from Lauder.
Undulating course.
9 holes, 6002 yards, S.S.S.70
Designed by W. Park of Musselburgh.
Founded 1896
Visitors: welcome.
Green Fee: apply for details.
Societies: book in advance.

P42 Liberton
☎(031) 664 3009 Sec, 664 8580 Clubhouse, 664 1056 Pro

297 Gilmerton Rd, Edinburgh EH16 5UJ
S of Edinburgh on A7.
Parkland course.
18 holes, 5299 yards, S.S.S.66
Founded 1920
Visitors: welcome except after 5pm on Mon, Wed, Fri.
Green Fee: on application.
Societies: welcome weekdays.
Catering: full facilities available.

P43 Linlithgow
☎(0506) 842585 Sec, 671044 Clubhouse/bar, 844356 Pro
Braehead, Linlithgow, W Lothian EH49 6QF
Approx 10 miles from Edinburgh on M9; proceed W along High Street, left at Preston Road (opposite Black Bitch pub), signposted from there.
Undulating parkland course.
18 holes, 5729 yards, S.S.S.68
Designed by Robert Simpson of Carnoustie.
Founded 1913
Visitors: welcome except Sat.
Green Fee: £12/round, £17/day WD; £17/round, £22/day WE (approx).
Societies: by arrangement with Sec.
Catering: curtailed in winter, every day except Tues during season.
Hotels: Star & Garter; West Port.

P44 Lochmaben
☎(0387) 810552
Castlehill Gate, Lochmaben, Dumfries DG11 1NT
On A709 between Dumfries and Lockerbie.
Undulating parkland course.
9 holes, 5304 yards, S.S.S.66
Designed by James Braid.
Founded 1926
Visitors: welcome except competition days.
Green Fee: apply for details.
Societies: catered for on weekdays.
Catering: by arrangement for meetings. Fishing, sailing.

P45 Lockerbie
☎(0576) 23363, 202462
Corrie Rd, Lockerbie, Dumfriesshire DG11 2ND

A74 to Lockerbie, take Langholm road, turn left at T-junction towards Corrie, club 0.25 mile on right; signposted from town centre. Parkland course. 18 holes, 5327 yards, S.S.S.66 Designed by James Braid (original 9). Founded 1889 **Visitors:** welcome, pre-booking available. **Green Fee:** £15 WD, £18 Sat, £16 Sun. **Societies:** by arrangement; weekday package for groups of 20+, £20 (36 holes, meal etc.). **Catering:** full bar and catering service during summer. **Hotels:** Queens; Lockerbie Manor; Blue Bell; Kings Arms; Ravenshill.

P46 Longniddry
☎(0875) 852141, 852228 Starter Links Rd, Longniddry, E Lothian EH32 0NL A1 from Edinburgh, at Wallyford roundabout take A198, turn left at Longniddry down Links Rd. Links/parkland course. 18 holes, 6219 yards, S.S.S.70 Designed by Harry Colt. Founded 1921 **Visitors:** welcome excluding weekends, competition days and public holidays, unless with member; phone starter. **Green Fee:** £25/round, £35/day. **Societies:** Mon to Thurs. **Catering:** dining room excluding Fri, bar service, snacks available. **Hotels:** Marine (N Berwick); Kilspindie House (Aberlady).

P47 Lothianburn
☎(031) 445 2206 Clubhouse, 445 5067 Sec, 445 2288 Pro 106 Biggar Rd, Edinburgh EH10 7DU S boundary of Edinburgh, adjacent to Edinburgh by-pass. Panoramic hillside course. 18 holes, 5750 yards, S.S.S.69 Designed by James Braid. Founded 1893 **Visitors:** welcome weekdays only. **Green Fee:** £11/round, £16/day. **Societies:** welcome by arrangement with Sec on weekdays. **Catering:** lunch, bar meals, high tea; dinners by arrangement (not Wed). **Hotels:** Braid Hills.

P43 Luffness New
☎(0620) 843336 Sec, 843114 or 843376 Clubmaster, 842933 Fax

Aberlady, E Lothian EH32 0QA 1 mile outside Aberlady on the Gullane road, A198. Links course. 18 holes, 6122 yards, S.S.S.69 Designed by Tom Morris (1894). Founded 1894 **Visitors:** Mon to Fri only, except public and Bank Holidays; introduction by member or by own club Sec, h/caps to 24, ladies after 10am, jackets and ties obligatory in club rooms. **Green Fee:** £27/round, £40/day. **Societies:** welcome midweek by prior arrangement; no special terms. **Catering:** smoke room, dining room, coffee, lunch (2/3 course) daily, no snacks, high tea/dinner (min 10) by arrangement. Practice gound, 5-hole course. **Hotels:** Marine(N Berwick); Golf, Greywalls (Gullane).

P49 Melrose
☎(089 682) 2855, 2391 Sec. Dingleton, Melrose, Roxburghshire Off A68 Carlisle-Edinburgh road, 0.5 mile S of Melrose. Parkland course. 9 holes, 5464 yards, S.S.S.68 Founded 1880 **Visitors:** April-Oct, weekdays before 4pm and some Sun; Oct-Mar virtually any day. **Green Fee:** apply for details. **Societies:** by arrangement. **Catering:** snacks available; by arrangement for parties. Pool.

P50 Merchants of Edinburgh
☎(031) 447 1219 10 Craighill Gardens, Edinburgh EH10 5PY S side of Edinburgh off A701. Hilly parkland course. 18 holes, 4889 yards, S.S.S.64 Founded 1907 **Visitors:** weekdays before 4pm. **Green Fee:** £12/day WD. **Societies:** welcome on weekdays by arrangement with Sec. **Catering:** meals served if ordered in advance (except Wed and Thurs). **Hotels:** Braid Hills.

P51 Minto
☎(0450) 87220 Minto Village, by Denholm, Hawick, Roxburghshire 5 miles NE of Hawick off A698, turn left in Denholm for Minto.

Parkland course. 18 holes, 5460 yards, S.S.S.68 Founded 1926 **Visitors:** welcome most days, phone at weekends. **Green Fee:** £12/round, £18/day WD; £18/round, £25/day WE & BH. **Societies:** by arrangement. **Catering:** full catering and bar, except limited catering on Thurs. **Hotels:** Elm House; Kirklands.

P52 Moffat
☎(0683) 20020 Coatshill, Moffat, DG10 9SB On A701 between Moffat and Beattock, 1 mile off A74. Moorland course. 18 holes, 5218 yards, S.S.S.66 Designed by Ben Sayers. Founded 1884 **Visitors:** welcome; not Wed pm. **Green Fee:** £17/day WD, £25/day WE. **Societies:** welcome except Wed. **Catering:** bar, bar lunches, coffee daily. **Hotels:** Moffat House; Balmoral; Annandale Arms; Beechwood Country House; Auchen Castle.

P53 Mortonhall
☎(031) 447 6974 Sec. 231 Braid Rd, Edinburgh EH10 6PB 2 miles S of city centre on A702, situated on S of Braid Hills. Moorland course. 18 holes, 6557 yards, S.S.S.71 Designed by James Braid & Fred Hawtree. Founded 1892 **Visitors:** welcome weekdays. **Green Fee:** on application. **Societies:** welcome weekdays by arrangement. **Catering:** full bar and catering facilities. **Hotels:** Braid Hills.

P54 Murrayfield
☎(031) 337 3478 Murrayfield Rd, Edinburgh EH12 6EU 2 miles W of city centre. Parkland course. 18 holes, 5727 yards, S.S.S.68 Founded 1896 **Visitors:** welcome weekdays with letter of intro. **Green Fee:** on application. **Societies:** by arrangement. **Catering:** meals served except Mon. **Hotels:** Ellersly House; Murrayfield; Post House.

P55 Musselburgh

☎(031) 665 2005 Sec/forward
bookings, 665 7055 Pro/bookings on
the day
Monktonhall, Musselburgh, E Lothian
EH21 6SA
From the A1 end of the Edinburgh city
by-pass (A720) take B6415 to
Musselburgh.
Parkland course.
18 holes, 6614 yards, S.S.S.72
Designed by James Braid.
Founded 1938
Visitors: on application.
Green Fee: on application.
Societies: on application.
Catering: bar and restaurant
facilities, closed on Tues.

P56 Musselburgh Old Course

☎(031) 665 6981
Silver Ring Clubhouse, 3b Mill Hill,
Musselburgh, East Lothian EH21 7RG
7 miles E of Edinburgh.
Public seaside course.
9 holes, 5380 yards, S.S.S.67
Visitors: welcome weekdays and
Bank Holidays; weekends after 1pm.
Green Fee: apply for details.
Societies: by arrangement.

P57 New Galloway

☎(06443) 455 Sec
New Galloway, Castle Douglas,
Kirkcudbrightshire DG7 3RN
Easily located on way out of village
on A762.
Hilly panoramic moorland course.
9 holes, 5058 yards, S.S.S.65
Founded 1902
Visitors: welcome.
Green Fee: £10/day, jnrs (under 18)
£5.
Societies: apply to Sec.
Catering: bar; meals available in
village.
Hotels: Kenmure Arms; Kenbridge;
Leamington; Cairn Edward.

P58 Newbattle

☎(031) 663 2123, 660 1631 Pro,
663 1819 Sec
Abbey Rd, Dalkeith, Midlothian
7 miles SW of Edinburgh on A7, take
Newbattle exit at Esbank
roundabout, turn left opposite police
station, club 300 yards on right.
Undulating parkland course.
18 holes, 6012 yards, S.S.S.69
Founded 1935
Visitors: Mon-Fri except Public and
Local Holidays up to 4pm.

Green Fee: £14/round, £20/day.
Societies: Mon-Fri except holidays,
9-10am and 2-3pm.
Catering: full facilities on request.
Hotels: Lugton Inn; Stair Arms;
County.

P59 Newcastleton

☎(03873) 75257
Holm Hill, Newcastleton, Roxburgh
TD9 0QD
25 miles N of Carlisle; turn right off
A7 to Canonbie, 10 miles to
Newcastleton on B6357.
Hillside course.
9 holes, 5748 yards, S.S.S.68
Designed by J. Shade.
Founded 1894
Visitors: no restrictions.
Green Fee: £6/round/day.
Societies: welcome.
Catering: can be arranged.
Hotels: Grapes; Liddesdale.

P60 Newton Stewart

☎(0671) 2172
Kirroughtree Ave, Minnigaff,
Newton Stewart, DG8 6PF
Off A75.
Parkland course.
18 holes, 5970 yards, S.S.S.69
Founded 1981
Visitors: welcome.
Green Fee: £12/round, £16/day WD;
£16/round, £20/day WE.
Societies: by prior arrangement.
Catering: meals and bar lunches
during bar hours; other by
arrangement with Steward.
Hotels: Kirroughtree; Cally Palace.

P61 Niddry Castle

☎(0506) 891097
Castle Rd, Winchburgh, W Lothian
EH52 6RQ
2 miles NE of Broxburn.
Parkland course with large burn.
9 holes, 2757 yards, S.S.S.67
Designed by Derek Smith.
Founded 1984
Visitors: welcome except weekend
competition days.
Green Fee: £7.50/round WD,
£10/round WE.
Societies: booking only.
Catering: clubhouse.
Putting green, practice net.
Hotels: South Queensferry.

P62 North Berwick

☎(0620) 892135
Beach Rd, North Berwick EH39 4BB

23 miles E of Edinburgh on A198.
Seaside course.
18 holes, 6315 yards, S.S.S.70
Designed by Mackenzie Ross.
Founded 1832
Visitors: unrestricted.
Green Fee: £25/round, £35/day WD;
£35/round, £45/day WE & BH; under
16 half price.
Societies: unrestricted weekdays.
Catering: except Thurs, Mar-Oct
available all week.
Hotels: Marine; Royal; Point Gary;
Nether Abbey.

P63 Peebles

☎(0721) 720197
Kirkland St, Peebles EH45 8EU
NW of town off A72, signposted on
main roads into town; 23 miles S of
Edinburgh.
Undulating parkland course.
18 holes, 6137 yards, S.S.S.69
Designed by James Braid, with
alterations by H.S. Colt.
Founded 1892
Visitors: welcome; no denim or golf
footwear in clubrooms.
Green Fee: £13/round, £19.50/day
WD; £19/round, £26.50/day WE.
Societies: max 36.
Catering: bar and restaurant.
Hotels: Peebles Hydro; Park;
Kingsmuir.

P64 Polkemmet Country Park

☎(0501) 743905
Park Centre, Polkemmet Country
Park, Whitburn, Bathgate, W Lothian
EH47 0AD
On N side of B7066, midway
between Harthill and Whitburn; signs
from Whitburn exit M8.
Public parkland course (old private
estate).
9 holes, 2969 metres, S.S.S.37
Designed by W Lothian DC.
Founded 1981
Visitors: no restrictions; players
must have own clubs.
Green Fee: 9 holes, summer; £2.40
Mon-Sat, £3.10 Sun: winter; £1.90
all week; (not after 4.30pm WD or
before 12am Sat and 5pm Sun).
Societies: weekdays only.
Catering: bar snacks/meals, all day;
restaurant lunches/evening meals.
Driving range, bowls, play fort and
play area, riverside and woodland
walks.
Hotels: Whitdale (Whitburn); Golden
Circle, Dreadnought, Fairway,
(Bathgate).

P65 **Portobello**
☎(031) 669 4361
Stanley St, Portobello, Edinburgh
EH15 1JJ
E of Edinburgh on A1 to Milton Road.
Public parkland course.
9 holes, 2400 yards, S.S.S.32
Founded 1826
Visitors: no restrictions except for
Sat in summer (Medal Days).
Green Fee: £3.30 (9 holes).
Societies: no restrictions except Sat
in summer (Medal Days).
Hotels: Kings Manor.

P66 **Portpatrick (Dunskey)**
☎(0776 81) 273
Portpatrick, Stranraer, Wigtownshire
DG9 8TB
A77 follow signs to Stranraer, then
follow signs to Portpatrick, fork right
at War Memorial, 300 yards on right
signpost to club.
Links type course set on high
cliffs.
Dunskey, 18 holes, 5882 yards,
S.S.S.68; Dinvin, 9 holes, 1504
yards, S.S.S.27
Designed by Dunskey Estate.
Founded 1903
Visitors: welcome with h/cap cert
except competition days; best to
book.
Green Fee: Dunskey course,
£14/round, £21/day WD; £17/round,
£25/day WE; Dinvin course,
£5/round, £10/day.
Societies: welcome, must book in
advance with Sec.
Catering: all meals served in
season.
Hotels: Fernhill; Portpatrick; Crown
Golf; all offer concessionary golf
rates.

P67 **Powfoot**
☎(0461) 202866
Cummertrees, Annan, Dumfriesshire
3 miles W of Annan, off B724.
Seaside course.
18 holes, 6266 yards, S.S.S.70
Designed by James Braid.
Founded 1903
Visitors: welcome weekdays any
time, no visitors Sat, Sun after
2.45pm only.
Green Fee: £24/day WD, £16/round
inc Sun.
Societies: welcome weekdays only
by arrangement.
Catering: full bar facilities; lunches
and teas by arrangement.
Hotels: Powfoot Golf; Queensberry
Arms; Cairndale (Dumfries).

P68 **Prestonfield**
☎(031) 667 1273, 667 9665
6 Priestfield Rd N, Edinburgh EH16
5HS
Near to Commonwealth Pool,
Dalkeith Rd.
Parkland course.
18 holes, 6216 yards, S.S.S.70
Designed by James Braid.
Founded 1920
Visitors: welcome any weekday; not
between 8-10.30am and
12am-1.30pm Sat; not before
11.30am Sun.
Green Fee: £15/round, £22/day WD;
£22/round, £30/day WE & BH.
Societies: weekdays starting from
9.30am and 2pm.
Catering: full facilities daily.
Hotels: Rosehall; March Hall.

P69 **Pumpherston**
☎(0506) 32869
Drumshoreland Rd, Pumpherston,
Livingston EH53 0LF
1 mile S of Uphall off A89.
Undulating parkland course with
water hazards.
9 holes, 5154 yards, S.S.S.65
Founded 1895
Visitors: only with member.
Green Fee: £4 WD, £6 WE.
Societies: weekdays only, max 24.
Catering: bar snacks.
Hotels: Houston House.

P70 **Ratho Park**
☎(031) 333 1752 Sec/Fax, 333 1252
Ratho, Newbridge, Midlothian EH28
8NX
8 miles W of Edinburgh on Glasgow
road, adjacent to Edinburgh Airport.
Parkland course.
18 holes, 5996 yards, S.S.S.68
Designed by James Braid.
Founded 1928
Visitors: any day by arrangement
with Pro.
Green Fee: £20/round, £30/day WD
and WE.
Societies: Tues, Wed, Thurs.
Catering: bars and restaurant.
Snooker.

P71 **Ravelston**
☎(031) 315 2486
24 Ravelston Dykes Rd, Blackhall,
Edinburgh EH4 5NZ
Turn S off A90 Queensferry road at
Blackhall, on Strachan Road.
Parkland course.
9 holes, 5200 yards, S.S.S.66
Designed by James Braid.

Founded 1912
Visitors: allowed during quiet
periods; h/cap certs preferred.
Green Fee: £15 (18 holes).
Catering: light snacks only.

P72 **Royal Burgess Golfing Society of Edinburgh**
☎(031) 339 2075 Reservations
181 Whitehouse Rd, Edinburgh EH4
6BY
W side of Edinburgh on Queensferry
road, 100 yards N of Barton
roundabout.
Parkland course.
18 holes, 6494 yards, S.S.S.71
Designed by Tom Morris.
Founded 1735
Visitors: weekdays only.
Green Fee: on application.
Societies: weekdays only.
Catering: lunches and bar snacks.
Hotels: Barnton; Royal Scot.

P73 **Royal Musselburgh**
☎(0875) 810276 Clubhouse,
810139 Pro
Prestongrange House, Prestonpans,
E Lothian EH32 9RP
7 miles E of Edinburgh, 1 mile from
Wallyford roundabout on A1, take
A198 North Berwick road.
Parkland course.
18 holes, 6237 yards, S.S.S.70
Designed by James Braid.
Founded 1774
Visitors: weekdays welcome, very
limited weekends.
Green Fee: £18/round, £30/day WD;
£30/round WE.
Societies: must book in writing in
advance.
Catering: coffee, lunches, high teas,
snacks; dinner by advance booking.
Snooker.
Hotels: Woodside; Ravelston House;
Kings Manor; Kilspindie House;
Maitland Field; Golf Inn; Marine.

P74 **St Boswells**
☎(0835) 22359
Ashleabank, St Boswells,
Roxburghshire TD6 0AT
A68 junction with B6404 opposite
Buccleuch Hotel, 0.25 mile along
banks of River Tweed.
Flat parkland course.
9 holes, 2625 yards, S.S.S.65
Designed by William Park, altered by
John Shade (1956).
Founded 1899
Visitors: unrestricted except for
competition days.

Southerness

Nothing like enough golfers are acquainted with the delights of Southerness which lies on the silent, sandy stretches of the Solway Firth about 15 miles south of Dumfries. This is largely because the south-west corner of Scotland is not the best known golfing area of a country that has so much to offer, although those aware of its charm find it rich in quality and enjoyment and, like me, hard to believe that its reputation has not spread further.

As with so many courses around our shores, much of its appeal lies in its out of the way position, but it still makes a convenient beginning or end to any golfing tour. The drive from Carlisle is by no means arduous but, by the time that one turns off the main road down a long, narrow lane towards the sea, there is a growing impatience to see what lies beyond.

Before the days of a new clubhouse built in 1974 close to the position of the old 6th hole, journey's end was less imposing. The small community dominated by the Paul Jones Hotel consisted of a field of caravans, a few shops and a clubhouse which had more the look of some rustic cricket pavilion. A notice invited visitors to settle green fees with the caretaker in the village shop across the road and the path to the first tee was through a quaint little paddock.

However, one round on the course laid out by Mackenzie Ross shortly after the last war, is sufficient to appreciate its merit and indicate, rather like Dornoch at the opposite end of the country, that it is well worthy of having won its championship spurs.

By a happy coincidence, Dornoch was awarded the British Amateur Championship in 1985, the same year in which the Scottish Golf Union took the Scottish Amateur to Southerness (which was constructed for a mere £2000 around 1947). The staging of the championship bestowed a posthumous tribute on Mackenzie Ross, who resurrected Turnberry at more or less the same time as he paid his regular visits to Southerness.

It is a course that would be well worthy of a professional tournament — an intriguing prospect to see Nick Faldo or Severiano Ballasteros pitting their wits against holes stiffened by a fresh wind.

There is a pleasant variety of shots to be played and nothing slavish about their pattern. There are days when shots can be pitched up to the flag, and others when the only means of holding a green is to chip and run.

By the current rating, there is only one par 5 but the weight of the challenge is marked by having eight holes between 405 and 470 yards, many with fine natural greens angled to ensure that the best chance of finishing near the hole comes from drives correctly positioned. There is no great feeling that the fairways are narrow but gorse and heather can swallow up wayward shots and there is a tough start including the longest hole, the 5th, with its elevated and quaintly shaped green.

The 8th, taking aim on the lighthouse, begins the stretch along the shore but the pick of the holes are the dogleg 12th and the 13th and the old 18th, a formidable 467 yards. The 17th green, perched above the beach, also gives the best view of the splendour of the setting. Leagues of golden sand slip westwards along the coast of Kirkcaudbright and the peaks of Cumberland stand strong against the peaceful waters of the Firth. Inland, the simple green landscape completes a feeling of escape that causes as much surprise as finding a golf course to match its majestic surroundings.

THE IMPERIAL HOTEL
35 King Street, Castle Douglas   S.T.B. 4 crowns commended; AA & RAC two star.
Ideally situated in the centre of Dumfries & Galloway, A perfect base for your golfing holiday (Southerness 17.mls).
The golf photos in the bar indicate that this is 'the' Golfing Hotel in the area. Comfortable, warm en-suite rooms. TVs, tea/coffee, hairdryers, radios. Early b'fast or late dinners to suit tee times, club storage, drying facilities. Good Scottish home cooking & hospitality – late bar. Special 3 day breaks available from £33.50 for dinner, bed & breakfast.
Send for brochure and golf fact sheet by telephoning 0556 502086 (Fax 0556 503009)

Green Fee: £10/round/day WD, £15/round/day WE.
Societies: welcome by prior booking.
Catering: at Buccleuch Hotel.
Hotels: Buccleuch; Dryburgh Abbey.

P75 St Medan
☎(09887) 358
Monreith, Newton Stewart, Wigtownshire DG8 8NJ
3 miles S of Port William on A747.
Seaside links course.
9 holes, 4452 yards, S.S.S.62
Founded 1905
Visitors: no restrictions except competitions.
Green Fee: £7 (9 holes), £12/day, £45/week (7 days).
Societies: welcome any day.
Catering: full bar and catering except Tues, Mar-Sept.
Hotels: Steam Packet; Corsemalzie.

P76 Sanquhar
☎(0659) 50577, 58181 Sec
Old Barr Rd, Sanquhar, Dumfries DG4 6JZ
Off A76 0.5 mile from Sanquhar.
Parkland course.
9 holes, 2572 yards, S.S.S.68.
Founded 1894
Visitors: welcome.
Green Fee: £10 WD, £12 WE.
Societies: by prior arrangement.
Catering: by prior arrangement.
Snooker, carpet bowling, darts etc.
Hotels: Blackaddie House; Glendyne; Nithsdale; Mennock Lodge.

P77 Selkirk
☎(0750) 20621, 20427
The Hill, Selkirk
1 mile S of Selkirk on A7 to Hawick.
Moorland course.
9 holes, 5640 yards, S.S.S.67
Founded 1883
Visitors: welcome weekdays, not Fri evenings and Mon after 3pm (ladies only).
Green Fee: £11/day.
Societies: by arrangement.
Catering: parties by arrangement.
Hotels: County; Glen.

P78 Silverknowes
☎(031) 336 5359
Silverknowes, Parkway, Edinburgh EH4 5ET
W end of Edinburgh, off Cramond Foreshore.
Municipal course.
18 holes, 6210 yards, S.S.S.70
Founded 1958
Visitors: with reservation only.
Green Fee: on application.
Hotels: Commodore, adjacent.

P79 Southerness
☎(0387) 88677
Southerness, Dumfries DG2 8AZ
16 miles SW of Dumfries off A710.
Links course.
18 holes, 6566 yards, S.S.S.72
Designed by Mackenzie Ross.
Founded 1947
Visitors: members of recognised clubs only; 10-12am and 2-4pm weekdays, 10-11.30am and 2.30-4pm weekends.
Green Fee: £24/day WD, £32/day WE; £96/week (Mon-Fri).
Societies: apply to Sec.
Catering: full bar and catering.
Hotels: Baron's Craig; Abbey Arms; Criffel Inn; Station; Cairndale; Clonyard; Cavenshouse.

P80 Stranraer
☎(0776) 87245
Creachmore, Stranrear DG9 0LF
Take A718 from Stranraer towards Leswalt, club is well signposted on right.
Parkland course.
18 holes, 6300 yards, S.S.S.71
Designed by James Braid.
Founded 1905
Visitors: welcome.
Green Fee: £15.75/round, £21/day WD; £21/round, £26.25/day WE.
Societies: catered for.
Catering: not Mon.
Hotels: North West Castle; Fernhill; Portpatrick.

P81 Swanston
☎(031) 445 2239, 445 4002 Pro
111 Swanston Rd, Edinburgh EH10 7OS
S side of city on lower slopes of Pentland Hills.
Hillside course.
18 holes, 5024 yards, S.S.S.65
Designed by Herbert More.
Founded 1927
Visitors: welcome weekdays and with restrictions at weekends.
Green Fee: £8/round, £12/day WD; £10/round, £15/day WE.
Societies: by arrangement.
Catering: meals served except Tues.
Hotels: Braid Hills.

P82 Thornhill
☎(0848) 30546
Blacknest, Thornhill, Dumfries-shire
14 miles N of Dumfries on A76 to Thornhill, turn right at cross, 1 mile on right.
Moorland/parkland course.
18 holes, 6011 yards, S.S.S.69
Founded 1893
Visitors: welcome without reservation except on Open Competition days.
Green Fee: apply for details.
Societies: welcome; contact Club Steward.
Catering: bar facilities available; catering except Mon.

P83 Torphin Hill
☎(031) 441 1100
Torphin Rd, Colinton, Edinburgh EH13 0PG
SW of Colinton, follow signposts.
Hillside course.
18 holes, 5030 yards, S.S.S.66
Founded 1895
Visitors: restricted competition days; no 4-balls at weekends.
Green Fee: £8.50 WD, £12.50 WE.
Societies: welcome weekdays.
Catering: full facilities except Tues.
Hotels: Braid Hills.

P84 Torwoodlee
☎(0896) 2660
Galashiels, Selkirkshire
On A7 Galashiels-Edinburgh road, 1 mile from town centre.
Parkland course.
9 holes (18 from 1994), 5800 yards, S.S.S.68

Designed by Willie Park (new layout, John Gurner).
Founded 1895
Visitors: welcome, restricted Sat and Thurs after 1pm.
Green Fee: £12 WD, £25 WE.
Societies: welcome on application.
Catering: full facilities except Tues.
Hotels: Burts; George & Abbotsford.

P85 Turnhouse
☎(031) 339 1014
154 Turnhouse Rd, Edinburgh EH12 0AD
W of city on A9080 near airport.
Parkland/heathland course.
18 holes, 6171 yards, S.S.S.69
Founded 1909
Visitors: only visiting clubs; not weekends; Hotel visitors contact Pro.
Green Fee: £14/round, £20/day.
Catering: lunch, high tea except Mon.
Hotels: Royal Scot.

P86 Uphall
☎(0506) 856404 Manager, 855553 Pro
Houston Mains, Uphall, W Lothian EH52 6JT
7 miles W of Edinburgh airport, on A89 Edinburgh-Glasgow road in village of Uphall.
Parkland course.
18 holes, 6268 yards, S.S.S.67
Founded 1895 (centenary 1995)
Visitors: welcome, weekends telephone Pro for booking.
Green Fee: £13/round, £18/day WD; £17/round, £25/day.
Societies: very welcome by arrangement with Manager.
Catering: full catering service, hot and cold snacks, high teas, 2 bars. Practice ground, putting green.
Hotels: Houston; Uphall, Border Course.

P87 Vogrie
☎(0875) 21716
Vogrie Estate Country Park, Gorebridge, Lothian

Off A68 Jedburgh road.
Public parkland course.
9 holes, 2530 yards, Par 33
Founded 1989
Visitors: welcome.
Green Fee: apply for details.

P88 West Linton
☎(0968) 660463 Clubhouse, 660970 Sec, 660256 Pro
West Linton, Peebleshire
15 miles from Edinburgh on A702.
Moorland course.
18 holes, 6132 yards, S.S.S.69
Founded 1890
Visitors: welcome weekdays and after 1pm weekends.
Green Fee: £15/round, £21/day WD; £24/round WE, week ticket Mon-Fri £75.
Societies: welcome weekdays except Tues.
Catering: full catering facilities except Tues.
Hotels: Gordon Arms; Raemartin; Linton.

P89 West Lothian
☎(0506) 826030 Clubhouse
Airngath Hill, Linlithgow, W Lothian
On hill separating Bo'ness and Linlithgow, marked by Hope Monument.
Undulating meadowland course.
18 holes, 6340 yards, S.S.S.71
Designed by Fraser Middleton.
Founded 1892
Visitors: no restrictions weekdays before 4pm; after 4pm and at weekends by arrangement only.
Green Fee: on application.
Societies: catered for weekdays and at weekends.
Catering: meals as requested.
Hotels: Earl O'Murray.

P90 Wigtown & Bladnoch
☎(0988) 403354
Lightlands Terrace, Wigtown, Galloway DG8 9EF
0.25 mile from town centre on A746, signposted Whithorn.

Parkland course, part hilly.
9 holes, 2731 yards, S.S.S.67
Founded 1960
Visitors: no restrictions.
Green Fee: £7/day WD, £10 (18 holes) WE; jnrs and OAPs half price.
Societies: welcome by prior arrangement.
Catering: bar and snacks 12am-2.30pm (June-Sept); evening meals and groups by arrangement.
Hotels: Conifers Leisure Park; Bruce; Hill o'Burns; all offer free golf.

P91 Wigtownshire County
☎(05813) 420
Mains of Park, Glenluce, Newton Stewart, Wigtownshire DG8 0NN
8 miles E of Stranraer on A75, 2 miles W of Glenluce.
Links course.
18 holes, 5823 yards, S.S.S.68
Designed by Gordon Cunningham.
Founded 1894
Visitors: no h/cap certificate required, members priority times 10.30-11am, 1-1.30pm weekdays; 8-9.30am, 1-1.40pm weekends.
Green Fee: £15/round, £19/day WD; £17/round, £21/day WE.
Societies: welcome at all times, preferably by prior booking; discount of £1 per head for parties of 10 or more.
Catering: available all year 9.30am-5pm and 8am-11pm during summer.
Hotels: North West Castle.

P92 Winterfield
☎(0368) 62280 Clubhouse, 63562 Pro shop/bookings, 65119 Sec (62564 home)
North Rd, Dunbar, E Lothian
W side of Dunbar.
Seaside course.
18 holes, 5035 yards, S.S.S.65
Founded 1935
Visitors: welcome.
Green Fee: on application to Pro.
Societies: welcome by arrangement with Pro.
Catering: 2 bars, restaurant.

Q

STRATHCLYDE

Strathclyde casts a comprehensive net over the golfing scene as well as providing more than its share of Britain's great courses. It encompasses the remote outposts of Machrie and Machrihanish, the whole of the area around Glasgow and the veritable treasure trove of Ayrshire, a county many claim possesses more glittering golfing jewels than any other in Britain.

Prime among its southern defences is Turnberry, one of the world's most spectacular settings for golf. It hosts its third open in 1994 with a magnificent new clubhouse and spa. There are few more stirring stretches than that between the short 4th and the short 11th on the Ailsa course, a testing clutch of holes graduating from the relative shelter of the dunes to the rugged, rocky promontory alongside the lighthouse. Wild westerly winds can be more than flesh, blood and balance can stand, one solution lying on the Arran, the Ailsa's neighbour, which is flatter, less exposed and little inferior.

Together, they comprise a wonderful day's golf, a comment pretty commonplace in Ayrshire. How about Old Prestwick and Royal Troon, Western Gailes and Glasgow Gailes, Barassie and Irvine or Ayr Belleisle together with Prestwick St Nicholas?;and a word for Brunston Castle in its lovely setting at Dailly.

As the birthplace of championship golf, Old Prestwick commands eminence, a course that has proved its freshness time and again in spite of accusations of being a relic of the past. There are few more daunting opening tee shots, few better dogleg holes than the 4th and few more sporting tests than the 13th and 17th. It faded as a staging ground for the Open championship on account of its difficulty in handling big crowds. Its demise coincided with the rise of Troon, although 27 years separated Troon's first and second Opens, a gap attributable in part to the war.

There are five or six courses in Troon, or on its doorstep, many shrewd judges rating Western Gailes on a par with Royal Troon. It certainly ranks extremely highly, with a greater share perhaps of spectacular holes and of interesting greens. At one end, it is possible to hit a shot over the railway onto Kilmarnock (Barassie) and, at the other, onto Glasgow Gailes, the country "seat", so to speak, of the Glasgow GC in the city district of Killermont.

On one of the approach roads to Glasgow from the south, Eastwood, East Renfrewshire and Whitecraigs are encountered in quick succession but Glasgow is surrounded on all sides by good golf. Names to note are West Kilbride, Renfrew, Gleddoch, Old Ranfurly, Ranfurly Castle, Helensburgh, Balmore and Cawder.

Nor must the other courses overlooking the Clyde be forgotten or those on Arran, an island once described to me as "paradise". But, if it is romance that you seek, head for Machrie on the Isle of Islay or Machrihanish on the Mull of Kintyre, both reachable by air on a short hop from Glasgow airport.

Machrie is an authentic links full of hidden dells and high hills — bordered on one side by lonely, sandy beaches and on the other by moor and hill.

Back on the mainland at Machrihanish, the beach comes into play on the opening drive, and a notice for non-golfers proclaims "Danger, First Tee Above, please move further along the beach"; an invigorating introduction to another superb tract of natural land which many regard as the only true setting to the game.

For those choosing the lengthy and circuitous route by road, Machrihanish rarely disappoints but journey's end is Dunaverty ten miles south of Campbeltown and home of Belle Robertson, who brought it fame and distinction. Its raw charm is hard to better, although its modest length can be dramatically magnified by the breezes that frequently graduate to raging winds.

Q1 Airdrie
☎(0236) 762195
Rochsoles, Airdrie ML6 0PQ
From Airdrie Cross in centre of town
travel N on Glenmavis Rd.
Parkland course.
18 holes, S.S.S.69
Designed by James Braid.
Founded 1877
Visitors: welcome with introduction
from own Sec.
Green Fee: £12/round, £20/day.
Societies: contact Sec, not
weekends or Bank Holidays.
Catering: full catering.
Snooker.
Hotels: Tudor; Kenilworth.

Q2 Alexandra Park
☎(041) 556 3991
Alexandra Golf, Alexandra Park,
Sannox Gdns, Glasgow G31 8SE
M8 cut off before fruit market.
Hilly municipal parkland course.
9 holes, 2800 yards, Par 34
Designed by Graham McArthur.
Founded 1818
Visitors: welcome at all times.
Green Fee: on application.
Societies: by arrangement.
Catering: facilities available.
Bowling greens.
Hotels: Hospitality Inn; Copthorne;
Hilton.

Q3 Annanhill
☎(0563) 21644
Irvine Rd, Kilmarnock KA1 4RT
Off main Kilmarnock-Irvine road.
Parkland course.
18 holes, 6118 yards, S.S.S.70
Designed by J. McLean.
Founded 1957
Visitors: welcome except Sat.
Green Fee: £8 WD, £12 WE.
Societies: by arrangement.
Catering: snacks at weekends; full
meals, breakfast, lunch, dinner or
high tea by arrangement.
Hotels: Howard Park; Holiday Inn.

Q4 Ardeer
☎(0294) 64542
Greenhead, Stevenston, Ayrshire
Follow A78 (signs for Largs and
Greenock), on High Rd by-passing
Stevenston, turn right into Kerelaw
Rd and continue for 1 mile.
Parkland course.
18 holes, 6630 yards, S.S.S.72
Founded 1880
Visitors: welcome except Sat.
Green Fee: apply for details.

Societies: catered for Mon-Sat.
Catering: full catering facilities
available.

Q5 Auchenharvie Golf Complex
☎(0294) 603103
Moor Park Rd West, Brewery Park,
Stevenston, Ayrshire KA20 3HU
Public links/parkland course.
9 holes (18 tees), 2642 yards,
S.S.S.33
Designed by Michael Struthers.
Founded May 1991
Visitors: welcome.
Green Fee: £2.50 (£1 jnrs) WD,
£4.50 WE.
Societies: welcome.
Catering: clubhouse bar.
Driving range.

Q6 Ayr Belleisle
☎(0292) 41258
Belleisle Park, Doonfoot Rd, Ayr
1.5 miles S of Ayr on A719.
Parkland course.
18 holes, 6540 yards, S.S.S.71
Designed by James Braid & Stutt.
Founded 1927
Visitors: welcome.
Green Fee: apply for details.
Societies: apply to Course
Administrator at address above.
Catering: meals and snacks
available in hotel.
Hotels: Belleisle House; Balgarth;
Old Racecourse.

Q7 Ayr Dalmilling
☎(0292) 263893, 610543
Westwood Ave, Ayr, Strathclyde KA8
0QY
1.5 miles from town centre on NE
boundary off A77.
Municipal meadowland course.
18 holes, 5752 yards, S.S.S.68
Founded 1960
Visitors: unrestricted; times
bookable in advance from 1994.
Green Fee: £10/round, £18/day.
Societies: by prior arrangement.
Catering: tea, coffee, lunches, high
teas, snacks daily except Tues;
licensed bar.
Hotels: Racers.

Q8 Ayr Seafield
☎(0292) 41258
Belleisle Park, Doonfoot Rd, Ayr
1.5 miles S of Ayr on A719.
Parkland/seaside course.
18 holes, 5650 yards, S.S.S.68

Founded 1927
Visitors: welcome.
Green Fee: apply for details.
Societies: apply to course
Administrator at address above.
Catering: meals and snacks in hotel.
Hotels: Belleisle House; Balgarth;
Old Racecourse.

Q9 Ballochmyle
☎(0290) 550469
Ballochmyle, Mauchline, Ayrshire
KA5 6LE
1 mile S of Mauchline on B705, off
A76(T) Dumfries-Kilmarnock road.
Parkland course.
18 holes, 5952 yards, S.S.S.69
Founded 1937
Visitors: welcome weekdays.
Green Fee: on application.
Societies: weekdays except Wed.
Catering: bar and restaurant.
Snooker, squash.

Q10 Balmore
☎(0360) 2120240
Balmore, Torrance, Stirlingshire
2 miles N of Glasgow on A803/A807.
Parkland course.
18 holes, 5516 yards, S.S.S.67
Designed by James Braid.
Founded 1906
Visitors: introduced by member.
Green Fee: apply for details.
Catering: full catering facilities.

Q11 Barshaw
☎(041) 889 2908, 889 5400, 884
2533 Sec
Barshaw Park, Glasgow Rd, Paisley,
Renfrewshire
A737 from Glasgow W to Paisley, 1
mile before Paisley Cross.
Municipal meadowland course.
18 holes, 5703 yards, S.S.S.67
Founded 1920
Visitors: welcome all week.
Green Fee: £6 (half price OAPs, jnrs
and unemployed).
Hotels: Water Mill; Brablock.

Q12 Bearsden
☎(041) 942 2351, 942 2381 Sec
Thorn Rd, Bearsden, Glasgow G61
4BP
1 mile N from Bearsden Cross on
Thorn Rd.
Parkland course.
9 holes, 6014 yards, S.S.S.69
Founded 1891
Visitors: to be introduced by and
play with member.

Green Fee: on application.
Catering: light meals, snacks.
Hotels: Black Bull; Burnbrae.

Q13 **Beith**
☎(0505) 503166
Threepwood Rd, Beith, Ayrshire,
KA15 2JQ
2 miles S of Linwood, about 1 mile E
of Beith.
Hilly parkland course.
9 holes, 5600 yards, S.S.S.67
Founded 1896
Visitors: welcome Mon-Fri, Sun am.
Green Fee: £8/round, £10/day WD,
£12 Sun.
Societies: welcome; book by letter.
Catering: full facilities.
Pool.

Q14 **Bellshill**
☎(0698) 745124
Orbiston, Bellshill, Lanarkshire ML4
2RZ

Right turn off Bellshill/Motherwell
road 10 miles SE of Glasgow.
Parkland course.
18 holes, 6604 yards, S.S.S.72
Founded 1905
Visitors: not between 4pm and 7pm,
May-Aug inclusive; otherwise
welcome.
Green Fee: £14/day WD, £20/day
WE & BH.
Societies: by prior arrangement; not
Sun.
Catering: licensed bar and lounge;
meals and snacks available.

Q15 **Biggar**
☎(0899) 20618
The Park, Broughton Rd, Biggar,
Lanarkshire ML12
1 mile E of Biggar on Broughton Rd,
opposite police station, signposted.
Municipal flat scenic parkland
course.
18 holes, 5416 yards, S.S.S.67
Designed by Willie Park.

Founded 1895
Visitors: unrestricted but telephone
(0899) 20319 in advance.
Green Fee: £9 WD, £12 WE & BH.
Societies: welcome 36 max,
advance booking essential.
Catering: all day licence and
catering except Mon (smart casual
dress, no jeans).
All weather tennis, boating,
childrens' play area, caravan park.
Hotels: Toftcombs; Elphinstone
(Biggar); Tinto (Symington).

Q16 **Bishopbriggs**
☎(041) 772 1810 Club, 772 8938
Sec
Brackenbrae Rd, Bishopbriggs,
Glasgow G64 2DX
4 miles N of Glasgow on A803, turn
left 200 yards short of Bishopbriggs
Cross.
Parkland course.
18 holes, 6041 yards, S.S.S.69
Designed by James Braid.

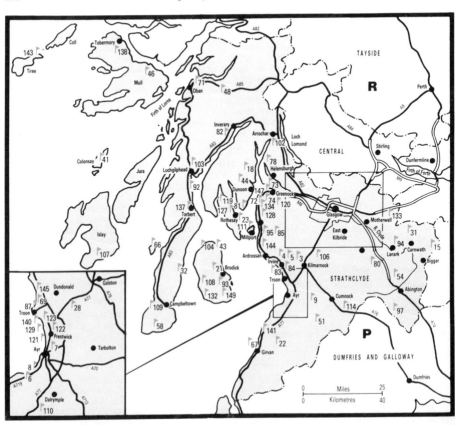

Founded 1906
Visitors: welcome with member or by application to Committee.
Green Fee: on application.
Societies: Tues, Wed, Thurs only; apply to Sec at least 1 month in advance.
Catering: meals and snacks served.

Q17 **Blairbeth**
☎(041) 634 3355
Fernhill, Rutherglen, Glasgow
2 miles S of Rutherglen via Stonelaw road, follow road signs.
Parkland course.
18 holes, 5448 yards, S.S.S.67
Founded 1910
Visitors: welcome with member.
Green Fee: on application.
Catering: by arrangement.

Q18 **Blairmore & Strone**
☎(036 984) 217
Strone, By Dunoon, Argyll PA23 8TJ
0.75 mile N of Strone on A880.
Undulating parkland/moorland course.
9 holes, 2112 yards, S.S.S.62
Founded 1896
Visitors: welcome; some delays Sat afternoons and Mon evenings.
Green Fee: apply for details.

Q19 **Bonnyton**
☎(03553) 2781, 2256 Pro
Eaglesham, Glasgow G76 0QA
City centre S of Eaglesham.
Moorland course.
18 holes, 6252 yards, S.S.S.71

Founded 1957
Visitors: welcome weekdays.
Green Fee: on application.
Societies: catered for by prior arrangement.
Catering: weekdays and Sun lunches and high teas; Sat lunches and dinner; bar lunches every day.

Q20 **Bothwell Castle**
☎(0698) 853177
Blantyre Rd, Bothwell, Glasgow G71
M74 junction 5 to A9071, 3 miles N of Hamilton.
Parkland course.
18 holes, 6240 yards, S.S.S.70
Founded 1922
Visitors: welcome weekdays 9.30am-3.30pm.
Green Fee: £18/round, £25/day.
Societies: weekdays by written application.
Catering: snacks, lunches, high teas, dinners daily.
Hotels: Silvertrees; Bothwell Bridge.

Q21 **Brodick**
☎(0770) 302349, 302513 Pro
Brodick, Isle of Arran
By car ferry from Ardrossan, Ayrshire (55 min); 0.5 mile from Brodick pier.
Seaside course.
18 holes, 4404 yards, S.S.S.62
Founded 1897
Visitors: welcome all week.
Green Fee: £9/round, £12/day.
Societies: by letter to Sec, catered for at all times.
Catering: light lunches, contact Steward (0770) 302349.

Q22 **Brunston Castle**
☎(0465) 81471, 81545 Fax
Bargany, Dailly, By Girvan, Ayrshire KA26 9RH
35 mins from Prestwick Airport, S of Ayr and Turnberry (4 miles); turn left off A77 just N of Girvan on to B741; after 6 miles turn left towards Dailly; signposted.
Parkland course beside Water of Girvan.
18 holes, 6790 yards, S.S.S.72
Designed by Donald Steel.
Founded 1992
Visitors: welcome any day unless course closed for tournaments; phone for booking.
Green Fee: £20/round, £30/day WD; £25/round, £35/day WE & BH.
Societies: welcome if times available.
Catering: clubhouse meals and snacks, bar facilities.
Practice area, putting green.
Hotels: Kings Arms (Girvan); Malin Court (Turnberry); Kings Arms (Ballantrae).

Q23 **Bute**
☎(070 083) 648 Sec
Kingarth, Isle of Bute, Strathclyde
In Stravanan Bay off A845
Rothesay-Kilchattan Bay road.
Links course.
9 holes, 2497 yards, S.S.S.64
Founded 1888
Visitors: welcome, not before 12.30pm Sat.
Green Fee: £5/day.
Hotels: Kingarth; St Blanes.

Q24 **Calderbraes**
☎(0698) 813425
57 Roundknowe Rd, Uddingston G71 7TS
Start of M74 to Carlisle, 4 miles from Glasgow.
Hilly parkland course.
9 holes, 5046 yards, S.S.S.67
Founded 1891
Visitors: weekdays only, off course by 5pm.
Green Fee: apply for details.
Societies: wekdays, max 20.
Catering: bar and catering available.
Hotels: Redstones.

Q25 **Caldwell**
☎(0505) 850329 Clubhouse, 850616 Pro
Uplawmoor, Renfrewshire
Off A736 5 miles SW of Barrhead, 12 miles NE of Irvine.

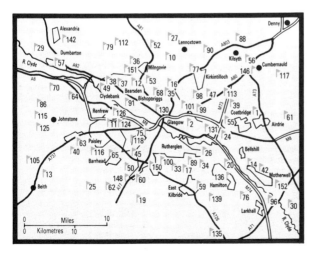

Moorland course.
18 holes, 6228 yards, S.S.S.70
Founded 1903
Visitors: welcome weekdays but
advisable to check in advance.
Green Fee: on application.
Societies: catered for on weekdays.
Catering: welcome weekdays.
Hotels: Uplawmoor; Dalmeny.

Q26 Cambuslang
☎(041) 641 3130
30 Westburn Drive, Cambuslang,
Glasgow
Off main Glasgow to Hamilton road at
Cambuslang.
Parkland course.
9 holes, 6072 yards, S.S.S.69
Founded 1891
Visitors: apply in writing to Sec.
Green Fee: on application.
Societies: weekdays except Tues.
Catering: full facilities.
Hotels: Cambus Court.

Q27 Campsie
☎(0360) 310244
Crow Rd, Lennoxtown, Glasgow G65
7HX
N of Lennoxtown on B822.
Hillside course.
18 holes, 5517 yards, S.S.S.67
Founded 1897
Visitors: welcome weekdays and by
prior arrangement at weekends.
Green Fee: on application.
Societies: apply to Sec.
Catering: bar snacks available;
meals by prior arrangement.
Hotels: Glazertbank; Kincaid House.

Q28 Caprington
☎(0563) 23702
Ayr Rd, Kilmarnock KA1 4UW
S of Kilmarnock on Ayr Rd.
Municipal parkland course.
18 holes, S.S.S.68
Visitors: welcome.
Green Fee: apply for details.

Q29 Cardross
☎(0389) 841213 Club, 841754 Sec,
841350 Pro
Main Rd, Cardross, Dumbarton G82
5LB
Between Dumbarton and
Helensburgh on A814.
Parkland course.
18 holes, 6469 yards, S.S.S.71
Designed by Willie Fernie of Troon
and James Braid.
Founded 1895

Visitors: welcome weekdays,
weekends introduced by member.
Green Fee: £18/round, £30/day.
Societies: by arrangement with Sec
(weekdays only).
Catering: bar snacks, teas except
Mon.
Hotels: Dumbuck; Commodore;
Cameron House.

Q30 Carluke
☎(0555) 771070
Hallcraig, Mauldslie Rd, Carluke ML8
5HG
1.5 miles from lights at town centre
on road to Hamilton and Larkhall.
Tree-lined parkland course with
views over Clyde valley.
18 holes, 5800 yards, S.S.S.68
Founded 1894
Visitors: weekdays only until
4.30pm; not public holidays.
Green Fee: £15/round, £20/day.
Societies: by written request to Sec.
Catering: full facilities.
Hotels: Popinjay (3 memberships).

Q31 Carnwath
☎(0555) 840251
1 Main St, Carnwath, Strathclyde
5 miles NE of Lanark.
Undulating course.
18 holes, 5860 yards, S.S.S.69
Founded 1907
Visitors: any day except Sat or after
4pm; no parties on Tues or Thur.
Green Fee: £18 WD, £22 Sun & BH.
Societies: catered for.
Catering: meals (snacks only Tues
and Thurs).
Hotels: Tinto (Symington).

Q32 Carradale
☎(05833) 387
Carradale, Campbeltown, Argyll
PA28 6QX
In Kintyre, Argyll, off B842 from
Campbeltown.
Difficult, scenic seaside course.
9 holes, 2392 yards, S.S.S.63
Founded 1906
Visitors: welcome at all times, no
introduction necessary.
Green Fee: £6/day; extended terms
on application.
Catering: at both hotels (below).
Hotels: Carradale; Ashbank.

Q33 Cathcart Castle
☎(041) 638 9449
Mearns Rd, Clarkston, Glasgow G76
7YL

1 mile from Clarkston on B767.
Undulating parkland course.
18 holes, 5832 yards, S.S.S.68
Founded 1895
Visitors: introduced by member.
Green Fee: £17/round, £25/day.
Societies: by arrangement with Sec,
Tues and Thurs only.
Catering: snacks, meals, bar.
Hotels: Redhurst; McDonald.

Q34 Cathkin Braes
☎(041) 634 6605, 634 0650 Pro
Cathkin Rd, Rutherglen, Glasgow
G73 4SE
SE of Glasgow on B759 between
A749 and B766.
Moorland course.
18 holes, 6208 yards, S.S.S.71
Designed by James Braid.
Founded 1888
Visitors: Mon-Fri by prior
arrangement.
Green Fee: £20/round, £30/day.
Catering: full catering to order.
Hotels: Stuart; Bruce; Burnside;
Busby.

Q35 Cawder
☎(041) 772 5167, 772 7101
Clubhouse, 772 7102 Pro
Cadder Rd, Bishopbriggs, Glasgow
G64 3QD
0.5 mile E of Bishopbriggs cross, off
A803 Glasgow-Kirkintilloch road.
Parkland course.
Cawder, 18 holes, 6229 yards,
S.S.S.71; Keir, 18 holes, 5877 yards,
S.S.S.68
Designed by Donald Steel (Cawder
course), James Braid (Keir course).
Founded 1933
Visitors: welcome weekdays by
arrangement with Sec.
Green Fee: on application.
Societies: welcome weekdays by
arrangement with Sec.
Catering: full catering facilities
available.
Hotels: Black Bull; Glazertbank;
Crowood House.

Q36 Clober
☎(041) 956 1685, 956 6963
Craigton Rd, Milngavie G62 7HP
7 miles NW of Glasgow.
Parkland course.
18 holes, 5068 yards, S.S.S.65
Designed by Lyle Family.
Founded 1952
Visitors: Mon-Thurs before 4.30pm,
Fri before 4pm.
Green Fee: on application.

Societies: weekdays by prior arrangement.
Catering: available Tues, Wed, Fri, Sat and Sun; snacks Mon and Thurs.
Hotels: Black Bull; Thistle.

Q37 Clydebank & District
☎(0389) 72389, 78686 Pro
Hardgate, Clydebank,
Dunbartonshire G81 5QY
8 miles NW of Glasgow via Great Western Rd.
Parkland course.
18 holes, 5825 yards, S.S.S.68
Founded 1905
Visitors: welcome weekdays, weekends with member only.
Green Fee: on application.
Societies: by arrangement.
Catering: meals served.
Hotels: Cameron House; Boulevard; Pine Trees.

Q38 Clydebank Overtoun
☎(041) 952 6372 Pro shop
Overtoun Rd, Clydebank,
Dunbartonshire
5 minutes from Dalmuir station.
Municipal parkland course.
18 holes, 5643 yards, S.S.S.66
Founded 1928
Visitors: municipal rules apply.
Green Fee: apply for details.
Societies: 1st Mon evening of month.
Catering: café attached to Pro Shop.

Q39 Coatbridge
☎(0236) 428975
Townhead Rd, Coatbridge, Lanark
ML5 2HX
In Coatbridge town.
Public parkland course.
18 holes, 6026 yards, S.S.S.69
Founded 1971
Visitors: welcome.
Green Fee: apply for details.
Societies: welcome.
Catering: full facilities.
Driving range, putting green.
Hotels: Jordanian.

Q40 Cochrane Castle
☎(0505) 320146
Scott Ave, Craigston, Johnstone PA5
0HF
0.25 mile off Johnstone-Beith road to S of town, Bird in the Hand Hotel is good landmark near turning to club.
Parkland course.
18 holes, 6226 yards, S.S.S.70
Designed by Charles Hunter of Prestwick, altered by James Braid.

Founded 1895
Visitors: weekdays unrestricted, introduced by member weekends.
Green Fee: £15/round, £20/day.
Societies: max 32 players.
Catering: full facilities except Mon.
Pool, darts.
Hotels: Lynhurst.

Q41 Colonsay
☎(09512) 316
Isle of Colonsay, Argyll, PA61 7Y
Ferry from Oban Mon/Wed/Fri (2.5 hrs); course is 2 miles W of pier.
Primitive and challenging public course on natural Hebridean machair, bearing no resemblance to modern or mainland courses.
18 holes, 4775 yards, S.S.S.72
Founded Pre 1880 (reputedly over 200 years)
Visitors: membership open to all at £5 per family per year.
Green Fee: apply for details.
Hotels: Colonsay; farm guesthouse and self-catering details on request.

Q42 Colville Park
☎(0698) 263017
Jerviston Estate, Motherwell,
Lanarkshire ML1 4UG
On left hand side of A723, 1 mile N of Motherwell Cross.
Parkland course.
18 holes, 6280 yards, S.S.S.70
Designed by James Braid.
Founded 1922
Visitors: with member only; no weekend parties.
Green Fee: £20/day.
Societies: Mon-Fri day ticket only.
Catering: full facilities.
Hotels: Old Mill; Moorings; Popinjay.

Q43 Corrie
☎(0770) 810223
Sannox, Isle of Arran KA27 8JD
By A84 coast road from Brodick.
Undulating course.
9 holes, 3896 yards, S.S.S.61
Founded 1892
Visitors: welcome except Sat pm.
Green Fee: on application.
Societies: limited numbers.
Catering: light meals and snacks.
Hotels: Ingledene (Sannox); Corrie; Black Rock GH (Corrie).

Q44 Cowal
☎(0369) 5673
Ardenslate Rd, Kirn, Dunoon, Argyll
PA23 8LT

NE edge of Dunoon, 0.5 mile from A815 at Kirn.
Moorland course.
18 holes, 6251 yards, S.S.S.70
Designed by James Braid.
Founded 1891
Visitors: welcome.
Green Fee: £13/round, £20/day WD; £20/round, £30/day WE.
Societies: welcome by prior booking; Sat, Sun limit 33 players; terms available from Hon Sec.
Catering: full catering available.
International and 'Home from Home' membership available to golfers resident outside Scotland.
Hotels: Belmont; Esplanade; Mayfair; Rosscairn; Slatefield; St Ives; West End.

Q45 Cowglen
☎(041) 632 0556
301 Barrhead Rd, Glasgow G43
S side of Glasgow, following signs to Burrell Collection, opposite Pollok golf club.
Undulating parkland course.
18 holes, 6006 yards, S.S.S.69
Founded 1906
Visitors: introduced by member or by letter to Sec.
Green Fee: £18/round, £25/day.
Societies: apply to Sec.
Catering: lunch, dinner, bar snacks.
Hotels: Tinto Firs.

Q46 Craignure
☎(06802) 370 Sec
Scallastle, Graignure, Isle of Mull
PA64 5AP
1 miles from ferry at Craignure.
Links course.
9 holes, 2218 metres, S.S.C.32
Founded 1980
Visitors: welcome any time, no restrictions.
Green Fee: £6.

Q47 Crow Wood
☎(041) 779 4954 Sec, 779 2011 Club, 779 1943 Pro
Garnkirk House, Cumbernauld Rd, Muirhead, Glasgow G69 9JF
1 mile N of Stepps on A80.
Parkland course.
18 holes, 6249 yards, S.S.S.70
Designed by James Braid.
Founded 1925
Visitors: welcome midweek, subject to 24 hrs minimum notice to Sec.
Green Fee: £16/round, £24/day.
Societies: weekdays by prior arrangement.

Catering: meals served daily.
Snooker.
Hotels: Garfield; Crow Wood House;
Moodiesburn House.

Q48 Dalmally
☎(08382) 370
Old Saw Mill, Dalmally, Argyll PA33
1AS
1 mile W of Dalmally on A85.
Public flat parkland course by River
Orchy.
9 holes, 2277 yards, S.S.S.62
Founded 1987
Visitors: welcome.
Green Fee: £7/day.
Societies: welcome with prior
notice.
Catering: available with prior notice.
Hotels: Glen Orchy Lodge.

Q49 Dalmuir Municipal
☎(041) 952 8698 bookings
Overtoun Rd, Dalmuir, Clydebank,
Strathclyde
8 miles W of Glasgow.
Public parkland course.
18 holes, 5349 yards, S.S.S.67
Visitors: welcome.
Green Fee: apply for details.
Catering: café.
Practice nets.
Hotels: Radnor.

Q50 Deaconsbank
☎(041) 638 7044
Stewarton Rd, Thornliebank,
Glasgow G46
5 miles S of Glasgow near
Thornliebank.
Public parkland course.
18 holes, 4800 yards, S.S.S.63
Founded 1922
Visitors: welcome.
Green Fee: apply for details.
Societies: welcome.
Catering: full facilities.
Driving range, putting green, pool
tables.
Hotels: The MacDonalds.

Q51 Doon Valley
☎(0292) 531607
Hillside Park, Patna, Strathclyde
10 miles S of Ayr on A713,
signposted from village of Patna.
Municipal meadowland course.
9 holes, 5592 yards, S.S.S.68
Founded 1927
Visitors: welcome.
Green Fee: £5/round (annual
membership £30).

Societies: by arrangement.
Catering: bar; catering by
arrangement.
Pool, darts.
Hotels: Parsons Lodge.

Q52 Dougalston
☎(041) 956 5750
Strathblane Rd, Milngavie, Glasgow
G62
7 miles N of Glasgow city centre on
A879 and A81.
Public parkland course.
18 holes, 6683 yards, S.S.S.72
Designed by John Harris.
Founded 1976
Visitors: no restrictions.
Green Fee: apply for details.
Societies: with advance booking at
any time.
Catering: all types of catering.
Hotels: Burnbrae, 1 mile.

Q53 Douglas Park
☎(041) 942 2220
Hillfoot, Bearsden, Glasgow G61 2SJ
20 minutes by rail and road from
centre of Glasgow; course adjacent
to to Hillfoot Station.
Parkland course.
18 holes, 5957 yards, S.S.S.68
Founded 1897
Visitors: with member only.
Green Fee: on request.
Societies: apply to Sec.
Catering: meals by arrangement.

Q54 Douglas Water
☎(055 588) 361
Ayr Rd, Rigside, Lanark ML11 9NY
7 miles SW of Lanark on A70, 2 miles
E of A74, signposted Rigside.
Undulating parkland course.
9 holes, 2947 yards, S.S.S.69
Designed by striking coal miners
1921.
Founded 1922
Visitors: welcome.
Green Fee: apply for details.
Catering: by arrangement.

Q55 Drumpellier
☎(0236) 424139 Pro, 428723
Clubmaster
Drumpellier Ave, Coatbridge ML5
1RX
8 miles E of Glasgow on A89, 1 mile
from Coatbridge.
Parkland course.
18 holes, 6227 yards, S.S.S.70
Designed by W. Fernie.
Founded 1894

Visitors: welcome weekdays
excluding Bank Holidays.
Green Fee: £25/day, £15/round.
Societies: weekdays.
Catering: full catering except Thurs.
Pool.
Hotels: Coatbridge.

Q56 Dullatur
☎(02367) 23230
Dullatur, Glasgow G68 0AR
1.5 miles from Cumbernauld village.
Undulating moorland course.
18 holes, 6195 yards, S.S.S.70
Founded 1897
Visitors: welcome weekdays by
arrangement.
Green Fee: £25/day, £18/round,
from 1.30pm WD only; fri last tee-off
12 noon.
Societies: weekdays.
Catering: full facilities available,
prior notice.

Q57 Dumbarton
☎(0389) 32830
Broadmeadows, Dumbarton,
Dumbartonshire G82 2BQ
15 miles NW of Glasgow off A82.
Meadowland course.
18 holes, 5981 yards, S.S.S.69
Founded 1888
Visitors: welcome weekdays.
Green Fee: apply for details.
Societies: by arrangement.
Catering: lunches, snacks etc
except Tues.

Q58 Dunaverty
☎(055 588) 361
Southend, Campbeltown, Argyll
PA28 6RF
On B842, 10 miles S of
Campbeltown.
Undulating seaside course.
18 holes, 4597 yards, S.S.S.63
Founded 1889
Visitors: welcome.
Green Fee: apply for details.
Catering: snacks available.

Q59 East Kilbride
☎(03552) 20913, 47728 Sec
Chapelside Rd, Nerston, East Kilbride
G74 4PF
On Glasgow to E Kilbride road turn off
at Nerston opposite Commerce Park.
Undulating meadowland course.
18 holes, 6419 yards, S.S.S.71
Designed by Fred Hawtree.
Founded 1900
Visitors: accompanied by member
or by prior arrangement.

Green Fee: £14/round, £20/day.
Societies: Mon and Fri.
Catering: full catering except Tues and Thurs pm.
Hotels: Bruce; Stuart.

Q60 East Renfrewshire
☎(03555) 258 Clubhouse, 206 Pro
Loganswell, Pilmuir, Newton Mearns, Glasgow
A77, 1 mile from Mearns Cross.
Moorland course with panoramic views.
18 holes, 6097 yards, S.S.S.70
Designed by James Braid.
Founded 1926
Visitors: welcome by prior phone call
Green Fee: apply for details.
Societies: by arrangement.
Catering: meals served.

Q61 Easter Moffat
☎(0236) 842878
Mansion House, Plains, by Airdrie, Lanarkshire
2 miles E of Airdrie on the old Edinburgh-Glasgow road.
Moorland/parkland course.
18 holes, 6221 yards, S.S.S.70
Founded 1922
Visitors: welcome.
Green Fee: apply for details.
Societies: weekdays.
Catering: in playing season (Mar-Sept), otherwise by arrangement.

Q62 Eastwood
☎(03555) 261
Loganswell, Newton Mearns, Glasgow G77 6RX
On A77 from Glasgow, 3 miles S of Newton Mearns Cross at junction of Old Mearns Rd.
Moorland course.
18 holes, 5886 yards, S.S.S.68
Designed by J. Moon.
Founded 1893
Visitors: parties welcome by prior appointment with Sec.
Green Fee: £18/round, £26/day.
Societies: by arrangement.
Catering: full facilities.
Hotels: Redhurst; McDonald (Giffnock).

Q63 Elderslie
☎(0505) 323956
63 Main Rd, Elderslie, Renfrewshire PA5 9AZ
On A737 between Paisley and Johnstone.

Undulating parkland course.
18 holes, 6037 yards, S.S.S.69
Founded 1909
Visitors: full facilities Mon to Fri only.
Green Fee: £16.10/round, £22/day.
Societies: Mon, Wed, Fri by arrangement.
Catering: full facilities.
Snooker.
Hotels: Excelsior, Glasgow Airport.

Q64 Erskine
☎(0505) 862108
Bishopton, Renfrewshire PA7 5PH
N of M8 leave Erskine Toll Bridge and turn left along B815 for 1.5 miles.
Parkland course.
18 holes, 6287 yards, S.S.S.70
Founded 1904
Visitors: welcome if introduced by or playing with a member.
Green Fee: on application.
Societies: welcome by prior arrangement.
Catering: meals served to members and guests only, otherwise by arrangement.
Hotels: Erskine; Crest.

Q65 Fereneze
☎(041) 881 1519, 221 6394 Sec, 881 7058 Pro
Fereneze Ave, Barrhead, Glasgow G78 1HJ
9 miles SW of Glasgow near Barrhead station.
Moorland course.
18 holes, 5821 yards, S.S.S.68
Founded 1904
Visitors: by application to Pro, Sec, or accompanied by member.
Green Fee: apply for details.
Societies: weekdays only, apply to Sec.
Catering: lunches, bar snacks, evening meals all day Sat/Sun, usually by booking weekdays.
Hotels: Dalmeny Park.

Q66 Gigha
☎(05835) 287
Isle of Gigha, Kintyre, Argyll
By ferry from Tayinloan (ring Whitehouse (088 073) 253/4 for times); 2.5 hours drive from Glasgow.
Links course.
9 holes, 5026 yards, S.S.S. 66
Visitors: welcome.
Green Fee: £5 day (honesty box).
Catering: at Boat House and Gigha Hotel.
Hotels: Gigha.

Q67 Girvan
☎(0465) 4346
Girvan, Ayrshire KA26 9HW
Off A77, main Stranraer to Ayr road.
Seaside links/parkland course.
18 holes, 5078 yards, S.S.S.65
Designed by James Braid.
Founded pre-1877
Visitors: welcome.
Green Fee: £10/round, £18/day.
Societies: welcome by arrangement.
Catering: meals served by arrangement (0465) 4272.
Hotels: Kings Arms; Turnberry.

Q68 Glasgow
☎(041) 942 2011 Sec, 942 0770 Fax
Killermont, Bearsden, Glasgow G61 2TW
6 miles NW of Glasgow near Killermont Bridge on A81 or A806 (Maryhill road).
Parkland course.
18 holes, 5968 yards, S.S.S.69
Designed by Tom Morris Snr.
Founded 1787 (Killermont 1905)
Visitors: catered for by application.
Green Fee: £30/round.
Societies: on application.
Catering: lunches, high teas served by prior arrangement.
Hotels: Grosvenor; Burnbrae; Black Bull; Stakis Pond.

Q69 Glasgow (Gailes)
☎(0294) 311347, (041) 942 2011 Sec, (041) 942 0770 Fax
Gailes, by Irvine, Ayrshire KA11 5AE
2 miles S of Irvine on A78.
Seaside links course.
18 holes, 6502 yards, S.S.S.72
Designed by Willie Park Jr.
Founded 1787 (Gailes 1892)
Visitors: on application to Sec, or introduction by member.
Green Fee: £27/round WD, £30/round WE, £33/day.
Societies: on application to Sec.
Catering: lunches and high teas; also bar snacks.
Hotels: Hospitality Inn (Irvine); Marine (Troon).

Q70 Gleddoch Country Club
☎(047 554) 304, 704 Pro
Langbank, Renfrewshire PA14 6YE
M8 to Greenock, first turning to Langbank Houston (B789).
Parkland/moorland course.
18 holes, 5661 yards, S.S.S.67
Designed by Hamilton Stutt.

Founded 1975
Visitors: welcome by arrangement with Pro, Keith Campbell.
Green Fee: on application.
Societies: welcome.
Catering: meals and snacks.
Hotels: Gleddoch House.

Q71 **Glencruitten**
☎(0631) 62868
Glencruitten Rd, Oban, Argyll PA34 5PU
1 mile from town centre off A816; follow road signs for Rare Breeds Park.
Hilly parkland/moorland course.
18 holes, 4452 yards, S.S.S.63
Designed by James Braid.
Founded 1908
Visitors: welcome weekdays, with restrictions on Thurs and Sat.
Green Fee: £9.50/round, £11.50/day
Societies: limited number of societies accepted.
Catering: meals and snacks available, licenced bar.
Pool tables.

Q72 **Gourock**
☎(0475) 31001
Cowal View, Gourock, Renfrewshire PA19 6HD
2 miles up hill from Gourock station.
Moorland course.
18 holes, 6492 yards, S.S.S.71
Designed by Henry Cotton.
Founded 1896
Visitors: by letter to Sec, weekdays only.
Green Fee: £12/round, £18/day.
Societies: by arrangement.
Catering: bar lunches, high teas, dinner by arrangement.
Hotels: Gantock; Castle Levan.

Q73 **Greenock**
☎(0475) 720793
Forsyth St, Greenock, Renfrewshire PA16 8RE
1 mile SW of town centre, main road to Gourock away from River Clyde.
Moorland course.
18 holes, 5838 yards, S.S.S.68; 9 holes, 2149 yards, S.S.S.32
Designed by James Braid.
Founded 1890
Visitors: welcome except Sat.
Green Fee: on application.
Catering: full catering service except Mon.
Hotels: Tontine.

Q74 **Greenock Whinhill**
☎(0475) 24694
Beith Rd, Greenock, Renfrewshire
23 miles W of Glasgow, Renfrewshire.
Moorland course.
18 holes, 5454 yards, S.S.S.68
Founded 1908
Visitors: welcome.
Green Fee: apply for details.
Societies: by arrangement.
Catering: meals by arrangement.

Q75 **Haggs Castle**
☎(041) 427 1157
70 Dumbreck Rd, Glasgow G41 4SN
At end of M77 off M8.
Parkland course.
18 holes, 6466 yards, S.S.S.71
Designed by Peter Allis & Dave Thomas.
Founded 1910
Visitors: only with member.
Green Fee: £24/round, £36/day.
Societies: Wed only by prior arrangement.
Catering: all types available.
Snooker.
Hotels: Sherbrooke Castle.

Q76 **Hamilton**
☎(0698) 282872, 286131 Sec
Riccarton, Ferniegair, Hamilton, Lanarkshire
Off A74 between Larkhill and Hamilton.
Parkland course.
18 holes, 6264 yards, S.S.S.70
Designed by James Braid.
Founded 1892
Visitors: welcome with member, others by arrangement.
Green Fee: apply for details.
Societies: by arrangement with Sec.
Catering: snacks daily, meals served by arrangement.

Q77 **Hayston**
☎(041) 776 1244, 775 0882 Pro, 775 0723 Sec
Campsie Rd, Kirkintilloch, Glasgow G66 1RN
NE from Glasgow via Bishopbriggs and Kirkintilloch, 1 mile N of Kirkintilloch.
Parkland course.
18 holes, 6042 yards, S.S.S.69
Designed by James Braid.
Founded 1926
Visitors: weekdays only with letter of intro.
Green Fee: on application.
Societies: Tues and Thurs.

Catering: full service from 9am; lunch, bar snacks, high tea, dinner if ordered in advance.

Q78 **Helensburgh**
☎(0436) 74173
25 East Abercromby St, Helensburgh, Dunbartonshire G84 9JD
21 miles W of Glasgow on A82.
Moorland course.
18 holes, 6053 yards, S.S.S.69
Designed by Tom Morris.
Founded 1893
Visitors: welcome weekdays.
Green Fee: £15/round, £23/day, jnrs £6/round.
Societies: by arrangement.
Catering: bar lunches, evening meals by arrangement.
Hotels: Commodore.

Q79 **Hilton Park**
☎(041) 956 4657
Stockiemuir Rd, Milngavie, Glasgow G62 9HB
8 miles N of Glasgow on A809.
Moorland courses.
Allander, 18 holes, 5374 yards, S.S.S.69; Hilton, 18 holes, 6054 yards, S.S.S.70
Designed by James Braid.
Founded 1927
Visitors: welcome weekdays by prior arrangement.
Green Fee: £18/round, £25 2 rounds.
Societies: weekdays.
Catering: full facilities.
Hotels: Kirkhouse; Black Bull; Country Club.

Q80 **Hollandbush**
☎(0555) 893484
Acretophead, Lesmahagow, Strathclyde
Off A74 between Lesmahagow and Coalburn.
Parkland/moorland course.
18 holes, 6110 yards, S.S.S.70
Designed by Ken Pate.
Founded 1954
Visitors: welcome.
Green Fee: on application.
Catering: full catering facilities.
Large practice ground.
Hotels: Station (Coalburn).

Q81 **Innellan**
☎(0369) 83242, 5758 Supervisor (home)
Knockamillie Rd, Innellan, Argyll

4 miles S of Dunoon.
Parkland course.
9 holes, 4878 yards, S.S.S.63
Founded 1891
Visitors: anytime except Mon
evenings.
Green Fee: £8 WD, £10 WE.
Societies: catered for weekdays and
weekends.
Catering: available (new Clubhouse
Mar 1994).
Hotels: Esplanade; Slatefield;
Rosscairn.

Q82 Inverary

No telephone as yet
Inverary, Argyll, Scotland
SW corner of town on Lochgilphead
Rd.
Parkland course.
9 holes, 5700 yards, S.S.S.67
Designed by Watt Landscaping.
Founded June 1993
Visitors: welcome any time except
during club competitions.
Green Fee: £6 WD, £8 WE; jnrs half
price.
Societies: welcome by prior
arrangement.
Nets, small practice area.
Hotels: Loch Fyne; George; The
Great Inn.

Q83 Irvine

☎(0294) 275979
Bogside, Irvine KA12 8SN
On road from Irvine to Kilwinning,
turn left after Ravenspark Academy
and carry straight on for 0.5 mile over
railway bridge.
Links course.
18 holes, 6454 yards, S.S.S.71
Designed by James Braid.
Founded 1887
Visitors: welcome weekdays and
after 3pm weekends.
Green Fee: £25/round, £35/day WD;
£35 WE.
Societies: welcome on application
to Sec.
Catering: meals and snacks served.
Hotels: Hospitality Inn; Redburn;
Eglinton Arms; Golf; Annfield.

Q84 Irvine Ravenspark

☎(0294) 271293, 276467 Pro
13 Kidsneuk Lane, Irvine, Ayrshire
KA12 8SR
On A78 midway between Irvine and
Kilwinning.
Municipal parkland course.
18 holes, 6496 yards, S.S.S.71
Founded 6 June 1907

Visitors: welcome every day except
Sat until 2.30pm.
Green Fee: £4/round, £8/day WD,
£8/round, £14/day WE.
Societies: catered for Mon-Fri, Sun
by arrangement with Sec.
Catering: bar open all day every day;
lunches and high teas.
Hotels: Hospitality Inn; Annfield;
Redburn; Golf Inn.

Q85 Kilbirnie Place

☎(0505) 683398
Largs Rd, Kilbirnie, Ayrshire
On outskirts of Kilbirnie on main
Largs road.
Parkland course.
18 holes, 5511 yards, S.S.S.67
Founded 1922
Visitors: welcome weekdays and
Sun.
Green Fee: apply for details.
Societies: weekdays and Sun, apply
in writing to Sec.
Catering: every day.

Q86 Kilmacolm

☎(050 587) 2139
Porterfield Rd, Kilmacolm,
Renfrewshire PA13 3PD
A740 to Linwood, then A761 to
Bridge of Weir.
Moorland course.
18 holes, 5964 yards, S.S.S.68
Designed by James Braid.
Founded 1890
Visitors: welcome weekdays;
weekends accompanied by member
only.
Green Fee: £20/round, £26/day.
Societies: by arrangement.
Catering: available.
Hotels: Gryffe (Bridge of Weir).

Q87 Kilmarnock (Barassie)

☎(0292) 311077 Club, 313920
Sec's office
29 Hillhouse Rd, Barassie, Troon,
Ayrshire KA10 6SY
Off A78 just N of Troon opposite
Barassie station.
Seaside course.
18 holes, 6473 yards, S.S.S.71
Designed by Matthew M. Monie.
Founded 1887
Visitors: welcome Mon, Tues, Thurs,
Fri only.
Green Fee: on application.
Societies: Tues and Thurs by prior
arrangement.
Catering: full catering facilities
available.
Hotels: Marine (Troon).

Q88 Kilsyth Lennox

☎(0236) 823525 (temporary
number pending reinstallation of
phone line)
Tak-Ma-Doon Rd, Kilsyth, Glasgow
G65 0HX
12 miles from Glasgow on A80.
Moorland/parkland course.
18 holes, Par 70, in play from spring
1994
Founded 1907
Visitors: details of new layout and
visitor restrictions still to be
confirmed; apply for information.
Green Fee: £8/round WD, £10/round
WE.
Societies: on application.
Catering: clubhouse burned to the
ground in 1993, replacement due
Autumn 1994.

Q89 Kirkhill

☎(041) 641 3083, 641 8499 Sec
Greenlees Rd, Cambuslang, Glasgow
G72 8YN
Follow East Kilbride road from
Burnside, take first turning on left
past Cathkin by-pass roundabout.
Meadowland course.
18 holes, 5862 yards, S.S.S.69
Designed by James Braid.
Founded 1910
Visitors: by arrangement with Sec.
Green Fee: £12/round, £20/day.
Societies: welcome by prior
arrangement in writing.
Catering: bar snacks, full meals by
arrangement with Clubmistress.
Hotels: Kings Park; Burnside; Stuart;
Bruce.

Q90 Kirkintilloch

☎(041) 776 1256 Club, 775 2387
Sec
Todhill, Campsie Rd, Kirkintilloch,
Glasgow G66 1RN
1 mile from Kirkintilloch on road to
Lennoxtown.
Meadowland course.
18 holes, 5269 yards, S.S.S.66
Designed by James Braid.
Founded 1895
Visitors: only if introduced.
Green Fee: £12/round, £17/day.
Societies: by advance booking.
Catering: full except Mon and Tues.
Hotels: Garfield (Stepps).

Q91 Knightswood

☎(041) 959 2131
Lincoln Ave, Knightswood, Glasgow
Off Dumbarton Rd from city centre.
Parkland course.

9 holes, 2717 yards, S.S.S.64
Founded 1920s
Visitors: welcome.
Green Fee: apply for details.
Societies: welcome by arrangement.

Q92 Kyles of Bute
☎(0700) 811603
Tighnabruaich, Argyll
B836 from Dunoon to Tighnabruaich, through village to Kames Cross, then B8000 to Millhouse, club entrance on left at top of 1st rise.
Undulating moorland course.
9 holes, 2389 yards, S.S.S.32
Founded 1907
Visitors: welcome except Sun am.
Green Fee: £5/day; £2.50 under 18.
Societies: by arrangement.
Catering: tea, coffee, snacks when available.
Hotels: Royal; Kames; Kyles of Bute.

Q93 Lamlash
☎(0770) 600296 Clubhouse, 600196 Starter
Lamlash, Brodick, Isle of Arran KA27 8JU
3 miles S of Brodick Pier on A841.
Undulating heathland.
18 holes, 4681 yards, S.S.S.63
Founded 1889
Visitors: welcome, no restrictions.
Green Fee: £9/day WD; £11/day WE.
Societies: booking by letter.
Catering: tearoom, club bar.
Hotels: Glenisle; Marine (unlicenced).

Q94 Lanark
☎(0555) 663219
The Moor, Whitelees Rd, Lanark ML11 7RX
Off A73 or A72, turn left in Lanark into Whiteleees Rd, for 0.5 mile.
Moorland course.
18 holes, 6423 yards, S.S.S.71
Designed by Ben Sayers and James Braid.
Founded 1851
Visitors: welcome weekdays.
Green Fee: on application.
Societies: Mon-Wed only.
Catering: full, resident chef.
Hotels: Tinto; The Popinjay.

Q95 Largs
☎(0475) 673594
Irvine Rd, Largs, Ayrshire KA30 8EU
1 mile S of Largs on A78, 28 miles from Glasgow.
Parkland course with sea views..

18 holes, 6220 yards, S.S.S.70
Founded 1891
Visitors: welcome.
Green Fee: £18/round, £24/day.
Societies: Tues and Thurs, small groups on Fri.
Catering: full facilities.
Hotels: Elderslie; Haylie; South Bay; Brisbane.

Q96 Larkhall
☎(0698) 881113
Burnhead Rd, Larkhall, Lanarkshire SW on B7019.
Municipal course.
9 holes, 6236 yards, S.S.S.70
Visitors: all welcome.
Green Fee: apply for details.
Societies: by arrangement.

Q97 Leadhills
☎(0659) 74222
Leadhills, Biggar, Lanarkshire ML12 6XR
On B797, 6 miles from A74 at Abington, course behind hotel within Leadhills village.
Moorland course; highest course in Great Britain.
9 holes, 4100 yards, S.S.S.62
Founded 1935
Visitors: welcome anytime.
Green Fee: apply for details.
Societies: welcome.
Catering: at local hotel.
Hotels: Hopetoun Arms.

Q98 Lenzie
☎(041) 776 1535, 776 6020 Sec/bookings
19 Crosshill Rd, Lenzie, Glasgow G66 3DA
A80 to Stepps, Lenzie road turn left at traffic lights.
Moorland course.
18 holes, 5984 yards, S.S.S.69
Founded 1889
Visitors: welcome with member.
Green Fee: on application.
Societies: welcome weekdays.
Catering: meals and snacks available except Mon.

Q99 Lethamhill
☎(041) 770 6220
Cumbernauld Rd, Glasgow G33 1AH
On A80 adjacent to Hogganfield Loch.
Municipal course.
18 holes, 6073 yards, S.S.S.68
Visitors: welcome.
Green Fee: £3.40/round summer, £4/round winter.

Q100 Linn Park
☎(041) 637 5871
Simshill Rd, Glasgow G44
Off M74 S of Glasgow.
Public parkland course.
18 holes, 4952 yards, S.S.S.65
Designed by Glasgow Parks.
Founded 1925
Visitors: welcome.
Green Fee: apply for details.
Catering: teas and snacks.
Wildlife park 200 yards from clubhouse.

Q101 Littlehill
☎(041) 772 1916
Auchinairn Rd, Bishopbriggs, Glasgow
3 miles N of city centre.
Municipal parkland course.
18 holes, 6228 yards, S.S.S.70
Designed by James Braid.
Founded 1924
Visitors: no restrictions.
Green Fee: apply for details.
Societies: apply to Glasgow Corporation Parks Dept.
Catering: lunches except Mon.

Q102 Loch Lomond
☎(043) 686 223, 686 265 Fax
Rossdhu House, Luss, Dunbartonshire G83 8NT
On W bank of Loch Lomond on A82.
Parkland course.
18 holes, 7053 yards, S.S.S.72 (provisional)
Designed by Tom Weiskopf.
Founded Opening 1994/5
Visitors: write for details of course availability and fees.

Q103 Lochgilphead
☎(0546) 2340
Blarbuie Road, Lochgilphead, Argyll PA31 8LD
A82 and A83 from Glasgow to Lochgilphead; 1 mile from parish church on Hospital Rd.
Hilly parkland course.
9 holes, 4484 yards, S.S.S.63
Designed by Dr Ian MacCammond.
Founded 1891
Visitors: welcome weekdays, members competitions weekends.
Green Fee: £8/day WD, £10/day WE; £30/week (Mon-Fri); jnrs and OAPs half price.
Societies: by arrangement.
Catering: bar available evenings and weekends; catering by arrangement.
Hotels: Stag; Argyll; Lochgair; Castleween Caravan Park; (free golf).

Q104 Lochranza

☎(077 083) 273
Lochranza, Isle of Arran, KA27 8HL
In village of Lochranza at N of island.
Grassland course with river and
trees, 3 holes adjacent seashore.
9 holes (18 flags, 18 tees), 5500
yards, Par 70
Designed by Iain M. Robertson.
Founded course laid 1991.
Visitors: welcome 7 days.
Green Fee: £4.50 (9 holes), £7 (18
holes), £9.50/day.
Societies: welcome any time.
Catering: tea room, home baking;
not licensed.
Hotels: caravan park adjacent (vans
for hire); weekly golf packages inc
outings to other courses; hotel/guest
house packages on request.

Q105 Lochwinnoch

☎(0505) 842153
Burnfoot Rd, Lochwinnoch,
Renfrewshire PA12 4AN.
On A760 about 10 miles S of Paisley,
1st on right after Struthers Garage,
400 yards along Burnfoot Rd.
Parkland course.
18 holes, 6243 yards, S.S.S.70
Founded 1897
Visitors: weekdays till 4pm, no
visitors weekends.
Green Fee: on application.
Societies: by arrangement.
Catering: full meals except Mon and
Thurs.
Hotels: Lindhurst.

Q106 Loudoun

☎(0563) 821993 Sec, 820551 Club
Galston, Ayrshire KA4 8PA
A77 to Kilmarnock, take Edinburgh
road, club lies on main road between
Galston and Newmilns.
Parkland course.
18 holes, 5844 yards, S.S.S.68
Founded 1909
Visitors: welcome weekdays.
Green Fee: £15/round, £25/day.
Societies: welcome.
Catering: facilities available.
Hotels: Broomhill; Foxbar.

Q107 Machrie

☎(0496) 2310, 2404 Fax
The Machrie Hotel & Golf Course,
Port Ellen, Isle of Islay, Argyll PA42
7AN
30 mins by air from Glasgow, 4 miles
from Port Ellen.
Traditional links course.
18 holes, 6226 yards, S.S.S.70

Designed by Willie Campbell,
redesigned by Donald Steel.
Founded 1891
Visitors: welcome.
Green Fee: apply for details.
Societies: at any time by
arrangement.
Catering: bar lunches, grill, table
d'hôte, à la carte.
Banqueting. conferences, company
days, own beach, salmon/sea trout
fishing, snooker.
Hotels: Machrie Hotel; leisure/golf
packages on request.

Q108 Machrie Bay

☎(0770) 850261
c/o Sec, Oakdene, Pirnmill, Brodick,
Isle of Arran KA27 8HP
Ferry to Brodick and via String Rd to
Machrie.
Fairly flat seaside course.
9 holes, 2123 yards, S.S.S.32
Designed by William Fernie.
Founded 1900
Visitors: welcome.
Green Fee: £4/round/day, £12/week.
Catering: snacks served April-Sept.
Tennis.

Q109 Machrihanish

☎(0586 81) 213
Machrihanish, Campbeltown, Argyll
PA28 6PT
5 miles W of Campbeltown on B843.
Seaside links course.
18 holes, 6228 yards, S.S.S.70; also
9 hole course
Founded 1876
Visitors: welcome at all times;
golf/flight day package available
through Logan Air, Glasgow.
Green Fee: £16/round, £22/day.
Societies: welcome, certain
weekends available also.
Catering: full facilities.

Q110 Maybole

Memorial Park, Maybole, Ayrshire
KA19
9 miles S of Ayr on Stranraer route.
Public hillside course with splendid
views.
9 holes, 2652 yards, S.S.S.65
Founded 1905
Visitors: no restrictions; booking
available through Kyle and Carrick
Parks Recreation and Leisure Dept
tourist schemes.
Green Fee: apply for details.
Societies: booking as for visitors.
Hotels: many in Ayr offering golf
packages.

Q111 Millport

☎(0475) 530311
Golf Rd, Millport, Isle of Cumbrae
KA28 0BA
Cal-Mac car ferry Largs Slip to
Cumbrae (7 minutes), thence 3 miles
by car or public transport.
Seaside moorland course.
18 holes, 5828 yards, S.S.S.68
Founded 1888
Visitors: welcome at all times.
Green Fee: £20/day max.
Societies: welcome, including
weekends.
Catering: full facilities, including
licensed bar.
Large practice area.
Hotels: Royal George; Islands.

Q112 Milngavie

☎(041) 956 1619
Laighpark, Milngavie, Glasgow G62
8EP
Off A809 NW of Glasgow.
Moorland course.
18 holes, 5818 yards, S.S.S.68
Founded 1895
Visitors: only with member at any
time.
Green Fee: apply for details.
Societies: catered for weekdays
except Mon and Tues.
Catering: by arrangement.
Hotels: Black Bull; Burnbrae.

Q113 Mount Ellen

☎(0236) 872277
Johnston Rd, Johnstone House,
Gartcosh, Glasgow
Off A80 Glasgow-Stirling road.
Parkland course.
18 holes, 5525 yards, S.S.S.68(66)
Founded 1905
Visitors: by appointment.
Green Fee: apply for details.
Catering: full facilities.
Pool.

Q114 New Cumnock

☎(0290) 32037
Lochill, Cumnock Rd, New Cumnock,
Ayrshire KA18 4BQ
0.5 mile N of New Cumnock.
Parkland course.
9 holes, 5176 yards, S.S.S.65
Founded 1901
Visitors: welcome, not before 4pm
Sun; restricted on competition days.
Green Fee: £8/day.
Societies: welcome with application
in writing.
Catering: snacks.
Hotels: Lochside House.

Machrie

Machrie's charm lies in its out of the way setting. Lapped on one side by the Atlantic and separated from the mainland by a sea voyage (or a short aeroplane hop from Glasgow), its delights are little known.

They are certainly not as well known as they deserve to be, because the course is in the very best tradition of seaside links. However, by developing its assets a little more than in the past, the Island of Islay is putting itself far more on the map; and without wishing to spoil a way of life by causing a golfing invasion to its shores, the recommendation for its golf is based on happy personal experience that it would be churlish not to pass on.

After years of acting as co-tenants to grazing sheep and cattle, golfers owe something of a transformation to the former owners of Bowmore Distillery, who bought the course and hotel, and added a cluster of cottages alongside which are an ideal base for whatever form of holiday you seek on Islay.

It is a wide choice but, as golfers have supported the distillers' product ever since man first took three putts, there is a delicious aptness about the change. However, Machrie's new look was not confined to new management. It has six new holes which add enormously to its rating as a test of golf. Some of the eccentricities that grew up before there was much in the way of machinery or golf course architects have been reduced; gone are one or two, though not all, of the blind shots into crater-like greens — a type of hole not so favourably looked upon as it once was; in their place have arisen a new 2nd, 10th, 11th, 12th, 13th and 14th that offer, in distillers' language, a smoother blend.

The 1st, a gentle opener, has an inviting drive from a raised tee, but the 2nd quickly gets down to the real golfing business. The first of the alterations, it is a winding dogleg to the left, the dogleg taking the form of a fast flowing brook; there are plans for extending the hole to par 5.

Anyone with aspirations of getting home in two will need a strong nerve as well as two good shots, although the 3rd and 4th are less stern. The 5th is a fine short hole and the 6th typical of Machrie's natural blessings with a drive to the left providing the correct approach and view of a green in a dell.

In its early days in the last century, the drive at the 7th over a vast sandhill was rather more formidable than it is now; all the same, it can still strike fear at the beginning of a stretch of three holes, all par 4s, which follow the line of a glorious sandy beach. These emphasise the remoteness and the beauty and the fact that, unlike many famous seaside courses, here is the opportunity really to see the sea.

The 10th tee is a notable example, even if it is not the time to be distracted. A marvellous natural short hole at the furthest limit of the course marks the introduction to the new golfing country; this is nicely demanding but, at the same time, there is a pleasant scenic change to the hills and the lonely peat moors.

The 11th requires a strong second to a long green with a heathery drop to the left, and the not so short par 3 12th is even tougher. The main feature of the 13th, a par 5 bending left, is the amphitheatre in which the green is situated, while the 14th is perhaps the hardest of all the par 4s. A long drive is necessary for the proper view of the flag outlined against the skyline.

After a spell where stout hitting is essential, the last four holes are not quite as severe; nevertheless, the need for good judgment is paramount and, against any sort of wind, the 16th and 18th, in particular, can pose considerably greater problems. However, if your score doesn't turn out quite the way you planned (how many do?), there are ample consolations.

There is no shortage of spirituous assistance to help forget the bad round — and celebrate the good — and the atmosphere of the Club and hotel, as of the island as a whole, is wonderfully friendly and informal.

Q115 Old Course Ranfurly

☎(0505) 613612 Club, 613214 office/Sec
Ranfurly Place, Bridge of Weir, Renfrewshire PA11 3DE
7 miles W of Paisley, 10 mins from Glasgow airport.
Moorland course.
18 holes, 6089 yards, S.S.S.69
Founded 1905
Visitors: welcome weekdays by introduction and weekends with member.
Green Fee: £15/round, £25/day.
Societies: catered for by special arrangement.
Catering: morning coffee, bar lunches, high tea, dinner.
Hotels: Gryffe Arms.

Q116 Paisley

☎(041) 884 4114 Pro shop
Braehead, Paisley PA2 8TZ
From Glasgow, A737 to Paisley, 3 miles S of Paisley centre.
Moorland course.
18 holes, 6424 yards, S.S.S.71
Founded 1895.
Visitors: weekdays before 4pm, h/cap cert or prior arrangement with Sec.
Green Fee: £16/round, £24/day.
Societies: by arrangement; not weekends or Bank Holidays.
Catering: full catering available. Snooker.
Hotels: Watermill; Excelsior.

Q117 Palacerigg

☎(0236) 734969
Palacerigg Country Park, Cumbernauld G67 3HU
Take A80 to Cumbernauld, follow signs to Country Park.
Parkland course.
18 holes, 6408 yards, S.S.S.71
Designed by Henry Cotton.
Founded 1975
Visitors: welcome weekdays.
Green Fee: £6.50 WD, £7.50 WE.
Societies: welcome weekdays.
Catering: lunches and high teas except Mon, Tues.
Hotels: Castlecary.

Q118 Pollok

☎(041) 632 1080
90 Barrhead Rd, Glasgow G43 1BG
On A736, 4 miles S of city centre.
Wooded parkland course.
18 holes, 6257 yards, S.S.S.70
Founded 1892
Visitors: men only Mon-Fri.

Green Fee: apply for details.
Societies: by letter to Sec.
Catering: full dining facilities.
Hotels: Albany; Macdonald; Holiday Inn; Forum.

Q119 Port Bannatyne

☎(0700) 502009
Bannatyne Mains Rd, Port Bannatyne, Isle of Bute
2 miles N of Rothesay on A845.
Hilly seaside course.
13 holes, 4654 yards, S.S.S.63
Designed by James Braid.
Founded 1968
Visitors: unrestricted.
Green Fee: £7.50/day, £30/week; jnrs £4/day, £15/week.
Societies: welcome.
Catering: by arrangement.
Hotels: Ardmory House; Port Royal; Ardbeg Lodge; Port Bannatyne Inn.

Q120 Port Glasgow

☎(0475) 704181
Devol Farm Industrial Estate, Port Glasgow, Renfrewshire PA14 5XE
SW of Glasgow on M8 towards Greenock; in town of Port Glasgow.
Undulating course.
18 holes, 5712 yards, S.S.S.68
Founded 1895
Visitors: weekdays until 3.55pm; at all other times only with introduction.
Green Fee: apply for details.
Societies: catered for on non-competition days (Sun-Fri).
Catering: meals served on request.
Hotels: Clune Brae; Star.

Q121 Prestwick

☎(0292) 77404
2 Links Rd, Prestwick, KA9 1QG
1 mile from Prestwick Airport adjacent to Prestwick station.
Seaside links course.
18 holes, 6544 yards, S.S.S.72
Founded 1851
Visitors: by arrangement; prior booking essential.
Green Fee: on application.
Societies: by arrangement.
Catering: dining room, men only; Cardinal room, mixed, casual dress, light lunches.
Hotels: Parkstone; Fairways; Golf View; North Beach.

Q122 Prestwick St Cuthbert

☎(0292) 77101 Sec
East Rd, Prestwick, Ayrshire KA9 2SX

Off main Ayr to Prestwick Rd, at Bellevue Rd.
Parkland course.
18 holes, 6470 yards, S.S.S.71
Designed by Stutt & Co.
Founded 1899
Visitors: welcome weekdays, weekends if introduced by member.
Green Fee: £18/round, £24/day.
Societies: by arrangement, not weekends or Bank Holidays.
Catering: lunch, bar lunches, dinner.
Hotels: Carlton; St Nicholas; Parkstone.

Q123 Prestwick St Nicholas

☎(0292) 77608
Grangemuir Rd, Prestwick, Ayrshire KA9 1SN
Off A79, from Main St turn into Grangemuir Rd running down to sea.
Links course.
18 holes, 5952 yards, S.S.S.69
Designed by C. Hunter.
Founded 1851
Visitors: welcome weekdays.
Green Fee: £18/round, £30/day WD.
Societies: weekdays.
Catering: bar lunch, high tea, dinner.
Hotels: Parkstone; St Ninians; North Beach.

Q124 Ralston

☎(041) 882 1349
Strathmore Ave, Ralston, Paisley, Renfrewshire PA1 3DT
Off main Paisley to Glasgow road.
Parkland course.
18 holes, 6100 yards, S.S.S.69
Founded 1904
Visitors: organised parties only.
Green Fee: on application.
Catering: meals served, bar snacks.
Hotels: Glynhill; Pines; Watermill; Crookston.

Q125 Ranfurly Castle

☎(0505) 612609
Golf Rd, Bridge of Weir, Renfrewshire PA11 3HN
Off M8 at sign for Linwood.
Undulating moorland course.
18 holes, 6284 yards, S.S.S.70
Designed by Andrew Kirkcaldy & Willie Auchterlonie.
Founded 1889
Visitors: weekdays by introduction.
Green Fee: £22/round, £27/day.
Societies: certain Tues only.
Catering: snacks, lunches, high teas.
Hotels: Gryffe Arms.

Q126 Renfrew
☎(041) 886 6692
Blythswood Estate, Inchinnan Rd, Renfrew
Off A8 at Normandy Hotel.
Parkland course.
18 holes, 6818 yards, S.S.S.73
Designed by John Harris.
Founded 1894
Visitors: introduced by member.
Green Fee: apply for details.
Societies: welcome by arrangement, max 30.
Catering: full catering.
Hotels: Normandy; Glynehill; Dean Park.

Q127 Rothesay
☎(0700) 503554
Canada Hill, Rothesay, Isle of Bute PA20 7HN
30 minutes by steamer from Wemyss Bay (30 miles from Glasgow).
Undulating parkland course.
18 holes, 5440 yards, S.S.S.67
Designed by James Braid.
Founded 1892
Visitors: welcome, bookings advisable Sat/Sun.
Green Fee: on application.
Societies: by arrangement.
Catering: full catering all week, April-Sept.

Q128 Routenburn
☎(0475) 673230
Largs, Ayrshire KA30 9AH
1 mile N of Largs; 1st major left turn coming into Largs from Greenock.
Seaside hill course.
18 holes, 5604 yards, S.S.S.67
Designed by James Braid.
Founded 1914
Visitors: welcome weekdays.
Green Fee: on application.
Societies: welcome weekdays.
Catering: full catering facilities except Thurs.
Hotels: Willowbank; Glen Eldon.

Q129 Royal Troon
☎(0292) 311555 Office, 317578 Club Steward, 313281 Pro, 318204 Fax
Craigend Rd, Troon, Ayrshire KA10 6EP
3 miles from Prestwick Airport.
Seaside links courses.
Old Course (championship), 18 holes, 6641 yards (6070 metres), S.S.S.73; Portland Course, 18 holes, 6274 yards (5738 metres), S.S.S.71
Designed by Cotton, Pennink, Lawrie.

Founded 1878
Visitors: Mon, Tues and Thurs only with starting time restriction; max h/cap 18; no Ladies on Old Course; letter of intro required with h/cap cert.
Green Fee: £78/day; Portland £48/day; only 1 round permitted on Old Course; lunch etc included.
Societies: max 24 persons.
Catering: full restaurant service and bar snacks by arrangement.
Hotels: Marine Highland; Piersland.

Q130 Ruchill
Brassey Street, Maryhill, Glasgow G20
2.5 miles NW of Glasgow off Bearsden road.
Municipal parkland course.
9 holes, 2240 yards, S.S.S.31
Founded 1928
Visitors: welcome.
Green Fee: apply for details.
Societies: contact Glasgow Parks Dept.

Q131 Sandyhills
☎(041) 778 1179
223 Sandyhills Rd, Glasgow G32 9NA
E side of Glasgow, from Tollcross Rd, left at Killin St and right into Sandyhills Rd.
Parkland course.
18 holes, 6253 yards, S.S.S.70
Founded 1905
Visitors: welcome by arrangement.
Green Fee: apply for details.
Societies: welcome by arrangement.
Catering: full catering except Mon.

Q132 Shiskine
☎(077 086) 293 Sec, 346 Treasurer
Blackwaterfoot, Isle of Arran KA27 8HA
300 yards off A841 in Blackwaterfoot.
Seaside course.
12 holes, 3000 yards, S.S.S.42
Founded 1896
Visitors: welcome.
Green Fee: apply for details.
Societies: catered for, write or phone Hon Sec or Hon Treasurer.
Catering: snacks, June-Sept.
Tennis, bowling.

Q133 Shotts
☎(0501) 820431, 822658 Pro shop
Blairhead, Shotts ML7 5BJ
Off M8 junction 5, B7057 Benhar road for 2 miles.

Undulating moorland course.
18 holes, 6125 yards, S.S.S.70
Designed by James Braid.
Founded 1895
Visitors: unlimited during week.
Green Fee: £15/day WD, £18 WE.
Societies: weekdays only by prior booking.
Catering: full catering April-Oct.
Practice area.
Hotels: Station; Travel Inn (4 miles).

Q134 Skelmorlie
☎(0475) 520152
Skelmorlie, Ayrshire PA17 5ES
1 mile from Wemyss Bay station.
Parkland/moorland course.
13 holes, 5104 yards, S.S.S.65
Designed by James Braid.
Founded 1891
Visitors: welcome except Sat from Mar to Oct.
Green Fee: on application.
Societies: welcome except Sat.
Catering: lunches, dinners and teas served.

Q135 Strathaven
☎(0357) 20539 or 20421
Overton Ave, Glasgow Rd, Strathaven ML10 6NL
Situated on outskirts of town on A726.
Parkland course.
18 holes, 6226 yards, S.S.S.70
Designed by William Fernie of Troon, extended to 18 holes by J.R. Stutt.
Founded 1908
Visitors: weekdays, parties Tues only.
Green Fee: on application.
Societies: Tues only.
Catering: catering facilities available all day.
Hotels: Strathaven.

Q136 Strathclyde Park
☎(0698) 266155 Ext 154, 283994 Pro
Mote Hill, Hamilton, Lanarkshire
Take Hamilton turn off M74 (heading N towards Glasgow), 0.5 mile on to roundabout, 2nd exit (straight through), to next roundabout and turn right into Mote Hill, past ice rink on left, course immediately ahead; 1.5 miles from M74.
Public parkland course.
9 holes, 3175 yards, S.S.S.70
Visitors: booking system; book same day, in person 7am, phones open 8.45am.
Green Fee: £2.25 (9 holes).

Catering: bar lunches and dinners served.
Driving range, putting green, practice area.
Hotels: Travel Lodge.

Q137 Tarbert
☎(0880) 820565
Kilberry Rd, Tarbert, Argyll PA29 6XX
1 mile on A83 to Campbeltown from Tarbert, turn right onto B8024 for 0.25 mile.
Hilly seaside course.
9 holes, 2230 yards, S.S.S.64
Visitors: welcome with restrictions.
Green Fee: £5 (9 holes), £8 (18 holes), £10/day.
Societies: by arrangement.
Hotels: Stonefield Castle; Tarbert; West Loch Tarbert.

Q138 Tobermory
c/o Sec, (0688) 2013, 2275
Erray Rd, Tobermory, Isle of Mull PA75 6PS
A848 to Tobermory, course past Police Station.
Clifftop heathland course; panoramic views over Sound of Mull.
9 holes, 4474 metres, S.S.S.64
Designed by David Adams.
Founded 1896
Visitors: welcome.
Green Fee: apply for details.
Societies: welcome.
Hotels: Western Isles.

Q139 Torrance House
☎(03552) 33451 Club, 48638
Starter's Office (bookings)
Strathaven Rd, East Kilbride, Glasgow G75 0QZ
On A726 on outskirts of East Kilbride travelling S to Strathven; course in country park.
Municipal parkland course.

18 holes, 6640 yards, S.S.S.71
Designed by Hawtree & Sons.
Founded 1969
Visitors: welcome, may book up to 6 days in advance.
Green Fee: £11.50/round.
Societies: visiting parties to book in advance (03552) 71225.
Catering: available in clubhouse.
Practice/driving area c.1 mile from club.

Q140 Troon Municipal
☎(0292) 312464
Harling Drive, Troon, Ayrshire KA10 6NE
100 yards from railway station.
Links course.
Lochgreen, 18 holes, 6687 yards, S.S.S.72; Darley, 18 holes, 6327 yards, S.S.S.70; Fullerton, 18 holes, 4784 yards, S.S.S.63
Founded 1905
Visitors: welcome.
Green Fee: apply for details.
Societies: welcome.
Catering: full catering.

Q141 Turnberry Hotel
☎(0655) 31000, 31706 Fax
Turnberry Hotel, Turnberry, Ayrshire KA26 9LT
0.25 mile off A77 from Glasgow, 15 miles south of Ayr.
Seaside links courses.
Ailsa, 18 holes, 6408 yards, S.S.S.72; Arran, 18 holes, 6014 yards, S.S.S.69
Designed by Mackenzie Ross.
Founded 1897
Visitors: principally reserved for Hotel residents; non-residents must apply in writing.
Green Fee: on application.
Societies: written applications.
Catering: clubhouse restaurant and bar open all day.

Wide range of facilities within Turnberry Hotel and Spa.
Hotels: Turnberry.

Q142 Vale of Leven
☎(0389) 52351, 52508 Sec
Northfield Rd, Bonfield, Alexandria, Dunbartonshire G83 9EP.
Turn right from A82 at Bonhill; course signposted from here.
Moorland course overlooking Loch Lomond and Ben Lomond.
18 holes, 5962 yards, S.S.S.66
Founded 1907
Visitors: welcome except Sat during April-Oct; parties welcome on application to Sec.
Green Fee: £12/round, £16/day WD; £16/round, £20/day WE.
Societies: welcome except Sat.
Catering: full bar and catering facilities except Tues.
Hotels: Balloch; Tullichewan; Lomond Park; Duck Bay Marina; Dumbuck; Dumbarton.

Q143 Vaul
☎(08792) 339
Scarinish, Isle of Tiree, Argyll PA77 6XH
50 miles west of Oban by ferry; 40 minute flight from Glasgow Airport.
Public seaside course on east coast of island.
9 holes, 5822 yards, S.S.S.70
Founded 1920
Visitors: welcome; no Sun golf.
Green Fee: apply for details.
Societies: by arrangement.
Catering: available at Lodge Hotel.
Hotels: Lodge Hotel (19th).

Q144 West Kilbride
☎(0294) 823911
33-35 Fullerton Drive, Seamill, W Kilbride, Ayrshire KA23 9HS

On A78 Ardrossan to Largs road at Seamill.
Seaside/links course.
18 holes, 6452 yards, S.S.S.71
Designed by Tom Morris.
Founded 1893
Visitors: welcome weekdays with introduction; not Bank Holidays or weekends.
Green Fee: on application.
Societies: Tues and Thurs.
Catering: bar and lunches, high teas and dinners.
Hotels: Seamill Hydro; Hospitality Inn.

Q145 Western Gailes
☎(0294) 311649
Gailes, Irvine, Ayrshire KA11 5AE
5 miles N of Troon on A78.
Links course.
18 holes, 6664 yards, S.S.S.72
Founded 1897
Visitors: welcome Mon, Tues, Wed and Fri (no Lady visitors on Tues); advisable to book in advance.
Green Fee: £38/round, £50/day.
Societies: welcome by arrangement Mon, Tues, Wed, Fri.
Catering: lunches, snacks and high teas available.

Q146 Westerwood Hotel Golf & Country Club
☎(0236) 457171, 452772 Tee-off times, 738478 Fax
St Andrews Drive, Cumbernauld, G68 0EW
Signposted off A80 13 miles from Glasgow.
Parkland course.
18 holes, 6721 yards, S.S.S.73.
Designed by Seve Ballasteros and Dave Thomas.
Founded May 1989
Visitors: welcome, no restrictions.
Green Fee: £22.50/round, £35/day WD; £27.50/round, £45/day WE.
Societies: by prior arrangement.
Catering: lunch, dinner and bar snacks available in clubhouse.
Indoor golf facility, driving range, putting green, bowls, tennis, croquet, boules, swimming, jacuzzi, gym etc.

Hotels: 49 bed hotel with business and conference facilities. Reduced green fees for residents; golfing packages available.

Q147 Whinhill
☎(0475) 21064
Beith Road, Greenock, Renfrewshire, Strathclyde
Just outside Greenock on old Largs road.
Municipal parkland course.
18 holes, 5434 yards, S.S.S.68
Visitors: welcome.
Green Fee: apply for details.
Catering: small clubhouse for members only. Putting green.

Q148 Whitecraigs
☎(041) 639 4530
72 Ayr Rd, Giffnock, Glasgow G46 6SW
7 miles S of Glasgow on A77.
Parkland course.
18 holes, 6230 yards, S.S.S.70
Founded 1905
Visitors: by introduction only.
Green Fee: apply for details.
Societies: Wed only.
Catering: lunches except Mon.
Hotels: Macdonald.

Q149 Whiting Bay
☎(0770) 700487
Golf Course Rd, Whiting Bay, Isle of Arran, Strathclyde
8 miles S of Brodick.
Heathland and hilly, levelling out from 4th.
18 holes, 4405 yards, S.S.S.66
Founded 1895
Visitors: welcome, no restrictions.
Green Fee: £6/day.
Societies: on application to Sec.
Catering: bar and catering from Easter to end Oct. Snooker, pool.
Hotels: Cameronia; Grange House; Kiscadale; Viewbank; Royal.

Q150 Williamwood
☎(041) 637 1783
Clarkston Rd, Netherlee, Glasgow G44

5 miles S of Glasgow.
Wooded parkland course.
18 holes, 5808 yards, S.S.S.68
Designed by James Braid.
Founded 1906
Visitors: by introduction only.
Green Fee: on application.
Societies: weekdays by arrangement.
Catering: lunch and evening meals.
Hotels: MacDonald (Giffnock); Redhurst (Clarkston).

Q151 Windyhill
☎(041) 942 7157 Pro shop, 942 2349 Clubhouse
Baljaffray Rd, Bearsden, Glasgow G61 4QQ
A739 from Glasgow, after 8 miles turn right onto A809, after 1 mile turn left onto A810, club 1 mile on right.
Undulating moorland course.
18 holes, 6254 yards, S.S.S.70
Designed by James Braid.
Founded 1908
Visitors: welcome on weekdays; weekends only with member.
Green Fee: day ticket £15.
Societies: only by prior arrangement with Sec.
Catering: full catering facilities except Tues.
Hotels: Burnbrae; Black Bull (Milngavie).

Q152 Wishaw
☎(0698) 372869 Sec/bookings, 358270 Pro
55 Cleland Rd, Wishaw, Lanarkshire ML2 7PH
15 miles SW of Glasgow, 5 miles from M74 (Motherwell Junction).
Parkland course.
18 holes, 6167 yards, S.S.S.69
Designed by James Braid.
Founded 1897
Visitors: welcome weekdays before 4pm; no visitors on Sat.
Green Fee: £12/round, £20/day; £25 Sun.
Societies: welcome weekdays, Sun by arrangement; not Sat.
Catering: lunches, bar snacks, high tea, dinner until 9pm.
Hotels: Wishaw Town.

R
TAYSIDE, CENTRAL REGION, FIFE

St Andrews, Carnoustie, Gleneagles and Blairgowrie — a vivid cross section of the many varied attractions that bring golfers by the thousand every year. Fife itself, quite apart from St Andrews, is as full of good things as a Christmas hamper, the magic carpet ride concentrating on the coastal sweep round past Kirkcaldy to the point near the lovely Balcomie links at Crail and then on still further to the shores of St Andrews Bay.

Burntisland and Kinghorn are the first of note although Leven and Lundin Links start the historians dipping into the archives to remind the modern golfer that he is on hallowed ground. The low boundary fence shared by the two Clubs reflects the days when Leven extended as far as the present clubhouse at Lundin. Later, it found spare land nearer home to the north of the old railway thus allowing Lundin to come into being in 1857.

Now, the railway has ceased to function but the line of the track remains a feature of both courses, a little more forbidding perhaps at Lundin. Scenic landmarks are Largo Bay and the opposite shore of East Lothian but the best view of that is from the 10th green of the Golf House Club, Elie, a course in the best holiday traditions and a notable favourite.

There are good practice facilities at Elie Sports Club where children are welcome, but St Andrews now has a permanent driving range as an accompaniment to the new Strathtyrum and revised Balgove courses. Meanwhile the updated versions of Jubilee and Eden help divert the demands on the Old and New, but before focusing attention on the other side of the Tay, mention must be made of Scotscraig and Ladybank.

Downfield, home of championships, is the finest of the courses in the immediate vicinity of Dundee but, by now, sights are set on Carnoustie, although not at the cost of by-passing Monifieth or Panmure at Barry, which overlap on either side of the Aberdeen railway line.

Carnoustie's absence from the Open championship rota since 1975, the year of Tom Watson's first victory, is no sign of declining powers. Very much the opposite. It housed the Amateur championship in 1992 and remains as formidable a challenge as any. And a word for Montrose, which hosted the 1991 British Boys championship, and for Letham Grange near Arbroath. Letham Grange, a relative newcomer, is a worthy addition to a famous area, a soothing contrast to the links lining its coastline.

For overseas visitors who tend to prefer inland golf, Gleneagles is still an automatic favourite, with its new Jack Nicklaus creation, called the Monarch. Almost as popular is Blairgowrie at Rosemount in a setting that is almost as glorious.

King James VI, an island retreat in the centre of the River Tay in the middle of Perth, is a must for romantics and historians while Glenbervie between Falkirk and Stirling is a regular staging post for important events.

Further afield, the charms of Central Region are epitomised by Buchanan Castle, Callander, Crieff, Dalmunzie, Alyth, Taymouth Castle and Edzell, a gentle way of breaking travellers in to the beautiful, rugged highland country to the north.

R1 Aberdour
☎(0383) 860256, 860080 Sec, 860688 Clubmaster
Seaside Place, Aberdour, Fife KY3 0TX
Right off A921 in Aberdour village travelling from Inverkeithing; by coast route to Burntisland.
Parkland/seaside course with extensive views over River Forth.
18 holes, 5460 yards, S.S.S.67
Designed by Peter Robertson & Joe Anderson.
Founded 1896
Visitors: welcome weekdays; casual visitors phone Pro for tee reservation.
Green Fee: £17/round, £28/day WD.
Societies: visiting clubs by prior booking with Sec, except Sat.
Catering: by arrangement with Clubmaster.
Hotels: Woodside.

R2 Aberfeldy
☎(0887) 820535
Taybridge Rd, Aberfeldy, Perthshire PH15 2BH
10 miles off A9 at Ballinluig.
Parkland course.
9 holes, 2733 yards, S.S.S.67
Designed by Kirkcaldy.
Founded 1895
Visitors: welcome.
Green Fee: on application.
Societies: small society meetings can be arranged.
Catering: snacks available.
Hotels: Weem; Crown; Guinach; Breadalbane; Ailean Chraggan; Station; Balnearn.

R3 Aberfoyle
☎(08772) 382493
Braeval, Aberfoyle, Stirling FK8 3RL
1 mile from Aberfoyle on A81 Stirling road.
Heathland course.
18 holes, 5204 yards, S.S.S.66
Designed by James Braid.
Founded 1890
Visitors: limited at weekends.
Green Fee: £12 WD, £16 WE.
Societies: welcome by arrangement.
Catering: full facilities.

R4 Alloa
☎(0259) 722745
Schawpark, Sauchie, Clackmannanshire FK10 3AX
On A908 1 mile N of Alloa; 8 miles E of Stirling.
Undulating parkland course.
18 holes, 6230 yards, S.S.S.70
Designed by James Braid.
Founded 1891
Visitors: welcome.
Green Fee: £12/round, £20/day WD; £24 WE.
Societies: weekdays only.
Catering: full facilities.
Snooker.
Hotels: Bruce; Royal Oak; Dunmar House; Claremont Lodge.

R5 Alva
☎(0259) 60431
Beauclerc St, Alva, Clackmannanshire FK12 5LE
On A91 Stirling-St Andrews road, 7 miles from Stirling.
Undulating course at foot of Ochil Hills.
9 holes, 2423 yards, S.S.S.64
Founded 1900
Visitors: welcome.
Green Fee: on application.
Catering: bar snacks.
Pool table.
Hotels: Alva Glen; Johnstone Arms.

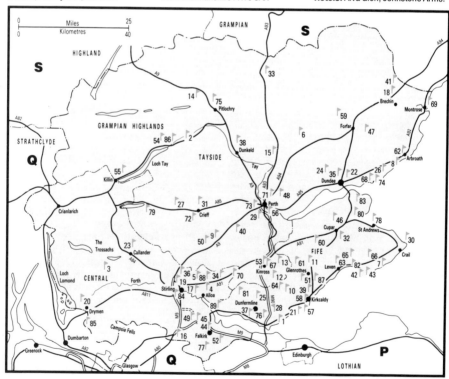

R6 Alyth
☎(08283) 2268 Sec and Steward, 2411 Starter/Pro
Pitcrocknie, Alyth, Perthshire PH11 8JJ
On B954 Alyth to Glenisla road about 0.5 mile from major roundabout on A926 Blairgowrie-Kirriemuir road. Heathland course.
18 holes, 6226 yards, S.S.S.70
Designed by James Braid.
Founded 1894
Visitors: welcome.
Green Fee: on application.
Societies: welcome by arrangement with Sec.
Catering: full catering facilities available.
Hotels: Alyth; Lands of Loyal; Losset Inn.

R7 Anstruther
☎(0333) 310956 Clubhouse, (0333) 312283 Sec
Marsfield, Shore Rd, Anstruther, Fife KY10 3DZ
Turn right off main road at Craw's Nest Hotel.
Seaside course.

9 holes, 4144 yards, S.S.S.63
Founded 1890
Visitors: welcome except on competition days.
Green Fee: £11/day WD, £15/day WE.
Societies: by arrangement.
Catering: snacks and lunches served.
Hotels: Craw's Nest; Royal; Smugglers Inn.

R8 Arbroath
☎(0241) 75837 Pro, 72069 Clubhouse
Elliot, Arbroath, Angus DD11 2PE
On A92, 1 mile S of Arbroath.
Public seaside links course.
18 holes, 6090 yards, S.S.S.69
Designed by James Braid.
Founded 1905
Visitors: unrestricted but should be a member of a golf club; not weekends am.
Green Fee: £10/round, £16/day WD; £15/round, £24/day WE.
Societies: by arrangement.
Catering: full bar and catering.
Hotels: North Sea; Hotel Seaforth.

R9 Auchterarder
☎(0764) 662804, 663711 Pro shop
Orchil Rd, Auchterarder, Perthshire PH3 1LS
On A9 between Stirling and Perth. Woodland and heathland course.
18 holes, 5778 yards, S.S.S.68
Designed by Bernard Sayers.
Founded 1892
Visitors: welcome but advisable to pre-book; phone Pro shop 1 week ahead.
Green Fee: £14/round, £20/day WD; £21/round WE; £28/day Sat, £30/day Sun.
Societies: must be booked by letter to secretary.
Catering: full catering and bar facilities.
Hotels: Golf Inn; Morven; Cairn Lodge (adjoining course).

R10 Auchterderran
☎(0592) 721579 Clubhouse; (0592) 720457 Sec
Woodend Rd, Cardenden, Fife KY5 0NH
On main Lochgelly to Glenrothes road at N end of Cardenden.

Public parkland course.
9 holes, 5250 yards, S.S.S.66
Founded 1904
Visitors: welcome.
Green Fee: apply for details.
Societies: welcome by advance booking.
Catering: bar facilities available.
Hotels: Bowhill; Central.

R11 Balbirnie Park
☎(0592) 752006
Balbirnie Park, Markinch,
Glenrothes, Fife KY7 6DD
2 miles E of Glenrothes.
Scenic parkland course.
18 holes, 6210 yards, S.S.S.70
Founded 1983
Visitors: unrestricted, but advisable to book beforehand.
Green Fee: £18/round, £25/day WD; £26/round, £32/day WE.
Societies: welcome.
Catering: coffee, lunches, snacks, high teas; dinners by arrangement.

R12 Ballingry
☎(0592) 860086
Lochore Meadows Country Park,
Crosshill, Ballingry, Fife KY5 8BA
Between Lochgelly and Ballingry, W of M90.
Public parkland course.
9 holes, 6488 yards, S.S.S.71
Founded 1981
Visitors: welcome.
Green Fee: apply for details.
Societies: welcome by arrangement.
Catering: cafeteria.
Angling, wind-surfing, pony trekking.

R13 Bishopshire
☎(0592) 780203
Kinnesswood by Kinross, Tayside, Scotland
3 miles E of Kinross off M90.
Upland course.
10 holes, 4700 yards, S.S.S.64
Designed by W. Park.
Founded 1903
Visitors: welcome, no restrictions.
Green Fee: £5 WD, £6 WE.
Societies: by arrangement.
Catering: by arrangement.
Hotels: Lomond; Scotlandwell Inn.

R14 Blair Atholl
☎(0796) 481407
Blair Atholl, Perthshire PH18 5TG.
On A9 5 miles N of Pitlochry.
Parkland course.
9 holes, 5710 yards, S.S.S.69

Founded 1896.
Visitors: welcome.
Green Fee: £10/day WD, £12/day WE.
Societies: bookings only.
Catering: bar snacks and meals.
Hotels: Atholl Arms; Tilt.

R15 Blairgowrie
☎(0250) 872594, 872622
Rosemount, Blairgowrie, Perthshire
PH10 6LG
A93 from Perth.
Moorland course.
Rosemount, 18 holes, 6588 yards,
S.S.S.72; Lansdowne, 18 holes,
6895 yards, S.S.S.73; Wee, 9 holes,
2307 yards, S.S.S.32.5
Designed by James Braid,
Thomas/Alliss, Peter Chalmers.
Founded 1889
Visitors: advance booking Mon,
Tues, Thur; through starter Wed, Sat,
Sun; no parties Wed, Sat, Sun.
Green Fee: £32/round, £45/day; WE £34/round.
Societies: Mon, Tue, Thur; book through (0250) 872622.
Catering: full facilities.
Hotels: Kinloch House; Rosemount Golf; Altamount House.

R16 Bonnybridge
☎(0324) 812645
Larbert Rd, Bonnybridge,
Stirlingshire FK4 1NY
On B816, 3 miles W of Falkirk.
Undulating moorland course.
9 holes, 6060 yards, s.S.S.69
Founded 1925
Visitors: welcome with member only.
Green Fee: apply for details.
Catering: meals served, limited in winter.

R17 Braehead
☎(0259) 722078
Cambus, by Alloa
On A907 on Stirling-Alloa road, about
1.5 miles W of Alloa.
Parkland course.
18 holes, 6013 yards, S.S.S.69
Founded 1891
Visitors: welcome unrestricted, advised to phone for start time.
Green Fee: £12/round, £18/day WD;
£18/round, £24/day WE.
Societies: welcome 7 days; prior booking required in writing.
Catering: April-Oct, lunch, high tea 7 days. Practice area.
Hotels: Royal Oak; Dunmar House.

R18 Brechin
☎(0356) 622326
Trinity, by Brechin, Angus DD9 7PD
Take B966 out of Brechin toward
Aberdeen, course is 1 mile from
Brechin and is clearly signposted.
Parkland/meadowland course.
18 holes, 6200 yards, S.S.S.69
Designed by James Braid.
Founded 1893
Visitors: welcome at any time;
parties welcome by prior
arrangement; restricted on Weds
(Ladies Day).
Green Fee: £11/round, £16/day WD;
£15/round, £26/day WE.
Societies: always welcome, parties
over 8 must book through Sec.
Catering: full catering and lounge
bar refreshments.
Squash.
Hotels: Northern (Brechin); Glenesk,
Panmure, Central (Edzell).

R19 Bridge of Allan
☎(0786) 832332
Sunnlaw, Bridge of Allan, Stirling
3 miles N of Stirling, at bridge over
River Allan turn up hill to course for 1 mile.
Undulating course.
9 holes, 4932 yards, S.S.S.65
Founded 1895
Visitors: welcome weekdays and Sun.
Green Fee: apply for details.
Catering: bar snacks at weekends
and after 7.30pm weekdays.
Hotels: Royal.

R20 Buchanan Castle
☎(0360) 60369 Clubmaster, 60330 Pro
Drymen, Glasgow
Off A809, 17 miles NW of Glasgow.
Parkland course.
18 holes, 6086 yards, S.S.S.69
Designed by James Braid.
Founded 1936
Visitors: by arrangement (limited).
Green Fee: £25/round, £35/day.
Societies: by arrangement with Sec
(0360) 60307.
Catering: by arrangement with
Clubmaster.
Hotels: Buchanan Highland.

R21 Burntisland
☎(0592) 874093 Manager, 873247
Starter and Pro.
Dodhead, Burntisland, Fife KY3 9EY
On B923, 0.5 mile E of Burntisland.
Parkland course.

Buchanan Castle

Scotland's celebrated reputation for the variety and quality of its golf courses is centred very largely around its coastline. Apart from Gleneagles, Blairgowrie and, more recently, Loch Lomond, there are few hidden jewels in its central heartland but the joy of exploring fresh territory lies in the pleasant surprises it brings forth.

The name of Buchanan Castle had been familiar to me for years. In the heyday of Eric Brown, the Club and his association with it was mentioned every time he played. Going back further, the connection of John M. Bannerman was even better known as the factor for the Estate of the Dukes of Montrose who allowed the course, designed by James Braid, to be opened in 1936.

Bannerman who, for a long time, held the record for the most number of Scottish rugby caps, was later Lord Bannerman after standing for Parliament as a Liberal. However, it was his influence which helped Buchanan Castle to flourish amid the scenic glories of the Trossachs, which receive thousands of visitors each year. For most, there is little thought of golf but it is a convenient port of call to those heading north and one that would grace the most distinguished itinerary. It can be an easy run from Glasgow Airport by way of the Erskine Bridge.

Its charms are gentler than the championship links, its overall length, in fact, being modest by modern standards. Its character is that of a peaceful parkland with an air of antiquity lent by some handsome trees and the Castle that is reminiscent of Brancepeth in Durham.

For those with a lively imagination, there is the belief that the course might be in the grounds of your country home. This complies with the feeling of intimacy, but it would be wrong to suggest that it is devoid of demand or challenge. It requires thought and decision as well as the shotmaking ability and control

to avoid the snares that line its path.

The 1st is a case in point, the opening drive having to negotiate the giant tree that forms the right angled dogleg. Confidence is not always an abundant commodity on the first tee and it is easy to play too safe, leaving the green out of reach although there is no respite on the 2nd and 3rd which are similarly testing par 4s, the 3rd with a stream crossing the fairway.

It is a course of fast flowing brooks, attractive bridges and strategic trees or copses, the stream on the 3rd reappearing to tease on the drive and pitch 5th which follows the first of the short holes. A drive that tempts you to cut the corner is the best feature of the par 5 6th which is a little dull near the green. However, the scene is quickly transformed on the 7th which is a classic dogleg round a majestic wood, only the most solid drive bringing the green into view or range. Fours are greatly to be prized.

Good judgement and a sound nerve are requirements of the short 8th where the tee shot is over water, and then follow two more attractive fours, the 9th curving right.

The 12th returns close to the clubhouse, leaving a finishing loop of six holes that offer variety, and opportunity as well as a capacity to come to grief. Length is supplied by the 13th and 14th but there is considerably less freedom on the 15th where the gap between trees on either side of the tee can seem alarmingly narrow.

There is a rural tinge to the setting of the green but the 16th, which turns about, is an excellent short hole while the 17th and 18th maintain the need for strong hitting. Nevertheless, there is nothing too daunting on a course so eminently suitable for the vast legions of golfers whose enjoyment is so often eroded elsewhere by an impression of mission impossible.

18 holes, S.S.S.69
Designed (and redesigned) by James
Braid.
Founded 1897
Visitors: welcome; contact Manager
for starting times; £5 per head
deposit on application.
Green Fee: on application.
Societies: snacks and meals served.
Catering: morning coffee, lunch, bar
lunch, high tea, dinner.
Hotels: Inchview; Kingswood.

R22 Caird Park
☎(0382) 453606
Mains Loan, Dundee, Tayside DD4
9BX
Via Kingsway to NE of town.
Municipal parkland course.
18 holes, 6303 yards, S.S.S.70
Founded 1926
Visitors: welcome.
Green Fee: on application.
Societies: book via Dundee District
Council.
Catering: by arrangement with club;
bar and spacious lounge.

R23 Callander
☎(0877) 330090 Clubhouse/Sec
Aveland Rd, Callander, Perthshire
FK17 8EN
A84 from Stirling, turn right at Roman
Camp Hotel about 0.5 mile from Main
St, car park and clubhouse
signposted.
Parkland course.
18 holes, 5125 yards, S.S.S.66
Designed by Tom Morris.
Founded 1890
Visitors: welcome any time.
Green Fee: £14/round, £18/day WD;
£18/round, £22/day WE; jnrs (under
18) half price.
Societies: welcome any time,
contact Sec.
Catering: full catering every day, bar
open all day.
Hotels: Abbotsford Lodge; Roman
Camp; Dalgair House; The Coppice.

R24 Camperdown Municipal
☎(0382) 623398; (0382) 23141
Bookings
Camperdown Park, Dundee, Tayside
Coupar-Angus road, at Kingsway
junction.
Championship parkland course.
18 holes, 6305 yards, S.S.S.72
Designed by Eric Brown.
Founded 1959
Visitors: bookings only.

Green Fee: apply for details.
Societies: by arrangement.
Catering: bar facilities in clubhouse.
Tennis.
Hotels: Swallow.

R25 Canmore
☎(0383) 724969
Venturefair Ave, Dunfermline, Fife
On A823, 1 mile N of Dunfermline.
Undulating parkland course.
18 holes, 5474 yards, S.S.S.66
Founded 1897
Visitors: welcome weekdays, Sat
after 4pm.
Green Fee: apply for details.
Societies: welcome by prior
arrangement.
Catering: full catering.

R26 Carnoustie Golf Links
☎(0241) 53789 Reservations,
53249 Starter, 52720 Fax
Links Parade, Carnoustie, Angus
DD7 7JE
On A630, 12 miles E of Dundee.
Seaside course.
Championship, 18 holes, 6936
yards, S.S.S.74; Burnside, 18 holes,
6020 yards, S.S.S.69; Buddon Links,
18 holes, 5420 yards, S.S.S.66
Visitors: welcome with reservation,
deposit required; h/cap certs
required on Championship Course.
Green Fee: Championship,
£36/round, £63/day; Burnside,
£14/round, £21/day; Buddon Links,
£10/round, £15/day; jnrs half-price;
combination, 3-day and weekly
tickets available.
Societies: welcome by prior
arrangement.
Catering: available.
Hotels: Glencoe; Station; Kinloch;
Carlogie.

R27 Comrie
☎(0764) 670055 Clubhouse.
c/o Sec, Donald C. McGlashan, 10
Polinard, Comrie, Perthshire PH6 2HJ
On A85 6 miles W of Crieff.
Highland course.
9 holes, 5962 yards, S.S.S.69
Founded 1891
Visitors: welcome; tee reserved
from 4.30pm Mon/Tues and 4.30pm
to 6.30pm Fri.
Green Fee: £10 WD & WE.
Societies: by arrangement with Sec,
numbers restricted to 20.
Catering: coffee, light snacks during
summer season.
Hotels: Comrie; Royal; Mossgeil GH.

R28 Cowdenbeath
☎(0383) 511918
Seco Place, Cowdenbeath, Nr
Dunfermline, Fife KY4 8JPA
6 miles E of Dunfermline.
Municipal parkland course.
9 holes, 6552 yards, S.S.S.71
Founded 1990
Visitors: welcome, no restrictions.
Green Fee: £8/day.
Societies: welcome, phone in
advance.
Catering: licensed bar, light snacks.
Practice area.

R29 Craigie Hill
☎(0738) 20829 Sec, 22644 Pro,
24377 Clubhouse
Cherrybank, Perth PH2 0NE
About 1 mile W of Perth, easy access
from A9 and M90.
Hilly course.
18 holes, 5386 yards, S.S.S.66
Designed by W. Fernie and J.
Anderson.
Founded 1909
Visitors: Mon to Fri unlimited;
weekends telephone bookings.
Green Fee: on application.
Societies: available weekdays and
Sun.
Catering: full except Mon and Tues.

R30 Crail
☎(0333) 50278 Clubhouse, 50686
Sec, 50960 Pro.
Balcomie Clubhouse, Fifeness, Crail
KY10 3XN
11 miles SE of St Andrews on A917.
Seaside links/parkland course.
18 holes, 5720 yards, S.S.S.68
Designed by Tom Morris.
Founded 1786
Visitors: welcomed, restrictions only
on main competition days and
members priority times.
Green Fee: £17/round, £25/day WD;
£22/round, £33/day WE.
Societies: entertained as for visitors.
Catering: full service of quality
catering.
Hotels: Balcomie Links; Golf; Croma;
Marine (Crail); Craw's Nest,
(Anstruther).

R31 Crieff
☎(0764) 652909 Bookings, 652397
Office/Catering/Sec
Perth Rd, Crieff, Perthshire PH7 3LR
From Edinburgh M9 to Dunblane;
from Glasgow A80/M80/M9 to
Dunblane then A9 for 5km and A822
to Crieff; take A85 at town centre for

1km, course on left; from Perth A85, course at entry to Crieff on right. Parkland course.
Ferntower, 18 holes, 6402 yards, S.S.S.71; Dornock, 9 holes, 2386 yards, S.S.S.63
Founded 1891
Visitors: welcome, advance booking advisable, must book for weekends.
Green Fee: Ferntower, £16/round, £27/day WD, £20/round WE: Dornock, £11 (18 holes) WD, £13 WE.
Societies: welcome but must book well in advance.
Catering: full restaurant facilities, advisable to book; bar meals also available.
Hotels: Crieff Hydro; Murray Park; Arduthie.

R32 Cupar
☎(0334) 53549
Hilltarvit, Cupar
10 miles from St Andrews off A91.
Hillside/parkland course.
9 holes, 5074 yards, S.S.S.65
Founded 1855
Visitors: welcome weekdays.
Green Fee: £10/day WD, £12/day WE.
Societies: weekdays and Sun.
Catering: lunches and high teas by arrangement.

R33 Dalmunzie
☎(025 085) 226
Spittal of Glenshee, Blairgowrie, Perthshire PH10 7QG
On A93 Blairgowrie-Braemar road, 18 miles N of Blairgowrie, adjacent to Dalmunzie Hotel.
Undulating course.
9 holes, 2035 yards, S.S.S.60
Designed by Alister Mackenzie.
Founded 1922
Visitors: welcome any day.
Green Fee: apply for details.
Societies: please book, all welcome.
Catering: facilities in hotel.
Hotels: Dalmunzie House.

R34 Dollar
☎(0259) 42400
Brewlands House, Dollar, Clackmannanshire
On A91, 13 miles E of Stirling.
Hillside course.
18 holes, 5144 yards, S.S.S.66
Founded 1890
Visitors: welcome.
Green Fee: £7/round, £11/day WD; £15/day WE.

Societies: by arrangement.
Catering: meals served daily except Tues.
Hotels: Strathallan.

R35 Downfield
☎(0382) 825595 Office, 89246 Pro, 813111 Fax
Turnberry Ave, Dundee DD2 3QP
Turn off Kingsway (signposted A923 Coupar Angus), right at mini roundabout into Faraday St (signposted Clatto Country Park), 100 yards turn left into Harrison Rd, at T-junction turn left into Dalmahoy Drive, 0.5 mile to clubhouse.
Parkland course.
18 holes, 6899 yards, S.S.S.73
Designed by C.K. Cotton.
Founded 1932
Visitors: weekdays 9.30-11.48am and 2.18-3.48pm; weekends call Pro on day of play.
Green Fee: £24/round, £36/day.
Societies: as for visitors Mon-Fri, Sun 2-3pm must be pre-booked through Sec.
Catering: full catering and bar facilities.
Snooker, extensive practice area.
Hotels: Stakis Earl Grey; Swallow; Angus Thistle.

R36 Dunblane New
☎(0786) 823711
Perth Rd, Dunblane FK15 0LJ
On old A9 at Fourways roundabout, 6 miles N of Stirling.
Parkland course.
18 holes, 5863 yards, S.S.S.68
Founded 1923
Visitors: Mon-Fri, advisable to pre-book with Pro.
Green Fee: £16/round, £23/day.
Societies: Mon and Thurs only.
Catering: full bar and restaurant facilities.
Tennis and squash adjacent.
Hotels: Dunblane Hydro; Stirling Arms.

R37 Dunfermline
☎(0383) 723534
Pitfirrane, Crossford, Dunfermline KY12 8QV
2 miles W of Dunfermline on road to Kincardine Bridge, A994, on S side of main road between Crossford and Cairney Hill.
Parkland course.
18 holes, 6237 yards, S.S.S.70; Short 9 hole Par 3 course
Designed by J.R. Stutt & Sons.

Founded 1887 (course 1952)
Visitors: Mon to Fri before 5pm subject to availability.
Green Fee: £25/day, £18/round.
Societies: Mon-Fri by arrangement.
Catering: bar and restaurant, not Mon unless previous notice.
Snooker.
Hotels: Keavil; Pitfirran Arms; The Maltings.

R38 Dunkeld & Birnam
☎(0350) 727524, 727564 Sec
Fungarth, Dunkeld, Perthshire PH8 0HY
1 mile N of Dunkeld on A923 Blairgowrie road.
Heathland course.
9 holes, 5240 yards, S.S.S.66
Founded 1892
Visitors: welcome.
Green Fee: on application.
Societies: catered for.
Catering: full facilities.

R39 Dunnikier Park
☎(0592) 261599, 205916 Pro, 200627 Sec/booking
Dunnikier Way, Kirkcaldy, Fife KY1 3LP
N boundary of town.
Parkland course.
18 holes, 6601 yards, S.S.S.72
Founded 1963
Visitors: no restrictions.
Green Fee: £9/round WD, £11/round WE.
Societies: on application to Sec.
Catering: full catering facilities.
Hotels: Dunnikier House.

R40 Dunning
☎(0764) 684747
Rollo Park, Dunning, Perth
Off A9, 9 miles SW of Perth.
Parkland course.
9 holes, 4836 yards, S.S.S.64
Visitors: welcome.
Green Fee: £8/day (£4 jnrs), £30/week.
Societies: by application to Sec, Mr J. Slater, Kirkgate House, Tron Square, Dunning, Perth PH2 0RG.
Catering: tea, coffee, soft drinks available in clubhouse; meals and refreshments in village.

R41 Edzell
☎(0356) 648235 Clubhouse, 647283 Sec, 648094 Fax
High St, Edzell, by Brechin, Angus DD9 7TF

Take A94 N from Forfar and turn left at N end of Brechin by-pass onto B966.
Moorland/parkland course.
18 holes, 6348 yards, S.S.S.70
Designed by Bob Simpson.
Founded 1895
Visitors: weekdays excluding 4.45-6.15pm, weekends 7.30-10am and 12am-2pm.
Green Fee: £16.50/round, £24/day WD; £22/round, £33/day WE.
Societies: by arrangement with Sec.
Catering: bar 11am-11pm, light refreshments 9am-9pm, restaurant 12am-9pm in season.
Hotels: Glenesk; Central; Panmure Arms.

R42 **Elie**
☎(0333) 330301 Sec, 330327 Clubhouse
Golf House Club, Elie, Leven, Fife KY9 1AS
12 miles from St Andrews on A915, 6 miles from Leven on A917.
Seaside links course.
18 holes, 6241 yards, S.S.S.70
Founded 1875
Visitors: welcome.
Green Fee: £22/round, £30/day WD; £33/round, £42/day WE.
Societies: by arrangement with Sec; not June, July, Aug, public holidays or weekends.
Catering: lunches, soups, sandwiches, high teas by arrangement with Steward.
Hotels: Craw's Nest; Old Manor; Golf.

R43 **Elie Sports Club**
☎(0333) 330955 Pro, (0334) 870907 Sec
Elie, Fife KY9 1AG
10 miles S of St Andrews on A917.
Seaside course.
9 holes, 5800 yards, S.S.S.64
Visitors: welcome.
Green Fee: on application.
Societies: by arrangement.
Catering: meals served April-Oct.
Driving range, tennis, bowling, putting green.
Hotels: Golf; Victoria; Elms GH.

R44 **Falkirk**
☎(0324) 611061, 612219
136 Stirling Rd, Falkirk FK2 7YP
1.5 miles W of Falkirk centre on A9.
Parkland course.
18 holes, 6282 yards, S.S.S.69
Designed by James Braid.

Founded 1922
Visitors: weekdays to 4pm; not Sat; Sun by arrangement.
Green Fee: £12/round, £20/day; £25/round, £30/day Sun.
Societies: not Wed or Sat.
Catering: full facilities.
Hotels: Stakis Park; Red Lion.

R45 **Falkirk Tryst**
☎(0324) 562415
86 Burnhead Rd, Larbert FK5 4BD
3 miles NW of Falkirk on outskirts of Stenhousemuir, close to A9, 0.75 mile from Larbert Station.
Flat links course.
18 holes, 6053 yards, S.S.S.69
Founded 1885
Visitors: no unintroduced visitors Sat or Sun.
Green Fee: £12/round, £17/day.
Societies: Mon-Fri only.
Catering: full facilities.
Hotels: Red Lion; Commercial; Park.

R46 **Falkland**
☎(0337) 57404
The Myre, Falkland, Cupar, Fife KY7 7AA
In The Howe of Fife near to villages of Freuchie and Auchtermuchty.
Parkland course.
9 holes, 5216 yards, S.S.S.65
Founded 1976
Visitors: all welcome.
Green Fee: apply for details.
Societies: by prior arrangement.
Catering: morning coffee, lunch, high tea available by arrangement; bar lunchtime and summer evenings and weekends; restricted in winter.

R47 **Forfar**
☎(0307) 62120
Cunninghill, Arbroath Rd, by Forfar, Angus DD8 2RL
1 mile from town on road to Arbroath.
Undulating moorland course.
18 holes, 6012 yards, S.S.S.69
Designed by James Braid.
Founded 1871
Visitors: welcome.
Green Fee: £15/round, £20/day WD; £25 Sun.
Societies: welcome by arrangement with Sec.
Catering: meals served.
Hotels: Royal; James House.

R48 **Glenalmond**
☎(073 888) 270
Glenalmond, Perthshire, Tayside

Moorland course.
9 holes, 2900 yards, S.S.S.68
Founded 1923
Visitors: members only.
Green Fee: apply for details.

R49 **Glenbervie**
☎(0324) 562605 Sec, 562725 Pro
Stirling Rd, Larbert, Stirlingshire FK5 4SJ
On A9 between Falkirk and Stirling.
Parkland course.
18 holes, 6469 yards, S.S.S.71
Designed by James Braid.
Founded 1932
Visitors: no visitors at weekends.
Green Fee: on application.
Societies: Tues and Thurs.
Catering: lunches, high teas, dinner.
Hotels: Park (Falkirk).

R50 **Gleneagles Hotel**
☎(0764) 663543, 662231, 662134 Fax
Auchterarder, Perthshire PH3 1NF
Half-way between Perth and Stirling on A9.
Undulating moorland courses.
Kings, 18 holes, 6471 yards, S.S.S.71; Queens, 18 holes, 5965 yards, S.S.S.69; Monarchs, 18 holes, 7081 yards, S.S.S.72
Kings and Queens courses designed by James Braid.
Founded 1908
Visitors: restricted to members and hotel residents.
Green Fee: £50/round.
Societies: welcome if resident.
Catering: meals and snacks available; 4 restaurants and bars.
9 hole Par 3 course; Country Club; health spa; clay target shooting school; equestrian centre.
Hotels: Gleneagles.

R51 **Glenrothes**
☎(0592) 754561, 756941
Golf Course Rd, Glenrothes, Fife KY6 2LA
W end of town 8 miles from M90 junction 3, A92.
Public, undulating parkland course.
18 holes, 6449 yards, S.S.S.71
Designed by J.R. Stutt.
Founded 1958
Visitors: no restrictions except parties of 12 and more to book in advance through Sec.
Green Fee: £8.50/round WD, £10/round WE.
Societies: by arrangement with Sec 1 month in advance, min 12 max 40.

Catering: all types of catering available 7 days.
Hotels: Forum; Stakis Albany; Rescobie; Balgedie; Balbirnie.

R52 Grangemouth

☎(0324) 711500
Polmonthill, Polmont, Stirlingshire FK2 0YA
M9 junction 4, follow signpost to Polmont Hill.
Public parkland course.
18 holes, 6,330 yards, S.S.S.71
Designed by Sportwork.
Founded 1973
Visitors: welcome.
Green Fee: apply for details.
Societies: by arrangement.
Catering: meals by arrangement.
Hotels: Inchrya Grange; Lea Park.

R53 Green Hotel

☎(0577) 863467 Hotel, 863407
Bookings, 865125 Pro shop
Green Hotel, Kinross KY13 7AS
0.5 mile from M90 junction 6
(Kinross), 27 miles from Edinburgh and 16 miles from Perth; opposite Green Hotel in centre of Kinross.
Parkland course.
Red, 18 holes, 6257 yards, S.S.S.70;
Blue, 18 holes, 6456 yards, S.S.S.71
Founded 1970/1991
Visitors: welcome, booking advised.
Green Fee: £14/round, £20/day WD; £20/round, £30/day WE; reductions for jnrs and Hotel residents.
Societies: by arrangement.
Catering: meals served in Hotel and Clubhouse by arrangement.
Swimming, squash, sauna, tennis at Green Hotel.
Hotels: Green Hotel, 200 yards from course.

R54 Kenmore Golf Course

☎(0887) 830226, 830211 Fax
Kenmore, Aberfeldy, Perthshire PH15 2HN
W off A9 at Ballinluig to Aberfeldy; 6 miles past Aberfeldy on A827 through village of Kenmore, over river on right.
Public, mildly undulating, parkland course beside Loch Tay.
9 holes, 6052 yards, S.S.S.69
Designed by D. Menzies and Partners.
Founded 1992
Visitors: welcome any time, no beginners.
Green Fee: £7 (9 holes), £10 (18 holes) WD; £8 (9 holes), £11 (18 holes) WE; £40/week; £55/fortnight.

Societies: welcome by prior booking.
Catering: bar, lounge and restaurant. Boules.
Hotels: Guinach House (Aberfeldy); self-catering cottages on site.

R55 Killin

☎(0567) 820312
Killin, Perthshire FK21 8TX
On outskirts of village on Aberfeldy road going E.
Parkland course.
9 holes, 2508 yards, S.S.S.65
Designed by John Duncan of Stirling.
Founded 1913
Visitors: welcome weekdays and weekends.
Green Fee: £9/round, £12/day.
Societies: welcome, max 24 per party.
Catering: bar and full range of meals and snacks.

R56 King James VI

☎(0738) 32460 and 25170
Moncreiffe Island, Perth PH2 8NR
On island in centre of Perth (River Tay); access by footbridge (15 min walk).
Inland parkland course.
18 holes, 5664 yards, S.S.S.68
Founded 1858
Visitors: welcome; not Sat.
Green Fee: £12/round, £18/day WD; £24/day, £15 after 10am Sun.
Societies: by arrangement.
Catering: yes.
Hotels: Salvation; Isle of Skye.

R57 Kinghorn

☎(0592) 890345
Macduff Crescent, Kinghorn, Fife KY3 9RE
Off A92 3 miles W of Kirkcaldy (A921).
Municipal undulating links course.
18 holes, 5269 yards, S.S.S.67
Layout recommended by Tom Morris.
Founded 1887
Visitors: welcome.
Green Fee: £8/round, £13.50/day WD; £10/round, £15.50/day WE.
Societies: application for parties 12-30 in writing to Sec.
Catering: full catering by arrangement, snacks at weekends.
Hotels: Kingswood; Longboat.

R58 Kirkcaldy

☎(0592) 260370
Balwearie Rd, Kirkcaldy, Fife KY2 5LT
On A92 at W end of town.

Parkland course.
18 holes, 6004 yards, S.S.S.70
Founded 1904
Visitors: welcome any day except Sat.
Green Fee: apply for details.
Societies: any day except Tues and Sat.
Catering: full catering every day.
Hotels: Parkway.

R59 Kirriemuir

☎(0575) 72144, 73317 Pro, 74608 Fax
Northmuir, Kirriemuir, Angus DD8 4PN
1 mile N of town centre.
Parkland and heathland course.
18 holes, 5510 yards, S.S.S.67
Designed by James Braid.
Founded 1908
Visitors: weekdays only; available from 9.30am for individual players but not for parties.
Green Fee: £13/round, £18/day.
Societies: parties can be booked for weekdays.
Catering: full catering at clubhouse.
Hotels: Dykehead; Ogilvy Arms; Airlie Arms; Thrums Hotel.

R60 Ladybank

☎(0337) 830814 Sec, 830725 Starter
Annsmuir, Ladybank, Fife KY7 7RA
6 miles W of Cupar on main Kirkcaldy to Dundee road.
Heathland course.
18 holes, 6641 yards, S.S.S.72
Designed by Tom Morris.
Founded 1879
Visitors: at any time (no booked parties at weekend).
Green Fee: £25/round, £34/day WD; £27/round, £37/day WE.
Societies: welcome by arrangement with Sec.
Catering: full catering services.
Practice ground.
Hotels: Fernie Castle; Lomond Hills.

R61 Leslie

☎(0592) 620040
Balsillie, Leslie, Fife KY6 3EZ
Leave M90 at junctions 5/7 to Leslie 11 miles.
Undulating course.
9 holes, 4940 yards, S.S.S.64
Founded 1898
Visitors: welcome.
Green Fee: on application.
Hotels: Rescobie; Balgedie; Station; Greenside.

R62 Letham Grange

☎(0241) 890373, 890377 Pro shop, 890414 Fax
Letham Grange, Colliston, by Arbroath, Angus DD11 4RL
A92 Dundee to Arbroath, at Arbroath take A933 to Brechin, at Colliston (4 miles) turn right, signposted.
Public parkland/woodland course.
Old course, 18 holes, 6954 yards, S.S.S.73; New course, 18 holes, 5528 yards, S.S.S.68
Designed by Donald Steel & G.K. Smith (Old course), T. MacAuley (New course).
Founded 1985 (Old), 1988 (New).
Visitors: welcome, not before 10.30am Sat/Sun/Tues on Old course; not before 10am Sat/Sun/Fri on New course.
Green Fee: Old, £20/round, £30/day WD, £25/round WE; New, £12/round, £18/day WD, £15/round WE: both courses, £26 WD, £35 WE.
Societies: welcome every day subject to availability.
Catering: bars and restaurants within hotel.
Practice ground, putting green, chipping green.
Hotels: Letham Grange.

R63 Leven

☎(0333) 428859 Sec
Links Rd, Leven, Fife KY8 4HS
Travel E along Promenade, turn left into Church Rd, turn right into Links Rd, clubhouse at end of road on right.
Seaside course.
18 holes, 6434 yards, S.S.S.71
Founded 1820
Visitors: welcome weekdays but some restrictions at weekends; for parties of 12 or under phone (0333) 421390, over 12 in number, (0333) 428859.
Green Fee: £18/round, £24/day WD; £24/round, £36/day WE.
Societies: contact Mr B Jackson, Links Secretary, c/o Starters Box, Leven Links, Promenade, Leven, Fife.
Catering: full meals at any time, bar snacks etc.
Snooker table.
Hotels: Old Manor; Lundin Links; Caledonian.

R64 Lochgelly

☎(0592) 780174
Cartmore Rd, Lochgelly, Fife
On A910 2 miles NE of Cowdenbeath.
Parkland course.
18 holes, 5768 yards, S.S.S.67
Founded 1911

Visitors: welcome.
Green Fee: on application.
Catering: facilities available.

R65 Lundin

☎(0333) 320202; Pro 320051
Golf Rd, Lundin Links, Fife KY8 6BA
In an easterly direction from Kirkcaldy, 14 miles; from Leven 3 miles.
Seaside course.
18 holes, 6377 yards, S.S.S.71
Designed by James Braid.
Founded 1857
Visitors: Mon to Fri 9-15 (booking system operates) Sat afternoon only after 2.30pm.
Green Fee: apply for details.
Catering: during playing season Mon-Fri.
Hotels: Old Manor.

R66 Lundin Ladies

☎(0333) 320832, 320022
Woodielea Road, Lundin Links, Fife KY8 6AR
On N side of A915 in middle of Lundin Links (100 yards W of Lundin Links Hotel).
Short, challenging, parkland course.
9 holes, 4730 yards, S.S.S.67 (LGU criteria)
Designed by James Braid.
Founded 1891
Visitors: welcome; Wed in summer may be difficult (medal).
Green Fee: £6 WD, £7.50 WE.
Societies: tee booking through Sec for parties.

R67 Milnathort

☎(0577) 864069
South St, Milnathort KY13 2AW
Off M90 1.5 miles N of Kinross.
Parkland course.
9 holes, 5669 yards, S.S.S.69
Founded 1890
Visitors: welcome except on competition days.
Green Fee: £10/day WD, £15/day WE.
Societies: welcome by prior arrangement with Hon Sec.
Catering: meals and snacks available by prior arrangement.
Hotels: Royal; Thistle.

R68 Monifieth

☎(0382) 532767, 535553 Sec
c/o Sec H.R.Nicoll, Medal Starter's Box, Princes St, Monifieth, Dundee DD5 4AW

6-7 miles E of Dundee along A930 to Monifieth High St; signposted to golf courses thereafter.
Seaside courses.
Medal, 18 holes, 6657 yards, S.S.S.72; Ashludie, 18 holes, 5123 yards, S.S.S.66
Visitors: welcome by arrangement with Starter; Sat after 2pm; Sun after 10am; party bookings through Sec; parties of 12 and over must have h/cap certs.
Green Fee: Medal, £22/round, £32/day WD; £24/round, £36/day WE; Ashludie, £14/round, £20/day WD; £15/round, £22/day WE; both courses £24 WD, £28 WE.
Societies: welcome by arrangement with Sec, subject to weekend restrictions as above.
Catering: every day.
Hotels: Panmure; Woodlands.

R69 Montrose Links Trust

☎(0674) 72932, 671800 Fax
Traill Drive, Montrose, Angus DD10 8SW
Off A92 Dundee-Aberdeen road, 1 mile from town centre.
Seaside courses.
Medal, 18 holes, 6443 yards, S.S.S.71; Broomfield, 18 holes, 4765 yards, S.S.S.63
Records of golf being played at Montrose in 1562.
Visitors: welcome.
Green Fee: Medal, £13/round, £22/day WD; £19/round, £30/day WE; £70/week; Broomfield, £8/round £12/day WD; £12/round, £18/day WE; £46/week; reductions for jnrs, member's guests and unemployed.
Societies: welcome.
Catering: can be arranged in one of the member Golf Clubs (Montrose Caledonia GC (0674) 72313; Montrose Mercantile GC 72408; Royal Montrose GC 72376).
Hotels: Park (offers golfing package holidays); Links; George.

R70 Muckhart

☎(025 981) 423
Drumburn Rd, Muckhart, Dollar, Clackmannanshire FK14 7JH
Between A91 and A823 S of Muckhart, signposted.
Undulating moorland course.
18 holes, 6034 yards, S.S.S.70
Founded 1908
Visitors: welcome, phone call advisable at weekends.
Green Fee: £12.50/round, £18/day WD; £18/round, £24/day WE.

Societies: every day, contact Club Manager.
Catering: lunches every day, evening meals by arrangement.
Hotels: B&B on perimeter of course.

R71 **Murrayshall**

☎(0738) 52784 Pro Shop, 51171
Scone, Perthshire PH2 7PH
Signposted off A94 from Perth/Coupar Angus, 4 miles from Perth city centre.
Parkland course.
18 holes, 6420 yards, S.S.S.71
Designed by J. Hamilton Stutt.
Founded 1981
Visitors: no restrictions.
Green Fee: apply for details.
Societies: welcome by prior arrangement.
Catering: full clubhouse catering.
Tennis, bowls, croquet.
Hotels: Murrayshall House on course.

R72 **Muthill**

☎(0764) 653319 Sec, 681523 Clubhouse
Peat Rd, Muthill, Crieff PH5 2AD
500 yards off Stirling-Crieff road A822, signposted at foot of road at W end of village.
Parkland course.
9 holes, 2371 yards, S.S.S.63
Founded 1935
Visitors: restricted evenings and days when club matches taking place.
Green Fee: £8 WD, £12 WE.
Societies: not encouraged.
Hotels: Drummond Arms.

R73 **North Inch**

☎(0738) 39911 Council, 36481 Starter
c/o Perth & Kinross District Council, Old Council Chambers, 3 High Street, Perth PH1 5JU
On open space to N of central Perth, adjacent to Gannochy Trust Sports Complex.
Public course, tree- and river-lined parkland.
18 holes, 5178 yards, S.S.S.65
Tom Morris involved in original design.
Founded 18 holes since 1927
Visitors: pay as you play policy.
Green Fee: up to £5.40 depending on season/day.
Societies: in summer tee occasionally reserved for local clubs.
Catering: at adjacent sports complex.

R74 **Panmure**

☎(0241) 853120, 855120
Burnside Road, Barry, Angus DD7 7RT
Off A930, 2 miles W of Carnoustie.
Seaside course.
18 holes, 6317 yards, S.S.S.70
Founded 1845
Visitors: welcome except Sat.
Green Fee: £23/round, £35/day.
Societies: by arrangement.
Catering: full facilities 7 days.
Hotels: Carlogie; Woodlands.

R75 **Pitlochry**

☎(0796) 2792 Pro and Starter
Golf Course Rd, Pitlochry
A9 to Pitlochry, then via Atholl Rd, Larchwood Rd, and Golf Course Rd.
Hill course.
18 holes, 5811 yards, S.S.S.68
Designed by W. Fernie, modernised by Major Cecil Hutchinson.
Founded 1908
Visitors: welcome.
Green Fee: £15/day WD, £18/day WE.
Societies: welcome by arrangement with Estate Office (0796) 472114.
Catering: meals and snacks served, breakfast and dinner by arrangement with Steward (0796) 472334.

R76 **Pitreavie (Dunfermline)**

☎(0383) 722591, 723151 Pro
Queensferry Rd, Dunfermline, Fife KY11 5PR
From A90(M) junction 2 turn off for Dunfermline onto A823, course between Rosyth and Dunfermline on E side of dual carriageway.
Undulating parkland course.
18 holes, 6086 yards, S.S.S.69
Designed by Dr Mackenzie.
Founded 1922
Visitors: welcome every day; small parties can reserve tees through Pro.
Green Fee: £14/round, £19/day WD; £25/day WE.
Societies: must be reserved in advance through Sec.
Catering: full catering facilities, parties to be booked in advance.
Hotels: King Malcolm (Thistle Inns); Pitbauchlie House.

R77 **Polmont**

☎(0324) 711277
Manuelrigg Maddiston, by Falkirk, Stirlingshire
4 miles S of Falkirk, 1st right after Central Region Fire Brigade HQ.
Undulating parkland course.
9 holes, 3044 yards, S.S.S.69
Founded 1904
Visitors: welcome, not on Sat.
Green Fee: £7 WD, £12/round Sun (£2.50/round with member).
Societies: by arrangement.
Catering: full catering, by arrangement with Sec.
Hotels: Inchyra Grange; Polmont.

R78 **St Andrews**

☎(0334) 75757 (all courses)
St Andrews Links Management Committee, Pilmour Cottage, St Andrews, Fife KY16 9JA
60 miles N of Edinburgh via A91 to St Andrews; by rail to Leuchars on Edinburgh-Dundee main line.
Public seaside courses.
Green Fee: apply for details.
Societies: welcome.
Catering: in nearby hotels.
Hotels: full range in St Andrews from B&B to 4-star international standard.

Old Course

18 holes, 6566 yards, S.S.S.72
Founded circa 1400
Visitors: welcome except Sun; only with letter of intro or h/cap cert; no bookings Sat, tee times allotted by ballott.

New Course

18 holes, 6604 yards, S.S.S.72
Founded 1896
Visitors: welcome; no tee reservations Sat, first come, first served.

Jubilee Course

18 holes, 6805 yards, S.S.S.72
Founded 1897
Visitors: welcome; book tee 24 hours in advance.

Eden Course

18 holes, 6112 yards, S.S.S.70
Founded 1914
Visitors: welcome; book tee 24 hours in advance.

Balgove Course

9 holes, 1530 yards, Par 30
Founded 1974
Visitors: welcome.

Strathtyrum Course

18 holes, 5094 yards, S.S.S.65
Founded 1993
Visitors: welcome.

R79 **St Fillans**
☎(0764) 85312
South Loch Earn Rd, St Fillans, Perthshire PH6 2NG
12 miles W of Crieff on A85 to Crianlarich.
Parkland course.
9 holes, 5268 yards, S.S.S.68
Designed by James Braid.
Founded 1903
Visitors: welcome any day.
Green Fee: apply for details.
Societies: any time except July and Aug (max 16).
Catering: unlicensed, snacks and light meals available.
Hotels: Achray House; Four Seasons; Drummond Arms; Comrie. Weekly holiday tickets to play 5 courses available.

R80 **St Michaels**
☎(0334) 839365
Leuchars, St Andrews, Fife
On A919 6 miles from St Andrews and Dundee, at W end of Leuchars village turn over railway bridge about 200 yards out of village.
Undulating parkland course.
9 holes, 5510 yards, S.S.S.68
Founded 1903
Visitors: welcome except Sun before 1pm.
Green Fee: on application.
Societies: welcome except Sun am by prior arrangement with Sec.
Catering: bar and lounge facilities, meals available except Wed.

R81 **Saline**
☎(0383) 852591
Kinneddar Hill, Saline, Fife KY12 9UN
M90 exit 4, travel 7 miles on B914 to Dollar, 5 miles NW of Dunfermline, on Stirling road A907, signposted.
Hillside course.
9 holes, 5302 yards, S.S.S.66
Founded 1912
Visitors: welcome without restriction except Sats April-Oct.
Green Fee: £8 WD, £10 Sun.
Societies: weekdays and Sun.
Catering: bar, snacks, full catering by prior arrangement.
Practice nets, putting area.
Hotels: Saline; Castle Campbell.

R82 **Scoonie**
☎(0333) 427057
North Links, Leven, Fife KY8 4SP
10 miles SW of St Andrews.
Flat municipal parkland course.
18 holes, 4967 metres, S.S.S.66
Founded 1951
Visitors: welcome by letter to Sec (except Thurs and Sat).
Green Fee: £8/round, £10/day WD, £12 Sat, £15 Sun.
Societies: welcome by appointment, letter to Sec, min 12 max 30.
Catering: bar, snacks and full meals.
Hotels: Caledonian (15 mins walk).

R83 **Scotscraig**
☎(0382) 552515
Golf Rd, Tayport, Fife DD6 9DZ
On B946 3 miles from S end of Tay Road Bridge, turn left 3rd street past petrol station.
Links/seaside course.
18 holes, 6496 yards, S.S.S.71
Founded 1817
Visitors: welcome weekdays and by arrangement at weekends.
Green Fee: on application.
Societies: welcome by arrangement.
Catering: meals served except Tues.
Hotels: Seymour; Pinewoods.

R84 **Stirling**
☎(0786) 464098 Office, 471490 Pro shop
Queens Rd, Stirling FK8 3AA
1 mile W of town centre on A811 on left hand side of ring road.
Parkland course.
18 holes, 6400 yards, S.S.S.71
Designed by James Braid/Henry Cotton.
Founded 1869
Visitors: welcome weekdays, restricted weekends.
Green Fee: £17/round, £23/day WD.
Societies: weekdays only.
Catering: lunches, high teas, dinner by arrangement. Pool table.
Hotels: Garfield; Golden Lion; Terraces.

R85 **Strathendrick**
☎(0360) 40582 Sec
Glasgow Rd, Drymen, Stirlingshire
17 miles NW of Glasgow off A809.
Hilly moorland course.
9 holes, 4962 yards, S.S.S.65
Founded 1901
Visitors: with member only.
Green Fee: apply for details.

R86 **Taymouth Castle**
☎(08873) 228
Kenmore, by Aberfeldy, Tayside PH15 2NT
6 miles W of Aberfeldy, large sign by castle gates on right of road.
Fairly flat parkland course.
18 holes, 6066 yards, S.S.S.69
Designed by James Braid.
Founded 1923
Visitors: unlimited, booking required.
Green Fee: apply for details.
Societies: welcome.
Catering: full catering, bar open all day from 11am.

R87 **Thornton**
☎(0592) 771111
Station Rd, Thornton, Fife KY1 4DW
1 mile E of A92 through Thornton.
Parkland course.
18 holes, 6177 yards, S.S.S.69
Founded 1921
Visitors: welcome.
Green Fee: £12/round, £17/day WD; £16/round, £27/day WE.
Societies: catered for.
Catering: lunches, snacks, high teas.
Hotels: Crown; Albany; Garl David.

R88 **Tillicoultry**
☎(0259) 50124 Sec, 51337 (Home)
Alva Rd, Tillicoultry, FK13 6BL
9 miles E of stirling on A91.
Undulating meadowland course.
9 holes, 5266 yards, S.S.S.66
Designed by Peter Robertson, Braids Hill G.C. Edinburgh.
Founded 1899
Visitors: welcome weekdays, weekends by arrangement; restrictions on jnrs (under 15).
Green Fee: £8/round WD; £13.50/round WE (no day tickets).
Societies: by arrangement, contact Sec, R. Whitehead, 12 Stalker Ave, Tillicoultry, FK13 6EY.

Catering: bar meals all year, catering for parties by prior arrangement.
Hotels: Castle Craig.

R89 **Tulliallan**
☎(0259) 730396

Alloa Rd, Kincardine on Forth, by Alloa FK10 4BB
1.5 miles N of Kincardine Bridge on Alloa road, next to Police College.
Parkland course.
18 holes, 5982 yards, S.S.S.69
Founded 1902

Visitors: welcome by arrangement with Pro.
Green Fee: apply for details.
Societies: welcome by prior arrangement except Sat; weekdays max 40, Sun max 30.
Catering: full meals and snacks served.

HIGHLANDS, GRAMPIAN

By far the fastest and most convenient road to Inverness is the much improved A9 which has no sooner bade farewell to Perth than it has, it seems, found Aviemore beckoning. The scenery along the way outshines even the postcards and calendars, although it is one journey in Scotland in which golf takes a back seat.

There are one or two courses that might tempt a stopover. Blair Atholl, Pitlochry and, on reaching Aviemore, Boat of Garten, an authentic classic in the short course mould. There has been a course of some sort at Boat of Garten for a hundred years, but it was the handiwork of James Braid which, by extending it to 18 holes, really put it on the map.

But the ardent connoisseur, who has had his card marked properly, will undoubtedly opt for the east coast route starting in Aberdeen and working north round Buchan Ness and then west along the Moray Firth to Inverness.

It will, in fact, be hard getting away from Aberdeen after acquaintance with Royal Aberdeen, with its valleyed fairways between dunes and an awareness that the Club, founded in 1780, is one of the oldest in the world. The nearby Kings Links is one of the country's busiest courses, while Murcar, which rubs shoulders with Royal Aberdeen, has a lot in common with its distinguished neighbour, although a number of holes in the second half occupy a lofty perch that marks a change in character.

A few miles to the north, Cruden Bay represents the model links with mountainous dunes and resplendent views worthy of comparison alongside Turnberry, Tralee and Pebble Beach. In prewar days, it had a luxury hotel, a railway link with the south and a glowing reputation. The hotel and public railway have disappeared but its reputation remains undimmed, an example of ingenuity guiding shotmaking and one or two old-fashioned blind shots that undoubtedly enhance that reputation.

All these courses deserve a long look, but time is often pressing and many good things lie ahead notably Peterhead, Fraserburgh, the Moray Club at Lossiemouth and Nairn, once known freely as the Brighton of the North. As with Cruden Bay, the scenic quality of Moray and Nairn is a major part of their attraction. Nairn opens with a number of holes along the shore but both have housed their championships and left their would-be conquerors suitably contrite and chastened.

Nairn lies close to Inverness Airport, providing easier access from London for those whose sights are set on Dornoch and who haven't the time to indulge in leisurely detours. It would be wrong to say that the aeroplane has been responsible for the discovery of Dornoch because its praises have been sung by many, not least Roger and Joyce Wethered who knew a thing or two about good courses.

However, it is perfectly true to say that the fashion for visiting Dornoch has grown significantly in the last 30 years particularly among Americans curious to see where Donald Ross, the most famous American golf course architect, was born, and what it was about the ancient links that influenced his work so enormously. This is not an attempt to betray the secret, simply a laying of the scent and an assurance that bridges over the Cromarty and Dornoch Firth have shortened the approach from Inverness.

Nor is Dornoch the end of the northern rainbow. It certainly lives up to its star billing but nearby Golspie is decidedly pleasant if less severe and Brora, a creation of James Braid, where the insomniac golfer can play in the famous midnight competition in June, provides the perfect foil for anyone seeking relief from trying to tame Dornoch. Even true lovers of art cannot look at one masterpiece all the time.

S1 Abernethy
☎(0479) 821305
Nethybridge, Inverness-shire
On B970 Grantown-on-Spey to
Coylum Bridge road, 0.25 mile N of
Nethybridge.
Undulating course.
9 holes, 2551 yards, S.S.S.66
Founded 1893
Visitors: welcome.
Green Fee: on application.
Societies: by arrangement.
Catering: meals served.
Hotels: Nethybridge; Mountview;
Heatherbrae.

S2 Aboyne
☎(03398) 86328
Formaston Park, Aboyne,
Aberdeenshire AB3 5HD
On A93 from Aberdeen, take 1st right
after entering village, signposted.
Undulating parkland course.
18 holes, 5910 yards, S.S.S.68
Founded 1883
Visitors: welcome.
Green Fee: on application.
Societies: welcome except Sun.
Catering: full catering service
available April-Oct.
Hotels: Charleston Hotel; Birse Lodge

S3 Alford
☎(09755) 62178
Montgarrie Rd, Alford, Nr
Aberdeenshire AB33 8AE

26 miles due W of Aberdeen on A944;
course in centre of village of Alford.
Parkland course.
18 holes, 5290 yards, S.S.S.66
Designed by David Hurd.
Founded 1982
Visitors: welcome; advised to
telephone for weekend play; h/cap
not required but practical knowledge
of the game preferred.
Green Fee: £8/round, £12/day WD;
£14/round, £18/day WE.
Societies: anytime by prior booking;
weekdays preferred; course usually
very busy weekends in summer.
Catering: bar, snacks, dining area
with meals booked in advance. Pool.
Hotels: Kildrummy Castle (8 miles);
hotels in village and Bridge of Alford.

S4 Alness
☎(0349) 883877
Ardross Rd, Alness, Ross-shire
On A9 10 miles N of Dingwall.
9 holes, 4718 yards, S.S.S.63
Designed by John Sutherland.
Founded 1904
Visitors: welcome at any time.
Green Fee: apply for details.
Catering: can be arranged.

S5 Askernish
Lochboisdale, Askernish, South Uist,
Western Isles
5 miles NW of Lochboisdale, ferry
terminal from Oban.

Seaside course.
9 holes, 5371 yards, S.S.S.61
Designed by Tom Morris.
Founded 1891
Green Fee: apply for details.
Societies: welcome.
Hotels: Borrodale; Lochboisdale.

S6 Auchenblae
☎(05617) 8869
Auchenblae, Laurencekirk,
Kincardineshire AB30 1BU.
2 miles off A94 W of Fordoun.
Parkland course.
9 holes, 2174 yards, S.S.S.30
Visitors: welcome anytime; Wed and
Fri competition nights for members
so restricted 5.30-9pm.
Green Fee: apply for details.
Catering: local shop selling golf
balls, snacks etc.
Hotels: Drumtochty Arms.

S7 Auchmill
☎(0224) 714577
Auchmill, Aberdeen
5 miles N of Aberdeen.
Municipal course.
18 holes, 5952 yards, S.S.S.69
Visitors: all welcome.
Green Fee: apply for details.

S8 Ballater
☎(03397) 55567 Sec, 55658 Pro
Victoria Rd, Ballater, AB3 5QX

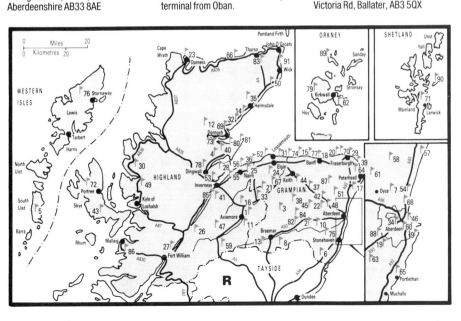

THE BOAT HOTEL
TEE BREAKS & MASTER CLASSES
AA ★★★ RAC

Situated overlooking the beautiful but challenging Boat of Garten
Golf Course – the 'Gleneagles' of the Highlands – the Boat Hotel offers
you Master Classes with our resident Professional, or the superb value
'Tee Break' holidays with golf on any of six local courses.

**Please contact: Golf Desk, The Boat Hotel, Boat of Garten,
Inverness-shire PH24 3BH
Telephone (0479) 831258 Fax (0479) 831414**

A93 on Deeside, 42 miles W of
Aberdeen, 62 miles from Perth.
Open flat, moorland course.
18 holes, 5638 yards, S.S.S.69
Designed by James Braid.
Founded 1891
Visitors: welcome, book weekends
and certain days during summer.
Green Fee: £15/round, £22.50/day
WD; £18/round, £27/day WE; jnrs
(under 18) half adult rate.
Societies: welcome by arrangement
with Sec.
Catering: full catering.
Putting green, tennis, bowls.

S9 Balnagask
☎(0224) 876407, 871286 (Nigg Bay)
St Fitticks Rd, Balnagask, Aberdeen
2 miles SE of city centre.
Public seaside course.
18 holes, 5986 yards, S.S.S.69
Designed by Hawtree & Son.
Founded 1955
Visitors: welcome.
Green Fee: apply for details.
Societies: by arrangement.
Catering: apply to Council.

S10 Banchory
☎(0330) 822365, 822447 Tee
reservations
Kinneskie Rd, Banchory,
Kincardineshire AB31 3TA
18 miles W of Aberdeen, on North
Deeside road; 100 yards SW of
Banchory shopping centre.
Parkland course.
18 holes, 5284 yards, Par 67
Founded 1905
Visitors: welcome, no intro required.
Green Fee: £18/day WD, £20/day
WE.
Societies: welcome by arrangement
Mon, Tues, Wed, Fri only.
Catering: full bar and restaurant.
Hotels: Tor-na-coille; Burnett Arms;
Banchory Lodge; Invery House;
Raemoir House.

S11 Boat of Garten
☎(047983) 1282 Golf Shop
Boat of Garten, Inverness-shire PH24
3BQ
5 miles N of Aviemore on old A9 road,
turn right onto B970.
Undulating, tree-lined fairways.
18 holes, 5837 yards, S.S.S.69
Designed by James Braid.
Founded 1898
Visitors: welcome.
Green Fee: £15 WD, £20 WE.
Starting sheet used every day.
Societies: must book in advance.
Catering: facilities available all day.
Hotels: Craigard; Moorfield; Boat.

S12 Bonar Bridge & Ardgay
☎(054 982) 248
Market Stance, Migdale Rd, Bonar
Bridge IV24 3EJ
Off A9 travelling N from Inverness.
Moorland course.
9 holes, 2313 yards, S.S.S.63
Founded 1901
Visitors: welcome at all times.
Green Fee: £8/day.
Societies: any weekday by prior
arrangement.
Catering: available May-Sept.
Hotels: Bridge; Dunroamin.

S13 Braemar
☎(03397) 41618
Cluniebank Rd, Braemar,
Aberdeenshire AB35 5XX
Signposted from village of Braemar,
club lies approximately 0.5 mile from
Braemar on Cluniebank.
Parkland/moorland course with River
Clunie running through.
18 holes, 4916 yards, S.S.S.64
Designed by Joe Anderson.
Founded 1902
Visitors: welcome by arrangement
(book 24 hours in advance).
Green Fee: £10/round, £14/day WD;
£13/round, £17/day WE; £48/week.

Societies: welcome, prior booking
required.
Catering: bar open 11am-11pm
(midnight Fri and Sat), lunch, snacks
and high teas available to 7pm.
Hotels: Fife Arms; Moorfield;
Invercauld Arms.

S14 Brora
☎(0408) 621417
Golf Rd, Brora, Sutherland KW9 6QS
75 miles N of Inverness on A9,
signposted in middle of village.
Seaside links course.
18 holes, 6110 yards, S.S.S.69
Designed by James Braid.
Founded 1891
Visitors: welcome, restrictions may
occur on tournament days.
Green Fee: £15/day; £65/week.
Societies: by written application.
Catering: available Easter to Oct.
Hotels: Links; Royal Marine;
Sutherland Arms; Braes; Bay View.

S15 Buckpool (Buckie)
☎(0542) 832236
Barhill Rd, Buckie, AB5 1DU
Leave A98 signposted Buckpool,
course 1 mile at end of road before
entering St Peters Rd.
Seaside links course.
18 holes, 6259 yards, S.S.S.70
Founded 1965
Visitors: welcome.
Green Fee: £8/round, £15/day WD;
£12/round, £20/day WE.
Societies: societies and groups
welcome by prior arrangement.
Catering: weekends and daily by
prior arrangement.Squash.
Hotels: St Andrews; Cluny;
Commercial.

S16 Carrbridge
☎(047 984) 623 Clubhouse
Carrbridge, Inverness-shire PH23
3AU

About 200 yards from village on A938.
Parkland/moorland course.
9 holes, 2633 yards, S.S.S.66
Founded 1980
Visitors: welcome; Sun limited due to competitions.
Green Fee: £9 WD, £10 WE.
Catering: tea, coffee, light snacks.
Hotels: Dalrachny Lodge; Carrbridge; Struan House; Cairns.

S17 Cruden Bay
☎(0779) 812285, 812414 Pro shop, 812945 Fax
Aulton Rd, Cruden Bay, Peterhead, Aberdeenshire AB42 7NN
23 miles N of Aberdeen on coastal route to Peterhead.
Seaside course.
9 holes, 4710 yards, S.S.S.62; 18 holes, 6370 yards, S.S.S.71
Designed by Tom Morris & Archie Simpson.
Founded 1899
Visitors: not on competition days before 3.30pm; restricted weekends.
Green Fee: £20/day WD, £28 WE.
Societies: on application, weekdays only.
Catering: full bar and restaurant.
Hotels: Kilmarnock Arms, Red House (Cruden Bay); Waterside Inn (Peterhead); Udny Arms (Newburgh).

S18 Cullen
☎(0542) 840685
The Links, Cullen, Buckie, Banffshire, Grampian AB56 2UU
200 yards from A98 on W of Cullen.
Links/parkland course.
18 holes, 4610 yards, S.S.S.62
Designed by Tom Morris (original 9).
Founded 1879
Visitors: welcome, time restrictions on application.
Green Fee: £9/day WD; £12/day WE.
Societies: all months except July/August, apply for details.
Catering: bar and catering April-Oct.
Practice nets, 18-hole putting green, sea swimming, fishing, bowls, tennis, pool, darts etc.
Hotels: Royal Oak; Waverley; Grant Arms; Seafields Arms; Three Kings Inn; Bayview; Cullen Bay; Moray Golf Rover scheme from Moray DC.

S19 Deeside
☎(0224) 869457 Sec, 861041 Pro
Bieldside, Aberdeen AB1 9DL
3 miles W of Aberdeen on A93 North Deeside road.

Parkland course.
18 holes, 5972 yards, S.S.S.69; 9 holes, 3316 yards, S.S.S.36
Founded 1903
Visitors: welcome if member of recognised golf club and with letter of intro from Sec.
Green Fee: £15/day WD, £17/day WE & BH.
Societies: welcome Thurs only.
Catering: full facilities.
Hotels: Cults; Bieldside Inn.

S20 Duff House Royal
☎(0261) 812062
The Banyards, Banff AB45 3SX
On A98 entering town from S.
Parkland course.
18 holes, 6161 yards, S.S.S.69
Designed by Dr A. and Major C.A. Mackenzie.
Founded 1909
Visitors: welcome at all times, h/cap cert preferred, tee times restricted at weekends and July/Aug.
Green Fee: £12/round, £16/day WD; £17/round, £22/day WE.
Societies: catered for at all times but weekends fully booked with waiting list.
Catering: full service.
Hotels: Banff Springs; County; Fife Lodge; Highland Haven; Carmelite.

S21 Dufftown
☎(0340) 20325
Tomintoul Road, Dufftown, Banffshire AB55 4BX
1 mile from Dufftown on B9009.
Family course with panoramic views.
18 holes, 5308 yards, S.S.S.67
Founded 1896
Visitors: unrestricted.
Green Fee: apply for details.
Societies: 7 days, by arrangement.
Catering: bar, snacks etc.

S22 Dunecht House
☎(0224) 487187
Dunecht, Skene, Aberdeenshire AB3 7AX
B944 to Dunecht, 1st left.
Parkland course.
9 holes, 6270 yards, S.S.S.78
Founded 1925
Visitors: with member only.
Green Fee: apply for details.

S23 Durness
☎(0971) 511364 Sec (home)
Balnakeil, Durness, Sutherland, IV27 4PN

57 miles NW of Lairg on A838.
Public seaside course with daring finishing hole.
9 holes, 5545 yards, S.S.S.68
Designed by F. Keith, L. Ross, I. Morrison.
Founded 1988
Visitors: welcome, occasionally restricted Sun am.
Green Fee: £8/day, £32/week.
Societies: any time.
Catering: snacks 12am-5pm, June-Sept.

S24 Elgin
☎(0343) 542338
Hardhillock, Birnie Rd, Elgin, Moray IV30 3SX
On S edge of Elgin, turn right into Birnie Rd from Rothes road going S.
Undulating sandy parkland course.
18 holes, 6401 yards, S.S.S.71
Founded 1906
Visitors: welcome after 9.30am weekdays, 10am weekends; book in advance.
Green Fee: £15/round, £22/day WD; £22/round, £30/day WE.
Societies: book with Sec.
Catering: full bar and catering.
Hotels: Eight Acres; Laich Moray; Rothes Glen; St Leonards.

S25 Forres
☎(0309) 72949
Muiryshade, Forres, IV36 0RD
1 mile S of clock tower in town centre, in St Leonards Rd and Edgehill Rd.
Undulating parkland course.
18 holes, 6203 yards, S.S.S.69
Designed by James Braid.
Founded 1889
Visitors: welcome.
Green Fee: £12/day WD, £16/day WE.
Societies: welcome by confirmation.
Catering: full catering facilities all year.
Hotels: Royal; Ramnee; Park.

S26 Fort Augustus
☎(0320) 6460 Sec, 6660 Clubhouse
Markethill, Fort Augustus, Inverness-shire PH32 4DT
Off A82, entrance beyond 30mph restriction S of village.
Moorland course.
9 holes, 5454 yards, S.S.S.68
Designed by Dr Lane.
Founded 1905
Visitors: tickets at clubhouse, minimum restrictions.

Green Fee: on application.
Societies: apply Sec, Glentarff, Fort Augustus.
Catering: self-catering facilities.
Hotels: Lovat Arms; Caledonian; Brae.

S27 Fort William

☎(0397) 4464
North Rd, Torlundy, Fort William PH33 6RD
On A82 Fort William to Inverness road, 2 miles N of Fort William.
Moorland course.
18 holes, 5640 yards, S.S.S.68
Designed by J.R. Stutt.
Founded 1975
Visitors: welcome any time.
Green Fee: apply for details.
Societies: welcomed.
Catering: full license, bar snacks.

S28 Fortrose & Rosemarkie

☎(0381) 620529 Sec (party bookings), 620733 Pro
Ness Rd East, Fortrose, Ross-shire IV10 8SE
On Cromarty road branching off A9 N out of Inverness, about 16 miles N of Inverness.
Seaside links course.
18 holes, 5973 yards, S.S.S.69
Re-designed by James Braid.
Founded 1888
Visitors: welcome at all times.
Green Fee: £12/round, £17/day WD; £17/round WE.
Societies: catered for if possible on written application.
Catering: available.
Hotels: Marine; Royal (Fortrose).

S29 Fraserburgh

☎(0346) 518287
Philorth, Fraserburgh AB43 5TL
1 mile E of Fraserburgh, on A92 Aberdeen-Fraserburgh road, turn off right on road to Cairnbulg.
Undulating seaside course.
18 holes, 6297 yards, S.S.S.70
Designed by James Braid.
Founded 1881
Visitors: no restrictions, all welcome.
Green Fee: £11 WD, £15 WE.
Societies: no restrictions weekdays and most Sun; small parties on Sat subject to Club commitments.
Catering: bar lunches daily, evening meals to order.
Hotels: Royal; Tufted Duck (St Combs).

S30 Gairloch

☎(0445) 2407
Gairloch, Ross-shire IV21 2BE
On main road A832, in Gairloch.
Seaside course.
9 holes, 2093 yards, S.S.S.63
Designed by Captain Burgess.
Founded 1898
Visitors: welcome all week.
Green Fee: £10/day.
Catering: shop with refreshments during season.

S31 Garmouth & Kingston

☎(034 387) 388
Garmouth, Fochabers, Moray IV32 7LU
Off A96 8 miles E of Elgin.
Seaside course.
18 holes, 5616 yards, S.S.S.67
Founded 1931
Visitors: welcome.
Green Fee: £10/round, £12/day WD; £14/round, £18/day WE.
Societies: by arrangement with Sec; deductions for parties over 20.
Catering: by arrangement with Sec.
Hotels: Gordon Arms; Garmouth.

S32 Golspie

☎(0408) 633266
Ferry Rd, Golspie, Sutherland KW10 6ST
First right in Golspie off A9 from Inverness.
Links/heathland/seaside/ meadowland course.
18 holes, 5836 yards, S.S.S.68
Founded 1889
Visitors: unrestricted.
Green Fee: £15/day.
Societies: welcome subject to tee reservations for competitions and tournaments.
Catering: all day during season (April-Oct).
Hotels: Stags Head; Sutherland Arms.

S33 Grantown-on-Spey

☎(0479) 2079 Clubhouse, 2715 Sec, 2398 Pro
Golf Course Rd, Grantown-on-Spey, Morayshire PH26 3HY
Leave A9 at Aviemore, take A939 to Grantown, situated at end of town.
Woodland/parkland course.
18 holes, 5715 yards, S.S.S.67
Designed by Willie Park and James Braid.
Founded 1890
Visitors: welcome, not before 10am Sat/Sun.

Green Fee: £13/day WD, £16/day WE & BH.
Societies: by arrangement, not before 10am Sat/Sun.
Catering: full facilities April-Oct.
Hotels: Grant Arms; Ben Mohr; Garth; Strathspey.

S34 Hazlehead

☎(0224) 317336 Pro
Hazlehead Park, Aberdeen AB1 8BD
4 miles NW of city centre.
Municipal moorland courses.
18 holes, 6045 yards, S.S.S.68; 18 holes, 6205 yards, S.S.S.70; 9 holes, 2770 yards, S.S.S.34
Visitors: all welcome.
Green Fee: £4.20 (18 holes), £2.15 (9 holes) winter; summer on application.
Catering: available nearby.

S35 Helmsdale

☎(04312) 339
Golf Rd, Helmsdale, Sutherland, KW8 6JA
Off A9 into village of Helmsdale.
Moorland course.
9 holes, 3720 yards, S.S.S.60
Founded 1895
Visitors: welcome.
Green Fee: £3/day, £10/week.
Societies: welcome.
Hotels: Navidale; Bridge; Belgrave.

S36 Hopeman

☎(0343) 830578
Hopeman, Moray IV30 2YA
7 miles N of Elgin on B9012.
Seaside links-type course.
18 holes, 5500 yards, S.S.S.67
Designed by J. McKenzie.
Founded 1923
Visitors: unrestricted weekdays, after 9.30am Sat/Sun.
Green Fee: £10 WD, £15 WE.
Societies: welcome.
Catering: bar and restaurant facilities.
Pool.
Hotels: Station; Neuk.

S37 Huntly

☎(0466) 792643, 794023 Shop
Cooper Park, Huntly, Aberdeenshire AB54 4SH
On A96 0.5 mile from town centre, through school arch.
Parkland course.
18 holes, 5399 yards, S.S.S.66
Founded 1892
Visitors: welcome except Thurs.

Green Fee: £10/day WD, £15/day
WE; £50 weekly.
Societies: by arrangement with Sec.
Catering: facilities by arrangement.
Practice area.
Hotels: Castle; Huntly; Gordon Arms.

S38 Insch
☎(0464) 20363
Golf Terrace, Insch, Aberdeenshire
28 miles NW of Aberdeen, off A96
Inverness road.
Parkland course with water hazards.
9 holes, 5488 yards, S.S.S.67
Visitors: welcome, no restrictions.
Green Fee: apply for details.
Catering: bar; catering on request.
Snooker, darts.

S39 Inverallochy
☎(0346) 582000
Inverallochy, Nr Fraserburgh,
Grampian
3 miles S of Fraserburgh on B9033.
Seaside links course.
18 holes, 5137 yards, S.S.S.65
Founded 1888
Visitors: welcome except
10.30am-2.30pm Sat.
Green Fee: £10.
Societies: welcome.
Catering: limited catering available.
Bowls.
Hotels: Tufted Duck (Fraserburgh).

S40 Invergordon
☎(0349) 852715
King George St, Invergordon,
Ross-shire
Off High St, Invergordon.
Parkland course.
9 holes (planned to increase to 18),
3014 yards, S.S.S.69
Designed by Mr J. Urquhart.
Founded 1893
Visitors: welcome at any time; (Mon
and Wed evenings Ladies
competitions; Tues and Thurs
evenings Men's competitions; all day
Sat Men's competitions).
Green Fee: £7.
Societies: by arrangement.
Hotels: Marine; Kincraig.

S41 Inverness
☎(0463) 239882 Sec, 231989 Pro
Culcabock Rd, Inverness IV2 3XQ
1 mile W of A9, near Raigmore
Hospital.
Parkland course.
18 holes, 6226 yards, S.S.S.70
Founded 1883

Visitors: welcome, restricted Sat.
Green Fee: £16/round, £22/day WD;
£20/round, £24/day WE.
Societies: limited; early booking
required; not Sat.
Catering: full bar facilities; no
catering Thurs unless pre-booked.
2 practice areas.
Hotels: Kingsmills; Craigmonie;
Caledonian.

S42 Inverurie
☎(0467) 24080
Blackhall Rd, Inverurie,
Aberdeenshire
On A96 Aberdeen-Inverness road, off
Blackhall Rd.
Wooded parkland course.
18 holes, 5096 yards, S.S.S.65
Designed by G. Smith and J.M. Stutt.
Founded 1923
Visitors: welcome but prior booking
on (0467) 20193 advisable.
Green Fee: apply for details.
Societies: welcome by prior
arrangement.
Catering: available daily.
Hotels: Kintore Arms; Gordon Arms;
Pittodrie House.

S43 Isle of Skye
☎(0478) 2000
Sconser, Isle of Skye, Inverness
Between Broadford and Portree (on
main road).
Seaside course.
9 holes, 4798 yards, S.S.S.63
Designed by Dr F. Deighton.
Founded 1964
Visitors: welcome at all times.
Green Fee: £7/day, £14/3 days,
£20/week.
Hotels: Sconser Lodge.

S44 Keith
☎(0542) 882469 Club, 886286 Sec
Fife Park, Fife-Kelth, Keith,
Banffshire AB55 3DF
0.5 mile off A96 on Dufftown road.
Undulating parkland course.
18 holes, S.S.S.68
Founded 1965
Visitors: welcome at all times,
advisable to phone during playing
season.
Green Fee: £9 WD, £12 WE.
Societies: welcome at all times by
prior arrangement with Hon Sec.
Catering: bar every evening 5-11pm
weekdays, 4-11pm weekends; full
catering by arrangement.
Pool table.
Hotels: Ugie House.

S45 Kemnay
☎(0467) 642225
Monymusk Road, Kemnay,
Aberdeenshire AB51 5RA
15 mile N of Aberdeen on A96, turn
onto B994.
Parkland course.
9 holes, 2751 yards, S.S.S.67; from
May 1994, 18 holes, 5903 yards,
S.S.S.68
Designed by Greens of Scotland Ltd
(New course).
Founded 1908
Visitors: welcome most times but
check in case tee booked for
competitions.
Green Fee: £10/round, £15/day WD;
£12/round, £18/day WE.
Socleties: welcome by arrangement.
Catering: bar, bar snacks.
Hotels: Park Hill Lodge; Grant Arms
(Monymusk).

S46 King's Links
☎(0224) 632269
King's Links, Aberdeen
E of city centre adjacent to Pittodrie
Stadium.
Municipal seaside course.
18 holes, 6384 yards, S.S.S.71
Visitors: all welcome.
Green Fee: municipal rates.
Societies: by arrangement.

S47 Kingussie
☎(0540) 661600 Sec, 661374
Clubhouse
Gynack Rd, Kingussie,
Inverness-shire PH21 1LR
Leave A9 at N end of village, drive
into village, turn right at Duke of
Gordon Hotel and continue to end of
road.
Hill course.
18 holes, 5555 yards, S.S.S.67
Designed by Vardon & Herd.
Founded 1891
Visitors: unrestricted.
Green Fee: £12/round, £15/day WD;
£14/round, £18/day WE.
Societies: by arrangement.
Catering: available May-Oct.

S48 Kintore
☎(0467) 32631
Balbithan Rd, Kintore, Inverurie,
Aberdeenshire
Off A96, 12 miles N of Aberdeen.
Undulating moorland course.
18 holes, 5985 yards, S.S.S.69
Founded 1911
Visitors: welcome daily except Mon,
Wed and Fri after 4pm.

Green Fee: apply for details.
Societies: welcome.
Catering: available if booked in advance.
Hotels: Crown; Torryburn.

S49 Lochcarron
☎(05202) 257 Sec.
Lochcarron, Rossshire
1 mile E of Lochcarron village.
Seaside/heathland course.
9 holes, 3578 yards, S.S.S.62
Founded 1910
Visitors: welcome except 1pm-6pm Sat; club hire.
Green Fee: apply for details.
Hotels: Lochcarron; Rock Villa; Strathcarron.

S50 Lybster
Main St, Lybster, Caithness KW1 6BL
13 miles S of Wick on A9, turn down village main street, golf course entrance opposite football pitch.
Moorland course.
9 holes, 1898 yards, S.S.S.62
Founded 1926
Visitors: welcome, pay before play in money box provided.
Green Fee: apply for details.
Societies: any group welcome anytime except Sat evenings (club competitions).

S51 McDonald
☎(0358) 720576
Hospital Rd, Ellon, Aberdeenshire AB41 9AW
Leave Ellon by A948 Auchnagatt road and take 1st turning on left.
Parkland course.
18 holes, 5986 yards, S.S.S.69
Founded 1927
Visitors: welcome.
Green Fee: on application.
Societies: by arrangement.
Catering: bar 7 days, full catering Tues-Sun.
Hotels: Buchan; New Inn; Station.

S52 Moray
☎(0343) 812018, 813330 Pro, 815102 Fax
Stotfield Rd, Lossiemouth, Moray IV31 6QS
From Elgin on A96
Aberdeen-Inverness road, travel on A941 Elgin-Lossiemouth road.
Links courses.
Old, 18 holes, 6643 yards, S.S.S.72;
New, 18 holes, 6044 yards, S.S.S.69
Founded 1889

Visitors: welcome; New Course any time; Old Course, weekdays after 9.30am, weekends after 10am, not 1pm-2pm any day, advance booking required.
Green Fee: on request.
Societies: reduction of 10% for parties of 12 or more.
Catering: full during summer, weekends Oct-Mar.
Hotels: Stotfield; Laverock Bank; Huntly House; Skerrybrae; Rock House.

S53 Muir of Ord
☎(0463) 870825 Administrator, 871311 Pro
Great North Rd, Muir of Ord, Ross-shire IV6 7SX
15 miles N of Inverness on either A862 or A9/A832.
Moorland/parkland course with links-type fairways.
18 holes, 5129 yards, S.S.S.65
Part designed by James Braid.
Founded 1875
Visitors: welcome, not before 11am weekends.
Green Fee: £12/day WD, £15/day WE.
Societies: welcome, book in advance.
Catering: bar, snacks, full meals April-Oct inc.
Practice area, putting green, snooker, pool.

S54 Murcar
☎(0224) 704354, 704370 Pro (Phone/Fax)
Bridge of Don, Aberdeen AB23 8BD
3 miles from Aberdeen on A92, Fraserburgh road.
Seaside course.
18 holes, 6240 yards, S.S.S.70
Designed by Archie Simpson.
Founded 1909
Visitors: welcome weekdays, h/cap cert required.
Green Fee: £16/round £20/day.
Societies: catered for weekdays.
Catering: snacks, lunches, dinners.

S55 Nairn
☎(0667) 53208, 56328 Fax
Seabank Rd, Nairn IV12 4HB
1 mile N of A96, W of Nairn, turn off onto Seabank Rd at church.
Seaside links course.
18 holes, 6722 yards, S.S.S.72
Designed by Tom Morris, James Braid.
Founded 1887

Visitors: welcome.
Green Fee: on application.
Societies: catered for.
Catering: summer full catering, winter restricted.
Snooker.
Hotels: Golf View; Royal Marine; Windsor; Newton; Alton Burn.

S56 Nairn Dunbar
☎(0667) 52741, 53964 Pro, 56897 Fax
Lochloy Rd, Nairn IV12 5AE
Off A96, 0.5 mile E of town.
Seaside course.
18 holes, 6431 yards, S.S.S.71
Founded 1899
Visitors: welcome.
Green Fee: £15 WD, £20 WE.
Societies: welcome.
Catering: available.
Hotels: Links; Golf View; Windsor.

S57 Newburgh-on-Ythan
☎(0358) 789438
C/o 51 Mavis Bank, Newburgh, Ellon, Aberdeen AB41 0FB
14 miles N of Aberdeen on Peterhead road, on entering village of Newburgh turn right at Ythan Hotel.
Seaside links course.
9 holes, 6348 yards, S.S.S.70
Founded 1888
Visitors: welcome except Tues after 4pm from May to Sept.
Green Fee: £10/day WD, £12/day WE.
Societies: apply to Sec.
Hotels: Ythan; Foveran House; Udny.

S58 Newmachar
☎(0651) 863002
Swailend, Newmachar, Aberdeen AB2 0UU
12 miles N of Aberdeen on A947.
Heathland course.
18 holes, 6605 yards, S.S.S.73
Designed by Dave Thomas.
Founded 1990
Visitors: welcome weekdays; h/cap cert required.
Green Fee: £16/round, £24/day WD; £20/round WE.
Societies: weekdays with prior booking.
Catering: full catering and bar facilities.

S59 Newtonmore
☎(05403) 328
Golf Course Rd, Newtonmore, Highland PH20 1AT

Leave A9 2 miles S of Newtonmore, course 150 yards from centre of village
Moorland/parkland course.
18 holes, 5890 yards, S.S.S.68
Designed by James Braid.
Founded 1893
Visitors: welcome, no restrictions.
Green Fee: apply for details.
Societies: apply to Sec.
Catering: meals and snacks served. Pool.
Hotels: Craigerne; Alvey; Glen; Balavil Sports; Braeriach; Mains; Highland.

S60 Northern
☎(0224) 636440
Golf Rd, Kings Links, Aberdeen AB2 1QB
E of city centre.
Municipal seaside course.
18 holes, 6700 yards, S.S.S.69
Visitors: welcome.
Green Fee: £6/round.
Societies: by arrangement.
Catering: at weekends, by arrangement during week.

S61 Oldmeldrum
☎(0651) 872648
Kirk Brae, Oldmeldrum, Aberdeen, AB51 0DJ
18 miles NW of Aberdeen on A947 Banff road; turn 1st right on entering village of Oldmeldrum.
Parkland course.
18 holes, 5988 yards, S.S.S.69
Founded 1885 extended 1990
Visitors: phone clubhouse for tee reservation (bar hours).
Green Fee: £10/round/day WD, £12/round/day WE.
Societies: contact Sec via clubhouse.
Catering: by arrangement; licensed bar, snacks available; (new clubhouse March 1994).
Practice area.
Hotels: Meldrum Arms; Morris's; Meldrum House.

S62 Orkney
☎(0856) 872457, 874165 Sec
Grainbank, Kirkwall, Orkney KW15 1RD
0.5 mile W of Kirkwall.
Parkland course.
18 holes, 5406 yards, S.S.S.68
Founded 1889
Visitors: at all times, some restrictions in summer due to competitions.

Green Fee: £10/day; weekly and fortnightly rates available.
Societies: at all times.
Catering: bar lunchtime and evening during week, all day weekends.
Games room.
Hotels: Ayre.

S63 Peterculter
☎(0224) 734994 (Tel/Fax)
Oldtown, Burnside Rd, Peterculter, Aberdeen AB1 0LN
On W side of Peterculter village, signposted from the main Deeside road.
Undulating, scenic parkland course.
18 holes, 5924 yards, S.S.S.69
Designed by E. Lappin.
Founded 1989
Visitors: welcome, Mon-Fri 9am-3pm and after 6.30pm every 20 mins, weekends and holidays after 9.15am, every 30 mins.
Green Fee: £15/day WD, £20/day WE.
Societies: Tues-Fri, formal bookings only.
Catering: meals daily except Mon. Practice ground.
Hotels: Ardoe House; Maryculter House; New Marcliffe.

S64 Peterhead
☎(0779) 72149
Craigewan Links, Peterhead, Aberdeenshire AB4 6LT
A92 and A975, 30 miles N of Aberdeen.
Seaside links course.
18 holes, 6100 yards, S.S.S.70; 9 holes, 2400 yards, S.S.S.60
Designed by Willie Park and James Braid.
Founded 1841
Visitors: weekdays few restrictions, weekend restrictions to tee times for competitions.
Green Fee: £12/day WD, £16/day WE.
Societies: by arrangement except Sat.
Catering: bar, meals by arrangement, snacks.
Pool table.
Hotels: Palace; Waterside Inn.

S65 Portlethen
☎(0224) 782575
Badentoy Rd, Portlethen, Aberdeen AB1 4YA
Alongside A92 6 miles S of Aberdeen.
Parkland course.
18 holes, 6735 yards, S.S.S.72

Designed by Donald Steel.
Founded 1981
Visitors: some restrictions weekends; dress, smart but casual.
Green Fee: £10/round, £15/day WD, £15/round WE.
Societies: by prior arrangement.
Catering: bar, restaurant 9am-9pm every day. Snooker.
Hotels: Hillside; Skean Dhu (Aberdeen).

S66 Reay
☎(084 781) 288
By Thurso, Caithness KW14 7RE
11 miles W of Thurso.
Most northerly links course on mainland Britain.
18 holes, 5865 yards, S.S.S.68
Founded 1893
Visitors: welcome anytime.
Green Fee: £10/round/day, £30/week.
Societies: not Sat.
Catering: bar; lunch during summer months only.
Hotels: Forss House; Meluich.

S67 Rothes
☎(0340) 831443
Blackhall, Rothes, Aberlour, Banffshire AB38 7AN
On S side of Rothes which lies on A941 about 10 miles W of Elgin; turn right by Glen Spey distillery and follow road past Rothes castle.
Moorland course, partly surrounded by pine forest.
9 holes, 5052 yards, S.S.S.64
Designed by John Souter.
Founded 1990
Visitors: welcome.
Green Fee: £8 per 18 holes WD, £10 WE.
Societies: welcome any time by arrangement subject to club/open competitions.
Catering: bar open evenings during summer and usually lunchtimes July/Aug; catering at weekends or by arrangement.
Hotels: Seafield Arms; Station; Eastbank; Rothes Glen; Craigellachie.

S68 Royal Aberdeen
☎(0224) 702571
Balgownie, Bridge of Don, Aberdeen AB2 8AT
2 miles N of Aberdeen on A92, cross River Don, turn right at 1st set of lights, then Links Rd to course.
Seaside links courses.

18 holes, 4066 yards, S.S.S.60; 18 holes, 6372 yards, S.S.S.71 Designed by Robert Simpson and James Braid.
Founded 1780
Visitors: welcome with letter of intro or h/cap cert; not before 3.30pm Sat.
Green Fee: apply for details.
Societies: weekdays and Sun by arrangement.
Catering: full facilities.
Hotels: Invery House; Udny Arms.

S69 Royal Dornoch
☎(0862) 810219, 810792 Fax
Golf Rd, Dornoch IV25 3LW
A9 from Inverness, via Tain and Dornoch Bridge.
Links course.
Championship 18 holes, 6581 yards, S.S.S.72; Struie 18 holes (6 from original course), 5500 yards, S.S.S.66
Designed by Tom Morris, John Sutherland, George Duncan.
Founded 1877
Visitors: welcome, tee reservations in advance; h/cap certs (max 24 Men, 35 Ladies) required for Championship course.
Green Fee: on request.
Societies: when requested except July/Aug; early reservations required.
Catering: full facilities except Mon.
Hotels: Burghfield House; Castle; Mallin House; Royal Golf.

S70 Royal Tarlair
☎(0261) 832897
Buchan St, Macduff AB4 1TA
On A98 48 miles from Aberdeen.
Seaside links course.
18 holes, 5866 yards, S.S.S.68
Designed by George Smith.
Founded 1923
Visitors: welcome any day.
Green Fee: £15/day WD, £19/day WE.
Societies: by arrangement.
Catering: full catering and bar.
Hotels: Knowes; Highland Haven.

S71 Shetland
☎(0595) 84369, 3065 Manager, 2691 Sec
Dale, Gott by Lerwick, Shetland
Road N from Lerwick, 3 miles.
Undulating moorland course.
18 holes, 5776 yards, S.S.S.70
Designed by Fraser Middleton.
Founded 1891
Visitors: welcome.

Green Fee: £8/day, £25/week.
Societies: by arrangement.
Catering: bar and snacks.
Hotels: Lerwick; Grand; Queens.

S72 Skeabost
☎(047 032) 202
Skeabost Bridge, Isle of Skye IV5 19NP
40 miles from Kyle of Lochalsh.
Parkland course.
9 holes Par 3, 1700 yards, S.S.S.29
Founded 1984
Visitors: welcome; no jeans or T-shirts, proper golf shoes.
Green Fee: apply for details.
Catering: bar and restaurant in hotel (April-Oct).
Hotels: Skeabost (26 beds).

S73 Skibo
☎(086 288) 250
Skibo Castle, Dornoch, Sutherland IV24 3RQ
Just off A9 immediately N of Dornoch Firth Bridge.
Seaside links course.
18 holes, 6650 yards, S.S.S.72
Designed by Donald Steel.
Founded 1994
Visitors: welcome on production of h/cap cert of 18 or less.
Green Fee: apply for details.
Societies: welcome by prior arrangement.
Catering: meals and snacks.

S74 Spey Bay
☎(0343) 820424
Spey Bay, Fochabers, Moray IV32 7JP
Turn off A96 near Fochabers Bridge, follow B9104 Spey Bay road to coast.
Links course.
18 holes, 6059 yards, S.S.S.69
Designed by Ben Sayers.
Founded 1907
Visitors: welcome.
Green Fee: apply for details.
Catering: meals and bar all day.
Driving range, tennis, petanque, putting, caravan site.
Hotels: Spey Bay, golf packages/golf outings arranged.

S75 Stonehaven
☎(0569) 62124
Cowie, Stonehaven AB3 2RH
On A92 1 mile N of town, new roundabout at Commodore Hotel, take second exit on left, pass Leisure Centre on right.

Seaside/parkland course.
18 holes, 5103 yards, S.S.S.65
Designed by A. Simpson.
Founded 1888
Visitors: welcome except Sat before 4pm.
Green Fee: £13/day WD, £18/day WE.
Catering: full.
Hotels: Commodore; St Leonards; Heugh; Royal.

S76 Stornoway
☎(0851) 702240
Castle Grounds, Stornoway, Isle of Lewis PA87 0XP
5 mins walk from town centre, just within main entrance to castle grounds.
Parkland/moorland course.
18 holes, 5178 yards, S.S.S.66
Designed by J.R. Stutt.
Founded 1890
Visitors: welcome from Mon to Sat.
Green Fee: £12/day, £35/week, £60/fortnight.
Societies: Mon-Fri, special rates apply.
Catering: bar snacks, full meals by arrangement.
Hotels: can be arranged, ring Sec.

S77 Strathlene
☎(0542) 31798
Portessie, Buckie, Banffshire AB5 2DJ
On A942, 2 miles E of Buckie Harbour, from main Banff-Inverness road, take turning to Strathlene 3 miles E of Buckie road sign.
Undulating moorland/seaside course.
18 holes, 6180 yards, S.S.S.69
Designed by Alex Smith.
Founded 1877
Visitors: welcome.
Green Fee: on application.
Societies: welcome.
Catering: available 9am-5pm.
Hotels: Commercial.

S78 Strathpeffer Spa
☎(0997) 421219, 421011 Sop
Strathpeffer, Ross-shire IV14 9AS
5 miles W of Dingwall, 0.25 mile N of village square (signposted).
Upland course, no sand bunkers.
18 holes, 4792 yards, S.S.S.65
Designed by W. Park.
Founded 1888
Visitors: welcome without reservation; tee reserved for members and guests to 10am Sun.

Skibo

Skibo is a highland paradise. It transports you to a world of peace and beauty, solitude and splendour. Andrew Carnegie fell in love with it at first sight and hundreds of others have done so since.

Carnegie, who left Dunfermline at the age of 13, to become the "Steel King" in America, holidayed in Scotland most summers, seeking a home for himself in old age and for his only daughter, Margaret, who was born in 1897. He renovated the Castle and Estate, building up the outdoor interests of hunting, fishing and shooting and even commissioning John Sutherland, Royal Dornoch's famous Secretary, to design a 9-hole golf course on the promontory of land nestling between Loch Evelix and the Dornoch Firth.

It is said that Carnegie had been asked to play at Dornoch but, being a non-golfer at that time, felt that he had better build his own course in order to learn to play first. After Carnegie's death in 1919, the golf course generally faded as one of Skibo's attractions, but in 1992 it was restored as the centre-piece of The Carnegie Club which Peter de Savary, who bought Skibo in 1990, established as a private residential sporting club.

In keeping with the natural glories of the surroundings, the course was made to blend with a landscape of exciting contrasts. It is part links, part heath and part meadowland, flanked on three sides by water and looked down upon by the brooding hills of Sutherland.

The course itself, which is designated a Site of Special Scientific Interest, is an object lesson of how a proper understanding can be forged between golfers and those wishing to preserve our rare, wildlife habitats. An independent voice, seeing the course at the end of construction, declared that it had transformed the appearance of the land and will certainly allow many more people to appreciate Skibo's wonders.

From the time that the second shot at the first hole merges with low dunes until the drive at the 7th scales an attractive ridge, the flavour is essentially seaside. The par 3 3rd is worthy of the delights of Rye's short holes and, while the 4th and 5th , on the other side of the little ferry road, are par 4s of modest length, correct placement from the tee is vital. They also bring the first of the water into close proximity although gorse is more of a menace on these holes.

Having negotiated the short 6th and the gentle climb to the 7th fairway, the next six or seven holes offer a little more shelter, but the 8th, which doglegs round the shores of Loch Evelix, is the favourite of many, before the 9th, 10th, 12th, 13th and 14th involve a bout of strong hitting.

The drive on the 14th passes the old boathouse on the right and the second shot the salmon ladder below the causeway road which meanders through the woodland back to the castle. It is a fact that the castle is only visible from the 17th and 18th but these holes are part of the scenic finish which really begins with the last of the short holes at the 15th.

The 15th and 18th greens sandwich the clubhouse which possesses a suitably warm, highland character in an enchanting spot that surveys the scene in all its moods. Not that the golfing challenge is done. Far from it. The last three holes form a triangle of equal proportions in the sense of devilment and daring.

From the 16th green in the low sandhills, the 17th and 18th favour the brave, the 17th bordered all too closely by the Firth once more and the par 5 18th , a replica of the last at Pebble Beach. There is a decided advantage in cutting off as much of the marsh as possible but there is a limit to how safely you can play to the right and, from the sloping fairway, it needs care and cunning with the second and third shots if the green on the water's edge is to be reached .

Green Fee: £10/round, £15/day WD; £15/round WE.
Societies: by arrangement.
Catering: licensed, meals, snacks 7 days.
Hotels: Craigdarroch Lodge; Dunraven Lodge; Holly Lodge; Richmond; Achilty; all offer package arrangements.

S79 Stromness

☎(0856) 850772, 850622 Sec
Ness, Stromness, Orkney K16 3DU
Bordering sea at S end of town.
Parkland course.
18 holes, 4672 yards, S.S.S.64
Founded 1890
Visitors: no restrictions, bookings not necessary.
Green Fee: £10/day.
Societies: welcome any time.
Catering: bar.
Tennis, pool, darts, bowls.
Hotels: Braes.

S80 Tain

☎(0862) 892314 Sec/bookings
Tain, Ross-shire IV19 1PA
A9 N of Inverness, 0.5 mile from town centre.
Seaside/parkland course.
18 holes, 6238 yards, S.S.S.70/69
Designed by Tom Morris.
Founded 1890
Visitors: welcome.
Green Fee: £12/round, £18/2 rounds WD; £18/round, £24/2 rounds WE.
Societies: welcome.
Catering: by arrangement with Club Steward.
Hotels: Royal; Morangie; Mansfield.

S81 Tarbat

☎(086 287) 236
Portmahomack, Ross-shire IV20 1YQ
B9165 off A9, 7 miles E of Tain.
Seaside links course.
9 holes, 2568 yards, S.S.S.66
Designed by J. Sutherland.
Founded 1910
Visitors: welcome at all times.
Green Fee: £5 WD, £6 WE & BH, £20/week (Mon-Fri).
Societies: welcome by prior arrangement.
Catering: tea and coffee.
Hotels: Castle; Caledonian.

S82 Tarland

☎(03398) 81413
Aberdeen Rd, Tarland, Aboyne, Aberdeenshire AB3 4YL

On A974, 30 miles W of Aberdeen, 6 miles N of Aboyne.
Parkland course.
9 holes, 5816 yards, S.S.S.68
Designed by Tom Morris.
Founded 1908
Visitors: no restrictions.
Green Fee: £10 WD, £12 WE.
Societies: not weekends.
Catering: June-Sept all day; April, May, Oct by arrangement.
Hotels: Aberdeen Arms; Balnacoil; Commercial; Pannanich Wells.

S83 Thurso

☎(0847) 63807, 65024 Sec
Newlands of Geise, Thurso, Caithness KW14 7XF
2 miles SW from centre of Thurso on B870.
Parkland course.
18 holes, 5841 yards, S.S.S.69
Designed by W. Stuart.
Founded 1893
Visitors: no restrictions.
Green Fee: on application.
Catering: all day bar, catering all day during summer.
Hotels: Pentland; John O'Groats House; (free golf for residents).

S84 Torphins

☎(03398) 82115, 82563 Sec
Bog Rd, Torphins, Banchory AB31 4JA
6 miles W of Banchory on A980.
Undulating heathland course.
9 holes, 2317 yards, S.S.S.63
Founded 1896
Visitors: unrestricted except during competitions.
Green Fee: £10/day WD, £12 WE.
Societies: weekdays only.
Catering: snacks only.
Hotels: Learney Arms.

S85 Torvean

☎(0463) 225651 Sec, 711434 Starter
Glenurquhart Rd, Inverness
On A82 Fort William road, 1 mile W of city centre, on W of Caledonian Canal.
Municipal parkland course.
18 holes, 5784 yards, S.S.S.68
Founded 1962
Visitors: welcome; booking advisable, contact Starter.
Green Fee: approx £8.50/round WD, £10/round WE.
Societies: welcome by arrangement with Inverness District Council.
Catering: meals by arrangement.
Hotels: Loch Ness House (opposite).

S86 Traigh

☎(06875) 234
Traig Farm, Arisaig, Inverness-shire
3 miles W of Arisaig on A830 Fort William-Mallaig road.
Links course.
9 holes, 2500 yards, S.S.S.68
Designed by John Salveson.
Redesigned 1993 (open July 1994)
Visitors: welcome, pay at course.
Green Fee: £6/day.
Catering: snacks at clubhouse.
Hotels: Cnoc-na-Faire.

S87 Turriff

☎(0888) 62745 Clubhouse, 62982 Sec, 63025 Pro
Rosehall, Turriff, Aberdeenshire AB53 7BB
On Aberdeen side of town, about 1 mile up Huntly Rd on B9024.
Meadowland/parkland course.
18 holes, 6145 yards, S.S.S.69
Founded 1896
Visitors: welcome with h/cap cert, book with Pro; not before 10am weekends unless with member.
Green Fee: £12/round, £15/day WD; £15/round, £20/day WE.
Societies: welcome by arrangement with Sec.
Catering: by arrangement.
Hotels: Union; Banff Spring.

S88 Westhill

☎(0224) 740159
Westhill Heights, Skene, Aberdeenshire AB3 6TY
6 miles from Aberdeen on A944 Aberdeen-Alford road, course to N of town overlooking it.
Undulating parkland/moorland course.
18 holes, 5921 yards, S.S.S.69
Designed by Charles Lawrie.
Founded 1977
Visitors: welcome except 4.30-7pm weekdays, not Sat.
Green Fee: £12/round, £16/day WD; £15/round, £20/day WE & BH.
Societies: weekdays and Sun.
Catering: bar, catering by arrangement.
Hotels: Westhill Inn.

S89 Westray

☎(08577) 373 Treasurer, 516 Sec
Tulloch's Shop, Westray, Orkney
In Westray.
Links course.
9 holes, 2405 yards, Par 33
Founded 1890s
Visitors: welcome 7 days.

Green Fee: £3/day (£1.50 jnrs),
£15/week (£7.50 jnrs).
Societies: welcome.
Hotels: Cleaton House.

S90 Whalsay
☎(08066) 481
Skaw Taing, Island of Whalsay,
Shetland
At N of island, ask directions from
ferry.
Moorland/parkland course, part
municipal.

18 holes, 6009 yards, S.S.S.70
Founded 1975
Visitors: welcome, unrestricted.
Green Fee: £5/day.
Societies: welcome, phone in
advance.
Catering: bar and snacks.

S91 Wick
☎(0955) 2726
Reiss, Wick, Caithness KW1 4RW
3 miles N of Wick on A9, turn right at
signpost, 0.75 mile to clubhouse.

Seaside links course.
18 holes, 5976 yards, S.S.S.69
Designed by McCulloch.
Founded 1870
Visitors: welcome subject to club
and open competitions.
Green Fee: apply for details.
Societies: welcome by prior
arrangement.
Catering: bar, snacks at weekends.
Pool.
Hotels: Queens; Nethercliffe;
Mackays (free golf for residents);
Rosebank; Mercury.

T

NORTHERN IRELAND

Discussion on comparative merits of golf courses is always fierce although rarely conclusive. Golfers are influenced by a multitude of factors from how they played to the condition of the greens and the beauty of the setting. Where the debate surrounds courses that are near neighbours, passions are liable to be even more frenzied but, whilst Royal Portrush and Royal County Down cannot quite be classed as neighbours, they lie roughly equidistant on either side of Belfast and, as a result, tend to split opinion nicely.

This is not the place to fuel the argument about their merits but there is not the slightest doubt that both are in the classic mould and nobody should visit Ulster and play one without the other. Few big cities can boast two championship links within such easy reach of its centre.

Royal County Down is at Newcastle, an attractive holiday town nestling in the romantic shadow of the Mountains of Mourne. Mountains make an imposing backcloth to golf anywhere and one is always aware of their brooding presence at Newcastle, sun and cloud casting ever changing patterns and colours. They make the 9th particularly imposing but an equally dominant impression of the course is forged by the massive sand dunes that line so many of the fairways, together with the heather and gorse that magnify and punish errant shots.

They place huge demands on bold, forceful driving, although the varied nature of the shots to the greens gives an important added dimension that increases the regret that circumstances beyond its control have denied Royal County Down more major championships. The British Amateur of 1970 and the Curtis Cup match two years earlier were events enhanced by the quality of its challenge; but the same applies to Royal Portrush — the only Irish Club to have housed the Open Championship — in 1951. It saw Max Faulkner emerge as champion, although his win marked the beginning of a drought where British victories were concerned, which lasted until Tony Jacklin won in 1969.

Portrush also saw the crowning of Catherine Lacoste as British Women's champion, many of the noble holes bringing out the best in a supreme striker, and in 1993 the British Men's Amateur Open returned after a gap of 33 years. The spectacular part is down by the shore, not far from the Giant's Causeway. Holes entitled Purgatory and Calamity convey the true picture.

However, it must not be thought that golf in the Province is confined to Newcastle and Portrush — superb as they are. Lovers of links golf have a splendid example in Portstewart and another in Castlerock — both close to Portrush. Belfast itself is well served, Royal Belfast, with excellent views of the city, and Malone, being the pick.

There is also Balmoral, home club of the late Fred Daly, Holywood and Shandon Park, which used to stage the Gallaher's Ulster Open at a time when a young Tony Jacklin was taking his first steps onto the world golfing stage.

Clandeboye and Bangor are towns on the fringe of the Belfast district with splendid courses and I well remember journeys to Lurgan when Frank Pennink was redesigning the course; and a sentimental mention for Warrenpoint near the border with the Republic, the course that raised Ronan Rafferty.

T1 **Aberdelghy**

☎(0846) 662738
Bell's Lane, Lambeg, Co Antrim, N
Ireland
Between Dunmurry and Lambeg, just
off main Belfast-Lisburn road.
Municipal parkland course.
9 holes, 4384 yards, S.S.S.65
Founded July 1986
Visitors: welcome any time.
Green Fee: £3.20 (9 holes), £6 (18
holes) WD; £3.70/£6.50 WE & BH;
reductions for jnrs, OAPs and
unemployed.
Societies: welcome, discount for 15
and over; tee times cannot be
reserved.
Hotels: Beechlawn, Forte Crest
(Dunmurry).

T2 **Ardglass**

☎(0396) 841219 Sec, 841022 Pro
Castle Place, Ardglass, Co Down
BT30 7TP.
On B1, 7 miles from Downpatrick.
Seaside course.
18 holes, 5498 metres, S.S.S.69
Founded 1896

Visitors: welcome.
Green Fee: £13 WD, £18 WE;
discount if playing with member.
Societies: welcome.
Catering: meals except Mon, bar.
Snooker.
Hotels: Abbey Lodge (Downpatrick).

T3 **Ballycastle**

☎(026 57) 62536
Cushendall Rd, Ballycastle, Co
Antrim BT54 6QP
About 40 miles along coast road, N of
Larne Harbour.
Undulating seaside course.
18 holes, 5882 yards, S.S.S.69
Founded 1890
Visitors: welcome weekdays and
weekends by arrangement.
Green Fee: £13 (£8 with member)
WD, £18 (£12 with member) WE.
Societies: catered for all year except
July/Aug (bookable).
Catering: bar snacks and meals
available.
Snooker.
Hotels: Antrim Arms; Hillsea;
Marine.

T4 **Ballyclare**

☎(0960) 322696, 342352
25 Springvale Rd, Ballycare, Co
Antrim
14 miles N of Belfast, off Larne road.
Parkland course.
18 holes, 5840 metres, S.S.S.71
Founded 1923
Visitors: welcome, not Sat.
Green Fee: £14/day WD, £20/day
WE & BH.
Societies: by arrangement.
Catering: restaurant and snacks.
Snooker, indoor bowls (winter).
Hotels: Chimney Corner; Dunadry
Inn.

T5 **Ballyearl Golf and Leisure Centre**

☎(0232) 848287
585 Doagh Rd, Newtownabbey,
Belfast BT36 8RZ
1 mile N of Mossley off B59.
Public parkland course.
9 holes Par 3, 2400 yards
Visitors: welcome.
Green Fee: £3 WD, £4 WE;
reductions for jnrs and OAPs.

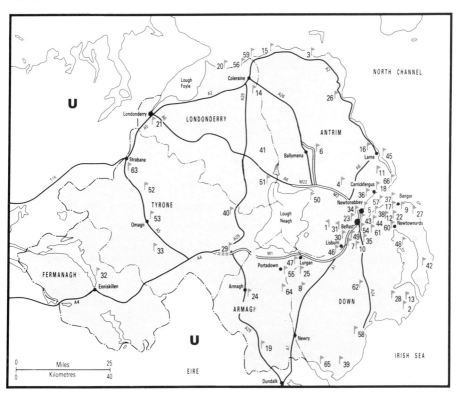

Societies: welcome.
Catering: bar and snacks.
Squash courts, fitness centre, driving range, 180-seat theatre.
Hotels: Chimney Corner.

T6 **Ballymena**

☎(0266) 861487
128 Raceview Rd, Ballymena, Co Antrim BT42 4HY
2.5 miles E of town on A42 to Brough Shane and Carnlough.
Heathland/parkland course.
18 holes, 5245 metres, S.S.S.67
Founded 1902
Visitors: welcome weekdays and Sun; not Sat.
Green Fee: apply for details.
Societies: recognised societies by arrangement with Hon Sec.
Catering: available daily.
Hotels: Adair Arms; Tullyglass House; Leighinmohr; Country House.

T7 **Balmoral**

☎(0232) 381514, 667747 Pro shop
518 Lisburn Rd, Belfast BT9 6GX
2 miles S of Belfast city centre; clubhouse is immediately beside King's Hall on Lisburn Rd, opposite Balmoral Halt railway station.
Flat parkland course.
18 holes, 5702 metres, S.S.S.70
Founded 1914
Visitors: welcome except Sat and after 3pm Sun.
Green Fee: £15/day WD, £18 Wed; £22.50 WE & BH.
Societies: Mon and Thurs by arrangement.
Catering: bar (0232) 668540; restaurant (0232) 664571.
Snooker.
Hotels: Conway; Europa; Plaza; York; Beechlawn; Balmoral.

T8 **Banbridge**

☎(08206) 62211/62342
Huntly Rd, Banbridge, Co Down BT32 3UR
About 0.5 mile from town along Huntly Rd, River Bann on right all the way.
Parkland course.
18 holes, 5376 metres, S.S.S.68
Founded 1913
Visitors: welcome; ladies preference Tues, men's competitions Sat.
Green Fee: apply for details.
Societies: welcome summer months.
Catering: arranged on request.
Hotels: Bannville House; Belmont; Downshire.

T9 **Bangor**

☎(0247) 270922, 462164 Pro
Broadway, Bangor, Co Down BT20 4RH
0.75 mile S from town centre.
Undulating parkland course.
18 holes, 6424 yards, S.S.S.71
Designed by James Braid.
Founded 1903
Visitors: welcome weekdays; weekends by prior arrangement.
Green Fee: £16 WD, £22 Sun.
Societies: Mon and Wed only by prior arrangement, min 20.
Catering: bar meals available 11.30am-2.30pm and 5.30-7.30pm; dining room available, contact caterer (0247) 270483; no catering Mon Oct-Mar.
Hotels: Royal; Crawfordsburn Inn.

T10 **Belvoir Park**

☎(0232) 491693 office, 641159 catering, 692817 bar, 646714 Pro
73 Church Rd, Newtownbreda, Belfast BT8 4AN
About 4 miles from centre of Belfast, off Ormean Rd which is main road to Saintfield and Newcastle.
Parkland course.
18 holes, 6516 yards, S.S.S.71
Designed by H.S. Colt.
Founded 1927
Visitors: welcome.
Green Fee: £30 WD except Wed, £35 WE, Wed and BH.
Societies: council permits 5 outings per month April/Sept, 24 or more £24 green fee.
Catering: excellent facilities by Parkview Catering.
Snooker.
Hotels: La Mon House; Stormont.

T11 **Bentra**

☎(09603) 78996
1 Slaughterford Rd, Whitehead, Co Antrim BT38 9TG
5 miles N of Carrickergus on road to Larne.
Municipal parkland course.
9 holes (planned extension to 18), 6084 yards, S.S.S.68
Visitors: welcome at any time.
Green Fee: £5.25/round (18 holes) WD, £7.50/round WE; reductions jnrs and OAPs.
Societies: welcome, tee times cannot be reserved.
Catering: bar and snacks at Bentra Roadhouse adjoining course, from 11.30am (12.30am Sun).
Hotels: Magheramorne House; Coast Road, Dobbins (Carrickfergus).

T12 **Blackwood**

☎(0247) 853581
150 Crawfordsburn Rd, Clandeboye, Bangor BT19 1GB
On A2 towards Bangor from Belfast turn for Newtownards. then left after 1 mile; course 500 yards on right.
Heathland/parkland course.
18 holes, c.6,500 yards, Par 72; 18 holes Par 3, c.2,500 yards.
Designed by Simon Gidman.
Founded Opening late summer 1994.
Visitors: always welcome, pay-and-play; advisable to phone in advance.
Green Fee: c. £12-15.
Societies: welcome, book in advance.
Catering: bar and snacks, restaurant, dining room.
Driving range.
Hotels: Clandeboye Lodge.

T13 **Bright Castle**

☎(0396) 841319
14 Coniamstown Rd, Bright, Co Down, N Ireland
5 miles S of Downpatrick.
Parkland course.
18 holes, 6900 yards, S.S.S.74
Designed by Arnold Ennis.
Founded 1971
Visitors: welcome, no restrictions.
Green Fee: £10 WD, £12 WE.
Societies: welcome, contact in advance.
Catering: bar, bar snacks.
Hotels: Abbey Lodge (Downpatrick).

T14 **Brown Trout**

☎(0265) 868209
209 Agivy Road, Aghadowey, Nr Coleraine, Co Londonderry
Intersection of the A54 and B66.
Parkland course.
9 holes, 2800 yards, S.S.S.68
Designed by Bill O'Hara Snr.
Founded 1984
Visitors: no restrictions.
Green Fee: £7 WD, £10 WE & BH.
Societies: very welcome, inc. Sat.
Catering: all-day catering, à la carte restaurant.
Horse riding, fishing.
Hotels: Brown Trout Golf and Country Inn on course.

T15 **Bushfoot**

☎(026 57) 31317
50 Bushfoot Rd, Portballintrae, Co Antrim BT57 8RR
4 miles E of Portrush on coast.
Seaside links course.

9 holes, 5572 yards, S.S.S.67
Founded 1890
Visitors: Welcome on weekdays and at weekends if no official club competitions.
Green Fee: on application.
Societies: welcome by arrangement; £12 weekdays, £15 weekends.
Catering: bar and restaurant facilities.
Snooker room, Pitch & Putt (summer), functions.
Hotels: Bayview; Beech; Bushmills Inn; Causeway.

T16 Cairndhu

☎(0574) 583324
192 Coast Rd, Ballygally, Larne, Co Antrim BT40 2QG
4 miles N of Larne.
Parkland course.
18 holes, 6122 yards, S.S.S.69
Designed by John S.F. Morrison.
Founded 1929
Visitors: welcome except Sat.
Green Fee: £12 WD, £18 Sun; ladies £6 WD, £9 Sun.
Societies: welcome.
Catering: meals and snacks weekdays 5pm-10pm, Sat 11.30am-8pm, Sun 12.30-6.30pm.
Snooker.
Hotels: Ballygally Castle; Halfway House; Drumnagreagh House.

T17 Carnalea

☎(0247) 270368, 273989 Fax
Station Rd, Bangor, Co Down BT19 1EZ
Adjacent to Carnalea railway station 1.5 miles from Bangor.
Seaside meadowland course.
18 holes, 5574 yards, S.S.S.67
Founded 1927
Visitors: welcome 7 days.
Green Fee: £11 (£9 with member) WD; £15 (£11 with member) WE & BH.
Societies: weekdays only.
Catering: full catering except Mon.
Hotels: Royal; Crawfordsburn Inn; Tedworth.

T18 Carrickfergus

☎(09603) 363713 Sec/office, 362203 Clubhouse, 51803 Pro
35 North Rd, Carrickfergus, Co Antrim BT38 8LP
Off A2, 9 miles NE of Belfast; on North Rd, 1 mile from Shore Rd.
Parkland/meadowland course.
18 holes, 5752 yards, S.S.S.68
Founded 1926
Visitors: welcome except Sat.

Green Fee: £13 WD, £18 WE.
Societies: Mon-Fri only.
Catering: full facilities.
Snooker.
Hotels: Coast Road; Dobbins Inn; Glenavna House.

T19 Castleblayney

☎(042) 40197 Sec
Onomy, Castleblayney, Co Monaghan, Ulster
Almost in Castleblayney town centre on Derry-Dublin road.
Parkland course.
9 holes, 2678 yards, S..S.S.66
Designed by Bobby Browne.
Founded 1985
Visitors: welcome.
Green Fee: £5 WD, £8 WE & BH.
Societies: welcome.
Catering: full facilities; Hope Castle restaurant and bar.
Hotels: Glencarn; Central.

T20 Castlerock

☎(0265) 848215 Members, 848314 Office
65 Circular Rd, Castlerock, Co Londonderry BT51 4TJ
Off A2, 6 miles W of Coleraine.
Seaside course.
18 holes, 6121 metres, S.S.S.72; 9 holes, 2457 metres, S.S.S.34
Designed by Ben Sayers.
Founded 1901
Visitors: welcome.
Green Fee: £15 (£8 with member) WD, £25 (£13 with member) WE & BH.
Societies: weekdays only.
Catering: franchise at club.
Snooker.
Hotels: Golf (Castlerock); Lodge (Coleraine).

T21 City of Derry

☎(0504) 46369
49 Victoria Rd, Londonderry BT47 2PU
On main Londonderry-Strabane road, 3 miles from Craigavon Bridge.
Parkland course.
Dunhugh, 9 holes, 4708 yards, S.S.S.63; Prehen, 18 holes, 6362 yards, S.S.S.71
Founded 1912
Visitors: welcome weekdays before 4.30pm unless with member; weekends by arrangement with Pro; Dunhugh course open at all times.
Green Fee: apply for details.
Societies: catered for on weekdays and possibly at weekends.
Catering: full facilities available.

Hotels: Everglades (bargain break packages); Broomhill House; White Horse Inn; Waterfoot.

T22 Clandeboye

☎(0247) 271767
Sec/Manager/bookings, 271750 Pro
Tower Rd, Conlig, Newtownards, Co Down BT23 3PN
Above Conlig village off A21 between Bangor and Newtownards.
Dufferin, parkland/heathland course; Ava, parkland/moorland course.
Dufferin, 18 holes, 5915 metres, S.S.S.71; Ava, 18 holes, 5172 metres, S.S.S.68
Designed by William Rennick Robinson and Dr Bernard von Limburger.
Founded 1933
Visitors: welcome weekdays; must be accompanied by member Sat and Sun; (Ladies Day Thurs).
Green Fee: £17.50/£14 WD (£9/£8 with member); £23/£17.50 WE & BH (£11/£10 with member).
Societies: by arrangement, Apr-Sept Mon, Tue, Wed, Fri; Oct-Mar Mon, Wed.
Catering: available, restaurant not open Mon Oct-Mar.
Hotels: Royal; Culloden; Crawfordsburn Inn; Strangford Arms.

T23 Cliftonville

☎(0232) 744158, 746595 Sec and catering
44 Westland Rd, Belfast BT14 6NH
From centre of Belfast take Antrim road, about 2 miles from centre, then Cavehill Rd on left and left again at Fire Station.
Parkland course.
9 holes, 3120 yards, S.S.S.70
Founded 1911
Visitors: welcome except Sat and Tues afternoons.
Green Fee: £12 (£8 with member) WD; £15 (£10 with member) Sun.
Societies: by arrangement with Council through Hon Sec, J.M. Henderson.
Catering: bar snacks available; meals by arrangement.
Hotels: Lansdowne Court.

T24 County Armagh

☎(0861) 522501, 525861 office, 525864 Pro
Demesne, Newry Rd, Armagh, Co Armagh
Off Newry Rd, 0.25 mile from city centre.

Parkland course.
18 holes, 6147 yards, S.S.S.69
Founded 1893
Visitors: welcome except
12am-2pm Sat and 12am-3pm Sun.
Green Fee: £10 WD, £15 WE & BH.
Societies: catered for except on Sat.
Catering: full facilities; by prior
arrangement Mon.
Hotels: Charlemont Arms; Drumsill
House.

T25 **Craigavon**
☎(0762) 326606
Golf and Ski Centre, Turmoyra Lane,
Silverwood, Lurgan, Craigavon, Co
Armagh
Off M1 from Belfast at A76 exit 10,
continue for 500 yards from sliproad,
take 1st right into Kiln Rd and 1st
right again.
Public parkland course.
18 holes, 6496 yards, Par 72; 9
holes, 1349 yards, Par 3.
Visitors: welcome any time,
advisable to ring in advance
weekends.
Green Fee: apply for details.
Societies: by arrangement, mainly
Sun, some Sat.
Catering: snacks, bar and restaurant
at Silverwood Golf & Ski Centre
adjacent to course.
12-hole Pitch & Putt, driving range
and putting green.
Hotels: Silverwood.

T26 **Cushendall**
☎(02667) 71318, 58366 Sec
Shore Rd, Cushendall, Ballymena, Co
Antrim BT44 0QQ
Turn right at Curfew Tower in village,
proceed 0.25 mile to Strand.
Seaside/parkland course.
9 holes, 2193 metres, S.S.S.63
Designed by Daniel Delargy.
Founded 1938
Visitors: welcome.
Green Fee: £8/day WD, £10/day WE
& BH.
Societies: weekdays.
Catering: summer, weekends
winter; or by prior arrangement at
any time.
Hotels: Thornlea.

T27 **Donaghadee**
☎(0247) 883624
84 Warren Rd, Donaghadee, Co
Down BT21 0PQ
On A2 18 miles E of Belfast.
Part links/part parkland.
18 holes, 5576 metres, S.S.S.69

Founded 1899
Visitors: welcome except Sat
(competition day), booking
advisable.
Green Fee: £13.50 WD; £17 WE.
Societies: Mon, Wed and Fri.
Catering: full facilities.
Snooker.
Hotels: Copelands; Dunallen.

T28 **Downpatrick**
☎(0396) 615947 Office; 612152
Clubhouse; 615244 Catering;
615167 Golf shop
43 Saul Rd, Downpatrick, Co Down
BT30 6PA
A24 and A7 23 miles SE of Belfast.
Parkland course.
18 holes, 6400 yards, S.S.S.69
Designed by Hawtree & Sons.
Founded 1932
Visitors: welcome, restricted at
weekends.
Green Fee: £14 WD, £18 WE & BH.
Societies: by arrangement.
Catering: full facilities.
Snooker.
Hotels: Denvir's; Abbey Lodge.

T29 **Dungannon**
☎(08687) 22098, 27338 Office
34 Springfield Lane, Mullaghmore,
Dungannon, Co Tyrone BT70 1QX
0.5 mile out of town on Donaghmore
Rd.
Parkland course.
18 holes, 5818 yards, S.S.S.68
Founded 1890
Visitors: welcome anytime.
Green Fee: £10 WD, £13 WE.
Societies: welcome by arrangement.
Catering: by arrangement.
Hotels: Dunowen; Inn on the Park;
Glengannon Inn.

T30 **Dunmurry**
☎(0232) 610834
91 Dunmurry Lane, Dunmurry,
Belfast BT17 9JS
Situated between Dunmurry village
and Upper Malone Rd, Belfast.
Parkland course.
18 holes, 5832 yards, S.S.S.68
Designed by T.J. McAuley.
Founded 1905
Visitors: not before 5pm Sat, after
5pm Tues and Thurs.
Green Fee: £14 WD, £20 WE & BH.
Societies: not Sat,
11.30am-12.30pm Sun.
Catering: each day except Mon.
Hotels: Conway; Beechlawn;
Balmoral.

T31 **Edenmore Golf Course**
☎(0846) 611310 Clubhouse,
619199 Restaurant
Edenmore House, 70 Drumnabreeze
Rd, Maralin, Co. Armagh, N Ireland
BT67 0RH
From Belfast take M1 motorway, turn
off at 5th exit for Moira; through
Moira to Maralin (1 mile); at Maralin
turn left into New Forge Rd, then 1st
left into Steps Rd; after small bridge
take 1st right into Orange Lane and
1st left into Drumnabreeze Rd.
Parkland course.
9 holes (18 by summer 1994).
Designed by Frank Ainsworth.
Founded June 1992
Visitors: welcome except Sun
(course closed); no h/cap
requirement; Club members have
priority booking for tee-off times on
Sat up to 12.30pm.
Green Fee: £5 (9 holes), £8 (18
holes) WD; £7 (9 holes), £10 (18
holes, with member) Sat & BH.
Societies: welcome any time by
prior arrangement.
Catering: excellent restaurant;
morning tea or coffee, lunch
(12-2pm), afternoon tea; private
functions in evenings by prior
arrangement (for 20-80).
Hotels: Seagoe (Portadown); White
Gables (Hillsborough); Silverwood
(Lurgan).

T32 **Enniskillen**
☎(0365) 25250
Castlecoole, Enniskillen, Co
Fermanagh
1 mile from Enniskillen off Tempo Rd.
Parkland course.
18 holes, 5420 metres, S.S.S.70
Designed by Dr Dixon & George
Mawhinney (1st 9), T.J. McAuley
(2nd 9).
Founded 1896
Visitors: unrestricted.
Green Fee: £10/day WD, £12 WE &
BH.
Societies: golfing societies welcome
if previous arrangements made with
Club Steward.
Catering: bar snacks daily, full
catering by prior arrangement.
Snooker.
Hotels: Killyhevlin; Fort Lodge;
Railway, Belmore Court.

T33 **Fintona**
☎(0662) 841480
Ecclesville Demesne, Fintona, Co
Tyrone

9 miles SW of Omagh.
Parkland course.
9 holes, 6251 yards, S.S.S.70
Founded 1896
Visitors: welcome.
Green Fee: £10/round.
Societies: by prior arrangement.
Catering: by prior arrangement.

T34 **Fortwilliam**
☎(0232) 370770
Downview Ave, Belfast B15 4EZ
On A2 3 miles N of Belfast.
Meadowland course.
18 holes, 5796 yards, S.S.S.67
Designed by Mr Buchart.
Founded 1891
Visitors: welcome except Sat.
Green Fee: apply for details.
Societies: welcome by arrangement
with Sec.
Catering: full service available.
Hotels: Lansdowne Court.

T35 **Gilnahirk**
☎(0232) 448477
Manns Corner, Upper Bramel Rd,
Gilnahirk, Castlereagh, Belfast
3 miles from Belfast off Ballygowan
road.
Public moorland course.
9 holes, 5398 metres, S.S.S.68
Founded 1984
Visitors: welcome.
Green Fee: apply for details.
Putting green.
Hotels: Stormont.

T36 **Greenisland**
☎(0232) 862236
156 Upper Rd, Grennisland,
Carrickfergus, Co Antrim BT38 8RW
About 9 miles N of Belfast.
Meadowland course.
9 holes, 5536 metres, S.S.S.69
Re-designed by H. Middleton.
Founded 1894
Visitors: welcome except Sat.
Green Fee: £10 WD, £15 Sun.
Societies: welcome by prior
arrangement.
Catering: full facilities.
Snooker.
Hotels: Glenavna, Newtownabbey.

T37 **Helen's Bay**
☎(0247) 852601
Golf Rd, Helen's Bay, Bangor, Co
Down BT19 1TL
Off A2, 9 miles E of Belfast.
Seaside course.
9 holes, 5176 metres, S.S.S.67

Founded 1896
Visitors: welcome Mon, Wed, Thurs
(before 2pm), Fri, Sun; with member
only Sat and Bank Holidays after
2.30pm.
Green Fee: on application.
Societies: Mon, Wed and Fri.
Catering: full facilities.

T38 **Holywood**
☎(0232) 422138
Nuns Walk, Demesne Rd, Holywood,
Co Down BT18 9LE
On A2 6 miles E of Belfast.
Undulating course.
18 holes, 5885 yards, S.S.S.68
Founded 1904
Visitors: welcome except Sat.
Green Fee: £15 WD, £21 Sun.
Societies: catered for except Thurs,
Sat and Bank Holidays.
Catering: full bar and catering
facilities.
Snooker.
Hotels: Culloden.

T39 **Kilkeel**
☎(06937) 62296, 65095, 63787 Sec
Mourne Park, Kilkeel, Co Down BT34
4LB
3 miles from Kilkeel on Newry road,
signposted.
Parkland course.
18 holes, 6625 yards, S.S.S.72
Designed by Lord Justice Babbington
(original 9), Eddie Hackett (new 9).
Founded 1948 on present site.
Visitors: welcome except Sat.
Green Fee: £16 WD, £18 WE & BH.
Societies: on application.
Catering: full facilities.
Snooker, pool.
Hotels: Kilmorey Arms; Cranfield
House.

T40 **Killymoon**
☎(06487) 62254 Members, 63762
Office, 63460 Pro
200 Killymoon Rd, Cookstown, Co
Tyrone BT80 8TW
0.5 mile off A29 on S side of
Cookstown.
Parkland course.
18 holes, 5498 metres, S.S.S.69
Designed by Hugh Adair.
Founded 1889
Visitors: all week except Sat, club
competition day.
Green Fee: £13 WD, £17 Sun & BH.
Societies: except Thurs and Sat.
Catering: bar, full catering facilities
available.
Hotels: Glenavon; Greenvale; Royal.

T41 **Kilrea**
☎(0265) 834738 Sec
38 Drumagarner Rd, Kilrea, Co
Londonderry, N Ireland
0.5 mile SW of Kilrea on road to
Maghera.
Inland links course, well-drained.
9 holes, 4326 yards, S.S.S.66
Founded 1920
Visitors: welcome 7 days, avoid
Tues, Wed evenings, Sat in summer.
Green Fee: £7.50/day.
Societies: welcome any day.

T42 **Kirkistown Castle**
☎(02477) 71233 Sec, 71353
Catering, 71004 Pro, 71699 Fax
142 Main Rd, Cloughey, Co Down
BT22 1JA
A20 from Belfast to Kircubbin, follow
signs to Newtownards and
Portaferry, then B173 to Cloughey.
Links course.
18 holes, 6157 yards, S.S.S.70
Designed by B. Polley.
Founded Oct 1902
Visitors: welcome.
Green Fee: £13 WD (£9 with
member); £25 WE & BH (£12 with
member); jnrs £5 WD, £10 WE.
Societies: welcome weekdays,
except Bank Holidays; society rates
available for 16 and over.
Catering: full facilities daily
11am-8pm.
Hotels: Portaferry.

T43 **The Knock**
☎(0232) 483251 Office, 483825
Pro, 482249 Club, 480519 Catering
Summerfield, Upper Newtownards
Rd, Dundonald, Belfast BT16 0QX
E out of Belfast towards Dundonald,
course on left 0.5 mile beyond
Stormont Houses of Parliament.
Parkland course.
18 holes, 6407 yards, S.S.S.71
Designed by Colt, McKenzie & Allison.
Founded 1895
Visitors: not Sat unless with
member.
Green Fee: £20 WD (£8 with
member); £25 WE & BH (£11 with
member).
Societies: Mon and Thurs.
Catering: full facilities all week.
Snooker.
Hotels: Stormont (within 1 mile).

T44 **Knockbracken G & CC**
☎(0232) 792108, 795666
Ballymaconaghy Rd, Knockbracken,
Belfast BT8 4SB

Near Four Winds restaurant on SE
outskirts of city.
Meadowland course.
18 holes, 5312 yards, S.S.S.68
Visitors: welcome any time but
priority tee times for members at
weekends.
Green Fee: apply for details.
Societies: by arrangement.
Catering: full bar and restaurant
facilities 7 days.
Driving range, putting greens, ski
slope.
Hotels: La Mon; Drumkeen.

T45 **Larne**
☎(09603) 382228
54 Ferris Bay Rd, Islandmagee,
Larne BT40 3RT
From Belfast, N to Carrickfergus, 6
miles from Whitehead; from Larne S
along coast road to Islandmagee; 23
miles from Belfast, 7 miles Larne.
Seaside course at N tip of
Islandmagee peninsula.
9 holes, 6082 yards, S.S.S.69
Designed by Babington.
Founded 1894
Visitors: weekdays; not Sat.
Green Fee: on application.
Societies: open; not Sat.
Catering: available.
Hotels: Magheramorne House.

T46 **Lisburn**
☎(0846) 677216
68 Eglantine Rd, Lisburn, Co Antrim
BT27 5RQ
3 miles S of Lisburn, 200 yards from
BBC radio transmitter mast.
Meadowland/parkland course.
18 holes, 5708 metres, S.S.S.72
Designed by Hawtree & Sons.
Founded 1905
Visitors: at specified times.
Green Fee: apply for details.
Societies: Mon, Thurs, Fri.
Catering: 7 days.
Hotels: White Gables (Hillsborough).

T47 **Lurgan**
☎(0762) 322087 Sec/Manager,
325306 Club, 321068 Pro
The Demesne, Lurgan, Co Armagh
BT67 9BN
Centre of Lurgan to Windsor Ave and
proceed past castle gates around
edge of lake.
Parkland course bordering on Lurgan
Park and lakes.
18 holes, 5836 metres, S.S.S.70
Designed by F. Pennink.
Founded 1894

Visitors: welcome except Sat.
Green Fee: £15 WD, £20 WE & BH;
Ladies £12, students £10, under 18s
£5.
Societies: on request, not Sat.
Catering: available except Mon.
Hotels: Silverwood; Carngrove;
Seagoe.

T48 **Mahee Island**
☎(0238) 541234
Comber, Newtownards, Co Down,
BT23 6ET
Turn left 0.5 mile from Comber on
Comber/Killyleagh road, keep
bearing left to Mahee Island, 6 miles.
Parkland/seaside course.
9 holes, 5588 yards, S.S.S.67
Founded 1929
Visitors: restricted after 4pm Wed
and until 5pm Sat.
Green Fee: £9 WD, £13 WE & BH.
Societies: alternate Sun, weekdays
except Mon; apply in writing to Sec.
Catering: by arrangement, no bar.
Pool.
Hotels: Balloo House; La Mon House;
Strangford Arms.

T49 **Malone**
☎(0232) 612758
240 Upper Malone Rd, Dunmurry,
Belfast BT17 9LB
5 miles from Belfast centre, take
Upper Malone Rd.
Parkland course.
18 holes, 6433 yards, S.S.S.71
Designed by Fred Hawtree.
Founded 1895
Visitors: welcome except Wed after
2pm and Sat before 5pm.
Green Fee: apply for details.
Societies: catered for Mon and
Thurs.
Catering: full facilities except Sun
after 2pm.

T50 **Massereene**
☎(0849) 428096
51 Lough Rd, Antrim
1 mile S of town, 3.5 miles from
Aldergrove Airport.
Parkland course.
18 holes, 6614 yards, S.S.S.71
Designed by F.W. Hawtree.
Founded 1895
Visitors: welcome weekdays and
weekends, Sat competition day.
Green Fee: £16 WD, £20 WE.
Societies: Tues, Thurs 9-12am and
2-3.30pm; Wed 9-11.30am.
Catering: full facilities.
Hotels: Dunadry; Deerpark.

T51 **Moyola Park**
☎(0648) 68468, 68830 Pro.
Shanemullagh, Castledawson,
Magherafelt, Co Londonderry BT45
8DG
Turn right half-way through
Castledawson village, along Curran
Rd, entrance 400 yards on right.
Parkland course.
18 holes, 6517 yards, S.S.S.71
Designed by Don Patterson.
Founded 1976
Visitors: welcome.
Green Fee: £12 WD, £20 WE.
Societies: welcome at all times
except Sat by prior arrangement.
Catering: full facilities, phone (0648)
68392. Snooker.
Hotels: Moyola Lodge.

T52 **Newtownstewart**
☎(06626) 61466, 61829
38 Golf Course Rd, Newtownstewart,
Omagh, Co Tyrone BT78 4HU
2 miles SW of Newtownstewart via
B84 Drumquin road.
Parkland course.
18 holes, 5341 metres, S.S.S.69;
Soc S.S.S.68
Designed by Frank Pennink.
Founded 1914
Visitors: welcome but advance
booking advisable.
Green Fee: £10 WD, £15 WE & BH.
Societies: by prior arrangement.
Catering: bar open normal hours,
meals by arrangement. Snooker.
Hotels: Hunting Lodge; Royal Arms;
Silver Birch; Fir Trees Lodge.

T53 **Omagh**
☎(0662) 243160, 241442
83a Dublin Rd, Omagh, Co Tyrone
BT78 1HQ
On A5 on outskirts of Omagh.
Parkland course.
18 holes, 5429 metres, S.S.S.69
Founded 1910
Visitors: welcome any day except
Tues, Sat and Sun.
Green Fee: £10/day WD, £15/day
WE & BH; £2 reduction with member,
senior citizens half price.
Societies: welcome weekdays.
Catering: available for societies.
Snooker.
Hotels: Royal Arms.

T54 **Ormeau**
☎(0232) 641069, 640700, 640999
50 Park Rd, Belfast BT7 2FX
2 miles from city centre on Ravenhill
Road.

Royal Portrush and Royal County Down

Old Tom Morris's achievement in laying out Royal County Down at a cost not to exceed £4.00 is part of golf's folklore and represented remarkably good value for money even in those far off days. However, not much of his original work survives in the modern version of a links that many now regard as perhaps the mightiest of them all.

If you are lucky enough to play golf on either of Northern Ireland's two great courses, Royal County Down and Royal Portrush, somebody, sooner or later, is bound to fuel the debate about which is the better.

Rather like being asked to decide whether Bobby Jones was superior to Ben Hogan, or Jack Hobbs a better batsman than Don Bradman, it is a provocative question, but one fact upon which nearly everyone is agreed is that both rank among the 10 best courses in Great Britain and Eire, and no self-respecting golfer visiting those parts for the first time should play the one and not the other.

Although the approach to Portrush along the coast road from Antrim can be spectacularly beautiful, one reason for giving County Down at Newcastle the edge is because its setting under the shadow of the Mountains of Mourne is so majestic and inspiring that nobody could fail to be moved by it. There is something special about playing against a backcloth of mountains, but even if you denied Newcastle the splendour of its distant views, the avenues forged by the fairways between high sandhills clad with gorse, would still be most beguiling.

The quiet seaside town of Newcastle lies on a narrow strip of dune country on the edge of Dundrum Bay, its fine, natural features combining to present the severest of championship tests in which there is a big demand on long, straight driving, and no end of challenging strokes onto the well protected greens.

It is sad that Ulster's problems have denied it more championship status

following its staging of the Curtis Cup in 1968 and the British Amateur Championship, won for the third successive year by Michael Bonallack, in 1970.

The first three holes along the shore make a stern beginning; then comes a long short hole from a high tee across the gorse and a classic par 4, the 5th doglegging round the hills. More holes linger in the mind notably the 9th which, following a blind drive, unveils the full panoply of the setting: it is one of the most photographed pictures in golf. The inward half continues the challenging trend, the least blemish being severely punished.

Not that Portrush offers any more relief. It, too, lies in the mist of some natural golfing country, north of Belfast, and, with the wind blowing in from the Atlantic and the rough in full bloom, good scoring is no light matter.

Bernard Darwin, on seeing it for the first time, wrote that its designer, Harry Colt, had built himself a monument more enduring than brass and it is certainly a thorough examination of a golfer's skill. The 5th, with its green by the water's edge looking away towards the giant's causeway, is particularly appealing, along with the magnificent one-shot 6th that follows.

Then, later on, there are holes aptly termed "calamity corner" and "purgatory" and all the time, to lend a historical, note the reminder that in 1951 Max Faulkner won the Open Championship on the only occasion in which it ventured outside Scotland or England. Similarly, in 1960, Joe Carr, perhaps the best known and most loved figure in all Ireland, stood 10 up and 10 to play in the final of the Amateur Championship.

These were the supreme moments of the lives of two players who, in their respective worlds, provided more colour and entertainment than any of their contemporaries. For them, Royal Portrush, which housed the British Amateur once again in 1993, must have a warm place in their hearts, and no wonder.

Parkland course.
9 holes, 2653 yards, S.S.S.65
Founded 1893
Visitors: welcome weekdays and
Sun.
Green Fee: on application.
Societies: Thurs and Sun on
application.
Catering: bar and restaurant.
Snooker.
Hotels: Drumkeen House.

T55 **Portadown**

☎(0762) 355356
192 Gilford Rd, Portadown,
Craigavon, Co Armagh BT63 5LF
On A59 2 miles SE of Portadown,
entrance 400 yards beyond Metal
Box factory on right.
Parkland course.
18 holes, 5621 metres, S.S.S.70
Founded 1900
Visitors: welcome except Tues and
Sat.
Green Fee: £15 (male) £12 (female)
WD; £18 (male), £15 (female) WE &
BH.
Societies: details on request.
Catering: bar daily, restaurant
except Mon.
Squash, snooker.
Hotels: Seagoe; Carn.

T56 **Portstewart**

☎(026583) 2015, 3839
117 Strand Rd, Portstewart, Co
Londonderry BT55 7PG
4 miles W of Portrush.
Links course.
Strand, 18 holes, 6714 yards,
S.S.S.72; Town, 18 holes, 4733
yards, S.S.S.62; Blue, 9 holes, 2662
yards, Par 32
Founded 1894
Visitors: weekdays on application.
Green Fee: apply for details.
Societies: welcome weekdays,
must book by phone.
Catering: every day.
Hotels: Edgewater.

T57 **Royal Belfast**

☎(0232) 428165, 428586 Pro
Station Rd, Craigavad, Holywood, Co
Down BT19 0BP
2 miles E of Holywood on A2.
Parkland course.
18 holes, 5963 yards, S.S.S.69
Designed by H.C. Colt, redesigned
(1988) Donald Steel.
Founded 1881
Visitors: except Wed and Sat before
4.30pm; letter of intro from own club.

Green Fee: £20/round WD,
£25/round WE & BH.
Societies: by arrangement.
Catering: full facilities.
Hotels: Culloden.

T58 **Royal County Down**

☎(03967) 23314, 26281 Fax
Newcastle, Co Down BT33 0AN
From Belfast take A24 to Carryduff,
A7 to Ballynahinch and A2 to
Newcastle, about 30 miles.
Links course.
18 holes, 6968 yards, S.S.S.73
Designed by Tom Morris Snr.
Founded 1898
Visitors: Mon, Tues, Thurs, Fri;
h/cap cert required.
Green Fee: summer, £43 WD, £55
WE & BH; winter, £32 WD, £43 WE &
BH.
Societies: by arrangement only.
Catering: Centenary Room open
Mon-Fri.
Hotels: Slieve Donard; Burrendale;
Glassdrumman Lodge.

T59 **Royal Portrush**

☎(0265) 822311, 823139 Fax
Bushmills Rd, Portrush, Co Antrim
BT56 8JQ
1 mile from Portrush town off A1.
Seaside links course.
Valley, 18 holes, 6273 yards,
S.S.S.70; Dunluce, 18 holes, 6784
yards, S.S.S.73
Designed by H.S. Colt.
Founded 1888
Visitors: welcome Mon, Tues, Thurs,
Fri am, Sun after 10am.
Green Fee: Dunluce, £35 WD, £40
WE; Valley, £15 WD, £20 WE.
Societies: catered for; on Dunluce
Mon, Tues, Thurs, Fri am, Sun
10.30-11.30am; on Valley every day
except Sat/Sun am.
Catering: full catering daily, snacks,
high tea and à la carte.
Hotels: Bayview (Portballatrae);
Magherabuoy House.

T60 **Scrabo**

☎(0247) 812355 Sec, 817848 Pro,
822919 Fax
233 Scrabo Rd, Newtownards, Co
Down BT23 4SL
Off A20 10 miles E of Belfast; near
Scrabo Tower.
Hilly parkland course.
18 holes, 5699 metres, S.S.S.71
Founded 1907
Visitors: weekdays except Wed.
Green Fee: £15 WD, £20 WE.

Societies: any day except Sat, not
during June.
Catering: full bar and restaurant.
Snooker.
Hotels: Strangford Arms; George; La
Mon House.

T61 **Shandon Park**

☎(0232) 793730
73 Shandon Park, Belfast BT5 6NY
3 miles from city centre via Knock
dual carriageway.
Parkland course.
18 holes, 6252 yards, S.S.S.70
Founded 1926
Visitors: welcome weekdays.
Green Fee: apply for details.
Societies: Mon and Fri only by
arrangement.
Catering: meals and snacks.
Hotels: Stormont; Drumkeen.

T62 **Spa**

☎(0238) 562365
20 Grove Rd, Ballynahinch, Co Down
BT24 8PN
A24, 1 mile from Ballynahinch, exit at
sign for Spa or Dromara.
Parkland course.
18 holes, 5938 metres, S.S.S.70
Founded 1907
Visitors: welcome.
Green Fee: on application.
Societies: Mon-Thurs and some
Sun; 1st tee 10.30-11.45am.
Catering: bar; meals by
arrangement.
Snooker, pool, bowls.
Hotels: Millbrook Lodge; White
Horse.

T63 **Strabane**

☎(0504) 382271, 382007
Ballycolman, Strabane, Co Tyrone
BT82 9PH
1 mile from Strabane on Dublin road
beside church and three schools.
Parkland course.
18 holes, 5865 yards, S.S.S.69
Designed by Eddie Hackett.
Founded 1909
Visitors: welcome.
Green Fee: £10 WD (£8 with
member), £12 WE (£10 with
member).
Societies: apply to Sec.
Catering: by arrangement.
Hotels: Fir Trees Lodge.

T64 **Tandragee**

☎(0762) 841272 office, 840727
Club, 841761 Pro

Market Hill Rd, Tandragee, Co
Armagh BT62 2ER
A27 from Portadown towards Newry
and Dublin, right on B3 in Tandragee
towards Market Hill and Clare Glen,
course 200 yards on right.
Hilly parkland course.
18 holes, 5519 metres, S.S.S.69
Designed by F. Hawtree.
Founded 1920
Visitors: Mon-Wed before 4pm,
Thurs before 2pm (Ladies Day), Fri
before 1pm, Sun 10.30-11.30am
and after 3pm.
Green Fee: £10 WD, £15 WE & BH.
Societies: Sun 10.30-11.30am,
Mon-Wed before 12am and after
2pm, Fri before 12am.
Catering: full service from 12.30pm
daily; normal bar facilities 7 days.

Snooker, large function room.
Hotels: Seagoe, Carn Grove
(Portadown).

T65 **Warrenpoint**
☎(06937) 53695, 52371 Pro
Lower Dromore Rd, Warrenpoint, Co
Down BT34 3LN
5 miles from Newry on main
Warrenpoint road.
Parkland course.
18 holes, 5626 metres, S.S.S.70
Founded 1893
Visitors: by appointment.
Green Fee: on application.
Societies: by prior arrangement.
Catering: full facilities.
Snooker, squash.
Hotels: Carlingford Bay.

T66 **Whitehead**
☎(09603) 53631 Sec, 53792 Club
McCrae's Brae, Whitehead, Co
Antrim BT38 9NZ
Take turning into Whitehead off main
Carrickfergus-Larne road to
Islandmagee road, signposted at
bottom of McCrae's Brae to club.
Undulating parkland course.
18 holes, 6426 yards, S.S.S.71
Founded 1904
Visitors: any day except Sat.
Green Fee: £11 WD, £17 Sun and
BH.
Societies: Mon to Fri 9am-12.30pm,
1.30pm-4.30pm (Fri until 4pm), Sun
10.30-12am.
Catering: available by arrangement
with Steward.
Hotels: Magheramorne House.

U

EIRE

The first lesson that has to be learned about golf in Ireland is that, in order to derive the greatest benefit, it is better not to be in too much of a hurry. Settle in to the pace of life. Don't plan an impossible itinerary. Travel can be slow and golfing destinations remote but that is undoubtedly part of their attraction and you will soon adapt.

This certainly applies to the coastal sweep that begins in Dublin and ends in Galway, a journey that incorporates many wonderful courses, particularly out west where giant dunes, lonely beaches and wild winds lend an accompaniment to the play that is quite uplifting. Ballybunion, Lahinch, Tralee and Waterville are fit for giants, places that pose the ultimate in challenge although beguiling enough to soften failure.

For those arriving at Shannon Airport, the decision is whether to head north or south of the great estuary which runs into Limerick. Greater by far is the number of courses to the south-west but Lahinch, called the St Andrews of Ireland because of its discovery by officers of the Black Watch, is as fine an example of links golf as could be imagined.

Ballybunion's Old course is an undoubted monument that has brought deserved fame to the little seaside town. It involves a little more climbing than on other links, but some of the high spots enhance the spectacular views. Herbert Warren Wind, the American writer, puts it on an exalted pinnacle but fiercer debate involves the New course whose design and construction led to the building of a newly positioned clubhouse.

Nearby Tralee, the work of Arnold Palmer, is a course of two parts, a front 9 of more open land and a back 9 dominated by majestic dune country involving many demanding strokes.

Some of the greens on the outward half enjoy settings on the edge of the sea which are captivating if the wind is not severe. But the beauty of the settings is a recurring theme all over the south-west of Ireland, and it certainly applies to Waterville, the inspiration of a local man, J.A. Mulcahy.

I never think the golf at Killarney quite matches the surroundings but that may be because Killarney is inland and my leanings are more seaside, but there are other inland delights such as Little Island (Cork), Carlow, set in a lovely old deer park, and three new creations, St Helen's at Rosslare, Faithlegg in County Waterford, and the European Club in County Wicklow. Further up the east coast, Baltray represents as fine a tract of natural terrain as exists in a country renowned for its great courses.

The Irish course which has seen more great events than any other is Portmarnock, a few miles south of Baltray. Many Irish Opens, the Canada Cup, British Amateur and the Walker Cup, head the impressive list, a tribute to a formidable test of golf.

Royal Dublin, older than Portmarnock, is another noble links and a word for Sutton, the 9-hole course famous for its association with Joe Carr. It stands on Cush Point looking across the narrow estuary to Portmarnock where Carr was born. It is such a short, compact little course that it used to be said that if Carr shouted "Fore", everybody ducked; but if it is enchantment that you want, the Island at Malahide offers the perfect retreat among its lonely dunes.

Many of Dublin's other courses are more parkland in character, but out on the west coast the feature of the courses is again one of grandeur and beauty. Connermara, Donegal, Rosapenna and Westport are the main attractions, and there are few lovelier spots where the game is played than County Sligo at Rosses Point, home of the late Cecil Ewing, another giant of Irish golf. Last year, the Club housed the Home Internationals, a wonderfully friendly environment for a unique gathering.

U1 Abbeyleix
☎(0502) 31450
Abbeyleix, Co Laois
Within 0.5 mile of Main St on
Stradbally Rd.
Parkland course.
9 holes, 5680 yards, S.S.S.68
Founded 1895
Visitors: welcome.
Green Fee: £6 WD, £8 WE if
available.
Societies: usually on Sat.
Catering: by arrangement for
societies.
Hotels: Hibernian; Killeshin;
Montague (Portlaoise); Globe House
(Ballinakill).

U2 Achill Island
☎(098) 43202
Keel, Achill, Co Mayo
Via Castlebar or Westport.
Public seaside course.
9 holes, 2723 yards, S.S.S.66
Designed by P. Skerrit.
Founded 1951
Visitors: welcome.
Green Fee: £4/round, £16/week.
Societies: monthly (approx).
Hotels: Achill Sound; Wavecrest;
Atlantic; Gray's; McDowell's;
Slievemore; Achill Head; Clew Bay;
The Strand; Stellamaris GH.

U3 Adare Manor
☎(061) 396204
Adare, Co Limerick
10 miles from Limerick city on main
Killarney road.
Parkland course built round castle
and friary ruins.
18 holes, 6000 yards, S.S.S.69
Designed by Eddie Hackett.
Founded 1900
Visitors: welcome weekdays,
weekends with member or by prior
arrangement.
Green Fee: £15.
Societies: on club notice board;
book well in advance.
Catering: limited to chicken, fish etc
in basket; sandwiches, tea, coffee
etc available.
Hotels: Dunranen Arms; Woodlands.

U4 Ardee
☎(041) 53227, 56283, 56137 Fax
Town Parks, Ardee, Co Louth
0.25 mile N of town on Mullinstown
Road.
Parkland course.
18 holes, 6046 yards, S.S.S.69
Designed by Eddie Hackett.

Founded 1911
Visitors: welcome at all times,
Mon-Fri.
Green Fee: £15.
Societies: Mon-Sat.
Catering: facilities available at
all times.
Hotels: Gables B&B; Nuremore.

U5 Arklow
☎(0402) 32401
Abbeylands, Arklow, Co Wicklow
0.5 mile from Arklow town centre.
Seaside course.
18 holes, 5963 yards, S.S.S.68
Designed by Hawtree & Taylor.
Founded 1927
Visitors: welcome except Sun.
Green Fee: £13 WD, £18 Sat.
Societies: welcome except Sun.
Catering: by arrangement.
Hotels: Arklow Bay; Royal; Hoynes.

U6 Ashford Castle
☎(092) 46003
Cong, Co Mayo, EIRE
27 miles N of Galway on shores of
Lough Corrib.
Parkland course.
9 holes, 4506 yards, Par 70
Designed by Eddie Hackett.
Founded 1972
Visitors: welcome, phone for tee
times.
Green Fee: £15/day.
Societies: welcome by prior
arrangement.
Catering: bar and snacks.

U7 Athenry
☎(091) 94466
Palmerstown, Oranmore, Co Galway
5 miles from Athenry on
Galway-Dublin route N6 at junction
with Athenry road.
Parkland course.
18 holes, 6100 yards, S.S.S.69
Designed by Eddie Hackett.
Founded 1902
Visitors: welcome Mon-Sat.
Green Fee: £12.
Societies: welcome if booked in
advance.
Catering: full bar and catering
facilities.

U8 Athlone
☎(0902) 92073, 92235
Hodson Bay, Athlone, Co
Roscommon
3 miles from Athlone on Roscommon
road on shores of Lough Ree.

Undulating parkland course.
18 holes, 6518 yards, S.S.S.70
Designed by Fred Hawtree.
Founded 1892
Visitors: welcome every day except
Sun; booking advisable.
Green Fee: £12/WD, £15 WE.
Societies: welcome all week except
Sun.
Catering: bar and restaurant
facilities.
Snooker; driving range 2 miles from
course.
Hotels: Hodson Bay; Prince of Wales;
Royal Hoey; Shamrock Lodge.

U9 Athy
☎(0507) 31729
Geraldine, Athy, Co Kildare
On T6, 2 miles N of Athy.
Undulating parkland course.
9 holes, 3079 yards, S.S.S.69
Founded 1906
Visitors: welcome weekdays.
Green Fee: apply for details.
Societies: catered for Sat am by
arrangement.
Catering: by arrangement with Club
Steward; ring after 7.30pm.
Hotels: Leinster Arms; Kilkea Castle

U10 Balbriggan
☎(01) 841 2173, 841 2229
Sec/Manager
Blackhall, Balbriggan, Co Dublin
0.5 mile S of town on main
Belfast-Dublin road, 17 miles from
Dublin.
Parkland course.
18 holes, 5881 metres, S.S.S.71
Designed by R. Stilwell, J. Paramour.
Founded 1945
Visitors: welcome weekdays.
Green Fee: £14 WD, £18 WE & BH.
Societies: weekdays.
Catering: full restaurant facilities
available.
Hotels: Holmpatrick House;
Skerries; Old Well; Julianstown.

U11 Ballaghaderreen
☎(0907) 60295
Aughalista, Ballaghaderreen, Co
Roscommon
3 miles from Ballaghaderreen.
Parkland course.
9 holes, 4663 yards, S.S.S.66
Visitors: welcome.
Green Fee: £6/day.
Societies: welcome, phone in
advance.
Catering: snacks, meals by
arrangement.

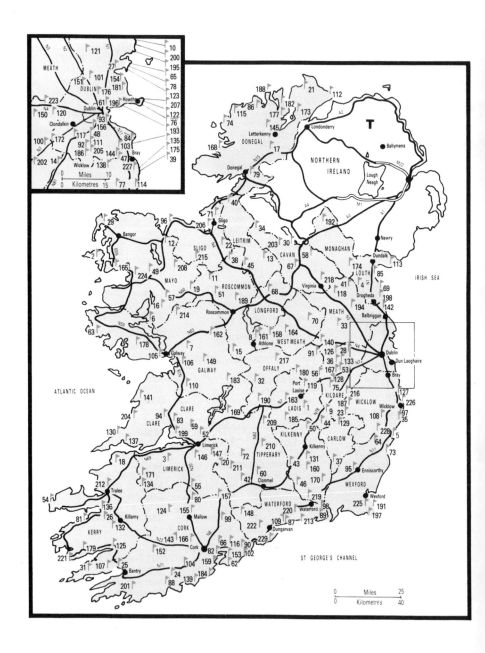

U12 Ballina

☎(096) 21050
Mossgrove, Shanaghy, Ballina, Co Mayo
On outskirts of town on road to Bonniconlon.
Inland, undulating course.
9 holes, 5700 yards, S.S.S.67
Designed by Eddie Hackett.
Founded 1910
Visitors: welcome.
Green Fee: £10.
Societies: by arrangement with Sec or Steward.
Catering: bar, meals by arrangement.
Hotels: Downhill; American; Bartra House.

U13 Ballinamore

☎(078) 44346
Creevy, Ballinamore, Co Leitrim
1 mile from town centre, sign at bridge.
Moorland/parkland course.
9 holes, 5680 yards, S.S.S.67
Founded 1939
Visitors: welcome except some Sun.
Green Fee: apply for details.
Societies: welcome by arrangement.
Catering: bar, coffee, soup etc.
Hotels: Slieve-an-Iaraim; Commercial; McAllisters.

U14 Ballinascorney

☎(01) 512516
Bohernabreena, Tallaght, Dublin 24
10 miles SW of Dublin.
18 holes, 5464 yards, S.S.S.67
Founded 1971
Visitors: welcome weekdays.
Green Fee: apply for details.
Catering: bar.

U15 Ballinasloe

☎(0905) 42126, 42538 Fax
Rossgloss, Ballinasloe, Co Galway
Turn left opposite Garbally College gates on Ballinasloe-Portumna road, 1 mile from there.
Parkland/meadowland course.
18 holes, 6445 yards, S.S.S.70
Designed by Eddie Hackett.
Founded 1894
Visitors: welcome 7 days except major competitions on Sun.
Green Fee: £10/day WD, £12 WE & BH.
Societies: welcome 7 days.
Catering: bar and full catering facilities available.
Hotels: Haydens; Lerridges Country.

U16 Ballinrobe

☎(092) 41448
Castlebar Road, Ballinrobe, Co Mayo
30 miles from Galway, 30 miles from Knock Airport.
Public parkland course set amid beautiful scenery.
9 holes, 5790 yards, S.S.S.68; new 18 hole course scheduled for 1995.
Founded 1905
Visitors: welcome all week except Tues after 5.00pm and Sun during competitions.
Green Fee: £10/day, £40/week.
Societies: welcome weekdays.
Catering: bar and restaurant; good food also at Red Door restaurant and several pubs.
Fishing in some of best lakes in Ireland.
Hotels: Lakeland; Valkenberg.

U17 Ballybofey & Stranorlar

☎(074) 31093, 31104 Sec
Stranorlar, Ballybofey, Co Donegal
14 miles from Strabane, club 500 yards off Strabane-Balleybofey main road on outskirts of Stranorlar village, signposted.
Parkland course.
18 holes, 5922 yards, S.S.S.69
Designed by P.C. Carr.
Founded 1958
Visitors: welcome except major competitions; check with Steward.

Green Fee: £12.
Societies: by arrangement with Sec or Steward (074) 31033; fee £10.
Catering: bar facilities; snacks and meals by arrangement.
Hotels: Kee's; Jackson's.

U18 **Ballybunion**
☎(068) 27146, 27387 Fax
Sandhill Rd, Ballybunion, Co Kerry
In Ballybunion, 20 miles from Tralee, 40 miles from Killaney.
Links course.
Old, 18 holes, 6542 yards, S.S.S.72;
Cashen, 18 holes, 6477 yards, S.S.S.71
Designed by Simpson McKenna (Old), R. Trent Jones Snr (Cashen).
Founded 1896
Visitors: welcome, book in advance; min h/cap 24 (men), 36 (ladies).
Green Fee: Old, £30/round; Cashen, £20/round; £45/day both courses.
Societies: welcome Mon-Fri.
Catering: snacks, meals, dining room, restaurant.
Practice green, steam room etc.
Hotels: Golf; Marine; Cliff House.

U19 **Ballyhaunis**
☎(0907) 30014, 30013 Sec (business), 30143 (home)
Coolnaha, Ballyhaunis, Co Mayo
2 miles N of Ballyhaunis on Sligo road, 6 miles from Horan International Airport; on main rail line from Dublin; main bus routes Galway/Derry, Dublin/Westport.
Undulating course.
18 holes, 5887 yards, S.S.S.68
Founded 1929
Visitors: welcome; Ladies Day Thurs, Club competitions on Sun.
Green Fee: £6/day.
Societies: catered for; contact Hon Sec 1 week in advance.
Catering: on notification.
Fishing, shooting, clay pigeon shoot, snooker, bridge etc.
Hotels: Central; Manor House; Westway; Orina; International; also local B&B.

U20 **Ballykisteen Golf & Country Club**
☎(062) 51439
Ballykisteen, Co Tipperary, EIRE
On Limerick road, 3 miles from Tipperary town.
Parkland course.
18 holes, Par 72
Designed by Des Smyth.
Founded April 1994

Visitors: welcome all week.
Green Fee: £18-22.
Societies: welcome.
Catering: full bar and restaurant.
Hotels: Ballykisteen (on site).

U21 **Ballyliffin**
☎(077) 76119
Ballyliffin, Carndonagh P.O., Co Donegal
8 miles from Buncrana, 6 miles from Carndonagh.
Seaside links course.
18 holes, 6384 yards, S.S.S.72
Founded 1947
Visitors: welcome.
Green Fee: apply for details.
Societies: welcome by booking.
Catering: bar, snacks and meals during summer (or by arrangement).
Hotels: Strand; Ballyliffin; (free golf for residents).

U22 **Ballymote**
☎(071) 83460
Carrigans, Ballymote, Co Sligo
1 mile N of Ballymote.
Parkland course.
9 holes, 2576 yards, S.S.S.66
Founded 1966
Visitors: welcome at any time.
Green Fee: apply for details.
Hotels: Castle.

U23 **Baltinglass**
☎(0508) 81350
Baltinglass, Co Wicklow
40 miles S of Dublin.
Parkland course.
9 holes, 6070 yards, S.S.S.69
Designed by Dr. W.G. Lyons, Hugh Dark and Col. Mitchell.
Founded 1928
Visitors: welcome.
Green Fee: apply for details.
Societies: 3 outings per month.
Catering: meals by arrangement.

U24 **Bandon**
☎(023) 41111, 42224
Castlebernard, Bandon, Co Cork
1.5 miles W of Bandon town, 15 miles from Cork Airport.
Parkland course.
18 holes, 5496 yards, S.S.S.69
Founded 1909
Visitors: welcome every day.
Green Fee: apply for details.
Societies: welcome weekdays.
Catering: full facilities.
Tennis.
Hotels: Munster Arms.

U25 **Bantry Park**
☎(027) 50372
Donemark, Bantry, Co Cork
1 mile from Bantry on Glengariff road.
9 holes, 6436 yards, S.S.S.70
Founded 1975
Visitors: welcome; club h/cap required.
Green Fee: £10/day.
Societies: apply in writing.
Catering: bar, snacks, lunches available.
Hotels: West Lodge, Bantry Bay, Sea View, Reendesert, Dromkeal; all have special arrangements with club.

U26 **Beauford**
☎(064) 44440
Churchtown, Beauford, Killarney, Co Kerry, EIRE
7 miles W of Killarney.
Parkland course.
18 holes, 7000 yards, Par 71
Designed by Arthur Spring.
Opening Sept 1994
Visitors: welcome, phone in advance.
Green Fee: £25/round.
Societies: welcome, phone in advance.
Catering: tea, coffee, soup and sandwiches.

U27 **Beaverstown**
☎(01) 436439
Beaverstown, Donabate, Co Dublin
24km (15 miles) N of Dublin, 5km N of Dublin Airport.
Parkland course.
18 holes, 5855 metres, S.S.S.71
Designed by Eddie Hackett.
Founded 1985
Visitors: welcome weekdays, with member at weekends.
Green Fee: £12 WD, £20 WE & BH.
Societies: by prior arrangement.
Catering: bar, restaurant, (snacks, lunches, evening meals).
Snooker.

U28 **Beech Park**
☎(01) 580522, 580100, 588365 Fax
Johnstown, Rathcoole, Co Dublin
2 miles from Rathcoole village on Kilteel road.
Parkland course.
18 holes, 5738 metres, S.S.S.70
Designed by Eddie Hackett.
Founded 1983
Visitors: welcome on Mon, Thurs, Fri, subject to course availability.

Green Fee: £16 (£7 with member).
Societies: by arrangement with Sec/Manager.
Catoring: full bar and catering facilities. Snooker.
Hotels: Greenisle; Ambassador.

U29 Belmullet
☎(097) 81266
Carne, Belmullet, Co Mayo
1.5 miles W of Belmullet.
Seaside links course.
18 holes, 6016 metres, S.S.S.72
Designed by Eddie Hackett.
Founded 1925
Visitors: welcome
Green Fee: £8/day, £35/week.
Hotels: Western Strands.

U30 Belturbet
☎(049) 22210
Erne Hill, Belturbet, Co Cavan
0.5 mile on Cavan road from Belturbet, on left.
Parkland course.
9 holes, 5230 yards, S.S.S.65
Founded 1950
Visitors: welcome weekdays and weekends.
Green Fee: apply for details.
Societies: most welcome at all times by appointment with Sec.
Catering: full catering on request. Snooker.
Hotels: Seven Horseshoes; Slieve Russell.

U31 Berehaven
☎(027) 70469
Millcove, Castletownbere, Co Cork
On main Glengariff-Castletownbere road, 3 miles before Castletownbere.
Public seaside course.
9 holes, 2257 metres, S.S.S.66
Founded 1902
Visitors: welcome at all times with valid h/cap.
Green Fee: £8 WD, £10 WE.
Societies: welcome at all times.
Catering: available.
Tennis, swimming, fishing, sailing.

U32 Birr
☎(0509) 20082
Glenns, Birr, Co Offaly
2 miles from Birr on road to Banager.
Undulating parkland course.
18 holes, 6262 yards, S.S.S.70
Founded 1893
Visitors: welcome, check on Sun.
Green Fee: apply for details.
Societies: every day except Sun.

Catering: by arrangement except Tues.
Hotels: County Arms, Doolys (Birr); Shannon (Banager).

U33 The Black Bush
☎(01) 250021
Thomastown, Dunshaughlin, Co Meath
0.5 mile E of Dunshaughlin on Ratoath road.
Parkland course with panoramic views.
18 holes, 7000 yards, S.S.S.73; 9 holes, 3400 yards, S.S.S.71
Designed by Robert Brown.
Founded 1988
Visitors: welcome, 9 hole course any time; 18 hole course any weekday, check for availability weekends.
Green Fee: apply for details.
Societies: welcome weekdays.
Catering: bar and restaurant 11.00am-11.00pm daily.
Driving range.
Hotels: Gaulstown House.

U34 Blacklion
☎(072) 53024
Toam, Blacklion, Co Cavan, via Sligo
W on A4 from Enniskillen to Sligo; E on N16 from Sligo to Enniskillen; located beside Blacklion village.
Parkland course.
9 holes, 5614 yards, S.S.S.69
Designed by E. Hackett.
Founded 1962
Visitors: welcome except on President's/Captain's days etc.
Green Fee: £5 WD, £7 Sun; £4 WD, £5 Sun with member.
Societies: by arrangement.
Catering: bar, bar snacks, meals by arrangement; clubhouse open from 1.30pm daily. Fishing.
Hotels: guest houses in Blacklion, Belcoo and Florencecourt.

U35 Blainroe
☎(0404) 68168
Blainroe, Co Wicklow
3 miles S of Wicklow on coast road.
Seaside course.
18 holes, 6681 yards, S.S.S.72
Designed by Hawtree & Sons.
Founded 1978
Visitors: ring for times.
Green Fee: £18 WD, £25 WE.
Societies: catered for 6 days.
Catering: lunch, dinner and bar food.
Hotels: Arklow Bay; Grand; Hunter's; Tinakilly House.

U36 Bodenstown
☎(045) 97096
Bodenstown, Sallins, Co Kildare
5 miles N of Naas via N7 and R407.
Parkland course.
Old Course, 18 holes, 6132 metres, S.S.S.72; New Course, 18 holes, 5278 metres, S.S.S.71
Founded 1972 (Old), 1983 (New)
Visitors: welcome; members only on Old Course weekends.
Green Fee: Old £10, New £9 (£8 WE)
Societies: by arrangement.
Catering: full facilities. Snooker.
Hotels: Ambassador (Kill).

U37 Borris
☎(0503) 73143
Deer Park, Borris, Co Carlow
Drive S from Carlow via Begenalstown; drive E from Kilkenny via Gowran and Goresbridge.
Parkland course.
9 holes, 6041 yards, S.S.S.69
Founded 1908
Visitors: welcome weekdays and with member on Sun.
Green Fee: on application.
Societies: catered for on weekdays and Sat am between 10.00am and 12.00am.
Catering: catering available for societies by arrangement.
Hotels: New Park, Springhill, Clubhouse, Hotel Kilkenny (all Kilkenny); Royal, Seven Oaks, Lane Court (all Carlow).

U38 Boyle
☎(079) 62594
Boyle, Co Roscommon
1.5 miles from Boyle on Roscommon road.
Undulating parkland course.
9 holes, 5450 yards, S.S.S.66
Designed by Eddie Hackett.
Founded 1911
Visitors: welcome.
Green Fee: apply for details.
Societies: welcome.
Catering: bar facilities and snacks.
Hotels: Royal; Forest Park.

U39 Bray
☎(01) 286 2484 Sec, 286 2092 Public
Ravenswell Rd, Bray, Co Wicklow
L29 from Dublin, turn left at bridge entering town.
Parkland course.
9 holes, 2866 metres, S.S.S.70
Founded 1897

Visitors: welcome weekdays except Mon.
Green Fee: £17/day.
Societies: societies affiliated to Golfing Union catered for.
Catering: limited catering available.
Snooker.
Hotels: Royal; Westbourne.

U40 **Bundoran**
☎(072) 41302
Bundoran, Co Donegal
32 miles W of Enniskillen, 25 miles N of Sligo.
Links/parkland course.
Championship 18 holes, 5785 mtrs, S.S.S.71
Designed by Harry Vardon.
Founded 1894
Visitors: welcome, book in advance.
Green Fee: apply for details.
Societies: welcome but advance booking required.
Catering: snacks, meals in hotel.
Hotels: Great Northern on course; Holyrood; Imperial; Maghery; Atlantic.

U41 **Cabra Castle**
☎(042) 67030
Kingscourt, Co Cavan, Eire
6 miles S of Carrickmacross.
Parkland course.
9 holes, 2654 metres, S.S.S.68
Visitors: welcome, only with member Sun.
Green Fee: £9/day.
Societies: welcome except Sun, phone in advance.
Catering: full facilities.
Snooker, horse riding.

U42 **Cahir Park**
☎(052) 41474
Kilcommon, Cahir, Co Tipperary.
1 mile S of Cahir on Clogheen road.
Parkland course.
9 holes, 5696 metres, S.S.S.69
Designed by Eddie Hackett.
Founded 1965
Visitors: welcome; advisable to check at weekends.
Green Fee: apply for details.
Societies: catered for on Sat.
Catering: bar; group meals at 3 days notice.
Hotels: Cahir House; Castle Court; Kilcoran Lodge.

U43 **Callan**
☎(056) 25136
Geraldine, Callan, Co Kilkenny

10 miles S of Kilkenny, 0.5 mile from Callan.
Parkland course.
9 holes, 6258 yards, S.S.S.70
Designed by Des Smyth.
Founded 1929
Visitors: welcome.
Green Fee: apply for details.
Societies: welcome weekdays and Sat am.
Catering: bar daily, food by arrangement.
Hotels: Somers; Newpark; Hotel Kilkenny; Club House.

U44 **Carlow**
☎(0503) 31695 office, 41745 Pro, 40065 Fax
Deerpark, Dublin Rd, Carlow, Co Carlow
1 mile from Carlow station, take Naas road from Dublin (52 miles).
Undulating parkland course.
18 holes, 5844 metres, S.S.S.70
Designed by Tom Simpson.
Founded 1899
Visitors: welcome.
Green Fee: £20 WD, £25 WE.
Societies: weekdays only, advance booking required.
Catering: full catering available.
Hotels: Seven Oaks; Royal; Lane Court.

U45 **Carrick-on-Shannon**
☎(079) 67015
Woodbrook, Carrick-on-Shannon, Co Roscommon.
3 miles W of Carrick on N4 route.
Parkland course.
9 holes, 5545 yards, S.S.S.68
Designed by E. Hackett.
Founded 1910
Visitors: welcome at all times.
Green Fee: £10/day, reduced over winter months.
Societies: on request to Sec.
Catering: bar facilities and snacks, catering on request.
Hotels: County; Bush.

U46 **Carrick-on-Suir**
☎(051) 40047
Garravoone, Co Tipperary
Approx 2 miles from Carrick-on-Suir on main road to Dungarvan; signposted on right side of road.
Undulating parkland course.
9 holes, 5948 yards, S.S.S.68
Designed by Edward Hackett.
Founded 1939
Visitors: welcome except Sun.
Green Fee: apply for details.

Societies: welcome except Sun.
Catering: by advance booking.
Hotels: Carraig; Cedarfield House.

U47 **Carrickmines**
☎(01) 295 5972
Off Glenamuck Rd, Carrickmines, Dublin 18
T43, 7 miles S of Dublin, left at Sandyford.
Heathland course.
9 holes, 6078 yards, S.S.S.69
Founded 1900
Visitors: welcome weekdays & Sun; Sat, Bank Holidays only with member.
Green Fee: £15 WD, £18 Sun.
Catering: very limited.

U48 **Castle**
☎(01) 904207
Woodside Dr, Rathfarnham, Dublin 14
From city turn left after Terenure and 2nd right.
Parkland course.
18 holes, 6240 yards, S.S.S.69
Designed by H.S. Colt.
Founded 1913
Visitors: welcome weekdays.
Green Fee: apply for details.
Societies: applications considered.
Catering: full lunch and dinner.
Hotels: Orwell Lodge.

U49 **Castlebar**
☎(094) 21649
Rocklands, Castlebar, Co Mayo
1.25 miles from town centre.
Parkland course.
18 holes, 6229 yards, S.S.S.69
Founded 1910
Visitors: welcome weekdays.
Green Fee: £10.
Societies: welcome except Sun.
Catering: available, 3 hours notice.
Hotels: Welcome Inn; Breaffy House; Travellers Friend; Imperial.

U50 **Castlecomer**
☎(056) 41139
Drumgoole, Castlecomer, Co Kilkenny
On N7 10 miles N of Kilkenny.
Parkland course.
9 holes, 6450 yards, S.S.S.71
Designed by Pat Ruddy.
Founded 1935
Visitors: welcome Mon to Sat, book in advance.
Green Fee: £10 WD, £12 WE & BH.
Societies: Mon-Sat.
Catering: snacks; lunches to order.
Hotels: Newpark (Kilkenny).

U51 Castlerea

☎(0907) 20068
Clonalis, Castlerea, Co Roscommon
On main Dublin-Castlebar road,
course just outside town on
Castlebar side.
Parkland course.
9 holes, 4974 yards, S.S.S.66
Founded 1905
Visitors: welcome.
Green Fee: apply for details.
Societies: welcome by arrangement.
Catering: available by arrangement
for societies.

U52 Castletroy

☎(061) 335261, 335753 Sec
Castletroy, Limerick
3 miles from Limerick city on Dublin
road, turn right at signpost in
Castletroy, course 300 yards on left.
Parkland course.
18 holes, 6340 yards, S.S.S.71
Founded 1937
Visitors: weekdays unlimited,
weekends with member only.
Green Fee: £20 (£12 with member).
Societies: Mon, Wed, Fri by
arrangement.
Catering: full catering service.
Hotels: Two Mile Inn; Castletroy
Park; Royal George.

U53 Castlewarden Golf & Country Club

☎(01) 589254 (Phone/Fax)
Castlewarden, Straffan, Co Kildare,
EIRE
Between Rathcoole and Kill; 2nd turn
after Blackchurch Inn.
Moorland course.
18 holes, S.S.S.69
Designed by Tommy Halpin;
re-designed by R.J. Browne (1992)
Founded 1989
Visitors: welcome Mon. Thurs, Fri;
weekends with member only.
Green Fee: £12 WD, £8 with
member, £10 WE with member.
Societies: welcome Mon, Thurs, Fri;
some Sats if no Medals or Majors.
Catering: bar, snacks, lunch, dinner.
Practice area.
Hotels: Ambassador (Kill).

U54 Ceann Sibeal (Dingle)

☎(066) 56255, 56408, 56409 Fax
Ballyferriter, Co Kerry
Follow Ballyferriter signs from
Dingle, turn right 0.5 mile after
Ballyferriter.
Seaside links course; most westerly
golf course in Europe..
18 holes, 6440 yards, S.S.S.71
Designed by Eddie Hackett.
Founded 1924
Visitors: welcome at all times.
Green Fee: £18.
Societies: welcome with advance
booking.
Catering: full bar and restaurant.
Sea fishing, practice ground.
Hotels: Granville, Ostan Golf Dun an
Oir (Ballyferriter); Benners, Skellig
(Dingle)

U55 Charleville

☎(063) 81257 Office, 81274 Fax
Smiths Rd, Ardmore, Charleville, Co
Cork
On main road from Cork to Limerick,
about 35 miles from Cork, 25 miles
from Limerick.
Parkland course.
18 holes, 6430 yards, S.S.S.70
Founded 29 July 1941
Visitors: welcome weekdays;
contact office in advance.
Green Fee: £12/day.
Societies: any day except Sun, £10
per person; contact office.
Catering: full bar and restaurant.
Hotels: Deer Park.

U56 Cill Dara

☎(045) 21433
Kildare, Co Kildare
1 mile E of Kildare.
Moorland course.
9 holes, 6196 yards, S.S.S.66
Visitors: welcome.
Green Fee: apply for details.
Societies: meals by arrangement.

U57 Claremorris

☎(094) 71527
Rushbrook, Castlemagarett,
Claremorris, Co Mayo
1.5 miles from Claremorris town on
Galway road.
Parkland course.
9 holes, 5898 yards, S.S.S.69
Founded 1927
Visitors: welcome except Sun.
Green Fee: on application.
Societies: catered for on weekdays.
Catering: by arrangement.
Hotels: Dalton Inn; Western.

U58 Clones

☎(047) 56017
Hilton Park, Clones, Co Monaghan
3 miles S of Clones towards
Scotshouse.
Parkland course.
9 holes, 5788 yards, S.S.S.68
Founded 1913
Visitors: welcome, restricted Sun.
Green Fee: £6 WD, £10 WE.
Societies: welcome, except Sun;
societies of 15 or more £5.
Catering: available at all times.
Hotels: Creighton; Hibernian;
Lennard Arms; White Horse,
Cootehill.

U59 Clonlara

☎(061) 354141
Clonlara Golf and Leisure, Clonlara,
Co Clare, EIRE
7 miles W of Limerick.
Parkland course.
9 holes, 2549 yards, Par 34
Visitors: welcome.
Green Fee: £8/round.
Societies: welcome weekdays,
phone in advance.
Catering: bar and bar meals.
Tennis, sauna.
Hotels: cottages and apartments let.

U60 Clonmel

☎(052) 21138, 24050 Sec and Pro
Lyreanearla, Mountain Rd, Clonmel,
Co Tipperary
On road to Comeragh Mountains, 2
miles SE of Clonmel.
Parkland course.
18 holes, 5875 metres, S.S.S.70
Designed by Eddie Hackett.
Founded 1911
Visitors: phone Sec for details.
Green Fee: £12 WD, £15 WE.
Societies: welcome by arrangement.
Catering: full facilities.
Snooker, pool, table tennis.
Hotels: Hotel Minella; Clonmel Arms;
Hearns.

U61 Clontarf

☎(01) 331892 Office, 331877 Pro,
331520 Bar
Donnycarney House, Malahide Rd,
Dublin 3
NE of city centre, proceed for 2.5
miles from city centre via North
Strand and Fairview to Lower
Malahide Road.
Parkland course.
18 holes, 5459 metres, S.S.S.68
Founded 1912
Visitors: welcome weekdays, check
with Sec for times.
Green Fee: £21.
Societies: Tues and Fri.
Catering: full facilities.
Bowling green; snooker.
Hotels: Skylon; Hollybrook; Marine.

U62 Cobh
☎(021) 812399
Ballywilliam, Cobh, Co Cork
1 mile E of Cobh.
Public parkland course.
9 holes, 4606 metres, S.S.S.63
Designed by Eddie Hackett.
Founded 1987
Visitors: welcome weekdays,
booking at weekends.
Green Fee: £8 WD, £9 WE, £5 with
member.
Societies: welcome Mon-Sat.
Catering: bar, snacks.
Putting and pitching green.
Hotels: Commodore, Rinn Ronain
(free golf).

U63 Connemara
☎(095) 23502/23954, 23662 Fax
Ballyconneely, Clifden, Co Galway
9 miles S of Clifden.
Links course on edge of Atlantic set
amidst mountain scenery.
18 holes, 6620 metres, S.S.S.75
(Championship); 9 hole course under
development.
Designed by Eddie Hackett.
Founded 1973
Visitors: welcome all year; must
have h/cap cert.
Green Fee: July/Aug £18, May/June,
Sept/Oct £16, March/April £14,
Nov-Feb £10.
Societies: welcome except
July/Aug.
Catering: full bar and à la carte
restaurant.
Hotels: Allbey Glen; Rock Glen;
Clifden Bay; Ballynahynch Castle.

U64 Coolattin
☎(055) 29125, 26302 Sec
Coolattin, Shillelheh, Co Wicklow
12 miles SW of Aughrim.
Parkland course.
9 holes, 6203 yards, S.S.S.70
Visitors: welcome Mon-Fri.
Green Fee: £10/day.
Societies: welcome weekdays by
prior arrangement.
Catering: bar and snacks; full meals
by arrangement, phone (055) 29207.
Pool table.

U65 Corballis
☎(01) 436583
Dunabate, Co Dublin
Off main Dublin-Belfast road.
Public seaside links course.
18 holes, 4543 metres (4971 yards),
S.S.S.64
Founded 1971

Visitors: welcome, golf clubs for
each player, no other restrictions.
Green Fee: apply for details.
Societies: welcome by arrangement
except Sun.
Catering: no bar, limited facilities.
Pool.
Hotels: Dunes; Swords.

U66 Cork
☎(021) 353451, 353421 Pro,
353410 Fax
Little Island, Cork, Co Cork
5 miles E of Cork on N25.
Championship parkland course.
18 holes, 6115 metres, S.S.S.72
Designed by Alister Mackenzie.
Founded 1888
Visitors: welcome Mon, Tues, Wed,
Fri except 12.30-2pm or after 4pm;
weekends after 2.30pm.
Green Fee: £23/day WD, £26 WE,
(£8 with member).
Societies: as for visitors; groups of
20 or more £18 WD, £20 WE.
Catering: full catering facilities
available.
Hotels: Silver Springs; Ashbourne
House; John Barleycorn;
Commodore; Metropole.

U67 County Cavan
☎(049) 31283
Arnmore House, Drumelis, Cavan, Co
Cavan
1 mile from Cavan town on
Killeshandra road.
Parkland course.
18 holes, 6030 yards, S.S.S.69
Founded 1894
Visitors: welcome 7 days per week,
restricted days Wed and Sun.
Green Fee: apply for details.
Societies: welcome, Mon-Fri
preferred.
Catering: full catering.
Snooker.
Hotels: Kilmore; Farnham Arms.

U68 County Longford
☎(043) 46310
Glack, Longford
Off Dublin to Sligo road (N4) E of
town, signposted.
Undulating course.
18 holes, 6028 yards, S.S.S.68
Designed by E. Hackett.
Founded 1894
Visitors: welcome.
Green Fee: apply for details.
Societies: welcome by prior
arrangement.
Catering: meals served.

U69 County Louth
☎(041) 22329
Baltray, Drogheda, Co Louth
4 miles NE of Drogheda, follow N
bank of River Boyne to Baltray village.
Seaside links course.
18 holes, 6763 yards, S.S.S.72
Designed by Tom Simpson.
Founded 1892
Visitors: on request, not Tues.
Green Fee: £27 WD, £33 WE.
Societies: on application.
Catering: full facilities.
Tennis, snooker.
Hotels: Glenside; Neptune; Boyne
Valley.

U70 County Meath (Trim)
☎(046) 31463, 31438 Sec
Newtownmoynagh, Trim, Co Meath
3 miles from Trim on Longwood road.
Parkland course.
18 holes, 6720 yards, S.S.S.72
Designed by Eddie Hackett.
Founded 1898
Visitors: welcome weekdays,
restrictions Thurs, Sat, Sun.
Green Fee: £12 WD, £15 WE & BH.
Societies: Mon-Sat inc, enquiries
welcome; £11 WD, £14 WE.
Catering: bars, restaurant; new
clubhouse.
Hotels: Wellington Court (Trim);
Harry's (Kinnegad); Wells (Enfield).

U71 County Sligo
☎(071) 77186, 77460 Fax
Rosses Point, Sligo
5 miles W of Sligo, off N15 at N edge
of town; signposted Rosses Point.
Seaside links championship course.
18 holes, 6003 metres, S.S.S.72
Designed by Colt & Alison.
Founded 1894
Visitors: welcome weekdays;
limited times weekends and Bank
Holidays, booking essential.
Green Fee: £16/round WD,
£22/round WE.
Societies: welcome by prior
arrangement subject to availability.
Catering: bar, bar food, restaurant.
Practice areas.
Hotels: Yeats Country; Ballincar
House; Sligo Park; Silver Swan;
Markree Castle; Southern.

U72 County Tipperary Golf & Country Club
☎(062) 71116, 71366 Fax
Dundrum, Cashel, Co. Tipperary
1 mile from Dundrum village, 6 miles
W of Cashel off Dublin/Cork road.

County Louth

There are certain courses throughout Britain and Ireland where a sense of expectancy reaches a peak at a specific point near journey's end; when turning off the main road at Wadebridge for St Enodoc, for instance, or when a long drive nears its end along the only road to Southerness, a superb links on the Solway Firth, which in 1985 hosted the Scottish Amateur for the first time.

A similar sense of anticipation accompanies the last lap to Brancaster which takes you past the church and down through the marsh lined by tall rushes; and there is a less glamorous approach beyond the level crossing to the Royal Cinque Ports Golf Club at Deal. The twisty conclusion to the journey to Rye is another example. But there can be few sights as thrilling as the links of County Louth at Baltray at last coming into view.

It is a fine, challenging course in the traditional mould of dunes, undoubtedly one of my favourites and one whose rating within Ireland is not as high as it should be. It is worthy of the best, full of variety and contrast with always the magnificence of its distant views.

Although there have been modifications, one or two made necessary by moving the clubhouse some years ago, there is still an authentic touch of Tom Simpson about it that bears the unmistakable mark of quality. If I had to exemplify it, I would point to the long 3rd which, after a reasonably straight forward drive, reveals hidden talents once the brow of dunes has been scaled. Beautifully natural humps and hollows make careful placing of the second shot essential and, for those attempting to get home in two, there is only a narrow path between salvation and ruin. An attractive small green is not easy to hit.

The curving 1st and testing 2nd make a nice introduction but the 4th, a short par 4, offers some relief before the first of four first class short holes. The 5th and 7th, sandwiched around another fine par 5, demand well-controlled, truly hit iron shots while the 8th and 9th are no easy 4s.

A sense of space becomes more apparent on the second half which, having begun with a hole alongside the clubhouse, works its way towards the sea by means of the dogleg par 5 11th. It is then that a special character is lent by the 12th, 13th and 14th which, from a combination of factors, comprise a notable trio. They emphasise the merit of great par 4s, not perhaps daunting in terms of yardage but rewarding in the satisfaction they give by being played properly, as they must be if they are to yield a par or a birdie.

Changes to the course have resulted in two short holes in the last four but the 16th is appealing and the 18th the last of five par 5s.

Baltray, as the course is more conveniently called after the local fishing village, has a championship cloak without a doubt and it also has its less forbidding side which makes it so popular for a day out.

Harry Bradshaw's winning aggregate of 291 in the 1947 Irish Professional championship tells a tale or two about its full blown potential. It is also rare among Irish clubs in having two legendary Irish women golfers as members. Val Reddan, as Clarrie Tiernan, won the Irish title twice and was also the first Irish woman to play in the Curtis Cup. After the war, she was confronted by her new local rival Philomena Garvey in the final of the Irish, not, as would have been most appropriate, at Baltray, but at Lahinch. After the longest final, Garvey won at the 39th, the first of her 15 victories.

Continuing the feminine influence, Mrs Josephine Connolly founded the East of Ireland Men's championship played annually at Baltray, an event by which Irish golfers set great store. It can claim father and son winners in Joe and Roddy Carr, but when you speak of the course you speak of distinction. Its list of champions is no more than it deserves.

Courtown Golf Club
Kiltennel, Gorey, Co Wexford, Tel: 055-25166

Parkland course with some spectacular views of the nearby
sea through tree lined fairways.

Green Fees
High Season (June, July, August) £15 mid week £20 weekend
Remaining 9 months £13 midweek £17 weekend

Full catering facilities available. Sets of golf clubs can be hired.

Parkland course.
18 holes, 6682 yards, S.S.S.72
Designed by Philip Walton.
Founded 1993
Visitors: welcome.
Green Fee: £15 WD, £20 WE & BH.
Societies: welcome by arrangement.
Catering: 2 bars, 2 restaurants, snack bar. Snooker.
Hotels: Dundrum House on site.

U73 **Courtown**
☎(055) 21533
Kiltennel, Gorey, Co Wexford
3 miles from Gorey off
Dublin-Rosslare road.
Parkland course.
18 holes, 6398 yards, S.S.S.70
Designed by Harris & Associates.
Founded 1936
Visitors: welcome except on major competition days.
Green Fee: June-Aug, £15 WD, £20 WE; Sept-May, £12 WD, £17 WE.
Societies: by prior arrangement except June-Aug.
Catering: snacks and full catering.
Hotels: Bayview; Marlfield House.

U74 **Cruit Island**
☎(075) 43296
Kincasslagh, Co Donegal, EIRE
6 miles N of Dungloe adjacent to
Viking House Hotel.
Scenic seaside links course.
9 holes, 4833 metres, S.S.S.68
Founded 1985
Visitors: welcome.
Green Fee: £7/day; July/Aug £9/day;
Societies:
Catering: bar and snacks weekends; daily in summer.

U75 **Curragh**
☎(045) 41714, 41238
Curragh, Co Kildare
3 miles S of Newbridge, 28 miles SW
of Dublin.

Parkland course.
18 holes, 6001 metres, S.S.S.71
Designed by David Ritchie (1852).
Founded 1883
Visitors: weekdays only; required to
contact Sec before attending.
Green Fee: £13/round WD,
£16/round WE & BH.
Societies: weekdays, limited
number of weekends; apply to Sec in
advance.
Catering: full facilities.
Hotels: Hotel Keadeen; Lumville
House.

U76 **Deer Park Hotel**
☎(01) 832 2624, 839 2405 Fax
Deer Park Hotel, Howth, Co Dublin
9 miles E of city centre via Fairview,
Clontarf and Sutton; 3rd turn right
after Sutton Cross.
Public parkland courses.
18 holes, 6647 yards (6778 from
May 1994), Par 72; 9 holes, 3130
yards, Par 35; 12 holes Par 3, 1810
yards; new 9 hole 3373 yard course
opening May 1994
Designed by Fred Hawtree.
Founded 1973
Visitors: welcome all week;
weekends expect delays.
Green Fee: £9.50.
Societies: Welcome weekdays.
Catering: full facilities, lounge,
snack bar, restaurant.
Snooker, function room.
Hotels: Deer Park Hotel on site;
golfing specials available.

U77 **Delgany**
☎(01) 287 4536 Office, 287 4697 Pro
Delgany, Co Wicklow
Adjacent to village of Delgany off
main road to Wexford.
Parkland course.
18 holes, 5454 metres, S.S.S.69
Founded 1908
Visitors: welcome except
competition days.

Green Fee: £17 WD, £20 WE.
Societies: welcome.
Catering: full catering facilities.
Hotels: Wicklow Arms; Glenview.

U78 **Donabate**
☎(01) 436346, 436001
Donabate, Balcarrick Co Dublin
1st right 1 mile N of Swords on Dublin
to Belfast road.
Parkland course.
18 holes, 5679 metres, S.S.S.69
Visitors: welcome.
Green Fee: apply for details.
Societies: welcome by arrangement.
Catering: meals served.

U79 **Donegal**
☎(073) 34054, 34377 Fax
Murvagh, Laghey, Co Donegal
About 6 miles S of Donegal via N15.
Seaside links course.
18 holes, 6867 yards, S.S.S.73
Designed by Eddie Hackett.
Founded 1960, opened 1973
Visitors: welcome, no restrictions.
Green Fee: £14/£18.
Societies: catered for daily.
Catering: bar and restaurant; buffet
service. Snooker.
Hotels: Sandhouse (Rossnowlagh);
Abbey, Highland Central (Donegal).

U80 **Doneraile**
☎(022) 24137
Doneraile, Co Cork
Off T11, 28 miles N of Cork.
Parkland course.
9 holes, 5528 yards, S.S.S.66
Visitors: welcome.
Green Fee: apply for details.
Societies: welcome.
Catering: meals served.

U81 **Dooks**
☎(066) 68205
Glenbeigh, Co Kerry

4 miles W of Killonglin, at bridge between Killonglin and Glenbeigh. Seaside course.
18 holes, 6021 yards, S.S.S.68
Designed by Eddie Hackett.
Founded 1889
Visitors: welcome, check at weekends; evidence of handicap required.
Green Fee: £16/day.
Societies: welcome.
Catering: restaurant facilities.
Hotels: Glenbeigh; Towers; Bianconi Inn; Canagh Lodge; Mount Brandon; And ns Si; Castlerosse; Village House.

U82 Douglas
☎(021) 891086, 895297
Sec/Manager
Douglas, Cork
Within 3 miles of Cork city, 0.5 mile beyond Douglas village.
Parkland course.
18 holes, 5294 metres, S.S.S.68
Founded 1910
Visitors: welcome, with reservation at weekends.
Green Fee: on application.
Societies: by arrangement before start of season.
Catering: snacks and meals served.

U83 Dromoland Castle
☎(061) 368444, 368144
Newmarket-on-Fergus, Co Clare
On main Limerick-Galway road, 1.5 miles through Newmarket-on-Fergus.
Public parkland course.
18 holes, 6098 yards, S.S.S.71
Designed by Whittaker (USA).
Founded 1964
Visitors: welcome.
Green Fee: £18/day WD, £20/day WE.
Societies: welcome, fees negotiable.

Catering: available.
Tennis, banqueting.
Hotels: Dromoland Castle.

U84 Dun Laoghaire
☎(01) 280 3916, 280 4868 Fax
Eglinton Park, Tivoli Rd, Dun Laoghaire, Co Dublin
7 miles from Dublin, 0.5 mile from Dun Laoghaire centre and ferry port.
Parkland course.
18 holes, 5478 metres, S.S.S.69
Founded 1910
Visitors: Mon, Tues, Wed am, Fri; reserved for members 12.30-2pm.
Green Fee: £20.
Societies: Tues and Fri by prior booking only.
Catering: full service during season.
Hotels: Royal Marine; Fitzpatricks Castle; Hotel Victor.

U85 Dundalk
☎(042) 21731 Office, 22102 Pro, 22270 Members.
Blackrock, Dundalk, Co Louth
Off T1 3 miles S of Dundalk on Dundalk Bay.
Parkland course.
18 holes, 6740 yards, S.S.S.72
Designed by Thomas & Allis.
Founded 1905
Visitors: welcome except Sun (competition day).
Green Fee: on application.
Societies: booking essential.
Catering: full catering, dinners, snacks every day.
Hotels: Fairways; Imperial; Ballymascanlon; Derryhale; Carrickdale; Lorne.

U86 Dunfanaghy
☎(074) 36335 Sec/bookings
Dunfanaghy, Letterkenny, Co Donegal

On main Letterkenny-Dunfanaghy road 0.5 mile E of Dunfanaghy.
Public seaside links course.
18 holes, 5006 metres, S.S.S.66
Founded 1906
Visitors: welcome except Sun.
Green Fee: £10 WD, £12 WE.
Societies: by arrangement.
Catering: bar, snacks.
Hotels: Arnold's; Shandon; Carrig Rua; Port-na-blagh.

U87 Dungarvan
☎(058) 41605/43310
Knocknagranagh, Dungarvan, Co Waterford
Take N25, approx 2 miles E of Dungarvan turnright to club.
Meadowland course.
18 holes, 6134 metres, S.S.S.73
Designed by Maurice Fives.
Founded 1924
Visitors: welcome any time.
Green Fee: £12 WD, £15 WE.
Societies: welcome, apply in advance.
Catering: full catering and dining facilities.
Hotels: Clonea Strand; Gold Coast Holiday Homes; Park.

U88 Dunmore
☎(023) 33352
Dunmore House, Muckross, Clonakilty, Co Cork
3 miles from Clonakilty, clearly signposted.
Hilly open course.
9 holes, 4464 yards, S.S.S.61
Designed by E. Hackett.
Founded 1967
Visitors: welcome any time.
Green Fee: apply for details.
Societies: welcome by prio arrangement.
Catering: bar and restaurant facilities in Dunmore House.

U89 Dunmore East Golf & Country Club
☎(051) 83151
Dunmore East, Co Waterford
Take 1st left at entrance to Dunmore village, left at the strand, then 1st right; course signposted.
Parkland course.
18 holes, 6236 yards, Par 72; 9 holes, 4756 yards, Par 66
Designed by Eamon Condon & Assoc.
Founded 1993
Visitors: welcome.
Green Fee: £10 WD, £15 WE.
Societies: welcome by arrangement.
Catering: bar and snacks all day; meals arranged at local hotels.

U90 East Cork
☎(021) 631687
Gortacrue, Midleton, Co Cork
On main Cork to Waterford road 10 miles E of Cork city, turn left at roundabout in Midleton, signposted about 1.5 miles.
Parkland course.
18 holes, 4874 yards, S.S.S.69
Designed by Edward Hackett.
Founded 1970
Visitors: welcome except Sun am.
Green Fee: apply for details.
Societies: phone for details.
Catering: lunches served except Sun.
Snooker, horse riding etc, details on request.
Hotels: Commodore, Garryvoes (special golf packages); Middleton Park.

U91 Edenderry
☎(0405) 31072
Kishavanny, Edenderry, Co Offaly
1 mile before town on road from Dublin; turn right just before River Boyne, clubhouse 0.5 mile on left.
Public parkland/moorland course, quick drying.
18 holes, 5531 metres, S.S.S.69
Founded 1947
Visitors: restricted Thurs and weekends; apply for details.
Green Fee: apply for details.
Societies: except Sun and Thurs.
Catering: bar, good quality catering by arrangement.

U92 Edmondstown
☎(01) 493 2461 Club, 493 1082 Sec, 494 1049 Pro, 493 3205 Restaurant, 493 3152 Fax
Rathfarnham, Dublin 16
T42 S of Dublin, Rathfarnham 1 mile.
Parkland course.
18 holes, 5663 metres, S.S.S.69
Designed by Eddie Hackett.
Founded 1944
Visitors: welcome, dress code in operation.
Green Fee: £20 WD, £40 WE by arrangement.
Societies: Mon, Thurs, Fri, Sat, to 11.30am.
Catering: full facilities. Snooker.
Hotels: Jury's; Christchurch; Orwell Lodge.

U93 Elm Park
☎(01) 269 3438, 269 3014, 269 4505 Fax
Nutley Lane, Donnybrook, Dublin 4
2 miles from city centre beside Montrose television studios and St Vincents Hospital.
Parkland course.
18 holes, 5422 metres, S.S.S.68
Designed by Fred Davies.
Founded 1927
Visitors: welcome but phone in advance.
Green Fee: on application.
Societies: catered for Tues only.
Catering: full facilities.

U94 Ennis
☎(065) 24074 Office, 20690 Pro.
Drumbiggle, Ennis, Co Clare
1 mile W of N18 Limerick-Galway at Ennis.
Gently rolling parkland course.
18 holes, 5316 metres, S.S.S.68
Founded 1907
Visitors: not before 12.00am Sun; please book in advance.
Green Fee: £14.
Societies: not Sun.
Catering: bar, excellent daylong catering. Snooker.
Hotels: Auburn Lodge; Queens; West County; Old Ground; (concessionary green fee scheme).

U95 Enniscorthy
☎(054) 33191, 33135
Knockmarshal, Enniscorthy, Co Wexford
1.5 miles from town on New Ross road.
Parkland course.
18 holes, 5697 metres, C.S.S.70
Designed by E. Hackett.
Founded 1924
Visitors: welcome except Tues (Ladies Day); prior arrangement at weekends.
Green Fee: £10 WD, £12 WE & BH.
Societies: most welcome.
Catering: full catering.
Hotels: Murphy Floods.

U96 Enniscrone
☎(096) 36297, 36657 Fax
Enniscrone, Co Sligo
8 miles N of Ballina, 0.5 mile from Enniscrone.
Seaside course.
18 holes, 6487 yards, S.S.S.72
Designed by E. Hackett.
Founded 1918
Visitors: weekdays unrestricted, phone for weekend times.
Green Fee: 1st April-31st Oct £15/day WD, £18/round WE, husband and wife £20/day; 1st Nov-31st March, £10/day WD, £12/round WE.
Societies: welcome if arranged in advance, phone (096) 36335; fees from £8 to £13 per day..
Catering: bar and restaurant facilities, order before play.
Hotels: Atlantic, Benbulben, Castle Arms, (Enniscrone); Downhill, Imperial, Beleek Castle, (Ballina).

U97 European Club The
☎(0404) 47415, 47346 Fax, (01) 280 8457 Fax
Brittas Bay, Co Wicklow
N11 S from Dublin; turn left for Brittas Bay at Jack White's Inn; turn right at beach and proceed 1.5 miles.
Links course.
18 holes, 6750 yards, S.S.S.71
Designed by Pat Ruddy
Founded 1989
Visitors: welcome every day; h/cap cert desired.
Green Fee: £20 WD, £25 WE.
Societies: welcome every day; 10% discount on 20+ players.
Catering: light refreshments. Practice range.
Hotels: Grand (Wicklow); Tinakilly House (Rathnew); Glenview (Glen of Downs); Jack White's Inn (Brittas Bay).

U98 Faithlegg
☎(010 353 51) 82241, 82688, 82664 Fax
Faithlegg House, Co. Waterford
6 miles from Waterford city centre, on banks of River Suir; from Waterford, take Dunmore East Rd towards Cheekpoint village.
Parkland course.
18 holes, 6633 yards, S.S.S.72

Designed by Patrick Merrigan.
Founded May 1993
Visitors: always welcome.
Green Fee: £23/day, £16 before 9am, £27 for golf and dinner; group rates available.
Societies: always welcome, rates negotiable.
Catering: full bar and restaurant facilities; phone (051) 82155.
Practice area and putting green.
Hotels: Tower; Jury's; Granville; Dooley's; Candlelight; B&B readily available.

U99 Fermoy
☎(025) 31472
Fermoy, Co Cork
2 miles from Fermoy off Cork-Dublin road.
Undulating course.
18 holes, 5550 yards, S.S.S.70
Designed by Commander Harris.
Founded 1892
Visitors: welcome weekdays.
Green Fee: apply for details.
Societies: welcome weekdays and Sat am.
Catering: snacks served.
Hotels: Grand.

U100 Finnstown Fairways
☎(01) 628 0644
Finnstown Fairways Country House Hotel and Golf Course, Newcastle Rd, Lucan, Co Dublin
From Dublin take M50 for 7 miles to Lucan crossroads, then left onto Newcastle Rd.
Parkland course.
9 holes, 5190 yards, S.S.S.66
Designed by Bobby Brown.
Founded 1988
Visitors: welcome with h/cap cert.
Green Fee: £10/day WD, £12/day WE.
Societies: welcome, phone in advance.
Catering: bar and restaurant.
Gym.

U101 Forrest Little
☎(01) 401763 or 401183
Forest Little, Cloghran, Co Dublin
0.5 mile beyond Dublin Airport on Dublin-Belfast road; take 1st turn left.
Parkland course.
18 holes, 5865 metres, S.S.S.70
Designed by Fred Hawtree.
Founded 1940
Visitors: welcome weekdays.
Green Fee: apply for details.

Societies: catered for on Mon and Thurs afternoons.
Catering: snacks always available; à la carte menu from 5pm daily.

U102 Fota Island
☎(353 21) 883710 Bookings, 883713 Fax
Fota Island, Carrigtwohill, Co Cork
9 miles E of Cork City on N25 Waterford and Roslaire road; take right turn at sign for Fota Island and Cobh, entrance immediately over bridge on right.
Gently rolling parkland course set amidst woodland; traditional design with pot bunker, double greens etc.
18 holes, S.S.S.72
Designed by Peter McEvoy and Christy O'Connor Jnr.
Founded Sept 1993
Visitors: welcome 9am-12.30pm and 2-5pm weekdays, 10.30am-12.30pm and 2-5pm weekends and holidays; h/caps not required but visitors must be golfers.
Green Fee: £27 WD, £30 WE.
Societies: welcome, £24 WD, £26 WE (20-50) discounts for larger groups.
Catering: bar and light meals, full restaurant.
Driving range.
Hotels: Ashbourne House; Silver Springs; Ballymaloe House; Arbutus Lodge.

U103 Foxrock
☎(01) 289 3992 Office, 289 3414 Shop, 289 5668 Catering, 289 4943 Fax
Torquay Rd, Dublin 18
About 6 miles from Dublin; turn right off T7 just past Stillergan on to Leopardstown Rd, then left into Torquay Rd.
Parkland course.
9 holes, 5439 metres, S.S.S.69
Founded 1893
Visitors: welcome Mon, Wed am, Thurs, Fri; Sun only with member.
Green Fee: £20.
Societies: catered for Mon and Thurs.
Catering: soup, sandwiches, coffee.

U104 Frankfield
☎(021) 361199
Frankfield, Douglas, Co Cork
10 miles S of Cork.
Parkland course.
9 holes, 5352 yards, Par 68
Visitors: welcome.

Green Fee: £5/day.
Societies: phone in advance.
Catering: lunch served Mon-Fri.

U105 Galway
☎(091) 23038 Pro, 21827 Catering, 22169 Sec/Manager
Blackrock, Salthill, Co Galway
On L100 2 miles W of Galway.
Tight, tree-lined, parkland course.
18 holes, 5815 metres, S.S.S.71
Founded 1895
Visitors: welcome Mon, Wed, Thurs, Fri.
Green Fee: £15.
Societies: accepted, with advance booking.
Catering: full facilities.
Snooker.

U106 Galway Bay Golf & Country Club
☎(091) 90500
Renville, Oranmore, Co Galway
From Galway take coast road through Oranmore, signposted from there.
Seaside parkland course.
18 holes, 6453 metres, S.S.S.73
Designed by Christy O'Connor Jnr.
Founded 1993
Visitors: welcome, must have h/cap cert.
Green Fee: April-Sept, £25/round WD, £30/round WE; Oct-March, £20/round WD, £25/round WE.
Societies: welcome, phone in advance.
Catering: restaurant, bar, spikes bar.
Practice bays.

U107 Glengarriff
☎(027) 63150
Glengarriff, Co Cork
On T65, 55 miles W of Cork.
Seaside course.
9 holes, 2042 metres, S.S.S.62
Founded 1936
Visitors: welcome.
Green Fee: apply for details.
Societies: special rates for societies.

U108 Glenmalure
☎(0404) 46679
Greenan, Rathdrum, Co. Wicklow
2 miles W of Rathdrum, towards the Glenmalure.
Moorland course.
18 holes, S.S.S.69
Designed by Pat Suttle.
Founded May 1992
Visitors: welcome, no restrictions.

Green Fee: £12 WD, £15 WE and BH.
Societies: welcome, no restrictions.
Catering: bar lunches, no dinner as yet. Hard tennis courts.
Hotels: Vale View, Woodenbridge (Avoca).

U109 Gold Coast Golf and Leisure
☎(058) 42416, 42880 Fax
Ballinacourty, Dungarvan, Co. Waterford
On the edge of Dungarvan Bay.
Links course
9 holes, 6327 yards, S.S.S.70
Designed by Capt. R. Hewson
Founded 23 April, 1939
Visitors: any time, subject to availability; official h/cap cert required.
Green Fee: £10-£12.
Societies: any time subject to availability.
Catering: at Gold Coast Restaurant (on course) or Clonea Strand Hotel.
Driving range; indoor leisure centre at Clonea Strand Hotel.
Hotels: Clonea Strand; Gold Coast Cottages; Gold Coast Golf Hotel due to open June 1994.

U110 Gort
☎(091) 31336
Laughty Shaughnessy, Gort, Co Galway
Tubber road, Gort, 24 miles S of Galway.
Parkland course.
9 holes, 5174 metres, S.S.S.67
Designed by E. Hackett.
Founded 1924
Visitors: welcome all week except Wed evenings and Sun am; Ladies' Day Thurs.
Green Fee: £7.
Societies: apply to Hon Sec or bar manager.
Catering: light snacks April-Sept.
Hotels: Sullivans; Glynn's; O'Gradey's Rest.

U111 Grange
☎(01) 932832, 932889 or 935800 (locker room)
Grange Rd, Rathfarnham, Dublin 16
7 miles S from city centre, near Rathfarnham village.
Parkland course.
18 holes, 5517 yards, S.S.S.69
Designed by James Braid.
Founded 1910
Visitors: welcome weekdays except Tues and Wed afternoons.

Green Fee: apply for details.
Societies: welcome Mon and Thurs.
Catering: full facilities.

U112 Greencastle
☎(077) 81013
Greencastle, Moville, Co Donegal
On L85 23 miles NE of Londonderry through Moville.
Public seaside course.
18 holes, 5211 metres, S.S.S.67
Designed by Eddie Hackett (new 9 holes).
Founded 1892
Visitors: welcome.
Green Fee: £9 WD (£7 with member), £13 WE & BH (£9 with member).
Societies: by arrangement.
Catering: bar and catering facilities.
Hotels: Fort; McNamaras, Foyle (Moville).

U113 Greenore
☎(042) 73212 Members, 73678 Office phone/Fax
Greenore, Co Louth
From Belfast, take 1st left on Dundalk road out of Newry to Omeath and Carlingford, course 2 miles on from Carlingford; from Dublin, through Drogheda, take 1st right on Newry road out of Dundalk, then 15 miles to Greenore.
Wooded seaside course.
18 holes, 6506 yards, S.S.S.71
Designed by Eddie Hackett.
Founded 1896
Visitors: welcome weekdays and most weekends; advisable to phone Sec at weekends.
Green Fee: £12 WD, £18 WE & BH.
Societies: welcome any day.
Catering: daily.
Hotels: Ballymascanlon; McKevitts Village; Park; Granvue.

U114 Greystones
☎(01) 287 6624, 287 4136
Greystones, Co Wicklow,
N11 out of Dublin towards Wexford, signposted.
Parkland course.
18 holes, 5175 metres, S.S.S.68
Founded 1895
Visitors: welcome Mon, Tues, Fri; phone in advance.
Green Fee: £20/round.
Societies: by arrangement, phone in advance.
Catering: full facilities; summer every day, winter Wed-Sun inclusive.
Hotels: La Touche.

U115 Gweedore
☎(075) 31140
Derrybeg, Letterkenny, Co Donegal
L82 from Letterkenny or T72 from Donegal.
Seaside course.
18 holes, 6873 yards, S.S.S.73
Designed by Eddie Hackett.
Founded 1923
Visitors: always welcome.
Green Fee: apply for details.
Societies: catered for weekends.
Catering: lunches at weekends.

U116 Harbour Point
☎(021) 353094
Little Island, Cork, Co Cork
Take Rosslare road out of Cork; after 2.5 miles at 2nd roundabout take Little Island exit and watch for 'Harbour Point' signposts.
Undulating parkland championship course overlooking harbour.
18 holes (2 natural loops of 9), 6800 yards, S.S.S.72
Designed by Paddy Merrigan.
Founded June 1991
Visitors: welcome any time.
Green Fee: £20/day, £10 befoe 11am Mon, Wed, Thurs, Fri.
Societies: by arrangement.
Catering: full bar and restaurant.
Driving range.
Hotels: Fitzpatricks Silversprings; Ashbourne House; John Barleycorn.

U117 Hazel Grove
☎(01) 520911
Mt Seskin Rd, Jobstown, Tallaght, Dublin 24
On Blessington road, 2.5 miles from Tallaght.
Parkland course.
9 holes, 5030 metres, S.S.S.67; extending to 18 holes.
Designed by Jim Byrne.
Founded 1988
Visitors: welcome Mon, Wed, Fri; not after 12am Tues, not after 11am Sat, not Sun; Thurs Ladies' Day.
Green Fee: apply for details.
Societies: by arrangement max 50 (Sat am max 40).
Catering: bar, function room (140); catering by arrangement.
Large practice area.

U118 Headfort
☎(046) 40146, 40639 Pro shop/bookings
Kells, Co Meath
0.25 mile from Kells on main Kells-Dublin road.

Parkland course.
18 holes, 6543 yards, S.S.S.70
Founded 1930
Visitors: welcome Mon, Wed, Thurs,
Fri; limited weekends.
Green Fee: £15 WD, £18 WE & BH.
Societies: mornings only weekdays
(except Tues); limited number of Sat
mornings.
Catering: full catering service
available.
Hotels: Headfort Arms.

U119 Heath
☎(0502) 46533
The Heath, Portlaoise, Co Laois
4 miles NE of Portlaoise, just off main
Dublin to Cork/Limerick road.
Heathland course.
18 holes, 5721 metres, S.S.S.70
Founded 1930
Visitors: welcome, by arrangement
with Hon Sec at weekends.
Green Fee: apply for details.
Societies: welcome by arrangement,
apply to Sec.
Catering: full facilities available by
arrangement with Steward.
Driving range.
Hotels: Killeshin; Montague;
Regency.

U120 Hermitage
☎(01) 626 8491, 626 5049
Lucan, Co Dublin
T3 W from Dublin, 1 mile from Lucan.
18 holes, 6034 metres, S.S.S.71
(Championship)
Founded 1905
Visitors: welcome Mon, Thurs, Fri
most mornings.
Green Fee: apply for details.
Societies: weekdays.
Catering: every day.
Hotels: Ashling; Spa; Springfield.

U121 Hollywood
☎(01) 433406, 433113 after hours
Hollywood, Ballyboughal, Co Dublin
12 miles N of Dublin city off
Dublin/Belfast road.
Public parkland course with
all-weather elevated greens.
18 holes, 7146 yards, S.S.S.72
Designed by Mel Flanagan.
Founded 1990
Visitors: welcome any time.
Green Fee: apply for details.
Societies: booking necessary.
Catering: bar, restaurant.
Hotels: Trust House Forte (Dublin
Airport); Grand (Malahide); Skylon
(Drumcondra).

U122 Howth
☎(01) 323055, 393895/322844
Pro, 321793 Fax
Carrickbrack Rd, Sutton, Dublin 13
9.5 miles NE of city centre, 1.5 miles
from Sutton Cross towards Howth
summit.
Heathland course.
18 holes, 5618 metres, S.S.S.69
Designed by James Braid.
Founded 1916
Visitors: welcome weekdays.
Green Fee: £16 Mon-Thur, £18 Fri.
Societies: weekdays except Wed.
Catering: snacks and bar service.
Hotels: Marine; Howth Lodge.

U123 Island
☎(01) 843 6104 Public, 843 6205
Office, 843 6462 Sec/Manager, 843
6860 Fax
Corballis, Donabate, Co Dublin
From Dublin leave N1 approx 1 mile
beyond Swords at Donabate sign,
then L91 for 3 miles and right at sign.
Seaside course.
18 holes, 6053 metres, S.S.S.72
Designed by F. Hawtree & Eddie
Hackett.
Founded 1890
Visitors: weekdays.
Green Fee: £27 WD.
Societies: Mon, Tues, Fri.
Catering: available.
Hotels: Grand (Malahide); The Dunes
(Donabate).

U124 Kanturk
☎(029) 50534
Fairyhill, Kanturk, Co Cork
Parkland course
9 holes, 5508 metres, S.S.S.69
Founded 1974
Visitors: welcome any time.
Green Fee: £8.
Catering: bar refreshments.

U125 Kenmare
☎(064) 41291
Kenmare, Co Kerry
On N71, 20 miles S of Killarney, 100
yards out of town.
Parkland course.
18 holes, 5950 yards, S.S.S.68
(provisional)
Designed by Eddie Hackett.
Founded 1903, extended 1993
Visitors: welcome, no restrictions.
Green Fee: approx £12.50.
Societies: apply to Sec.
Catering: bar, snacks on request.
Hotels: Park; Sheen Falls Lodge;
Kenmare Bay.

U126 Kilcock
☎(01) 628 7283
Gallow, Kilcock, Co Meath
2 miles N of Kilcock.
Parkland course.
18 holes, 5775 metres, S.S.S.71
Designed by Eddie Hackett.
Founded 1984
Visitors: welcome weekdays
unrestricted, weekends by prior
arrangement.
Green Fee: £9/day WD, £10/day WE.
Societies: welcome, £20 deposit;
phone in advance.
Catering: bar snacks.
Hotels: The Wells (Enfield).

U127 Kilcoole
☎(01) 287 2066
Kilcoole, Co Wicklow
21 miles S of Dublin on E coast.
Parkland course.
9 holes, 6000 yards, Par 70
Visitors: welcome except Sat and
Sun am.
Green Fee: £10 (18 holes).
Societies: welcome, book in
advance.
Catering: drinks, snacks, meals by
arrangement.

U128 Kildare Hotel & Country Club
☎(01) 627311
Straffan, Co Kildare
22 miles from Dublin city centre via
N7 Naas dual carriageway, or
Lucan/Celbridge route.
Parkland course.
18 holes.
Designed by Arnold Palmer.
Founded 1991
Visitors: welcome, booking
essential.
Green Fee: £77 WD, £85 WE.
Societies: by arrangement.
Catering: restaurant, snack bar, full
bar facilities.
Indoor and outdoor tennis, river and
lake fishing, exercise centre,
croquet.
Hotels: Hotel on site.

U129 Kilkea Castle
☎(0503) 45156
Castle Dermot, Co Kildare
40 miles from Dublin.
Parkland course.
9 holes, 2978 metres, Par 71
Designed by McDadd & Cassidy.
Founded summer 1994
Visitors: welcome but advisable to
book.

Green Fee: £25/round Mon-Thurs, £30/round, Fri-Sun.
Societies: book in advance.
Catering: full facilities.
Leisure centre, tennis, horse riding, clay shooting, archery.

U130 **Kilkee**
☎(065) 56048
East End, Kilkee, Co Clare
Within 400 metres of town.
Meadowland course.
9 holes, 6185 yards, S.S.S.69
Designed by McAllister.
Founded 1892
Visitors: welcome.
Green Fee: apply for details.
Societies: May, June and from mid-Aug to end of Sept.
Catering: snacks always available; meals for societies by arrangement.
Hotels: Strand; Victoria; Stella Maris; Bay View.

U131 **Kilkenny**
☎(056) 22125, 65400
Sec/Manager, 61730 Pro
Glendine, Kilkenny, Co Kilkenny
1 mile NW of mediaval city of Kilenny off the Castlecomer road.
Parkland course.
18 holes, 6450 yards, S.S.S.70
Founded 1896
Visitors: welcome, few restrictions.
Green Fee: £15 WD, £17 WE & BH.
Societies: catered for, mostly Sat mornings.
Catering: at clubhouse.
Snooker and pool.
Hotels: Newpark; Hotel Kilkenny; Springhill Court.

U132 **Killarney**
☎(064) 31034/31242/33899
Sec/Reservations, 31615 Pro
Mahoney's Point, Killarney, Co Kerry
3 miles W of Killarney on Killorglin road.
Parkland/lakeside courses.
Killeen, 18 holes, 7122 yards, S.S.S.73; Mahony's Point, 18 holes, 6734 yards, S.S.S.71
Designed by Eddie Hackett and Dr W. Sullivan (Killeen), Sir Guy Campbell (Mahony's).
Founded 1893
Visitors: welcome, h/cap cert required.
Green Fee: £26.
Societies: at all times.
Catering: all day every day.
Hotels: green fee discounts at numerous local hotels.

U133 **Killeen**
☎(045) 66003, 75881 Phone/Fax
Kill, Co Kildare
N7 to Kill village, turn right off carriageway leading for Straffan, turn left at next junction, 2 miles on left.
Parkland course.
18 holes, 5445 yards, S.S.S.66
Founded 1986
Visitors: Welcome weekdays and weekends.
Green Fee: £11 WD, £13 WE.
Societies: welcome.
Catering: full bar and catering facilities.
Hotels: Green Isle; Ambassador.

U134 **Killeline**
☎(069) 61600 Clubhouse, 62117 Manager (home), 62853 Fax
Newcastle West, Co. Limerick
On the town (Newcastle West) boundary, 500 yards off main Limerick-Killarney road.
Parkland course.
9 holes (extending to 18 in 1994/5)
Founded 1938
Visitors: welcome all day Mon-Sat, Sun by arrangement only.
Green Fee: £10 (18 holes).
Societies: all days except Sun, £7 per member.
Catering: lounge bar and restaurant facilities.
Hotels: River Room; Devon Inn.

U135 **Killiney**
☎(01) 285 1983, 285 2823 Fax
Ballinclea Rd, Killiney, Co Dublin
3 miles from Dun Laoghaire town centre.
Parkland course.
9 holes, 5626 metres, S.S.S.69
Founded 1903
Visitors: welcome; not Thurs, Sat, Sun am.
Green Fee: £18 WD, £20 Sun and BH.
Societies: by arrangement only.
Catering: snacks at all times, full catering by arrangement.
Hotels: Killiney Castle; Killiney Court; Victor.

U136 **Killorglin**
☎(066) 61979, 61437 Fax
Steelroe, Killorglin, Co. Kerry, EIRE
3km from Killorglin on raod to Tralee; 25km from Tralee, 22km from Killarney.
Parkland course.
18 holes, S.S.S.72

Designed by Eddie Hackett.
Founded 1992
Visitors: welcome at all times; pre-booking advisable at weekends.
Green Fee: IR£12
Societies: society/group rates available on request.
Catering: bar, restaurant, meals and snacks.
Hotels: numerous in area; details on request by fax.

U137 **Kilrush**
☎(065) 51138
Parknamoney, Kilrush, Co Clare
On main road into town from Ennis, Co Clare.
Parkland course.
9 holes, 2793 yards, S.S.S.67
Founded 1934
Visitors: welcome.
Green Fee: apply for details.
Societies: catered for by arrangement.
Catering: bar facilities only.

U138 **Kilternan Golf & Country Club**
☎(01) 955542, 955559
Kilternan Hotel, Enniskerry Road, Co Dublin
10 miles S of Dublin centre.
Hilly course.
18 holes, 5413 yards, S.S.S.66
Founded 1977
Visitors: welcome weekdays, and afternoon weekends; restricted Mon (Ladies').
Green Fee: apply for details.
Societies: welcome by prior arrangement.
Catering: full facilities.
Extensive leisure and health facilities.
Hotels: Own hotel on site; special packages for individuals and societies.

U139 **Kinsale**
☎(021) 772197
Ringenane, Belgooly, Co Cork
On main Cork-Kinsale road, 2 miles short of Kinsale signposted on left, 10 miles from Cork Airport.
Parkland course.
9 holes, 5332 yards, S.S.S.68
Founded 1912
Visitors: welcome weekdays.
Green Fee: apply for details.
Societies: welcome by appointment.
Catering: bar and full catering.
Hotels: Trident, Actons, Blue Hand; (reduced green fees for residents).

U140 Knockanally Golf & Country Club
☎(045) 69322
Donadea, North Kildare
3 miles off main Dublin-Galway road between Kilcock and Enfield.
Parkland course.
18 holes, 6484 yards, S.S.S.72
Designed by Noel Lyons.
Founded 1985
Visitors: welcome, no restrictions.
Green Fee: £16 WD, £20 WE & BH.
Societies: every day.
Catering: full catering facilities available.
Hotels: Moyglare Manor (Maynooth); Curryhills House (Prosperous); Wells (Enfield).

U141 Lahinch
☎(065) 81003 Sec/Pro, 81592 Fax
Lahinch, Co Clare
34 miles from Shannon Airport.
Seaside courses.
Old, 18 holes, 6123 metres, S.S.S.73; Castle, 18 holes, 5138 metres, S.S.S.69
Designed by Tom Morris, revised by Dr A. MacKenzie; Castle Course, Commander J.D. Harris, revised by Donald Steel.
Founded 1892
Visitors: welcome weekdays; weekends except from 9-10am and 1-2pm Sat; 9-10.30am and 1-2pm Sun.
Green Fee: on application to Sec or Pro.
Societies: Old, Mon-Sat; Castle, every day.
Catering: full catering facilities available.
Hotels: Aberdeen Arms; Sancta Maria; Liscannor Golf; Atlantic; Claremont; Falls.

U142 Laytown & Bettystown
☎(041) 27170 office, 27563 locker room
Bettystown, Co Meath
On L125 off T1, 26 miles N of Dublin, 4 miles from Drogheda.
Seaside links course.
18 holes, 5652 metres, S.S.S.69
Founded 1909
Visitors: welcome weekdays.
Green Fee: apply for details.
Societies: most days; every effort made.
Catering: full bar and restaurant facilities.
Hotels: Neptune; Boyne Valley; Rosnaree; Mosney Holiday Centre.

U143 Lee Valley
☎((021) 331721
Clashanure, Ovens, Co Cork, EIRE
On main Cork-Killarney road.
Parkland course.
18 holes, 6800 yards, Par 72
Designed by Christy O'Connor Jnr.
Founded 1993
Visitors: welcome.
Green Fee: £20/round.
Societies: welcome by prior arrangement.
Catering: bar and restaurant.
Driving range.

U144 Leopardstown Golf Centre
☎(01) 289 5341
Foxrock, Dublin 18
5 miles S of Dublin.
Public parkland course.
9 holes.
Visitors: welcome.
Green Fee: apply for details.
Societies: Sun am only.
Catering: café, restaurant.
Driving range.
Hotels: Fitzpatricks Castle.

U145 Letterkenny
☎(074) 21150, 24319 Sec.
Barnhill, Letterkenny, Co Donegal
On T72, 2 miles N of Letterkenny.
18 holes, 6299 yards, S.S.S.69
Designed by E. Hackett
Visitors: welcome.
Green Fee: apply for details.
Societies: welcome.
Catering: snacks served, meals by arrangement.

U146 Limerick
☎(061) 414083 Catering, 415146 Office, 412492 Pro
Ballyclough, Limerick
Take Fedamore road S of city.
Parkland course.
18 holes, 6483 yards, S.S.S.71
Founded 1891
Visitors: welcome before 4pm Mon, Wed, Thurs, Fri; no visitors weekends.
Green Fee: £20/day.
Societies: Mon, Wed, Fri before lunch.
Catering: full facilities.
Hotels: Woodfield House.

U147 Limerick County Golf & Country Club
☎(061) 351881
Bellyneety, Co Limerick

5 miles from Limerick on Kilmallock road.
Parkland course.
18 holes, 6712 yards, S.S.S.72
Designed by Des Smith.
Founded 1994
Visitors: welcome 9am-5pm weekdays, 10am-1.30pm weekends.
Green Fee: £28/round.
Societies: very welcome, phone in advance.
Catering: full facilities.
Golf school, putting greens, 3 practice holes.
Hotels: 12 holiday cottages to let.

U148 Lismore
☎(058) 54026
Lismore, Co Waterford
0.5 mile from Lismore on Killarney road.
Parkland course.
9 holes, 5127 metres, S.S.S.67
Designed by Eddie Hackett.
Founded 1965
Visitors: welcome all days, some Sun reserved.
Green Fee: apply for details.
Societies: all days except Sun.
Catering: prior booking needed.
Hotels: Lismore; Ballyraeter House.

U149 Loughrea
☎(091) 41049
Loughrea, Co Galway
On L11, 1 mile N of Loughrea.
Meadowland course.
9 holes, 5578 yards, S.S.S.67
Designed by Eddie Hackett.
Founded 1924
Visitors: unrestricted.
Green Fee: apply for details.
Societies: welcome.
Catering: by prior arrangement.
Hotels: O'Deas; Meadow Court.

U150 Lucan
☎(01) 628 2106, 628 0246, 628 2929 Fax
Celbridge Rd, Lucan, Co Dublin
0.5 mile past Lucan village on road to Celbridge from Dublin.
Parkland course.
18 holes, 6000 yards, S.S.S.71
Founded 1897
Visitors: weekdays only, Wed to 1pm.
Green Fee: £16.
Societies: welcome Mon, Wed and Fri.
Catering: full bar and restaurant service.

U151 Luttrellstown Castle
☎(01) 821 3237
Clonsilla, Dublin 15
W of Co Dublin.
Parkland course.
18 holes, 6981 yards, Par 72
Designed by Dr Nick Bielenberg.
Founded 1993
Visitors: welcome.
Green Fee: £30-£35.
Societies: welcoem, phone in
advance.
Catering: full facilities.

U152 Macroom
☎(026) 41072 Clubhouse, 334 123
Bookings
Lackaduv, Macroom, Co Cork
Situated on outskirts of town on main
Cork/Killarney road; entrance to
clubhouse through cattle gates in
centre of Macroom town.
Parkland course.
18 holes, 5598 metres, S.S.S.70
Designed by J. Kennealy (new 9
holes)
Founded 1924
Visitors: welcome except specified
weekends, phone to check; prior
booking during golf season
recommended.
Green Fee: £12/day.
Societies: by prior booking or
arrangement with Sec; £10 per
player, £50 booking deposit
(deductable).
Catering: full facilities.
Hotels: Castle, Victoria (reduced
green fees for residents).

U153 Mahon
☎(021) 362480
Blackrock, Co Cork
2 miles SE of Cork on Douglas road.
Municipal course.
18 holes, Par 67
Visitors: welcome weekdays,
advance booking weekends.
Green Fee: apply for details.
Catering: bar, snacks, lunch, dinner
by arrangement.

U154 Malahide
☎(01) 846 1611 Sec/Manager, 846
0002 Pro, 846 1270 Fax
Beechwood, The Grange, Malahide,
Co Dublin
1 mile off coast road at Portmarnock,
15 mins by road from Dublin Airport.
Parkland course.
3 x 9 holes, 3 courses with
S.S.S.70/70/71
Designed by Eddie Hackett.

Founded 1892 (new course 1990).
Visitors: welcome at all times but
please book in advance; jacket and
tie after 7.30pm.
Green Fee: £21 WD, £31 WE & BH.
Societies: on application.
Catering: bar and restaurant
facilities.
Snooker.
Hotels: Grand, Grove (Malahide);
Sands, Country Club (Portmarnock).

U155 Mallow
☎(022) 21145, 42501 ans service
Ballyellis, Mallow, Co Cork
1 mile from town on Killavullen road.
Public parkland course.
18 holes, 5874 metres, S.S.S.71
Designed by Commander J.D. Harris.
Founded 1947
Visitors: weekdays except Tues
(Ladies Day), weekends members
only.
Green Fee: £15/round WD, £18 WE.
Societies: prior booking, not Sun.
Catering: bar and restaurant.
Tennis, squash, snooker.
Hotels: Longueville House; Central;
Hibernian; Springport Hall.

U156 Milltown
☎(01) 497 6090
Lower Churchtown Rd, Dublin 14
3 miles S of city centre, via Ranelagh
village.
Parkland course.
18 holes, 5703 metres, S.S.S.69
Founded 1907
Visitors: welcome except Tues, Wed
pm and Sat.
Green Fee: on application.
Societies: by arrangement.
Catering: lunch and dinner served.
Hotels: Orwell Lodge; Montrose;
Jurys; Berkley Court.

U157 Mitchelstown
☎(025) 24072
Mitchelstown, Co Cork
1 mile from Mitchelstown off N1
Dublin to Cork road.
Parkland course.
15 holes (due to extend to 18), 5057
metres, S.S.S.67
Designed by David Jones.
Founded 1908
Visitors: welcome.
Green Fee: £10.
Societies: welcome except Sun.
Catering: full catering for societies
by arrangement.
Hotels: Clongibbon House; Firgrove;
Castle Park.

U158 Moate
☎(0902) 81271
Moate, Co Westmeath
On T4, 8 miles E of Athlone.
Parkland course.
9 holes, 5348 yards, S.S.S.66
Founded 1942
Visitors: welcome.
Green Fee: apply for details.
Societies: catered for.
Catering: meals by arrangement.

U159 Monkstown
☎(021) 841376 Phone/Fax Manager
Parkgariffe, Monkstown, Co Cork
On L68 7 miles SE of Cork; on
entering Monkstown village from
Cork, turn right up hill at signpost to
club, at crossroads at top of hill turn
left, Club 200 yards on right.
Parkland course (89 new bunkers).
18 holes, 5669 metres, S.S.S.69
Founded 1908
Visitors: welcome except Tues.
Green Fee: £20 WD, £23 WE.
Societies: welcome, £18.
Catering: full meals all day; phone
(021) 841089.
Practice ground.
Hotels: Rochestown Park; Norwood
Court.

U160 Mount Juliet
☎(056) 24725, 24828 Fax
Thomastown, Co Kilkenny
1 mile from Thomastown on main
Dublin-Waterford road.
Parkland course.
18 holes, 7142 yards, Par 72; 3 hole
Teaching Academy
Designed by Jack Nicklaus.
Founded 1991
Visitors: welcome every day, please
book in advance.
Green Fee: £60 non-resident,
£35-£45 resident.
Societies: every day, book in
advance.
Catering: full bar and restaurant.
Driving range, riding, fishing, clay
shooting, archery, tennis, swimming
pool, spa and leisure centre.
Hotels: Mount Juliet House.

U161 Mount Temple
☎(0902) 81545 Home, 81841 Office
Campfield Lodge, Moate, Co
Westmeath
In Mount Temple village just off main
Dublin/Galway N6 Route, 5 mile from
Athlone, 4 miles from Moate.
Parkland course, built in old
traditional style.

18 holes, 6421 yards, S.S.S.68
Designed by Robert J. Brown and
Michael Dolan.
Founded Oct 1991
Visitors: all welcome, open
competitions available throughout
the year; Sat play by arrangement.
Green Fee: £8 WD, £10 WE.
Societies: welcome by prior
acknowledgement to management.
Catering: home-cooked farmhouse
refreshment; bar; village pub 100
yards.
Hotels: Grand (Moate); Prince of
Wales, Hudson Bay, Royal (Athlone).

U162 Mountbellew

☎(0905) 79259
Shankhill, Mountbellew, Co Galway
On T4, 28 miles E of Galway
Undulating meadowland course.
9 holes, 5649 yards, S.S.S.66
Founded 1927
Visitors: welcome.
Green Fee: apply for details.
Societies: by arrangement with Sec.
Catering: teas, soup, sandwiches,
full meals on notification.

U163 Mountrath

☎(0502) 32558
Knockinina, Mountrath, Co Laois
1.5 miles on Limerick side of
Mountrath off Dublin-Limerick road.
Undulating parkland course.
9 holes (18 from June 1994), 5300
yards, S.S.S.66
Founded 1929
Visitors: welcome.
Green Fee: £8/day.
Societies: contact Sec.
Catering: on request for outings etc.
Hotels: Killeshin; Leix County.

U164 Mullingar

☎(044) 48366, 48629
Belvedere, Mullingar, Co Westmeath
3 miles from Mullingar on Tullamore
road.
Parkland course.
18 holes, 6450 yards, S.S.S.71
Designed by James Braid.
Founded 1894 (1994 centenary
year).
Visitors: welcome any time, no
restrictions.
Green Fee: on application.
Societies: welcome by prior
arrangement.
Catering: full bar and restaurant
facilities.
Hotels: Bloomfield House; Greville
Arms.

U165 Mulrany

☎(098) 36262 (day)
Mulrany, Westport, Co Mayo
N59, 10 miles W of Newport.
Undulating seaside links.
9 holes, 6383 yards, S.S.S.69
Founded 1896
Visitors: welcome.
Green Fee: on application.
Societies: welcome.
Catering: at Mulrany Bay Hotel.
Hotels: Mulrany Bay; Newport
House; Achill Sound.

U166 Muskerry

☎(021) 385297 Sec, 385104 Pro,
Carrigrohane, Co Cork
7 miles W of city centre, near Blarney
village.
Parkland course.
18 holes, 5786 metres, S.S.S.70
Founded 1897
Visitors: welcome on weekdays
except Wed afternoons, Thurs
mornings before 12.30pm and Fri
after 3.30pm; advisable to phone in
advance.
Green Fee: £17.
Societies: as for visitors.
Catering: snacks available; meals by
arrangement before play.
Hotels: Christys; Blarney Park.

U167 Naas

☎(045) 97509
Kerdiffstown, Naas, Co Kildare
On road between Johnstown and
Sallins.
Parkland course.
9 holes (18 from May 1992), 5792
metres, S.S.S.70
Designed by Arthur Spring.
Founded 1896
Visitors: Mon, Wed, Fri and Sat.
Green Fee: apply for details.
Societies: Mon, Wed, Fri and Sat
am.
Catering: bar; meals by prior
arangement.
Snooker.
Hotels: Harbour View; Town House;
Ambassador.

U168 Narin & Portnoo

☎(075) 45107
Portnoo, Co Donegal
From Donegal via Ardara, then 6
miles N.
Seaside course.
18 holes, 5976 yards, S.S.S.68
Founded 1930
Visitors: welcome, restricted
July/Aug.

Green Fee: apply for details.
Societies: by arrangement.
Catering: bar and light snacks.
Snooker.
Hotels: Nesbitt Arms; Highlands

U169 Nenagh

☎(067) 31476 Club, 33242 Pro.
Beechwood, Nenagh, Co Tipperary
4 miles NE of Nenagh town, well
signposted.
Parkland course.
18 holes, 5491 metres, S.S.S.68
Designed by Alister Mackenzie
(original 9), E. Hackett (additional 9).
Founded 1929, extended 1972
Visitors: welcome every day but
advisable to ring Steward for
availability on Sat/Sun.
Green Fee: £12 WD, £15 WE.
Societies: by prior arrangement.
Catering: full facilities.
22-acre practice ground.
Hotels: Nenagh Lodge; Lakeside
(Killalde).

U170 New Ross

☎(051) 21433
Tinneanny, New Ross, Co Wexford
From town centre take Waterford Rd,
right at Albatros factory, about 1 mile.
Parkland course.
9 holes, 6133 yards, S.S.S.69
Founded 1904
Visitors: welcome except Sun if
there is a competition.
Green Fee: apply for details.
Societies: by arrangement.
Catering: snacks always available,
meals by arrangement.

U171 Newcastle West

☎(069) 62105, 76104, 72142 Sec
Ardagh, Co Limerick
2 miles off main Limerick/Killarney
roadway N21, 23 miles from
Limerick city.
Parkland course.
18 holes, Par 71 (new course from
April 1994)
Designed by Arthur Spring.
Founded 1938, 1994 on present site.
Visitors: welcome most times by
arrangement; not Sun.
Green Fee: £16 approx.
Societies: welcome most days
except Sun; reduced green fees
subject to numbers.
Catering: bar and bar snacks
(restaurant under construction).
Hotels: Dunraven Arms, Woodlands
(Adare); River Room (Newcastle
West); Devon (Templeglantine).

U172 Newlands
☎(01) 459 3157 Sec/Office, 459
2903 Bar, 459 3498 Fax
Clondalkin, Dublin 22
6 miles from city centre on main
southern Cork road.
Parkland course.
18 holes, 5696 metres, S.S.S.70
Designed by James Braid.
Founded 1926
Visitors: welcome weekdays.
Green Fee: £27 (18 holes), £10 with
member.
Societies: welcome weekdays.
Catering: full catering facilities
available.
Hotels: Green Isle.

U173 North West
☎(077) 61027
Lisfannon, Fahan, Co Donegal
2 miles S of Buncrana.
Seaside links course.
18 holes, 6203 yards, S.S.S.69
Founded 1891
Visitors: welcome at any time, no
restrictions.
Green Fee: £10 WD, £15 WE.
Societies: welcome weekdays,
weekends in summer.
Catering: bar and restaurant every
day.
Snooker room.
Hotels: White Strand; Roneragh
House; Lake of Shadows.

U174 Nuremore
☎(042) 61438, 61853 Fax
Carrickmacross, Co Monaghan
1 mile S of Carrickmacross on main
Dublin to Derry road.
Parkland course.
18 holes, 6138 metres, S.S.S.71
Designed by Eddie Hackett.
Founded 1964, new course opened
July 1991
Visitors: welcome any time, no
restrictions.
Green Fee: £15 WD, £18 WE.
Societies: welcome any time.
Catering: meals and snacks at hotel
or clubhouse.
Hotels: Nuremore.

U175 Old Conna
☎(01) 282 6055
Ferndale Road, Bray, Co Dublin
12 miles from Dublin city.
18 holes, Par 72
Visitors: welcome Mon, Thurs, Fri.
Green Fee: apply for details.
Catering: bar, snacks, lunches and
dinners served.

U176 The Open Golf Centre
☎(01) 864 0324
Newtown House, St Margaret's, Co
Dublin
6 miles from city centre on main
Derry road, adjacent to Dublin
Airport.
Public parkland course.
18 holes, 6533 yards
Designed by Martin Hawtree.
Founded May 1993
Visitors: all welcome.
Green Fee: £7.25 WD, £10.75 WE.
Societies: welcome.
Catering: snacks.
Driving range.

U177 Otway
Rathmullan, Co Donegal
On W shore of Loch Swilly.
Seaside course.
9 holes, 4134 yards, S.S.S.60
Visitors: welcome.
Green Fee: £5.
Societies: welcome.
Hotels: Pier; Rathmullan House; Fort
Royal.

U178 Oughterard
☎(091) 82131, 82733 Fax
Oughterard, Co Galway
1 mile from Oughterard on N59, 15
miles from Galway.
Mature parkland course with
elevated greens.
18 holes, 6256 metres, S.S.S.69
Designed by Hawtree/Hackett.
Founded 1973
Visitors: welcome.
Green Fee: £12 WD, £15 WE & BH.
Societies: welcome weekdays
(avoid Wed).
Catering: bar, snacks, lunch,
dinners, full à la carte menu daily.
International Angling and Golf
competition held annually during 1st
weekend in May.
Hotels: Connemara Gateway;
Rosslake; Boat Inn; Corrib; Lake;
Mountain View.

U179 Parknasilla
☎(064) 45233
Parknasilla, Sneem, Co Kerry
2 miles E of Sneem on Ring of Kerry
road.
Undulating seaside course.
9 holes, 4894 yards, S.S.S.65
Founded 1976
Visitors: welcome.
Green Fee: £10.
Hotels: Parknasilla Great Southern.

U180 Portarlington
☎(0502) 23115
Garryhinch, Portarlington, Co Offaly
3 miles from Portarlington on
Mountmellick road.
Tree-lined parkland course.
9 holes (18 holes from May 1992),
5598 yards, S.S.S.66
Founded 1908
Visitors: welcome.
Green Fee: apply for details.
Societies: welcome except Sun.
Catering: bar and restaurant
facilities.
Snooker.
Hotels: East End (for special
arrangements phone 23225); Hazel;
Montague.

U181 Portmarnock
☎(01) 846 2968 Office, 846 2979
Caddymaster, 846 2794 Bar, 846
2634 Pro, 846 2601 Fax
Portmarnock, Co Dublin
From Dublin along coast road to
Baldoyle, on to Portmarnock, right at
Jet Garage, 1 mile up private road.
Seaside links course.
3 x 9 holes; Green, 18 holes, 6064
yards, S.S.S.73; White, 18 holes,
6276 yards, S.S.S.74; Yellow, 18
holes, 6489 yards, S.S.S.75
Designed by W.G. Pickeman &
George Ross.
Founded 1894
Visitors: welcome, 12am-2pm each
day reserved for members.
Green Fee: £40 (Men), £30 (Ladies)
WD; £50 WE & BH.
Societies: welcome by arrangement
Mon, Tues, Fri according to
availability.
Catering: full facilities; jackets and
ties must be worn.
Hotels: Portmarnock Country Club.

U182 Portsalon
☎(074) 59459
Portsalon, Fanad, Co Donegal
Letterkenny to Ramelton to Milford to
Kennykeel to Portsalon.
Seaside links course.
18 holes, 5878 yards, S.S.S.68
Designed by Mr Thompson of
Portrush.
Founded 1891
Visitors: welcome.
Green Fee: £11/day.
Societies: welcome booked in
advance; £8.50 WD, £11 WE.
Catering: bar and restaurant.
Hotels: Claggan House; Portsalon
House; Fort Royal, Rathmullan
House, Pier (Rathmullan).

U183 Portumna
☎(0509) 41059
Woodford Rd, Portumna, Co Galway
1.5 miles from Portumna on
Woodfood road.
Parkland course.
18 holes, 5205 metres, S.S.S.69
Founded 1913
Visitors: welcome.
Green Fee: apply for details.
Societies: by arrangement.
Catering: light refreshments, dinner
by arrangement.
Hotels: Westpark; Clonwyn House;
Portland House.

U184 Raffeen Creek
☎(021) 378430
Ringaskiddy, Co Cork
1 mile from Ringaskiddy (Cork)
Ferryport.
Seaside/parkland course with water.
9 holes, 5800 yards, S.S.S.68
Designed by Eddie Hackett.
Founded 1989
Visitors: unrestricted weekdays,
afternoons at weekends.
Green Fee: apply for details.
Societies: By arrangement.
Catering: bar food.
Snooker.

U185 Rathdowney
☎(0505) 46170
Rathdowney, Portlaoise
N7 to Abbeyleix, turn left for
Rathdowney, follow signposts from
square in Rathdowney.
Meadowland course.
9 holes, S.S.S.69
Designed by Eddie Hackett.
Founded 1931
Visitors: welcome.
Green Fee: apply for details.
Societies: by arrangement.
Catering: by arrangement with Hon
Sec giving one week notice.

U186 Rathfarnham
☎(01) 493 1201
Newtown, Rathfarnham, Dublin 16
2 miles from Rathfarnham village.
Parkland course.
9 holes, 3173 yards, C.S.S.70
Designed by John Jacobs.
Founded 1899
Visitors: welcome except Tues, Sat,
Sun.
Green Fee: £20 (£8 with member).
Societies: by arrangement only.
Catering: lunch and dinners by
arrangement.
Hotels: Marley Park.

U187 Rathsallagh House
☎(045) 53112
Dunlavin, Co Wicklow
32 miles SW of Dublin.
Parkland course.
18 holes, 7017 yards, Par 72
Designed by Peter McEvoy.
Founded 1994
Visitors: welcome, especially
weekdays.
Green Fee: £30/round.
Societies: by arrangement.
Catering: full facilities.
Practice range, snooker, pool, tennis.

U188 Rosapenna
☎(074) 55301
Rosapenna, Downings, Co Donegal
25 miles N of Letterkenny.
Championship links course.
18 holes, 6271 yards, S.S.S.71
Designed by Tom Morris (1893),
Braid & Vardon (1906)
Visitors: welcome.
Green Fee: apply for details.
Catering: at Rosapenna Hotel.
Hotels: Rosapenna; Carrigart.

U189 Roscommon
☎(0903) 26382
Mote Park, Roscommon, Co
Roscommon
On N61, 95 miles W of Dublin, 0.5
mile S of Roscommon town.
Public parkland course.
9 holes (extending to 18 summer
1995), 5784 metres, S.S.S.70
Founded 1903
Visitors: welcome.
Green Fee: £10/day, £40/week.
Societies: by arrangement with Sec
(0903) 26100 office, 26062 home.
Catering: bar and limited restaurant
facilities.
Practice area.
Hotels: Royal; Abbey.

U190 Roscrea
☎(0505) 21130
Derryvale, Roscrea, Co Tipperary
2 miles E of Roscrea on N7 Dublin
road.
Public parkland course.
18 holes, 6283 yards, S.S.S.71
Designed by A. Spring.
Founded 1891
Visitors: no restrictions.
Green Fee: apply for details.
Societies: by appointment.
Catering: bar and restaurant.
Snooker.
Hotels: Racket Hall; Pathe; Leix
County.

U191 Rosslare
☎(053) 32203 (Phone/Fax) Office,
32113 Bar, 32238 Pro
Rosslare Strand, Co Wexford
10 miles S of Wexford, 6 miles N of
Rosslare Harbour.
Seaside links course.
Old course, 18 holes, 6564 yards,
S.S.S.71; New, 9 holes, 3153 yards,
S.S.S.70
Designed by Hawtree & Taylor (Old),
Christy O'Connor Jnr (New).
Founded 1908 (Old), 1992 (New).
Visitors: welcome most days, ring
for availability; time sheets in
operation Tues (Ladies Day), Sat,
Sun.
Green Fee: Old, £18 WD, £23 WE
(high season), £15 WD, ₤20 WE
(winter); New £12/round (18 holes)
all year.
Societies: ring office for bookings.
Catering: full bar and restaurant
facilities.
Practice ground, snooker.
Hotels: Kellys Strand; Cedars;
Burrow Park; (4-day packages in off
season).

U192 Rossmore
☎(047) 81316
Rossmore Park, Monaghan
About 2 miles from Monaghan on
Cootehill road.
Undulating parkland course.
18 holes, 6000 yards, S.S.S.68
Designed by Des Smyth.
Founded 1916
Visitors: welcome; check by phone
at weekends.
Green Fee: £8 WD, £10 WE & BH.
Societies: catered for.
Catering: full facilities 7 days.
Snooker, bridge club.
Hotels: Hillgrove; Four Seasons;
Westenra; Lakeside.

U193 Royal Dublin
☎(01) 336346 Sec/Manager,
337153 Club, 336504 fax.
Bull Island, Dollymount, Dublin 3
4 miles NE of city centre on coast
road to Howth.
Seaside links course.
18 holes, 6858 yards, S.S.S.73
Designed by H.S. Colt.
Founded 1885
Visitors: welcome weekdays;
weekends and Bank Holidays by
arrangement with Sec/Manager.
Green Fee: apply for details.
Societies: weekdays except Wed.
Catering: full service.
Hotels: Marine; Howth Lodge.

U194 Royal Tara
☎(046) 25244, 25508
Bellinter, Navan, Co Meath
30 miles N of Dublin off N3.
Public parkland course.
18 holes, 5757 yards, S.S.S.70; 9
holes, 3184 yards, S.S.S.35
Designed by Des Smyth Golf Design.
Founded 1923
Visitors: welcome by arrangement.
Green Fee: apply for details.
Societies: Mon, Thurs, Fri, Sat by
arrangement.
Catering: full facilities.

U195 Rush
☎(01) 437548, 438177 Office
Rush, Co Dublin
Dublin to Belfast road, turn right at
Blakes Cross.
Seaside links course.
9 holes, 5598 metres, S.S.S.69
Founded 1943
Visitors: preferably not Wed, Thurs,
Sat, Sun and Bank Holidays.
Green Fee: apply for details.
Societies: catered for.
Catering: full facilities.
Hotels: Argyle Lodge B&B.

U196 St Annes
☎(01) 332797 Club, 336471
Sec/bookings
North Bull Island, Dollymount, Dublin
5
4 miles NE of Dublin off coast road to
Howth.
Seaside course.
18 holes, 5660 metres, S.S.S.69
Designed by Eddie Hackett
Founded 1921
Visitors: no restrictions except
competitions; prior enquiry advised.
Green Fee: £16 WD, £20 WE & BH.
Societies: on application.
Catering: by arrangement.

U197 St Helen's Bay
☎(053) 33669, 33234, 33803 Fax
St Helen's, Kilrane, Rosslare
Harbour, Co Wexford
On main Wexford/Rosslare Harbour
road, 1.5 miles from Rosslare
Harbour.
Links and parkland course.
18 holes, 6091 metres, S.S.S.72
Designed by Philip Walton.
Founded 1993
Visitors: welcome all times
including weekends.
Green Fee: Low season, £15 WD,
£18 WE; high season, £17 WD, £22
WE.

Societies: welcome at all times.
Catering: full time catering and bar
available.
Practice and tuition area.
Hotels: 6 local hotels are corporate
members; own accommodation on
site.

U198 Seapoint
☎(353 41) 22333, 22331 Fax
Termonfeckin, Co Louth
35 mins from Dublin Airport, 70 miles
from Belfast; from Dublin, take N1 to
Drogheda, cross Boyne river and turn
right for Termonfeckin; in
Termonfeckin turn right after bridge
for Seapoint.
Championship links course.
18 holes, S.S.S.71
Designed by Des Smyth, Declan
Branigan
Founded June 1993
Visitors: welcome at all times;
booking required.
Green Fee: £17 WD, £22 WE.
Societies: most welcome weekdays,
reduced rates for groups.
Catering: bar; restaurant from June
1994.
Driving range, putting green.
Hotels: Westcourt; Boyne Valley.

U199 Shannon
☎(061) 61020
Shannon Airport, Co Clare
0.5 mile from Shannon Airport
terminal.
Woodland/parkland course.
18 holes, 6854 yards, S.S.S.73
Founded 1966
Visitors: welcome weekdays.
Green Fee: apply for details.
Societies: by arrangement.
Catering: bar, snacks, lunch and
dinner served.

U200 Skerries
☎(01) 491567, 491204
Hacketstown, Skerries, Co Dublin
Take Belfast road N out of Dublin,
past Airport and Swords, fork right
for Lusk and Skerries after end of
Swords by-pass.
Undulating parkland course.
18 holes, 6174 metres, S.S.S.72
Founded 1906
Visitors: welcome.
Green Fee: apply for details.
Societies: welcome Mon, Thurs and
Fri.
Catering: full facilities.
Snooker.
Hotels: Pier House; Anna Villa.

U201 Skibbereen & West Cabbery
☎(028) 21227, 22340 Clubhouse
Licknavar, Skibbereen, Co Cork
Off T65, 52 miles SW of Cork City.
Moorland course.
18 holes, 5900 metres, S.S.S.68
Designed by Eddie Hackett.
Founded 1905
Visitors: welcome, advisable to ring
in advance.
Green Fee: £12 (£15 July and Aug),
£7 with member.
Societies: welcome by
arrangement.
Catering: bar, pub food at all times.
Driving net, putting green.
Hotels: West Cork; Eldon.

U202 Slade Valley
☎(01) 582207, 582183, 582739
Lynch Park, Brittas, Co Dublin
Off N1 Dublin to Naas road.
Undulating course.
18 holes, 5337 metres, S.S.S.68
Designed by W.D. Sullivan and D.
O'Brien.
Founded 1971
Visitors: welcome by arrangement
with Sec.
Green Fee: apply for details.
Societies: apply to Sec.
Catering: meals at weekends, also
Tues and Wed during summer.
Hotels: Green Isle; Downshire House
(Blessington).

U203 Slieve Russell
☎(049) 26444
Ballyconnell, Co Cavan
Approx 90 miles SW of Belfast.
Parkland course.
18 holes, 7013 yards, S.S.S.74
Designed by Paddy Merrigan.
Founded 1992
Visitors: visitors always welcome,
but book in advance.
Green Fee: £22/round Sun-Fri,
£30/round Sat & BH.
Societies: welcome, booking
required.
Catering: full facilities.

U204 Spanish Point
☎(065) 84198
Spanish Point, Miltown Malbay, Co
Clare
2 miles from Milton Malbay, 8 miles
from Lahinch.
Seaside course.
9 holes, 3470 metres, S.S.S.58
Founded 1896
Visitors: welcome.

Green Fee: apply for details.
Societies: welcome except Sun.
Catering: only on special occasions; light snacks at bar (eg sandwiches).
Hotels: Central.

U205 Stackstown

☎(01) 942338, 941993
Kellystown Road, Rathfarnham, Dublin 16
8 miles S of Dublin via N81 and R115.
Hilly course with panoramic views.
18 holes, 5925 metres, S.S.S.72
Founded 1975
Visitors: welcome weekdays; ? weekends
Green Fee: apply for details.
Societies: by arrangement.
Catering: bar, snacks, lunch, dinner.

U206 Strandhill

☎(071) 68188
Strandhill, Co Sligo
5 miles W of Sligo city, 1 mile from Strandhill Airport; course is situated in resort of Strandhill and is well signposted.
Seaside links course.
18 holes, 5950 yards, S.S.S.69
Founded 1931
Visitors: welcome weekdays and most weekends.
Green Fee: £12 WD, £14 WE.
Societies: welcome, group rates available.
Catering: snacks available, meals by arrangement.
Sea fishing, surfing.
Hotels: Ocean View (Strandhill); Southern, Silver Swan, Yeats Country Ryan, Sligo Park (Sligo town).

U207 Sutton

☎(01) 323013
Cush Point, Sutton, Dublin 13
7 miles NE of city centre.
Seaside links course.
9 holes, 5522 yards, S.S.S.67
Designed by Donald Steel.
Founded 1890
Visitors: welcome except competition days (Tues and Sat).
Green Fee: apply for details.
Societies: by arrangement only.
Catering: by arrangement only.

U208 Swinford

☎(094) 51378, 51183 Sec
Brabazon Park, Swinford, Co Mayo
Beside town, opposite Western Health Board complex; 3.5 hours W of Dublin on N5.

Public parkland course.
9 holes, 2950 yards, S.S.S.68
Founded 1922
Visitors: welcome any time.
Green Fee: £6/day, £30/week.
Societies: welcome at all times.
Catering: bars, bar snacks.
Hotels: Heather Lodge.

U209 Templemore

☎(0504) 31400, 31720 Sec.
Manna South, Templemore, Co Tipperary
0.5 mile from town centre beside the Thurles road.
Parkland course.
9 holes, 5112 metres, S.S.S.67
Founded 1972
Visitors: no restrictions except on special event days.
Green Fee: £5/day WD, £10 WE & BH.
Societies: by appointment with Hon Sec.
Catering: no bar, light refreshments on request, catering at local Inns. Hayes, Anner (Thurles).

U210 Thurles

☎(0504) 21983, 23787 Sec
Turtulla, Thurles, Co Tipperary
1 mile S of Thurles on Cork road.
Parkland course.
18 holes, 6300 yards, S.S.S.70
Founded 1909
Visitors: welcome except Sat/Sun.
Green Fee: £13 WD. £15 WE.
Societies: catered for weekdays and Sat.
Catering: full catering.
Driving range, championship squash courts.
Hotels: Hayes; Anner; Hotel Munster.

U211 Tipperary

☎(062) 51119
Rathanny, Tipperary
1 mile from town on Glen of Aherlow road.
Parkland course.
9 holes, 5805 metres, S.S.S.70
Founded 1896
Visitors: welcome weekdays, Sun by prior arrangement.
Green Fee: apply for details.
Societies: by arrangement.
Catering: bar, snacks.
Hotels: Glen; Royal; Aherlow House.

U212 Tralee

☎(066) 36379 Sec, 36008 Fax
West Barrow, Ardfert, Co Kerry

8 miles NW of Tralee; from Tralee through villages of Spa and Churchill to Barrow.
Links course.
18 holes, 5961 metres, S.S.S.71
Designed by Arnold Palmer Design.
Founded 1896
Visitors: welcome weekdays by arrangement with Sec; not Weds during June, July, Aug; weekends 11am-12.30pm; h/cap certs may be required, max 28 men, 36 ladies..
Green Fee: £25/round WD, £30/round WE.
Societies: weekdays; 10% discount for 20 or more.
Catering: full facilities.
Hotels: Mount Brandon; Grand.

U213 Tramore

☎(051) 86170
Newtown Hill, Tramore, Co Waterford
Via Waterford, 1 mile beyond Tramore.
Parkland course.
18 holes, 6660 yards, S.S.S.73
Designed by Tibbett (1936/7)
Founded 1894
Visitors: welcome.
Green Fee: on application.
Societies: by arrangement.
Catering: meals served.
Hotels: Majestic; Grand; Sea View.

U214 Tuam

☎(093) 28993
Barnacurragh, Tuam, Co Galway
1.5 miles from town on the Athenry road which is off Dublin road.
Parkland course.
18 holes, 5944 metres, S.S.S.71
Founded around 1910
Visitors: welcome weekdays.
Green Fee: approx £10.
Societies: catered for on weekdays and Sat by arrangement.
Catering: full restaurant and bar facilities.
Hotels: Hermitage; Imperial.

U215 Tubbercurry

☎(071) 85849
Tubbercurry, Co Sligo
Within 1.5 miles of Tubercurry on Ballymote road.
Parkland course.
9 holes, 5478 metres, S.S.S.69
Designed by Eddie Hackett.
Founded 1991
Visitors: welcome at all times.
Green Fee: £6
Catering: new clubhouse under construction (1994).

U216 Tulfarris Hotel & Country Club
☎(045) 64574
Blessington, Co Wicklow
Turn left 6 miles from Blessington off N81.
9 holes, 5612 metres, S.S.S.69
Designed by Eddie Hackett.
Founded 1987
Visitors: welcome; limited Sun.
Green Fee: apply for details.
Societies: by arrangement.
Catering: restaurant, bar, bar snacks.
Banqueting, conference centre, tennis, indoor swimming pool, gym, snooker.
Hotels: Tulfarris Hotel & CC, special golfing packages on request.

U217 Tullamore
☎(0506) 21439
Brookfield, Tullamore, Co Offaly
2.5 miles from town centre, 1 mile off Birr road, on Kinnity road.
Parkland course.
18 holes, 6322 yards, S.S.S.70
Designed by James Braid.
Founded 1896
Visitors: welcome except during club competitions on Sun.
Green Fee: £12/round WD, £15/round WE & BH.
Societies: weekdays and Sat.
Catering: readily available, large numbers (eg societies) by prior arrangement.
Hotels: Phoenix Arms.

U218 Virginia
☎(049) 47235
Virginia, Co Cavan
50 miles N of Dublin on main Cavan-Dublin road, within Park Hotel, by Lough Ramor.
Meadowland course.
9 holes, 4139 metres, S.S.S.62
Founded 1946
Visitors: welcome.
Green Fee: apply for details.
Catering: in Park hotel.
Hotels: Park.

U219 Waterford
☎(051) 76748 Sec, 54256 Pro, 53405 Fax
Newrath, Waterford
0.25 mile from city centre.
Parkland course.
18 holes, 6237 yards, S.S.S.70
Designed by Cecil Barcroft and Willie Park.
Founded 1912

Visitors: welcome weekdays.
Green Fee: £15 WD, £18 WE.
Societies: catered for weekdays.
Catering: full facilities available.
Hotels: Jurys; Bridge; Granville; Dooleys; Tower.

U220 Waterford Castle Golf & Country Club
☎(051) 71633, 79316 Fax
The Island, Co Waterford
Approx 2 miles out of Waterford City on Dunmore East road; take 4th left after Regional Hospital roundabout; own car ferry to island.
Parkland course on island in River Suir.
18 holes, 6209 yards, Par 72
Designed by Des Smyth and Declan Brannigan.
Founded 1991
Visitors: welcome; book in advance.
Green Fee: £25/round; 4 or more in party, £20.
Societies: welcome by arrangement.
Catering: teas, coffee, snacks; meals by prior arrangement.
Tennis, indoor swimming pool.
Hotels: Waterford Castle (051) 78203.

U221 Waterville House & Golf Links
☎(066) 74102, 74545, 74482 Fax.
Rink of Kerry, Waterville, Co Kerry
N70 to Waterville, then coastal road for 1 mile W of town.
Seaside links course.
18 holes, 7184 yards, S.S.S.74
Designed by E. Hackett.
Founded 1889
Visitors: welcome at all times except major tournaments; all players must produce h/cap cert before signing in.
Green Fee: £35/round.
Societies: group rates available, 7 days; society must be affiliated and members must have club h/caps.
Catering: bar and restaurant.
Practice range, putting green.
Hotels: Waterville House; Butlers Arms; Bay View; Jolly Swagman; Villa Maria; Club Med.

U222 West Waterford
☎(058) 43216, 44343 Fax
Coolcormack, Dungarvan, Co Waterford
2.5 miles W of Dungarvan off N25 on Aglish Road.
Parkland course.
18 holes, 6771 yards, S.S.S.74
Designed by Eddie Hackett.

Founded July 1993
Visitors: welcome.
Green Fee: £15WD, £20 WE.
Societies: welcome by arrangement, discount for goups.
Catering: bar and restaurant all day every day.
Practice ground; guest house.

U223 Westmanstown
☎(01) 205817
Clonsilla, Dublin 15
Coming from Dublin to Lucan village turn right and follow sign for Clonsilla, course on right.
Flat parkland course.
18 holes, 5819 metres, S.S.S.70
Designed by Eddie Hackett.
Founded 1989
Visitors: welcome Mon-Fri.
Green Fee: apply for details.
Societies: welcome by prior arrangement.
Catering: available when clubhouse completed.
Hotels: Spa (Lucan).

U224 Westport
☎(098) 25113, 27070, 27481 Pro, 27217 Fax
Carrowholly, Westport, Co Mayo
2 miles from Westport, continue for 0.5 mile on Newport road then left.
Parkland course.
18 holes, 7606 yards, S.S.S.71
Designed by Hawtree & Son.
Founded 1973 (present course)
Visitors: welcome.
Green Fee: April-Sept, £15 WD, £18 WE & BH; Oct-March, £12 WD, £15 WE & BH.
Societies: welcome; special rates by arrangement.
Catering: lounge bar; snacks and meals in dining room.
Hotels: Railway; Clewbay; Central; Castlecourt; Woods; Hotel Westport.

U225 Wexford
☎(053) 42238
Mulgannon, Wexford
Within Wexford town.
Parkland course.
18 holes, 6100 yards, S.S.S.70
Designed by J. Hamilton Stutt & Co (original), Des Smyth (new course).
Founded 1961
Visitors: welcome weekdays; avoid Wed evening and Thurs (Ladies Day).
Green Fee: £14 WD, £15 WE.
Societies: welcome by booking; reduced green fees depending on numbers.

Catering: bar and snacks.
Pool table, darts.
Hotels: Talbot· Whites; Kelly's
Strand; Cedars.

U226 **Wicklow**
☎(0404) 67379
Dunbur Rd, Wicklow, Co Wicklow
On L29 32 miles from Dublin.
Seaside course.
9 holes, 2633 yards, S.S.S.67
Founded 1904
Visitors: welcome weekdays.
Green Fee: apply for details.
Catering: meals served except Tues.

U227 **Woodbrook**
☎(01) 282 4799
Dublin Rd, Bray, Co Wicklow
11 miles S of Dublin centre on N11.
Parkland course.

18 holes, 6540 yards, S.S.S.71
Founded 1921
Visitors: by arrangement.
Green Fee: £26 WD, £35 WE & BH.
Societies: Mon, Thurs, Fri by
arrangement.
Catering: bar, snacks, dinner, à la
carte.
Hotels: Royal; Victor; Killiney Castle.

U228 **Woodenbridge**
☎(0402) 35202
Woodenbridge, Arklow, Co Wicklow
45 miles S of Dublin on route N11 to
Arklow; 4 miles NW of Arklow.
Parkland course.
9 holes (extending to 18 by Aug
1994), 6104 yards, S.S.S.68
Founded 1884
Visitors: welcome except Thurs and
Sat.
Green Fee: approx £15 WD, £20 Sun.

Societies: welcome weekdays by
arrangement.
Catering: full restaurant facilities
generally available.
Practice ground.
Hotels: Woodenbridge; Valley; Vale
View.

U229 **Youghal**
☎(024) 92787
Knockaverry, Youghal, Co Cork
Overlooking Youghal town and bay.
Meadowland course.
18 holes, 6206 yards, S.S.S.69
Designed by Commander Harris.
Founded 1898
Visitors: welcome.
Green Fee: apply for details.
Societies: welcome by prior
arrangement.
Catering: full bar and restaurant
facilities.

DRIVING RANGES

Driving ranges are listed alphabetically within the county groups used in the main part of the Guide (see the map on p4). If a driving range is attached to a golf course covered in the main part of the book, a reference to the course is given so that further relevant information, including the address, can be found. In each case, the entry indicates in this order: the number of bays available; the opening hours; and the charges.

A1 **Bowood**
☎(0840) 213017 · See **A6** · 12 · 9am-9pm.
A2 **Central Park GC**
☎(0752) 509391
Central Park, Plymouth, Devon
9am-dusk.
A3 **China Fleet Country Club**
☎(0752) 848668 · See **A11** · 28 ·
8am-10pm · £3.50, £2.25.
A4 **Cornwall Golf Centre**
☎(0208) 77588
Clifton Park, Carminow Cross, Bodmin, Cornwall
8 covered, floodlit · Mon-Fri
10.30am-9.30pm; Sat 10am-1pm; Sun
10am-5.30pm · £1.60/60.
A5 **Dinnaton**
☎(0752) 892512, 691288 · See **A17** · 6
covered, floodlit · 9am-9pm · £2/50.
A6 **Fingle Glen**
☎(0647) 61817 · See **A23** · 12 covered, floodlit.
A7 **Ilfracombe & Woolacombe GR**
☎(0271) 866222
Woolacombe Rd, Ilfracombe, Devon EX34 7HF
12 covered, 6 open · June/July/August
8am-8pm; winter ring to check · £2/50.
A8 **Killiow**
☎(0872) 70246 · See **A31** · 9 covered, floodlit · 9.30am-9pm · £1.30/50.
A9 **Les Mielles Golf Centre (Western Golf Range)**
☎(0534) 482629 · See **A35** · 30 open ·
dawn-dusk · £2.20/84.
A10 **Libbaton**
☎(0769) 60269, 60167 · See **A36** · 7
covered, floodlit · 9am-9pm · £1.50/50.
A11 **Merlin**
☎(0841) 540222 · See **A40** · 6 covered,
floodlit, main-dark · £1.20/40, £2.50/120.
A12 **Newton Abbot Golf Range**
☎(0626) 64885
The Racecourse, Newton Abbot TQ12 3AF
10 open, 10 grass · winter 9.30am-dusk;
summer 9.30am-7.30pm; closed on race
days · £1.50/40, £2/40 best balls.
A13 **Otter Valley Golf Centre**
☎(0404) 86266
Upottery, Honiton, Devon EX14 9QP
4 · 8am-9pm.
A14 **Radnor Golf Centre**
☎(0209) 211059 · See **A50** · 12 covered,
floodlit; 6 open · 8.30am-9pm (6pm WE) ·
£1.50/50.
A15 **Royal Guernsey**
☎(0481) 46523 · See **A51** · 20 · 8am-dark ·
50p/25-30.

A16 **Saint Pierre Park Hotel**
☎(0481) 727039 · See **A59** · 9 · 8am to 2
hrs before dusk · £1.50/50.
A17 **Thorn Park Golf Range**
☎(0395) 579564
Salcombe Regis, Sidmouth EX10 0JH
9 covered, floodlit · winter 10am-6.30pm,
summer 10am-dusk · £1.80/50+.
A18 **Torbay Golf Centre**
☎(0803) 528728
Grange Rd, Clennan Valley, Goodrington,
Paignton TQ4 7JY
24 covered, floodlit; · 11.30am-9pm WD,
10am-6pm WE · £2.10/50; £2.40 9 holes;
£3.20 18 holes.
A19 **Woodbury Park G & CC**
☎(0395) 233382, 233384 · See **A77** · open
· 7am-dusk · £1/25.

B20 **Bournemouth GDR**
☎(0202) 593131 · See **B59** · 23 covered,
floodlit · 9am-9pm · £1.60/50.
B21 **Bowood G & CC**
☎(0249) 822228 · See **B5** · 10 covered, 8
open · 8am-10pm (4.30pm winter) · £3/55.
B22 **Broome Manor**
☎(0793) 532403 · See **B12** · 35 covered,
floodlit · 8am-9.30pm · £2.75/large,
£2/medium, £1.20/small.
B23 **Cheddar Valley GDR**
☎(0934) 742727
Penstone, Lyppiatt Lane, Cheddar,
Somerset BS27 3QT
10 covered, floodlit · 7.30am-9pm · £1/30.
B24 **Crane Valley**
☎(0202) 814088 · See **B21** · 10 covered ·
7.30am-9pm · £1/30.
B25 **Dudsbury**
☎(0202) 594448 · See **B24** · 10 · daylight
hours · £1/30.
B26 **East Dorset**
☎(0929) 472272 · See **B25** · 22 floodlit, 12
covered · 8am-9pm · £2/bucket.
B27 **Farrington**
☎(0761) 241274 · See **B29** · 16 covered, 8
off grass, floodlit · 8am-8pm · £1/25.
B28 **Halstock**
☎(0935) 891689 · See **B32** · 12 covered,
floodlit · 9am-dusk (7.30pm winter) ·
£1.65/bucket.
B29 **Iford Bridge Sports Complex**
☎(0202) 473817 · See **B38** · 15 open ·
8am-dark · £1.50/50, £3/100.
B30 **Long Sutton**
☎(0458) 241017 · See **B45** · 12 · 8am-9pm
· £2.50/100.
B31 **Mendip Spring**
☎(0934) 853337 · See **B50** · 15 covered,
floodlit · 8.30am-9pm · £2.50/100.
B32 **Oake Manor**
☎(0823) 461993 · See **B56** · 10 covered ·
dawn-dusk · apply.
B33 **Oaksey Park**
☎(0666) 577995 · See **B57** · 10 · daylight
hours · £2.50/40, £1.50/20.
B34 **Solent Meads Par 3**
☎(0202) 420795 · See **B68** · 10 open · 8am
to 1 hour before sunset · £1.80/50,
£1.10/25.
B35 **Stockwood Vale**
☎(0272) 866505 · See **B69** · 12 covered, 4
open · 8.30am-dark · £2.50/75.

B36 **Swingrite Golf Centre**
☎(0823) 442600
Haydon Lane, Holway, Taunton TA3 5AB
12 covered, floodlit, 6 open · 9am-9pm
(7pm WE & winter) · £1.80/60; £1.20/60
jnrs, unemployed etc.
B37 **Thoulstone Park**
☎(0373) 832825 · See **B75** · 20 covered,
floodlit · 8am-9pm (6pm Sun) · £2/50,
£3.50/100.
B38 **Wessex Golf Centre**
☎(0305) 784737 · See **B80** · 20 open · 9am
to 1 hr before dusk · £1.80/40, £3/90.
B39 **Wingfield GDR**
☎(0225) 776365
Wingfield Rd, Trowbridge, Wilts BA14 9LW
28 covered, floodlit · 9.30am-9.30pm (6pm
Sun) · £2/50, £3/100.
B40 **Wrag Barn G & CC**
☎(0793) 766027 · See **B87** · 10 open ·
7am-dark · £1.50/bucket.

C41 **Aldershaw**
☎(0424) 870898 · See **C1** · 24 covered ·
8am-9.30pm · £2/50.
C42 **Basingstoke Golf Centre**
☎(0256) 50054 · See **C11** · 24 indoor ·
8.30am-9.30pm (9am-6pm Fri-Sun winter)
· £1/26.
C43 **Bishopswood**
☎(0734) 815213, 812200 · See **C12** · 12 ·
8am-9pm · £1/30, £2.80/90.
C44 **Botley Park Hotel & CC**
☎(0489) 780888 · See **C15** · 12 · 8am to
1hr before dark · £1/40.
C45 **Brookfield Farm**
☎(0403) 891568 · See **C19** · 6 covered, 6
open, floodlit · 24 hours · membership
£60/year.
C46 **Chichester Golf Centre**
☎(0243) 533833 · See **C22** · 27 floodlit ·
7am-9pm summer, 9am-6pm winter ·
£2.50/60, £1/20.
C47 **Dibden**
☎(0703) 845596 · See **C33** · 19 · 8am-8pm
(6pm WE) · 80p/26.
C48 **Hastings**
☎(0424) 852981 · See **C51** · 14 · 9am-9pm
· £2/50.
C49 **Horam Park**
☎(0435) 813477 · See **C58** · 16 floodlit ·
8am-10.30pm · £2/bucket.
C50 **Moors Valley Country Park**
☎(0425) 479776 · See **C68** · 14 ·
10am-8pm WD, 8am-6pm WE;
10am-10pm summer · £1.50/45.
C51 **Old Thorns**
☎(0428) 724555 · See **C72** · 3 · 8am-4pm ·
£2/bucket.
C52 **Osiers Farm**
☎(0798) 44097 · See **C74** · 6 open · dawn
to dusk · £3/120, £2/60.
C53 **Paultons Golf Centre**
☎(0703) 813345 · See **C75** · 20 covered,
floodlit; 10 open · 7am-8pm · £1/25, £2,60.
C54 **Pease Pottage**
☎(0293) 521706 · See **C78** · 36 · 8am-9pm
(10pm summer) · £2.30/60, £3.80/120.
C55 **Portsmouth Golf Centre**
☎(0705) 664549, 699519 · See **C48** · 25
covered, floodlit · 8am-9pm WD, 7am-8pm
(6pm winter) WE · £1.80/50.

C56 **Singing Hills GC**
☎(0273) 835353 · See **C96** · 15 · dawn-dusk
· £2/55.

C57 **Sinfold Park G & CC**
☎(0403) 791555 · See **C97** · 19 covered,
floodlit · 8am-9pm.

C58 **Southampton GR**
☎(0703) 740544 · See **C100** · 30 covered,
floodlit · 8am-9pm (6pm WE) · £1.50/50.

C59 **Tilgate Forest Golf Centre**
☎(0293) 530103 · See **C107** · 35 floodlit ·
8.30am-10pm · £2.70/bucket.

C60 **Wellshurst G & CC**
☎(04353) 813636 · See **C113** · 16 floodlit ·
7.30am-9.30pm · £2/50.

C61 **West Chiltington**
☎(0798) 812115 · See **C114** · 8 open, 5
covered · dawn-dusk · £1.60/50.

D62 **Beverley Park Golf Range**
☎(081) 949 9200
Beverley Way, New Maldon, Surrey KT3 4PH
60, 2 tier, covered, floodlit · 8am-10pm
(9.30pm WE) · £2/50.

D63 **Birchwood Park**
☎(0322) 660554 · See **D15** · 30 covered, 8
open, floodlit · 10am-10pm · £2/.51.

D64 **Bramley**
☎(0483) 893685 · See **D16** · 7 · dawn-dusk ·
£1/35; members only.

D65 **Broadwater Park**
☎(0483) 429955 · See **D17** · 16 covered,
floodlit · 8am-10pm · £2.25/55.

D66 **Chatham Golf Centre**
☎(0634) 848925
Street End Rd, Chatham, Kent ME5 0BG
30 covered, floodlit · 10am-10pm · £1.80/50.

D67 **Chessington**
☎(081) 391 0948 · See **D25** · 18 covered,
floodlit · 9am-10pm (9pm WE) · £1/35.

D68 **Chiswick Bridge GR**
☎(081) 995 0537/0539 · See **Dnew** · 50
covered, floodlit · 9.30am-10pm (9pm Sun) ·
£2.50/56.

D69 **Croydon GDR**
☎(081) 656 1690
175 Long Lane, Addiscombe, CR0 7TE
24 covered, floodlit · 9am-10pm (9pm WE) ·
£2/40, £3.75/80.

D70 **Edenbridge G & CC**
☎(0732) 865097 · See **D46** · 14 covered,
floodlit · 7.30am-9pm (8pm WE) · £1.70/50.

D71 **Fairmile Driving Range**
☎(0932) 864419
Portsmouth Rd, Cobham, Surrey
24 covered floodlit · 10am-10pm WD,
9am-9pm WE · £2/70, £2.50/100,
£3.75/150.

D72 **Foxhills**
☎(0932) 872050 · See **D54** · 10 · dawn-dusk
· £2/65; members only.

D73 **Herne Bay GDR**
☎(0227) 742742
Bullockstone Rd, Herne Bay, Kent CT6 7TL
15 covered, floodlit · 9am-10pm · £2/50,
£3/100.

D74 **Hewitts Golf Centre**
☎(0689) 896266 · See **D63** · 40 covered,
floodlit · 8am-10pm winter, 6am-10pm
summer · £2.20/40, £3.80/80; off peak
£1.70/£3.

D75 **Hoebridge Golf Centre**
☎(0483) 722611 · See **D66** · 25 covered,
floodlit · 7am-11pm · £2/£3/£3.75 buckets.

D76 **Langley Park Driving Range**
☎(0622) 863163
Langley Park, Sutton Rd, Langley, Maidstone,
Kent ME17 3NQ
25 covered, floodlit · 10am-10pm (9pm WE,
7.30pm winter) · £1.50/40.

D77 **Lingfield Park**
☎(0342) 834602 · See **D80** · 10 open ·
8am-dusk · £2/£3/£4 buckets.

D78 **Oak Park (Crandall)**
☎(0252) 850880, 850000 · See **DOC** · 16
covered, floodlit · dawn-dusk · £1/small,
£2/large.

D79 **Oaks Sports Centre**
☎(081) 643 8363 · See **D97** · 16 covered,
floodlit · 9am-10pm · £1/bucket.

D80 **Oast Golf Centre**
☎(0795) 473527
West Tonge Farm, Church Rd, Tonge ME9 9AR
17 covered, floodlit; 9-hole Par 3 course ·
10am-10pm (11pm WE) · £1/30; £2.50 18
holes before 12am.

D81 **Pachesham Golf Centre**
☎(0372) 843453 · See **D99** · 33 covered,
floodlit · 9am-10pm (9pm WE) · £1/30,
£1.75/60, £2.50/90.

D82 **Pine Ridge Golf Centre**
☎(0276) 20770 · See **D100** · 36 covered,
floodlit · 9am-10pm · £2.30/50.

D83 **Prince's**
☎(0304) 613797 · See **D102** · 4, plus open
range · dawn-dusk · £3.50/100, £2/50.

D84 **Richmond Golf Range**
☎(081) 332 9200
The Athletic Ground, Kew Foot Rd, Richmond
23 covered, floodlit · 9.30am-9.30pm WD,
9am-5pm WE · £1.50/small; £2.20/large.

D85 **Richmond Park**
☎(081) 876 3205/1795 · See **D110** · 15 open
· 715am-4pm · £1/25, £1.75/50.

D86 **Ridge The**
☎(0622) 844243 · See **D111** · 10 open ·
dawn-dusk · £2/bucket.

D87 **Riverside**
☎(081) 310 7975 · See **D112** · 31 covered,
floodlit · 8am-11pm · £2/52.

D88 **Rusper**
☎(0293) 871871 · See **D122** · 12 covered
dawn-dusk · £1/51.

D89 **Ruxley**
☎(0689) 871490 · See **D123** · 29 covered,
floodlit · dawn-10pm · £1.70/50 (£2 WE),
£3/100 (£3.50 WE).

D90 **Sandown Golf Centre**
☎(0372) 463340, 465921 · See **D126** · 33
covered, floodlit · 10am-10pm (9pm WE) ·
£2/70.

D91 **Sandwich GDR**
☎(0304) 612812
Ash Rd, Sandwich, Kent CT13 9XX
9 covered, floodlit bays · 10am-10pm ·
£2.50/65, £1.25/35.

D92 **Selsdon Park Hotel and GC**
☎(081) 657 8811 · See **D127** · 4 open ·
8.30am-4pm · £2/bucket.

D93 **Silvermere**
☎(0932) 867275 · See **D135** · 32 covered,
floodlit · 8am-10pm · £2.50/£1.50.

D94 **Sunbury**
☎(0932) 772898 · See **D138** · 32 floodlit ·
10am-10pm · £2/bucket.

D95 **Swanley Golf Centre**
☎(0322) 669201
Beechenlea Lane, Swanley, Kent BR8 8DR
15 open, 18 covered, floodlit · 10am-11pm ·
£1/50 WD, £2/50 WE.

D96 **Upchurch River Valley**
☎(0634) 360626, 379592 · See **D149** · 16
covered, floodlit · 7am-9pm · £1/30.

D97 **Windlemere**
☎(0276) 858727 · See **D165** · 12 covered,
floodlit · 9am-9.45pm · £2.30/50.

E98 **Airlinks**
☎(081) 561 1418 · See **E3** · 36 covered,
floodlit · 10am-10pm · £1/45, £2/100.

E99 **Belhus Park (Thurrock)**
☎(0708) 852248 · See **E12** · 11 covered,
floodlit · 8am-9pm WD, 9am-5pm Sat,
8am-7pm Sun · £1.50/100, £1/50.

E100 **Belvedere Golf Range**
☎(0268) 286612, 522828
Hardings Elms Road, Crays Hill, Billericay,
Essex CM11 2UH
28 covered, floodlit · 10am-10pm (9pm WE) ·
£2/50.

E101 **Benton Hall**
☎(0376) 502454 · See **E14** · 20 floodlit ·
7am-9pm · £2/40, £3.50/80.

E102 **Brentwood Park**
☎(0277) 211994
Brentwood Park, Warley Gap, Brentwood,
Essex CM13 3LG
23 covered, floodlit · 7.30am-10pm · £2/45,
£4/90.

E103 **Bunsay Downs**
☎(0245) 222648 · See **E27** · 4 indoor ·
7am-6pm (9pm Sat), closed Fri · £1.50/50.

E104 **Bushey G & CC**
☎(081) 950 2215 · See **E31** · 30 covered,
floodlit · 9am-10pm · £2/60.

E105 **Castle Point**
☎(0268) 510830 · See **E35** · 18 covered,
floodlit · 7am-9pm.

E106 **Chingford Golf range**
☎(081) 529 2409
Waltham Way, Chingford, London E4 8AQ
23 covered, floodlit · 9.30am-10pm ·
£1.50/40, £1.95/60; £2.75/100.

E107 **Colchester Golf range**
☎(0206) 230974
Old Ipswich Road, Ardleigh, Colchester, Essex
12 covered, floodlit · 10am-9pm (5pm WE) ·
£1.25/30, £1.75/50.

E108 **Ealing Golf Range**
☎(081) 845 4967
Rowdell Rd, Northolt, Middx UB5
36 covered, floodlit · 10am-10pm · £2/50.

E109 **Earls Colne G & CC**
☎(0787) 224466 · See **E49** · 20 covered,
floodlit · 9am-10pm WD, 8am-9pm WE ·
£1.75/50.

E110 **Elstree**
☎(081) 207 5680 · See **E52** · 60 covered,
floodlit · 7am-10pm · £2/60.

E111 **Fairlop Waters**
☎(081) 500 9911 · See **E55** · 32 covered,
floodlit · 9.30am-9pm · £2.50/100.

E112 **Fairways Golf Range**
☎(081) 531 5126
Walthamstow Avenue, N Circular Rd, E4 8TA
31 covered, floodlit · 10am-10pm · £2/60.

E113 **Family Golf Centre The**
☎(0462) 482929 · See **E56** · 25 covered,
floodlit · 8am-10pm · £2/60.

E114 **Gosling Sports Park**
☎(0707) 331056
Stanborough Rd, Welwyn Garden City, Herts
AL8 6XE
24 covered floodlit · 10am-10pm WD,
9am-8pm WE · £1.90/50.

E115 **Hockley Golf Range**
☎(0702) 207218/201008
Aldermans Hill, Hockley, Nr Southend, Essex
16 covered, floodlit · 9am-9pm · £1.75/46.

E116 **Langdon Hills**
☎(0268) 548444 · See **E89** · 22 covered,
floodlit · 7.45am-9.30pm WD, 7.30am-8pm
WE · £1.20/bucket.

E117 **Lee Valley**
☎(081) 803 3611, 345 6666 · See **E90** · 20
covered, floodlit · 8am-9.30pm · £2/70.

E118 **Leigh GDR**
☎(0702) 710586
Leigh Marshes, Leigh-on-Sea, Essex
18 covered, floodlit · 10am-9.30pm (not
Christmas) · £1.60/50.

E119 **Little Hay Golf Complex**
☎(0442) 833798 · See **E92** · 25 covered,
floodlit · 10am-9pm · £1.50/bucket.
E120 **London Golf Centre**
☎(081) 845 3180 · See **E93** · 20 covered,
floodlit · 10am-10pm · £1/25, £2/75.
E121 **Pipps Hill**
☎(0268) 533212 · See **E111** · 20 covered,
floodlit · 9am-9.30pm · £2/50, £3/75.
E122 **Redbourn**
☎(0582) 793493, 792150 · See **E115** · 20
covered, floodlit · 7.30am-7.30pm ·
£1.80/40.
E123 **Regents Park Golf Centre**
☎(071) 724 0643 · See **Enew** · 11 covered,
floodlit · 8am-9pm · £2/50 (daily membership
£3, annual £60)·
E124 **Ruislip**
☎(0895) 638835 · See **E121** · 40 covered,
floodlit · 8am-10pm · £1/32, £2/64.
E125 **Stevenage**
☎(0438) 880424 · See **E128** · 22 covered,
floodlit · dawn-10.30pm · £1/40.
E126 **Tiptree GDR**
☎(0621) 819374
Newbridge Road, Tiptree, Essex CO5 OHS.
12 covered, floodlit · 10am-9pm (6pm WE) ·
£1.50/50.
E127 **Top Meadow**
☎(0708) 852239 · See **E140** · 10 covered,
floodlit · 5-10pm · £1.50/50.
E128 **Towerlands**
☎(0376) 326802 · See **E141** · 6 open ·
8.30am-dusk · £1.25/50.
E129 **Trent Park**
☎(081) 366 7432 · See **E142** · 24 covered,
floodlit · 9am-11pm · £2.50/45.
E130 **Twickenham Park**
☎(081) 783 1698 · See **E144** · 23 covered, 4
open, floodlit · 9am-10pm · £2/60.
E131 **Warren Park Golf Centre**
☎(081) 597 1120
Whalebone Lane North, Chadwell Heath,
Romford, Essex RM6 6SB
27 covered, floodlit · 9am-10pm (9pm Sat) ·
£1.70/35, £3.50/110.
E132 **Watford Golf Driving range**
☎(0923) 675560
Sheepcot Lane, Garston, Watford, Herts
20 covered, floodlit · 9am-10pm · £1/35
approx.
E133 **Whitehill**
☎(0920) 438495 · See **E156** · 24 covered,
floodlit · dawn-9.30pm (6pm WE, dusk in
summer) · £1.50/45, £2.50/85.
E134 **Woodham Mortimer GR**
☎(0245) 222276
Burnham Road, Woodham Mortimer, Maldon,
Essex CM9 6SR
14 covered, floodlit, 7 open; snack bar ·
10am-9pm WD; 9am-5pm (7pm Sat, 8pm
Sun in summer) WE · £2.80/60, £3.50/100;
Pitch & Putt (18 holes) £3.50 adult, £1.50
child.

F135 **Aylesbury Golf Centre**
☎(0296) 393644 · See **F3** · 30 covered,
floodlit · 8am-10pm WD, 7am-10pm WE ·
£2/bucket.
F136 **Aylesbury Vale**
☎(0525) 240196 · See **F4** · 9 covered,
floodlit · 8am-10pm · £2/bucket.
F137 **Bird Hills (Hawthorn Hill)**
☎(0628) 75588, 771030 · See **F9** · 38
covered, floodlit · 9.30am-10pm · £2.30/55.
F138 **Blue Mountain Golf Centre**
☎(0344) 300200 · See **F10** · 33 covered,
floodlit · 8am-9pm · £2.
F139 **Braywick Golf Range**
☎(0628) 76910

Braywick Rd, Maidenhead, Berks SL6 1DH
45 bays (grass and mats) · 9am to 1 hr before
dusk · £2.30/40.
F140 **Colnbrook GDR**
☎(0753) 682670
Galleymead Rd, Old Bath Rd, Colnbrook,
Slough SL3 OEN
14 covered, floodlit, 10 open ·
9.30am-10.30pm · £1/36.
F141 **Drayton Park**
☎(0235) 550607 · See **F28** · 21 covered,
floodlit · 8am-9pm · £2/45, £3/75.
F142 **Heathfield GDR**
☎(0869) 350626
Heathfield G & CC, Bletchingdon, Oxfordshire
12 covered, floodlit, 25 grass tees ·
10am-9pm · £3.50/100.
F143 **Hennerton**
☎(0734) 401000, 404778 · See **F40** · 7
floodlit · 8am-9pm · £2/50.
F144 **Hillside Farm GDR**
☎(0295) 720361
Bloxham, Banbury, Oxon OX15 4PF
15 covered floodlit · 8am-8pm · £1.30/40,
£3/120.
F145 **Lavender Park Golf Centre**
☎(0344) 886096 · See **F45** · 27 covered,
floodlit · 9.30am-10.30pm · £1.90/small,
£3/large.
F146 **Lyneham**
☎(0993) 831841 · See **F47** · 12 open ·
8am-5pm · £2/70.
F147 **Oxford Golf Centre**
☎(0865) 721592
Binsey Lane, Botley, Oxford OX2 0EX
19 covered, floodlit, 8 open · 10am-9pm
(7.30pm Sat, 8.30pm Sun) · £3/90, £2/40.
F148 **Silverstone**
☎(0280) 850005 · See **F58** · 12 covered,
floodlit · dawn-10pm · £1/42.
F149 **Sindlesham Golf Range**
☎(0734) 788494
Mole Rd, Sindlesham, Berks RG11 5DJ
24 covered, floodlit · 7am-10.30pm · £2/50.
F150 **Waterstock**
☎(0844) 338093 · See **F68** · Practice range,
floodlit (from June 1994) · 8am-10pm
(provisional) · £1.20/30, £2/60.
F151 **Wavenden Golf Centre**
☎(0908) 281811 · See **F69** · 36 covered,
floodlit · 8am-10pm · £1.60/small,
£2.85/large.
F152 **Windmill Hill**
☎(0908) 378623 · See **F75** · 27 covered,
floodlit · 9am-9pm WD, 8am-8pm WE ·
£1.60/48, £3/96.
F153 **Woodcote GDR**
☎(0491) 681188
Reading Rd, Woodcote, Nr Reading, Berks
RG8 0RB
12 covered · 9.30am-dusk, (12am-dusk Mon)
· £2/48.
F154 **Wycombe Heights Golf Centre**
☎(0494) 816686, 812862 · See **F78** · 24
covered, floodlit · dawn-10.30pm ·
£2/bucket.

G155 **Abbotsley**
☎(0480) 215153, 474000 · See **G1** · 24
covered, floodlit · 7.30am-9pm · £2/bucket.
G156 **Beadlow Manor Hotel, G & CC**
☎(0525) 860800 · See **G4** · 25 covered,
floodlit · apply for details.
G157 **Blaby**
☎(0533) 784804 · See **G8** · 27 covered,
floodlit · 9am-9pm · £1/bucket.
G158 **Charnwood Golf Centre**
☎(0509) 610022
Derby Road Sports Ground, Loughborough,
Leics LE11 0SS

24 covered, floodlit; 9-hole Pitch & Putt ·
8am-10pm · £1.95/60;·
G159 **Collingtree Park**
☎(0604) 700000, 702600 · See **G14** · 15
covered, floodlit · dawn-dusk · £2/50.
G160 **Daventry District Council
Pitch & Putt**
☎(0327) 71100 ext 413
Lodge Rd, Daventry, Northants
9 hole Pitch & Putt · 12am-dusk WD,
10am-dusk WE and school hols · £1.40
adults.
G161 **Delapre Park**
☎(0604) 764036 · See **G19** · 38 covered,
floodlit · 9am-10pm · £2/60.
G162 **Edrich Range**
☎(0487) 815622, 813519 · See **G63** · 12
covered, 12 open, floodlit · 10am-10pm
(earlier by arrangement · £1/30.
G163 **Golf Link**
☎(0530) 836591
Snibston Heritage Centre, Ashby Rd, Coalville,
Leics LE6 2LN
20 covered, floodlit; 200 grass tees ·
10am-9.30pm (6pm Sat, 7pm Sun) winter,
9am-10pm summer · £2/75; £2.50/9 holes,
£3.50/18.
G164 **Greetham Valley**
☎(0780) 460444, 460666 · See **G28** · 15
covered, 6 open, floodlit · 8am-9pm WD,
7.30am-9pm WE · £1.50/48, £2.50/96.
G165 **Hellidon Lakes Hotel & CC**
☎(0327) 62550 · See **G30** · 8 covered bays ·
8am-6pm · £2.50/60.
G166 **Hemingford Abbots**
☎(0480) 495000 · See **G31** · 30 covered,
floodlit · 10am-9.30pm (8.30pm WE) ·
£1.70/small, £2.80/large.
G167 **Ivinghoe Golf Range**
☎(0296) 662720
Cheddington Rd, Ivinghoe, Nr Leighton
Buzzard, Beds LU7 9JY
33 covered, floodlit · 10am-9pm (8pm WE
winter, 7pm WE summer) · £2/75, £1/35.
G168 **Kibworth**
☎(0533) 792301 · See **G38** · 8 · 9am-dusk ·
£1/30, £1.50/50.
G169 **Kilworth Springs**
☎(0858) 575082 · See **G39** · 18 floodlit ·
6am-11pm · £2/bucket.
G170 **Kingstand**
☎(0533) 387908 · See **G40** · 14 covered,
floodlit · 7am-10pm · £1/35.
G171 **Kingsway**
☎(0763) 262727 · See **G42** · 40 covered,
floodlit · 8.30am-10pm · £1/£2 baskets.
G172 **Lakeside Lodge**
☎(0487) 740540, 741541 · See **G44** · 11 ·
dawn-dusk · £2/100.
G173 **Leicestershire Forest Golf
Centre**
☎(0455) 824800 · See **G47** · 16 floodlit ·
8am-9pm · £2/bucket.
G174 **Mowsbury**
☎(0234) 771041, 216374 · See **G59** · 12
covered, floodlit · dawn-10pm ·
£1.50/bucket.
G175 **Stockwood Park**
☎(0582) 413704 · See **G82** · 20 covered,
floodlit · 7am-9pm · £1.70/50, £2.55/100.
G176 **Thorney Golf Centre**
☎(0733) 270570 · See **G83** · 13 floodlit ·
8am-9.30pm (6pm Sun) · £1.50/55.
G177 **Tilsworth**
☎(0525) 210721 · See **G85** · 30 covered,
floodlit · 10am-9.30pm · £1.35/50,
£2.25/100.
G178 **West Park G & CC**
☎(0327) 858092 · See **G89** · 300 yard range,
floodlighting and bays under construction ·
dawn-dusk · £1/bucket.

G179 **Whaddon Golf Centre**
☎(0223) 207325 · See **G91** · 20 covered,
floodlit · 8am-9pm · £1/50.
G180 **Whetstone**
☎(0533) 861424 · See **G92** · 20 turf ·
8.30am-4.30pm WD, 7am-4.30 WE ·
£1.70/70.

H181 **Bawburgh**
☎(0603) 746390, 42323 · See **H4** · 14
covered · 8am-9pm (7pm WE) · £2/80.
H182 **Browston Hall Driving Range**
☎(0493) 603511
Browston Green, Great Yarmouth, Norfolk
NR31 9DW
13 covered, floodlit, 13 open; 9 hole Pitch &
Putt · 8am-10pm · £1/44; £2/88.
H183 **Diss**
☎(0379) 642847, 644399 · See **H10** · 10
indoor, 10 outdoor · 9am-dusk · £1/40,
£2/90.
H184 **Eagles**
☎(0553) 827147 · See **H11** · 18 floodlit
(some covered) · 8am-9pm · £1.90/50.
H185 **Fynn Valley**
☎(0473) 785463 · See **H18** · 10 covered,
floodlit; 13 open · summer 7am-9.30pm
(7pm WE), winter 8am-9.30pm (7.30am-6pm
WE) · £1.50/50, £2.20/100.
H186 **Middleton Hall**
☎(0553) 841800 · See **H29** · 10 covered,
floodlit · 7am-9pm · £1/basket.
H187 **Richmond Park**
☎(0953) 881803 · See **H33** · 3 · 8am-dusk ·
£1/50.
H188 **St Helena**
☎(0986) 875567 · See **H41** · 10 covered, 8
open · 8am-dusk · £1.85/large, £1.25 small.
H189 **Seckford**
☎(0394) 388000 · See **H42** · 12 open ·
8am-9pm · £2.50/large, £1.75 small.
H190 **Sprowston Park**
☎(0603) 410657, 417264 · See **H45** · 27
covered, floodlit · 7.30am-8.30pm · £1/£2
buckets.
H191 **Ufford Park Hotel**
☎(0394) 383555 · See **H50** · 9 open ·
7.30-dusk · £1/40.
H192 **Wensum Valley**
☎(0603) 261012 · See **H52** · 6 open ·
7am-8pm · £2/80.

I193 **Abbey Park G & CC**
☎(0527) 63918 · See **I1** · 12 covered ·
dawn-dusk · £1.50/50, £2.50/100.
I194 **Ansty Golf Centre**
☎(0203) 602671 · See **I2** · 18 open ·
dawn-dusk · £1/45.
I195 **Bransford (Pine Lakes)**
☎(0886) 833551 · See **I9** · 20 · 8am-dusk ·
£1/30.
I196 **Bromsgrove Golf Centre**
☎(0527) 575886, 570505 · See **I11** · 41
covered, floodlit · 9am-10pm (6pm WE) ·
£1.10/35, £1.45/50, £2.20/100.
I197 **City of Coventry (Brandon Wood)**
☎(0203) 543141 · See **I16** · 11 covered,
floodlit; 8 open · 9am-9pm WD, 8am-5pm WE
· £1.20/60.
I198 **Four Ashes Golf Centre**
☎(0564) 779055
Four Ashes Rd, Dorridge, Solihull, W Midlands
B93 8NQ
28 covered, floodlit · 10am-10pm (6pm WE) ·
£2.30/90; £1.30/45.
I199 **Gloucester Hotel & CC**
☎(0452) 411331 · See **I33** · 12 floodlit ·
10am-9.30pm · £1/40.

I200 **Halesowen Golf Range**
☎(021) 550 2920
Quarry Lane, Halesowen, B63 4PB.
14 open bays · 9.30am-dusk · £1.50/50;
£2.60/100.
I201 **John Reay Golf Centre**
☎(020333) 3920, 8071, 3405
Sandpits Lane, Keresley, Coventry CV7 8NJ
30 covered, floodlit · 9am-10pm WD,
9.30am-10pm WE · £1/45.
I202 **Lea Marston Hotel & Leisure Complex**
☎(0675) 470468 · See **I52** · 30 covered,
floodlit · 10am-10pm · £2.20/65.
I203 **Leominster**
☎(0568) 611402 · See **I54** · 14 covered,
floodlit; 4 open · 8am-9pm · £1/30.
I204 **M.J.M. GDR**
☎(052 785) 7129
Brickyard Lane, Studley, Warwicks B78 7EE.
14 covered, floodlit; 6 open, floodlit ·
10am-9pm (6pm W E) . £1.40/50, £2/90,
£2.90/150.
I205 **Ombersley**
☎(0905) 620747 · See **I72** · 36 open ·
dawn-dusk · £1.40/40.
I206 **Purley Chase G & CC**
☎(0203) 395348 · See **I76** · 13 covered,
floodlit · 7am-9.30pm · £1.25/bucket.
I207 **Sapey Golf**
☎(0886) 853288, 853567 · See **I83** · 6 open
· dawn-dusk · £1.25/50, £2.25/100.
I208 **Stratford Oaks**
☎(0789) 731571, 731700 · See **I90** · 26
covered, floodlit · 9am-9pm · £2.50/50.
I209 **Thornbury Golf Centre**
☎(0454) 281144 · See **I95** · 24 covered,
floodlit · 7.30am-10pm · £2/50, £3/75,
£3.75/100.
I210 **Vale G & CC The**
☎(038 682) 781, 520 · See **I98** · 20 open ·
8am-8.30pm (dusk Sun/Mon) · £1.80/50,
£3/100.
I211 **Warwick**
☎(0926) 494316 · See **I101** · 23 covered,
floodlit · 10am-9pm (4.30pm WE) ·
£1.20/small, £2.30/large.
I212 **Whitelakes Golf Centre**
☎(0564) 824460
Tilehouse Lane, Wythall, Solihull, W Midlands
15 covered, floodlit; 9 hole Par 3 golf course ·
8am-9pm · £2/100.
I213 **Worcester Golf Range**
☎(0905) 421213
Weir Lane, Lower Wick, Worcester WR2 4AY.
26 covered, floodlit; 9 hole pitch & putt ·
10am-9pm (5.30pm W E) . 85p/25,
£1.50/45.

J214 **Bannel Golf Range**
☎(0244) 544639
Chester Road, Penymynydd, Nr Chester,
Clwyd CH4 0EN
10 covered, floodlit, 3 open · 10am-8.30pm
WD, 9.30am-6.30pm (4.30pm winter) WE ·
£2/50.
J215 **Caerleon**
☎(0633) 420342 · See **J23** · 16 covered,
floodlit, 4 open · 10am-4pm & 5pm-9pm
(8pm WE); from 8am in summer ·
£1.30/small, £1.85 large.
J216 **Dewstow**
☎(0291) 430444 · See **J38** · 26 floodlit ·
9am-9pm · £1/50.
J217 **Kinmel Park Golf Complex**
☎(0745) 833548 · See **J54** · 25 covered,
floodlit · 10am-late · from £1.50/bucket.
J218 **Lakeside**
☎(0639) 893232 · See **J56** · 20 floodlit ·
9am-8.30pm · £2/70.

J219 **Llannerch Park**
☎(0745) 730805 · See **J63** · 14 floodlit ·
10am-9pm · £1/36, £3/108.
J220 **Mayfield Golf Range**
☎(0437) 890308
Clareston Hall, Freystrop, Haverfordwest,
Pembrokeshire
12 covered, floodlit · 10am-9.30pm (8pm
winter WE) · £2.50/80, £1.25/40.
J221 **Mid-Wales Golf Centre**
☎(0686) 688303 · See **J71** · 12 covered,
floodlit; 4 open · 8.30am-9pm · £1.20/35,
£2/75.
J222 **Mountain Lakes**
☎(0222) 861128 · See **J79** · z20 covered,
floodlit · 9am-9pm · £1/40.
J223 **Oakdale**
☎(0495) 220044 · See **J86** · 18 floodlit ·
9.30am-9.30pm (8pm Sat) · £1.30/50.
J224 **Parc Golf**
☎(0633) 680933 · See **J92** · 38 covered,
floodlit · 7am-10pm · £1/basket.
J225 **Penrhos G & CC**
☎(0974) 202999 · See **J95** · 3 · 8am-dusk ·
£1.50/60.
J226 **South Wales Golf Range**
☎(0446) 742434
101 Port Road East, Barry, CF6 7PX
16 covered, floodlit; 9-hole course ·
9am-8pm (5pm WE) · £2/65, £3.30/130.
J227 **Virginia Park DR**
☎(0222) 863919 · See **J132** · 20 floodlit ·
7am-10pm · £1.50/basket.
J228 **Welsh Border Golf Complex**
☎(0743) 884247 · See **J133** · 10 floodlit ·
8.30am-10pm · £2/70.
J229 **Wernddu Golf Centre**
☎(0873) 856223 · See **J136** · 26 covered, 10
open, floodlit · 8am-9pm · £1.50/50.

K230 **Alvaston Hall Golf Centre**
☎(0270) 629444
Alvaston Hall, Middlewich Rd, Nantwich,
Cheshire CW5 6PD.
16 covered, floodlit; 9 hole Par 3 golf course ·
9am-9pm · £2/34.
K231 **Carden Park**
☎(0829) 731000 · See **K27** · 13 covered ·
8am-dusk · £2/50.
K232 **Cranford GDR**
☎(061) 432 8242
Harwood Road, off Didsbury Road, Heaton
Mersey, Stockport, Cheshire SK4 3AW
40 covered, 2 open, floodlit; refreshments ·
10.30am-11pm · £2.50/50, £4.80/100.
K233 **Craythorne Golf Centre**
☎(0283) 64329, 37992, 33745 · See **K35** ·
14 · 9.30am-4pm & 5pm-9pm WD, 9am-1pm
& 2pm-dusk WE · £1/40.
K234 **Croft Golf Centre**
☎(0925) 763741
Cross Lane, Croft, Cheshire WA3 7AW
20 floodlit; practice greens, cafe · 9am-9pm
(7pm Fri-Sun winter) · £1/35.
K235 **Fishley Park Golf Range**
☎(0922) 685279
Fishley Lane, Pelsall, Walsall, WS3 5AE.
12 covered, floodlit; 9 hole pitch & putt; bar ·
9am-9pm · £1.20/40, £3.50/110.
K236 **Hartford Golf Range**
☎(0606) 871162
Burrows Hll, Hartford, Northwich CW9 3AA
30 covered, floodlit; 9 hole course ·
10am-9pm (7pm Sat) · £1.50/45, £3/100.
K237 **Ketley Golf & Squash Centre**
☎(0952) 251618
Holyhead Road, Ketley, Telford, TF3 1ED
12 covered, floodlit · 10am-2pm, 4pm-10pm
WD winter, 3pm-10pm WE;
11.30am-2.30pm, 5.30pm-10pm WD

summer, 6pm-10pm WE · £2.35/80,
£2.75/100; 6 hole Par 3 course £2.15.

K238 **Newcastle Municipal**
☎(0782) 627596 · See **K88** · 26 floodlit ·
9am-10pm · £2/60, £3/95.

K239 **Oswestry GDR**
☎(0691) 670580, 671246 · See **K85** · 12
floodlit · 8.30am-dusk (6pm winter) · £1/30.

K240 **Perton Park Golf Centre**
☎(0902) 380073 · See **K98** · 12 indoor, 12
outdoor · 8am-dusk · £1.50/48, £3/100.

K241 **Sandfield GDR**
☎(0244) 301752
Ince Lane, Bridge Trafford, Nr Chester, CH2
4JR
12 covered, floodlit ; 3 open · 10am-9pm
(6pm WE) · £1.70/50; £3/100.

K242 **Sedgley Golf Centre**
☎(0902) 880503 · See **K115** · 10 covered,
floodlit; 6 open · 9.30am-9pm WD, 8am-5pm
WE winter only · £1.20/small, £2/large.

K243 **Seedy Mill**
☎(0543) 417333 · See **K116** · 26 covered,
floodlit · 9am-9.30pm · £2/60.

K244 **Shrewsbury**
Telford Way, Shrewsbury, Shropshire.
28 covered, floodlit · 10am-9pm · £2/70
approx.

K245 **Shropshire The**
☎(0952) 677866 · See **K121** · 30 covered,
floodlit · 7am-10pm · £1/30, £2/65.

K246 **Swindon**
☎(0902) 897031 · See **K127** · 20 covered,
floodlit, 7 open · 9am-9pm (6pm WE) ·
£1.40/small, £2.95 large.

K247 **Three Hammers Golf Complex**
☎(0902) 790428 · See **K130** · 23 covered,
floodlit · 9.30am-10pm · £2/small, £4/large.

K248 **Wirral Golf and Drive Centre**
☎(051) 677 6606
Tarran Way, Moreton, Wirral, Merseyside L46
4TP
20 covered, floodlit · 10am-8.30pm · £1/30,
£2/65.

L249 **Belton Woods Hotel & CC**
☎(0476) 593200 · See **L7** · 24 covered,
floodlit · 10am-10pm · £1/48.

L250 **Bondhay G & CC**
☎(0909) 723608 · See **L10** · 30 covered,
floodlit · 8am-10pm · £1.99/bucket.

L251 **Carlton Forum Golf Range**
☎(0602) 612949
Foxhill Road, Carlton, Nottingham NG4 1RL
28 covered, floodlit · 9.30am-10pm
(12am-10pm Mon) · from £2.10/75.

L252 **Cotgrave Place G & CC**
☎(0602) 335500 · See **L27** · 12 covered,
floodlit · 9.30am-9pm WD, 7am-9pm WE ·
£1.50/50.

L253 **Elms Golf Range, The**
☎(0754) 881230
Croft, Nr Wainfleet, Skegness, PE24 4AW
20 covered, floodlit; 6 hole course ·
10am-10pm · £1.70/50;·

L254 **Four Seasons Golf Centre**
☎(0335) 60096
Hall Lane, Brailsford, Ashbourne, Derby DE6
3BX
15 floodlit · dawn-10pm · £2/60.

L255 **Gainsborough**
☎(0427) 613088 · See **L33** · 20 covered,
floodlit · 8am-9pm (dusk WE) · £1/46.

L256 **Gedney Hill**
☎(0406) 330922 Pro · See **L34** · 10 open ·
8am-10pm · £1/35.

L257 **GDR**
☎(0472) 698131
Mini Golf House, Kings Road, Cleethorpes,
Humberside DN35 0QG

8 covered, floodlit; open grass area; 9 hole
Pitch & Putt · 10am-8pm (6pm winter) ·
£1.20/50.

L258 **Grange Park**
☎(0724) 762945 · See **L36** · 20 covered,
floodlit · 9am-9.30pm (8.30pm WE) ·
£1.25/50, £2.50/100.

L259 **Grassmoor Golf Centre**
☎(0246) 856044 · See **L37** · 26 covered,
floodlit · 8am-9.30pm · £2/80.

L260 **Horncastle**
☎(0507) 526800 · See **L40** · 25 covered,
floodlit · 9am-9.30pm · £2.50/bucket.

L261 **Horsley Lodge**
☎(0332) 780838, 781400 · See **L41** · 10
covered, floodlit · dawn-10pm · £2/52.

L262 **Lenton Lane GDR**
☎(0602) 862179
Lenton Lane, Nottingham
24 coverd, floodlit; 9 hole Pitch & Putt ·
10am-10pm (7pm WE) · £2/80.

L263 **Lincoln Golf Range**
Washingborough Rd, Washingborough,
Lincoln
25 covered, floodlit; 9 hole Par 3 course ·
10am-8.30pm (8pm WE)·

L264 **Millfield**
☎(0427) 718255 · See **L62** · 8 floodlit ·
dawn-dusk · £2/100.

L265 **Oakmere Park (Oxton)**
☎(0602) 653545 · See **L68** · 30 covered,
floodlit · 7.30am-9pm · £2.50/90.

L266 **Ramsdale Park Golf Centre**
☎(0602) 655600 · See **L73** · 25 covered,
floodlit · 7.30am-10pm · £2/£3/£3.75
buckets.

L267 **Trent Lock Golf Centre**
☎(0602) 464398 · See **L91** · 24 covered,
floodlit · 8am-10pm · £1.75/51, £3/102.

M268 **Bardsley Park Golf Centre**
☎(061) 627 2463
Knott Lanes, Bardsley, Oldham, Lancs OL8
3JD
17 covered, floodlit · 10am-9pm WD,
9am-6pm WE · £2.20/46.

M269 **Beacon Park**
☎(0695) 622700 · See **M11** · 24 covered,
floodlit · 9am-9.30pm · £2/50.

M270 **Blackburn GDR**
☎(0254) 581996
Queens Park Playing Fields, Haslingden Road,
Blackburn, Lancs BB2 3HJ
27 covered, floodlit · 10am-9pm WD,
9am-7pm WE · £3/100.

M271 **Bowlee GDR**
☎(061) 653 1603
Heywood Old Road, Middleton, Manchester
M24
16 covered, floodlit · 10am-7.30pm WD,
9am-4.30pm WE · £2.25/60.

M272 **Brayton Park GC**
☎(069 73) 20840 · See **M23** · 9 floodlit ·
8am-9pm · £1.50/70.

M273 **Castle Hawk**
☎(0706) 59995 · See **M29** · 10 covered, 5
open · 9am-9pm · £1.50/50.

M274 **Eden**
☎(0228) 573003 · See **M47** · 20 covered,
floodlit · 8.30am-5.30pm · £1.50/50.

M275 **Euxton Park Golf Range**
☎(0257) 261601
Euxton Lane, Chorley, Nr Preston, Lancs
30 covered, floodlit, 10 open, 10 grass; 9 hole
course · 10am-9.15pm WD, 9am-7.15pm WE
· £1.75/50.

M276 **Fore'Long GDR**
☎(0228) 49583
Carlisle Racecourse, Durdar, Carlisle,
Cumbria

6 covered, floodlit; bar/restaurant · Closed
Mon and race days; Tues-Fri 10am-8pm;
Sat/Sun 10am-4pm · £1.10/small,
£1.40/large.

M277 **Formby Golf Range**
☎(07048) 75952
Moss Side, Formby, Merseyside L37 0AF
14 covered, floodlit, 7 open · 9.30am-9.30pm
(8.30pm winter WD and summer WE, 5.30pm
winter WE) · £1.50/45, £3/90.

M278 **Indoor Golf Driving Range**
☎(0253) 893150 · See **M108** · 4 indoor ·
8am-7.30pm (3.30pm winter) · £2.50 per 30
mins.

M279 **Kearsley Driving Range**
☎(0204) 75726
Moss Lane, Kearsley, Bolton, Lancs BL4 8SF
10 covered, floodlit,18 open grass; 9 hole
Pitch & Putt · 11am-10pm (5pm WE) ·
£1.25/25; £2.50/50.

M280 **Leisure Lakes GDR**
☎(0772) 815842
Tabby Nook, Mere Brow, Tarleton, Lancs PR4
6LA
20 covered, floodlit · 9am-8.30pm (5pm WE) ·
£1.50/50.

M281 **Manchester**
☎(061) 643 3202 · See **M92** · 4 covered ·
8.30-5.30 · £1.50/50, £3/110.

M282 **Newby Grange Hotel & GC**
☎(0228) 573003 · See **M98** · 20 covered ·
9am-9pm · £1.50/55.

M283 **Phoenix GDR**
☎(0253) 854846
Phoenix Sporting & Leisure Centre, Fleetwood
Road, Norbreck, Blackpool, Lancs FY5 1RN.
17 covered, 10 open, floodlit; 9 hole Par 3
course · 9am-9pm (7pm Fri/Sat/Sun) ·
£1.70/50.

M284 **Preston GDR**
☎(0772) 861827
Preston Grasshoppers, Lightfoot Lane,
Fulwood, Preston, Lancs PR4 0AE.
23 covered, floodlit · 9.30am-9pm (12am
winter Sun, 6pm summer Sat/Sun) · £2/45,
£3.50/105.

M285 **Solway Village Golf Centre**
☎(06973) 31236 · See **M129** · 13 floodlit ·
9am-dusk, March-Oct · £1/40.

N286 **Arnold Palmer Golf Range**
☎(0742) 361195
Bradway Rd, Bradway, Sheffield S17 4QU.
23 covered, floodlit bays · 9am-9pm · £2/65,
£2.50/85, £3.50/120.

N287 **Austerfield Park**
☎(0302) 710841, 710850 · See **N5** · 10
covered, floodlit · 8am-9.30pm (or dusk in
summer) · £1.50/45.

N288 **Bradley Park**
☎(0484) 539988 · See **N17** · 14 covered,
floodlit · 9am-9.30pm (7pm weekends in
winter) · £2.50/80, £1.30/40.

N289 **Darrington Golf Academy**
☎(0977) 704522 · See **N87** · 30 floodlit ·
8.30am-8pm (6pm WE) · £1/30.

N290 **Forest Park**
☎(0904) 400425 · See **N46** · 7 open ·
8am-5pm · £1.50/50.

N291 **Hull Golf Centre**
☎(0482) 492720
National Avenue, Hull, N Humberside HU5 4JB
23 covered, floodlit; 9 hole Pitch & Putt ·
9.30am-9pm (7.30pm WE) · £1/40, £2/90.

N292 **Leeds Golf Centre**
☎(0532) 886186 · See **N78** · 20 floodlit ·
9am-10pm (9pm Sun) · £2/50.

N293 **Oulton Park**
☎(0532) 823152 · See **N95** · 22 covered,
floodlit · dawn-10pm · £2.50/65, £3.50/90.

N294 **Phoenix Driving Range**
☎(0709) 364669
Grange Lane, Brinsworth, Rotherham, S Yorks
20 covered, floodlit · 8am-9pm · £2/50
£3/100.
N295 **Rudding Park**
☎(0423) 872100 · See **N114** · 14 open ·
dawn-dusk.
N296 **Sandhill**
☎(0226) 753444 · See **N117** · 18 floodlit ·
9.30am-8pm (6pm WE) · £1.60/50, £3/100.
N297 **Scotton GDR**
☎(0423) 868943
Low Moor Lane, Scotton/Lingerfield, Nr
Knaresborough, W Yorks HG5 9HZ
14 covered, floodlit; 6 open · 10am-dusk ·
£2/50.
N298 **Swallow Hall**
☎(0904) 448889 · See **N135** · 7 covered ·
8am-dusk · £1.50/50.
N299 **York GDR**
☎(0904) 690421
Wigginton Road, Wigginton, York YO3 3RJ
20 covered, floodlit bays · 10am-5pm;
7pm-10pm · £1.50/40, £2/60, £2.50/80.

O300 **Belford**
☎(0668) 213433 · See **O11** · 10 floodlit ·
7am-9pm · £1/35.
O301 **Knotty Hill Golf Centre**
☎(0740) 620320 · See **O41** · 14 covered,
floodlit · 8am-9pm · £2/small, £3 large.
O302 **Middlesbrough Municipal**
☎(0642) 315533 · See **O44** · 12 floodlit ·
9am-9pm (5pm WE) · £2.05/60.
O303 **Oak Leaf Golf Complex**
(Aycliffe)
☎(0325) 310820 · See **O51** · 18 covered,
floodlit · 10am-9pm (7pm WE) · £1.75/45,
£2/75.
O304 **Parklands**
☎(091) 236 4480, 417 2626 · See **O52** · 45
covered, floodlit · 8.30am-10pm · £2/75.
O305 **Roseberry Grange**
☎(091) 370 2047, 370 0660 · See **O56** · 17
covered, floodlit · 8am-9pm · £2/75.
O306 **Wallsend**
☎(091) 262 1973 · See **O74** · 24 floodlit ·
8am-9pm · £2/bucket.
O307 **Washington GR**
☎(091) 417 2626 · See **O76** · 21 covered,
floodlit · 9am-10pm · £1.50/50.

P308 **Gretna**
☎(0461) 338464 · See **P27** · 7 covered, 7
open · 10am-dusk · £1/60.
P309 **Polkemmet DR**
☎(0501) 743905 · See **P64** · 15 floodlit ·
12am-8.30pm WD, 10am-4.30pm WE ·
£1/50, £1.70/100 winter; £1.60/50,
£2.60/100 summer.
P310 **Port Royal Golf Range**
☎(031) 333 4377
Ingliston, Edinburgh, Midlothian EH28 8TR
24 covered, floodlit; 9 hole Pitch & Putt ·
10am-10pm · £1.60/50.

Q311 **Auchenharvie Golf Complex**
☎(0294) 603103 · See **Q5** · 18 covered,
floodlit · 9am-9pm (5pm WE) · £1.30/50,
£2.50/100.
Q312 **Brunston Castle**
☎(0465) 81471 · See **Q22** · 8 open ·
8am-5pm · £1/20.
Q313 **Clydeway Golf Centre**
☎(041) 641 8899
Blantyre Farm Rd, Uddingston, Glasgow G71
7RR

25 covered, floodlit · 9.30am-9pm (8.30pm
Sat), 10am-8.30pm Sun · £1.70/50.
Q314 **Coatbridge**
☎(0236) 421492 · See **Q39** · 18 covered,
floodlit · 11am-8.30pm · £1.06/50.
Q315 **Deaconsbank**
☎(041) 638 7044 · See **Q50** · 15 covered,
floodlit · 10am-8.30pm (7.30pm WE) · £2/50,
£3/100.
Q316 **Normandy Golf Range**
☎(041) 886 7477
Inchinnan Road, Renfrew, Strathclyde PA4
9EG
4 open; 20 covered, floodlit · 9.30am-10pm
(9pm winter WD, 6pm winter WE) · £1.50/48
(coin operated) ·
Q317 **Prestwick Golf Range**
☎(0292) 79849
Monkton Road, Prestwick, Ayrshire KA9
20 covered, floodlit · 9am-9pm (6pm Sat,
8pm Sun) · 80p/30.
Q318 **Strathclyde Park**
☎(0698) 283994 · See **Q136** · 24 covered,
floodlit · 10am-9pm · £2.20/small, £2.70
large.

R319 **Elie Sports Club**
☎(0333) 330955 · See **R43** · 8 · 8am-7pm
summer, 9am-2pm winter · £2/50.
R320 **Glenrothes GDR**
☎(0592) 775374 · See **R51** · 24 covered,
floodlit · 10am-8.30pm (5.30pm WE) ·
£1.50/50.
R321 **Middlebank GDR**
☎(0821) 670320
Middlebank, Errol, Tayside PH2 7SX.
7 covered, floodlit · 9am-9pm (8pm winter) ·
£1.40/50.
R322 **St Andrews Links DR**
☎(0334) 74489 · See **R78** · 12 covered, 12
open, floodlit · 8am-9pm · £1.70/50.

S323 **Fairways Leisure Park**
☎(0463) 713335
Castle Heather, Inverness IV1 2AA
22 covered, floodlit · 9am-10.00pm · £1/24.
S324 **Spey Bay**
☎(0343) 820424 · See **S74** · 16 covered,
floodlit · 10am-10.30pm · £1/30.

T325 **Ballyearl G & LC**
☎(0232) 848287 · See **T5** · 26 covered,
floodlit · 9am-10pm · £2/70, £2.70/110.
T326 **Ballymena GDR**
☎(0266) 40654
Warden Street, Ballymena, Co Antrim, N
Ireland
7 covered, floodlit · 12am-8.30pm WD,
10.30am-3.30pm Sat, closed Sun · £1.55/50,
£2.35/100.
T327 **Blackwood**
☎(0247) 853581 · See **T12** · 20 covered,
floodlit; 4 open · 8am-10pm · £2.50/60.
T328 **Craigavon**
☎(0762) 326606 · See **T25** · 14 covered,
floodlit · 8.30am-9pm · £1.60/50.
T329 **Downpatrick Golf Range**
☎(0396) 613558
86 Ardglass Rd, Downpatrick, Co Down BT30
7DX
14 covered, floodlit · 9am-9pm · £2/85,
£1.25/45.
T330 **Knockbracken G & CC**
☎(0232) 792108, 795666 · See **T44** · 24
covered, floodlit · 8am-11pm · £1.40/40.
T331 **Newry and Mourne Golf**
Centre
☎(06937) 73247

45 Milltown Street, Burren, Warrenpoint, Co
Down BT34 3RJ
10 covered, floodlit; grass facilities ·
10am-10pm (8pm WE) · £1.30/50, £2/80,
£2.50/120.

U332 **Black Bush The**
☎(01) 250021 · See **U33** · 6 covered, floodlit ·
dawn-dusk. £1/35.
U333 **Fota Island**
☎(353 21) 8837 · See **U102** · off natural
grass · 9am-6pm . £2/bucket.
U334 **Gold Coast Golf and Leisure**
☎(058) 42416 · See **U109** · 10 floodlit · all
day . £1/20.
U335 **Harbour Point**
☎(021) 353719 · See **U116** · 21 covered,
floodlit · 9.30am-9.30pm · £2/small,
£3.50/large.
U336 **Heath**
☎(0502) 46533 · See **U119** · 10 covered,
floodlit · 9am-10pm · £1 50/75.
U337 **Lee Valley GDR**
☎(021) 331721 · See **U143** · 23, covered,
floodlit · 9am-9pm · £1/30.
U338 **Leopardstown Golf Centre**
☎(01) 289 5341 · See **U144** · 33 covered,
floodlit, 25 open · 9.30am-10pm (9.15pm
winter).
U339 **Limerick County G & CC**
☎(061) 351881 · See **U147** · 20 covered, 20
open, floodlit · 10am-10pm · £4/100.
U340 **Mount Juliet**
☎(056) 24725 · See **U160** · open · 8am-7pm
· £3/small, £5/large.

INDEX